T0205258

Lecture Notes in Computer Science 13096

More information about this subseries at http://www.springer.com/series/7409

Constantine Stephanidis ·
Don Harris · Wen-Chin Li ·
Dylan D. Schmorrow · Cali M. Fidopiastis ·
Margherita Antona · Qin Gao ·
Jia Zhou · Panayiotis Zaphiris ·
Andri Ioannou · Robert A. Sottilare ·
Jessica Schwarz · Matthias Rauterberg (Eds.)

HCI International 2021 - Late Breaking Papers

Cognition, Inclusion, Learning, and Culture

23rd HCI International Conference, HCII 2021
Virtual Event, July 24–29, 2021
Proceedings

 Springer

Editors
Constantine Stephanidis
University of Crete and Foundation
for Research and Technology – Hellas
(FORTH)
Heraklion, Crete, Greece

Wen-Chin Li
Cranfield University
Cranfield, UK

Cali M. Fidopiastis
Design Interactive, Inc.
Orlando, FL, USA

Qin Gao
Tsinghua University
Beijing, China

Panayiotis Zaphiris
Cyprus University of Technology
Limassol, Cyprus

Robert A. Sottilare
Soar Technology Inc.
Orlando, FL, USA

Matthias Rauterberg
Eindhoven University of Technology
Eindhoven, Noord-Brabant, The Netherlands

Don Harris
Coventry University
Coventry, UK

Dylan D. Schmorrow
Soar Technology Inc.
Orlando, FL, USA

Margherita Antona
Foundation for Research and Technology –
Hellas (FORTH)
Heraklion, Crete, Greece

Jia Zhou
Chongqing University
Chongqing, China

Andri Ioannou ⓘ
Cyprus University of Technology
Limassol, Cyprus

Research Center on Interactive Media,
Smart Systems and Emerging Technologies
(CYENS)
Limassol, Cyprus

Jessica Schwarz
Fraunhofer FKIE
Wachtberg, Nordrhein-Westfalen, Germany

ISSN 0302-9743   ISSN 1611-3349   (electronic)
Lecture Notes in Computer Science
ISBN 978-3-030-90327-5   ISBN 978-3-030-90328-2   (eBook)
https://doi.org/10.1007/978-3-030-90328-2

LNCS Sublibrary: SL3 – Information Systems and Applications, incl. Internet/Web, and HCI

This Springer imprint is published by the registered company Springer Nature Switzerland AG
The registered company address is: Gewerbestrasse 11, 6330 Cham, Switzerland

Foreword

Human-Computer Interaction (HCI) is acquiring an ever-increasing scientific and industrial importance, and having more impact on people's everyday life, as an ever-growing number of human activities are progressively moving from the physical to the digital world. This process, which has been ongoing for some time now, has been dramatically accelerated by the COVID-19 pandemic. The HCI International (HCII) conference series, held yearly, aims to respond to the compelling need to advance the exchange of knowledge and research and development efforts on the human aspects of design and use of computing systems.

The 23rd International Conference on Human-Computer Interaction, HCI International 2021 (HCII 2021), was planned to be held at the Washington Hilton Hotel, Washington DC, USA, during July 24–29, 2021. Due to the COVID-19 pandemic and with everyone's health and safety in mind, HCII 2021 was organized and run as a virtual conference. It incorporated the 21 thematic areas and affiliated conferences listed on the following page.

A total of 5222 individuals from academia, research institutes, industry, and governmental agencies from 81 countries submitted contributions, and 1276 papers and 241 posters were included in the volumes of the proceedings that were published before the start of the conference. Additionally, 174 papers and 146 posters are included in the volumes of the proceedings published after the conference, as "Late Breaking Work" (papers and posters). The contributions thoroughly cover the entire field of HCI, addressing major advances in knowledge and effective use of computers in a variety of application areas. These papers provide academics, researchers, engineers, scientists, practitioners, and students with state-of-the-art information on the most recent advances in HCI. The volumes constituting the full set of the HCII 2021 conference proceedings are listed in the following pages.

I would like to thank the Program Board Chairs and the members of the Program Boards of all thematic areas and affiliated conferences for their contribution towards the highest scientific quality and overall success of the HCI International 2021 conference.

This conference would not have been possible without the continuous and unwavering support and advice of Gavriel Salvendy, founder, General Chair Emeritus, and Scientific Advisor. For his outstanding efforts, I would like to express my appreciation to Abbas Moallem, Communications Chair and Editor of HCI International News.

July 2021   Constantine Stephanidis

HCI International 2021 Thematic Areas and Affiliated Conferences

Thematic Areas

- HCI: Human-Computer Interaction
- HIMI: Human Interface and the Management of Information

Affiliated Conferences

- EPCE: 18th International Conference on Engineering Psychology and Cognitive Ergonomics
- UAHCI: 15th International Conference on Universal Access in Human-Computer Interaction
- VAMR: 13th International Conference on Virtual, Augmented and Mixed Reality
- CCD: 13th International Conference on Cross-Cultural Design
- SCSM: 13th International Conference on Social Computing and Social Media
- AC: 15th International Conference on Augmented Cognition
- DHM: 12th International Conference on Digital Human Modeling and Applications in Health, Safety, Ergonomics and Risk Management
- DUXU: 10th International Conference on Design, User Experience, and Usability
- DAPI: 9th International Conference on Distributed, Ambient and Pervasive Interactions
- HCIBGO: 8th International Conference on HCI in Business, Government and Organizations
- LCT: 8th International Conference on Learning and Collaboration Technologies
- ITAP: 7th International Conference on Human Aspects of IT for the Aged Population
- HCI-CPT: 3rd International Conference on HCI for Cybersecurity, Privacy and Trust
- HCI-Games: 3rd International Conference on HCI in Games
- MobiTAS: 3rd International Conference on HCI in Mobility, Transport and Automotive Systems
- AIS: 3rd International Conference on Adaptive Instructional Systems
- C&C: 9th International Conference on Culture and Computing
- MOBILE: 2nd International Conference on Design, Operation and Evaluation of Mobile Communications
- AI-HCI: 2nd International Conference on Artificial Intelligence in HCI

Conference Proceedings – Full List of Volumes

38. CCIS 1420, HCI International 2021 Posters - Part II, edited by Constantine Stephanidis, Margherita Antona, and Stavroula Ntoa
39. CCIS 1421, HCI International 2021 Posters - Part III, edited by Constantine Stephanidis, Margherita Antona, and Stavroula Ntoa
40. LNCS 13094, HCI International 2021 - Late Breaking Papers: Design and User Experience, edited by Constantine Stephanidis, Marcelo M. Soares, Elizabeth Rosenzweig, Aaron Marcus, Sakae Yamamoto, Hirohiko Mori, P. L. Patrick Rau, Gabriele Meiselwitz, Xiaowen Fang, and Abbas Moallem
41. LNCS 13095, HCI International 2021 - Late Breaking Papers: Multimodality, eXtended Reality, and Artificial Intelligence, edited by Constantine Stephanidis, Masaaki Kurosu, Jessie Y. C. Chen, Gino Fragomeni, Norbert Streitz, Shin'ichi Konomi, Helmut Degen, and Stavroula Ntoa
42. LNCS 13096, HCI International 2021 - Late Breaking Papers: Cognition, Inclusion, Learning, and Culture, edited by Constantine Stephanidis, Don Harris, Wen-Chin Li, Dylan D. Schmorrow, Cali M. Fidopiastis, Margherita Antona, Qin Gao, Jia Zhou, Panayiotis Zaphiris, Andri Ioannou, Robert A. Sottilare, Jessica Schwarz, and Matthias Rauterberg
43. LNCS 13097, HCI International 2021 - Late Breaking Papers: HCI Applications in Health, Transport, and Industry, edited by Constantine Stephanidis, Vincent G. Duffy, Heidi Krömker, Fiona Fui-Hoon Nah, Keng Siau, Gavriel Salvendy, and June Wei
44. CCIS 1498, HCI International 2021 - Late Breaking Posters (Part I), edited by Constantine Stephanidis, Margherita Antona, and Stavroula Ntoa
45. CCIS 1499, HCI International 2021 - Late Breaking Posters (Part II), edited by Constantine Stephanidis, Margherita Antona, and Stavroula Ntoa

http://2021.hci.international/proceedings

HCI International 2021 (HCII 2021)

The full list with the Program Board Chairs and the members of the Program Boards of all thematic areas and affiliated conferences is available online:

http://www.hci.international/board-members-2021.php

HCI International 2022

The 24th International Conference on Human-Computer Interaction, HCI International 2022, will be held jointly with the affiliated conferences at the Gothia Towers Hotel and Swedish Exhibition & Congress Centre, Gothenburg, Sweden, June 26 – July 1, 2022. It will cover a broad spectrum of themes related to Human-Computer Interaction, including theoretical issues, methods, tools, processes, and case studies in HCI design, as well as novel interaction techniques, interfaces, and applications. The proceedings will be published by Springer. More information will be available on the conference website: http://2022.hci.international/.

General Chair
Prof. Constantine Stephanidis
University of Crete and ICS-FORTH
Heraklion, Crete, Greece
Email: general_chair@hcii2022.org

http://2022.hci.international/

Contents

Cultural Experiences

Cognition and Cognitive Modelling

Situational States Influence on Team Workload Demands in Cyber Defense Exercise

Torvald F. Ask[1,2](✉) 🆔, Stefan Sütterlin[2,3,4] 🆔, Benjamin J. Knox[1,2] 🆔,
and Ricardo G. Lugo[1,2] 🆔

[1] Norwegian University of Science and Technology, Gjøvik, Norway
[2] Østfold University College, Halden, Norway
[3] Tallinn University of Technology, Tallinn, Estonia
[4] Albstadt-Sigmaringen University, Sigmaringen, Germany

Abstract. Cyber operations are increasingly automated processes that can occur at computational speed with the intent of reducing, or denying time for good decision making or time to ground communication between human agents. There is a lack of performance measures and metrics in cyber operation settings. One potential setting describing human performance could be emotional stability under stress. Measures of higher individual affective variability indicate more emotional adaptability and allows for measuring individuals as dynamic systems. Previous research in other security-sensitive high-stake situations has shown that individuals with less emotional adaptability display maladaptive behaviors while individuals with more emotional adaptability can adapt more efficiently to changing situations, show more confidence in their own abilities and skills, and display better performance. We hypothesized that measurements of affective variability during a cyber defense exercise will be associated with team workload demands. Data was collected from 13 cadets during the Norwegian Defence Cyber Academy's annual Cyber Defense Exercise. Three indicators of individual affective variability were measured daily with the Self-Assessment Manikin and compared to scores on the Team Workload Questionnaire. We found that affective variability was negatively associated with team workload demands. Participants with higher affective variability, as measured by the Self-Assessment Manikin, will impose less workload demands on the team, which can lead to better outcomes. This is the first study to assess how individual emotional adaptability affects team dynamics in a cyber defense setting. Future research should include variable measurements as they may have better explanatory power for performance measurements.

Keywords: Affective states · Team workload demands · Cyber defense exercise

1 Introduction

Cyber operations are increasingly automated processes that can occur at computational speed with the intent of reducing, or denying time for good decision making or time to ground communication between human agents. One of the most persistent issues in studying cyber defense individuals and teams is that there is a general lack of performance

© Springer Nature Switzerland AG 2021
C. Stephanidis et al. (Eds.): HCII 2021, LNCS 13096, pp. 3–20, 2021.
https://doi.org/10.1007/978-3-030-90328-2_1

metrics and measures in such a setting. In recent years, there has been an increase in research evaluating the performance of cyber defenders in teams, but few studies have looked at individual aspects that may influence team performance [1].

Cyber operations are high-stake situations and COs are under heavy cognitive load for prolonged periods of time. Security Operations Centers (SOCs) consist of teams that work around the clock to prevent, detect, and respond to cyber threats and incidents [2]. SOC teams monitor large and continuous streams of network data to detect potential threats. Operative cyber personnel (Cyber Operators; COs) make up the technical staff of SOC teams and are responsible for threat detection, data analysis, digital forensics, network security and cyber intelligence, as well as communicating with SOC decision-makers and clients. Thus, the task-environment that COs are working within spans the cyber, physical, and social domain [3] and creates a complex socio-technical system (STS)[4] where humans and machines interact to maintain cyber resilience in civil and military sectors.

The cognitive challenges SOC teams face while operating in a STS span a wide range of domains from complex problem-solving, to asset prioritization and protection, intra- and inter-team communication, decision-making based on high uncertainty, leadership efficiency, collaboration and coordination efficiency, constant acquisition of technical and threat competence, updating situational awareness, risk management, problem detection, and information seeking, and more [3]. Developing applicable solutions to these challenges such that SOC team performance can be improved will require scientific approaches at both the team- [3] and individual level [3, 5].

Communication problems are listed as one of the main challenges facing SOC teams [6] but individual factors that affect communication and coordination in cyber teams are poorly understood. Due to the cognitive load associated with cyber operations, the ability to adaptively regulate stress and emotions may serve as relevant individual level indicators of performance.

1.1 The Relationship Between Affective States and Adaptive Performance

Higher affective variability (RMSSD)[7] is defined as "relatively short-term changes that are construed as more or less reversible and that occur more rapidly" [8]. Indices of affective variability allows for the measurement of individuals as dynamic systems where neither trait nor state measurements are able to access changes during specific situations [9] and has been shown to predict higher maladaptive behaviors [10] and higher variability in perceived control predicted earlier mortality [11].

Interpreting stress reactions and tension has effects on perceiving one's state and adaptation ability [12, 13]. Research has shown that positive moods improved confidence [14], while despondent moods decreased feelings of self-efficacy [15, 16]. Research on affective states and their influence on behaviors in cyber security is scarce. Research in other domains has shown that affective states can influence performance [17, 18] and this could lead to targeted interventions to help learning [18].

Situational stressors, whether environmental, emotional, or cognitive, increase physiological arousal to prepare the individual to adapt to the environment, and all stressor categories essentially work on the same biological systems to activate the individual for action. Theories for optimal arousal suggest that there is an individual sweet spot for every person where arousal levels matched to a task maximizes performance, and arousal levels below or above this sweet spot is an impediment to performance (Yerkes-Dodson law [19, 20]). Arousal levels change with shifts in attention but are dependent on the emotional valence of stimuli [21] and optimal attention-allocation for task-related performance appears to be associated with proxies for regulation of arousal that are also associated with affective variability [22]. This suggests that the neural components responsible for regulating affective states are intertwined with performance-related factors associated with attention and arousal. Cognitive- and behavioral neuroscience approaches to problems facing the field of cybersecurity are currently under-explored. To fully appreciate why the regulation of affective states can be important for cyber team performance, it is necessary to first understand the central and peripheral psychophysiological correlates of affective regulation, communication and coordination, and complex problem solving, and how these abilities rely on the same neural systems. Thus, in the three following sections we will detail the underlying neural components of these abilities and how they are related.

1.2 Neural Correlates of Affective Control and Variability and Relationships with Regulation of Physiological Arousal

The primary neural structure that is responsible for an individual's ability to regulate their own affective states is the prefrontal cortex (PFC). The PFC exerts top-down control on emotional states in part via a prefrontal sub-structure called the dorsolateral PFC (DLPFC) which is involved in regulating both neutral and negative emotions [23]. In addition to affective regulation, the DLPFC also plays an important role in other executive functions such as planning and attention control. During conscious regulation of one's own affective states, activity in the DLPFC increases while activity in the Amygdala, a structure associated with arousal and negative affect, decreases along with self-reports of negative affect [23, 24].

For an individual to consciously regulate their own affective states, the DLPFC must first be engaged to allocate attention to the individual's emotional state then decide how to regulate it. The role of the DLPFC in affective regulation is lateralized, with the left DLPFC (lDLPFC) being involved in affective regulation while increased right DLPFC (rDLPFC) activity is associated with affective dysregulation and deficits in emotional attention regulation [25, 26]. The PFC receives signals about emotional- and physiological arousal through a process called interoception (sensing the activity in your organs; gut feelings) [27] and the PFC integrates this information when deciding how to regulate affective states.

The DLPFC regulates physiological- and emotional arousal in part by (1) increasing activity in the vagal branch of the autonomic nervous system (ANS), and (2) inhibiting activity in the sympathetic branch of the ANS [28–30]. Both branches of the ANS innervate all the organs of the body, and this DLPFC-to-ANS pathway of stimulation will lead to reduced arousal, characterized by decreased activity in organs such as the heart and lower heart rate. As opposed to the constant and high heart rate resulting from sympathetic input to the heart, the increased DLPFC modulated vagal input to the heart causes the length and variations in the intervals between each heart beat to increase, increasing heart rate variability (HRV). This mechanism is what allows the DLPFC to aid the individual in adapting their emotional and stress responses to situations with varying levels of stress [31]. Higher vagally mediated HRV (vmHRV) reflects higher vagal input to the heart at rest, lower heart rate, and higher affective variability, while lower vmHRV reflects lower vagal input to the heart at rest, higher heart rate, and lower affective variability. Higher affective variability means higher regulatory range thus higher capacity for adaptive emotional responding, while lower affective variability means lower regulatory range thus lower capacity for adaptive emotional responding.

Evidence for top-down control of the PFC on stress- and emotional arousal was found in a study where transcranial direct current stimulation (tDCS) to the left DLPFC reduced was associated with increased vmHRV, higher mood scores, and reduced levels of cortisol, the latter being a hormonal biomarker of stress [28]. Further evidence for the coupling of cognitive function, affective variability, and physiological adaptive ability was demonstrated in a study showing that cognitive flexibility along with higher vmHRV predicted ability to regulate arousal during prolonged stressors [32]. As COs operating in teams can be exposed to heavy stress and cognitive load for long periods of time [5, 33] it suggests that affective regulation capacity can be vital to cyber team performance. Furthermore, affective regulation ability is related to the degree individuals can emotionally detach from work-related stress, with lower affective regulation ability being associated with lower ability to detach, indicated by higher levels of work-related perseverative cognitions [34]. The temporal intensity of affective states may increase allocation of attentional resources to attentional states resulting in perseverative cognition [35]. Given the tendency for SOC team members to work 12-h shifts [2], the ability to detach from work may be important to reduce work-stress load on COs, although our previous research show that indicators of affective intensity are not related to perseverative cognitions in cyber officer cadets [36]. This may suggest that the selection process for COs result in cognitive and emotional profiles that differ from the general population, which in turn could downplay the effect of affective variability on cyber team dynamics.

1.3 Neural Correlates of Affective Variability and Control Overlaps with Neural Correlates of Social Coherence, Coordination, and Communication

vmHRV and its relation to affective regulation is suggested to be important for interpersonal functioning [37] arguing for its relevance in collaborative settings such as cybersecurity. Studies on socio-emotional problems in children suggest that they co-occur with communication problems [38] and continuous measures of vmHRV suggest that reduced affective and arousal regulation is associated with communication problems in adults [39]. Moreover, vmHRV is associated with proxies of social cognitions. This includes personal indicators of ability to adapt to the environment in the face of adverse conditions such as feelings of trust and social relatedness among adolescents and young adults [40] as well as social orientation values in male adults such as preference for cooperation [41]. Being able to regulate one's own affective states during social interactions may result in experiencing social interactions as low-stress, thus, for individuals working in high-stress social settings and in teams, affective regulatory capacity could possibly aid cooperation by facilitating pro-social cognitions.

A wide range of data from various settings suggest that for humans to coordinate and communicate successfully in dyads and in groups, it requires the synchronization of various physiological systems in both the central and peripheral nervous system [42–51]. One simple example of how disruptive asynchrony can be to communication is if you are trying to maintain a conversation with someone who is shouting when you are talking calmly or if they are not walking at your pace. The same is true for affective states and physiological arousal, indicated by studies assessing vmHRV synchrony with respect to social coherence and communication [39, 48]. Coordinating and communicating with an individual that is in a different and perhaps unpredictable affective state compared to one's own can be challenging during exposure to prolonged stressors.

Communication is a complex social interaction, with contextually guided predictions and mental models of speakers and listeners contributing to message comprehension as much as the actual words that are shared. In studies using functional magnetic resonance imaging, spatial and temporal neural coupling (brain-to-brain synchrony) between speaker and listener is important for the success of communication with respect to whether the listener comprehends what the speaker is trying to convey [47, 51]. Both mirroring and predictive synchronous activity was observed in the listener with respect to the brain activity of the speaker, with greater neural coupling being related to greater understanding of the conveyed message. In naturalistic studies of groups of high-school students, attentional effort appears to be a determinant of brain-to-brain synchrony [44]. A recent review found that optimizing attentional efforts for task-related processing is positively associated with vmHRV [22].

The pupil of the eye has been used as a physiological system to study synchrony with respect to communication [52]. Pupil dilation is under control of the sympathetic nervous system, with reduced sympathetic activity resulting in wider pupil diameter [53, 54]. Under constant luminance conditions, pupil dilation is positively associated with emotional arousal, cognitive load, mental effort, conflict processing, and emotion regulation efforts [55–57]. tDCS of the DLPFC during processing of emotional stimuli has opposite effects on pupil diameter depending on whether the lDLPFC or rDLPFC is stimulated, with tDCS of the lDLPFC being associated with increased pupil diameter [58]. Similarly, chronic vagus nerve stimulation, a safe treatment for affective dysregulation, increases resting pupil diameter without affecting light reflexes [59]. Spontaneously synchronized pupil dilation patterns across individuals (speaker-and-listener dyads) has been shown to be a marker of joint attention, with higher pupillary synchrony occurring during emotional peaks in communication [52]. Individual factors such as level of expressiveness in the speaker and level of empathy in the listener is positively associated with degree of synchrony, thus greater brain-to-brain coupling. For high-school students, silent gazing into a randomized peer's eyes for 2 min prior to class predicted greater brain-to-brain synchrony during class, as measured with electroencephalogram [44]. Together, the above data suggest that the neural mechanisms responsible for successful affective regulation is, at least in part, responsible for successful coordination and communication.

1.4 Neural Correlates of Affective Variability and Control Overlaps with Neural Correlates of Complex Problem-Solving

Being involved in executive functioning, the DLPFC is also a central structure involved in working memory [60, 61] which is a resource with limited capacity that individuals use for problem solving. In line with this notion, complex problem solving is dependent brain networks where the DLPFC is a central component in breaking the problem up in individual tasks [62–64], representing contextual task-demands [65], and cognitive control of perceptual information during loss of situational awareness [66]. Taken together with the fact that optimal allocation of attention to task-related stimuli is associated with psychophysiological proxies of DLPFC functioning and affective variability [22], this can potentially have important implications for cyber operations. If cybersecurity personnel are simultaneously exposed to (1) complex technical problem solving, (2) stressors that require conscious regulation of affective states, and (3) challenges related to communication, this will arguably tax the DLPFC and plausibly result in a conflict of information processing that can affect priorities and be detrimental to team performance.

Together, the above studies suggest that there is a significant overlap in the neural substrates that affect success in both communication and affective control as well as problem solving. If DLPFC task-load reaches an individual's capacity threshold in one domain (e.g. affective regulation), functioning in the other domains (problems solving or communication) may break down. Thus, measures of indicators of affective variability at the level of the individual may provide important performance metrics related to inter-individual cooperation and coordination in collaborative settings such as cyber defense.

1.5 How Affective States May Relate to the Hybrid Space Framework and the Orienting, Locating, Bridging (OLB) Model

As the challenges that COs face span the cyber, physical, and social realm, COs must skillfully apply a wide range of cognitive abilities to flexibly transition between these contexts. To conceptualize the cognitive complexity and communicative challenges that COs face, work conducted in collaboration with our lab proposed the Hybrid Space (HS) framework [3]. The HS framework is based on cognitive engineering and focuses on the interconnectedness between cyber- and physical space, and the tension between tactical and strategic goals in decision-making to illustrate the cognitive landscape that COs must navigate (Fig. 1,a). Knowing where you are in the HS requires the ability to observe your own mental state, termed metacognitive awareness, and to move within the HS requires cognitive agility (Fig. 1,b) [5]. When individuals such as team members or superordinates and subordinates are located in different quadrants of the HS, competencies, goals, and proximity to situational stressors may differ between them, making the nature of communication more difficult thus increasing the cognitive load on COs (Fig. 1,c) [33]. When information is relayed back and forth across individuals with different locations in the HS, cognitive complexity increases (Fig. 1,d) [33] and may require constant re-adjustment of message content and mental representation of the recipient. During prolonged high-stress cyber threat situations, increased efforts to regulate affective arousal may also be necessary. Knowing how to navigate and communicate in hierarchical social structures requires an accurate model of one's own position in the social network relative to others. Recent fMRI studies on accurate neural representation of social network position (e.g. social distance between individuals) show that these representations occur spontaneously in the brain when an individual enters a social context (e.g. is shown a picture of a peer) [67] and that this encoding rely on prefrontal structures involved in affective regulation [30]. If affective variability is an indicator of prefrontal cortical function, then lower affective variability may indicate reduced prefrontal functioning thus ability to accurately represent one's own position in a social setting which may be detrimental to social cohesion.

To accurately locate other individuals in the HS requires perspective taking [68, 69]. Taking the perspective of other individuals is partly dependent on empathy. Empathy is reliant on PFC structures [70], is positively associated with psychophysiological proxies of affective regulation such as vmHRV [41] and may in part explain some of the ways the PFC aids the individual in navigating a social network.

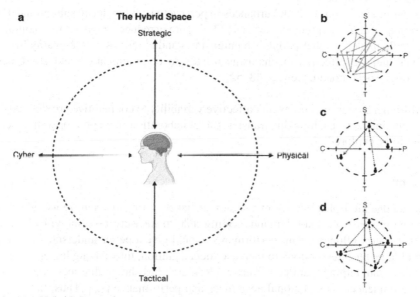

Fig. 1. The Hybrid Space framework conceptualizing the cognitive and communicative challenges of cyber operations [3, 5, 33]. **a** The Hybrid Space. Created with BioRender.com. **b** Cognitive agility. **c** Hierarchical structure, complicated relations. **d** Hierarchical structure, complex relations.

Our lab recently proposed the Orienting, Locating, Bridging (OLB) model [68], a three-stage pedagogic tool to foster metacognitive awareness for improved communication flow in the HS. The OLB model explicates the steps an individual must take to facilitate communication and coordination across levels of expertise, hierarchical layers, and professional backgrounds. First, an individual must apply metacognition to find their own location in the HS (Orienting), then the individual must apply perspective taking to find the communication partner's location in the HS (Locating), then the individual must adapt their communication style and content to the partner depending on their own and the partner's location in the HS (Bridging).

Affective dysregulation could potentially prevent successful OLB-ing, either by forcing the individual to allocate attentional resources to their own affective states thus preventing them from engaging in model application (or communication in general), or at individual stages of the model depending on the timing of situational and affective challenges. For example, affective dysregulation could lead to problems with:

1. Orienting, via conflicts or deficits in shared mechanisms that relate affective regulation to metacognition [71] or deficits in neurocognitive processing related to self-regulation such as being aware of and aligning emotional responses, cognitions, and behaviors to goals [72]. If you are not aware of whether your mental state is aligned with your goals then, arguably, you may not successfully self-locate in the HS. Your goals may be oriented towards the cyber operation, but your affective and cognitive states and behaviors may be focused on your arousal levels in the physical and social domains.
2. Locating, for example by disturbances in perspective taking due to suboptimal development of self-other representations [73–75] or via reduced capacity for maintaining a stable model of other people's mental states and emotions with empathy [41].
3. Bridging, via affective mechanisms related to communication and coordination through social coherence [39, 48, 52].

Although numerous studies link affective variability to cooperative proxies and optimal social interactions, how this translates to collaboration in a cyber operation setting has yet to be explored.

1.6 Aim

We argue that multiple affective measurements taken during an exercise would be associated with team workload demands. Being able to measure how individual variable affective states influence team performance would give a better understanding of how to develop better interventions to increase metacognition, thus having better situational awareness and helping team performance. Research has shown that metacognition has positive influences on situational awareness and performance [76]. Thus, in this paper we examine the relationship between affective variability and team workload demands.

2   Methods

2.1   Participants and Procedure

Data was collected during the Norwegian Defense Cyber Academy's (NDCA) annual Cyber Defense Exercise (CDX). This arena facilitates the opportunity for students to train in tactics, techniques and procedures for handling various types of cyberattacks. The exercise contributes to improving appreciation for the human and technical competences necessary to establish, manage and defend a military digital information infrastructure under simulated operational conditions. The exercise lasted five days. Before each day, the participants were asked to rate their affective states. At the end of the day the participants were asked to assess team performance. A total of 13 cadets participated in the research.

2.2 Measurements

The Self-assessment Manikin (SAM; [77]) was used to measure affective states. The SAM is a 3-item 9-point Likert-scale (1 to 9) that measures mood (negative to positive), physiological activation (PA; little to much), and control (little to much). The SAM is a validated culture- and language independent visual scale that is used in performance [18] research in different domains and populations including cyber environments [77–79].

Both mean and variability scores were computed. Affective variability was computed for the three aspects of the SAM using the formula:

$$RMSSD = \sqrt{\frac{1}{(N-1)} \sum_{j=0}^{n} (RR_{j+1} - \overline{RR})}$$

where N is the total number of R peaks, RR_j is the jth RR interval, RR is the mean of the RR intervals, j denotes the average of the RR intervals up to the jth. This resulted in three independent variables: Mood, Activation and Control. Higher mood indicates more positive mood, higher activation indicates more arousal, and higher control indicates higher self-efficacy.

For this study, the SAM showed good reliability for each subscale (Mood Cronbach's a = .633; Activation Cronbach's a = .891; Control Cronbach's a = .928).

The Team Workload Questionnaire (TWLQ)[80] was used to assess the workload demand in team tasks. Items are scored on an 11-point Likert scale (range: very low – very high) with high scores indicating higher levels of subjective workload. Average scores for team workload performance were computed on the subscales of the two dimensions, the Teamwork component (communication, coordination, team performance monitoring) and Task-Team component (time-share, team emotion, team support).

The TWLQ has shown good reliability on all subscales (Cronbach's a > .70) [80] and also for this research (Teamwork Cronbach's a = .847; Task-team Cronbach's a = .624).

2.3 Ethical Considerations

The study conformed to institutional guidelines and was eligible for automatic approval by the Norwegian Social Science Data Services' (NSD) ethical guidelines for experimental studies. Participants gave their informed consent verbally prior to the study and were informed that they could withdraw from participation at any time and without any consequences.

2.4 Data Analysis

Statistical analysis was done with JASP version .14.1 [81]. All variables were centered and standardized for analysis. Alpha levels for hypothesis testing were set at the 0.05 level. A multiple linear regression was computed with affective state measures (SAM) entered as predictors and the subscales of the TWLQ as criterion variables.

3 Results

Descriptive statistics and correlations among the variables are given in Table 1. From the initial correlation analysis, separate regressions were computed on each of the relevant TWLQ subscales.

Only the SAM Activation average score had any association with teamwork components of the TWLQ (Team Performance Monitoring; $r = .828, p < .01$) but not with any of the Team-task components.

For calculated variability SAM scores for workload demands focusing on Teamwork aspects; communication, coordination and performance monitoring workloads, only higher variable control was associated with less team performance monitoring ($\beta = -.558, p = .048, R^2 = .311, F = 4.96$).

For calculated variability SAM scores for team workload demands focusing on Tasks-team workloads, higher mood variability ($\beta = -.322$) and higher activation (more aroused; $\beta = -.511$) predicted less team support demands ($R^2 = .448, F = 4.058, p = .026$ 1-tailed).

Higher variability for mood ($\beta = -.423$), activation ($\beta = -.282$), and control ($\beta = -.323$) predicted less team support demands ($R^2 = .523, F = 3.29, p = .036$ 1-tailed).

For team emotional support, higher variable control was associated with lower team emotional support but this was not significant ($r = -.473, p = .051$ 1-tailed).

Table 1. Descriptive statistics and correlations ($N = 13$)

	Scale	M	SD	1	2	3	4	5	6	7	8	9	10	11	12
1	Mood	6.38	.75	—											
2	Activation	4.36	1.44	-.428	—										
3	Control	5.65	1.31	.238	-.412	—									
4	R-Mood	1.38	.54	-.569**	.241	.245	—								
5	R-Activation	1.37	.73	-.460	.158	-.202	.251	—							
6	R-Control	1.07	.44	-.019	-.300	.334	.132	.301	—						
7	TWLS Communication	5.60	.70	.010	.133	-.195	.144	.274	.237	—					
8	TWLS Coordination	5.16	.92	.367	.364	-.036	-.117	.046	-.082	.675*	—				
9	TWLS TPM	4.04	1.06	-.161	.828***	-.337	.124	-.056	-.558**	-.114	.218	—			
10	TWLS TSD	4.12	1.26	.366	-.019	-.255	-.450	-.592*	-.290	.187	.345	.067	—		
11	TWLS Team Emotion	2.91	1.08	-.315	.295	-.163	-.187	.118	-.374	-.320	.066	.193	.177	—	
12	TWLS Team Support	3.86	1.24	.201	-.331	-.372	-.538**	-.488*	-.473	-.144	-.264	-.050	.604*	.128	—

R: RMSSD (variability); TWLQ: Team Workload Questionnaire; TPM: Team Performance Monitoring; TSD: Time Share Demand.
*p < .1, ** p < .05, *** p < .01,

4   Discussion and Conclusion

Recent research indicated that there is a scarcity of studies in cybersecurity that simultaneously assess team and individual factors [1]. In this study, we set out to assess the association between individual measurements of affective variability (Mood, Physiological Activation, and Control) on team workload demands (teamwork demands, task-team demands).

We found that higher affective variability could predict better teamwork behaviors (team performance monitoring) as well as decreasing the task-team workload demands. Participants with higher affective variability, as measured by the Self-Assessment Manikin, will impose less workload demands on the team, which can lead to better outcomes [7, 82]. Previous studies showed that more flexible intra-individual psychological processes (i.e. variable self-efficacy) could predict better team outcomes [82].

On a neurological level, while being important for regulating affective states [23], the DLPFC is also important for complex and technical problem solving such as understanding computer code [63, 64] and perceptual tasks such as sorting through perceptual stimuli [83, 84]. Moreover, psychophysiological proxies for DLPFC functioning are associated with a sense of mastery as an adaptive individual trait [40]. In our study, we found that higher variable Control, an indicator of self-efficacy, was associated with less performance monitoring and less team support demands. In previous research, we showed that interoceptive ability, an indicator related to the cognitive perceptions of emotions and arousal, was moderated by self-efficacy during counterintuitive decision-making in officer cadets [85]. Self-efficacy may facilitate better cyber oriented decision-making in certain situations [86] and is negatively associated with stress arousal during task-engagement [87]. Higher Control variability in our sample may be indicative of the level of expertise among COs, and recent research seems to suggest that cybersecurity experts need less intra-team communication and coordination compared to novices [88, 89].

A previous study suggested that increasing cybersecurity alerts were associated with drops in team performance [90]. The authors suggested that team dynamics were affected at the structural level with communication breaking down due to cognitive fatigue. As lower affective variability is due to limited capacity of prefrontal structures such as the DLPFC to exert top-down control on emotional states [23] then it is possible that the (1) arousal was higher than participants were comfortable with (i.e. past optimal arousal levels) such that attention was focused inwards, (2) that affective states were competing with problem solving (3) and sorting between task-related perceptual stimuli to maintain situation awareness [66]. Thus, lower affective variability in our sample may reflect reduced capacity for situational load thus higher team support demands.

Inability to regulate one's own affective states will also affect the capacity to help regulate other individual's affective states due to low tolerance for cognitive-emotional load [91, 92]. If an individual must spend cognitive effort on regulating their own stress- and affective arousal, less cognitive capacity can be allocated to help handle other people's stress levels. If communication dyads are significantly stressed without capacity to down-regulate their own arousal, this may result in a positive feedback loop elevating arousal-related conflict levels during communication [39]. A recent preliminary report on US army computer network defense teams participating in a CDX reported that arguing in cyber defense teams was negatively associated with team performance [93]. The authors reported that frequent arguing was negatively associated with two performance measures: (1) the time between start of an inject to returned rapport approval by team controller, and (2) the percentage of category of injects correctly identified by the blue team. The study did, however, not report p-values for this relationship. This can have major consequences in high-stress, high time-pressure social settings such as cyber threat situations. The relationship between affective variability, characteristics of communication among cyber team members, and performance in a CDX should be assessed in future studies.

This is the first study to assess how individual emotional adaptability affects team dynamics in a cyber defense setting. Our findings suggest avenues for metacognitive training on self-regulation strategies as well as advocating the need for neuroergonomic approaches to understanding how the interrelatedness between different domains of challenge to individual CO performance might affect team performance in cybersecurity.

4.1 Limitations

There are several limitations for the study. An a priori power analysis (G*Power [94]) showed that the minimum number of participants needed ($N = 17$) to achieve medium effect sizes ($f^2 = .25$), our study only had 13, but was the full cohort of the group. This, alongside that the study is correlational in nature and all variables are self-reported, meaning the results need to be interpreted with caution as type I and II error may occur since several results were near significance levels.

5 Conclusion

Future research on team performance in cybersecurity should include variable measurements of individual factors as they are more sensitive and may have better explanatory power for performance measurements than team-level measures alone.

Funding. This study was conducted as part of the Advancing Cyber Defense by Improved Communication of Recognized Cyber Threat Situations (ACDICOM; #302941) project. ACDICOM is funded by the Norwegian Research Council.

References

1. Ask, T.F., et al.: Human-Human Communication in Cyber Threat Situations: A Systematic Review, N.U.o.S.a. Technology, Editor. p. 20 (2021)
2. Muniz, J., McIntyre, G., AlFardan, N.: Security Operations center: Building, Operating, and Maintaining your Soc. Cisco Press (2015)
3. Jøsok, Ø., Knox, B.J., Helkala, K., Lugo, R.G., Sütterlin, S., Ward, P.: Exploring the hybrid space: theoretical framework applying cognitive science in military cyberspace operations. In: Schmorrow, D.D., Fidopiastis, C.M. (eds.) Foundations of Augmented Cognition: Neuroergonomics and Operational Neuroscience: 10th International Conference, AC 2016, Held as

Part of HCI International 2016, Toronto, ON, Canada, July 17-22, 2016, Proceedings, Part II, pp. 178–188. Springer International Publishing, Cham (2016). https://doi.org/10.1007/978-3-319-39952-2_18

4. Zanenga, P.: Knowledge eyes: nature and emergence in society, culture, and economy. In: 2014 International Conference on Engineering, Technology and Innovation (ICE). IEEE (2014)

5. Knox, B.J., Lugo, R.G., Jøsok, Ø., Helkala, K., Sütterlin, S.: Towards a cognitive agility index: the role of metacognition in human computer interaction. In: Stephanidis, C. (ed.) HCI International 2017 – Posters' Extended Abstracts: 19th International Conference, HCI International 2017, Vancouver, BC, Canada, July 9–14, 2017, Proceedings, Part I, pp. 330–338. Springer International Publishing, Cham (2017). https://doi.org/10.1007/978-3-319-58750-9_46

6. Agyepong, E., et al.: Challenges and performance metrics for security operations center analysts: a systematic review. J. Cyber Secur. Technol. **4**(3), 125–152 (2020)

7. Koval, P., Ogrinz, B., Kuppens, P., Van den Bergh, O., Tuerlinckx, F., Sütterlin, S.: Affective instability in daily life is predicted by resting heart rate variability. PLoS ONE **8**(11), e81536 (2013). https://doi.org/10.1371/journal.pone.0081536

8. Nesselroade, J.R.: Interindividual differences in intraindividual change. In: Collins, L.M., Horn, J.L. (eds.) Best methods for the analysis of change: Recent advances, unanswered questions, future directions., pp. 92–105. American Psychological Association, Washington (1991). https://doi.org/10.1037/10099-006

9. Molenaar, P.C., Campbell, C.G.: The new person-specific paradigm in psychology. Curr. Dir. Psychol. Sci. **18**(2), 112–117 (2009)

10. Timmermans, T., Van Mechelen, I., Kuppens, P.: The relationship between individual differences in intraindividual variability in core affect and interpersonal behaviour. Eur. J. Pers. **24**(8), 623–638 (2010)

11. Boehm, J.K., et al.: Variability modifies life satisfaction's association with mortality risk in older adults. Psychol. Sci. **26**(7), 1063–1070 (2015)

12. Hoffman, R.R., Hancock, P.A.: Measuring resilience. Hum. Factors **59**(4), 564–581 (2017)

13. Kahneman, D., Klein, G.: Conditions for intuitive expertise: a failure to disagree. Am. Psychol. **64**(6), 515 (2009)

14. Kavanagh, D.J., Bower, G.H.: Mood and self-efficacy: impact of joy and sadness on perceived capabilities. Cogn. Ther. Res. **9**(5), 507–525 (1985)

15. Bandura, A.: Perceived self-efficacy in the exercise of personal agency. J. Appl. Sport Psychol. **2**(2), 128–163 (1990)

16. Caprara, G.V., et al.: Mastery of negative affect: a hierarchical model of emotional self-efficacy beliefs. Psychol. Assess. **25**(1), 105 (2013)

17. González-Ibáñez, R., Shah, C.: Performance effects of positive and negative affective states in a collaborative information seeking task. In: Baloian, N., Burstein, F., Ogata, H., Santoro, F., Zurita, G. (eds.) Collaboration and Technology, pp. 153–168. Springer International Publishing, Cham (2014). https://doi.org/10.1007/978-3-319-10166-8_14

18. Lugo, R.G., et al.: Impact of initial emotional states and self-efficacy changes on nursing students' practical skills performance in simulation-based education. Nurs. Rep. **11**(2), 267–278 (2021)

19. Corbett, M.: From law to folklore: work stress and the Yerkes-Dodson law. J. Manag. Psychol. **30**(6), 741–752 (2015). https://doi.org/10.1108/JMP-03-2013-0085

20. Yerkes, R.M., Dodson, J.D.: The relation of strength of stimulus to rapidity of habit-formation. Punishment Issues Exp. p. 27–41 (1908)

21. Fernandes, M.A., et al.: Changing the focus of attention: the interacting effect of valence and arousal. Vis. Cogn. **19**(9), 1191–1211 (2011)

22. Khoshnoud, S., Igarzábal, F.A., Wittmann, M.: Peripheral-physiological and neural correlates of the flow experience while playing video games: a comprehensive review. Peer J. **8**, e10520 (2020)
23. Golkar, A., et al.: Distinct contributions of the dorsolateral prefrontal and orbitofrontal cortex during emotion regulation. PLoS ONE **7**(11), e48107 (2012)
24. Banks, S.J., et al.: Amygdala–frontal connectivity during emotion regulation. Soc. Cognitive Affect. Neurosci. **2**(4), 303–312 (2007)
25. De Raedt, R., Koster, E.H.: Understanding vulnerability for depression from a cognitive neuroscience perspective: a reappraisal of attentional factors and a new conceptual framework. Cogn. Affect. Behav. Neurosci. **10**(1), 50–70 (2010)
26. De Raedt, R., Vanderhasselt, M.-A., Baeken, C.: Neurostimulation as an intervention for treatment resistant depression: from research on mechanisms towards targeted neurocognitive strategies. Clin. Psychol. Rev. **41**, 61–69 (2015)
27. Thayer, J.F., Lane, R.D.: A model of neurovisceral integration in emotion regulation and dysregulation. J. Affect. Disord. **61**(3), 201–216 (2000)
28. Brunoni, A.R., et al.: Polarity-and valence-dependent effects of prefrontal transcranial direct current stimulation on heart rate variability and salivary cortisol. Psychoneuroendocrinology **38**(1), 58–66 (2013)
29. Nikolin, S., Boonstra, T.W., Loo, C.K., Martin, D.: Combined effect of prefrontal transcranial direct current stimulation and a working memory task on heart rate variability. PLoS ONE **12**(8), e0181833 (2017)
30. Thayer, J.F., et al.: A meta-analysis of heart rate variability and neuroimaging studies: implications for heart rate variability as a marker of stress and health. Neurosci. Biobehav. Rev. **36**(2), 747–756 (2012)
31. Appelhans, B.M., Luecken, L.J.: Heart rate variability as an index of regulated emotional responding. Rev. Gen. Psychol. **10**(3), 229–240 (2006)
32. Hildebrandt, L.K., et al.: Cognitive flexibility, heart rate variability, and resilience predict fine-grained regulation of arousal during prolonged threat. Psychophysiology **53**(6), 880–890 (2016)
33. Jøsok, Ø., Knox, B.J., Helkala, K., Wilson, K., Sütterlin, S., Lugo, R.G., Ødegaard, T.: Macrocognition applied to the hybrid space: team environment, functions and processes in cyber operations. In: Schmorrow, D.D., Fidopiastis, C.M. (eds.) Augmented Cognition. Enhancing Cognition and Behavior in Complex Human Environments: 11th International Conference, AC 2017, Held as Part of HCI International 2017, Vancouver, BC, Canada, July 9-14, 2017, Proceedings, Part II, pp. 486–500. Springer International Publishing, Cham (2017). https://doi.org/10.1007/978-3-319-58625-0_35
34. Cropley, M., et al.: The association between work-related rumination and heart rate variability: a field study. Front. Hum. Neurosci. **11**, 27 (2017)
35. Résibois, M., et al.: The relation between rumination and temporal features of emotion intensity. Cogn. Emot. **32**(2), 259–274 (2018)
36. Lugo, R.G., et al.: Interoceptive sensitivity as a proxy for emotional intensity and its relationship with perseverative cognition. Psychol. Res. Behav. Manag. **11**, 1 (2018)
37. Porges, S.W.: The polyvagal perspective. Biol. Psychol. **74**(2), 116–143 (2007)
38. Prizant, B.M., Meyer, E.C.: Socioemotional aspects of language and social-communication disorders in young children and their families. Am. J. Speech Lang. Pathol. **2**(3), 56–71 (1993)
39. Wilson, S.J., et al.: When couples' hearts beat together: synchrony in heart rate variability during conflict predicts heightened inflammation throughout the day. Psychoneuroendocrinology **93**, 107–116 (2018)
40. Sætren, S.S., et al.: A multilevel investigation of resiliency scales for children and adolescents: the relationships between self-perceived emotion regulation, vagally mediated heart rate variability, and personal factors associated with resilience. Front. Psychol. **10**, 438 (2019)

41. Lischke, A., et al.: Heart rate variability is associated with social value orientation in males but not females. Sci. Rep. **8**(1), 1–9 (2018)
42. Bertollo, M., Robazza, C., Comani, S.: The juggling paradigm: a novel social neuroscience approach to identify neuropsychophysiological markers of team mental models. Front. Psychol. **6**, 799 (2015)
43. Bourguignon, M., et al.: The pace of prosodic phrasing couples the listener's cortex to the reader's voice. Hum. Brain Mapp. **34**(2), 314–326 (2013)
44. Dikker, S., et al.: Brain-to-brain synchrony tracks real-world dynamic group interactions in the classroom. Curr. Biol. **27**(9), 1375–1380 (2017)
45. Lindenberger, U., et al.: Brains swinging in concert: cortical phase synchronization while playing guitar. BMC Neurosci. **10**(1), 1–12 (2009)
46. Filho, E., et al.: Shared mental models and intra-team psychophysiological patterns: a test of the juggling paradigm. J. Sports Sci. **35**(2), 112–123 (2017)
47. Hasson, U., et al.: Brain-to-brain coupling: a mechanism for creating and sharing a social world. Trends Cogn. Sci. **16**(2), 114–121 (2012)
48. McCraty, R.: New frontiers in heart rate variability and social coherence research: techniques, technologies, and implications for improving group dynamics and outcomes. Front. Public Health **5**, 267 (2017)
49. Müller, V., Lindenberger, U.: Cardiac and respiratory patterns synchronize between persons during choir singing. PLoS ONE **6**(9), e24893 (2011)
50. Reed, K.B., et al.: Haptic cooperation between people, and between people and machines. In: 2006 IEEE/RSJ International Conference on Intelligent Robots and Systems. IEEE (2006)
51. Stephens, G.J., Silbert, L.J., Hasson, U.: Speaker–listener neural coupling underlies successful communication. Proc. Natl. Acad. Sci. **107**(32), 14425–14430 (2010)
52. Kang, O., Wheatley, T.: Pupil dilation patterns spontaneously synchronize across individuals during shared attention. J. Exp. Psychol. Gen. **146**(4), 569 (2017)
53. Beatty, J., et al.: Handbook of Psychophysiology. Cambridge University Press Cambridge. pp. 142–162 (2000)
54. Loewenfeld, I.E.: The Pupil: Anatomy, Physiology, and Clinical Applications. Vol. 2. Iowa State University Press (1993)
55. Johnstone, T., et al.: Failure to regulate: counterproductive recruitment of top-down prefrontal-subcortical circuitry in major depression. J. Neurosci. **27**(33), 8877–8884 (2007)
56. Kinner, V.L., et al.: What our eyes tell us about feelings: tracking pupillary responses during emotion regulation processes. Psychophysiology **54**(4), 508–518 (2017)
57. Van Steenbergen, H., Band, G.P.: Pupil dilation in the Simon task as a marker of conflict processing. Front. Hum. Neurosci. **7**, 215 (2013)
58. Allaert, J., Sanchez-Lopez, A., De Raedt, R., Baeken, C., Vanderhasselt, M.-A.: Inverse effects of tDCS over the left versus right DLPC on emotional processing: A pupillometry study. PLoS ONE **14**(6), e0218327 (2019)
59. Jodoin, V.D., et al.: Effects of vagus nerve stimulation on pupillary function. Int. J. Psychophysiol. **98**(3), 455–459 (2015)
60. Goldman-Rakic, P.S.: Cellular basis of working memory. Neuron **14**(3), 477–485 (1995)
61. Wang, M., et al.: NMDA receptors subserve persistent neuronal firing during working memory in dorsolateral prefrontal cortex. Neuron **77**(4), 736–749 (2013)
62. Duncan, J.: The multiple-demand (MD) system of the primate brain: mental programs for intelligent behaviour. Trends Cogn. Sci. **14**(4), 172–179 (2010)
63. Ivanova, A.A., et al.: Comprehension of computer code relies primarily on domain-general executive brain regions. Elife **9**, e58906 (2020)
64. Liu, Y.-F., et al.: Computer code comprehension shares neural resources with formal logical inference in the fronto-parietal network. Elife **9**, e59340 (2020)

65. Jiang, J., et al.: Prefrontal reinstatement of contextual task demand is predicted by separable hippocampal patterns. Nat. Commun. **11**(1), 1–12 (2020)
66. Catherwood, D., et al.: Mapping brain activity during loss of situation awareness: an EEG investigation of a basis for top-down influence on perception. Hum. Factors **56**(8), 1428–1452 (2014)
67. Parkinson, C., Kleinbaum, A.M., Wheatley, T.: Spontaneous neural encoding of social network position. Nat. Hum. Behav. **1**(5), 1–7 (2017)
68. Knox, B.J., et al.: Socio-technical communication: the hybrid space and the OLB model for science-based cyber education. Mil. Psychol. **30**(4), 350–359 (2018)
69. Shamay-Tsoory, S.G., et al.: Characterization of empathy deficits following prefrontal brain damage: the role of the right ventromedial prefrontal cortex. J. Cogn. Neurosci. **15**(3), 324–337 (2003)
70. Koenigs, M.: The role of prefrontal cortex in psychopathy. Rev. Neurosci. **23**(3), 253–262 (2012)
71. Meessen, J., Sütterlin, S., Gauggel, S., Forkmann, T.: Learning by heart—the relationship between resting vagal tone and metacognitive judgments: a pilot study. Cogn. Process. **19**(4), 557–561 (2018). https://doi.org/10.1007/s10339-018-0865-6
72. Kelley, N.J., et al.: Stimulating self-regulation: a review of non-invasive brain stimulation studies of goal-directed behavior. Front. Behav. Neurosci. **12**, 337 (2019)
73. Beeney, J.E., et al.: Self–other disturbance in borderline personality disorder: neural, self-report, and performance-based evidence. Personal. Disord. Theory Res. Treat. **7**(1), 28 (2016)
74. Frith, U., Frith, C.D.: Development and neurophysiology of mentalizing. Philos. Trans. Royal Soc. London. B Biol. Sci. **358**(1431), 459–473 (2003)
75. Preston, S.D., De Waal, F.B.: Empathy: its ultimate and proximate bases. Behav. Brain Sci. **25**(1), 1–20 (2002)
76. Hamilton, K., et al.: Skilled and unaware: the interactive effects of team cognition, team metacognition, and task confidence on team performance. J. Cognitive Eng. Deci. Making **11**(4), 382–395 (2017)
77. Bradley, M.M., Lang, P.J.: Measuring emotion: the self-assessment manikin and the semantic differential. J. Behav. Ther. Exp. Psychiatry **25**(1), 49–59 (1994)
78. DeFalco, J.A., et al.: Detecting and addressing frustration in a serious game for military training. Int. J. Artif. Intell. Educ. **28**(2), 152–193 (2018)
79. Paquette, L., et al.: Sensor-Free or Sensor-Full: A Comparison of Data Modalities in Multi-Channel Affect Detection. International Educational Data Mining Society (2016)
80. Sellers, J., et al.: Development of the team workload questionnaire (TWLQ). In: Proceedings of the Human Factors and Ergonomics Society Annual Meeting. SAGE Publications Sage CA: Los Angeles, CA (2014)
81. Goss-Sampson, M.: Statistical analysis in JASP: A guide for students. JASP (2019)
82. Lugo, R.G., Knox, B.J., Josøk, Ø., Sütterlin, S.: Variable self-efficacy as a measurement for behaviors in cyber security operations. In: Schmorrow, D.D., Fidopiastis, C.M. (eds.) HCII 2020. LNCS (LNAI), vol. 12197, pp. 395–404. Springer, Cham (2020). https://doi.org/10.1007/978-3-030-50439-7_27
83. Nakajima, M., Ian Schmitt, L., Halassa, M.M.: Prefrontal cortex regulates sensory filtering through a basal ganglia-to-thalamus pathway. Neuron **103**(3), 445-458.e10 (2019)
84. Phillips, J.M., Kambi, N.A., Saalmann, Y.B.: A subcortical pathway for rapid, goal-driven, attentional filtering. Trends Neurosci. **39**(2), 49–51 (2016)
85. Lugo, R.G., et al.: The moderating influence of self-efficacy on interoceptive ability and counterintuitive decision making in officer cadets. J. Mil. Stud. **7**(1), 44–52 (2016)

86. Choi, M., Levy, Y. Hovav, A.: The role of user computer self-efficacy, cybersecurity counter-measures awareness, and cybersecurity skills influence on computer misuse. In: Proceedings of the Pre-International Conference of Information Systems (ICIS) SIGSEC–Workshop on Information Security and Privacy (WISP) (2013)
87. Lan, L.Y., Gill, D.L.: The relationships among self-efficacy, stress responses, and a cognitive feedback manipulation. J. Sport Exerc. Psychol. **6**(2), 227–238 (1984)
88. Buchler, N., et al.: Mission command in the age of network-enabled operations: social network analysis of information sharing and situation awareness. Front. Psychol. **7**, 937 (2016)
89. Lugo, R., et al.: Team workload demands influence on cyber detection performance. In: Proceedings of 13th International Conference on Naturalistic Decision Making (2017)
90. Champion, M.A., et al.: Team-based cyber defense analysis. In: 2012 IEEE International Multi-Disciplinary Conference on Cognitive Methods in Situation Awareness and Decision Support. IEEE (2012)
91. Reeck, C., Ames, D.R., Ochsner, K.N.: The social regulation of emotion: an integrative, cross-disciplinary model. Trends Cogn. Sci. **20**(1), 47–63 (2016)
92. van't Wout, M., Chang, L.J., Sanfey, A.G.: The influence of emotion regulation on social interactive decision-making. Emotion **10**(6), 815 (2010)
93. Henshel, D.S., et al.: Predicting proficiency in cyber defense team exercises. In: MILCOM 2016–2016 IEEE Military Communications Conference. IEEE (2016)
94. Faul, F., Erdfelder, E., Buchner, A., Lang, A.-G.: Statistical power analyses using G*Power 3.1: tests for correlation and regression analyses. Behav. Res. Methods **41**(4), 1149–1160 (2009)

Human-Human Communication in Cyber Threat Situations: A Systematic Review

Torvald F. Ask[1,2(✉)] ⬤, Ricardo G. Lugo[1,2] ⬤, Benjamin J. Knox[1,2] ⬤,
and Stefan Sütterlin[2,3,4] ⬤

[1] Norwegian University of Science and Technology, Gjøvik, Norway
[2] Østfold University College, Halden, Norway
[3] Tallinn University of Technology, Tallinn, Estonia
[4] Albstadt-Sigmaringen University, Sigmaringen, Germany

Abstract. In cyber threat situations, decision-making processes within organizations and between the affected organization and external entities are high-stake. They require human communication entailing technical complexity, time pressure, interdisciplinary factors, and often an insufficient information basis. Communication in cyber threat situations can thus be challenging and has a variety of implications for decision-making. The cyber-physical system is a rapidly changing socio-technical system that is understudied in terms of how cyber events are communicated and acted upon to secure and maintain cyber resilience. The present study is the first to review human-to-human communication in cyber threat situations. Our aims are to outline how human-human communication performance in cybersecurity settings have been studied, to uncover areas where there is potential for developing common standards for information exchange in collaborative settings, and to provide guidance for future research efforts. The review was carried out according to the PRISMA guidelines and articles were searched for on scientific databases. Articles focusing on human-human communication in cyber threat situations published in peer reviewed journals or as conference papers were included. A total of 17 studies were included in the final review. Most of the studies were correlational and exploratory in nature. Very few studies characterize communication in useful goal-related terms. There is a need for more collaboration between cyber defense exercise-organizers and cognitive scientists. Future studies should assess how team mental model-development affects team communication and performance in cyber defense exercises.

Keywords: Cyber threat communication · Human factor · Systematic review

1 Introduction

A Cyber Threat Situation (CTS) is the potential occurrence of a cyber-attack aiming to damage, disrupt, or steal a cyber asset. A cyber asset can be understood as a completely or partly digitized protected organizational resource (Whitman and Mattord 2012). With the increased digitization of society and global network coverage, the cyber threat landscape is evolving and so is the need for research on the prevention and effective handling

© Springer Nature Switzerland AG 2021
C. Stephanidis et al. (Eds.): HCII 2021, LNCS 13096, pp. 21–43, 2021.
https://doi.org/10.1007/978-3-030-90328-2_2

of cyber threats. Organizations often assign their cybersecurity operations to Security Operation Centers (SOCs). SOCs are teams and organizational units that cover multiple security activities such as preventing, detecting, assessing, and responding to cyber threats and incidents (Muniz et al. 2015). Within the SOC organizational structure, technical tasks such as asset monitoring, detection, analysis, forensics, network security, intelligence, and communicating suggestions for cyber threat- and cyber incident response are assigned to technical staff while subsequent decision-making tasks such as how to act on threat and incident reports are assigned to other individuals (decision-makers; Muniz et al. 2015). Consequently, there is a potential knowledge gap between technical personnel and decision-makers.

Cyber professionals, known as cyber operators in military sectors and cyber analysts in civil sectors (interchangeably referred to as COs), make up the technical personnel in SOCs and face a unique set of challenges spanning the cyber, physical, and social domain (Jøsok et al. 2016). This cyber-physical working environment of human-machine and human-human interaction creates a complex Socio-Technical System (STS) that is subject to high rates of innovation, increasing network interconnectedness, and rapid flow of information (Zanenga 2014). Decision-making in STSs has its own set of challenges. In cyberspace, the impact of decisions and actions on own- and third-party infrastructure is influenced by connectivity between different decision-making agents (Tikk-Ringas et al. 2014). In a cybersecurity setting, there is a persisting element of uncertainty regarding the presence, persistence, and consequences of adversarial behavior. This suggests that decision-makers need to prioritize multiple assets based on known and unknown risk and cognitively transition between cyber and physical contexts when estimating the impact of their decisions (Jøsok et al. 2016).

Due to the multiple impact-dimensions of cyber defense decisions, communication between human agents is at the core of good cyber defense decision-making (Knox et al. 2018). Strategic-level decision-making and tactical-level technical developments need simultaneous integration but are usually distributed over different roles, both vertically and horizontally within an organization. Since CO activity and decision-making is distributed among different roles within the SOC (Muniz et al. 2015), there are multiple dyadic relationships that simultaneously influence the information requirements of cyber threat communication. The information communicated from a CO during a CTS must be available for interpretation by all dyads. This can be challenging when stakeholders belong to non-technical sectors or lack technical skills. In a recent review, Agyepong et al. (2020) identified communication as one of the challenges facing SOCs. How cyber events are communicated and acted upon in the physical domain to secure and maintain cyber resilience is currently not well understood. In this paper, we systematically review the literature on human-human communication in CTSs.

1.1 An Accurate Recognized Cyber Picture is Critical for Effective Cyber Defense Decisions

Successful decision-making based on human interaction requires a shared situational awareness (SA) of the CTS. This includes a mutual understanding of what caused the situation, the current state of assets, potential adversaries, how the situation is evolving, and which actions to take to mitigate detrimental outcomes. An organization's Cyber

Situational Awareness (CSA) influences whether an organization maintains control in its cyberspace (Franke and Brynielsson 2014). Seven requirements that need to be met to have full CSA for cyber defense have been suggested (Barford et al. 2009): (1) awareness of the current situation, (2) awareness of the impact of the attack, (3) awareness of how situations evolve, (4) awareness of adversarial behavior, (5) awareness of why and how the current situation is caused, (6) awareness of the quality and trustworthiness of the CSA information, and (7) assessment of plausible outcomes. Having an accurate Recognized Cyber Picture (RCP; or Cyber Common Operational Picture) is crucial to achieve CSA. While CSA can be understood as being aware of the underlying state of a specific cyber environment at any given moment (Franke and Brynielsson 2014), RCPs consist of actively selected and actionable information specifically pertaining to cyber threats (Cyber Threat Intelligence; CTI) and aim to update stakeholders CSA and support their decision-making. To achieve this goal, RCPs should contain the information suggested by Barford et al. (2009).

In the process of cyber threat communication, the CO must first investigate the threat to create the initial RCP, then it is shared (shared RCP; sRCP) across platforms, in differing modalities, and often across organizations, hierarchical layers, professional backgrounds, and societal sectors. When the CO shares the RCP, the CO must translate information that is often inherently complex and at times vague. The receiving partner may lack the expertise of the CO and have a mindset that is oriented towards action in the physical world (Knox et al. 2018). Thus, the cyber-to-physical relay of RCPs is subject to many challenges which may render the sRCP inaccurate, losing critical information. Consequently, the sociocognitive demands of the tasks performed by COs are complex, demanding high cognitive load, and require both technical (e.g. digital forensic analysis) and non-technical skills (e.g. communication; Jøsok et al. 2017).

1.2 Cognitive Aspects of Cybersecurity Performance and Implications for Cyber Threat Communication

Through enhanced information flow, cyber increases human operative abilities (Buchler et al. 2016) while simultaneously creating an environment at odds with human cognition (Zachary et al. 2013). Due to high levels of social barriers, situational shift, and uncertainty, COs must understand and skillfully apply a variety of cognitive processes to adapt to complex and changing task demands (Jøsok et al. 2016, 2017, Knox et al. 2019a). Although these challenges are acknowledged by the adoption of science-based educational approaches to meet the cognitive demands of cyber (e.g. Knox et al. 2019a), common best practices to meet these demands currently do not exist.

Research conducted in collaboration with our lab put forward the Hybrid Space (HS; Fig. 1,a) framework (Jøsok et al. 2016) to conceptualize the cognitive landscape COs must navigate. The HS framework focuses on the interconnectedness between cyber- and physical space, and the tension between tactical and strategic goals in decision-making. If a CO is more oriented towards cyber, communicative challenges may arise when the COs communicates with someone located in the strategic-physical quadrant who in turn must relay the information to an individual with orientation in another quadrant (Fig. 1,b; Jøsok et al. 2017). Further socio-cognitive complexity is added when a group of individuals in different hierarchical layers and different tasks all communicate with each other, requiring constant re-adjustment of communication style and message content (Fig. 1,c; Jøsok et al. 2017). From the perspective of the CO, locating your own current cognitive focus within the HS requires metacognitive awareness (Knox et al. 2017). When other individuals enter the HS, the CO needs to be aware of their presence in the space and adopt perspective taking to understand their CSA, their grasp of the RCP, and to communicate efficiently one's own RCP understanding. This helps facilitate that involved partners can develop and calibrate shared CSA so that decisions incorporate both tactical and strategic approaches in both the physical and cyber domain (Knox et al. 2018).

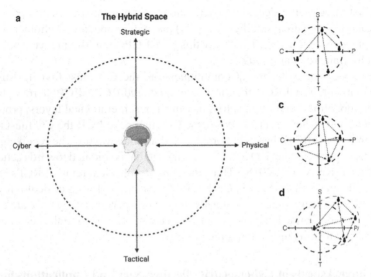

Fig. 1. a The Hybrid Space Framework (Jøsok et al. 2016, 2017) conceptualizing the cognitive landscape cyber operators must navigate. Created with BioRender.com **b** Hierarchical structure, complicated relations. **c** Hierarchical structure, complex relations. **d** Sliding space. C = Cyber. S = Strategic. P = Physical. T = Tactical.

Good cyber defense relies on effective team coordination (Forsythe et al. 2013) and COs working in teams must actively engage in dynamic problem solving to acquire knowledge from each other and the environment (Jøsok et al. 2017). In line with the shifting task demands of the HS, the HS might move along its axis as the focus of the team changes (Fig. 1, d; Jøsok et al. 2017) thus changing communicational needs.

1.3 Current Approaches to Solving Communication Problems in the Hybrid Space: The Orienting, Bridging, Locating (OLB) Model

The process of communication from threat detection to the CO submitting the RCP to a decision-maker is subject to many iterative sub-processes and factors that affect the sRCP and decision-making. Building on the HS framework, our lab proposed the Orienting, Locating, Bridging (OLB) model (Fig. 2; Knox et al. 2018) as a tool to improve communication flow. Although metacognitive awareness is associated with movements in the HS (Knox et al. 2017) and the OLB model provides guidelines for how to apply the HS framework to improve communication (Knox et al. 2018), more research on HS movements and subsequent communication efficiency is needed.

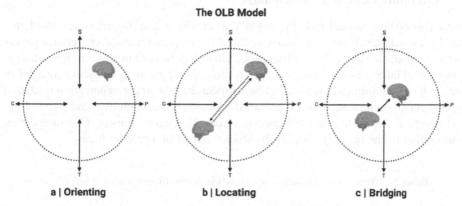

Fig. 2. Orienting, Bridging, Locating (OLB) model. The OLB model (Knox et al. 2018) is a three-stage pedagogical tool to ground communication between cyber operators and their communication partners. C = cyber. S = strategic. P = physical. T = tactical.

1.4 Aim

Given the lack of knowledge regarding human cyber threat communication, in this paper, we review the literature on communication in CTSs. Our aims are to (1) outline how human-human communication performance in cybersecurity settings has been studied, (2) to uncover areas where there is potential for developing common standards for information exchange in collaborative settings, and (3) to provide guidance for future research efforts. While laws and regulations can both be promoters and impediments to information sharing practices (see Pala and Zhuang 2019), reviewing laws are currently outside the scope of this article.

2   Methods

The systematic review was carried out according to the PRISMA guidelines (Moher et al. 2009). We wanted to review qualitative and quantitative original research articles and reviews that studied human-human communication of cyber threat information.

2.1   Review Procedure

1. Identify literature on human-human communication in CTSs through database searches.
2. Categorize the publications according to type and methodological approaches.

3. Provide a summary of the selected articles in order of methodological approaches and which aspect of communication that was studied.
4. Synthesis and discussion of findings followed by suggestions for future research.

2.2 Literature Collection Methodology

There was no limit to publication year. Only articles written in English were considered. Databases and search terms are listed in Table 1. Any peer reviewed conference papers and journal articles that either: (1) described characteristics of human communication of cyber threat information, (2) suggested ways to improve the relay of cyber threat information between humans, (3) assessed how aspects of human communication related to cybersecurity performance, or (4) assessed neuroscientific, cognitive, and psychological constructs related to communication were considered for inclusion. Communication could either be the primary focus of the studies or part of a broader focus.

Table 1. Overview of databases, search terms, filters, hits, and date of last search

Database	Search terms	Filters	Hits	Date of last search
Google Scholar	"communication", "cyber threat", "human-interaction experiment", "recognized cyber picture", "cyber common operational picture", "cyber threat communication"	None	590	Feb. 11. 2021
ScienceDirect	"communication", "cyber threat", "human-interaction experiment", "recognized cyber picture", "cyber common operational picture", "cyber threat communication"	Reviews and research articles	1251	Feb. 11. 2021
IEEE	"communication", "cyber threat", "human-interaction experiment", "recognized cyber picture", "cyber common operational picture", "cyber threat communication"	None	388	Feb. 11. 2021
Taylor & Francis	"communication", "cyber threat", "human-interaction experiment", "recognized cyber picture", "cyber common operational picture", "cyber threat communication"	None	11	Feb. 13. 2021

2.3 Descriptive Information and Statistics

Characteristics of each study such as literature type and methodology, results and out-comes including statistics, and studied population were summarized and presented in tables.

3 Results

The phases of the review are depicted in the flow diagram in Fig. 3. Of studies assessed for eligibility, 13 were excluded due to: (1) proposing technical tools for improved CSA without assessing effects on human communication, (2) only focusing on organization-media communication after a security breach, (3) focusing on increasing the frequency of threat reporting without suggesting ways to organize cyber threat information or mak-ing human-to-human communication more effective, (4) not studying human-to-human relay of cyber threat information or associated human factors, (5) applying mathematical modeling of communication and collaboration without human subjects. A total of 17 studies were included in the final review. Twelve of the selected articles studied some aspect of cognition and its role in cybersecurity performance. Six of the studies were con-ducted on team-based cyber defense exercises (CDXs), Table Top Exercises (TTXs) or Cyber Defense Games (CDGs). There were not enough data to conduct a meta-analysis. None of the studies were published prior to 2012, average publication year was 2016. Overview of the identified publications according to type and methodology is provided in Table 2.

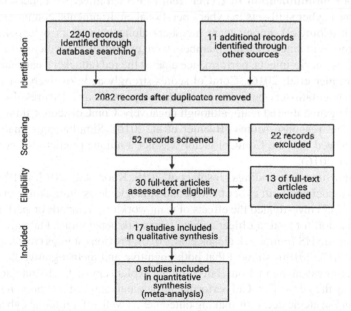

Fig. 3. Flow diagram depicting different phases of the systematic review.

Table 2. Overview of the selected publications according to type and methodology

Type	Methodology			
	Qualitative	Quantitative	Mixed	Total
Conference paper	3	2	3	8
Journal article	6	3		9
Knowledge type				
Empirical	5	5	3	13
Theoretical	4			4
Total	9	5	3	17

3.1 Quantitative and Mixed Studies on Cyber Threat Communication

Five studies examined communication in cyber teams during CDXs, TTXs, or CDGs (Buchler et al. 2016, Champion et al. 2012, Finomore et al. 2013, Henshel et al. 2016, Lugo et al. 2017). One study assessed the role of expectations on security information sharing (Mermoud et al. 2018). One study assessed the role of beliefs on knowledge absorption of cyber threat information (Percia David et al. 2020). One study assessed the knowledge requirements of strategic level decision makers (Garcia-Granados and Bahsi 2020). Table 3 summarizes the selected quantitative/mixed articles.

The Role of Communication in Cyber Team Performance. To understand how to develop human cyber skill-sets in cyber operational environments, communication and collaboration (ComCol) among team members along with years of experience, and number of roles inhabited by team members were examined as predictors of maintain-service tasks, scenario-injects, performance against the red (attacker) team, and incident response (Buchler et al. 2016). ComCol scores strongly and positively predicted performance on maintain-service tasks and scenario-injects. ComCol scores also predicted performance against the red team, although negatively. ComCol scores did not strongly predict incident response scores (Buchler et al. 2016). Simultaneous analysis of all predictors showed that the ComCol factor was not a unique predictor of performance (Buchler et al. 2016).

As a follow-up to no-findings (Jøsok et al. 2019, Knox et al. 2017, 2019b) on individual traits associated with cyber tactical and strategic decision-making performance, Lugo et al. (2017) investigated the effects of team workload demands on performance in a CDX simulation for testing officer cadets' teamwork perceptions. Outcome measures were based on the HS framework (Jøsok et al. 2016). Previous studies (Jøsok et al. 2019, Knox et al. 2017, 2019b) showed that both cognitive and metacognitive factors could explain cyber-physical interactions, but could not explain any tactical-strategic decision-making during the CDX. ComCol performance demands showed increased involvement on tactical and strategic decision-making outcomes as well as facilitating cyber-physical transitions (Lugo et al. 2017). Only dissatisfaction with team performance was identified as a negative team factor. The results suggested that situational and team factors need to

Table 3. Overview of quantitative and mixed studies included in the review

First author, year	Design	Effect sizes	Results	Outcome	Population (N; sex)	Comments
Buchler (2016)	Correlational; naturalistic: Survey, structured observation	ComCol on: Maintain services: R2 = 0.42 (−0.13, 1.00); Scenario injects: R2 = 0.54 (−0.03, 1.13); Red team: R2 = 0.27 (−0.23, 0.79)	Maintain services: $\beta1$ = 0.65 (−0.21, 1.54)*; Scenario injects: $\beta1$ = 0.74 (−0.04, 1.53)**; Red team: $\beta0$ = −0.00 (−0.94, 0.90)*	ComCol joint positive predictor of maintain services, scenario injects, and joint negative predictor of scores against red team	Students in cyber defense competition (N = 64; sex not reported)	
Garcia-Granados (2020)	Correlational; Literature review, expert panel survey	Not applicable	45 topics identified. SLDM must know all of them. ART had highest average ranking	Overview of which topics SLDM must have knowledge about and ranked order of priority	CISOs (N = 10; sex not reported)	
Champion (2012)	Correlational: Unstructured interview, observation, TTX	Not reported	$(F, 1,15)$ = 4.584*); 60.17% correctly classified	Number of security alerts reduce team effectiveness and CTSA	Proprietary sample (N = 24; sex not reported)	Cognitive load = NASA-TLX
Finomore (2013)	Experiment; naturalistic, within-subjects design	Not reported	Correct: $F(2, 11.06)$ = 9.(0*; None (M = 87.5%), Medium (M = 87.5%), High (M = 37.5%). Time: $F(2, 9.88)$ = 14.10*; Medium (M = 15 min, Medium (M = 15 min, 30 s), None (M = 16 min, 54 s), High (M = 27 min, 48 s) inject	Untruthful statements diminish team performance	Paid participants (N = 24, m = 9)	

(continued)

Table 3. (continued)

First author, year	Design	Effect sizes	Results	Outcome	Population (N; sex)	Comments
Henshel (2016)	Correlational; naturalistic	Not reported	Average arguing 2.05 of 7; Average task redistribution 5.66 of 7	Arguing negatively correlated with TTP and Correct categorization of NIST event	US army's Computer Network Defense Teams (N = 446; M = 96%)	
Lugo (2017)	Correlational; naturalistic	X-axis: ($R2 = .245$**); Y-axis: ($R2 = .124$*)	Communication demands associated with cyber-physical actions (X) and tactical-strategic decision-making (Y)	Hybrid space performance movements operationalized (4 variables) as DV	Cyber defense cadets (N = 31; sex not reported)	IV: TWLS; DV: Hybrid space
Mermoud (2018)	Correlational survey	Spearman's p Frequency: .184–.244** Intensity: .169–.275**	Value of info, social reciprocity, institutional design, and trust associated with SIS	2 DV: Frequency & Intensity of information sharing	MELANI-net cybersecurity managers (N = 262; sex not reported)	6 hypotheses tested
Percia David (2020)	Correlational; questionnaire	Spearman's p: Resource = 0.2860; Usefulness = 0.2779; Reward = 0.0258; Reciprocity = 0.3543	Resource belief***, usefulness belief***, and reciprocity belief*** positively associated with knowledge absorption	Knowledge about which beliefs are associated with knowledge absorption of cyber threat information	MELANI-net cybersecurity managers (N = 262; sex not reported)	Follow-up of Mermoud (2018)

Notes. $P < .05 = *$, $P < .01 = **$, $P < .001 = ***$. ART = Advanced persistent threat. CDX = Cyber defense exercise. CISO = Chief information security officer. ComCol = Communication and Collaboration. CTSA = Cyber team situational awareness. DV = dependent variable. IV = independent variable. NIST = National Institute of Standards and Technology. SIS = Security information sharing. SLDM = Strategic level decision-maker. TTP = Time between start of inject to returned approval by team controller. TTX = Tabletop exercise. TWLS = Team workload scale be taken into consideration alongside individual factors to explain performance (Lugo et al. 2017).

Several factors influence cyber team SA (CTSA) among COs. Based on the observation that intra-team communication problems were fundamental challenges to CTSA among COs participating in CDXs (Champion et al. 2012), a TTX pilot study was conducted. Team performance dropped by 0.42% per security alert added, affecting perceived attack path, collaborative team report detailing the order and specifics of security breaches, and CTSA. Mental demands were somewhat high and CTSA was moderate to low and declined with increased information (Champion et al. 2012). The authors suggested that information overload drive abnormalities in both team structure and team communication, and that team cyber defense processes must be restructured to facilitate sharing of workload and information. Lack of communication was suggested to be one of the most important contributors to the findings (Champion et al. 2012). The authors did not correlate mental fatigue scores with communication metrics.

In line with findings regarding the challenges associated with communication problems in cyber teams (Champion et al. 2012), detrimental effects of arguments on team performance were reported in initial findings from a study on predictors of cyber team proficiency in CDXs (Henshel et al. 2016). The effect of communication on the following Blue Team proficiency metrics were assessed: (1) Time-to-Detect: Time between start of inject and first validated detection report, (2) Time-to-apProval (TTP): Time between start of inject to returned approval by team controller, (3) Time-to-End (TTE): Time between start of inject to blue team filing close out report, and (4) Category Correct (CatCorrect): Percent of National Institute of Standards and Technology (NIST) category of inject correctly identified by the blue team. Frequent arguing was found to be significantly and negatively correlated with TTP as well as CatCorrect. Task redistribution when necessary was significantly and positively correlated with TTE and CatCorrect (Henshel et al. 2016). The authors did not report correlation coefficients or p-values but note that most of the data will be reported elsewhere (Henshel et al. 2016).

While other studies (Champion et al. 2012, Henshel et al. 2016) mainly looked at communication with respect to cyber-attacks aimed at assets, one study (Finomore et al. 2013) sought to study the influence of human-directed cyber-attacks on team communication and performance. Distributed team members in a CDG were exposed to misleading information and effects on team processes and decision-making were measured. They all received unique factoids and had to compare them to the factoids received by other team members through communication over a shared radio channel (Finomore et al. 2013). Within-subjects design was employed and divided in conditions None, Medium, and High. For the Medium condition, the inject was suggestive and contradicted supportive information. In the High condition the injects contradicted expert factoids and were phrased as facts. There were no injects in the None condition. Injects in the High condition had the most detrimental effect on team performance both on number of correct answers as well as time spent on completion. How the injects affected communication specifically was not assessed (Finomore et al. 2013).

Knowledge Requirements of Strategic-Level Decision-Makers (SLDMs). To tackle communication problems between SLDMs and their CO teams, a study (Garcia-Granados and Bahsi 2020) tried to identify topics of knowledge requirements that could serve as basis for training or CDXs for SLDMs without IT or security background. A literature search identified 43 topics of knowledge that were sorted based on incident rate to assess their emphasis in the literature. 10 chief security information officers from different industries rated the topics on the level of knowledge needed. A higher rank meant that the topics were attributed a higher knowledge priority (Garcia-Granados and Bahsi 2020). Although having a low incident rate in the literature, "Advanced Persistent Threat" had the highest average ranking. The lowest ranked topic was "Access control models". No topic was rated as 'no knowledge' meaning that the participants meant SLDMs needed some knowledge about all the topics that were identified (Garcia-Granados and Bahsi 2016). Topics associated with third party security attained a lower average rank.

The Role of Expectations on Sharing of Cyber Threat Information. The role of incentives for Security Information Sharing (SIS) between human agents working in institutions were assessed to see if expectations of usefulness, reciprocity, institutional barriers, reputation, and trust would affect SIS (Mermoud et al. 2018). A questionnaire was administered to participants of the closed user group of the Swiss Reporting and Analysis Center for Information Assurance (MELANI) which is a government organization that provides a platform to facilitate SIS between Critical Infrastructures (Mermoud et al. 2018). Six hypotheses were tested regarding the effect of expectations on frequency and intensity of SIS, and the moderating role of trust. They found that the value of information a human agent expects to receive from SIS significantly increases the intensity of SIS, but not frequency. Expectancy of social reciprocity significantly increased both intensity and frequency of SIS, as did expectations that SIS would be facilitated by their institution. Both transactional reciprocity and trust between human agents significantly increased frequency of SIS but not intensity. Reputation was not a significant predictor of SIS. They found partial support for their hypothesis regarding the moderating role of trust. It negatively and significantly moderated the relationship between value and the intensity, but not the frequency of SIS. Trust negatively and significantly moderated the relationship between transactional reciprocity and SIS (Mermoud et al. 2018). Education was negatively associated with the frequency of SIS. Gender, age, length of membership in MELANI, and industry affiliation were not significant predictors of SIS.

The Role of Beliefs on Knowledge Absorption of Cyber Threat Information. Building on the previous findings of Mermoud et al. (2018) regarding the role of incentives on SIS, Percia David et al. (2020) assessed the relationship between various resource beliefs and tacit cybersecurity knowledge absorption in a study of cybersecurity managers participating in MELANI (the same closed user-group as in Mermoud et al. 2018). Knowledge absorption was not tested directly, but measured through participants rating the amount of exclusive information they received through SIS. They found that the belief that valuable knowledge could be acquired (resource belief), expectations of augmenting efficiency of cybersecurity production (usefulness belief), and willingness to reciprocate when receiving valuable information (reciprocity belief) were all positively associated with cybersecurity knowledge absorption. The belief that participation in knowledge-transfer processes would result in reward (reward belief) was not associated with knowledge absorption. Neither were any control variables except prior participations in ISAC events (Percia David et al. 2020).

3.2 Qualitative Studies on Cyber Threat Communication

Three studies examined the collaborative and information sharing practices of COs and made suggestions for how to improve the information sharing practice (Ahrend et al. 2016, Skopik et al. 2018, Staheli et al. 2016). One study examined the information requirements different stakeholders had to find an RCP useful (Varga et al. 2018). Two studies researched the role of team mental models (TMMs) in team communication (Hámornik and Krasznay 2018, Steinke et al. 2016). One study assessed the role various aspects of communication had on performance during CDXs (Jariwala et al. 2012). One study examined how communication impacts the level of trust given to individuals and how it affects cybersecurity risk assessment (Henshel et al. 2015). One study surveyed the literature on Technical Threat Intelligence (TTI) to define what it entails (Tounsi and Rais 2018). Table 4 summarizes the selected qualitative articles.

Table 4. Overview of qualitative studies included in the review

First author, year	Design	Results	Outcome	Population (N, sex)	Comments
Ahrend (2016)	Exploratory: semi-structured interview, user diary, thematic analysis	6 themes, 5 subthemes	Knowledge about how COs collaborate to organize threat and defense information and tailor it to the needs of the client	Threat intelligence service providers (N = 5; m = 4)	Supports Staheli (2016)
Hámornik (2018)	Exploratory: semi-structured interviews	TMM is developed and updated by both internal and external communication	Good TMMs may reduce need for communication during high-risk incident responses and under high time pressure	Industry experts operating SOCs or performing SOC related activities (N = 13; sex not reported)	Similar communication methods as reported by Ahrend (2016)
Henshel (2015)	Exploratory: review and synthesis	Trust framework with four subcategories of communication: 'accuracy', 'thoroughness or completeness', 'timeliness', and 'honesty'	Trust framework for risk assessment related to human factors in the cyber domain	Not applicable	

(*continued*)

Table 4. (*continued*)

First author, year	Design	Results	Outcome	Population (N, sex)	Comments
Jariwala (2012)	Exploratory: observation, questionnaires, focus group	Distributed leadership, open task communication, active feedback, asking for help, offering aid crucial in cyber team performance	Communication aspects relevant for cyber team performance	Computer security students (N = 20; m = 18)	
Skopik (2016)	Exploratory: review/survey	Suggestions to increase and optimize information sharing among COs and stakeholders	Structural overview of the dimensions of cyber threat information sharing	Not applicable	
Staheli (2016)	Exploratory; semi-structured interviews	COs collaborate and communicate more with each other than decision-makers. COs are dis-incentivized to share CTI	A user-centered collaborative system for COs called Cyber Analyst Real-Time Integrated Notebook Application	Cybersecurity personnel spanning several job junctions and 8 sectors (N = 37; sex not reported)	Supports Ahrend et al. (2016)
Steinke (2015)	Exploratory: review	Methods for improving communication and developing TMMs for CERTs	Suggestions for enhancement of CERT communication	EMS teams, MR teams, NPPO teams	
Tounsi (2018)	Exploratory: review	Trust is an important factor for successful sharing of threat intelligence	Identification of factors when sharing threat intelligence	Not applicable	Supports Henshel (2015) and Steinke (2015)

(*continued*)

Table 4. (*continued*)

First author, year	Design	Results	Outcome	Population (N, sex)	Comments
Varga (2018)	Exploratory: open-ended survey	Enriched, non-speculative information about an event and how to mitigate it in the short- and long-term. No one requested information on adversarial behavior	RCP Information elements that are useful for stakeholder's CSA	National government agencies, regional county administrative boards, county council, local municipal actors, commercial companies that mainly operate nation-wide infrastructure (N = 28; Sex not reported)	

Notes. CERT = Cyber emergency response team. CO = Cyber operator. CSA = Cyber situational awareness. EMS = Emergency medical systems. MR = Military response. NPPO = Nuclear power plant operating. RCP = Recognized cyber picture. SOC = Security operation center. TMM = Team mental model.

Interviews on the SIS Practices of COs. Analyst level COs engage in several informal collaborative and coordination practices when gathering CTI (Ahrend et al. 2016, Staheli et al. 2016). The information needed about a threat differ between clients, thus, RCPs need to be enriched with client-specific information (Ahrend et al. 2016, Staheli et al. 2016). COs communicate through email and phone calls with clients to identify their CTI needs, which is done through onboarding procedures and ongoing communication centered around CTI reports (Ahrend et al. 2016). Gathering information on similar threats that occurred in the past is called gathering Threat and Defense Knowledge (TDK). If a CO was not the one investigating the original cyber threat, COs communicate with the CO who did to gather TDK (Ahrend et al. 2016). This is done by requesting artifacts and information either by face-to-face communication or over email. COs learn about who have encountered similar threats through team meetings, conferences, blogs, and eavesdropping on conversations in and around the office (Ahrend et al. 2016). If COs cannot find information about threats they often assume it does not exist. Existing databases for SIS is circumvented due to not meeting the needs of the COs (Ahrend et al. 2016). COs are often de-incentivized to share data or interim analyses as their reputation as experts is built upon being the one to uncover cyber threats (Staheli et al. 2016) and not sharing information is common (Skopik et al. 2018).

The collaborative ecosystem may involve many organizations with CSA being distributed across COs but the collaborative practices are less common higher up in the SOC hierarchy (Staheli et al. 2016). A typical decision-making hierarchy can be structured with analyst level COs at the bottom, then further up you have supervisors, managers, and then directors at the top (Staheli et al. 2016). While analyst level COs make decisions about what information to include in the RCP, strategic level COs make decisions about whether to send or revise RCPs. Interaction is often uni-dimensional with information being 'pushed up' and decisions being 'pushed down' the hierarchy (Staheli et al. 2016). A centralized system that incentivizes documenting, SIS and that allows for organizing files to avoid 'cluttering' is needed to facilitate communication of CTI between COs (Ahrend et al. 2016, Staheli et al. 2016). Staheli et al. (2016) proposed a user-centered collaborative system for COs but it needs testing.

Review on the SIS Practices of COs. In their extensive survey, Skopik et al. (2016) identify five primary dimensions of information sharing: (1) Efficient cooperation and coordination, (2) Legal and regulatory landscape, (3) Standardization efforts, (4) Regional and International implementations, and (5) Technology integration into organizations (Skopik et al. 2016). The authors discuss two taxonomies for information and note that TS-CERT taxonomy (Kácha 2014) is more convenient due to the main categories being universal while sub-categories being part of the description rather than a classification schema. The authors also identify 4 scenarios where cybersecurity information is shared; (1) SIS about recent or ongoing incidents; (2) SIS about service dependencies; (3) SIS about the technical service status, and; (4) when requesting assistance of organizations (Skopik et al. 2016). Shortcomings regarding SIS practices concern Cyber Emergency Response Teams (CERTs) not sharing incident data with other CERTs (ENISA 2011). Recommendations were made to enrich incident information with additional metadata to provide insights into observed events (ENISA 2011) and to develop verification methods and criteria for assessing the quality of the data sources. There was demand for establishment of SIS communities with defined scopes (ISO 2012). A CTI exchange (ITU-T 2012) model was proposed.

Interview on Stakeholder's RCP Information Requirements. Most of the reviewed studies approach RCPs from the perspective of SOCs. To address the limited research on stakeholder's RCP needs, one study examined the information elements an RCP must contain to be perceived as relevant for the stakeholder's CSA (Varga et al. 2018). Respondents said RCPs needed non-speculative factual descriptions of the events leading up to an incident and that information came from multiple trustworthy sources; otherwise the quality of the information had to be explicitly stated (Varga et al. 2018). The RCP needed information on the internal state of one's own organization, correct time stamps of events, affected location, size of event, up-to-date picture of organizational stance, all taken and planned actions, explicit view of one's own information requirements, communication plan with approved messages, whom to coordinate responses with, and list of available resources. Difficulties regarding information sharing such as adaptation of information to the situation and receivers were mentioned. The information needed in a RCP depended on the situation but included operational information (Varga et al. 2018). Most wanted information on the consequences an incident had to one's own organization and how it would evolve; few wanted to know the impact on other organizations. Differences were seen between regional and service-specific actors, where regional actors need RCPs to facilitate crisis management collaboration while service-specific actors use RCPs to maintain continuity in a service (e.g. electricity) provided to customers and to inform governments agencies with information for a broader perspective. No one asked for information about adversarial behavior (Varga et al. 2018).

Interview on the Role of TMMs in SOC Team Communication. Due to the known role of TMMs on team performance, Hámornik and Krasznay (2018) explored the role of team communication on TMMs in SOC teams. Communication facilitating team-level cognitive processes needs to be explicit and is more effective prior to security events. When security events occur, cognitive load is high, capacity for effective communication is low, and coordination is implicit (Hámornik and Krasznay 2018). 13 industry experts who are operating a SOC or performing tasks related to SOCs were interviewed using a semi-structured approach. They reported that local team members communicate within the team verbally or by using email, chat, or ticketing systems. Remote teams communicate via computer-mediated channels, phone calls, and occasional but rare face-to-face meetings (Hámornik and Krasznay 2018). The TMMs are developed and updated by both internal and external communication. If the mental models are well functioning, explicit communication and coordination activities may not be required during high-risk incident responses and under high time pressure. The authors propose that team cognitions such as constructing and updating TMMs via communication is key in SOC team performance and suggest that research should be focused on measuring the effect of communication on TMMs (Hámornik and Krasznay 2018).

Review on the Role of TMMs in Team Communication. CERTs are composed of two or more individuals who prepare for and respond to cybersecurity incidents. By examining other emergency response team's methods of adaptation to incidents, Steinke et al. (2015) identified 5 areas that could be improved to increase CERTs effectiveness. One area concerned enhancement of communication. Information richness and reduction in complexity of interaction was important for effective communication; more one-way communication and less two-way exchanges of information. All necessary information should be communicated at once. The authors (Steinke et al. 2015) propose that CERTs can develop TMMs and transactive memory through cross-training, guided team self-correction training, role identification behaviors, pre-mission communication briefings, individual and team after-action reviews and debriefings pointing to where communication broke down, where interactions and coordination did not occur where they should have, and by making electronic knowledge maps displaying team member roles and expertise (Steinke et al. 2015). The authors note that the dynamic and evolving nature of cyber can make it hard to adopt strategies from other incident response teams and must therefore be experimentally tested on CERTs.

Observation and Focus Group on the Role of Communication on Team Performance During CDXs. Among all the studies on cyber team communication, only one detailed the goal of communication within teams (Jariwala et al. 2012). Two cybersecurity teams, Team A and Team B were observed to assess the influence of team communication and coordination on performance. Team A outperformed Team B. Team A had distributed leadership among three members which facilitated sharing of completed tasks and information. Team B had one leader who at times was uncertain about what the team was working on. Team A openly discussed each other's tasks and provided feedback. When

Team A members needed help with a task, the team adjusted and assisted the team member until they could resume independence. Team A members asked for and offered aid more than they planned and assigned roles. When a task could not be completed, leaders would instruct members to pick up another task where completion was feasible. Team B had members that never spoke during the length of the CDX, partly attributed to cultural and language barriers (Jariwala et al. 2012).

Review on the Impacts of Communication on the Level of Trust Given to COs and How It Affects Cybersecurity Risk Assessment. In their review of trust as a human factor in cybersecurity risk assessment, Henshel et al. (2015) describes how their 'trust framework' relates to communication in cyber defense situations. According to their framework, trust is increased by a CO who can effectively communicate with superiors and other COs, log incident reports with minimal false negatives and false positives, communicate information in a timely manner, and employ competency when applying cyber defense tools (Henshel et al. 2015). Communication is efficient when there is common ground and it is built on shared mental models. Based on the concept of defender trust, they divide communication in four subcategories; 'accuracy', 'thoroughness or completeness', 'timeliness', and 'honesty' (Henshel et al. 2015). Effective communication for cyber defenders requires timeliness as any amount of wasted time will increase the window for attackers to do damage or go undetected. Honesty is integral to trust whilst dishonest communication harms both team effectiveness and the accuracy of defensive efforts in the cyber domain (Henshel et al. 2015).

Review on Subdivisions of Technical Threat Intelligence. In response to the diversity of CTI research and subsequent lack of consensus of what CTI is, Tounsi and Rais (2018) reviewed the literature on TTI, a subset of CTI, and its multiple sources, the gathering methods, information lifespan, and intended receivers. The authors found that fast sharing of CTI alone was not sufficient to avoid targeted attacks (Tounsi and Rais 2018). In support of the framework suggested by Henshel et al. (2015), trust was identified to be an important factor for successful SIS; trusted environments and anonymous sharing were listed as possible solutions when organizations engage in SIS (Tounsi and Rais 2018). The interconnectedness of organizational SIS is increased through the recent use of portals and blogs to exchange semi-automatic threat information. When the quantity of threat information is large, security teams must contextualize the threat data they collect with the specific vulnerabilities and weaknesses they have internally (Tounsi and Rais 2018). As in the reports of Ahrend et al. (2016) and Staheli et al. (2016), a need for common standards for information sharing were expressed (Tounsi and Rais 2018).

4 Discussion

The aim of this paper was to: (1) outline how human-human communication performance in cybersecurity settings have been studied, (2) uncover areas where there is potential for developing common standards for information exchange, and (3) provide guidance for future research efforts. We found that very little research has been done on human-human communication in CTSs and most of the current studies are correlational and exploratory in nature. One study assessed what kind of information that was deemed useful for stakeholders' RCP (Varga et al. 2018). None of the stakeholders interviewed listed adversarial behavior as useful. This could indicate that stakeholders are more oriented towards action in the physical world than in cyber. This can be useful knowledge for COs and suggest use cases for the HS framework (Jøsok et al. 2016, 2017) and the OLB model (Knox et al. 2018) which address these potential problems at both a theoretical-conceptual and practical level, respectfully. The HS framework might be a useful tool for stakeholders to become aware of their own cognitive 'blind spots', while the OLB model can be used by COs to enrich CTI with information on adversarial behavior and make salient how this behavior contributes to the evolution of the CTS.

Steinke et al. (2015) suggested that enriched, one-way communication of cyber threat information where all necessary information is communicated once would enhance CERTs cybersecurity performance. The relevance of these findings is addressed in the HS framework (Fig. 1, a–d; Jøsok et al. 2016, 2017) which illustrates how communication between individuals located across the HS gets increasingly complex when information is relayed across the space and individuals. When cyber threats occur, timely responses are often key, especially during cyber threat incidents with high time pressure. For one-way communication to be effective, updated and effective TMMs are necessary (Hámornik and Krasznay 2018, Steinke et al. 2015). Cyber TMMs that are updated through communication and coordination prior to the occurrence of cyber incidents may allow for less communication during high-risk incidents with high time pressure (Hámornik and Krasznay 2018, Steinke et al. 2015). Cyber teams perform better in CDXs when they spend more of their time communicating help needs and aid-offerings than planning and role-assigning (Jariwala et al. 2012). Based on these findings, longitudinal studies on cyber TMMs and how they relate to the evolution of communication practices could provide novel insights into how and when cyber threat communication can be optimized for performance.

Support for the notion that too much communication during cyber threat incidents can be detrimental to performance is seen in naturalistic studies showing that ComCol negatively predict scores against attacker teams (Buchler et al. 2016). This, however, might depend on the quality and type of communication, the aspect of performance that is in question (Buchler et al. 2016, Champion et al. 2012, Henshel et al. 2016, Jariwala et al. 2012), and level of expertise (Lugo et al. 2017, Buchler et al. 2016). For example, communication positively predicts handling of both maintenance tasks and scenario injects (Buchler et al. 2016) and productive communication regarding task progress-updates and stating the need of help can enhance incident handling (Jariwala et al. 2012). Under-communication can also be detrimental to team performance by leading to team members working on the same tasks without knowing (Champion et al. 2012). Distributed team leadership might mitigate these issues if individuals holding leadership positions also spend time communicating with team members to know which tasks they are working on (Jariwala et al. 2012). Indeed, the dynamic and evolving nature of cyber and the broad demands of expertise might favor distributed leadership (Jøsok et al. 2017). ComCol performance demands influence tactical and strategic decision-making outcomes and cyber-physical transitions in the HS (Lugo et al. 2017). As opposed to the Buchler et al. (2016) study on CO experts, these cadets were novices. ComCol demands might be necessary in training and development, but may become less relevant with experience.

To update their own and clients CSA, COs enrich RCPs with useful TDK by communicating with both team members and COs from other organizations as well as their clients when investigating a cyber incident (Ahrend et al. 2016, Staheli et al. 2016). This practice is most common for analyst level COs but less and less common higher up in the decision-making hierarchy (Staheli et al. 2016). Albeit making decision-making more effective, these structural inefficiencies can be detrimental to CSA and shared mental models in the organization, cause communication and coordination problems, and potentially reduce creativity among COs (Staheli et al. 2016). This can be illustrated with the HS framework (Jøsok et al. 2016) when COs and SLDMs are in different quadrants of the HS without knowing where the other organizational members are. Studies assessing or manipulating the RCP-related resource-beliefs of COs and SLDMs (Mermoud et al. 2018, Percia David et al. 2020) may be useful in determining the effect of shared mental models on the resulting RCP.

The reviewed literature has several limitations. Most of the studies were the first to assess the relationships they studied and have thus not been replicated, although they seem to converge on some common principles. Half of quantitative studies (Buchler et al. 2016, Lugo et al. 2017, Mermoud et al. 2018, Percia David et al. 2020) report effect sizes and one study did not report effect sizes nor p-values (Henshel et al. 2016). Sensitivity issues might be the reason why few studies report participant characteristics such as which sector respondents belong to. The Varga et al. (2018) study was conducted exclusively on Swedish participants with a large disproportion of respondents belonging to national agencies and critical infrastructure operators, meaning that the robustness of the findings may vary according to which sector provided the answers. This issue is discussed by the authors (Varga et al. 2018). In general, cybersecurity personnel are hard to access, and naturalistic studies are tricky to conduct because contextual variables are hard to manipulate partly due to restricted collaboration with CDX organizers. This is apparent in the reviewed literature and is a barrier that needs to be overcome. Few studies (Jariwala et al. 2012, Steinke et al. 2015) elaborate on the quality and characteristics of communication. A focused effort is needed to develop quantitative measures of communication that can be readily applied in CDXs in addition to measures of TMM development. Moreover, only two studies assessed individual and team measures (Champion et al. 2012, Lugo et al. 2017) although only one study assessed the relationship between these measures (Lugo et al., 2017). Thus, there is also a need for studies simultaneously assessing individual and team factors related to communication and performance.

4.1 Conclusion

Communication in CTSs has not received much attention and the nature and quality of studies vary. Studies assessing both team factors and individual factors simultaneously are almost non-existent. We found only one study where variables were manipulated to see their effects on communication and more basic and experimental studies are needed. CDX organizers could benefit from collaborating with cognitive scientists to experimentally manipulate aspects of the CDX such that new insights can be achieved.

It would be useful to manipulate and quantify TMM development prior to and during a CDX or TTX to measure the effect on communication. Standards for characterizing and assessing cyber team communication need to be developed and implemented in studies.

Funding. This study was conducted as part of the Advancing Cyber Defense by Improved Communication of Recognized Cyber Threat Situations (ACDICOM; project number 302941) project. ACDICOM is funded by the Norwegian Research Council.

References

Agyepong, E., et al.: Challenges and performance metrics for security operations center analysts: a systematic review. J. Cyber Secur. Technol. **4**(3), 1–28 (2020). https://doi.org/10.1080/237 42917.2019.1698178

Ahrend, J.M., et al.: On the collaborative practices of cyber threat intelligence analysts to develop and utilize tacit threat and defence knowledge. In: 2016 International Conference on Cyber Situational Awareness, Data Analytics and Assessment (CyberSA) (2016). https://doi.org/10. 1109/cybersa.2016.7503279

Barford, P., et al.: Cyber SA: situational awareness for cyber defense. In: Cyber Situational Awareness, pp. 3–13. Springer, Cham (2009). https://doi.org/10.1007/978-1-4419-0140-8_1

Buchler, N., et al.: Mission command in the age of network-enabled operations: social network analysis of information sharing and situation awareness. Front. Psychol. **7**, 937 (2016)

Champion, M.A., et al.: Team-based cyber defense analysis. In: 2012 IEEE International Multi-Disciplinary Conference on Cognitive Methods in Situation Awareness and Decision Support (2012). https://doi.org/10.1109/cogsima.2012.6188386

ENISA: Proactive detection of network security incidents (2011). https://www.enisa.europa.eu/ activities/cert/support/proactive-detection/survey-analysis. Accessed 20 Mar 2021

Finomore, V, et al.: Effects of cyber disruption in a distributed team decision making task. In: Proceedings of the Human Factors and Ergonomics Society Annual Meeting, vol. 57, no. 1, pp. 394–398 (2013)

Forsythe, C., Silva, A., Stevens-Adams, S., Bradshaw, J.: Human dimension in cyber operations research and development priorities. In: Schmorrow, D.D., Fidopiastis, C.M. (eds.) AC 2013. LNCS (LNAI), vol. 8027, pp. 418–422. Springer, Heidelberg (2013). https://doi.org/10.1007/ 978-3-642-39454-6_44

Franke, U., Brynielsson, J.: Cyber situational awareness – a systematic review of the literature. Comput. Secur. **46**, 18–31 (2014). https://doi.org/10.1016/j.cose.2014.06.008

Garcia-Granados, F. Bahsi, H.: Cybersecurity knowledge requirements for strategic level decision makers. In: International Conference on Cyber Warfare and Security 2020 (2020). https://doi. org/10.34190/ICCWS.20.102

Hámornik, B.P., Krasznay, C.: A team-level perspective of human factors in cyber security: security operations centers. In: Nicholson, D. (ed.) AHFE 2017. AISC, vol. 593, pp. 224–236. Springer, Cham (2018). https://doi.org/10.1007/978-3-319-60585-2_21

Henshel, D., et al.: Trust as a human factor in holistic cyber security risk assessment. Procedia Manuf. **3**, 1117–1124 (2015)

Henshel, D.S., et al.: Predicting proficiency in cyber defense team exercises. In: MILCOM 2016 - 2016 IEEE Military Communications Conference (2016). https://doi.org/10.1109/milcom. 2016.7795423

ISO: ISO/IEC27010: Information technology – security techniques –information security management for inter-sector and interorganizational communications (2012)

ITU-T: Recommendation ITU-T x.1500 cybersecurity information exchange techniques (2012)

Jariwala, S., et al.: Influence of team communication and coordination on the performance of teams at the iCTF Competition. In: Proceedings of the Human Factors and Ergonomics Society Annual Meeting, vol. 56, no. 1, pp. 458–462 (2012)

Jøsok, Ø., Knox, B.J., Helkala, K., Lugo, R.G., Sütterlin, S., Ward, P.: Exploring the hybrid space. In: Schmorrow, D.D.D., Fidopiastis, C.M.M. (eds.) AC 2016. LNCS (LNAI), vol. 9744, pp. 178–188. Springer, Cham (2016). https://doi.org/10.1007/978-3-319-39952-2_18

Jøsok, Ø., Knox, B.J., Helkala, K., Wilson, K., Sütterlin, S., Lugo, R.G., Ødegaard, T.: Macrocognition applied to the hybrid space: team environment, functions and processes in cyber operations. In: Schmorrow, D.D., Fidopiastis, C.M. (eds.) AC 2017. LNCS (LNAI), vol. 10285, pp. 486–500. Springer, Cham (2017). https://doi.org/10.1007/978-3-319-58625-0_35

Jøsok, Ø., et al.: Self-regulation and cognitive agility in cyber operations. Front. Psychol. **10**, 875 (2019)

Kácha, P.: Idea: security event taxonomy mapping. In: 18th International Conference on Circuits, Systems, Communications and Computers, 2014 (2014)

Knox, B.J., et al.: Socio-technical communication: the hybrid space and the OLB model for science-based cyber education. Mil. Psychol. **30**(4), 350–359 (2018)

Knox, B.J., Lugo, R.G., Jøsok, Ø., Helkala, K., Sütterlin, S.: Towards a cognitive agility index: the role of metacognition in human computer interaction. In: Stephanidis, C. (ed.) HCI 2017. CCIS, vol. 713, pp. 330–338. Springer, Cham (2017). https://doi.org/10.1007/978-3-319-58750-9_46

Knox, B.J., et al.: Cognisance as a human factor in military cyber defence education. IFAC-PapersOnLine **52**(19), 163–168 (2019)

Knox, B.J., et al.: Slow education and cognitive agility: improving military cyber cadet cognitive performance for better governance of cyberpower. Int. J. Cyber Warfare Terrorism (IJCWT) **9**(1), 48–66 (2019)

Lugo, R., et al.: Team workload demands influence on cyber detection performance. In: 13th International Conference on Naturalistic Decision Making 2017, pp. 223–225 (2017)

Mermoud, A., et al.: Incentives for human agents to share security information: a model and an empirical test. In: 2018 Workshop on the Economics of Information Security (WEIS), Innsbruck (2018)

Moher, D., et al.: Preferred reporting items for systematic reviews and meta-analyses: the PRISMA statement. J. Clin. Epidemiol. **62**(10), 1006–1012 (2009). https://doi.org/10.1016/j.jclinepi.2009.06.005

Muniz, J., et al.: Security Operations Center: Building, Operating, and Maintaining Your SOC. Cisco Press, Indianapolis (2015)

Pala, A., Zhuang, J.: Information sharing in cybersecurity: a review. Decis. Anal. (2019). https://doi.org/10.1287/deca.2018.0387

Percia David, D., et al.: Knowledge absorption for cyber-security: the role of human beliefs. Comput. Hum. Behav. **106**, 106255 (2020). https://doi.org/10.1016/j.chb.2020.106255

Skopik, F., et al.: A problem shared is a problem halved: a survey on the dimensions of collective cyber defense through security information sharing. Comput. Secur. **60**, 154–176 (2016). https://doi.org/10.1016/j.cose.2016.04.003

Staheli, D., et al.: Collaborative data analysis and discovery for cyber security. In: SOUPS 2016: Twelfth Symposium on Usable Privacy and Security (2016)

Steinke, J., et al.: Improving cybersecurity incident response team effectiveness using teams-based research. IEEE Secur. Priv. **13**(4), 20–29 (2015). https://doi.org/10.1109/msp.2015.71

Tikk-Ringas, E., et al.: Cyber security as a field of military education and study. Joint Forces Q. **75**(4), 57–60 (2014)

Tounsi, W., Rais, H.: A survey on technical threat intelligence in the age of sophisticated cyber attacks. Comput. Secur. **72**, 212–233 (2018)

Varga, S., et al.: Information requirements for national level cyber situational awareness. In: 2018 IEEE/ACM International Conference on Advances in Social Networks Analysis and Mining (ASONAM) (2018)

Whitman, M.E., Mattord, H.J.: Principles of Information Security, 4th edn. Course Technology, Boston (2012)

Zachary, W., et al.: Context as a cognitive process: an integrative framework for supporting decision making. In: The 8th International Conference on Semantic Technologies for Intelligence, Defense, and Security (STIDS 2013) (2013)

Zanenga, P.: Knowledge eyes: Nature and emergence in society, culture, and economy. In: 2014 International Conference on Engineering, Technology and Innovation (ICE) (2014)

Monitoring Attention of Crane Operators During Load Oscillations Using Gaze Entropy Measures

Jouh Yeong Chew[1,2(✉)], Koichi Ohtomi[1], and Hiromasa Suzuki[1]

[1] Department of Precision Engineering, The University of Tokyo, 7-3-1 Hongo, Bunkyo-ku, Tokyo 113-8656, Japan
koichi.ohtomi@delight.t.u-tokyo.ac.jp,
suzuki@den.t.u-tokyo.ac.jp
[2] National Institute of Advanced Industrial Science and Technology, AIST Tsukuba Central 1, 1-1-1 Umezono, Tsukuba, Ibaraki 305-8560, Japan
jy.chew@aist.go.jp

Abstract. This study evaluates mobile crane operator's gaze pattern to discriminate effects of skills and performance. Scalar variables define the degree of disorder and distribution of gaze fixations between discrete Area-of-Interests (AOI). A field experiment was carried out to measure gaze behavior of operators from two skill categories. Gaze fixations on discrete Area-of-Interests (AOIs) are analyzed using the first order Markov transition matrix. Matrix elements are mapped to scalar variables such as gaze entropy for statistical analysis. The conventional mapping method is revised to accommodate sparse transition matrix resulting from large number of AOIs. The results suggest the revised scalar variables can be interpreted like those for non-sparse transition matrices. More importantly, the findings suggest statistically significant correlations between operators' gaze patterns and performance. Therefore, operator attention is well-defined by these variables which are promising for development of work support or guidance system to facilitate crane operation.

Keywords: Load oscillation · Gaze entropy · Attentional control · Work performance · Expert-novice differences · Sparse Markov chains

1 Introduction

1.1 Mobile Crane Operation

Basic crane operation consists of four independent inputs such as slew, boom length, boom angle, and hoist, as shown in Fig. 1(a). Despite this, crane operation is not easy. The challenges are load oscillations [1, 2] and lag of control input [3]. Most studies focus on addressing load oscillation because lag of control input is naturally addressed when operators become accustomed with the delay [3]. Input shaping control [4] and second order sliding mode control [5] were proposed to overcome load oscillations. However, these solutions are black box to operators and provide little information to help them

© Springer Nature Switzerland AG 2021
C. Stephanidis et al. (Eds.): HCII 2021, LNCS 13096, pp. 44–61, 2021.
https://doi.org/10.1007/978-3-030-90328-2_3

improve their skills. Operators depend on practice to slowly get accustomed to these challenges.

Since safety is paramount in operation of heavy machineries, it is desirable for novice operators to work efficiently in the shortest time possible. This paper presents a novel approach to decipher gaze behavior of operators to understand expert-novice differences. Findings from this study serve as groundworks of future studies to develop work support system to facilitate crane operation. The primary crane-operator interaction is visual and motor (hand manipulation of operation levers). Figure 1(b) shows the operator's view from work cabin, and Fig. 1(c) shows the layout of operation levers labelled according to Fig. 1(a). A typical gaze representation tend to cover the interior cabin layout and the exterior work environment.

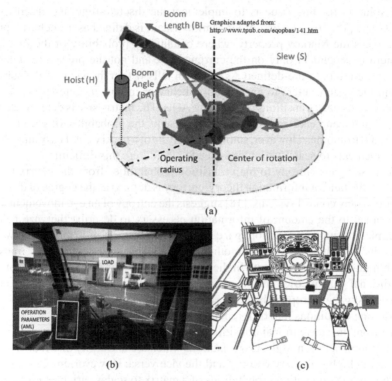

Fig. 1. Crane (a) operation, (b) the operator's view, and (c) the layout of operation levers.

1.2 Quantitative Representation of Gaze Behavior

Gaze behavior analyses are promising to address the difficulties facing crane operators because visual information constitutes a significant part of the information necessary for operators to control load oscillations. Experienced operators typically monitor fluctuation of the load during crane operation to maintain its stability. [6] investigated pilots' monitoring strategies and their performance. It suggests monitoring failures contribute to communication break-down between pilot and automation. This finding indicates the significance of visual input in decision making. Several studies also evaluated relationship between gaze and different mental modes - task load [7], fatigue [8], curiosity [9], and skills [10].

Other applications of gaze behavior analyses are in Kansei engineering [11] and medicine [12]. Gaze behavior analyses are commonly carried out using scan paths [8, 13] and fixation frequency [14]. Other metrics such as dwell time and pupil diameter were used by [6, 10]. However, these measures are inadequate to provide a telegraphic representation of gaze behavior to facilitate statistical analyses. For example, dwell time and fixation frequency are commonly calculated for each area-of-interest (AOI). Therefore, it is not easy to carry out statistical analyses for gaze behavior because representation becomes more complex with higher number of AOIs.

One solution for this issue is to implement the discrete-time and discrete-space Markov Chain [15, 16]. The first order Markov Chain is defined as a stochastic process which satisfies the Markov property, where conditional probability of the future state of a system is dependent only on the current state, and not the preceding states. The discrete-space refers to pre-defined AOIs which falls within the view of the subject of study, and the system refers to gaze fixation behavior in this discrete-space. A square matrix represents gaze transitions on different AOIs. The matrix size is determined by the number of AOIs, and each matrix element represents the probability of gaze transition from one AOI to another. However, statistical analysis of a matrix is not easy and mapping of matrix elements to scalar variables is needed to address this difficulty.

[7, 17] used gaze entropy to map transition probabilities from the matrix to scalar variables. In the field of information theory, entropy is defined as the degree of disorder or uncertainty of any control systems. [18] suggests the entropy of an eye movement system is proportional to the amount of information necessary to describe the gaze behavior. For example, a dynamic or random gaze with equal transition probabilities between all AOIs results in high entropy. On the other hand, a stable gaze without any transitions results in minimal or zero entropy. In the same study [18], gaze entropy was compared with traditional gaze metrics such as dwell time and mean saccade amplitude, and the results suggest gaze entropy is better at sorting drivers into different age groups, and at sorting driving conditions into different task load.

Apart from the conventional transition entropy, [9] used stationary entropy to define gaze distribution between AOIs. Gaze fixations which are uniformly distributed between AOIs result in high stationary entropy and the vice versa. However, implementation of this method to map transition probabilities of a matrix to scalar variables is constrained to non-sparse matrices, which do not consist of zero elements. Consequently, application is limited to cases with small number of AOIs because sparseness of a transition matrix increases proportionally with the number of AOIs. Prior knowledge of gaze distribution is required for AOI definition to avoid defining AOIs with zero gaze fixations. Use of dynamic AOIs is also not feasible because of the same reason. Thus, solution to facilitate implementation of gaze entropy for sparse transition matrices is necessary because it increases the flexibility of AOI definition in different case studies.

1.3   Objectives

This study extends some findings from [19, 20] to map transition probabilities of a sparse transition matrix to scalar variables, hereafter referred to as gaze metrics. The following extensions address the insufficiencies in the preceding works. (1) Gaze entropies are adapted for sparse transition matrices and the results are consistent with the original interpretation in different experiment settings using different types of eye tracking devices. Generalization of the solution provides flexibility in defining type and size of AOIs. (2) Gaze metrics are revised to better represent continuous gaze fixations and operator attention is defined using summation of these metrics. (3) The expert-novice differences of gaze behavior are evaluated using statistical tests and the responses are consistent with their performance. The following null and alternative hypotheses are tested.

H_0: Non-beginner crane operators will exhibit gaze attention like beginners when facing difficulties during work
H_1: Non-beginner crane operators will exhibit unique gaze attention distinct from beginners to detect and handle difficulties during work

2   Methodology

2.1   Gaze Metrics

The first order Markov Chain is used to represent gaze behavior. AOIs are modeled as state space $S = \{s_1, s_2, \ldots, s_M\}$, where M represents total number of AOIs. Gaze behavior measured using the Tobii Glasses 2 eye tracker are down sampled before being used to model the Markov Chain. Given X_n is the AOI at n th time step and $i, j \in S$, transition from state i to state j is represented by $P(X_{n+1} = j | X_n = i) = p_{ij}$, where p_{ij} is an element of transition matrix. Transition and stationary probability are calculated by $p_{ij} = n_{ij} / \sum_j n_{ij}$ and $\pi_i = n_i / \sum_i n_i$, respectively. Variable n_{ij} represents transition count from state i to j, and $n_i = \sum_j n_{ij}$. The model considers additional rules $p_{ij} = 0$ and $p_{ii} = 1$ when $n_i = 0$ based on [21]. Therefore, $\sum_j^M p_{ij} = 1$. Although Markov Chain was used in [15, 16], there are inadequate works to map transition probabilities of the matrix to scalar variables. [9] introduced entropy measures for non-sparse and small model (three AOIs) and cited higher number of AOIs and model sparseness as challenges. [20] used gaze metrics to evaluate gaze pattern in virtual environment on a screen using fixed type eye-tracker.

This study proposes a method to address the challenge cited in [9] and generalizes the solution to evaluate gaze pattern in different environment settings and devices. An arbitrary small variable α is added to the *log* term in Eqs. (1) and (2) to calculate zero elements of sparse Markov model. Stationary and transition entropies are represented by H_s and H_t, respectively. This adaptation results in interpretation of entropies that is like the original ones. A more uniformly distributed gaze results in larger H_s, and a more random gaze results in larger H_t. From the perspective of information theory, H_s and H_t refer to the degree of disorder of a system. In layman terms, they indicate the number of configurations which could be derived from a system. Larger amount of random data tends to result in larger entropies, and vice versa. This adapted method is more pragmatic to compute gaze entropies because implementations of gaze behavior analyses in real environment commonly require large number of AOIs. In addition, gaze attention on these AOIs is usually not known, leading to sparse transition matrices.

$$H_s = -\sum_{i \in X} \pi_i \log(\pi_i + \alpha). \tag{1}$$

$$H_t = -\sum_{i \in X} \pi_i \sum_{j \in X} p_{ij} \log(p_{ij} + \alpha). \tag{2}$$

Other gaze metrics are also derived from sparse transition matrix. Metric D indicates continuous gaze fixations (duration). In the preceding work [19], this metric was calculated using norm-2 of eigenvalues $\|\lambda\|_2$ of the transition matrix. However, this value is biased when the number of gaze samples is small. Therefore, it is not an ideal representation of continuous gaze fixations. As the solution, this study uses the proportion of gaze fixations on each AOI as weights in Eq. (3). Thus, a stable gaze on the same AOI results in smaller metric D. Continuous fixations on the same AOI results in higher transition probabilities for diagonal elements of a transformation matrix. Intuitively, this information is a good indicator of gaze stability. Metric den in Eq. (4) indicates sparseness of the transition matrix. A larger value suggests presence of transitions between more AOIs during the experiment. Introduction of these metrics is useful to better interpret enlarged and sparse Markov model common for real environments. This study defines operator attention as the summation of gaze metrics represented by metric sum in Eq. (5).

$$D = \left| \sqrt{M} - \sqrt{\sum_{i \in X} (\pi_i \lambda_i)^2} \right|. \tag{3}$$

$$den = \frac{\#Non - zero\ matrix\ elements}{M^2}. \tag{4}$$

$$sum = H_s + H_t + D + den. \tag{5}$$

2.2 Grid-Based AOI Definition

This section discusses the correlation of gaze metrics with randomness and uniformity using examples of a simple gaze experiment. It is noteworthy that this experiment focuses on discussing the behavior of gaze metrics given any gaze patterns. Individual difference is not the subject of interest. Figure 2(a) shows the Tobii Pro X3–120 used to measure gaze behavior. The digital reproduction of "The Tempest" oil painting in Fig. 2(b) is used as the stimulus. The distance of the participant's eye from the screen is approximately 750 mm and the size of the stimulus is 215 mm × 240 mm. One participant carried out two tasks to entice varying gaze behavior to explain the gaze metrics. One of them is a 'search' task, hereafter referred to as Task A, where the participant searched for three attractive objects and simultaneously said their names aloud. The other one is a 'describe' task, hereafter referred to as Task B, where the participant verbally described appeal of the most attractive object.

Gaze plots in Figs. 3(a) to (b) suggest gaze of task A is more uniformly distributed and random compared to B. This behavior is consistent with time plots in Figs. 3(e) to (f), where gaze of task A fixates evenly on all AOIs with short delay compared to B, which focuses on one AOI with long delay. Figures 3(c) and (d) show the corresponding transition matrices. Diagonal elements are probabilities of gaze fixating on the same AOI, which are an implicit representation of gaze duration. Non-diagonal elements are probabilities of gaze fixating on different AOIs. Gaze metrics - D, den, H_s and H_t, are shown on top of Figs. 3(a) to (b).

It is noteworthy that all gaze metrics of task A are larger than those of B. This indicates random gaze transition and uniformly distributed gaze result in larger H_t and H_s. Metric *den* represents sparseness of gaze transitions and uniformity of the distribution of attention. It is larger for task A because gaze is more random and covers all but one matrix element in Fig. 3(c). Metric D is an implicit representation of fixation duration. Compared to [19], this study corrects the bias resulting from small number of fixations on an AOI. Referring to Fig. 3(f), small number of fixations on AOI2 causes bias in transition probabilities on the second row of Fig. 3(d). The transition probability is small, and it is not an ideal representation because of the small samples. Thus, Eq. (3) uses the proportion of fixation on each AOI as weights. As the result, stable gaze with longer fixation duration in Fig. 3(b) is represented by smaller D.

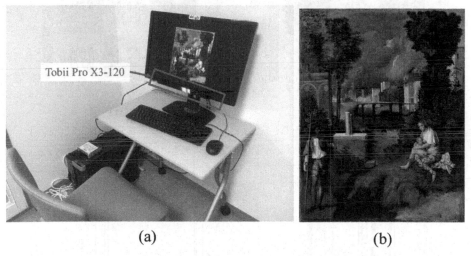

(a)   (b)

Fig. 2. (a) Experiment setup using Tobii Pro X3–120 eye tracker. (b) Stimulus - "The Tempest" oil painting. (Source: https://en.wikipedia.org/wiki/The_Tempest_(Giorgione))

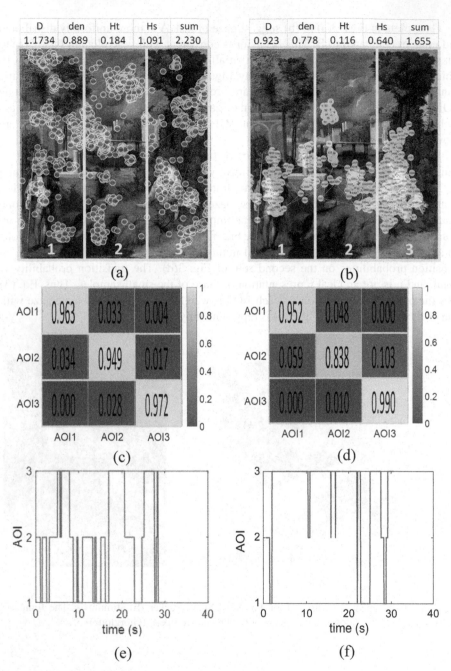

Fig. 3. (a) Grid-based AOIs and gaze plots on the stimulus for task A, and (b) B. (c) Markov transition matrix for task A, and (d) B. (e) Time plot of gaze transition between AOIs for task A, and (f) B.

2.3 Experiment Conditions

This section explains the experiment setup which is used to evaluate gaze strategies of crane operators. The objective is to study correlations of gaze behavior to skills, performance, and load oscillation, which is regarded as one of the major difficulties faced by crane operators. The experiment protocol of this study is approved by the ethics committee of the University of Tokyo and informed consent is obtained from each participant. This experiment uses large number of dynamic AOIs, which results in sparse Markov model. This demonstrates implementation of gaze metrics in real environment, which is lacking in previous studies. Seven crane operators took part in this experiment and each carried out several trials. Results of the first two trials are used for analysis to minimize the training effect. For this same reason, one participant is excluded from the analysis because he is responsible for the experiment setup and had more opportunities to operate the crane before the actual test. As such, this participant is more familiar with the experimental conditions compared to others.

Performance of crane operators is evaluated using the demerit scoring system, which is a subjective evaluation method currently used by the training center of one crane maker. The score sheet covers multiple criteria such as load oscillation and operation duration. An experienced trainer carried out the scoring and the demerit scores are used to separate the operators into two groups – Beginners and Non-Beginners, each consisting of three participants. Gaze fixations are measured using the Tobii Pro Glasses 2 in Fig. 4(a) and each operator carried out the same task in Fig. 4(b). The yellow-colored donuts represent obstacles. The cyan and blue arrows represent crane operation in the clockwise and counterclockwise directions, respectively.

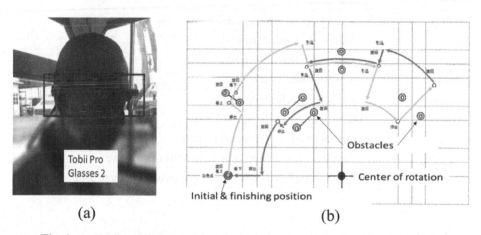

Initial & finishing position

(a)   (b)

Fig. 4. (a) Tobi Pro Glasses 2 is used to record gaze data. (b) The experiment task.

The original scene and the scene with AOIs overlaid on it are shown in Figs. 5(a) and (b). Table 1 explains the nine AOIs which are used in this study. One of the challenges of this study is the difficulty in getting participants because crane operation is regarded as a highly specialized task. Safety elements need to be considered during the experiment. Another challenge is the dominant and dynamic background, which makes grid based

AOI analysis difficult. Content-based AOIs analysis is used to limit spatial information to area around the load and to filter gaze fixations on the background.

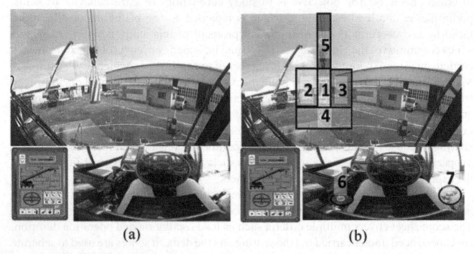

(a)   (b)

Fig. 5. (a) The original scene and (b) the content based AOIs overlaid on it.

Table 1. Content-based AOIs definition for crane operation analysis.

AOIs	Definition
Load (1)	The object that is being lifted by the crane
West (2)	Area on the right of the load
East (3)	Area on the left of the load
South (4)	Area below the load
Winch (5)	The hook/winch above the load
Left (6)	Control levers on the operator's left
Right (7)	Control levers on the operator's right
NoAOI (8)	Gaze fixations on areas other than AOIs listed above
NoFix (9)	Eye movements excluding fixations (includes missing data)

3   Results

3.1   Interpretation of Gaze Metrics

This section discusses the behavior of gaze metrics using different types of gaze sequence. The number of transitions and AOI hits are used as simple representation of randomness and uniformity. Figure 6 shows four types of gaze sequence, where the corresponding number of AOI hits, transitions and gaze metrics are listed in Table 2.

Figure 6 is a uniformly distributed gaze sequence which results in high H_s. Figure 6 is like (a), except for the extended fixation, which results in lower D, as discussed in Sect. 2.1. Correlations between gaze metrics also result in smaller H_t and H_s because they are dependent on π_i, which is the proportion of fixations on each AOI. Figure 6(c) shows reduction in AOI hits which reduces H_s and den. The attention is focused on fewer AOIs which is consistent with lower D. Figure 6(d) shows frequent transitions which results in high H_t. It also results in higher den and decreases the possibility of continuous fixations as shown by higher D.

Table 2. Gaze metrics of different types of AOI sequences.

Case	AOI hits	Transition	D	den	Ht	Hs	Sum
8(a)	6	5	2.058	0.306	0.164	1.792	2.362
8(b)	6	5	1.950	0.306	0.148	1.520	2.176
8(c)	4	5	1.878	0.278	0.171	1.238	1.759
8(d)	4	9	1.934	0.333	0.296	1.238	1.989

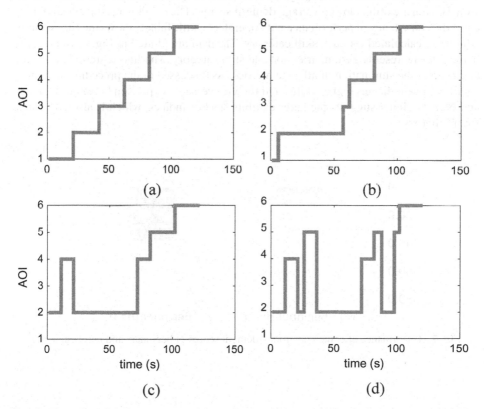

Fig. 6. Time plot of AOI sequences with varying transition number (randomness) and AOI hits (uniformity). The corresponding gaze metrics are given in Table 2.

As the rule of thumb, smaller metrics indicates 'stable gaze with focus' and larger metrics indicates 'random gaze without focus'. In this study, operator attention is reasonably represented by 'stable gaze with focus' or smaller gaze metrics. The summation of gaze metrics, as indicated by the last column of Table 2, is used to represent operator attention. This is reasonably illustrated by this example, where the summation is the largest for a uniformly distributed gaze in Fig. 6(a). On the other hand, the summation is the smallest for a gaze which focuses longer on fewer AOIs in Fig. 6(c).

3.2   Expert-Novice Difference of Crane Operators

This section explains the implementation of gaze metrics to evaluate the difference between skills of crane operators. The experimental setup in Sect. 2.3 is used for this purpose. Gaze data of the whole experiment task is used to calculate gaze metrics because gaze behaviour is expected to be task dependent. Task-based analysis is preferred because it averages the operators' gaze behaviour while they are carrying out multiple sub-tasks. This provides a more general approximation of gaze behaviour to evaluate expert-novice differences.

Result of the demerit scoring system (see Sect. 2.3) is summarized in Fig. 7, where Non-Beginner exhibits lower average demerit scores. The result is reasonable and indicates the consistency of performance with operators' skill. Table 3 shows the gaze metrics which are calculated for each skill category. The data are plotted in Fig. 8, where each bar cluster represents gaze metrics for one skill category. The line represents operator attention or the summation of all gaze metrics. As discussed in the preceding section, a smaller value indicates higher skills, and the vice versa. Comparison between Beginner and Non-Beginner suggests the latter exhibits smaller indices, which is also consistent for all metrics.

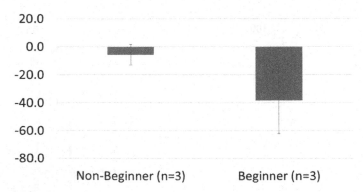

Fig. 7. Performance of crane operators – demerit scores of beginners and non-beginners.

Table 3. Gaze metrics of crane operators for the experiment task.

	Non-beginner		Beginner	
	μ	σ	μ	σ
D	2.424	0.019	2.554	0.005
den	0.259	0.000	0.294	0.026
H_t	0.521	0.112	0.587	0.104
H_s	1.253	0.135	1.484	0.124
sum	4.458	0.135	4.919	0.221

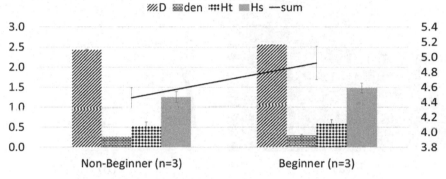

Fig. 8. Gaze metrics of crane operators for the experiment task.

The two sample t-test is used to test the null hypothesis that population mean of Non-Beginner is the same as those of Beginner. Table 4 shows that all the gaze metrics reject the null hypothesis at different significance level, except for H_t. More importantly, operator attention represented by sum rejects the null hypothesis at 0.05 significance level. This indicates gaze behavior of Non-Beginner and Beginner is statistically significant different and the proposed gaze metrics are useful to define skills of crane operators.

Table 4. Two sample t-test to evaluate gaze metrics of Non-Beginner and Beginner (degree-of-freedom = 4).

	D	den	H_t	H_s	Sum
P-value	3.27E-04	0.0780	0.4950	0.0940	0.0369
tstat	−11.50	−2.36	−0.75	−2.18	−3.08
Significance	0.01	0.10	–	0.10	0.05

3.3   Expert-Novice Difference During Load Oscillations

This section extends gaze metrics analysis to focus on expert-novice differences during load oscillations, which is one of the main difficulties facing new operators. The basis of this study relies on the observation that Non-Beginner can estimate oscillation and coordinate the operation to minimize it. However, it appears that Beginner does not possess this instinct. Slewing is identified as the sub-task with high tendency to cause tangential load oscillations, as in Fig. 9. This sub-task is highlighted by red in Fig. 9(b). Like the preceding section, gaze metrics are calculated for each skill category and shown in Table 5, and the data are plotted in Fig. 10.

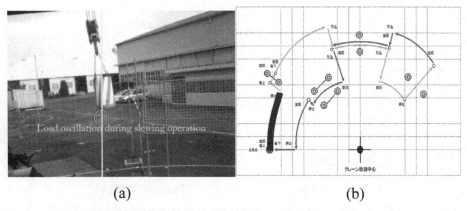

(a)   (b)

Fig. 9. (a) Difficult operation – load oscillations when slewing the load (supplementary material – Video A). (b) Sub-task of the experiment.

Table 5. Gaze metrics of crane operators during the slewing sub-task.

	Non-beginner		Beginner	
	μ	σ	μ	σ
D	2.398	0.078	2.549	0.021
den	0.214	0.007	0.224	0.016
H_t	0.520	0.088	0.568	0.053
H_s	1.111	0.049	1.321	0.029
sum	4.242	0.163	4.662	0.109

Referring to Fig. 10, the result exhibits similar pattern as those in Sect. 3.2. This indicates the possibility of Non-Beginner focusing on selected areas during the slewing operation and coordinates the operation to minimize oscillations. Results of the two sample t-test in Table 6 reject the null hypothesis of D and H_s at different significance levels. More importantly, operator attention represented by sum rejects the null hypothesis at 0.05 significance level. This result is consistent with those in Sect. 3.2 and suggests crane operators exhibit different gaze behavior during crane operations, which is also evident when handling load oscillations. This finding suggests the feasibility of further investigating the correlation of gaze behavior with crane operation strategy, especially those of Non-Beginners. This is promising to unearth the knacks of crane operation to assist Beginners.

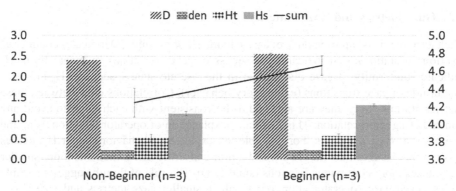

Fig. 10.   Gaze metrics of crane operators during the slewing sub-task.

Table 6.   Two sample t-test to evaluate gaze metrics of Non-Beginner and Beginner for the slewing sub-task (degree-of-freedom = 4).

	D	dcn	H_t	H_s	Sum
P-value	3.11E-02	0.3560	0.4579	0.0032	0.0208
tstat	−3.26	−1.04	−0.82	−6.33	−3.70
Significance	0.05	–	–	0.01	0.05

4   Discussions

4.1   Implications of Model Sparseness and Enlarged Base

This study adapts gaze entropies from preceding studies and introduces novel metrics to better interpret sparse gaze transition matrices. This simple adaptation yields significant advantages. First, it allows greater flexibility in the definition of AOIs, where larger size and different types of AOIs can be used. Second, it facilitates implementation of gaze metrics to solve real problems without prior knowledge of gaze behavior. In preceding methods, AOIs and length of gaze observation must be defined cautiously to avoid AOIs with zero fixations. Results in this study provide the evidence that gaze behavior is well-defined using D, den, H_s and H_t. Although the solution is dependent on AOIs definitions, interpretation of gaze transitions between any discrete spaces is expected to be the same, as illustrated by the consistency between grid-based (Sects. 3.1) and dynamic content-based (Sects. 3.2 and 3.3) AOI definitions. Different experimental conditions using fixed-typed eye-trackers and eye-tracking glasses also demonstrates the flexibility and repeatability of the solution in solving real problems, which commonly require large and sparse transition matrices. The contribution is significant compared to [7, 9], which evaluated problems with non-sparse matrices and smaller number of AOIs in laboratory environment.

4.2 Gaze Metrics and Gaze Pattern

Each gaze metric is representative of a gaze feature. For example, D indicates continuous fixations (duration), den indicates sparseness of gaze transitions in binary term, H_s indicates uniformity of gaze distribution in the discrete state space, and H_t indicates magnitude of gaze transitions (exploratory behavior). Correlations exist between these metrics. In this study, they are adjusted to be consistent with each other to avoid any contradicting interpretation. This facilitates explanation of operator attention using the summation of gaze metrics. For example, an exploratory behavior (larger H_t) causes less continuous fixations (larger D), and a non-uniformly distributed attention (smaller H_s) causes more continuous fixations (smaller D). The rule of thumb suggests a stable and focused gaze (operator attention) result in smaller gaze metrics and vice versa. Compared to [19], D is revised in this paper to correct bias resulting from unequal gaze fixation proportion. Results in Sect. 3 suggest the revised D successfully represented gaze behavior in terms of fixation duration.

4.3 Performance and Gaze Metrics

Results also suggest gaze behavior of Non-beginner is non-uniformly distributed and less random because of smaller H_s and H_t. This results in continuous fixations which is consistent with smaller D. This behavior can be observed from time plot of gaze fixations in Fig. 11(a), where the Non-beginner exhibited less uniform gaze which covered only four AOIs, resulting in smaller metrics which correspond to 'stable gaze with focus'. On the other hand, the Beginner gazed at six AOIs in Fig. 11(b) and exhibited higher metrics for 'random gaze without focus'. This behavior is consistent with those of [22, 23], where expert tennis players exhibited consistent gaze because they knew where to focus during the game. [10] also concluded expert surgeons exhibited higher fixation frequency and dwell time on operative sites. Such behavior corresponded to the definition of 'stable gaze with focus'. In other words, the correlation between skill and gaze has been observed in other tasks. Therefore, operator attention as a single index derived from summation of gaze metrics can be a valid representation of expert-novice differences.

4.4 Task Load, Attention, and Anxiety

Comparison between Tables 3 and 5 suggests all operators exhibited smaller gaze metrics during the slewing operation, where tangential load oscillations are more evident and tends to result in higher task load. This is consistent with findings from [17, 18], which suggested an increase in cognitive demand or task load results in decrease of gaze randomness or complexity. However, this interpretation is not plausible in this study because it is not a task-to-task comparison. Gaze behavior of the whole task is observed from multiple operations which naturally results in higher randomness and uniformity.

Nonetheless, it is noteworthy that Non-beginner consistently exhibited the smallest gaze metrics. [10, 17] suggested similar findings from the evaluation of expert and junior surgeons. Thus, it is plausible to deduce that Non-beginner exhibited unique attention during difficult operations to detect and handle abnormalities such as load oscillations, which possibly resulted in better performance. The poor performance of Beginner can be related to the lack of such ability or knowledge. [7] also found that attentional control and performance of student pilots are negatively affected by anxiety. This could be another reason for the poor performance of Beginner. In short, the lack of attention by Beginner could have contributed to the poor performance, and this could be related to anxiety.

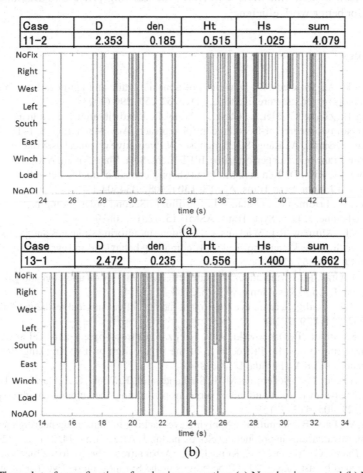

Fig. 11. Time plot of gaze fixations for slewing operation (a) Non-beginner, and (b) Beginner.

5 Conclusions and Future Works

Gaze behavior is well-defined using novel gaze metrics which are introduced to address the challenges of large and sparse Markov transition matrices. The solution provides significant flexibility in the definition of discrete spaces to observe gaze behavior in varying problem settings. Evaluations of the proposed method using different experiment conditions and devices show good consistency, suggesting gaze metrics are a valid index for attention of expert-novice differences and performance.

For the future work, the unique attention of Non-beginner at difficult work conditions is expected to facilitate development of work support or guidance systems based on visual motor coordination. Such system is expected to facilitate detection, handling, and prevention of abnormalities. Therefore, the learning process of Beginner can be improved for better work efficiency.

References

1. Maczynski, A., Wojciech, S.: Dynamics of a mobile crane and optimization of the slewing motion of its upper structure. Nonlinear Dyn. **32**, 259–290 (2003)
2. Ouyang, H., Zhang, G., Mei, L., Deng, X., Wang, D.: Load vibration reduction in rotary cranes using robust two-degree-of-freedom control approach. Adv. Mech. Eng. **8**, 1–11 (2016)
3. Vaughan, J., Smith, A., Kang, S.J., Singhose, W.: Predictive graphical user interface elements to improve crane operator performance. IEEE Trans. Syst. Man Cybern. A **41**, 323–330 (2011)
4. Singhose, W., Kim, D., Kenison, M.: Input shaping control of double-pendulum bridge crane oscillations. J. Dyn. Syst. Trans. ASME, **130** (2008). 034504-1-7
5. Vazquez, C., Fridman, L., Collado, J., Castillo, I.: Second-order sliding mode control of a perturbed-crane. J. Dyn. Syst. Trans. ASME **137** (2015). 081010-1-7
6. Sarter, N.B., Mumaw, R.J., Wickens, C.D.: Pilots' monitoring strategies and performance on automated flight decks: an empirical study combining behavioral and eye-tracking data. Hum. Factors **49**, 347–357 (2007)
7. Allsop, J., Gray, R.: Flying under pressure: effects of anxiety on attention and gaze behavior in aviation. J. Appl. Res. Memory Cogn. **3**, 63–71 (2014)
8. DiStasi, L.L., et al.: Saccadic eye movement metrics reflect surgical residents' fatigue. Ann. Surg. **259**, 824–829 (2014)
9. Krejtz, K., Smidt, T., Duchowski, A.T., Krejtz, I.: Entropy-based statistical analysis of eye movement transitions. In: Proceedings of the Symposium on Eye Tracking Research and Applications (ETRA), Florida, USA (2014)
10. Tien, T., Pucher, P.H., Sodergren, M.H., Sriskandarajah, K., Yang, G.Z., Darzi, A.: Differences in gaze behavior of expert and junior surgeons performing open inguinal hernia repair. Surg. Endosc. **29**, 405–413 (2015)
11. Kohler, M., Falk, B., Schmitt, R.: Applying eye-tracking in Kansei engineering methodology for design evaluations in product development. Int. J. Affect. Eng. **14**, 241–251 (2015)
12. Mello-Thoms, C., Nodine, C.F., Kundel, H.L.: What attracts the eye to the location of missed and reported breast cancers? In: Proceedings of the Symposium on Eye Tracking Research and Applications (ETRA), New Orleans, USA (2002)
13. DeBruin, J.A., Malan, K.M., Eloff, J.H.P.: Saccade deviation indicators for automated eye tracking analysis. In: Proceedings of the 2013 Conference on Eye Tracking South Africa (ETSA), Cape Town, South Africa (2013)

14. Grindinger, T., Duchowski, A.T., Sawyer, M.: Group-wise similarity and classification of aggregate scanpaths. In: Proceedings of the Symposium on Eye Tracking Research and Applications (ETRA), Austin Texas, USA (2010)
15. Goldberg, J.H., Kotval, X.P.: Computer interface evaluation using eye movements: methods and constructs. Int. J. Ind. Ergon. **24**, 631–645 (1999)
16. Otsuka, K., Yamato, J., Takemae, Y., Murase, H.: Quantifying interpersonal influence in face-to-face conversations based on visual attention patterns. In: Human Factors in Computing Systems, Quebec, Canada (2006)
17. DiStasi, L.L., et al.: Gaze-entropy as a task load index for safety-critical operators: military pilots and surgeons. J. Vis. **16**, 1341 (2016)
18. Schieber, F., Gilland, J.: Visual entropy metric reveals differences in drivers' eye gaze complexity across variations in age and subsidiary task load. In: Human Factors and Ergonomics Society Annual Meeting Proceedings, New York, USA (2008)
19. Chew, J.Y., Ohtomi, K., Suzuki, H.: Skill metrics for mobile crane operators based on gaze fixation pattern. Adv. Hum. Aspects Transp. Adv. Intell. Syst. Comput. **484**, 1139–1149 (2016)
20. Chew, J.Y., Ohtomi, K., Suzuki, H.: Glance behavior as design indices of in-vehicle visual support system: a study using crane simulators. Appl. Ergon. **73**, 183–193 (2018)
21. Teodorescu, J.: Maximum likelihood estimation for Markov Chains. *arXiv*, 0905.4131v1 (2009)
22. Ward, P., Williams, A.M., Bennett, S.J.: Visual search and biological motion perception in tennis. Res. Q. Exerc. Sport **73**, 107–112 (2002)
23. Button, C., Dicks, M., Haines, R., Barker, R., Davids, K.: Statistical modelling of gaze behavior as categorical time series: what you should watch to save soccer penalties. Cogn. Process **12**, 235–244 (2011)

Uncertainty of Skill Estimates in Operational Deep Knowledge Tracing

David R. King[(⊠)] [iD], Ziwei Zhou [iD], and Windy Therior

Edmentum, Bloomington, MN 55437, USA
david.king@edmentum.com
https://www.edmentum.com

Abstract. This paper reviews challenges and opportunities of using deep knowledge tracing (DKT) in a production hybrid instructional and assessment system (HIAS) for measuring learner skills. An empirical data analysis using K-12 Mathematics practice data from an operational HIAS showed that the DKT estimates in the training set were well calibrated, although the estimates in a holdout set overestimated student skill mastery at lower ability levels and underestimated mastery at higher ability levels. Examination of expected vs. observed plots across ability levels provided a means for evaluating the generalizability of the predictions to new students and suggested a stratified sampling approach may be needed for creating training and validation sets that better represented the full practice data. Estimation accuracy was further examined in a parameter recovery study, with response data simulated from patterns in the empirical data. The study showed that in general, the DKT procedure had high estimation accuracy, with an absolute mean difference of approximately 0.03 units on the [0, 1] probability scale and a Pearson correlation of +0.89 between true and estimated values. To examine uncertainty in the estimates, 80% and 95% confidence intervals were constructed around the mean estimate for each true ability level. As expected, results showed less uncertainty at ability levels where more response data were generated, indicating the DKT approach is sensitive to ability level information in the training data. Finally, the DKT approach was able to detect learning across attempts within a skill, suggesting this approach may be preferred over traditional measurement approaches in scenarios where ability levels change over time.

Keywords: Deep knowledge tracing · LSTM · Recurrent neural networks · Measurement precision · Adaptive instructional systems

1 Introduction

In a hybrid instructional and assessment system (HIAS), students are both instructed and measured on new skills. The instruction presents a measurement challenge because most students learn from the instruction and their skills change over time. Measurement of learning is important because it shows the

© Springer Nature Switzerland AG 2021
C. Stephanidis et al. (Eds.): HCII 2021, LNCS 13096, pp. 62–76, 2021.
https://doi.org/10.1007/978-3-030-90328-2_4

effectiveness of instructional content and provides useful information about skill mastery and gaps to the student, educator, and school administrators. Despite its importance, learning is difficult to measure using traditional approaches such as item response theory (IRT) [8], which typically assumes that student skills are fixed and measured at a single point in time. To measure skill changes over time using IRT, a new test would need to be given after each piece of instructional content; a format that is inefficient and unrealistic for an HIAS. A better approach for measuring skill changes over time is knowledge tracing, which estimates skills from sequential (i.e. time series) data. Two knowledge tracing methods that have been examined in the research literature are Bayesian knowledge tracing (BKT) [1] and deep knowledge tracing (DKT) [11], with DKT generally outperforming BKT in prediction accuracy [9]. Given the accuracy of the skill predictions, DKT might be used in a HIAS for measuring and reporting skill changes over time, although reporting skill estimates requires an understanding of the uncertainty (or measurement precision) of the estimates.

DKT uses recurrent neural networks with long short-term memory units (RNN-LSTM) [4] for estimating skills, a method which does not produce estimates of the uncertainty of the skills. Although inferences are made on the skill estimates, DKT performance is commonly evaluated with the AUC statistic, which measures binary classification accuracy of item scores and not the estimation accuracy of learner skills.

Using a variational dropout technique, the current paper examines skill estimation accuracy and the associated uncertainty of the skill estimates through a parameter recovery study and an empirical data analysis on data from an operational HIAS. The parameter recovery study explores how uncertainty changes as the learner completes activities and whether measurement precision is consistent across ability levels. The empirical data analysis investigates practical issues of implementing DKT in a production system including the specification of new skills and evaluation of model performance.

1.1 Evaluating Estimation Accuracy

The primary metric used to evaluate model performance in the knowledge tracing literature is AUC (Area Under the Curve), where the curve is a receiver operating characteristic curve derived from examining the classification accuracy of a binary predictor across all possible threshold values.

In DKT, an RNN-LSTM network provides an estimate for the probability of a correct response to the next item associated with a given skill. To calculate AUC, these continuous estimates are converted to discrete 0/1 values depending on whether the estimate is below or above a given threshold value. For a threshold value of 0.8, a skill estimate of 0.85 is converted to 1 and an estimate of 0.75 is converted to 0. For a threshold value of 0.9, both skill estimates of 0.85 and 0.75 are converted to 0. The receiver operating characteristic curve is then derived by comparing the converted (expected) values against the empirical (observed) values. The observed 0/1 values indicate incorrect (0) and correct (1) responses to an item associated with a skill. Higher consistency of expected and observed values across thresholds increases AUC, with perfect consistency having an AUC of 1.0, perfect inconsistency an AUC of 0.0, and random guessing an AUC of 0.5 [10]. Namely, to achieve an AUC of 1.0, all probability estimates must be either 0.0 or 1.0, with the 0.0 and 1.0 estimates associated with observed incorrect and correct responses respectively.

The model predictions in DKT are assumed to depend on an underlying ability level associated with the skill the item is measuring. A student may have a 0.5 probability of correctly responding to the next problem based on her or his ability level, although a model prediction of 0.5 does not provide information about whether the student is more likely to get the next problem correct or incorrect. Therefore a prediction of 0.5 has high accuracy if the student's actual probability of correctly responding to the next item is 0.5, although this prediction contributes to a low AUC. This scenario arises in adaptive testing, where items with an expected response probability of 0.5 are typically selected because these items provide the most information about student ability. A DKT model that perfectly predicts response probabilities of 0.5 would have high estimation accuracy, although the AUC value would be no higher than the AUC value of a model with no information about student ability.

When using DKT to estimate student skill proficiencies, AUC may not be the most useful metric for evaluating the model's predictive power. Alternatively, expected vs observed plots at each interval of the [0, 1] scale provide practical information about estimation accuracy at each ability level.

1.2   Calibrating Results

Although RNN-LSTMs have high accuracy in predicting a binary outcome, the estimated probabilities may not be representative of the observed probabilities [7]. Namely, after binning skill estimates by probability level (e.g., 0.0–0.1, 0.1–0.2, ..., 0.9–1.0), the average observed item score in each level may not match the average estimate. To correct this issue, probability estimates may be calibrated after the RNN-LSTM is trained using a holdout validation data set. Two popular calibration approaches are logistic regression and isotonic regression [5].

The logistic regression approach fits the pre-calibrated skill estimates to the observed 0/1 item scores. The parameter estimates from the fit model can then be used to transform the pre-calibrated estimates to calibrated estimates that better represent the observed probabilities. The isotonic regression approach is similar although more flexible because it does not depend on parametric modeling assumptions and finds a monotonic, non-decreasing function that minimizes the distance between the pre-calibrated estimates and the observed probabilities.

1.3   Approximating Uncertainty in the Skill Estimates Through Variational Dropout

To obtain uncertainty estimates for the predicted probabilities, a variational dropout technique [3] may be implemented at inference time. Namely, after an RNN-LSTM network has been trained, the network can be used to make skill predictions for new student response data. This approach makes multiple predictions for each student skill at each time point. For each iteration, some portion of the nodes in the LSTM layer are removed randomly, and this produces a different prediction each time. After a large number of iterations of this process, uncertainty can be approximated by the empirical distribution of the predicted probabilities. According to [3], this distribution approximates the posterior predictive distribution integrated over multiple neural networks under a Bayesian framework.

2   Method

2.1   Empirical Data Analysis

Data were obtained from an operational HIAS developed and maintained by an educational technology company operating in the Midwest region of the United States. Although the HIAS included instructional, practice, and assessment data in three subject areas (language arts, mathematics, and reading), only Mathematics practice data from students in grades K-12 were used in this study.

In the HIAS, practice problems were selected for students based on placement in a linear progression of skills, which had been vertically articulated across grade level. Student placement in the learning progression was determined by performance on a diagnostic assessment.

Item score data from 18,750 students using the HIAS in the 2019–2020 school year were used to create training (n = 15,000) and validation (n = 3,750) sets for the DKT analysis. Note that this was a small subset of the 389,990 total students with practice data. In the sample, students completed an average of 10 items per skill for 4 skills (out of 164 total skills). The mean number of item responses was 39, although the median was much lower at 21, suggesting the response vector lengths were asymmetrically distributed across students.

The train and validate sets had discrepancies in average item score and average number of responses after a naive partitioning strategy was performed that did not take into account skill distributions, student grade level, time of year or other key variables for obtaining representative samples. Namely, average item score was approximately 0.88 in the training set and 0.82 in the validation set, and average number of responses was approximately 39 in the training set and 27 in the validation set.

A separate test set was created using 3,750 students from the 2020–2021 school year (from a total of 505,234 students) to examine the feasibility of using a trained RNN-LSTM from the previous school year to estimate skills for students in the new school year. Data characteristics were similar, with an average item score of 0.86 although these data had 160 skills, 4 of which were not present in the 2019–2020 data. New skills in the test set were retained to examine prediction challenges in an operational setting when new skills are added to a HIAS.

2.2   Parameter Recovery Study

To directly examine the accuracy of skill estimates and associated uncertainty, data were generated based on characteristics of the empirical data. Student ability was sampled from a standard normal distribution, and 50 skill difficulty means were equally spaced from -1.5 to 0.5. An error term was sampled from a normal distribution with a mean of zero and a standard deviation of 0.05 to represent variation in item difficulty associated with skills. Students were placed in the learning progression based on ability level and were administered 10 practice items per skill for 1 to 10 skills. After each item response within a skill, student ability level was increased by 0.1 on the logit scale (approximately 0.015 on the probability scale) to represent learning gains. Learning gains were removed when the student moved to the next skill. Item scores were generated for each student from a one-parameter logistic IRT model. Data for 15,000 students were generated for the training set and 3,750 students for the validation set. Data for an additional 3,750 students were generated for a test set. Similar to the empirical data, the test set included 5 skill IDs that were not present in the training and validation sets. Out of 50 skills, 45 were common across the training, validation, and test sets, with five skills unique to the training and validation sets and five skills unique to the test set. Average item score was approximately 0.8 across all data sets.

2.3   Variational Dropout Procedure

The variational dropout procedure was implemented for obtaining skill estimates and associated uncertainty on simulated and empirical data from an operational HIAS. For each student, skill, and time point, 100 iterations of the dropout procedure were performed at inference time to construct empirical predictive distributions. For hyperparameter tuning, various dropout rates were explored for input, output, and recurrent layers. The preliminary analysis indicated that the dropout rate 0.1 appeared to lead to slightly better parameter recovery (e.g., AMD between true and estimated probabilities), this dropout rate was adopted at the input, output, and recurrent layers. Namely, 10% of the nodes in the RNN-LSTM were dropped at each layer.

Using the input data that included both item scores and associated skill IDs, a regularized version of DKT[1] was implemented [12], which was shown to produce more consistent predictions due to applying regularization to the loss function in the original specification of the DKT [11]. The neural network was trained and later loaded to perform the variational dropout experiment in order to obtain uncertainty estimates around the predicted probabilities. The experimental setup in training the neural network followed [12] closely, including setting a batch size of 32, learning rate of 0.01, training dropout rate of 0.5, a single-layer RNN-LSTM with a state size of 200, weights initialization from Gaussian distribution with mean of 0 and small variance, and the maximum

---

[1] https://github.com/ckyeungac/deep-knowledge-tracing-plus.

gradient norm clipping value of 5. Moreover, this study trained the network in 10 epochs and directly used the best hyperparameters reported in [12] ($\lambda_r = 0.05, \lambda_{w1} = 0.03, \lambda_{w2} = 0.3$).

2.4 Skill Estimation

After training the RNN-LSTM, network weights were used to predict the next item score for each student and for each item. These predictions were compared to the observed data to calculate AUC, which was recorded as an overall measure of model classification accuracy.

After performing the dropout procedure to get a predictive distribution of 100 values for each student, skill, and time point, the value at the 50th percentile was defined as the skill estimate and values at the 2.5th and 97.5th percentiles were defined as the lower and upper bounds of the 95% confidence interval. (For 100 values, the second and third values were averaged to obtain the value at the 2.5th percentile and the 97 and 98th values were averaged to obtain the value at the 97.5th percentile).

2.5 Skill Estimation Accuracy

For the empirical data, true skill probabilities were assumed as drivers of the student's response process, although these true skill probabilities were not observable and could only be estimated. Therefore, skill estimation accuracy was evaluated at an aggregated level across students by comparing binned skill estimates (i.e., mean predicted values) against observed probabilities (i.e. fraction of positives). Namely, skill estimates were divided into 10 bins and plotted against binned observed probabilities for the validation and test sets. The logistic regression and isotonic regression calibration techniques described in the introduction were then applied to the pre-calibrated skill estimates. For the validation and test sets, the binned skill estimates and observed probabilities from the training set were used to develop the transformation functions.

For the simulated data, skill estimation accuracy was directly examined because the true skill probabilities were known. Estimation accuracy was assessed by comparing the skill estimates against the true skill values and calculating root mean square deviation (RMSD), absolute mean difference (AMD), variance ratio (VR), and Pearson correlation. RMSD provided an overall statistic of recovery performance. AMD examined the magnitude of the difference between true and predicted values in the same unit of measurement as the skill probabilities. VR examined how much variation exists in the true values compared to the predicted values, and the Pearson correlation examined the linear relationship between the true and predicted values.

2.6 Skill Uncertainty Accuracy

Skill uncertainty accuracy was only examined for the simulated data. Uncertainty accuracy was examined by comparing the 95% confidence intervals approximated from the variational dropout procedure with the percentage of true values contained in these intervals.

Uncertainty was also examined by computing AMD by true value and attempt number within a skill.

3 Results

3.1 Classification Accuracy

In the production HIAS data, AUC was higher for the test set (AUC = 0.83) than for the validation set (AUC = 0.74). The validation and test sets included the same number of students (n = 3,500), although the validation set was sampled from the same school year as the training set (2019–2020) and the test set was sampled from the next school year (2020–2021). This suggests that performance should have been worse in the test set than the validation set and systematic sampling error may have contributed to decreased performance in the validation set.

The lower AUC in the validation set is likely due to the lower average item score (0.82 vs 0.86) and lower average number of responses (27 vs 36). Previous research [6] found a strong relationship between AUC and average number of item responses. As noted in the introduction, AUC may not be a good predictor of skill estimation accuracy, although it is reported here because of the popularity in the DKT literature.

In the simulated data, AUC was higher in the validation set (AUC = 0.64) than in the test set (AUC = 0.62), although both were lower than the AUCs observed in the empirical data. The simulated validation and test sets were generated under the same assumptions, although the test set included five new skills not present in the training set used to optimize the network weights. The additional error from the new skills likely resulted in lower classification accuracy.

3.2 Skill Estimation Accuracy

The logistic and isotonic calibration transformations were performed on the training estimates to determine if the predictions could be better matched to the observed probabilities at each ability level. Figure 1 shows the expected vs observed plot for the pre-calibrated and calibrated estimates. The dotted black line shows perfect fit of the model to the data (i.e. accurate average estimate at each ability level). Results showed the initial LSTM estimates in the training set were well calibrated, although the estimates in the validation set overestimated student skill mastery at lower ability levels and underestimated mastery at higher ability levels. The isotonic calibrated estimates appeared to fit the data slightly better than the pre-calibrated estimates, although the logistic estimates appeared to fit the data worse. The calibration analysis on the validation set is shown in Fig. 2.

Lastly, the logistic and isotonic transformation functions were applied to the test data. The test set was used to assess how well the transformation functions

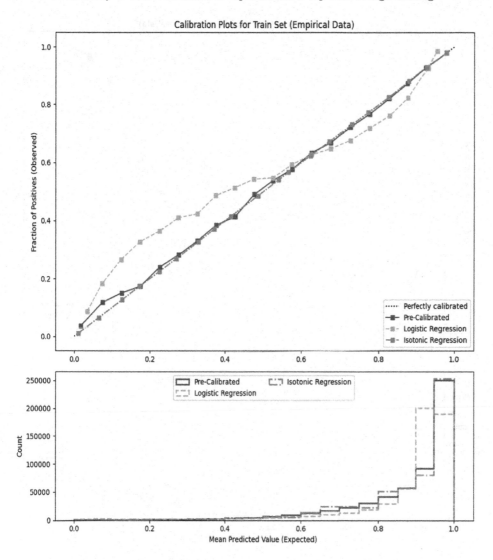

Fig. 1. Calibration plots and histograms of resulting distributions for the empirical training data

from the previous school year could be applied to data in the new school year. Figure 3 shows the calibration results for the test set were similar to the results for the validation set, although with less severe overestimation of ability at lower ability levels than in the validation set.

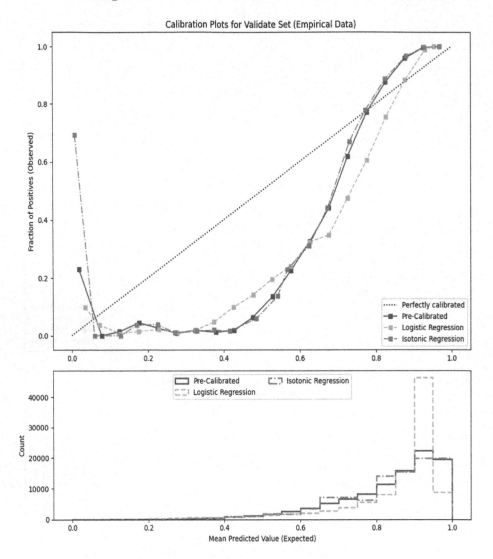

Fig. 2. Calibration plots and histograms of resulting distributions for the empirical validation data

3.2.1 Parameter Recovery

A parameter recovery study was performed on the simulated data to better understand the skill estimation accuracy of the DKT approach. Results are shown in Table 1 for the recovery of the true skill ability values in the validation and test sets. Student skill ability estimates for the validation and test sets were obtained using the prediction model developed from the training set.

Overall, estimation accuracy was high. Namely, the estimated values were approximately 0.03 units away from the true values on the [0, 1] probability

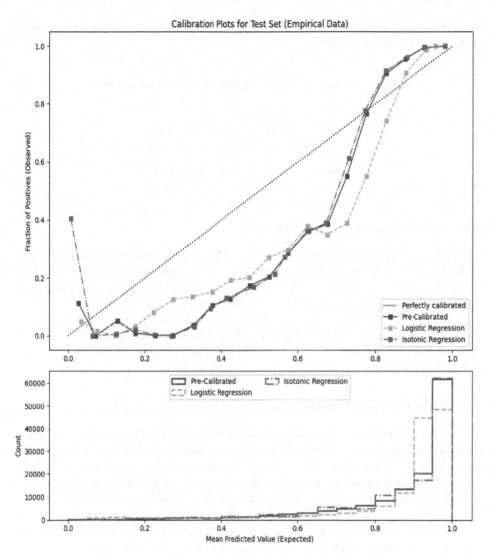

Fig. 3. Calibration plots and histograms of resulting distributions for the empirical test data

scale for the pre-calibrated estimates. The true values had slightly less variation than the estimated values (VR = 0.84) and there was a strong, positive linear relationship between the true and estimated values (Pearson correlation = 0.89).

As expected, estimation accuracy decreased for the test set (AMD = 0.06), with all statistics showing worse recovery accuracy in the test set than in the validation set due to the error introduced by the five new skills not present in the training set. However, despite the noise, the DKT approach was still able to produce estimates that had a moderate linear relationship with the true values (Pearson correlation = 0.56).

Table 1. Parameter recovery results for the simulated data

	Statistic			
	RMSD	AMD	VR	Corr
Validation	0.05	0.03	0.84	0.89
Test	0.12	0.06	0.50	0.56

3.3   Recovery of Learning Gains

The data generation algorithm incorporated learning gains by increasing learner skill ability by 0.1 on the logit scale after the learner completed each practice problem within a skill. Across 10 problems, the probability of a correct response increased by approximately 0.15 for the true response probabilities.

The pre-calibrated estimates consistently identified the learning gains, although underestimated the absolute gain (probability increase of 0.11). Mean estimates across attempts are shown in Fig. 4. The confidence bars are discussed in the next section.

3.4   Skill Uncertainty Accuracy

For the simulated data, the confidence intervals constructed from the variational dropout procedure (i.e. ordering the dropout samples and taking the values at the 2.5th and 97.5th percentiles as the lower and upper bounds of the confidence interval) were examined to determine the percentage of true skill values they contained. A well performing 95% confidence interval should contain approximately 95% of the true values. Unfortunately, the coverage rate was much lower at about 68% in the validation set and 60% in the test set. Attempts were made to rescale the intervals, although there were inconsistent percentages of true values contained in the intervals across true ability levels.

3.4.1   Uncertainty by Attempt Number
Measurement uncertainty was examined as a function of attempt number to determine if error bars decreased as the learner responded to more problems associated with a given skill.

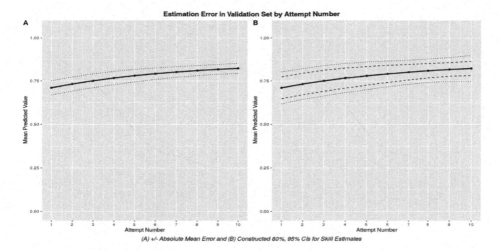

(A) +/- Absolute Mean Error and (B) Constructed 80%, 95% CIs for Skill Estimates

Fig. 4. Constructed confidence intervals based on absolute differences in the simulated data across attempts in the validation set

Figure 4 shows constructed confidence intervals for the pre-calibrated estimates. Confidence intervals consistently tightened across attempts, although the reductions in error were small and may be the result of the learner moving to ability levels with smaller mean errors.

The error bars in plot 4A show the average estimate at each true ability level, with the absolute mean difference at the ability level added above and below the estimate. The 80% and 95% boundaries in plot 4B show the absolute differences between true and estimated ability at the 95th and 80th percentile for each ability level. Namely, 80% and 95% of the absolute differences between true and estimated ability were equal to or less than the differences shown by the boundaries. Note that these confidence intervals were constructed through calculation of the AMD between true skills and associated estimates, and therefore could not be calculated for empirical data. However, the derived confidence intervals allowed for measurement uncertainty to be examined directly in the simulated data.

3.4.2 Uncertainty by True Ability Level

Measurement uncertainty was further assessed by plotting the AMD at each true ability level, as well as deriving empirical confidence intervals that contained 95% and 80% of the true values.

Figure 5 shows estimation error in the validation set across true skill values. Figure 5A shows the average skill estimate at each true ability level with a confidence interval derived by adding and subtracting the AMD from the average skill estimate. Figure 5B shows the empirical 95% and 80% confidence intervals. The estimates had less average error at the upper ability levels where there was more information in the data given the average item score of approximately 0.8.

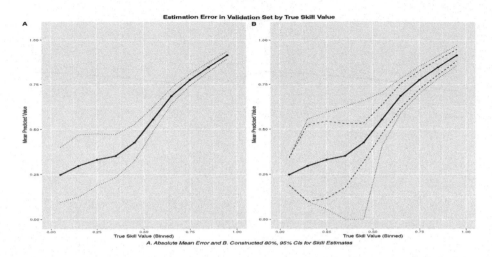

Fig. 5. Constructed confidence intervals based on absolute differences in simulated data across true ability in the validation set

There was a clear monotonic relationship between true skill value and mean predicted value, although the DKT prediction model tended to overestimate skill level at the lower ability levels, with an average estimate of 0.25 corresponding with a true skill value of 0.05.

The estimation accuracy analysis on the test data showed similar results as the validation data, although the constructed confidence intervals were larger due to the additional error from the new skills added to the test set.

4   Discussion

This paper reviewed challenges and opportunities of using deep knowledge tracing (DKT) in a production hybrid instructional and assessment system (HIAS) for measuring learner skills. An empirical data analysis using K-12 Mathematics practice data from an operational HIAS showed that the DKT estimates in the training set were well calibrated, although the estimates in a holdout set overestimated student skill mastery at lower ability levels and underestimated mastery at higher ability levels. Examination of expected vs. observed plots across ability levels provided a means for evaluating the generalizability of the predictions to new students and suggested a stratified sampling approach may be needed for creating training and validation sets that better represented the full practice data. Estimation accuracy was further examined in a parameter recovery study, with response data simulated from patterns in the empirical data. The study showed that in general, the DKT procedure had high estimation accuracy, with an absolute mean difference of approximately 0.03 units on the [0, 1] probability scale and a Pearson correlation of +0.89 between true and estimated values. To examine uncertainty in the estimates, 80% and 95% confidence intervals were constructed around the mean estimate for each true ability level. As expected, results showed less uncertainty at ability levels where more response data were generated, indicating the DKT approach is sensitive to ability level information in the training data. Finally, the DKT approach was able to detect learning across attempts within a skill, suggesting this approach may be preferred over traditional measurement approaches in scenarios where ability levels change over time.

4.1 Limitations of the Current Study

A naive data partitioning strategy that did not take into account characteristics of the data such as number of item responses, skill sequences, student grade level, and time of year was used in the current study to create the training and validation sets. Descriptive statistics showed systematic differences between these sets and expected vs observed plots of learner skills showed a large decrease in estimation accuracy from the training to the validation set.

An RNN-LSTM network trained from representative data should perform similarly on the training and validation sets if the network is not overfit to the training data. In the current study, the variational dropout method was used to prevent overfit of the network to the data. Given the complexity of the data and variation in key sample characteristics (e.g., skill sequences), a more thorough stratified sampling technique should be performed to ensure the training and validation sets are representative of the full data.

The current study only used a fraction of the full data for the training and validation sets (<4%) to decrease runtime costs. Increasing sample sizes may lead to improved model performance and better representation of the full data.

4.2 Next Steps

For DKT to be implemented in a production setting and used for reporting of learner skill estimates, the prediction model must provide reasonable changes in skill updates. [3] proposed regularization terms that reduce drastic changes in skill estimates from a single response and improve the consistency of updates with the previous item score (i.e. skill increases for a correct response, skill decreases for an incorrect response). These regularization terms were used in the current paper, although more attention needs to be paid to student-level results to better understand practical issues such as the number of practice problems that need to be answered correctly for a student to achieve a skill estimate of 0.8.

Efficiency of skill estimation is also important given the limited interactions of many students in the system. Providing the network with more sources of information during training, such as instructional content completed or learning aids used, has been shown to increase estimation accuracy [13]. Further research could explore which sources of information from a HIAS provide reliable increases in the estimation accuracy of skill proficiency beyond correct/incorrect response data.

For score reporting, estimates of uncertainty provide useful information for interpreting the reliability of a score. The dropout technique explored in the current paper did not produce useful approximations of uncertainty, although other approaches such as Bayesian DKT [2] are more theoretically grounded and may produce better results.

Beyond skill estimation and reporting, DKT skill estimates may also be used for personalized content recommendation. Future research could explore the utility of constructing knowledge graphs from the skill relationships identified by the network.

References

1. Corbett, A.T., Anderson, J.R.: Knowledge tracing: modeling the acquisition of procedural knowledge. User Model. User-Adap. Inter. **4**(4), 253–278 (1994). https://doi.org/10.1007/BF01099821
2. Donghua, L., Yanming, J., Jian, Z., Wufeng, W., Ning, X.: Deep knowledge tracing based on Bayesian neural network. In: Xhafa, F., Patnaik, S., Tavana, M. (eds.) IISA 2019. AISC, vol. 1084, pp. 29–37. Springer, Cham (2020). https://doi.org/10.1007/978-3-030-34387-3_4
3. Gal, Y., Ghahramani, Z.: A theoretically grounded application of dropout in recurrent neural networks. Adv. Neural Inf. Process. Syst. **29**, 1019–1027 (2016)
4. Graves, A., Mohamed, A.R., Hinton, G.: Speech recognition with deep recurrent neural networks. In: 2013 IEEE International Conference on Acoustics, Speech and Signal Processing. pp. 6645–6649. IEEE (2013)
5. Guo, C., Pleiss, G., Sun, Y., Weinberger, K.Q.: On calibration of modern neural networks. In: International Conference on Machine Learning, pp. 1321–1330. PMLR (2017)
6. King, D.R.: Production implementation of recurrent neural networks in adaptive instructional systems. In: Sottilare, R.A., Schwarz, J. (eds.) HCII 2020. LNCS, vol. 12214, pp. 350–361. Springer, Cham (2020). https://doi.org/10.1007/978-3-030-50788-6_25
7. Kuleshov, V., Fenner, N., Ermon, S.: Accurate uncertainties for deep learning using calibrated regression. In: International Conference on Machine Learning, pp. 2796–2804. PMLR (2018)
8. Lord, F.M.: Applications of Item Response Theory to Practical Testing Problems. Lawrence Eribaum Associates Inc., Hillsdale (1980)
9. Mao, Y.: Deep learning vs. Bayesian knowledge tracing: student models for interventions. J. Educ. Data Min. **10**(2) (2018)
10. Narkhede, S.: Understanding AUC-ROC curve. Towards Data Sci. **26**, 220–227 (2018)
11. Piech, C., et al.: Deep knowledge tracing. arXiv preprint arXiv:1506.05908 (2015)
12. Yeung, C.K., Yeung, D.Y.: Addressing two problems in deep knowledge tracing via prediction-consistent regularization. In: Proceedings of the Fifth Annual ACM Conference on Learning at Scale, pp. 1–10 (2018)
13. Zhang, L., Xiong, X., Zhao, S., Botelho, A., Heffernan, N.T.: Incorporating rich features into deep knowledge tracing. In: Proceedings of the Fourth (2017) ACM Conference on Learning@ Scale, pp. 169–172 (2017)

Emerging Applications of Cognitive Ergonomics: A Bibliometric and Content Analysis

Anne Louise Roach$^{(\boxtimes)}$ and Vincent G. Duffy$^{(\boxtimes)}$

School of Industrial Engineering-Purdue University, West Lafayette, IN 47906, USA
{roach11,duffy}@purdue.edu

Abstract. With modern technological advancements building a dependency on computer systems, the need to understand how the human brain processes information and interacts with computers has facilitated the emergence of a new field of human factors engineering, cognitive ergonomics. As the field becomes more developed, its principles have been applied to many various fields. In this study, bibliometric data for research literature surrounding the term "cognitive ergonomics" was extracted from databases such as Web of Science, Scopus, and Google Scholar through Harzing's Publish or Perish. This data was then analyzed through tools such VOSviewer, BibExcel, MAXQDA, and Mendeley compare the emergence of cognitive ergonomics and its application in five main categories: Healthcare, Automation, Transportation, Language, and Production. The analysis showed strong growth in the field of cognitive ergonomics with Production and Healthcare being the two leading categories of practical application.

Keywords: Cognitive ergonomics · Human factors engineering · Automation · Harzing's Publish or Perish · MAXQDA · VOSviewer · Human-computer interaction · Bibliometric analysis · Content analysis · BibExcel

1 Introduction

Cognitive ergonomics is a growing field within human factors engineering. It takes the principles of classic ergonomics and applies them to human cognition to improve human performance as well as safety and mental wellbeing at work. Through studying human cognitive abilities and limitations, the interactions between humans and any other component of a system can be further understood and used as governing principles in the design of processes. This is an increasingly crucial problem as the relationship between humans and machines moves from a basis in operation to one in supervision [23]. A simple way to understand cognitive ergonomics is to describe humans in terms of data science. The mind is simplified to a data processing agent. The inputs come from the five senses- taste, sight, smell, touch, and hearing. Human cognitive processes define the transformation and translation of the data into actionable knowledge to further a specific goal. The purpose of cognitive ergonomics is to define how humans receive and process data to design systems around those capabilities to improve the productivity and safety

© Springer Nature Switzerland AG 2021
C. Stephanidis et al. (Eds.): HCII 2021, LNCS 13096, pp. 77–89, 2021.
https://doi.org/10.1007/978-3-030-90328-2_5

of worker performing their set of tasks. This research has applications in many fields. This study began through a literature review for examples of these practical and future applications of cognitive ergonomics.

2 Purpose of Study

The purpose of this study was to answer the research questions: "How is the field of cognitive ergonomics progressing human-computer interaction research and to what extent is the field catching on in various applications to improve the performance and safety of humans in the workforce?" This was accomplished through investigating the trends in the cognitive ergonomics research literature and comparing the new applications of cognitive ergonomics which pertain to safety in various professions. By studying human cognition and cutting down on the processing power necessary to complete tasks through automating some of the steps, reaction times to critical safety incidents can be shortened.

3 Research Methodology

The process followed in this study was derived from classwork in IE 558 Safety Engineering, taught by Dr. Vincent Duffy at Purdue University. As part of the coursework, examples of previous literature by Purdue students were shared and reviewed to aid in developing the method of analysis used in this study [10, 11]. The tools used in this study were introduced and demonstrated in class. The analysis began by searching "cognitive ergonomics" in the Purdue Libraries and using a method covered in the class called "List 10 ways" to reduce the number of articles to those most pertinent to the field of interest as well as reviewing common pitfalls of bibliometric studies to avoid them [21]. Those articles were used compiled using Mendeley and reviewed to refine the scope of the project. As lectures progressed, new tools were introduced, which further refined and progressed the study. The following study was conducted using the various tools introduced in class and analyzed below for this final report.

3.1 Relevant Literature

Transportation
The field of automated driving has grown substantially in recent years. This is partly because motor-vehicle accidents are the leading cause of work-related fatalities [6]. Researchers have mapped out the system network of automated cars and used cognitive ergonomics to characterize the interactions between components [3]. This information will be used in the design of the various component of the transportation network from signage to road to the automation logic control of the cars themselves. While transportation is a good opportunity to implement and showcase the benefits of automation, considering the payoff of lowering the number of motor-vehicle accident-related deaths, it will take a cultural change for the concept to firmly take root in society. Autonomous cars have become a reality; however, with every car failure comes added censure to

the field. Researchers have investigated the misuse and disuse of automation due to poor human-computer partnerships and the subsequent lack of trust many have toward safety-critical system functions [13]. The level of trust a user has will change the human-computer interaction. For example, if the user trusts an autonomous car too much, they may become distracted while being driven to a location and not intercede by taking over the manual operation (braking steering, etc.) in time to avoid a collision. Alternatively, if the level of trust is too low, fewer people will buy autonomous cars and the driving algorithms may be disrupted due to a higher level of poor drivers on the road. As automation becomes more commonplace in daily life, society will slowly become desensitized to it, until a level of generally accepted trust is established. Similar phenomena are the advent of social media and cellphones, which have transitioned from initial skepticism to a level of trust in which very few users even read the Terms and Conditions when downloading updates. Likely, each generation will push this cultural shift along for automation as well.

Automation
Cognitive ergonomics are key to designing efficient automation systems. This is important for not only implementing new systems but also optimizing well-established processes. An example of cognitive ergonomics being applied to automate a system is a recent study in fighter aircraft displays [2]. The purpose of the study was to improve pilot safety by controlling the information provided to the pilot depending on the circumstances. For example, if an engine stalls, the display changes to remove superfluous information which may distract the pilot from recovery. Such distractions include flashing lights, which can temporarily blind pilots in critical moments [7] By streamlining the information flow in a critical moment, the pilot can focus on the task and appropriately respond.

By implementing new automated systems, society is paving the way for far more complex systems. This is leading to challenges within the field of cognitive ergonomics as past performance indicators no longer accurately model systems with an ever-increasing, "swarm" level, number of agents [12]. Because of the capabilities unlocked by converting to automated systems, cognitive ergonomics will have a large role in the success of the complex, integrated systems of the future.

Language
With the increasing popularity of artificial intelligence, cognitive ergonomics has been applied to language. It has been applied to improve CAT tools used by professional translators, investigating natural language processing and cadence for predictive text algorithms [16]. Other examples of cognitive ergonomics applied to language are the communication patterns of common AI assistants such as Siri in Apple products or Alexa in Amazon. With each update, the language processing has become more "human", which has allowed user requests to have a more natural flow and to be interpreted with increasing accuracy. Whether providing convenience or translating contract negotiations, the applications of cognitive ergonomics will greatly ease the cross-cultural language barriers which are seen more often as the world's supply chains become more interconnected.

Production
As the production of goods has become dependent on computers, cognitive ergonomics has had a growing importance in understanding the human-computer interaction for better process design [1]. The operator of the future, or Operator 4.0, the concept has gained traction as researchers define what skills will be key in the production processes of tomorrow. A recent study recommends a design strategy centered on three modes of operation: learning, knowledge, and disruption [14]. The operator-automated system interaction must have a learning phase to define process conditions, a knowledge phase to perform under those conditions, and a disruption phase to correct for deviations from the normal flow. Automated production systems which have a similar design have been implemented to show proof of concept for cognitive control units, which can imitate human information processing and through a series of rules, control the system as an operator would [15]. This was accomplished by mapping human cognition and programing a two-robot automated assembly unit to follow a similar logic pattern.

Healthcare
Healthcare is an increasingly popular application of cognitive ergonomics. This has led to mixed responses from the UK Prime Minister wholeheartedly backing the enterprise, declaring in 2018 that the UK will be a leader in the field, to elderly patients that refuse care without the presence of a doctor [20]. Cognitive ergonomics improvements in healthcare have affected many aspects of the care process, changing handover of patient data between shifts, the patient-caregiver interaction, situational awareness, and introducing new automation bias [20]. Many of the recent applications in healthcare involved complex data processing in time-critical situations, specifically anesthesia [22]. While improvements have been made to automating the anesthesia process, most approaches so far have been focused on timesaving and have created localized solutions that have not spread among institutions [4]. As improvements to common processes are made, implementing them across multiple hospital networks will be the upcoming challenge in the field.

3.2 Data Collection

Once the scope of the study was defined, data collection was performed by searching keywords in three main databases: Google Scholar via Harzing's Publish or Perish, Web of Science, and Scopus. Categories were defined from the original literature list. The phrase "cognitive ergonomics" alone was used as the general category, and for each additional search, the phrasing followed the same pattern seen below in Table 1. Asterisks were used to avoid over constraining the Boolean search.

Because the field of cognitive ergonomics is relatively new with most of its growth being in the past 20 years (see Fig. 2), Fig. 1 was used to compare the emergence of cognitive ergonomics in each category. The leading category changes between Healthcare and Production depending on the database searched. This may be due to differences in keyword tagging of the metadata and the vocabulary used in the abstracts of each publication. It is also clear from Fig. 1 that not all categories of cognitive ergonomics were covered due to discrepancies between the general category versus the sum of the others included in the study. Further research would be needed to know the next categories to investigate.

Table 1. The number of publications per application search category found in each database.

Search term	Search category	Web of Science results	Scopus results	Google Scholar via Harzing results
"Cognitive ergonomics"	General	347	617	990
"Cognitive ergonomics" and transport**	Transportation	11	27	135
"Cognitive ergonomics" and automat**	Automation	40	69	168
"Cognitive ergonomics" and lang**	Language	21	31	254
"Cognitive ergonomics" and product**	Production	64	119	667
"Cognitive ergonomics" and health**	Healthcare	40	85	868

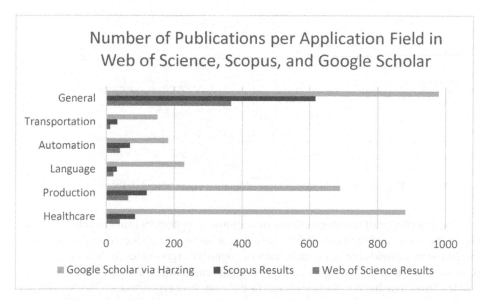

Fig. 1. Publications of "cognitive ergonomics" by application category

Figure 1 above clearly shows the vast difference among the database results. The number of Google Scholar results, extracted from Harzing's Publish or Perish, was consistently at least 150% more than those of Scopus and nearly 300% of Web of Science.

Scopus also consistently delivered more publications than Web of Science. Regardless of the database, it is clear that cognitive ergonomics an established with research impact in many fields.

3.3 Trend Analysis

A trend analysis was performed for the term "cognitive ergonomics" using Scopus. The resulting graph showing publications per year can be seen below in Fig. 2. The field has experienced steady growth; however, the sharp spike of interest in recent years bears further investigation in future literature reviews. This spike in interest shows that cognitive ergonomics is still an emerging field with a history of consistent growth. Because the spike is seen in 2020, the COVID-19 Pandemic may have contributed to the increased interest in cognitive ergonomics. Logically, with the increased reliance on technology experienced by all industries around the world due to international quarantine policies, it would raise further interest in how to optimize or improve human-computer interactions. Further investigation would be needed to pinpoint the reason for the pike in 2020, regardless, the field of cognitive ergonomics is experiencing significant growth as an emerging field of human factors engineering research.

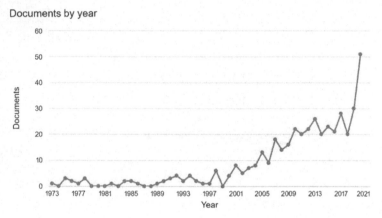

Fig. 2. Trends of search topic "cognitive ergonomics" in scopus

The emergence of new applications of cognitive ergonomics is also likely contributing to the growth of the field. While only five areas were considered in this literature review, as more fields apply the principles of cognitive ergonomics to their systems and processes, literature detailing the conjecture, implementation, and optimization of this will lead to increasing publications tagged with "cognitive ergonomics". Due to this phenomenon, it is expected that the field of cognitive ergonomics will continue the current growth trend seen in Fig. 1.

3.4 Leading Authors and Institutions

A brief study of the leading authors and institutions was conducted to better understand the increasing trend of cognitive ergonomics. Data was pulled from Google Scholar through Harzing's Publish or Perish by searching "cognitive ergonomics". The result-ing bibliometric metadata was then imported into BibExcel and refined to the leading authors with at least 8 publications in the field. The resulting PivotChart can be seen below in Fig. 3. The most prolific author, N. A. Stanton, was investigated further to understand the direction and impact of their research in the field. His work deals mainly in human factors engineering and developing theoretical systems thinking approaches to ergonomics. One of his most popular articles according to Google Scholar is "Distributed situation awareness in dynamic systems: theoretical development and application of an ergonomics methodology", which has experienced nearly 3,400 views and over 317 cita-tions according to Scopus [19]. It is noteworthy that not only is Stanton a prolific author but also a regularly cited perspective in cognitive ergonomics. Also, because the field has seen most of its growth within the past 20 years, to have amassed over 50 publications shows impressive dedication.

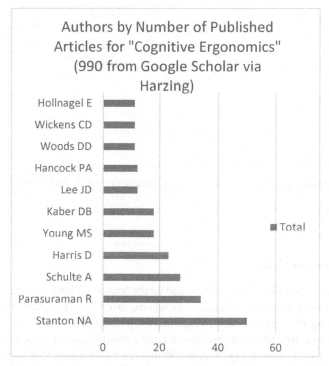

Fig. 3. Leading authors in cognitive ergonomics (Google Scholar, Harzing's Publish or Perish, BibExcel, n.d.)

In addition to the leading published authors, the leading institutions researching cog-nitive ergonomics were also investigated. This search was performed in Web of Science using the general search term "cognitive ergonomics". The resulting analysis can be seen below in Fig. 4. The top research institution by publications, CNRS, has published 25 articles, most of which have to do with the Language category investigated.. The research that CNRS is performing deals with the cognitive processes of dialogue-based learning, augmented by technology [8]. Their research is being used to further the Dialogue and Argumentation for Cultural Literacy Learning in Schools (DIALLS) programs in the EU. The program creates teaching materials to foster inclusion among school children of various cultures. Such experimental materials include wordless picture books and movies. Students are taught through dialogue-driven lectures with art projects to aid in sharing their perspectives on the chosen theme. The research performed by CNRS for the cognitive ergonomics of language and communication has greatly contributed to the success DIALLS has experienced.

Field: Organizations-Enhanced	Record Count	% of 367	Bar Chart
CENTRE NATIONAL DE LA RECHERCHE SCIENTIFIQUE CNRS	25	6.812 %	▮
UNIVERSITY OF LONDON	11	2.997 %	▮
UNIVERSITE PARIS VIII	7	1.907 %	▮
UNIVERSITY COLLEGE LONDON	7	1.907 %	▮
UNIVERSITY OF INDONESIA	7	1.907 %	▮
DELFT UNIVERSITY OF TECHNOLOGY	6	1.635 %	▮
HESAM UNIVERSITE	6	1.635 %	▮
ROYAL MELBOURNE INSTITUTE OF TECHNOLOGY RMIT	6	1.635 %	▮
UNIVERSITE DE TOULOUSE	6	1.635 %	▮
UNIVERSITY OF CAMBRIDGE	6	1.635 %	▮

Fig. 4. Leading institutions for cognitive ergonomics research (Web of science, n.d.)

4 Results

4.1 Co-citation Analysis

Once the data trends and leading authors and institutions were investigated, a co-citation analysis was conduction using metadata that was exported from Web of Science using the search term "cognitive ergonomics". This initial step resulted in 367 articles. VOSviewer was then used to refine the bibliometric data and extract the most shared citations. The final analysis, seen below in Fig. 5, resulted in three publications that had been cited a minimum of eleven times. Of the resulting three publications, *Human Error* by James Reason was the central link with connection to two other publications, one with a strong, red connection and the other with a weaker, green connection.

Fig. 5. Co-citation analysis results using bibliometric data from Web of Science (VOSviewer, n.d.)

To gain a general knowledge of the theme of the most popular publications, the central link, *Human Error* by James Reason [17], was further investigated. This was performed by downloading a pdf of the book, uploading it into MAXQDA, and creating a WordCloud to understand the high-level message and key terms of the book. The top words can be seen in Fig. 6. Through the WordCloud, it is clear that the book studies human cognition through mapping out common types of human errors that occur in man-machine interaction, particularly with computers. Through investigating these errors, systems can be designed to avoid the common pitfalls which reduce the cognitive ergonomics, productivity, and safety of human-computer processes.

Fig. 6. WordCloud of *human error* by James Reason [17] (MAXQDA, n.d.)

4.2 Content Analysis

Following the co-citation analysis and subsequent WordCloud, a similar content analysis was performed to identify keywords linked with the field of cognitive ergonomics. This study included a cluster analysis of the metadata previously extracted from Google Scholar via Harzing's Publish or Perish. This data was imported into VOSviewer to create a cluster analysis of key terms. The resulting five clusters can be seen below in Fig. 7. The five main clusters can be identified as automated systems and trust (green), human psychology and cognition (yellow), cognitive engineering and design decisions (blue), ergonomics (red), and human factors (purple). These data clusters are in line with the previous literature review conducted.

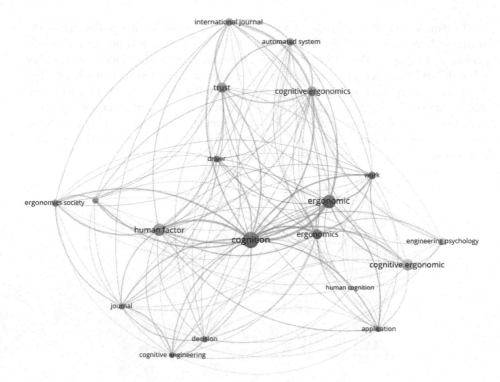

Fig. 7. Content analysis for "cognitive ergonomics" publications in Google Scholar (Harzing's Perish or Publish, n.d., VOSviewer, n.d.). (Color figure online)

4.3 Content Analysis Results from MAXQDA

An additional content analysis was conducted to compare the original literature review articles to the general metadata pulled from Google Scholar. The entire list of references for this paper was uploaded into MAXQDA to create the WordCloud below in Fig. 8 with the top 20 highest recurring words. The list was refined to take out common prepositions, helping verbs, and other non-definitive words. The resulting leading keywords from the MAXQDA can be seen in Fig. 9.

The content analysis from the literature review is consistent with the one found in Fig. 7. The main themes of trust, automation, human factors, ergonomics, and interactions remain the same. Most of the words are as expected; however, an interesting addition found in the WordCloud was the word "cat". Upon review, rather than a reference to felines or animal research, this is the acronym "CAT", which refers to computer-assisted translation (see 1.1 Relevant Literature-Language). Because the literature review articles follow the trend of the metadata from Google Scholar, it can be concluded that the review was an acceptable representation of current themes within the field of cognitive ergonomics.

Keywords such as "safety", "performance", and "tools" in Fig. 8 clearly indicate the benefits of applying cognitive ergonomics. The initial literature review accounts for most of the reference list, so it is logical that the benefits enumerated in those articles would

Fig. 8. Word cloud of keywords found in references (MAXQDA, n.d.)

Word	Word length	Frequency
trust	5	699
automation	10	590
human	5	302
research	8	302

Fig. 9. Leading words table output from MAXQDA content analysis (MAXQDA, n.d.)

spark keywords in Word cloud above. By applying cognitive ergonomics as discussed in the Relevant Literature section, tools were developed, and changes were made to improve the safety and performance of the humans involved in the systems and processes of the five study areas. Because the field of cognitive ergonomics has clear benefits when implemented, it is likely that more study areas will adopt its principles as it continues to grow in popularity as seen in the Trend Analysis.

5   Discussion

Cognitive ergonomics is a growing field within Human Factors Engineering. The number of research articles published per year has steadily increased over the past twenty years with the most dramatic growth in the past three years. It is becoming a pillar in the design of computer systems with its emphasis on understanding the human-automated system interaction. The consistent keywords of "trust", "automation", and "performance" clearly draw a connection between cognitive ergonomics and human-automation interaction.

Various applications of cognitive ergonomics to systems and processes within five areas of study—Transportation, Automation, Language, Production, and Healthcare—was found through the initial literature review. As more practical applications emerge within the field, further proof of concept will increase productivity and improve the safety of workers dealing with an ever-increasing number of automated processes. As society shifts the role of humans in the workforce from an operational to a supervisory role over machines, the need for cognitive ergonomics will also increase.

6 Future Work

There is a recent study that was awarded funding by the National Science Foundation due to their work tying cognitive ergonomics to language processing and translation. They managed to mathematically model eye movements while reading and correlate them to comprehension of the material [5]. This is a huge step forward in understanding how humans think, which will be valuable in designing computer systems to interact smoothly with the operator.

Another direction for future work within the field of cognitive ergonomics is designed while factoring in the mental health issues experienced by the general population. This research ranges from designing cognitive ergonomics for those with diagnosed mental disorders to designing systems to account for increased levels of stress [9, 18]. This research will create opportunities for those that otherwise may not have benefitted as much from the increase in automation seen in society. Additionally, it will pave the way for an inclusive work environment for all walks of life and cognitive patterns.

References

1. Akkari, A.C.S., da Rocha, M.F.M., de Farias Novaes, R.F.: Cognitive ergonomics and the industry 4.0. In: Iano, Y., Arthur, R., Saotome, O., Vieira Estrela, V., Loschi, H.J. (eds.) BTSym 2017, pp. 275–280. Springer, Cham (2019). https://doi.org/10.1007/978-3-319-93112-8_28
2. Alfredson, J., Holmberg, J., Andersson, R., Wikforss, M.: Applied cognitive ergonomics design principles for fighter aircraft. In: Harris, D. (ed.) EPCE 2011. LNCS (LNAI), vol. 6781, pp. 473–483. Springer, Heidelberg (2011). https://doi.org/10.1007/978-3-642-21741-8_50
3. Banks, V.A., Stanton, N.A., Burnett, G., Hermawati, S.: Distributed cognition on the road: using EAST to explore future road transportation systems. Appl. Ergon. 68(April), 258–266 (2018). https://doi.org/10.1016/j.apergo.2017.11.013
4. Beuscart-Zéphir, M C, Anceaux, F., Crinquette, V., Renard, J.M.: Integrating users' activity modeling in the design and assessment of hospital electronic patient records: the example of anesthesia. Int. J. Med. Inf. 64 (2001). www.elsevier.com
5. Bicknell, K., Levy, R.: The utility of modelling word identification from visual input within models of eye movements in reading. Vis. Cogn. 20(4–5), 422–456 (2012). https://doi.org/10.1080/13506285.2012.668144
6. Brauer, R.L.: Chapter 14: Transportation. In: Safety and Health for Engineers: Third Edition, 3rd ed., pp. 220–15 (2006). https://doi.org/10.1002/047175093X
7. Brauer, R.L.: Chapter 20: Visual Environment. In: Safety and Health for Engineers: Third Edition, 3rd ed., pp. 12–31 (2016). https://doi.org/10.1002/047175093X

8. Centre National de La Recherche Scientifique Archives - DIALLS. Dialls. 2020 (2020). https://dialls2020.eu/organisation/cnrs/
9. Crawford, J.R., Hubbard, E.-M., Goh, Y.M.: Mental health, trust, and robots: towards understanding how mental health mediates human-automated system trust and reliance. In: Ayaz, H. (ed.) AHFE 2019. AISC, vol. 953, pp. 119–128. Springer, Cham (2020). https://doi.org/10.1007/978-3-030-20473-0_13
10. Duffy, B.M, Duffy, V.G.: Data mining methodology in support of a systematic review of human aspects of cybersecurity. In: Digital Human Modeling and Applications in Health, Safety, Ergonomics and Risk Management. Human Communication, Organization and Work, Lecture Notes in Computer Science. pp. 242–253. Springer International Publishing, Cham (2020).https://doi.org/10.1007/978-3-030-49907-5_17
11. Duffy, G.A, Duffy, V.G.: Systematic literature review on the effect of human error in environmental pollution. In: Digital Human Modeling and Applications in Health, Safety, Ergonomics and Risk Management. Human Communication, Organization and Work, Lecture Notes in Computer Science. pp. 228–241. Springer International Publishing, Cham (2020). https://doi.org/10.1007/978-3-030-49907-5_16
12. Lee, J.D.: Emerging challenges in cognitive ergonomics: managing swarms of self-organizing agent-based automation. Theor. Issues Ergon. Sci. 2(3), 238–250 (2001). https://doi.org/10.1080/14639220110104925
13. Lee, J.D., See, K.A.: Trust in automation: designing for appropriate reliance human factors (In Press) n.d.
14. Mattsson, S., Fast-Berglund, Å., Li, D., Thorvald, P.: Forming a cognitive automation strategy for operator 4.0 in complex assembly. Comput. Ind. Eng. 139(January), 105360 (2020). https://doi.org/10.1016/j.cie.2018.08.011
15. Mayer, M.P., Odenthal, B., Wagels, C., Kuz, S., Kausch, B., Schlick, C.M.: Cognitive engineering of automated assembly processes. In: Harris, D. (ed.) EPCE 2011. LNCS (LNAI), vol. 6781, pp. 313–321. Springer, Heidelberg (2011)https://doi.org/10.1007/978-3-642-21741-8_34
16. O'Brien, S., Ehrensberger-Dow, M., Connolly, M., Hasler, M.: Irritating CAT Tool Features that matter to translators. HERMES – J. Lang. Commun. Bus. 56, 145–162 (2017). https://doi.org/10.7146/hjlcb.v0i56.97229
17. Reason, J.: Human Error. Cambridge University Press (1990)
18. Sauer, J., Schmutz, S., Sonderegger, A., Messerli, N.: Social stress and performance in human-machine interaction: a neglected research field. Ergonomics 62(11), 1377–1391 (2019). https://doi.org/10.1080/00140139.2019.1652353
19. Stanton, N.A., et al.: Distributed situation awareness in dynamic systems: theoretical development and application of an ergonomics methodology. Ergonomics 49(12–13), 1288–1311 (2006). https://doi.org/10.1080/00140130600612762
20. Sujan, M., et al.: Human factors challenges for the safe use of artificial intelligence in patient care. BMJ Health Care Inf. 26(1), 100081 (2019). https://doi.org/10.1136/bmjhci-2019-100081
21. Wallin, J.A.: Bibliometric methods: pitfalls and possibilities. Basic Clin. Pharmacol. Toxicol. 97, 261–275 (2005)
22. Webster, C.S., Weller, J.M.: Data visualisation and cognitive ergonomics in anaesthesia and healthcare. Brit. J. Anaesthesia 126(5), 913–915 (2021). https://doi.org/10.1016/j.bja.2021.01.009
23. Zohrevandi, E.: Visualization of complex situations to strengthen human-automation collaboration. In: ECCE 2019 - Proceedings of the 31st European Conference on Cognitive Ergonomics: "'Design for Cognition. pp. 14–18. New York, NY, USA, Association for Computing Machinery, Inc (2019). https://doi.org/10.1145/3335082.3335120

Total Learning Architecture (TLA) Data Pillars and Their Applicability to Adaptive Instructional Systems

Brent Smith[✉] and Laura Milham

Advanced Distributed Learning Initiative, Orlando, FL 32826, USA
{brent.smith.ctr,laura.milham}@adlnet.gov

Abstract. Since 2016, the Advanced Distributed Learning (ADL) Initiative has been developing the Total Learning Architecture (TLA), a 4-pillar data strategy for managing lifelong learning. Each pillar describes a type of learning-related data that needs to be captured, managed, and shared across an organization. Each data pillar is built on a set of international data standards that combine to increase the granularity and fidelity of learner data. Reusable Competency Definitions (IEEE 1484.20.1 RCD) are used to describe the Knowledge, Skills, Abilities, and Other behaviors (KSAOs) that are required in the workplace (e.g., the operational environment). Learning Activity Metadata (IEEE P2881 Learning Activity Metadata) is used to describe the various learning resources an organization uses to train and educate its people. The Experience API (IEEE 9274.1 xAPI) is used to track and manage learner performance both inside and outside a learning activity. An Enterprise Learner Record, currently an IEEE study group, is used to track and manage each learner's level of competency within the organization.

Together, this data enables a ledger of learner performance that ties all learning activities that a learner completes to competencies, credentials, and ultimately to the different career trajectories that a learner may pursue. The TLA data strategy includes linkages across the different standards listed above and collectively provide a data foundation for adaptive systems to build upon. This paper and discussion will walk viewers through the different data models that are being used to drive development of these standards.

Keywords: Total Learning Architecture · Adaptive instructional systems · Data strategy

1 Introduction to the TLA

The human capital supply chain is a complex system with inherent challenges to accommodating interoperability between organizations. The Advanced Distributed Learning (ADL) Initiative started the TLA project in 2016 with the goal of establishing a common data strategy across the education and training industry that enables lifelong learning. The TLA benefits from modern computing technologies, such as cloud-based deployments, microservices, and high Quality of Service (QoS) messaging services. Its capabilities come not from individual components or databases, but the enterprise-level collection, sharing, dissemination, and analysis of learner data [1].

The TLA defines a set of policies, specifications, and standards for enabling a future learning ecosystem. TLA standards help organize the learning-related data required to support lifelong learning and enable defense-wide interoperability across DoD learning tools, products, and data [2]. Business rules and governance strategies enable the management of this data across connected systems. The TLA relies on common data standards and exposed data interfaces to enable a wide range of functions. This abstracts away any dependencies on a single component and enables these functions to be performed by any connected component.

As a policy driven architecture, the TLA does not require any mandatory components. There are only required functions, organized into microservices and data stores. Each functional area must be exposed through common interfaces, asynchronous services, and standard data formats for communicating and storing data. Interfaces between components and data stores use the Secure Hypertext Transfer Protocol (HTTPS – part of an architectural pattern called Representational State Transfer or REST).

Message payloads are described using JavaScript Object Notation (JSON) and interfaces may be exposed at any point or points, depending on the physical components being used. The value of this strategy is that it supports the immediate and cost-effective reuse of legacy systems, while affording a gradual migration to a fully TLA compliant learning stack.

1.1 The TLA Data Strategy

Key to the human capital supply chain, learner data is a critical asset that enables effective decision making for both trainees to identify gaps in competencies, and for organizations to track employee capabilities across emerging needs. The key to managing lifelong learning data within the TLA is the interoperability afforded through the technical standards, specifications, and practices that underpin an integrated data strategy. The TLA Data Strategy is necessary to provide the semantic interoperability required for enterprise-level analysis and decision support. Data-driven decisions are enabled through enterprise-level analyses of learning data, supporting the continual refinement of occupational skills and the creation, selection, and maintenance of learning activities necessary to achieve proficiency.

The TLA Data Strategy provides a common set data standards and technical specifications designed to be implemented across DoD's education and training community. This overarching strategy will ensure that all data resources are designed in a way that they can be used, shared, and moved efficiently across the organization. The ADL Initiative is working with the Institute of Electrical and Electronics Engineers (IEEE), an internationally recognized standards-development organization, to formally establish the data standards required for successful TLA implementation. While these standards will continue to evolve, DoD education and training communities are urged to adopt and employ them now. These commercial standards describe the data within the four pillars of the TLA Data Strategy:

- **IEEE P9274.1 Experience API.** Learner performance tracking within different learning activities use the Experience API (xAPI) to capture learning activity streams [3]. This standard defines how learner performance is captured, communicated, and shared via a Learner Record Store (LRS), the server-side implementation of xAPI. The xAPI standard also includes xAPI profiles [4] such as cmi5 [5] and the TLA's Master Object Model. xAPI 2.0 is targeted for approval by IEEE in 2021.
- **IEEE P2881 Learning Activity Metadata.** Descriptions of learning activities and their associated content are stored in the TLA's Experience Index (XI). This draft standard builds upon IEEE 1484.12.1 Learning Object Metadata (LOM) to increase the granularity of how learning resources are defined [6]. It was developed by harmonizing with other educational data standards such as the Common Educational Data Standards (CEDS) project, the Postsecondary Educational Standards Council (PESC), Credential Engine's Learning Opportunity Type, the Learning Resource Metadata Initiative (LRMI), and Schema.org. The data model that informs the draft standard also includes numerous data types and properties that were derived from MILHDBK 29612, TRADOC FM 350–70, and the USAF 36–2235 Instructional Systems Design guidebook.
- **IEEE 1484.20.1 Reusable Competency Definitions.** The RCD standard enables a common approach for describing competencies, aligning competencies to other related competencies in the context of a framework, and defining the assessment and evaluation criteria for the evidence a learner must demonstrate to help measure proficiency [7]. This standard is being designed to facilitate a common language for describing the knowledge, skills, abilities, and other behaviors (KSAOs) required for performing different jobs, duties, and tasks associated with an occupational specialty. Competencies provide a common approach for aligning education and training activities to the desired operational performance expected from learners to perform with proficiency.
- **IEEE Enterprise Learner Records (Study Group).** This draft standard is built around a data model created by the ADL Initiative to meet DoD requirements on the Enterprise Learner Record Repository project [8]. This model was informed by the T3 Innovation Network's Learning and Employment Records (LER) Resource Hub and the Data Ecosystem Schema Mapper [9]. The data model builds upon the work performed by the T3 Innovation network to meet the evidentiary requirements (e.g., ownership, stewardship, and management of raw learner data) that many DoD organizations adhere to. It also supports future artificial intelligence/machine learning solutions that enable instructor support tools, intelligent tutoring, and additional insight into each learner that can be used to optimize and tailor their continuum of learning.

1.2   The TLA Reference Implementation

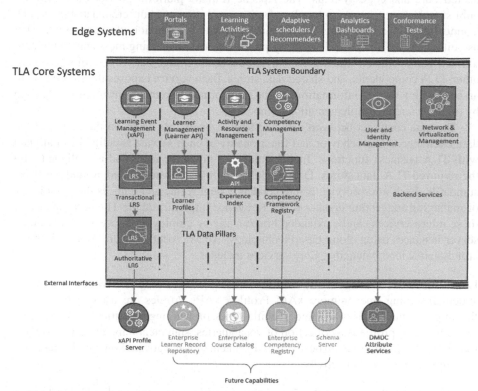

Fig. 1. Organization of Core and Edge Systems. The TLA's Core Services, required interfaces, and the data structures required for any TLA enclave align with the 4 TLA data pillars.

As shown in Fig. 1, the TLA Reference Implementation adopts a core/edge paradigm that deconstructs the learning environment into core services, core data, and edge systems [10]. Core systems replicate key functionality that typically resides in a Learning Management System (LMS), e.g., student registration, student tracking, content presentation, performance tracking, etc. that are necessary for any learning environment.

Core services manage the learner bookkeeping functions, while back-end core services manage the virtual network bookkeeping functions necessary to operate in a distributed, cloud-based environment. The edge systems are the devices used to provide learning, which may include traditional LMSs, as well as handheld devices, intelligent tutors, electronic publications, simulators, and any other evolving learning technologies. Ancillary functions, like an access portal, data visualization tools, adaptive algorithms, and any attached learning device, are also edge systems that communicate to the core.

The TLA reference implementation exists as a continuously evolving framework of software components designed and built to process large volumes of data from connected core and edge systems. The Apache Kafka® platform provides a distributed publish/subscribe messaging topology built around streams of different data topics [11]. Connected TLA components are instrumented with a collection of microservices that use either HTTP/S over TCP/IP or by producing and consuming messages to the centralized Kafka cluster. The services layer acts as the bridge between learning devices, other TLA components, and shared data stores. Each service exposes the stored data to an application so that information can be transformed into other meaningful data used by other Reference Implementation components.

The data contracts between data and service layers are based on the nature of the data exchanged. The behavior and functionality of each service is defined and aligned with TLA business functions. Input/output data flows are identified and aligned with the required TLA data stores. Data models and protocols are defined around the IEEE standards. Each microservice is independently deployable and reduces the complexity of managing and testing updates to the Reference Implementation. The performance of these microservices can be extended horizontally by cloning the processes on multiple server instances using cloud-based technology like Microsoft ®Azure Apache Hadoop and dynamic load balancing. Core services include:

Learning Event Management. Within the TLA, each learning activity generates xAPI statements using one or more xAPI Profiles. xAPI Profiles are used to help guide the implementation of xAPI into specific types of learning activities or for specific domains. Each profile is a collection of vocabularies, statement templates, and patterns that describe the relationship between xAPI statements and govern how xAPI statements are implemented into an activity.

Once an xAPI instrumented learning activity is connected to the TLA reference implementation (via the Learning Record Store (LRS)), other connected systems can glean insights from the learner performance data generated by that activity. The raw data collected in the LRS provides valuable insights into the learner pathways and decisions made within the context of each learning activity. This data can be used to provide adaptive feedback, remediation, instructor support, and can provide an understanding of how and why a learner performed the way they did within a single learning activity.

Given the diversity of different learning activities, occupational domains, and the xAPI Profiles that govern the xAPI Implementation within those systems, the TLA needs a way to normalize the data coming out of each activity. The TLA Master Object Model (MOM) is used to roll up the raw learner data into meaningful information that other connected systems can use [12]. The TLA MOM includes xAPI statements that describe key learner milestones for tracking and managing learner progression across all learning activities they encounter. The TLA MOM normalizes the xAPI statements coming out of a learning activity, as well as other learning systems such as schedulers, competency management systems, and career field planning tools.

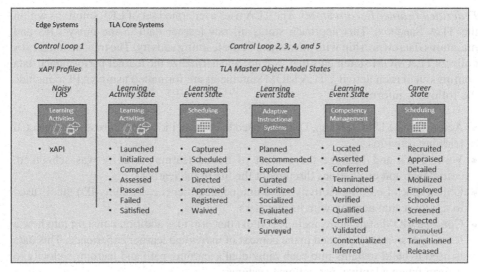

Fig. 2. TLA MOM Verbs. The TLA MOM defines the object life cycle of learners executing a single "thread of learning" that culminates in the reporting and evaluation of a learning event.

As shown in Fig. 2, the lifecycle of a learning event is defined by a series of learner-state transitions that are generated as a learner interacts with different systems used to schedule, deliver, and evaluate each instructional activity. The TLA MOM is implemented as an xAPI profile that generates xAPI statements at key points in the learner lifecycle and includes pointers to the raw learner data for systems that need it.

The TLA MOM's Learning Activity State defines the learner interactions a user will perform in a learning activity from initialization to completion or termination [13]. TLA MOM verbs in this state conform to the cmi5 Specification, which follows the lifecycle of the legacy SCORM cmi.core run-time data model. The use of cmi5 normalizes performance data and allows edge systems to perform their own adjudication so there are no conflicts within the TLA core data of what "correct performance" looks like.

The Learning Event State is associated with the activities that occur before a learner has interacted with a learning activity (e.g., requested, approved, scheduled, recommended, among others). It describes the context under which the learner pursued their learning. TLA verbs for this state are also generated after learner performance evidence has been generated or when an activity has been completed. These verbs are used to contextualize learner performance against a related set of competencies (e.g., validated, qualified, conferred, inferred, among others).

Career States are the verbs associated with moving to or progressing towards jobs on a career arc. These MOM statements would be generated by career field management tools, human resource systems, or other personnel systems. Career States change slowly over time as a learner moves from job to job and meets different career milestones (e.g., promoted, detailed, selected, among others).

Federated Learner Record Stores. The TLA uses a federated set of LRS solutions within the TLA Sandbox. This approach stores all raw learner data in the noisy LRS and maintains data ownership with the owners of the learning activity. The transactional LRS collects TLA MOM statements that 'roll up' and normalize the learner performance data coming out of each activity. TLA MOM statements are formatted using xAPI to include the following information:

- Actor: Unique User ID (e.g., DoD ID) used to track an individual across all connected learning activities.
- Verb: Track and Manage the context of how a learning activity was scheduled, completed, and evaluations throughout the life of the learner
- Object: Each Learning Activity has a unique identifier (i.e., Activity ID) that is used to associate that activity with its metadata.
- Context: MOM statements include context that provides additional insight into how a learning resources was used in the context of individual learner experience. This data is used to build insights into each individual's learning path and learning velocity to inform future adaptive instructional systems.

The authoritative LRS only includes verified competency assertions which will be discussed in the next chapter. This approach provides traceability of learner data for all learning activities that a learner encounters within an organization. Using this information, other connected systems can identify what training and education activities a learner has completed, use catalog descriptions to learn more about each activity, and evaluate learner performance in those activities.

Activity and Resource Management. Within the TLA, each learning resource (course, publication, activity) is described using the draft P2881 Learning Activity Metadata standard. Each learning activity has a unique, organizational identifier (ActivityID) that is used to update and manage these descriptions. As shown in Fig. 3, the draft P2881 standard includes data elements that enable other TLA systems to link learning outcomes to raw learner records (e.g., LRS endpoints, alignments, competencies). Other metadata elements are used to support lifecycle planning, adaptive instructional systems, and other elements that describe its fitness for use in an instructional setting.

Learning Activity Metadata is stored in an 'Experience Index'. Experience indices are maintained locally so that organizations can add additional metadata attributes as needed. P2881 Metadata governance allows for the promotion of locally created metadata attributes to the standard data model. Learning Activity Metadata attributes may be populated during development of the learning resource or they may be populated using values that are derived from other connects systems [14]. For example, a course survey system might allow a learner to rate their experience, when combined with other learner ratings, an 'AggregateRating' value can be calculated.

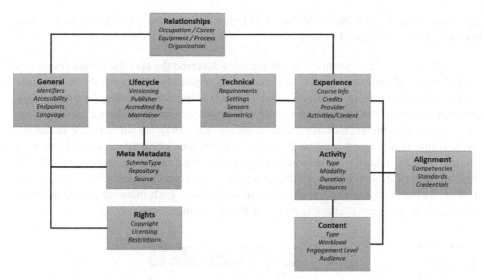

Fig. 3. Draft P2881 Learning Activity Metadata. The TLA uses a standardized data model for organizing one or more local course catalogs into a network of federated course catalogs.

The data model that the TLA's P2881 draft was derived from increases the granularity and fidelity for how we describe learning resources. Learning experiences (e.g., courses, seminars, classes) are decomposed into course sections, learning activities, and instructional content that comprise each course.

An Activity and Resource Management (ARM) service is associated with capturing, connecting, and sharing data about learning resources available within the TLA enclave. Key features include the ability to generate and manage metadata about each learning activity. The ARM functions of the TLA are associated with the creation, review, update, and deletion of Learning Activity Metadata (e.g., activities, courses), as well as the publishing those experiences to other connected systems (e.g., Enterprise Course Catalog). Learning experiences are initially defined as the different training and education resources that an organization has available; however, they may also represent other unique opportunities to enhance or demonstrate learning.

The Resource Management services are concerned with computational or physical assets, infrastructure, consumables, and staffing (e.g., observers, instructors) required to conduct a learning activity. Devices are registered as part of a Zero-Trust Network (ZTN) architecture. Device registration works with the identity and virtualization management services for security and integrity of the data generated and processed from each device. Devices include anything from an LMS or other Learning Experience Providers to mobile platforms and any number of future technologies. This allows users to use the organization's computational resources or their own personal devices once registered.

Competency Management. Competency management includes the process for evaluating learner performance and predicting proficiency levels for individual's teams, and organizations. Learner performance is collected using training and education activities that have been instrumented with the xAPI standard and the TLA MOM to federate learner data across multiple LRSs.

As shown in Fig. 4, competency definitions describe the specific details, contexts, related standards, mastery levels, and credentials required to successfully demonstrate the *knowledge, skills, abilities and other* (KSAO) behaviors necessary to successfully perform a job in an operational environment. Competency frameworks are used to define the relationships between defined competencies [15]. They are hierarchical in nature, but a single competency may be used across numerous occupations (e.g., jobs) so a 'many-to-many' relationship between many of the competency elements is required. The development of these models requires expertise in the science of learning, instructional design, and operational experience to accurately define each measure of competency, acceptable assessment strategies, and evidentiary requirements.

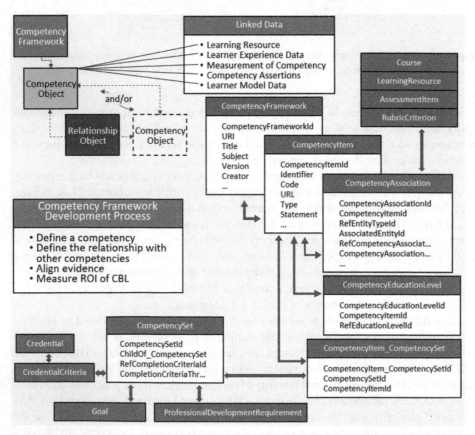

Fig. 4. Reusable Competency Definitions. RCDs formalize the way competencies, their relationships, and proficiency requirements are communicated to other TLA components.

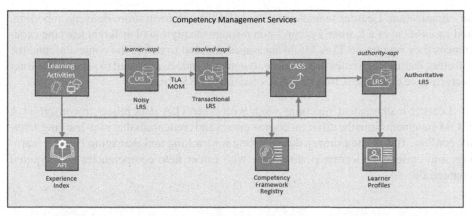

Fig. 5. Reusable Competency Definitions. RCDs formalize the way competencies, their relationships, and proficiency requirements are communicated to other TLA components.

Within the TLA, the competency management service manages evidence of an individual's knowledge, skills, abilities, attributes, experiences, personality traits, and motivators to predict their value toward effective performance. Figure 5 shows the flow of learner performance data from the learning activity to the noisy LRS, and over to the transactional LRS using the TLA MOM. The TLA MOM statements stored in the Transactional LRS provide the evidence upon which competency assertions are made.

To generate assertions of competency, the TLA's competency management service reads the TLA MOM statements that are stored in the Transactional LRS and parses each TLA MOM statement. The <xAPI Actor> field is correlated with the learner profile using the learner's UUID and the <API Object> field is correlated with the activity's metadata using the unique Activity ID. Each learning activity's metadata file includes unique competency identifiers that tells the competency services which competency definitions need to be pulled from the Competency Registry. Using the learner profile, learning activity metadata, and relevant competency definitions, The TLA competency management system can estimate proficiency levels for each competency.

A credential is issued by an entity with authoritative power and provides proof of an individual's qualification or competence in a subject. A network of competencies typically has varying mastery levels as part of its credentialing model. Previous levels contribute to the next level of mastery, and competency elements within the various levels may atrophy over time from disuse. Each credential is defined using the *Credential Transparency Description Language (CTDL)*. CTDL decomposes the credential into the competencies that it represents using the same unique identifiers for each competency definition [16]. These artifacts range widely from a college degree to a professional certificate to a badge or a micro-credential. Possessing a credential not only helps one to prove competency and capability within a field, but it also serves as verification that the individual is properly trained and equipped to carry out their duties within their specific vocations or disciplines.

Learner Management. The TLA's Learner Management functions are associated with the ledgering of all learning and development activities that a learner encounters within an organization. Learner management includes the administration, delivery, reporting, and assessment of a learner's progression through the myriad of different learning experiences they encounter. TLA MOM messages are used to define the context around the different learning activities that a learner completes and are also used to preserves learner performance evidence across the TLA's federated LRS structure.

Learner management functions work with other TLA data pillars to convert TLA MOM statements into the different competencies and credentials that each learning activity confers. This is the primary data pipeline for tracking and managing lifelong learning; and correlating learner performance with career field competencies and required credentials.

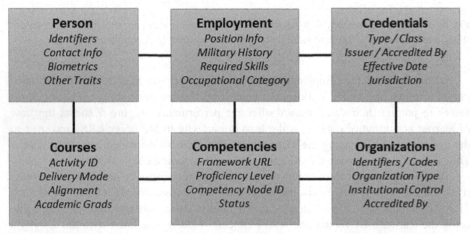

Fig. 6. Draft Enterprise Learner Record Data Model. Each learner record also includes a global registration of all places holding subordinate data about the learner, including learner attributes, learner performance records using xAPI, assessment data, and other related information.

A Learner Profile is used to record learner competency and credential history, aptitudes, local and global preferences, career trajectory and progress against learner goals. Figure 6 shows the different categories of data that are tracked within the Enterprise Learner Record data model. A unique user ID is used to track learner performance across all connected activities using xAPI statements. xAPI statements include linkages to the other core data repositories to provide additional information to any connected system that requires it.

A Learner profile is used to aggregate this information and a broad range of other data including demographic data, data about student interests, learning preferences, learning goals, career trajectories, and other relevant learner attributes. Connected TLA systems use the Learner API to communicate with the learner profile.

Learner profiles act as the data fabric "connector" and make learner records within the profile globally discoverable through an Enterprise Learning Record Repository (ELRR). The goal of the ELRR is to ensure globally relevant data about individual learners and teams is available to any command, learning system, or activity across the

DoD. These data may be used to support adaptive instruction, improved decision making, and analytical insights into learners and the systems they interact with. These data also facilitate the longitudinal analysis of a military career to evaluate systemic readiness issues, efficiency of education/training activities, completeness of standards, and media efficacy.

2 Supporting Adaptive Instructional Systems

Adaptive Instructional Systems, when developed with the TLA Data Pillars, can leverage the resultant data to support a number of different adaptive capabilities. Figure 7 describes these capabilities through a series of 'control loops'. At the first level, the learner's data can be used to adjust scaffolding within a specific learning activity (control loop 1). The activity may scale in difficulty, performance conditions, or the amount and type of feedback received. At a more complex level, learner data can be used to adapt across several different types of learning activities (control loop 2). For example, if there are identified gaps in learner knowledge, a path can be taken to provide supplemental learning activities before moving on to the next step towards achieving a credential.

Third, from an active learner's perspective, longitudinal data can be leveraged to compare several potential paths to get to a credential goal. Courses may vary in length, in ratings, or other factors that allow a learner to make decisions of how to structure their learning experience (control loop 3). Fourth (control loop 4), talent managers can work with learners to lay out long term plans to meet not only current career goals, but also to allow a career pivot to address emerging DoD mission needs (control loop 5), that leverages past learner credentials and competencies, or provides a new path.

The raw learner data from each learning activity can be connected to build learner insights beyond what a single learning activity is capable of. The TLA uses the concept of Control Loops, as shown in Fig. 7, to delineate how this 'lifelong' learner data might be used by different systems and at different levels of granularity across different time horizons. In other words, the same data collected from a learning activity may be used in different ways depending on the purpose for which it is being used.

The control loops show that learning data may be viewed from different perspectives requiring different levels of granularity and fidelity over different time horizons. For example, a learner may be pursuing a specific job credential required for promotion. They need to participate in one of more courses (e.g., a sequence of learning activities) in support of their career trajectory. This example can be viewed in the context of control loops 2, 3, and 4.

This approach to learner management enables a system of digital trust that provides auditability, privacy, and data integrity for the chain of evidence (e.g., raw learner performance data) used to assert proficiency levels for individuals or teams against one or more competencies. The five control loops in order of ascending time horizons address:

- **Control Loop 1**: Using learner performance data to optimize the transfer of learning within the current learning activity (e.g., Intelligent Tutoring, Instructor Support).
- **Control Loop 2**: Using learner performance data across numerous learning activities to optimize a learner's progress toward a credential.

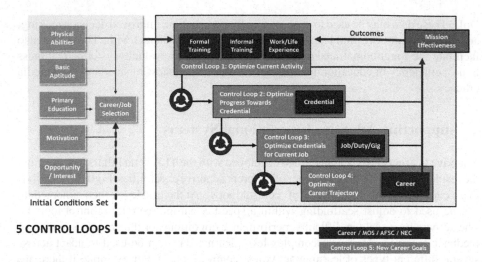

Fig. 7. TLA Control Loops. TLA MOM statements act as the sensors for the different control loops. The five control loops are constantly operating in parallel, but they provide a convenient way to categorize data.

- **Control Loop 3:** Using longitudinal learner data to prioritize the pursuit of credentials or activities to meet requirements for a potential job.
- **Control Loop 4:** Lifelong learning data to support career field management and the planning of education and training goals for an overall career trajectory.
- **Control Loop 5:** Lifelong learning data to support the establishment of a new career.

2.1   The Sum is Greater Than Its Parts.

Each TLA data pillar builds upon existing standards to increase the granularity and fidelity for how we describe learning resources, learners, their performance, and the competencies that need to be taught. The data models that drive the different TLA standards rely on other systems within the Human Capital Supply Chain to populate many of their data elements. Automation and a well-defined governance strategy are critical to updating and maintaining the data stored within each TLA data warehouse.

The TLA is asynchronous, and event driven. Every device or service in the ecosystem appears as either a learning record provider (LRP) and/or a learning record consumer (LRC). In many cases, a system may perform both roles (e.g., adaptive instructional systems). The use of APIs and microservices is designed to support modern high-performance messaging system and means that there is no single system responsible for coordinating the execution between components. This statelessness is essential for the loose coupling required to be a true ecosystem.

While most LRS solutions offer dashboards to view learner performance, they are commonly used to view xAPI statements that have been generated within a single learning activity. From an adaptation perspective, that data has great potential to automate remediation, feedback, or other optimizations that help expedite the transfer of learning.

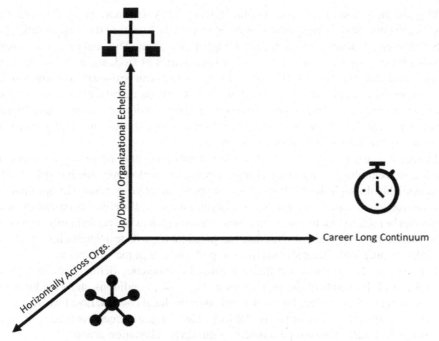

Fig. 8. Breadth and Scale of Learner Data. Learner data can be shared vertically within an organization, horizontally across other organizations, or longitudinally throughout a career.

The inclusion of the TLA MOM provides additional insights into how learning activities are used to support training and education within an organization. Tracking this information provides insights into learner path, learner velocity, and overall effectiveness. The addition of learning activity metadata and competency definitions enhance these capabilities by affording opportunities to tie training and education outcomes to key performance indicators in the operational environment.

The totality of this data promotes adaptive systems beyond training and education and afford new opportunities for career field management, workforce planning, and cross-training. Figure 8 shows the breadth and scale for how this data might be used to support the scope and breadth of DoD organizations from instructor dashboards to robust analytics for readiness and capable manpower. The data also supports the lifelong continuum of learning for all DoD personnel.

2.2 Data-Driven Adaptation

Artificial intelligence (AI) and Machine Learning (ML) are becoming powerful tools for adapting instructional content to increase motivation, autonomy, effectiveness, and efficiency of learners and teachers [17]. Data driven learning can take place in traditional face-to-face learning settings, as well as in the technology-enhanced learning settings. The scope and scale for how adaptation is implemented within a course or activity spans a wide range of use cases. Learning analytics have long been used to inform instructors, improve course content, or adjust how the course is delivered [18].

Beyond the scope of a single learning activity, TLA data may be used to provide insights into students' learning trajectories. Reeves (19) discussed three approaches for assessing online learning environments in higher education. The cognitive assessment focuses on measuring the higher order thinking abilities of students, achieved through means such as concept mapping. Performance assessment can be done by looking into the learner's ability to apply knowledge in realistic contexts, done by requiring students to demonstrate their capabilities directly through product creation or through engagement. Finally, a portfolio is where the work of the student is stored over time so that it can be reviewed with respect to both process and product.

In recent years, progress has been made towards providing adaptivity and personalization in technology-enhanced learning environments. However, the breadth of data made available through the TLA standards supports adaptive systems that optimize or tailor instruction to support the needs of the organization. Well-defined competency definitions can be used to link training and education resources to key performance measures in the operational environment. This data has potential to provide a longitudinal analysis that links training and education activities to performance in the workplace.

Competency frameworks and their associated competency definitions can also be adapted to suit the needs of the organization. The tasks, conditions, and standards for demonstrating proficiency are highly dependent on the local context. Local weather conditions, geographic location, or the availability of learning resources, coupled with organization goals and/or mission parameters might drive adaptation around the sequence of learning interventions that a learner is provided. Alternatively, performance support tools may also adapt to provide just-in-time support to learners while doing their jobs.

The TLA project has established a foundational data strategy that supports adaptation for learners, instructors, and organizational needs. TLA data standards will continue to evolve and adapt to better support the needs of the future learning ecosystem. As adaptive instructional systems mature and refine their algorithms, new data elements may be required within certain standards. This requires changes to how we develop standards so they can be continuously managed, refined, and updated through a well-defined governance strategy.

2.3 Conclusions and Next Steps

The aggregation of TLA data provides a baseline for continuous process improvement across all aspects of training and education from scheduling and planning activities to evaluating their effectiveness against key performance indicators in the operational environment.

Increased fidelity of learner data also provides insights into the different paths different learners take to achieve proficiencies in their chosen careers. Learning trajectories within career trajectories can be tailored to support different groups of learners and improved insights into career progressions can help expedite growth across different to present new opportunities for employees. Senior leaders within an organization may also use this information to evaluate readiness towards achieving mission outcomes. Workforce planning and cross-training opportunities will converge to help organizations adapt to evolving requirements.

The different IEEE standards that the TLA is built around are at different stages of the standardization pipeline. The IEEE's xAPI 2.0 standard is due to be released in 2021; the update to the Reusable Competency Definition Standard (IEEE 1484.20.1) is also expected in 2021; the IEEE P2881 Working Group is actively developing their draft standard for Learning Activity Metadata and the IEEE Enterprise Learner Record Study group is actively evaluating a draft data model to evaluate its potential as an IEEE standard.

These data standards should be viewed as a foundation to be continuously improved upon as the tools and technologies used for training and education evolve. The aggregation of data collected by these standards will have increasingly important roles across organizational boundaries, thus enabling the future learning ecosystem.

References

1. ADL Initiative: Total Learning Architecture Report (2019). https://www.adlnet.gov/assets/uploads/2019%20Total%20Learning%20Architecture%20Report.pdf
2. Barr, F., Morrison: Institute for Defense Analysis Report, The ADL's Total Learning Architecture (2020). https://www.adlnet.gov/assets/uploads/ADL%20TLA%20-%20IDA%20Report%202020.pdf
3. IEEE P9274 Experience Application Program Interface (xAPI) Standard. https://github.com/adlnet/xAPI-Spec
4. IEEE P9274.2.1 xAPI profile Specification. https://github.com/adlnet/xapi-profiles
5. cmi5 specification. http://aicc.github.io/CMI-5_Spec_Current/
6. IEEE P2881 Learning Metadata. https://standards.ieee.org/project/2881.html
7. IEEE 1482.20.1 Reusable Competency Definition Objects. https://standards.ieee.org/project/1484_20_1.html
8. Reardon, A., Gordon, J.: From silos to manifolds: strategies for improved learner records. In: Interservice/Industry Training, Simulation, and Education Conference (2020)
9. T3 Innovation Network, Data Ecosystem Schema Mapper (DESM), Learning and Employment Records Resource Hub. https://www.lerhub.org/s/curators/specs-0/s6wb9CdFi3qoxJQ48-0
10. 2020 TLA Reference Implementation Standup Guide, System/Subsystem Design Documentation, ADL Initiative
11. Apache Kafka 2.7 Documentation. https://kafka.apache.org/documentation/#design
12. TLA Master Object Model (MOM). https://github.com/adlnet/MasterObjectModel
13. Cmi5, EduTech wiki. http://edutechwiki.unige.ch/en/Cmi5
14. Liu, Y.: Metadata in the future learning ecosystem. In: Interservice/Industry, Training, Simulation, and Education Conference (2020)
15. Competency Framework Development Process Report. ADL Initiative (2020). https://www.adlnet.gov/assets/uploads/2020-03%20Competency%20Framework%20Development%20Process%20Report.pdf
16. Credential Engine Schemas Handbook. https://www.adlnet.gov/assets/uploads/2020-03%20Competency%20Framework%20Development%20Process%20Report.pdf
17. Foung, D., Chen, J.: A learning analytics approach to the evaluation of an online learning package in a Hong Kong University. Electron. J. e-Learn. **17**(1), 11–24 (2019)
18. Buckingham-Shum, S., Gasevic, D., Ferguson, R. (eds.) Lak '12: Proceedings of the 2nd International Conference on Learning Analytics and Knowledge. ACM, New York (2012)

19. Reeves, T.C.: Alternative assessment approaches for online learning environments in higher education. J. Educ. Comput. Res. **23**(1), 101–111 (2000)
20. Graesser, A.C., Greiff, S., Stadler, M., Shubeck, K.T.: Collaboration in the 21st century: the theory, assessment, and teaching of collaborative problem solving. Comput. Hum. Behav. (2019)

Effect of Image Captioning
with Description on the Working Memory

Nithiya Shree Uppara[1]([✉]), Troy McDaniel[2], and Hemanth Venkateswara[1]

[1] School of Computing, Informatics, and Decision Systems Engineering,
Arizona State University, Tempe, AZ, USA
{nuppara,hemanthv}@asu.edu
[2] The Polytechnic School, Arizona State University, Mesa, AZ, USA
troy.mcdanie@asu.edu

Abstract. Working memory plays an important role in human activities across academic, professional, and social settings. Working memory is defined as the memory extensively involved in goal-directed behaviors in which information must be retained and manipulated to ensure successful task execution. The aim of this research is to understand the effect of image captioning with image description on an individual's working memory. A study was conducted with eight neutral images comprising situations relatable to daily life such that each image could have a positive or negative description associated with the outcome of the situation in the image. The study consisted of three rounds where the first and second round involved two parts and the third round consisted of one part. The image was captioned a total of five times across the entire study. The findings highlighted that only 25% of participants were able to recall the captions which they captioned for an image after a span of 9–15 days; when comparing the recall rate of the captions, 50% of participants were able to recall the image caption from the previous round in the present round; and out of the positive and negative description associated with the image, 65% of participants recalled the former description rather than the latter.

Keywords: Working memory · Image captioning · Sentiment analysis

1 Introduction

The quest to understand the human brain and the workings of human memory has intrigued philosophers and researchers for centuries. Memory is one of the most important aspects of what makes us human, and yet it is one of the most elusive and misunderstood of human faculties. Memory can be pictured as a small filing cabinet with separate memory folders where information is kept, or as a brain supercomputer with enormous capacity and speed [31]. To retrieve a memory from the past, different areas of the brain collaborate. For example, let's consider the act of driving a car which is recreated by the brain from many

© Springer Nature Switzerland AG 2021
C. Stephanidis et al. (Eds.): HCII 2021, LNCS 13096, pp. 107–120, 2021.
https://doi.org/10.1007/978-3-030-90328-2_7

different areas: the memory of how to get from the current location to the end of the block, the memory of how to operate the car, and the memory of driving the car while following the safety rules, which all come from different parts of the brain. Each memory element (sights, sounds, phrases, and emotions) is encoded in the same portion of the brain that created that fragment in the first place, and recalling a memory effectively reactivates the neural patterns that were established during the original encoding [31]. A lasting memory in the brain is created when all the different types of memory work together to form it. The popular Atkinson-Shiffrin model defines a 3 step model for memory including sensory memory, short-term memory or working memory, and long-term memory [2].

Working memory, in particular, has been a fascinating area of research since its introduction in the 1960s [5,15]. Various studies about memory in the fields of psychology, biology or neuroscience have not been able to completely outline a categorization of memory in terms of its functionality and mechanism [4,11,33]. Working memory has been gaining a lot of importance in mundane human activities such as in academic, professional and social settings [25]. To understand the basic definition of working memory, one must first understand the difference between long-term memory and short-term memory. Long-term memory is defined as a vast store of knowledge and a record of prior events [11]. Long-term memory capacity varies from situation to situation and from person to person. Short-term memory is the ability of the human mind to hold a finite amount of information in a very accessible state, temporarily [2]. The main difference between long-term memory and short-term memory is the duration of the situation of information stored and the capacity of the information stored [7]. The former has a huge capacity to retain information for a long duration and the latter is limited by the total number of chunks of information that can be stored at a time [11].

Working memory is not completely different from short-term memory. Working memory is defined as the memory extensively involved in goal-directed behaviors in which information must be retained and manipulated to ensure successful task execution [9]. Miller et al. [32] proposed the term working memory to refer to memory as it is used to plan and carry out behavior. An example of a common use of working memory is recalling partial calculations while solving a mathematical problem. The information stored during this process is stored only for that instance of time and is discarded from memory when the purpose is served. The factors related to the amount of time the information is stored change depending on the situation in which the information is perceived. Working memory assessments have been found to correlate with intellectual aptitudes (particularly fluid intelligence) better than short-term memory measures, and possibly better than assessments of any other psychological process [13,14,19,28,33].

One of the most important characteristics of working memory is its limited capacity [3,12]. Working memory capacity helps to predict fluid intelligence and attentional control [20,22]. For visual objects, this value has been estimated to be three or four visual objects [30,34,39,40]. Studies which examine visual working memory by sequentially presenting items have shown that the information is either completely stored or entirely forgotten [27,37,41]. Many studies have shown that as the number of objects to be stored in working memory increases, the precision gradually decreases and it is worse for a sequential array of objects than a simultaneous array of objects [1,6,29].

An important question to examine is the effect of positive and negative information on visual working memory. Various studies have shown that emotional content increased the chances of retaining the information for a long period of time [8,17,24]. Various experiments conducted to examine the link between emotion and working memory by inducing a change in the mood of the participants have shown a change in cognitive task performance [18,23,38]. Spies et al. [38] and Cheng et al. [10] have demonstrated that negative mood hinders the performance on tests of problem solving, working memory and attention. This may be due to intrusive thoughts and worries which distract participants from the task at hand [21,36]. Individuals may be more likely to direct attention consciously toward emotional stimuli or to elaborate on emotional information because of its personal relevance [16,26]. Depending on the task at hand, having additional emotional stimuli can ease, if task-relevant information is processed, or weaken, if task-irrelevant information is processed, working memory capacity and performance of an individual. Perlstein et al. [35] have shown that emotional content has hindered the performance on working memory tasks.

In the proposed study we examine the effect of image captioning with description on the working memory of humans. We aim to understand the impact of positive and negative outcomes on working memory associated with a neutral image, and understand the impact on long-term memory as well. We hypothesize that positive descriptions will be retained for a longer period of time compared to negative descriptions associated with the outcome of an image. We would also like to understand if additional information associated with the image helps the participants in retaining the image captions for longer time in the working memory.

2   Experimental Setup and Methodology

2.1   Participants

The total number of participants enrolled in this IRB-approved study was 65 undergraduate and graduate students from Arizona State University between ages 17–27. All participants were well acquainted with the English language and had basic computer usage skills. We used data from 50 participants for the analysis after dropping records with missing entries.

2.2   Procedure

Eight neutral images were selected where each image could have a positive and negative outcome. All images comprise situations from everyday life. Each image is associated with two descriptions: a positive description, which is the result of a positive outcome of the situation shown in the image, and a negative description, which is the result of a negative outcome of the situation shown in the image.

The study consisted of three rounds performed with a minimum gap of three days to a maximum gap of five days between rounds. The first round consisted of two parts. In the first part, an image was randomly selected from the set of eight images, and was displayed to the subject to be captioned. In the second part of the round, the same image was displayed but along with a positive or negative description. The participant captioned the image again after reading the description associated with it. In addition, a question was asked to see if the participant understood the description correctly. The number of positive and negative descriptions were kept equal. Round 2 also consisted of two parts. The only difference between the first and second round was that the description in the first round was chosen at random for each participant whereas in the second round, the description was opposite of the description displayed in the first round. For the third or final round, the participants were given the same images without any descriptions and were asked to caption the image. The time taken to complete each round was noted (Fig. 1).

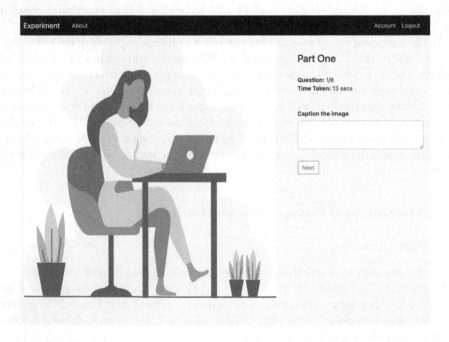

Fig. 1. Part-1 interface of Round-1 and Round-2 of the image captioning study.

Fig. 2. Part-2 interface of Round-1 and Round-2 of the image captioning study.

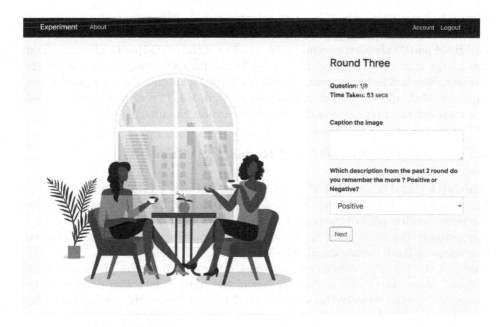

Fig. 3. Round-3 interface of the image captioning study.

2.3   Data Analysis

Each subject inputs 5 captions for each of the 8 images. The first caption is named Round-1 Part-1 (R1-P1), the second caption is named Round-1 Part-2 (R1-P2), the third caption is named Round-2 Part-1 (R2-P1), the fourth caption is named Round-2 Part-2 (R2-P2) and the fifth or final caption is named Round-3 (R3) (Figs. 2 and 3).

We propose to analyze the captions to test for similarity and to evaluate sentiment. It is possible that two captions from the same user are similar in context but differ in language. To account for such cases, we used the HuggingFace BERT Sequence Classification pre-trained model [42] to identify contextual similarity. We also used the HuggingFace BERT Sequence Classification pre-trained model to identify the sentiment of the caption.

The main purpose of conducting different rounds of the experiment with regular intervals of time is to observe the recall span and retention span of the image captions when additional information like description is provided with the image. The possible combinations for this purpose considered are the ability to remember captions from R1-P2 in R2-P1, from R2-P1 in R3 and from R1-P1 in R3.

3   Results

3.1   Round-1 Part-1 (R1-P1) vs. Round-3 (R3)

Figure 4 shows that only 25% of the captions, i.e., 101, were contextually the same, and 75% of the captions, i.e., 299, were contextually different for R1-P1 and R3. Figure 5 shows the trend in the number of the participants who captioned the image contextually the same and different for each image from the image dataset. It is interesting to note that even after looking at the same image five times in total, and captioning it four times before R3, 75% of participants could not recollect the first caption they used to caption the image.

3.2   Round-1 vs. Round-2 and Round-2 vs. Round-3

Round-1 (R1-P1 and R1-P2) vs. Round-2 Part-1 (R2-P1):
Figure 6 shows that of the participants who finished Round-1 (R1) and have seen the images twice, 36% of the participants, i.e., 143, captioned the image in R2-P1 contextually the same as in R1-P1; 13% of the participants, i.e., 54, captioned the image in R2-P1 contextually the same as in R1-P2; and the rest, 51%, of the participants, i.e., 203, captioned the image differently from the previous round. Figure 7 shows the trend in the number of the participants who captioned the image in R3 contextually the same as R1-P1, R1-P2, and the rest different for each image from the image dataset.

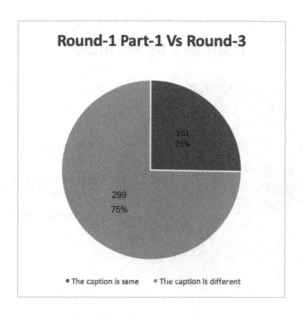

Fig. 4. Distribution of image captions from R1-P1 which are contextually the same as R3.

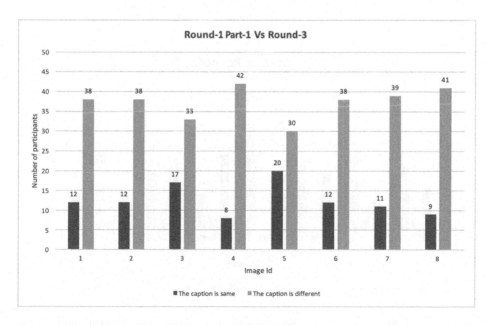

Fig. 5. Trend in the number of participants who captioned the image in R3 contextually the same as R1-P1 and different for each image from the image dataset.

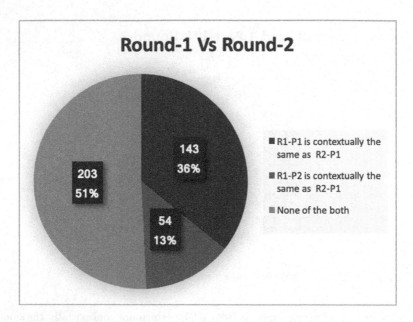

Fig. 6. Distribution of image captions from R1-P1 and R1-P2 which are contextually the same as R2-P1.

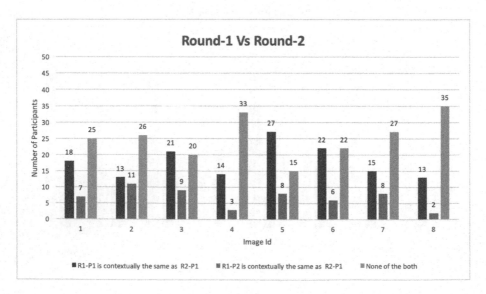

Fig. 7. Trend in the number of participants who captioned the image in R2 contextually the same as R1-P1, R1-P2 and not the same.

Round-2 (R2-P1 and R2-P2) vs. Round-3 (R3):
Figure 8 shows that of the participants who completed Round-2 (R2) and have seen the images four times, 37% of the participants, i.e., 146, captioned the image in R3 contextually the same as in R2-P1; 15% of participants, i.e., 61, captioned the image in R3 contextually the same as R2-P2; and the rest, 49%, of participants, i.e., 193, captioned the image differently from the previous round. Figure 9 shows the trend in the number of participants who captioned the image in R3 contextually the same as in R2-P1, R2-P2, and none of both, i.e., the rest are different for each image from the image dataset.

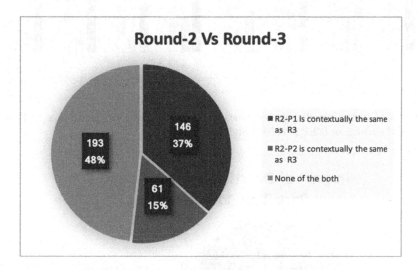

Fig. 8. Distribution of image captions from R2-P1 and R2-P2 which are contextually the same as R3.

An interesting observation is that even after seeing the image with extra information like the description associated with the image in R1 and R2, the majority of participants tend to remember the image caption they captioned in R1-P1 and R2-P2 respectively.

3.3   Trends in Round-1 Part-2 and Round-2 Part-2

Figure 10 shows that among the total number of participants whose image caption from R1-P2 is contextually the same as R1-P1, 67% of participants, i.e., 36, captioned the image with respect to the positive description associated to it, and 33% of participants, i.e., 18, captioned the image with respect to the negative description associated to it.

Figure 11 shows that among the total number of participants whose caption from R2-P2 is contextually the same as in R3, 56% of the participants, i.e., 34, captioned the image with respect to the positive description associated to it,

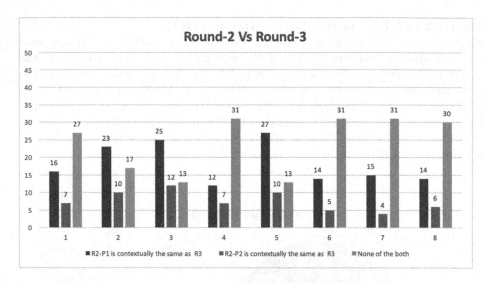

Fig. 9. Trend in the number of the participants who captioned the image in R3 contextually the same as R2-P1, R2-P2 and not the same.

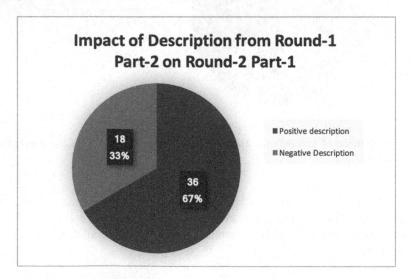

Fig. 10. Impact of positive and negative description from R1-P2 on R2-P1.

and 44% of the participants, i.e., 27, captioned the image with respect to the negative description associated to it.

It is interesting to note that out of the captions remembered by participants from R1-P2 and R2-P2, positive descriptions tend to have more impact on participants, causing them to remember the image caption for a longer duration compared to negative descriptions.

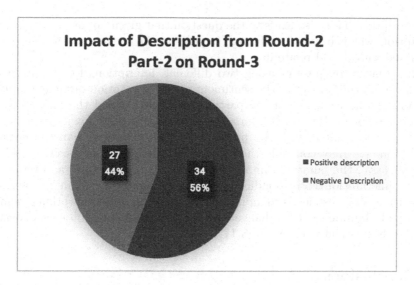

Fig. 11. Impact of positive and negative description from R2-P2 on R3.

4   Discussion

Only 25% of participants were able to recall the captions which they captioned for an image after a span of 9–15 days. It is interesting that even though the visual working memory capacity of a human is considered to be three to four objects, participants tended to retain some of the information for 9–15 days. This may be due to the fact that some participants were able to relate the situations from the images leading them to correlate the image with one or more experiences from their past, consistent with [16,26]. Due to this, even though the images were of no purpose to them, they tended to remember the captions for a long period of time, posing an interesting question to examine whether the image captions were saved to working memory or long-term memory. One other possible reason for retaining the image caption would be due to the additional information, i.e., the description, provided with the images. If providing description is a potential reason for participants to retain the information, it is fascinating to note that if the hypothesized reason behind remembering the image caption is that of the description, participants tended to recall the image caption which was captioned without the description.

When comparing the recall rate of the captions between the first and second rounds, and the second and third rounds, more than 50% of participants were able to recall the image caption from previous rounds. Out of the 50%, an average of 36% of the captions recalled were the image captions which were captioned without seeing the descriptions. This helps to understand that even after seeing extra description related to a given image, the first impression of the image made on participants has more impact and a higher chance to be retained in the working memory than the caption which had been captioned after seeing the description. This also leads to the question that given an image without any description, why is it easy for a human to perceive the image than the description associated with it and relate it.

The primary purpose of using two different descriptions for an image was to understand the impact of the sentiment of the description on image captioning. As hypothesized, out of the participants who recalled the image caption with description in R2 and R3, an average of 60% of participants remembered the caption associated with the positive description rather than the negative description. We may conclude that given two outcomes, one positive and the other negative, the human brain on average tends to remember and retain the positive information corresponding to the situation rather than the negative information. This also leads to an interesting question that the working memory capacity of a human tends to change with the sentiment of the objects associated with it, which is consistent with [8,17,24,35].

5   Conclusions

The findings from the results highlight that participants tend to retain information for longer periods than the expected duration for working memory, which may be because participants were able to relate the images with their everyday life scenarios. Figure 10 and Fig. 11 give insight that the positive description enabled participants to retain and recall more information than the negative description associated with the image. The inferences from this study are limited due to there being no evidence of the mood of each participant while participating in the study. Even though there are some limitations to this study, the results contribute to the growing research on working memory.

References

1. Allen, R., Baddeley, A., Hitch, G.: Is the binding of visual features in working memory resource-demanding? J. Exp. Psychol. Gen. **135**, 298–313 (2006). https://doi.org/10.1037/0096-3445.135.2.298
2. Atkinson, R.C., Shiffrin, R.M.: Human memory: A proposed system and its control processes. In: Psychology of Learning and Motivation, vol. 2, pp. 89–195. Elsevier (1968)
3. Baddeley, A.: Working memory: looking back and looking forward. Nat. Rev. Neurosci. **4**, 829–839 (2003). https://doi.org/10.1038/nrn1201
4. Baddeley, A.: Working memory. Curr. Biol. **20**(4), R136–R140 (2010)
5. Baddeley, A.: Working memory: theories, models, and controversies. Ann. Rev. Psychol. **63**(1), 1–29 (2012). https://doi.org/10.1146/annurev-psych-120710-100422. pMID: 21961947
6. Blalock, L., Clegg, B.: Encoding and representation of simultaneous and sequential arrays in visuospatial working memory. Q. J. Exp. Psychol. **2006**(63), 856–62 (2010). https://doi.org/10.1080/17470211003690680
7. Broadbent, D.E.: Percept. Commun. Pergamon Press, New York (1958)

8. Buchanan, T., Adolphs, R.: The role of the human amygdala in emotional modulation of long-term declarative memory. Adv. Cons. Res. **44**, 9–34 (2002). https://doi.org/10.1075/aicr.44.02buc
9. Chai, W.J., Abd Hamid, A.I., Abdullah, J.M.: Working memory from the psychological and neurosciences perspectives: a review. Front. Psychol. **9**, 401 (2018)
10. Cheng, P., Holyoak, K.: Pragmatic reasoning schemas. Cogn. Psychol. **17**, 391–416 (1985). https://doi.org/10.1016/0010-0285(85)90014-3
11. Cowan, N.: What are the differences between long-term, short-term, and working memory? Prog. Brain Res. **169**, 323–38 (2008)
12. Cowan, N.: The magical number 4 in short-term memory: a reconsideration of mental storage capacity. Behav. Brain Sci. **24**(1), 87–114 (2001). https://doi.org/10.1017/S0140525X01003922
13. Daneman, M., Carpenter, P.A.: Individual differences in working memory and reading. J. Verbal Learn. Verbal Behav. **19**(4), 450–466 (1980)
14. Daneman, M., Merikle, P.: Working memory and language comprehension: a meta-analysis. Psychon. Bull. Rev. **3**, 422–433 (1996). https://doi.org/10.3758/BF03214546
15. D'Esposito, M., Postle, B.R.: The cognitive neuroscience of working memory. Ann. Rev. Psychol. **66**(1), 115–142 (2015). https://doi.org/10.1146/annurev-psych-010814-015031. pMID: 25251486
16. Doerksen, S., Shimamura, A.: Source memory enhancement for emotional words. Emotion **1**, 5–11 (2001). https://doi.org/10.1037//1528-3542.1.1.5. (Washington, D.C.)
17. Dolan, R.: Emotion, cognition, and behavior. Science **298**, 1191–1194 (2002). https://doi.org/10.1126/science.1076358. (New York, NY)
18. Elliman, N., Green, M., Rogers, P., Finch, G.: Processing-efficiency theory and the working-memory system: Impairments associated with sub-clinical anxiety. Pers. Individ. Differ. **23**, 31–35 (1997). https://doi.org/10.1016/S0191-8869(97)00016-0
19. Engle, R., Tuholski, S.W., Laughlin, J., Conway, A.: Working memory, short-term memory, and general fluid intelligence: a latent-variable approach. J. Exp. Psychol. Gen. **128**(3), 309–331 (1999)
20. Engle, R., Tuholski, S., Laughlin, J., Conway, A.: Working memory, short-term memory and general fluid intelligence: a latent variable approach. J. Exp. Psychol. Gen. **130**, 169–183 (1999). https://doi.org/10.1037/0096-3445.128.3.309
21. Eysenck, M., Calvo, M.: Anxiety and performance: the processing efficiency theory. Cogn. Emot. **6**, 409–434 (1992). https://doi.org/10.1080/02699939208409696
22. Fukuda, K., Vogel, E., Mayr, U., Awh, E.: Quantity, not quality: the relationship between fluid intelligence and working memory capacity. Psychon. Bull. Rev. **17**, 673–679 (2010). https://doi.org/10.3758/17.5.673
23. Gray, J.: Emotional modulation of cognitive control: approach-withdrawal states double dissociate spatial from verbal 2-back task performance. J. Exp. Psychol. Gen. **130**, 436–52 (2001). https://doi.org/10.1037/0096-3445.130.3.436
24. Hamann, S.: Cognitive and neural mechanisms of emotional memory. Trends Cogn. Sci. **5**, 394–400 (2001). https://doi.org/10.1016/S1364-6613(00)01707-1
25. Harden, L.: A review of research on working memory and its importance in education of the deaf. Ph.D. thesis, Program in Audiology and Communication Sciences, Washington University (2011). http://digitalcommons.wustl.edu/pacs_capstones/627
26. Heuer, F., Reisberg, D.: Vivid memories of emotional events: the accuracy of remembered minutiae. Mem. Cogn. **18**, 496–506 (1990). https://doi.org/10.3758/BF03198482

27. Johnson, A., Miles, C.: Serial position effects in 2-alternative forced choice recognition: functional equivalence across visual and auditory modalities. Memory **17**, 84–91 (2008). https://doi.org/10.1080/09658210802557711. (Hove, England)

28. Kyllonen, P.C., Christal, R.E.: Reasoning ability is (little more than) working-memory capacity?! Intelligence **14**(4), 389–433 (1990)

29. Lecerf, T., de Ribaupierre, A.: Recognition in a visuospatial memory task: the effect of presentation. Eur. J. Cogn. Psychol. **17**, 47–75 (2005). https://doi.org/10.1080/09541440340000420

30. Luck, S., Vogel, E.: The capacity of visual working memory for features and conjunctions. Nature **390**, 279–81 (1997). https://doi.org/10.1038/36846

31. MacDonald, M.: Your Brain: The Missing Manual: The Missing Manual. O'Reilly Media, Sebastopol (2008)

32. Miller, G., Galanter, E., Pribram, K.: Plans and the structure of behavior. Am. J. Psychol. **75** (1960). https://doi.org/10.2307/1419559

33. Oberauer, K., Cowan, N.: Working memory capacity: (2005). Exp. Psychol. **54**, 245–246 (2007). https://doi.org/10.1027/1618-3169.54.3.245

34. Pashler, H.: Familiarity and visual change detection. Percept. Psychophys. **44**, 369–78 (1988)

35. Perlstein, W., Elbert, T., Stenger, V.: Dissociation in human prefrontal cortex of affective influences on working memory-related activity. In: Proceedings of the National Academy of Sciences of the United States of America, vol. 99, pp. 1736–41, March 2002. https://doi.org/10.1073/pnas.241650598

36. Seibert, P., Ellis, H.: Irrelevant thoughts, emotional mood states, and cognitive task performance. Mem. Cogn. **19**, 507–13 (1991). https://doi.org/10.3758/BF03199574

37. Smyth, M., Hay, D., Hitch, G., Horton, N.: Serial position memory in the visual-spatial domain: reconstructing sequences of unfamiliar faces. Q. J. Exp. Psychol. Hum. Exp. Psychol. **58**, 909–30 (2005). https://doi.org/10.1080/02724980443000412

38. Spies, K., Hesse, F., Hummitzsch, C.: Mood and capacity in baddeley's model of human memory. Zeitschrift für Psychologie mit Zeitschrift für angewandte Psychologie **204**, 367–381 (1996)

39. Vogel, E., Woodman, G., Luck, S.: Storage of features, conjunctions, and objects in visual working memory. J. Exp. Psychol. Hum. Percept. Perform. **27**, 92–114 (2001). https://doi.org/10.1037//0096-1523.27.1.92

40. William, P., Phillips, W.A.: on the distinction between sensory storage and short-term visual memory. Percept. Psychophys. **16**, 283–290 (1974). https://doi.org/10.3758/BF03203943

41. William, P., Christie, D.: Components of visual memory. Q. J. Exp. Psychol. **29**, 117–133 (1977). https://doi.org/10.1080/00335557743000080

42. Wolf, T., et al.: Transformers: state-of-the-art natural language processing. In: Proceedings of the 2020 Conference on Empirical Methods in Natural Language Processing: System Demonstrations, pp. 38–45. Association for Computational Linguistics, Online, October 2020. https://www.aclweb.org/anthology/2020.emnlp-demos.6

Adaptive Collaborative Intelligence: Key Strategies for Sensemaking in the Wild

Elizabeth S. Veinott[(✉)]

Michigan Technological University, Houghton, MI, USA
eveinott@mtu.edu

Abstract. In the real world, no one makes decision alone. Whether developing community responses during a pandemic, intelligence driven military operations, or business plans in turbulent economic times, effective collaboration and coordination between teams, across organizational levels, and organizations is often critical for success. For example, disaster response systems often require local personnel to estimate supply needs they have little or no experience with, resulting in wasted effort, wasted resources, or worse failure to deliver. To support adaptive systems for collaboration, one must first identify key dimensions of collaborative sensemaking that need to be adaptive. In this paper, I review several themes of collaboration from field studies we conducted against a literature review of ethnographic studies to highlight the role of adaptive collaborative intelligence in operational teams. Three collaborative themes are highlighted: coordinate through awareness of work progress, attention, while not disrupting, and supporting layers of context. They provide initial suggestions for where adaptive systems could support collaborative intelligence .

Keywords: Adaptive collaboration · Ethnographic methods · Sensemaking

1 Introduction

Teams in variety of settings must work together to solve hard problems and understanding how effective teams work has been a prominent topic in human-computer interaction research for the last 40 years in a variety of domains [5, 8, 10, 15, 21]. Making sense of information is a key component of team collaboration. There are many examples and case studies of expert teams, performing better than individuals [5], but reviews of controlled group decision making experiments indicate that nominal groups outperform collaborative groups under several conditions [c.f. 3]. By understanding collaboration and focusing on sensemaking in this paper, the goal is to contribute some new ideas regarding how adaptive systems could support teams, to more effectively leverage their collaborative intelligence.

Hackman [5] describes *collaborative intelligence*, as the way groups can work together effectively to improve performance relative to nominal teams. It should be noted this concept is different than the *collective intelligence* of a team, which has been defined

© Springer Nature Switzerland AG 2021
C. Stephanidis et al. (Eds.): HCII 2021, LNCS 13096, pp. 121–129, 2021.
https://doi.org/10.1007/978-3-030-90328-2_8

as the ability of a group to perform a variety of tasks, and analogous to general intelligence in individuals [24, 25]. Hackman and colleagues have conducted research on large and small teams from aviation to orchestras to identify teams that work, and describe collaborative intelligence as having six enabling characteristics on the team structure and mission (e.g., real team, compelling purpose, right people, norms of conduct, organizational support, timely coaching) [5]. For example, collaborative intelligence might involve focusing on the diverse ideas generated by team members during a brainstorming task. The current work complements this prior research by identifying sensemaking strategies pulled from a review of ethnographic research. It builds on our prior work in adaptive systems that has focused on adaptive learning in laboratory and field studies in the context of serious games [22] and intelligence analysis [13, 21].

Collaborative systems have unique challenges relative to well-defined single-user systems in that they impact a team in a dynamic, context dependent, and social environment. Due to the highly contextual and complex nature of team efforts, collaborative systems can violate people's mental models of their usefulness [16], and they can change the group process [1, 4, 8], both which could adversely impact collaborative intelligence.

There were three goals in this paper to extend the prior work. First, I describe several themes supporting collaborative sensemaking, pulled from ethnographic studies of collaboration in operational environments. Next, I provide some examples from field studies we have conducted in a disaster response that evaluate these ethnographic themes. Finally, I discuss how these themes could be used to support the design of adaptive collaborative intelligence approaches. The goal of this work is to develop ideas to harness the collaborative intelligence of teams.

2 Background Research

2.1 Collaboration Research

Research on computer supported cooperative work (CSCW), under which adaptive collaborative intelligence falls, has been a productive area of research for over 30 years. Collaboration can occur in the same time zone and place (e.g., face-to-face (F2F)) or it can be distributed in time (asynchronous), space (geographically distributed), or both. Because F2F collaboration tends to be the most effective, most research on collaborative systems focuses on making the experience as similar to F2F as possible [15].

Olson and Olson [15] in a review of collaboration at a distance, found that as teams become more distributed in physical space and time, collaboration becomes more difficult because the context changes, communication changes, coupling of the work changes, and incentives are affected. These challenges are areas where an adaptive system could provide support for the collaboration. It should be noted that the history of collaborative systems (e.g., shared video, social media, shared documents) suggests that simpler collaborative interaction has been more successful (e.g., Google classroom, YouTube, Twitter, Facebook). Ethnographic approaches to studying collaboration may provide new insights for supporting collaborative intelligence.

Collaboration is more complicated than a single person doing a single task, and managing the process between individual and group efforts is one natural area where to improve adaptive collaborative intelligence. This challenge was raised in [13], while developing a team tool to support multipath reasoning for improving forecasting. In that example, understanding where collaboration would be more effective was a challenge and is at the center of the collaborative intelligence idea.

2.2 Ethnographic Research on Collaboration

Workplace ethnographies typically involve observing people in their natural work settings accomplishing a set of tasks [7, 9–11, 14, 16, 18, 23]. They provide concrete, detailed descriptions of the context, but also examine how individuals and teams accomplish the tasks in that context. Ethnographic research typically provides more complete descriptions of the physical, socio-technical and cultural environment. However, ethnographic research takes time to conduct, time that design teams rarely have available when starting a project. Therefore, translating the results from existing ethnographic research is important to understand what should be adaptive in a collaborative system. There have been a few ethnographic frameworks proposed to integrate a socio-technical perspective with the front-end design requirements process [1, 18]. However, communicating the results from ethnographic studies to support design continues to be a challenge as has been discussed extensively in the literature [1, 2, 9].

Ethnographic studies of collaborative tools [6, 8, 16], capture the complexity of what was called *groupware tools* in context. Ethnographers have identified collaborative interaction themes before, but have not focused on sensemaking. By reviewing ethnographic findings of collaboration in a variety of workplace contexts, these could inform the development of adaptive collaborative intelligence by shedding light on what kinds of processes needed to be collaborative or strategies for making sense of information.

3 Methods

A review of ethnographic workplace studies uncovered several themes that could support collaborative sensemaking. These are not a complete description of all collaborative work, but provide the basis for the discussion of adaptive systems in collaborative sensemaking. Examples from prior field studies using collaborative technologies are provided to further unpack the ethnographic themes. We used the themes to evaluate examples from data collected on Twitter during the 2007 San Diego wildfires [20] and after an effective, state-wide flood response effort. In the later field study, we conducted interviews with military disaster response teams, civilian emergency managers (local and state), and volunteer coordinators about the 2009 North Dakota flood response. Our interviews focused on the nature of their collaborative work and the role of technology in support of collaboration.

4 Results

Three themes emerged from this literature review and are particularly relevant for sensemaking and collaborative intelligence: a) coordinating through close awareness of work progress, b) managing attention, while minimizing disruption, c) supporting layers of context for sensemaking. As mentioned, these themes provide a starting point for a discussion of adaptive collaboration to support better sensemaking. In addition, multiple themes were represented in each ethnographic study. Table 1 provides a summary of the themes identified in the literature review, each integrating the management of the work and the teams.

Table 1. Summary of three collaborative intelligence themes

Theme	Space	Time	Key Challenge
Coordinate through close awareness of work progress	Co-located, Distributed	Same Time (Synchronous) Different time (Asynchronous)	Workflow Communication Situation Awareness
Managing attention, minimizing disruption	Co-located, Distributed	Synchronous, Asynchronous	Communication Attention Management
Supporting layers of context	Co-located, Distributed	Synchronous, Asynchronous	Situation Awareness

4.1 Collaboration Themes

Theme 1: *Coordination Through Awareness of the Work* [6, 7, 9, 14]. Coordination often involves visual awareness the work, but it can be auditory too (e.g., commercial aviation pilots listening to air traffic control communicating with other aircrafts). This theme emerged from research in control rooms in operational environments, all involving co-located, synchronous work. Being aware of how others' work was unfolding over time allowed an individual to easily step in or out of the work with little or no explicit coordination.

One example of this theme comes from an ethnographic study of a subway control room [6]. In this situation, the primary controller was communicating with a train driver to diagnose a problem affecting train delays. A second controller in the room, overhearing the conversation, and directed track cameras to help provide additional information to the primary controller and made preliminary announcements to passengers at the affected stations. If the second controller had been working remotely this coordination would not be possible. If they had been working on a different problem, and had paused to listen to the first controller's conversation, it might have been disruptive. However, it highlights that in some cases, being able to collaborate through an awareness of the workflow can be effective.

Theme 2: *Managing Attention, While Minimizing Disruption* [1, 6, 10, 11]. This theme focuses on conventions that let people request help from each other. Often these requests are made unobtrusively at first. If the requester does not get the attention he or she feels is needed, then the requester can make a more explicit or demonstrative request. F2F work settings provide a rich collection of very lightweight ways of grabbing attention of others (e.g., thinking out loud, looking, knocking) and a repertoire of ways to escalate the request (e.g., gesturing, calling out). Adaptive strategies for this theme would benefit from focusing on managing attention.

Theme 3: *Supporting Layers of Context* [6, 7, 12, 16, 19] applies to many different aspects of sensemaking in teams. For example, an ethnographic study of two different oncology offices discussed strategies for making patient information available to the different users (e.g., doctors, nurses, respiratory therapists) to support their sensemaking and decision making [19]. More recently, research has focused on making medical record structures adapt to different users in the collaborative process to support each team member bringing their unique perspective and information to patient care. Adaptive systems could support collaborative intelligence with respect to this theme by representing different layers of contexts (e.g., using case-based reasoning).

4.2   Using Themes to Evaluate Collaborative Systems for Disaster Response

A brief comparison of these themes in two different disaster response contexts highlights different adaptive collaborative intelligence needs in the different contexts. The two contexts were Twitter usage during the 2007 San Diego, California wildfires [20] and a large scale, multi-organizational disaster response effort: the North Dakota 2009 Flood response [2].

In October, 2007, roughly 6000 firefighters, U.S. Armed Forces, and U.S. National Guard responded to the San Diego wildfires and facilitated the evacuation of more than 250,000 residents. Many civilians posted microblogs of disaster-related information (e.g., fire locations, status of roads, capacity at rescue centers) on Twitter (a new technology at the time) to help people make real time decisions. Twitter allows information to be crowd sourced in a sense with multiple people able to post. In this way, it could potentially support command and control in joint disaster response operations in several ways because it crosses platforms (e.g., cell phone, web) and can provide close to real-time information to support making sense of the situation. Table 2 lists the ethnographic themes and uses them to evaluate Twitter in the fire response context.

As can be seen in Table 2, only one of the collaborative themes was supported by Twitter. Because Twitter was limited to 140 characters at the time, it provides little context making it difficult to visualize the information. For example, if the fire had reached a certain block of a certain road, most users would need a map representation to interpret the tweets [20]. Without something like Google maps, the first theme was not supported. Interestingly, recognizing this need, Google started updating their maps with fire location information from different sources, including Twitter. The second theme was supported in Twitter, because the posts were passively received and managed by the user. The Twitter character limit reduces information overload, but at a cost of situation awareness. This wild fire example happened less than a year after Twitter first launched, at a time Twitter did not have widespread adoption. In either case, it was an interesting example of adaptive and distributed ad hoc collaboration. Though Twitter was not designed to be disaster response tool, soon after, researchers started focusing on it in crisis informatics [17].

Table 2. Adaptive collaborative analysis of light weight tool

Theme	Twitter evaluation
Coordinate through close awareness of work progress	Does not support. All information is pushed. However, many users provide information so the big picture of the work is possible
Managing attention while minimizing disruption	Supports. As tweets are passive, they do not disrupt. Users set up alerts to tweet hashtags #sandiegowildfire
Support layers of context	Does not support. Context not available due to limited characters space. Goggle maps provided needed layer of context by posting tweet info on the map

Adaptive collaborative intelligence of sensemaking during disaster response could focus on timing of the information, and the level of detail provided much as the Twitter use. In responding to disasters, people need lightweight, low bandwidth tools to provide information about current status of people, roads, electricity, traffic, and damages for effective decision making. Response teams and civilians need enough information about the situation to be useful, but not too much information to adversely impact their decisions as they may not have the time, bandwidth, or screen space to wade through mounds of information. Finally, people need to develop an appropriate picture of the nature of the situation. Social media tools support emergent distributed collaboration and decision making of civilians and first responders in unique ways.

For the second example, we reviewed data from a study of the effective 2009 flood response in North Dakota. We conducted interviews with the North Dakota National Guard, civilian emergency managers (local and state), and volunteer coordinators that involved a very large, coordinated response. Several collaborative tools were used (e.g., television, cell phones, a web-based resource and workflow management tool Twitter), and multiple organizations. Table 3 provides examples from the flood response for each theme.

In this example, two of the themes were demonstrated in the large-scale collaboration, while the third, supporting layers of context, was not. The last theme was interesting in the flood response context because disaster responses often require local personnel to estimate supply needs they have little or no experience with, which can result in wasted time or resources, or failure to receive much needed supplies. An adaptive system might be able to support this theme by providing historical information (from a previous flood or another town) or worked out examples to support the layers of context.

Table 3. Adaptive collaborative themes and flood response evaluation

Ethnographic theme	Fargo flood response examples
Coordinate through close awareness of work progress	Supported because centralized system of requests for supplies and personnel, joint command center, and daily standups meeting broadcast over public television
Managing attention while minimizing disruption	Supported. Video conferencing was used to provide a constant direct link between the disaster response command center and city engineers in several different cities addressing the flood. This allowed people on both sides to determine availability without disrupting
Support layers of context	Not supported. People making requests for personnel or supplies might not have all the available information to make requests (e.g., do not know how many National Guard might be needed to address flood problem in local area). Mismatched expectations of what is needed and what could be reasonably supplied

5 Conclusion

In this paper, three themes with examples of adaptive solutions were presented, Grudin [4] highlighted several challenges for collaborative systems 20 years ago that are still relevant today and could be supported by adaptive or intelligent systems. For example, Grudin described a *disparity in work and benefit* meaning that collaborative tools sometimes require additional work from individuals, who will not see a direct benefit from that additional work. It is possible an adaptive system could address this disparity by reducing it to some extent. Another challenge involved *disruptions to the social process*, such as lightweight communication systems (e.g., slack and discord) violating the norms of conversation (e.g., few acknowledgments, pushing tasking, but not being clear it was read, understood or accepted). An intelligent system could track those threads by providing context or a task list. Adaptive systems supporting collaborative intelligence could also address *exception handling* by identifying them, and providing a space for working out those ideas or improvisations.

Many collaborative tools have short lifecycles. Consequently, the design and use of such systems naturally co-evolves. For collaborative tools to be effectively used, the context, the social structures, and the collaborative situation need to be evaluated together. We were able to demonstrate these briefly in two disaster response contexts. These themes provide one method to work through some of the common issues found in different collaborative environments in order to determine what might be adaptive in a system to support a team's collaborative intelligence. Because ethnographic studies provide a detailed study of formal and ad hoc teams in context, they potentially provide information that currently is not being used by developers or available using other methods (e.g., experimental, questionnaires).

References

1. Ackerman, M.S., Halverson, C.A., Erickson, T., Kellogg, W.A. (eds.) Resources, Co-evolution and Artifacts: Theory in CSCW. Springer, London (2007). https://doi.org/10.1007/978-1-84628-901-9
2. Cox, D.A., Veinott, B.: Developing pattern languages: new ways of communicating naturalistic insights for system development and evaluation. In: 9th Bi-annual International Conference on Naturalistic Decision Making (NDM9), vol. 9, pp. 189–190, June 2009
3. DeRosa, D.M., Smith, C.L., Hantula, D.A.: The medium matters: mining the long-promised merit of group interaction in creative idea generation tasks in a meta-analysis of the electronic group brainstorming literature. Comput. Hum. Behav **23**(3), 1549–1581–239 (2007)
4. Grudin, J.: Interactive systems: bridging the gap between developers and users. In: Baecker, R., Grudin, J., Buxton, W., Greenberg, S. (eds.) Human Computer Interaction: Toward the Year 2000, 2nd Edn. pp. 293–304 (1999)
5. Hackman, J.R.: Collaborative Intelligence: Using Teams to Solve Hard Problems. Berrett-Koehler Publishers (2011)
6. Heath, C., Luff, P.: Collaboration and control: crisis management and multimedia technology in London underground line control rooms. Comput. Support. Coop. Work (CSCW) **1**(1–2), 69–941 (1992)
7. Hindmarsh, J., Pilnick, A.: The tacit order of teamwork: collaboration and embodied conduct in anesthesia. Sociol. Q. **43**(2), 139–164 (2002)
8. Hinds, P., Kiesler, S. (eds.) Distributed Work. MIT Press (2002)
9. Hughes, J.A., King, V., Rodden, T., Andersen, H.: Moving out from the control room: ethnography in system design. In: Proceedings of the 1994 ACM Conference on Computer Supported Cooperative Work, pp. 429–439, October 1994
10. Hutchins, E.: Cognition in the Wild. MIT Press (1995)
11. Kirk, D., Crabtree, A., Rodden, T.: Ways of the hands. In: Gellersen, H., Schmidt, K., Beaudouin-Lafon, M., Mackay, W. (eds.) ECSCW 200, pp. 1–21. Springer, Dordrecht (2005). https://doi.org/10.1007/1-4020-4023-7_1
12. Lauche, K.: Collaboration among designers: analyzing an activity for system development. Comput. Support. Coop. Work **14**, 253–282 (2006)
13. McDermott, A.F., et al.: Developing an adaptive framework to support intelligence analysis. In: Sottilare, R.A., Schwarz, J. (eds.) HCII 2021. LNCS, vol. 12792, pp. 550–558. Springer, Cham (2021). https://doi.org/10.1007/978-3-030-77857-6_39
14. Mondada, L.: Working with video: how surgeons produce video records of their actions. Vis. Stud. **18**(1), 58–73 (2003)
15. Olson, J.S., Olson, G.M.: Bridging distance. Human-computer interaction and management information systems: applications. In: Zwass, V. (ed.) Advances in Management Information Systems, pp. 101–118 (2014)
16. Orlikowski, W.: Learning from notes: organizational issues in groupware implementation. In: Proceedings of the 1992 ACM Conference on Computer-Supported Work, Toronto, Ontario, Canada, pp. 362–369 (1992)
17. Paylen, L., Liu, S.B.: Citizen communication in crisis: anticipating a future of ICT-supported public participation. In: Proceedings of the ACM CHI Conference on Computer Human Interaction, San Jose, Calif, USA, pp. 727–736 (2007)

18. Randall, D., Harper, R., Rouncefield, M.: Fieldwork for Design: Theory and Practice (2007). https://doi.org/10.1007/978-1-84628-768-8
19. Schmidt, K., Wagner, I., Tolar, M.: Permutations of cooperative work practices: a study of two oncology clinics. In: Proceedings of the 2007 International ACM Conference on Supporting Group Work, pp. 1–10, November 2007
20. Veinott, B., Cox, D., Mueller, S.: Social media supporting disaster response: evaluation of a lightweight collaborative tool. In: 9th Bi-annual International Conference on Naturalistic Decision Making (NDM9), vol. 9, pp. 307–308, June 2009
21. Veinott, E.S., Sestokas, J., Zimmerman, L., Bell, J., Manning, D.: Developing training tools for company intelligence support teams. In: Interservice/Industry Training, Simulation and Education Conference (I/ITSEC), Orlando, FL, December 2011
22. Whitaker, E., Trewhitt, E., Veinott, E.S.: Intelligent Tutoring, July 2019
23. Whitaker, E., Trewhitt, E., Veinott, E.S.: Intelligent tutoring design alternatives in a serious game. In: Sottilare, R.A., Schwarz, J. (eds.) HCII 2019. LNCS, vol. 11597, pp. 151–165. Springer, Cham (2019). https://doi.org/10.1007/978-3-030-22341-0_13
24. Wilkstrom, A., Larsson, U.: Technology-an actor in the ICU: a study in workplace research tradition. J. Clin. Nurs. **13**(5), 555–561 (2004)
25. Woolley, A.W., Aggarwal, I., Malone, T.: Collective intelligence and group performance. Curr. Dir. Psychol. Sci. **24**, 420–424 (2015)

Inclusive Design Approaches
and Applications

Analysis of Specialized Websites in Digital Libraries: Evaluation of UX with Blind Users

Teresita Álvarez-Robles[1](✉) ⓘ, Francisco Álvarez[2] ⓘ, Yadira Orozco[3] ⓘ,
and J. Andrés Sandoval-Bringas[1] ⓘ

[1] Universidad Autónoma de Baja California Sur, Sur KM5.5, La Paz 23080, Mexico
tj.alvarez@uabcs.mx
[2] Universidad Autónoma de Aguascalientes, Av. Universidad 940,
20131 Aguascalientes, Mexico
[3] Universidad de Guadalajara, Av. Juárez 976, 44160 Guadalajara, Jalisco, Mexico

Abstract. The main objective of this work is to carry out a deep analysis of the user experience (UX) of blind users when making use of specialized websites in digital libraries in order to know if they are usable, accessible, useful, easy to learn, among others.

Based on the foregoing, it is expected to know whether or not it is feasible to propose a general or specific support guide to make the corresponding modifications to a website and that it is easy to use by users with visual disabilities.

With the proposal of the guide, it is expected to achieve significant changes in the websites to be able to cover the characteristics and important needs for a blind person when making use of a specialized website.

To evaluate the websites, various user experience tests were carried out with both experts and the end user, within the tests carried out, the heuristic evaluation and the method of thinking aloud by dividing the tasks stand out. which are later evaluated based on specialized metrics to validate if the website is easy to learn, the actions are easy to remember, if the actions or information do not saturate the user, among others.

The research allows to conclude for a first stage that it is necessary to carry out adequate UX evaluations to guarantee that a product, system or service meets the necessary needs of the target users.

Keywords: Specialized websites · UX · Evaluation · Blind users

1 Introduction

In Mexico, the National Network of Public Libraries currently operates with 7,413 public libraries that are established in 2,282 municipalities [1].

In the State of Jalisco, Mexico, there are currently 282 libraries operating, of which only 23 are enabled to serve users with visual disabilities, it is worth mentioning that in the state of Jalisco the number of users with visual disabilities amounts to more than 30 thousand people, of According to 2004 figures from the National Institute of Statistics, Geography and Informatics (INEGI for its acronym in Spanish), [2].

© Springer Nature Switzerland AG 2021
C. Stephanidis et al. (Eds.): HCII 2021, LNCS 13096, pp. 133–146, 2021.
https://doi.org/10.1007/978-3-030-90328-2_9

Despite being 23 libraries that have various supports for people with visual disabilities, such as screen readers, amplifiers, braille printers, among others, there are few that manage Web sites and the number decreases when it comes to accessible Web sites; In this first study, the work focused on libraries that have websites that do not have an accessibility section, the reason for the above is because we can think that because libraries are physically accessible in their structure or service, the website will also accessible and easy to read by screen readers, among other functionalities suitable for people with this type of disability.

Based on the above, the final objective, once each of the UX tests has been analyzed is to be able to provide a guide that is useful to improve websites that are or are not focused on users with visual impairments.

In this way we will obtain websites that comply not only with the norms that the World Wide Web Consortium (W3C) establishes but that these sites obtain the certification of Web accessibility in a level if not AAA at least AA.

It is important to know that levels A, AA and AAA are composed of certain compliance criteria which indicate the accessibility impact of a specific website and these criteria are established within the Web Content Accessibility Guidelines (WCAG) which are a part of the W3C accessibility guidelines which ensure that the site is accessible [3].

Taking into account the above and based on the results obtained, we will be able to know if what is being offered to blind people meets the basic needs of users for easy handling and learning and therefore the website can be considered accessible and usable for a user with visual impairment when making use of a website specialized in the use of technologies focused on the field of libraries.

2   Websites Specialized in Digital Libraries

Borgman et al. [4] propose two definitions of digital libraries (1), are a set of electronic resources and associated technical capabilities for creating, searching and using information and (2) the digital libraries are constructed, collected and organized, by (and for) a community of users, and their functional capabilities support the information needs and uses of that community.

In the sense of the first one, they are an extension and enhancement of information storage and retrieval systems that manipulate digital data in any medium (text, images, sounds; static or dynamic images) and exist in distributed networks. In the sense of the second one, they are a component of communities in which individuals and groups interact with each other, using data, information and knowledge resources and systems. In this sense they are an extension, enhancement and integration of a variety of information institutions as physical places where resources are selected, collected, organized, preserved and accessed in support of a user community.

We focus more on the second definition since part of the work objective is to know if the existing digital libraries are or not accessible and usable for a specific group of people, in this case, people with visual disabilities, specifically people with total blindness. The foregoing based on the range covered by said definition since it focuses on a specific group.

In the case of the libraries we focus on, we know that not all have a website available so that a user can have access to the information at the time they need it and, if they have the website, they are commonly inaccessible to blind users because they are mostly not adapted to the screen readers commonly used by target users.

It is worth mentioning that despite being libraries that physically have the necessary support for a blind person, digitally access to information is not usually intuitive for said users.

Due to this last characteristic, the decision is made to carry out user experience (UX) tests to specialized websites in order to know whether or not they are accessible and if they are not, provide a guide that allows said site to have improvements so that in this way not only a blind user can have access but that it is accessible and therefore complies with the pertinent certifications not only of the WCAG but of the W3C and for this an evaluation of the usability of in a way that ensures the end user experience.

2.1   User Experience (UX)

Based on [5], it is known that there are three types of usability evaluation: (1) inspection, (2) inquiry and (3) test type. The first is normally carried out by experts in the field and the difference between the inquiry evaluation and the test type evaluation is that, although the two tests are carried out with users, the first is performed in early stages and the second once we have a prototype.

Table 1 shows some examples of usability evaluation methods, for this specific work, two precise methods are taken into account: (1) Heuristic evaluation and (2) Thinking aloud.

Table 1. Example of usability evaluation methods

1. Inspection	2. Inquiry	3. Test
Heuristic evaluation	Field observation	Thinking aloud
Cognitive tours	Focus group	Card sorting
Consistency inspection	Interviews	Retrospective tests

Within the field of computer science that studies the area of Human-Computer Interaction (HCI), one of its important aspects is the user experience evaluation (UX) which occurs once they are carried out various tests based on usability assessment methods.

In general, UX is defined as the sensation, feeling, emotional response, assessment and satisfaction of the user with respect to a product [6] and is made up of various factors which must be evaluated to guarantee the UX of the product, system or service.

Factors that Make up the UX. Among the models that work on UX, Peter Morville's (see Fig. 1.) is the best known and used today, this particular model is made up of seven factors, among them: usability, accessibility, utility, credibility, desirability, value, and ease of finding [7].

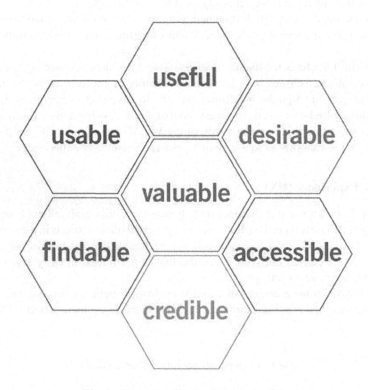

Fig. 1. Peter Morville model. Source: [7].

In particular, each factor ensures that the product, system or service is of quality for the end user, thereby obtaining a good user experience [7].

Based on the foregoing and considering that there are more than 86 UX evaluation methods [8], for this work two specifically were taken into account, the heuristic evaluation and the modified thinking aloud method [9], in this way two phases of Software engineering are evaluated, analysis and design, the most important thing about performing the UX is that by taking into account the opinion of the target users, the results will be satisfactory for the blind user.

3   Case Study: "Biblioteca Central Profesor García Ruiz"

As mentioned, in the city of Guadalajara, in the state of Jalisco in Mexico, there are about 12 libraries that have physical support for people with visual disabilities or blind users, most of these libraries have their own Web sites, in In some cases, the Web sites have the accessibility option and in others they do not, however, it is not known if they meet the needs of the blind user so that the UX is fulfilled.

Based on the above and, to carry out the corresponding tests, the user must be analyzed and a relevant user profile must be created which can be used to carry out the UX evaluation tests.

3.1   User Profile

For the UX tests, an association in the city of guadalajara was contacted. The association is called "organización de Invidentes Unidos de Jalisco AC", in this organization we have the support of five blind users (see Table 2).

Table 2. Users description

# User	Gender	Age	Blindness type
1	Male	24	Totally blind. Congenital
2	Female	26	Totally blind. Congenital
3	Female	40	Totally blind. Congenital
4	Male	56	Totally blind. Acquired
5	Male	60	Totally blind. Congenital

It is worth mentioning that all the users who participated in the evaluation tests are familiar with the use of screen readers, both JAWS and NVDA, however, it is important to note that they had never used a website that their focus was that of a Web catalog of a library as they normally exchange books through other digital media.

3.2   Biblioteca Central Profesor García Ruiz

The Library has an approximate collection of 50,000 volumes in circulation, which are available to users on the web through the Open Public Access Catalog (OPAC) system [10].

This site has an Accessibility section where the page format can be modified to its versions of large fonts, high contrast or text only (see Fig. 2 and Fig. 3).

It should be noted that even having an accessibility module, the library's website is complex. Based on the above, the heuristic evaluation was carried out to find "problems" that could confuse the end user.

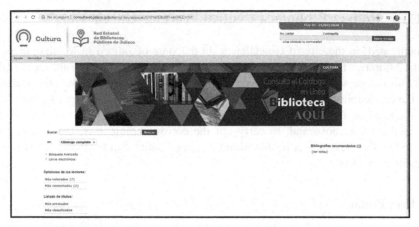

Fig. 2. Main page of the Central Library website. Source: [11].

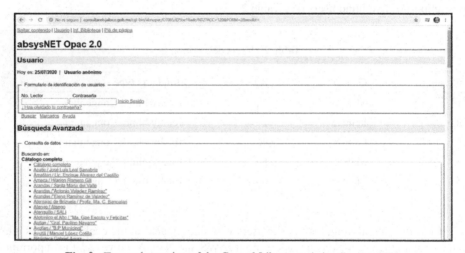

Fig. 3. Text-only version of the Central Library website. Source: [11].

3.3 Evaluation Methods

Heuristic Evaluation. As is known, the objective of heuristic evaluation is to measure the quality of the interface of any interactive system in relation to its ease of learning and ease of use by a specific group of users under a context of use [12].

Next, the 10 heuristics proposed by Nielsen [13] are taken as a basis, since being general they can be applied to any Web site, in this way each of the heuristics to be evaluated are listed:

- **H1.-** Visibility of system status
- **H2.-** Match between system and the real world
- **H3.-** User control and freedom
- **H4.-** Consistency and standards

- **H5.**- Error prevention
- **H6.**- Recognition rather than recall
- **H7.**- Flexibility and efficiency of use
- **H8.**- Aesthetic and minimalist design
- **H9.**- Help users recognize, diagnose, and recover from errors
- **H10.**- Help and documentation

This method, being inspection, allows experts to evaluate the website to determine subsequent tests with users, in the same test it is detected if the website is easy to learn and use by the target user.

Thinking Aloud Modified for Blind Users. For the test-type evaluation, we need the support of the users (see Table 1), in particular a modification to this method was used which is focused on blind users [9].

In general terms, it is a method that requires participants to verbalize what they are thinking while they carry out an activity to complement a task in the test, in this way they reveal aspects that they may like or not, confuse or even frustrate them.

The method is carried out as follows [14]:

1. An instructive practice is carried out with the blind user so that he understands what type of information is required to collect [15].
2. Users are provided with the prototype to be tested and an initial short task [5].
3. It is explained in detail and with terms that the user understands the task, as well as the operation of the device [9].
4. The initial task is carried out, if the user has problems / doubts, a change is made to the subsequent tasks to be able to apply them [15].
5. They are asked some questions and asked to explain what they think about it while they are working with the interface [5].
6. Continue in the same way with each of the tasks.
7. User participation is evaluated.

Once the process is followed, both quantitative and qualitative results are expected from the target user.

4   Application of UX Evaluation Methods

4.1   Heuristic evaluation

The heuristic evaluation tests were carried out using the text mode of the website in the accessibility section. The problems that were detected focus on the adaptation of labels for the easy interpretation of the screen reader, as well as the mobility presented when using the keyboard, in addition to problems detected when the user uses forms, the problems detected together with the heuristics that apply to each case, they can be viewed in Table 3.

Based on the problems detected, a group of tasks were established in order to be evaluated by the blind user.

Table 3. Heuristic problems identified on the Central Library Professor García Ruiz website

ID	Problem description	Unfulfilled Heuristic
P1	Notification missing when marking a book	H1
P2	Difficult access from the keyboard	H4
P3	No form filling instructions	H1
P4	The results section doesn't have the return button	H5
P5	SEARCH button displays the complete catalog (150 items)	H4 – H7 – H8
P6	Abbreviated words (Ind.Aut.)	H8
P7	Instructions to search appear at the end	H9
P8	The user section always appears at the beginning	H7
P9	Dropdown text not automatically read (comments)	H4
P10	Accessibility section is at the bottom of the page	H3 – H7
P11	Dropdown form is not read using pointer	H1 – H3
P12	The form doesn't clean itself	H5 – H9
P13	There are sentences that are not read in a row for the user	H3 – H4
P14	Button with abbreviation (Library Info)	H1 – H2 – H6
P15	The Library Info button doesn't seem to reach any special section	H7 – H4

5   Tasks and Results

The tasks that were established for this case study are listed below:

- **Task 1.** Find the accessibility section and select the text-only version
- **Task 2.** Search in the GDL/Central Library catalog by author, a book by "Juan Rulfo" published between 1950–1970 and mark a result
- **Task 3.** Search by subject "Mexico Culture" using the automatic index option. Open one of the results and open one of the books that appear on the screen, finally leaving a comment.
- **Task 4.** Search by title the book of "Pedro Paramo", select the type of collection as *sonoros*. Identify the options that the program offers in the face of the problem and return to the form to carry out a new search.

Each of the aforementioned tasks has its own objective which is carried out based on the procedure established in point 3.3.2, once the purpose of each task has been achieved, the user can continue with the next task until completion.

For each established task, both quantitative and qualitative results were obtained, due to the length of the document, results of each of the tasks are presented in a general way.

5.1 Task 1

The success criteria for this task was to find the accessibility button on the website and select the text-only option.

The qualitative results obtained by the users were:

- It is observed that the user has difficulties when using the keyboard to move within the website.
- They comment that it should be easier to get to the accessibility section and have to search for it until the end of the website.
- It was observed that for 60% of users it was difficult to complete the task because if they ignored the option they had to listen again to the entire tour of the site and its options, which was frustrating.

Within the quantitative results, in Graph 1 it is observed that for 20% of the participating users it was easy to carry out the task, for 60% despite achieving the task, it was difficult and they were on the verge of not doing it, while only 20% did not reach the goal.

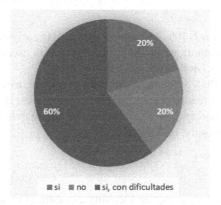

Graph 1. Compliance level of Task 1

Although most of the users managed to fulfill task 1 still with difficulties, it is concluded that the **accessibility** section does not have the best location because users prefer to abandon the test to continue trying to find the option.

5.2 Task 2

The evaluation criteria for task 2 were to consult the requested data in the library, search for the specified book and mark the result.

Within the qualitative evaluation, some of the user comments were the following:

- "I do not know when we can write in the form therefore we cannot complete the search"

- "The form should have notifications or sounds that allow us to know if we can write on the form or if we have already marked a book"

Based on the comments, we can conclude that the quantitative result was not what was expected, in general the results are shown in Graph 2.

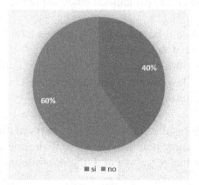

Graph 2. Compliance level of Task 2

As can be seen in Graph 2, 40% of the users managed to carry out the task successfully, however, they required support, while the remaining 60% of users had problems reaching the goal and made the decision to abandon it.

In this way, it is concluded that the form is deficient, the instructions for filling it are not clear using the screen reader because it does not notify users when they can write or if they have already written and in case of achieving the search, they are not sure when they mark an option due to the null feedback.

5.3   Task 3

In task 3, finding a book by subject and leaving a comment was taken as a criterion of success.

In general, in the qualitative aspect, all users agreed in the sense that they believe it is convenient that the form in this section should clean itself and also should be easier to use, since due to these details and the lack of feedback, no user was able to complete the task.

Therefore, from the quantitative aspect, 100% of the users could not fulfill the established task (see Graph 3).

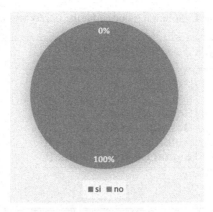

Graph 3. Compliance level of Task 3

In this way, it is concluded as in the case of Task 2 that the form does not provide the necessary elements for a blind user.

5.4   Task 4

For the last task, the success criterion was to search for a book in sound version and return to the search form.

Due to the characteristics of this task, the same case was presented as in Task 3, since the form in this section is not usable for the blind user, so they comment that *it is complex to fill out and when an error is made there is no any type of notice, in addition to the foregoing, this section does not have a "return" section either*. Therefore, the results of Graph 4 are similar to those of the previous case.

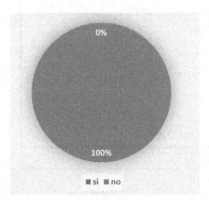

Graph 4. Compliance level of Task 4

It is concluded that the form should be easy to fill out, and that, when an error occurs, the screen reader should be able to read to the user the reason for said error, asking if they wish to return to a previous state of the system.

Table 4. Solution proposal for the library website.

Identified problem	Possible solutions	Observations
Notification missing when marking a book		The solution for the problem identified is to add an alternative text to the check which provides feedback to the user, depending on whether it is active or not.
Missing "back" button (return to search form)		The solution is to add a "back/return" button, possibly at the bottom so that you have a chance to evaluate all the options.
Accessibility section difficult to find		The accessibility button is included in the main menu.
The search form is not self-cleaning.		In this case, the form should clean itself after a search to avoid errors in the next query.
Scrolling through the keyboard is not good.		The user must be able to access all the information easily using the keyboard.

Therefore, we can conclude the section that, based on the results, the Web site of the *Biblioteca Central Profesor García Ruiz* does not comply with an accessible and usable design to be used by blind people.

5.5 Proposed Solution to the Case Study

To make a solution proposal to the case study of the *Biblioteca Central Profesor García Ruiz*, not only the opinions of blind users were taken into account when performing the thinking aloud test, but also the quantitative results obtained contemplating covering the problems detected when doing the heuristic evaluation.

Based on the above, changes are proposed that may be not only supportive but relevant for the use of a website of this type by blind users (see Table 4, the images within the proposal are in Spanish because the website of the case study only handles this language).

The small adjustments shown in Table 4 (when applied) are expected to significantly improve the experience of the blind user in consulting books on this particular website.

6 Conclusions and Future Works

The importance of taking into account today the end users in the development of any system, product or service is essential not only from the tests but from early phases such as the analysis of the development of what it is proposed to do. The objective of involving the target users from the early stages is precisely to avoid future problems, contemplating in each of their phases user experience evaluation tests to guarantee that we comply with all factors (which would be ideal) at least with most of them.

When it comes to accessibility and usability for visually impaired users and more precisely for blind users, the importance is even greater since as developers we must consider other aspects, as well as the needs of the end user.

As future work, it is proposed to make the modification (as a proposal) to the website of the case study in order to verify that the changes made are sufficient so that the blind user can use the website of the *Biblioteca Central Profesor García Ruiz* in a more agile way. On the other hand, it is expected to carry out more tests of this site with other case studies, either on library websites with or without an accessibility section, with the purpose of making a proposal for a design guide that can be taken into account. during the development of future Web sites that provide accessibility to this type of user.

In this way, the inclusion and participation of the target users will be encouraged throughout the software engineering process, waiting at the end of said product, system or service that complies with the UX factors that allow them to allow learnability and ease of use. suitable for blind users.

References

1. Cultura, S.d.: Red Nacional de Bibliotecas Públicas, México (2020)
2. Informador, E.: En Jalisco el 10% de las bibliotecas tiene un área para invidentes, Guadalajara (2010)

3. Alicante, U.d.: Niveles de adecuación de WCAG 2.0, Alicante (2018)
4. C. Borgman, M., et al.: Social aspects of digital libraries. Final report to the National Science Foundation (1996)
5. Granollers, J.L.y.J.C.T.: Diseño de sistemas interactivos centrados en el usuario. Editorial UOC, Barcelona (2011)
6. Álvarez-Robles, T.d.J.: Metodología Para La Evaluación De La Experiencia Del Usuario De Sistemas De Software Interactivos Para Usuarios Ciegos, Universidad Veracruzana Facultad de Estadistica e Informatica, Xalapa, Veracruz (2019)
7. Morville, P.: Semantic studios, 21 Juny 2004. [En línea]. https://semanticstudios.com/user_experience_design/
8. V. Roto, M.et al: All About UX, (2013). [En línea]. https://www.allaboutux.org/
9. Álvarez-Robles,T., Alvarez-Rodriguez, F., Benitez-Guerrero, y.E.: User experience evaluation method adapted and applied to blind users to evaluate the software's usability in mobile devices, DYNA, p. 488 (2019)
10. El Informador: Informador.Mx, 7 junio 2018. [En línea]. https://www.informador.mx/cultura/Un-espacio-renovado-para-la-lectura-20180606-0166.html
11. Red Estatal de Bibliotecas Públicas de Jalisco (2015). [En línea]. http://consultareb.jalisco.gob.mx/cgi-bin/abnopac/O7032/ID79ec65b3?ACC=101
12. Cespedes, D.: Heuristicas de Usabilidad y Experiencia del usuario en redes sociales, Valparaiso (2017)
13. Nielsen, J.: NN/g, 24 April 1994. [En línea]. https://www.nngroup.com/articles/ten-usability-heuristics/
14. Ericsson, K.A., Simon, y.H.A.: Verbal reports as data, Psychological review (1980)
15. Hughes, M.: Uxmatters, marzo 2012. [En línea]. https://www.uxmatters.com/mt/archives/2012/03/talking-out-loud-is-not-the-same-as-thinking-aloud.php. [Último acceso: agosto 2020]

When Worlds Collide: AI-Created, Human-Mediated Video Description Services and the User Experience

Sabine Braun[1]([✉]) [iD], Kim Starr[1] [iD], Jaleh Delfani[1] [iD], Liisa Tiittula[2] [iD],
Jorma Laaksonen[3] [iD], Karel Braeckman[4], Dieter Van Rijsselbergen[4],
Sasha Lagrillière[5], and Lauri Saarikoski[5]

[1] University of Surrey, Guildford GU2 7XH, UK
{s.braun,k.starr}@surrey.ac.uk
[2] University of Helsinki, Yliopistonkatu 4, 00100 Helsinki, Finland
[3] Aalto University, 02150 Espoo, Finland
[4] Limecraft, Sint-Salvatorstraat 18b/301, 9000 Gent, Belgium
[5] YLE, Media House Uutiskatu 5, 00240 Helsinki, Finland

Abstract. This paper reports on a user-experience study undertaken as part of the H2020 project MeMAD ('Methods for Managing Audiovisual Data: Combining Automatic Efficiency with Human Accuracy'), in which multimedia content describers from the television and archive industries tested *Flow*, an online platform, designed to assist the post-editing of automatically generated data, in order to enhance the production of archival descriptions of film content. Our study captured the participant experience using screen recordings, the User Experience Questionnaire (UEQ), a benchmarked interactive media questionnaire and focus group discussions, reporting a broadly positive post-editing environment. Users designated the platform's role in the collation of machine-generated content descriptions, transcripts, named-entities (location, persons, organisations) and translated text as helpful and likely to enhance creative outputs in the longer term. Suggestions for improving the platform included the addition of specialist vocabulary functionality, shot-type detection, film-topic labelling, and automatic music recognition. The limitations of the study are, most notably, the current level of accuracy achieved in computer vision outputs (i.e. automated video descriptions of film material) which has been hindered by the lack of reliable and accurate training data, and the need for a more narratively oriented interface which allows describers to develop their storytelling techniques and build descriptions which fit within a platform-hosted storyboarding functionality. While this work has value in its own right, it can also be regarded as paving the way for the future (semi)automation of audio descriptions to assist audiences experiencing sight impairment, cognitive accessibility difficulties or for whom 'visionless' multimedia consumption is their preferred option.

Keywords: Computer vision · Video description · Content description · Audiovisual translation · Archive retrieval · Audio description · Media accessibility

© Springer Nature Switzerland AG 2021
C. Stephanidis et al. (Eds.): HCII 2021, LNCS 13096, pp. 147–167, 2021.
https://doi.org/10.1007/978-3-030-90328-2_10

1   Introduction

1.1   Background

In the ongoing debate about the value of AI in human-dominated workstreams there are clearly tasks the human completes with greater compassion, empathy, subtlety and contextualisation than a machine, and these are skills which remain difficult to train into computer models (e.g. one which automates audio description or similar video description services). Yet the AI machine, programmed to operate dispassionately and with algorithmic efficiency, is capable of producing large volumes of data in a fraction of the time it would take human operatives (e.g. processing computer vision training data). While each of these methods offers benefits, they also present different challenges. Can automated video description ever match the expectations of audiovisual content creators and editors? Can human endeavour alone keep pace with the proliferation of new media resources requiring description? To what extent is quality negotiable in return for increased volumes and speed of output? And, most importantly, where do media access and the media consumer fit into the picture?

1.2   Study Aims and Structure

In the European MeMAD project (grant no. 780069), our primary focus has been on **developing semi-automated video description models** which replicate, as far as possible, the work of human describers of audiovisual content [1, 2]. This has been achieved using computer vision modelling, theories of human engagement with multimodal narrative, and the integration of machine-generated data within an editing platform, *Flow*, which draws together machine descriptions, named-entity recognition, metadata, transcriptions and translation services (Fig. 1). While the eventual aim is to **create a methodology** for achieving automated (or semi-automated) audio descriptions of high volume, low value media artefacts such as social media streams, it became clear early on in the MeMAD project that this goal is currently unattainable. Given the present level of sophistication achieved with machine-generated video captions [3–5], a more pragmatic approach was taken to produce baseline automated video descriptions and other metadata, which could be made available through an online editing platform. Human operatives would then use the machine-generated data as a starting point to create descriptions of archive film resources for future access and retrieval. As the accuracy of machine descriptions improves in the future, we anticipate the post-editing process will become less onerous for human content describers, freeing them to concentrate their efforts on the highest value audiovisual artefacts in their collections.

Fig. 1. Flow platform editing mode

This process has the potential to lead to the development of a system for the **semi-automation for audio description**, although suffice it to say this would require a seismic jump in functionality from the current state of affairs. Firstly, it would be necessary to integrate audio cue processing (using automatic speech recognition and topic detection) into the automated caption generation process, followed by identification of the available hiatuses in the original audio track, and subsequently, the application of text condensation techniques to match automated audio description scripts with gaps in the original audio track. Finally, a data prioritisation system or metric would have to be applied to order the narrative saliency of visual information. All of these complex audiovisual tasks are integral to the successful delivery of human-based audio description.

Within the above context, this paper reports the methodology and results of a recent study undertaken to test user experience on the *Flow* video description editing platform [6] with participants from the television and film archive industries. In particular, consideration was given to the commercial value of using an interface which offers a range of data and metadata from which the user may select and discard options in line with any given editing brief. In doing so, questions were raised about the **impact of semi-automation on workflows**, **data reliability**, and most importantly from the perspective of the end-consumer, **quality of outputs.**

Since our aim was to **assess the workflows** involved in editing automated and pre-packaged data within a platform environment, the quality of the machine descriptions and the users' output were not evaluated, nor did we measure or evaluate the speed of production. This was for several reasons: the novelty of the tool for users (lack of familiarity given that the users were new to this particular editing environment); our aim to include participants from different countries, which created some language barriers (the machine video captions were available only in English, whilst participants described the content in different languages); the quality of the sample content (i.e. our assumption, based on an earlier analysis of machine-derived video captions [1, 2], was that they are currently not sufficiently accurate or reliable to provide a realistic starting point for a simulation of true-to-life editing).

Having first outlined our research framework and methods, we will then present and extrapolate our results to consider the implications of harnessing human-machine interaction on editing platforms such as *Flow* in the context of future enhancements, as well as the possibility of extending accessibility beyond archive retrieval.

2 Methodology

2.1 Research Design

Due to the novelty of the workflows under evaluation, a mixed-methods approach to data collection was adopted. This comprised three phases: (i) **observation**, via screen recording software, of study participants undertaking hands-on work editing data on the platform; (ii) a validated **questionnaire**, the UEQ [7], used to evaluate user experience, complemented by specific questions about participants' experience of the *Flow* work environment; and (iii) **focus groups** to elicit participants' suggestions for further development of the platform and refinement of the features and functions of the prototype. In light of the Covid-19 pandemic, data collection was conducted through a series of online workshops with participants hosted via Zoom and the *Flow* platform, and chatroom technologies used for facilitating follow-up discussions.

Participants
Participants formed a convenience sample, with recruitment being conducted through organisations expressing an interest in the work of the MeMAD consortium. They were drawn from the broadcast and media archive industries including television production staff from a number of European broadcasters, and archivists from the Finnish national archive institution. Twenty-three participants were initially recruited to the study, with eighteen completing all three phases (four participants withdrew due to either time constraints or technical issues). Job descriptions of those whose finished all three phases (n = 18) included roles in television production, production coordinators, assistant producers, archive journalists and cataloguers. All participants had some previous experience describing filmed content. Recruitment took place across four countries (Finland, Sweden, Switzerland, Germany) with participant ages ranging from 30 to 69 years; 67% identified as female and 33% as male. The highest educational qualification participants held was a Master's degree (72%) with the remainder holding either first degrees or school leavers' qualifications (28%). They possessed between 1 and 10 + years' experience in the description of AV content in the television or archive industries. In terms of their expertise of working with similar editing platforms, the participants self-identified as expert (N = 2; 11.1%), advanced (N = 2; 11.1%), intermediate (N = 11; 61.1%), novice (N = 2; 11.1%) or inexperienced (N = 1; 5.6%) users of content editing platforms.

Study Design and Conduct
Participants were invited to an **evaluation workshop** during which they were given a hosted induction to the platform, followed by the opportunity to engage with the prototype in an individual, expert-led, hands-on session. Embedding the evaluation in a training workshop was regarded as the most effective way to introduce participants to the study, providing them a basic familiarity with the tool, while enabling the research

team to observe the process and elicit participants' initial views of the platform. As a consequence of the Covid-19 situation, several participants were working from home, using laptops. They were given access to the *Flow* platform through a private broadband connection; Zoom video conferencing software was used for the training workshop. Six workshops were held, each with up to five participants, all following the same pattern. The first segment comprised a 45-min introduction to the project and platform **induction** by the MeMAD project team including the software developers. Time was given for a brief Q&A. This was followed by a 45-min to one-hour **phase of individual work**, using the Zoom breakout rooms. Participants were given access to five short video clips, a mixture of both contemporary and heritage material (one clip was used as a "warm-up" exercise) and briefed on the content description task(s). To observe the video describers' approach to the content description task and their interaction with the prototype platform, participants were asked to share their screen in Zoom during the hands-on session. These sessions were video-recorded. The focus groups were also video-recorded using the Zoom platform. Participants worked at their own pace, according to experience and technical competence, with the result that the number of annotation tasks completed ranged from between one and five video clips per person. Three participants completed four clips, six participants completed three clips, a further six participants completed two clips; three participants worked on just one clip. Technical support was available to participants in Zoom breakout rooms throughout the hands-on session. After completion of the set tasks, a **questionnaire** was administered to elicit the participants' views on working with the platform. This was followed by a **focus-group** discussion, lasting between 33 and 71 min across the six workshops.

2.2 Data Collection

The questionnaire consisted of four sections: basic demographics; the standard User Experience Questionnaire (UEQ); and two additional sections comprising questions specific to the current study. The UEQ [7] is a widely adopted data collection instrument, used to elicit users' impressions, feelings and attitudes towards a range of interactive products similar to the *Flow* platform. It comprises twenty-six 7-point Likert-type questions, intended to measure usability and user experience across six dimensions. (Table 1).

Although the *Flow* platform is currently at an early stage of development, all components of the UEQ were used in this evaluation. The main focus was on **usability**, however, we also sought to elicit participants' views on **attractiveness** and **user experience** to inform future development. Interpretation of the outcomes for these components was conducted in a way that was mindful of the prototype nature of the platform.

The second part of the questionnaire contained two further sets of 7-point Likert-type questions, one relating to the **work environment** and the other eliciting users' preferences in relation to the particular **features and functions** of the *Flow* prototype. The work environment section interrogated participants' impressions of **process and workflows** (e.g. *"I felt comfortable working in this environment"*) and their perception of the opportunity to create more efficient or effective descriptions using the platform (e.g. *"I feel that the environment has helped me to produce good descriptions"*). The **preferences** section investigated the participants' attitudes towards specific characteristics of

Table 1. Dimensions of the UEQ (http://www.ueq-online.org)

Grouping	Dimension	Explanation
Overall	Attractiveness	Overall impression of the product. Do users like or dislike it?
Usability	Perspicuity	Is it easy to get familiar with the product and to learn how to use it?
	Efficiency	Can users solve their tasks without unnecessary effort? Does it react fast?
	Dependability	Does the user feel in control of the interaction? Is it secure and predictable?
User experience	Stimulation	Is it exciting and motivating to use the product? Is it fun to use?
	Novelty	Is the design of the product creative? Does it catch the interest of users?

the prototype (e.g. *"The 'adding a content description' feature was efficient/functional"*, *"The timeline lane showing places, persons, tags was useful"*).

2.3 Data Analysis

The standard sections of the UEQ **questionnaire** were analysed using an instrument integral to the package. This quantifies basic data on user experience by comparing participants' responses against a benchmark dataset, consisting of metrics from over 14000 participants evaluating more than 280 products (e.g. business software, web pages, online shops, social networks). From these studies, benchmarked mean scores for each of the six dimensions of the UEQ are supplied. The UEQ analysis was complemented by a statistical analysis of the overall experience questions, and the questions relating to specific features and functions, all of which were particular to this study. Answers to open-ended questions were analysed qualitatively with a focus on user preferences. To complement this data, **focus group discussions** were thematically analysed to compare and contrast participants' perceptions of the prototype. Wherever possible, references in the discussion were related to specific instances in the observed **hands-on sessions** and to the questionnaire responses of the respective participants. Our purpose was to use the focus groups to make a more granular study of the observed actions and questionnaire responses obtained in the earlier phases of the study.

2.4 Ethical Considerations

The study was approved by the University of Surrey Ethics Committee (Reference number: FASS 20–21 014 EGA). Participants were recruited from four nations, with most participants indicating that they were comfortable participating in English. The questionnaire was made available in English and Finnish to accommodate different language backgrounds. Focus groups were held in both Finnish and English.

3 Results

3.1 User Experience Questionnaire (UEQ)

Generic UEQ Questions. As illustrated in Table 1, the 26 items in the UEQ are grouped into six 'dimensions' representing usability and user experience. The results for each individual metric are presented as mean scores in Table 2; the scores for each of the six dimensions are shown in Table 3. UEQ scores range between −3 (extremely bad) and +3 (extremely good).

Table 2. UEQ mean scores for individual questions

Item	Mean	Variance	Std. Dev.	No.	Left	Right	Dimension
1	1.00	1.18	1.08	18	Annoying	Enjoyable	Attractiveness
2	1.06	1.23	1.11	18	Not understandable	Understandable	Perspicuity
3	1.17	0.85	0.92	18	Creative	Dull	Novelty
4	1.06	1.47	1.21	18	Easy to learn	Difficult to learn	Perspicuity
5	1.39	0.72	0.85	18	Valuable	Inferior	Stimulation
6	1.17	0.62	0.79	18	Boring	Exciting	Stimulation
7	1.94	0.41	0.64	18	Not interesting	Interesting	Stimulation
8	0.72	1.39	1.18	18	Unpredictable	Predictable	Dependability
9	1.28	1.74	1.32	18	Fast	Slow	Efficiency
10	1.17	2.03	1.42	18	Inventive	Conventional	Novelty
11	1.28	0.45	0.67	18	Obstructive	Supportive	Dependability
12	1.00	2.12	1.46	18	Good	Bad	Attractiveness
13	0.83	1.56	1.25	18	Complicated	Easy	Perspicuity
14	1.44	0.73	0.86	18	Unlikable	Pleasing	Attractiveness
15	0.94	0.41	0.64	18	Usual	Leading edge	Novelty
16	1.17	0.62	0.79	18	Unpleasant	Pleasant	Attractiveness
17	0.89	1.16	1.08	18	Secure	Not secure	Dependability
18	1.39	1.31	1.14	18	Motivating	Demotivating	Stimulation
19	0.94	1.35	1.16	18	Meets expectations	Does not meet expectations	Dependability
20	1.06	1.23	1.11	18	Inefficient	Efficient	Efficiency
21	1.00	1.53	1.24	18	Clear	Confusing	Perspicuity
22	1.33	0.94	0.97	18	Impractical	Practical	Efficiency

(continued)

Table 2. (*continued*)

Item	Mean	Variance	Std. Dev.	No.	Left	Right	Dimension
23	1.11	1.16	1.08	18	Organized	Cluttered	Efficiency
24	1.11	0.81	0.90	18	Attractive	Unattractive	Attractiveness
25	1.33	1.41	1.19	18	Friendly	Unfriendly	Attractiveness
26	1.44	0.85	0.92	18	Conservative	Innovative	Novelty

Table 3. UEQ 'Dimensions'

Dimension	Mean	Variance	Std. Dev.
Attractiveness	1.18	0.56	0.75
Perspicuity	0.99	1.09	1.04
Efficiency	1.19	0.86	0.93
Dependability	0.96	0.65	0.81
Stimulation	1.47	0.37	0.61
Novelty	1.18	0.57	0.76

However, the UEQ developers note that mean scores of above +2 or below −2 are unlikely to be observed due to a tendency for respondents to avoid both extremes when presented with a Likert scale survey. According to the UEQ development team, values between −0.8 and +0.8 represent a neutral evaluation of the corresponding item or dimension, values >0.8 represent a positive evaluation and values <0.8 indicate a negative evaluation. In line with this assessment, the mean scores recorded for both individual items and the six dimensions suggest that participants were rating the platform positively. The UEQ's rubric for estimating required sample size for generalisability, based on the level of precision E (i.e. difference between true scale mean in the population and estimated scale mean from the sample) and the standard deviation (in the sample), suggests that our sample size was large enough for E = 0.5 and for an error probability P = 0.05 for perspicuity and efficiency and P = 0.01 for attractiveness, dependability, stimulation, novelty.

In general, it can be observed that the mean scores for all six 'dimensions' fall above the >0.8 threshold identified by the UEQ development team as indicating positive feedback. Despite *Flow* still being in the prototype phase, *attractiveness* and the two *user experience* dimensions (*stimulation, novelty*) were evaluated very positively. Interestingly, the highest scores *(mean = 1.47)* relate to *stimulation* which, in the context of an industry where automation is often viewed with suspicion and perceived as a potential threat to job satisfaction, is highly encouraging. *Attractiveness (mean = 1.18)*, *efficiency (mean = 1.19)* and *novelty (mean = 1.18)* also score strongly. Unsurprisingly, for a new platform with a sharp learning curve, *perspicuity (mean = 0.99)* registered more modest (though still positive) scores, and dependability *(mean = 0.96)* while also an encouraging score, suffered from the vagaries of remote connectivity and, to some extent, the lack of reliability still evident in machine-generated descriptions.

In order to contextualise these scores, the study's UEQ results were benchmarked against an industry reference dataset made available by the UEQ developers. As noted above, this dataset is active and growing, but currently includes over 14000 questionnaire responses from 280 studies derived from a broad selection of interactive and digital product research studies. The benchmarked results for *Flow* are shown in Fig. 2. The classifications used in benchmarking are 'excellent' (meaning that the results are in the range of the 10% best results in the benchmark dataset), 'good' (10% of the results in the benchmark dataset are better and 75% are worse), 'above average' (25% of the results in the benchmark dataset are better and 50% are worse), 'below average' (50% of the results in the benchmark dataset are better and 25% are worse) and 'bad' (in the range of the 25% worst results).

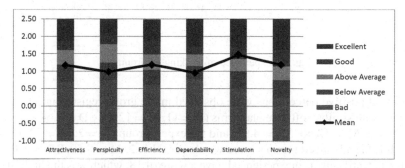

Fig. 2. Benchmarked UEQ scores compared with *Flow* mean scores

Figure 2 shows mean scores for *Flow* (marked in black) against benchmarked categories (excellent, good, above average etc.). Whilst two dimensions were slightly below the benchmarked average *(perspicuity* and *dependability)*, one scored above average *(efficiency)* and two were rated as good *(stimulation, novelty)*. The score of *attractiveness (mean = 1.18)* was good in absolute terms (as good as the score for *efficiency)*, but it was marginally lower (0.02) than the benchmarked average for this category, indicating that our evaluators found the platform attractive, but very marginally less attractive than the average product in the UEQ benchmark dataset. The two user experience dimensions *(stimulation, novelty)* benchmarked well against the reference dataset, which might be expected given that *Flow* offers a unique approach to archive development. The possible reasons for the ratings for *perspicuity* and *dependability* were outlined above. Further insights into the participants' perceptions can be derived from the 'Working environment' section of the questionnaire (below).

Working Environment. Participants' Responses regarding their general experience of the working environment – i.e. their interaction with the platform in their set-up, including their computer, workstation and internet connection – are presented as summative scores below (Fig. 3), based on the participants' perceptions of the naturalness in the use of the platform within their work environment, how comfortable they felt working in their environment, the impact that the work environment had on their performance, and whether the environment helped them to produce viable descriptions.

Based on these four questions, and using a 7-point Likert scale, the minimum and maximum scores were 1 and 28 respectively. The overall experience associated with the prototype was scored at M = 12.22 (SD = 3.54).

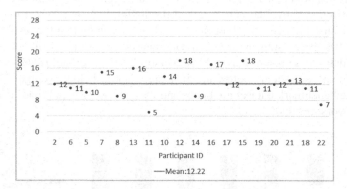

Fig. 3. Experience of working environment

The most positive perceptions were observed in the group registering intermediate experience with similar software platforms (N = 11; M = 12.36, SD = 3.64), the novice group (N = 2; M = 12.50, SD = 4.95) and the expert group (N = 2; M = 12.00, SD = 1.41), while the advanced group's score was lower (N = 2; M = 8.50, SD = 2.12). The participant identifying as inexperienced gave a score of 18, which was the highest score awarded. However, given the small participant numbers per group, these results need to be treated with caution.

The breakdown by years of experience creating content descriptions did not reveal large differences (1–5 years: N = 5, M = 11.2, SD = 2.86; 6–10 years: N = 3, M = 13.33, SD = 7.23; > 10 years: N = 10, M = 12.4, SD = 2.95). Stronger differences emerged in relation to the participants' professional affiliation. Participants from company A (N = 3) and company C (N = 4) scored their overall experience of working with the prototype at M = 15.33 (SD = 3.06) and M = 14.00 (SD = 4.24) respectively, whilst the scores given by participants from company B (N = 4) and D (N = 6) were M = 10.75 (SD = 2.63) and M = 10.67 (SD = 3.61). This is most likely linked to the companies' current workflows but it may in part be explainable by the fact that the organisations present different work environments, i.e. broadcaster vs. national archive.

For example, of the participants working in a **broadcasting environment**, those with intermediate expertise of using similar platforms commented that the tool was quite easy to handle and enjoyable, but that the combination of not knowing the context of the clips and not being familiar with the prototype interface made the specific task difficult, and that more time than available during the workshop would be needed to become familiar with the platform. Broadcaster-based participants with different levels of expertise (intermediate, expert) reported difficulties adjusting the time code of automatically pre-segmented segments, where they felt such adjustments were necessary. Furthermore, some individuals reported that text they had entered in the description fields seemed to disappear and had to be re-entered (intermediate, advanced). Other comments revealed problems with using the video player during the description, and problems with clearing data from some fields. Two participants had difficulty with playing the video clips on a Mac computer (expert) and processing the recorded video files from Zoom (intermediate). One participant (expert) thought that there was not enough automatic extraction of metadata to help description, especially with regard to face recognition [8]. Finally, the comments from the broadcaster-based participants also point to another source of difficulty: the participants' working environment, which was at home due to the pandemic. Whilst three of these participants did not have any technical problems, others felt that their (laptop) screen was too small, leading to them not being able to see all features of the interface at the same time.

Participants working in an **archival environment** reported relatively few technical problems. One participant from this group (novice) thought that moving the timeline was difficult, as the content moves while the track head stays in place, which was different from this participant's (limited) own practical experience. Another participant in this group (intermediate) felt that the user interface should communicate a little better, for example, warning the user when a description they produced would not be saved once they move to the timeline. One participant (intermediate) suggested that a list of terms to use could be helpful, depending on the purpose of the description.

Specific Features and Functions of the Prototype. The results of the specific features and functions of the prototype section are presented as measures of central tendency. Based on a 7-point Likert scale, eight of the sixteen items that participants were asked to score (Table 4) were rated average or above.

Table 4. Views about specific features of the *Flow* platform

Q#	Question	Mean	SD	Median	Mode
39	It was easy to access the application	2.67	1.41	2	2
40	The information provided in the application was not too technical	5.50	1.07	5.5	5
41	The 'adding a content description' feature was efficient/functional	3.22	1.31	3	3
42	The timeline was useful for navigating the clip	2.78	1.62	2	2
43	The timeline was useful for creating new content descriptions	3.28	1.97	3	2
44	The timeline zoom and pan was easy to use	3.89	1.59	4	4
45	Selecting a time range using the SET IN / SET OUT buttons was intuitive	3.39	1.60	3	5

(continued)

Table 4. (*continued*)

Q#	Question	Mean	SD	Median	Mode
46	The places, persons and other suggested tags were useful	3.50	1.21	3	3
47	The suggestion in the 'spoken text' field' was useful	3.44	1.61	3	3
48	The sidebar with existing content descriptions was clear	3.33	0.94	4	4
49	The timeline lane showing places, persons, tags was useful	3.56	1.71	3	3
50	The 'Deep Caption' timeline lane was useful	4.39	1.38	4	4
51	The 'Shots' timeline lane was useful	3.72	1.88	4	4
52	The 'Faces' timeline lane was useful	4.11	1.49	4	4
53	The 'OCR' (text detected in screen) timeline lane was useful	3.72	1.56	4	4
54	The 'Transcript' lane for the language spoken in the clip was useful	3.06	1.68	3	3

While the low scores for *access to the application* (Q39) require further scrutiny, the participants were generally appreciative of the way in which the information was presented on the platform (Q40). The scores for the core function of *adding a content description* (Q41) are average, but interestingly the various *support feeds* offered in the platform to enable the human operator to create (write) the descriptions were all perceived as being useful, especially the various timeline lanes (tiers) showing the *shot segmentation* (Q51), the *automated video captions* (Q50), the results of the *automatic face recognition* (Q52), *text detected in the AV content* (Q53), and the transcript (Q54). The various displays of *tags for persons, places and other features* were also deemed helpful (Q46, Q49) as was the *'spoken text' snapshot*, which highlighted quotes from the *transcript* (Q47). One participant with intermediate experience with editing platforms thought that the tag suggestions and the suggested (automatically generated) video descriptions were by far the most useful material; more useful than the timeline lanes. Another participant with intermediate experience commented that the tool as a whole is useful when there is enough time to learn how to use it and to work at one's own pace, without time pressure.

The perceptions of *working with the timeline* (Q42–45) were more mixed. In the feedback comments, one of the participants (with intermediate experience) noted that s/he did not fully understand how to move on the timeline. An advanced user stated that many points could be made about the timeline, but that its usefulness ultimately depends on the data available to be displayed in the timeline lanes. The feedback garnered in the focus group discussions (see Sect. 3.2) gives more insight into the participants' thoughts about the timeline features.

Further analysis shows that the reactions to the prototype's features and functions varied according to the participants' level of expertise with editing platforms (Fig. 4).

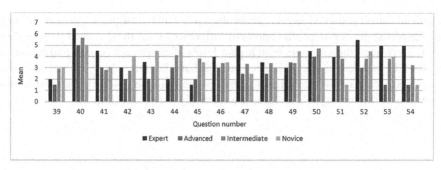

Fig. 4. Features and functions according to level of expertise (1)

Participants identifying as expert users of editing platforms (N = 2) had the most positive views on eight of the sixteen items (Table 5):

Table 5. Participants identifying as experts

Item#	Functionality
40	The information provided in the application was not too technical
41	The 'adding a content description' feature was efficient/functional
46	The places, persons and other suggested tags were useful
47	The suggestion in the 'spoken text' field' was useful
48	The sidebar with existing content descriptions was clear
52	The 'Faces' timeline lane was useful
53	The 'OCR' (text detected in screen) timeline lane was useful
54	The 'Transcript' lane for the language spoken in the clip was useful

Those identifying as beginners (N = 2) had the most positive views on five of the items (Table 6):

Table 6. Participants identifying as beginners

Item#	Functionality
39	It was easy to access the application
42	The timeline was useful for navigating the clip
45	Selecting a time range using the SET IN and SET OUT buttons was intuitive
49	The timeline lane showing places, persons, tags was useful

Furthermore, consistent with the assessment of the working environment, the expert, intermediate and novice groups were more positive in their assessment of the features than the advanced group. However, given the small number of participants in the individual expertise-level groups, the apparent differences need to be treated with caution. A breakdown according to users with higher levels of experience (expert and advanced, $N = 4$) and lower levels of experience (intermediate, beginner, $N = 13$) suggests that, with the exception of two technical features of the timeline (44, 45), the participants' perceptions of the prototype's features are relatively consistent (Fig. 5).

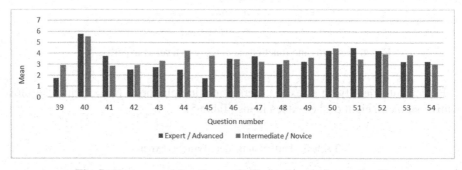

Fig. 5. Features and functions according to levels of expertise (2)

3.2 Focus Groups

Workshop and Prototype Evaluation. The focus groups (FG) largely corroborated the survey findings, revealing participants' **positive overall perceptions** of the workshop and the prototype. Most participants felt that the workshop was a good experience, and they described the prototype as interesting, novel, impressive, handy, intuitive, functional and logical. Consistent with the positive UEQ score for the effort required to learn how to work with the platform ($M = 1.1$, $SD = 1.2$), only a small number of participants reported in the FG that it was difficult to learn how to work with it. Some participants reported that they had **technical difficulties**, especially at the beginning of the hands-on session. Although these difficulties were resolved quickly, they may, in part, explain the low score for ease of access to the application in the specific features and functions section of the questionnaire (Q39: $M = 2.67$, $SD = 1.41$). In addition, the small screen size of the laptops that some participants used interfered with viewing the whole *Flow* platform at a glance. A recurrent theme across the focus groups was **familiarisation**. Several participants expressed regret at not having been given more time in the workshop to familiarise themselves with the tool. Some participants felt that this had made the evaluation somewhat difficult. Yet, participants who had seen earlier versions of the automatically generated metadata noted a clear progress, for example, in speech recognition.

Creating Content Descriptions from Machine-Generated Data. Participants' comments highlighted that their companies' archive systems are undergoing change (e.g. through the introduction of speech technology), and that they would welcome a tool with the functionalities offered by the *Flow* platform prototype, as it corresponds to **new**

ways of working in the broadcast industry. The participants acknowledged the potential of the **machine-enhanced human workflow** supported by the prototype, i.e. the creation of content descriptions based on machine-generated metadata/tags and video captions. Most participants felt that this workflow could, in principle, facilitate the content describers' task, for example by providing a starting point for a description and helping to increase the consistency of the descriptions. Interestingly, some of the highly experienced participants explained that they are so used to looking at the video footage in their normal practice that they initially ignored the automatic video captions. However, on closer inspection of the captions they felt that the captions could be helpful for **understanding unclear or highly unfamiliar content**, and that reading the captions enabled them to **identify information** they had missed in the video footage.

One participant felt that the automatic creation and ingestion of metadata is particularly relevant for legacy content without metadata, whilst for new productions, the production team would normally create basic metadata today (i.e. characters, places, keywords). In the case of new productions, metadata can be directly extracted from a planning/programming system, or this type of metadata can be combined with automatically created information.

As expected, however, the participants were critical of the **quality of the metadata and video captions** used in the evaluation, noting that this data was often flawed and that it is not possible to verify the information. Some participants thought that the video captions were more useful for the samples of contemporary video footage, and less effective for the legacy material. One participant pointed out that erroneous automated captions, which require much amendment, could be more trouble than they are worth. Another highlighted the potentially dire consequences of erroneous descriptions based on erroneous captions in some contexts. A further participant wondered at a machine's capability of identifying **salient or relevant information** in a video scene and contended that this requires human interpretation. Finally, some participants felt that the descriptions were **too detailed or fragmented** and that human describers would normally describe AV content at a higher level of abstraction. However, others pointed to the need for detail, explaining that from a search and retrieval perspective it would be more useful to be able to retrieve instances of "a playing child" rather than "a child". Options of this nature will, inevitably, reflect the video description protocols applied in each individual's place of work.

Overall Positive Aspects of the Prototype. In addition to the points outlined above, participants highlighted a number of positive aspects emerging from the prototype:

(i) the tool was commended for its **overall user-friendliness**, including its clear layout and ease of use (e.g. navigating through the video clips); (ii) the **presentation of data** was highlighted as a positive point, i.e. the fact that everything that is needed to create content descriptions was presented on one screen, obviating the need to search for metadata and enabling the user to choose and decide whether to use a given (machine-generated) description; (iii) the **timeline** was considered to be helpful, which is interesting to note in light of the mixed scores in the features and functions section of the questionnaire; (iv) the use of different **data lanes (tiers)** to display the various types of metadata was thought to be useful (this is corroborated by the ratings given in the features and functions section of the questionnaire); (v) the ability to **type a description**

while the video clip was running appealed to participants; (vi) the availability of **separate fields** for automatically generated data and human-made descriptions was deemed useful for accuracy and reliability; (vii) **traceability** (i.e. the possibility to see whether the material originated from another clip or program) was highlighted as important in the context of re-use rights, with participants pointing out that it can be problematic if re-use rights are not clear for a clip that is re-used or re-sold.

Aspects of the Prototype Requiring Improvement. Conversely, there were aspects of the prototype which participants considered could benefit from further improvements: (i) participants in one focus group felt that the platform should offer **more room to tell a story**, e.g. by incorporating a storyboard function; (ii) other participants queried the helpfulness of entering free keywords, suggesting that lists of **controlled vocabulary** would be more effective; (iii) another concern was that **repeated descriptions** were required across contiguous segments meaning that some labels had to be typed repeatedly, suggesting that a copy and paste functionality would be important; (iv) there was some uncertainty as to whether a description, tag or session had been **saved**, which led to re-entering descriptions repeatedly and (v) as was apparent from the specific features and functions section of the questionnaire, the **'set in set out' time feature** was difficult to use.

Principal Functions of the Prototype. Overall, all existing functionalities were considered useful but the detailed assessment and comments on some of the features varied in line with the practices and requirements of the participants' companies. This section summarises the main points made by the participants.

Content Descriptions. Asked how they would like to enter the content descriptions, i.e. whether they would prefer to edit/overwrite suggested descriptions or to write the descriptions from scratch, the participants said that this depends on the quality of the automated captions, as it would take time to edit highly incorrect descriptions. Some participants wondered whether this decision may also depend on the type of the content being described. A general view was that it would be useful and save time to have **suggestions** (of reasonable quality), as long as thcy can be easily and quickly deleted, if necessary. Paraphrased comments from participants also included the following, although they should be interpreted with caution, as they may have been influenced by the quality of the video captions in the sample material: (a) full sentences seem to be difficult to produce automatically; it would therefore be more helpful if the machine gave **keywords** which could be deleted or confirmed, as descriptive sentences are written; (b) writing content descriptions as **full sentences** meant it can take longer to correct the automated data than to write descriptions from scratch without automated prompts; (c) automatic suggestions are not always useful for content description, but **tags** may be useful to the end users; (d) for some users, since editing required both **deletion** and at other times **activation**, this increased the complexity of processing data (other participants, by contrast, regarded the way in which suggestions are now available as interesting and easy to use).

Segmentation and Shot Changes. Participants who describe shots or similarly short segments in their normal work practice found the video segmentation helpful and used it in the evaluation, while others who do not use it on a daily basis found it too detailed (the minimum length of a segment for description is normally five seconds). The segmentation feature was seen as particularly useful for programmes with several sub-topics, as it helped users move through the clip in an ordered fashion.

Transcription and Translation. Generally, participants found this feature useful as long as the transcript was accurate. Participants who do not normally describe speech said they would not need this feature in their own practice, but they could imagine cases where it could be useful, particularly for talk shows, factual programmes and noteworthy quotes. Transcription also enables the describer to **check names of persons and places and quotes**, and assists with (voiceover) **script writing**. Likewise, it would be very helpful for subtitling for the deaf and hard of hearing. Translations were found helpful for the description of **foreign-language programmes**, as a way of gisting. Interestingly, participants who describe the visual content only, without referring to any speech in the video clips, pointed out that they still need to understand what is said in the video clip, as context for the descriptions of the visuals. The translation feature was deemed to be particularly useful for broadcasters with multilingual programmes and archives.

Face Recognition. Participants found the idea of automatic face recognition [8] useful especially for describing **old material without metadata**, but questioned its reliability. Another use that was highlighted was the **identification of foreign names** through face recognition, as this would help with spelling if delivered as an editable functionality.

Tags. The automated tags were described as a very useful feature for both content description and retrieval. The general view was that the tags **save time** and **prevent typos** in the description. One participant also explained that the tag field enabled him/her to enter individual key words which would have been too fragmented in the description fields. S/he felt that tagging and content description supported each other. As with other automatically generated data, the problematic quality of some tags was highlighted (e.g. wrong place names and geodata lacking precision).

Additional suggestions for improvement made by participants. Finally, the participants also suggested functions and metadata that could be added into the tool (Table 7):

Table 7. Suggestions for additional functionalities and metadata

Feature	Notes
Storyboarding	For an 'at a glance' overview of segments
Topic capture	Speech alone may not contain a topic
Vocabulary or ontology	To assist with description creation
Supplementary speaker notes	E.g. to note when a speaker is not seen
Supplementary shot data	E.g. internal/external; type of shot/ratio

(continued)

Table 7. (*continued*)

Feature	Notes
Automatic music recognition	To assist with rights clearances
Automatic building identification	
Extra time lane/tier for subtitles	
Author field	
Confidence estimation for machine data	Automated caption reliability indicator
Provenance of data	Capacity to note origins of film material

4 Discussion

4.1 Considerations for Future User-Interface and User Experience Improvements

Clearly, this evaluation was primarily aimed at the *Flow* prototype, i.e. to explore the extent the prototype's *functionality* can support the production of AV content descriptions based on machine-generated metadata and video captions, human creation and human post-editing. As such, the evaluation reveals an overall very positive perception of the tool by professional content describers with different levels of experience and from different company backgrounds. Based on their own experience with similar platforms, the study participants engaged positively with the tool, highlighted benefits and made a number of suggestions for the further improvement of existing functionality and integration of additional functionality. In addition to the direct outcomes of the study, the high level of engagement can also be taken as a positive sign, which is in line with the changes currently taking place in the participants' work environments, including changes to archival systems, which in their view make the development of the *Flow* platform highly timely.

Beyond a functional evaluation of the platform's features, the study was also aimed at understanding the extent to which this novel **workflow** constitutes a viable way of producing AV content descriptions in the context of archive retrieval and re-sale. In this respect, the main finding emerging from the evaluation is that professional content describers acknowledge the benefits of this workflow as long as the machine-generated content is of a sufficient quality.

However, the evaluation also reveals broader conceptual issues about this workflow. One particularly interesting point is the perception by some of the study participants that a content editing platform should enable them to **"tell a story"** and, consequently, that a storyboard function would be helpful in achieving this aim, i.e. in gaining an overview of the entire video clip they are describing. This tallies with our earlier research [1, 2] on explicating the human process of discourse comprehension and production, which demonstrated that the process is holistic, requiring continuous attempts at creating a mental representation of the story emerging from any given (verbal or multimodal) text. As such, we use cues from this text to activate common knowledge which, in turn, helps us to integrate all elements present in a discourse to form a coherent storyline.

Familiar with describing video footage at this more abstract, integrated level, some describers took issue with the **amount of detail** the automated captions provided and with their fragmented, disjointed nature. This corresponds to our observation that video captions currently offer only basic descriptions of the visual content, as opposed to offering an event narration [1, 2]. Some participants did, however, point out that the creation of descriptions for archive retrieval/re-sale purposes requires them to focus on individual physical objects in the video footage.

In the short- to mid-term, one of the main benefits of the novel workflow could be that it helps a human describer deliver the required physical descriptions consistently and efficiently (provided that accuracy of object recognition can be further improved), whilst also supporting the human describer in **contextualising** and **interpreting** the material without which even the most accurate object recognition will fail to be meaningful. A useful next step for developing the editing platform may therefore be to provide support for the contextualisation work (that is, for "storytelling"), in the form of storyboarding tools or similar aids to holistic meaning-making.

Another implication from the participants' comments is that the **level of detail** included in any description and the decision about what constitutes the most useful combination of automation and human work is governed by the purpose of the description (and the audience) as well as the type of material (e.g. contemporary vs. legacy material). The immediate conclusion from this would appear to be that the editing platform would be most useful if it offered a high level of **customisation** to cater for different purposes and settings. Customisable options would also cater for **personalisation** to accommodate different working practices and styles, as well as the user's own preferences. Ultimately, customisation options in the tool should also pave the way for a future version of the editing platform that can cater for both the more object-oriented type of description mostly required for archival purposes, and the more narrative approaches required for other types of AV content description that this project has considered, namely audio description for visually/cognitively impaired audiences, which in addition to the differences in description style, also comes with a raft of technical requirements (e.g. fitting the description in silent moments in the audio track).

4.2 Limitations of the Study

Discrepancies in the data. Triangulation of the different sets of data suggests that there are some **discrepancies** between what participants reported in the FG and questionnaire, and what they actually did during the hands-on session. In some cases, participants seem to have misremembered or were not entirely clear about what they did when they worked with the prototype (for example, issues with saving content descriptions). Such problems were to be expected, given that the participants only learned how to use the prototype during the pre-study workshop.

Confounding Factors. Whilst the evaluation was focused on the usability and functionality of the prototype, many participants raised related topics such as the issue of **accuracy** and **reliability** of the automatically generated metadata and content descriptions. It is possible that the quality of the sample video captions and person/location [9, 10] content affected participants' perceptions of the prototype's usability and functions to some extent. The mismatch between the **language** in which the automatically generated video captions were presented (English) and the participants' native languages, may have been a further confound. Finally, as the study took place as virtual sessions, with participants working from home due to the Covid-19 pandemic, some reported problems with their technical set-up at home. This may have flavoured their opinions of the platform's useability.

5 Conclusions

The main aim of this evaluation was to find out to what extent, in the perception of professional content describers, the *Flow* prototype supports the creation of **viable video descriptions** and the way individual workflow and functionalities of the platform are perceived by professional describers. This was viewed as a preliminary step towards a secondary 'end-goal' of creating semi(automated) audio description which, it was acknowledged, is a considerably more complex task. Through a mixed method approach we have been able to measure the perceptions of the participants in relation to the key dimensions of **user experience** and **usability**, and **essential features** of the prototype, as well as capturing qualitative feedback on the **human-machine workflow** including suggestions for improvement. The prototype received an **overall positive evaluation** and was found to be capable of **supporting the task of describing AV content** for the specified purpose. As a **tool**, the prototype was found easy to use, intuitive, functional and logical. Regarding the validity of the **workflow** that the prototype has been developed to support, participants acknowledged that this was a useful way forward, i.e. a novel technology-enhanced human workflow. Looking to the future, **data quality** will be the primary driver of progress in this area, with automated captions playing a useful role in identifying aspects of the content that a human operator might overlook, as well as in improving consistency of description and bringing legacy material lacking metadata into the fold of digitally searchable media archives. It is also an early first step in developing a methodology for delivering **semi(automated) audio descriptions**. Whether such workflows would save time and improve the quality of the descriptions was not measured in this evaluation, due to the low quality of the automated data. Nevertheless, the present evaluation is the first of its kind (to the researchers' knowledge) – i.e. an evaluation of a prototype tool that supports post-editing of automatically generated textual content (including metadata and narrative), produced in an automated process of *intermodal* translation (images to text).

References

1. Braun, S., Starr, K.: Finding the right words: investigating machine-generated video description quality using a human-derived corpus-based approach. J. Audiov. Transl. **2**(2), 11–25 (2019). https://doi.org/10.47476/jat.v2i2.103
2. Starr, K., Braun, S., Delfani, J.: Taking a cue from the human: linguistic and visual prompts for the automatic sequencing of multimodal narrative. J. Audiov. Transl. **3**(2), 140–169 (2020). https://doi.org/10.47476/jat.v3i2.2020.138
3. Huang, T.H., et al.: Visual storytelling. In: Proceedings of NAACL-HLT, San Diego, California, 12–17 June, pp. 1233–1239 (2016). https://doi.org/10.18653/v1/N16-1147

4. Park, J.S., Rohrbach, M., Darrell, T., Rohrbach, A.: Adversarial inference for multi-sentence video description. In: Proceedings of the IEEE/CVF Conference on Computer Vision and Pattern Recognition (CVPR), pp. 6598–6608 (2019). https://doi.org/10.1109/CVPR.2019.00676
5. Laaksonen, J., Guo, Z.: PicSOM experiments in TRECVID 2020. In: TRECVID 2020 Workshop, 17–19 November, Online Conference (2020)
6. Limecraft homepage. https://www.limecraft.com/. Accessed 09 June 2021
7. Laugwitz, B., Held, T., Schrepp, M.: Construction and evaluation of a user experience questionnaire. In: Holzinger, A. (ed.) USAB 2008. LNCS, vol. 5298, pp. 63–76. Springer, Heidelberg (2008). https://doi.org/10.1007/978-3-540-89350-9_6
8. Lisena, P., Laaksonen, J., Troncy, R.: FaceRec: an interactive framework for face recognition in video archives. In: 2nd International Workshop on Data-driven Personalisation of Television (DataTV) Collocated with the ACM International Conference on Interactive Media Experiences (IMX 2021), 21–23 June 2021, forthcoming. https://doi.org/10.5281/zenodo.4764633
9. Harrando, I., Troncy, R.: Named entity recognition as graph classification. In: Verborgh, R., et al. (eds.) ESWC 2021. LNCS, vol. 12739, pp. 103–108. Springer, Cham (2021). https://doi.org/10.1007/978-3-030-80418-3_19
10. Porjazovski, D., Leinonen, J., Kurimo, M.: Named entity recognition for spoken finnish. In: Proceedings of 2nd International Workshop on AI for Smart TV Content Production Access and Delivery (AI4TV), pp. 25–29 (2020). https://doi.org/10.1145/3422839.3423066

Teaching Tablet Technology
to Older Adults

Beenish Chaudhry[1](✉), Dipanwita Dasgupta[2], Mona Mohamed[3],
and Nitesh Chawla[2]

[1] University of Louisiana, 301 E. Lewis Street, Lafayette, LA 70503, USA
beenish.chaudhry@louisiana.edu
[2] University of Notre Dame, 384D Nieuwland Science Hall, Notre Dame,
IN 46556, USA
nchawla@nd.edu
[3] Towson University, 8000 York Road, Towson, MD 21252, USA
mmohamed@towson.edu

Abstract. Tablets can open a new world for older adults and potentially improve their quality of life. We taught tablet skills to forty-two older adults, who were novice technology users. Sixteen socialized, group-based technology workshops were conducted and observational data was collected by the workshop facilitators. Thematic analysis revealed that older adults have some unique challenges with the tablet computer, including using its touchscreen and trusting the device with their personal information. Due to the absence of a mental model for using a tablet computer, older adults experience low self-confidence and require several iterations to master a new skill. Based on these observations, we devised some strategies that older adults found effective in developing technology skills. Pairing older adults with mentors and encouraging independent learning were the key teaching strategies. This work informs the development of a structured learning approach along with appropriate activities for future interventions and community programs targeted towards older adults.

Keywords: Tablet · Older adult · Teaching · Independent living

1 Introduction

The adoption of tablet PCs among the older adults has been steadily increasing. The most recent Pew Survey (2015) reported that 18% of older adults in United States owned a tablet personal computer (PC), which was slightly above half the national tablet ownership, i.e. 34% of all US adults in 2015 owned a tablet PC [1]. This is quite surprising, given that the tablets are recent in comparison to traditional desktop computers that still have not gained much popularity among seniors. Tablets may be more appealing to older people due to their ideal form factors. Firstly, tablets offer greater mobility due to their small sizes, low weight and compactness. Secondly, the absence of unattached hardware (keyboard and mouse) make them easier and more intuitive to use [2]. Finally, their optimal screen sizes favor reading and require less precise screen touches for selection.

© Springer Nature Switzerland AG 2021
C. Stephanidis et al. (Eds.): HCII 2021, LNCS 13096, pp. 168–182, 2021.
https://doi.org/10.1007/978-3-030-90328-2_11

Given the popularity of tablet PCs among older adults, it makes sense to use these devices to improve health literacy in this population. Many studies illustrate that technology based health interventions have a positive impact on the social, emotional and mental health of older people [3–5]. However, developing skills to fully engage in and benefit from such interventions is a major barrier for older adults. According to the 2014 Pew Survey, 59% of older adults (65+ years old) in United States use a computer to go online and 29% perceive that their physical limitations make technology use difficult [6]. Older adults also lack knowledge, resources and skills to make productive interactions with computers. This is problematic because older adults in general and low socioeconomic older adults in particular are susceptible to low health literacies [7,8]—a phenomenon that is associated with poorer health outcomes in general populations [9].

Many researchers have shared techniques they found useful in helping older adults overcome specific technology hurdles. Chaffin and Harlow developed a model that describes the process older adults use to learn computer skills. The model assumes that older adults' needs have been identified and teacher is motivated to address those needs. Overall, the model provides specific recommendations for addressing common technology challenges of the aged [10]. Fletcher-Watson and colleagues found that, in comparison to single or peer tutors, teams of tutors have a more positive impact on older adults' perceptions of self-efficacy of using a tablet [11]. Other researchers used learning theories such as social interdependence theory and cognitive theory of multimedia learning to improve technology literacy in older adults. However, some of the research shows that theory predicted outcomes are not always achieved. Moreover, the majority of research focuses on evaluation of technologies designed to address specific challenges in older adults' lives, e.g. medication management or physical activity [5]. There is a need to place an emphasis on teaching rather than technology itself. Without the awareness of techniques and strategies to pass down the use of these tools, it will not be possible to help those who may derive the most benefit from such innovation.

In this paper, we attempt to address this gap by sharing strategies that older adults found helpful in developing technology skills. We were inspired by existing research [10] and lessons learned from our trials and errors in the field. The study participants consisted of low-income older adults—a traditionally underserved population. Overall, we found study participants to be persistent and enthusiastic learners, who learned best with innovative and flexible teachers.

2   Context

We have developed a tablet-based mobile application called *seniorHealth* using a user-centered approach with community-dwelling low-income older adults [12]. The application integrates all components of successful aging, i.e. medication management, physical and mental health maintenance, and social engagement in one framework [13]. In collaboration with the Aging-in-Place (AiP) program designed by the local health system, Beacon Community Health, we conducted two pilot evaluations to examine the impact of *seniorHealth* on older adults' ability to self-manage their health and achieve successful aging. Participants were recruited from low-income independent living facilities where AiP was available free of cost to the residents. *seniorHealth* was offered as one of several projects of AiP aimed at providing health oversight and community resource navigation. Sixteen older adults volunteered to participate in the first pilot and thirty-seven in the second. Since the majority of study participants were novice computer users, we developed these technology workshops to teach them essential tablet skills.

3   Technology Workshops

The main goal of these workshops was to understand challenges faced by older adults in interacting with a tablet PC. Meanwhile, we wanted to gather older adults feedback on our teaching and learning strategies to so we could tailor them to maximize learning outcomes.

3.1   Participants

A total of 42 unique participants with an average age of 66 years (SD=9.2) participated in the two pilot studies. Fifteen participants were females and the remaining were males. Thirty-eight participants identified themselves as African American, three as non-Hispanic whites, and one as other. One participant was married and lived with her partner. The remaining were divorced/widowed/separated/single and lived alone. Six participants had less than eight years of education, thirteen had completed high school, sixteen had 1–2 years of vocational school, three were college graduates and one had an advanced degree. Thirty-four participants reported having at least one chronic condition. All participants were classified as low-income, since according to the living facility rules, only individuals with income at or below $25,380 (or $28,980 for a couple) could stay in the building. No participant had ever used a tablet or a smartphone in the first pilot. In the second pilot, five participants had prior experience with a tablet by the virtue of participating in the previous pilot and they considered themselves beginner to moderate users.

3.2   Workshop Facilitators

Pilot I. The first pilot study was During the first pilot study, two resident life assistants and a resident nurse conducted technology workshops with older adults located at one independent living facility. 10–12 seniors attended each tablet workshop. We conducted on workshop each. More specifically, the workshops were conducting once a week to once a month, depending on the schedule of participants and availability of the community room. The workshop topics were based on the needs and interests of the participants.

Pilot II. During the second pilot study, we solicited students from the Engineering and Technology Magnet Program of a local high school. The students in this program are expected to experience, create, design, build, discover and collaborate on real-life technology-related projects. We expected students to work closely with study participants to ultimately help minimize the trauma of a technology for senior participants.

Twenty students initially signed up to participate in the technology training workshops. The ages ranged from 15–18 years, and students ranged from being high school sophomores to seniors. Their technology experience was from using the technologies themselves and from coursework in their Engineering classes. Many students were also involved in sports and other clubs at school and in the community. No one had worked with a senior from the community or taught a senior how to use technology before.

We provided students with a list of topics to cover in each workshop. We also allocated a tablet to students so they could become familiar with it in preparation for running the workshops. The students were expected to prepare picture-based tutorials highlighting main ideas of each workshop so they could share them with seniors attending the workshop. A teacher from the school guided and mentored students to help them run the workshops effectively.

The workshops took place in the evening when students were done with their classes and extracurricular activities like football practice. Typically, 2–5 students led each workshop. Some students presented 2 or 3 times others presented once, and others didn't present at all but assisted in making workshop handouts. We had 16 participants at two locations and 5 at one. Typically, every senior from each location was present at the workshops. Students were assigned a location based on convenience. To maintain consistency, we attempted to keep students in the same location for each visit but sometimes they were moved to a different location for convenience reasons.

Students also provided printed manuals to older adults on topics covered during the workshops. Each workshop was conducted two times with each participant group because repetition has been identified as the key in increasing computer knowledge and decreasing computer anxiety in older adults. Two workshops were conducted at each location per month. Overall, students conducted four unique training sessions at each location.

3.3   Methods

Each study participants was provided a 7.0 inch Android tablet. We used Samsung Galaxy Tab 3 and 4 for pilot study 1 and 2 respectively. The workshops were conducted in the community rooms near/inside independent living facilities from where seniors were recruited for the studies. Each workshop lasted for at least one hour. We used the following setup in each workshop to maximize learning outcomes in older adults: (a) participants were seated in groups of fives for efficient management and targeted training; (b) facilitators gave an oral or digital presentation of the concepts; (c) facilitators demonstrated concepts on the tablet; and (d), finally, participants tried to develop competency by following the steps and getting help from the workshop facilitators.

During the first pilot, workshop facilitators took notes of their observations during the workshop. During the second pilot, we collected post-workshop reflections from both seniors and students using a paper-based survey that consisted of five open ended questions. The goal was identify challenges and successes of each workshop from both facilitators' and seniors' points of view to improve the quality of instruction and maximize learning outcomes in older adults.

3.4   Workshop Topics

Table 1. Topics covered in the workshops

Workshop #	Topics covered
Pilot I	
1	Tablet Basics (2)
2	Email (3)
3	Applications Store
4	Pandora, Pinterest and YouTube
5	Skype
Pilot II	
1	Tablet Basics (2)
2	Email and Applications Store (2)
3	Games (Bingo, Puzzles, Word Search) (2)
4	Calendar (Reminders/Events) (2)

Tablet Basics. This workshop's goal was to increase participants' comfort with the tablet. We started off with introducing by participants to the hardware of the tablet. The participants learned the functions of all the hard buttons (power on/off, volume controls, home and back). A participant mentioned wanting to know how to use the camera. The time was taken to show the participants how to use the camera and the video cam along with the various functions. One feature enjoyed by participants was the reverse camera option. They were enthused to discover that they could take "selfies". They enjoyed taking pictures of each other as well. We repeated this workshop one more time to ensure everyone has grasped the basic concepts of the workshop.

During the second pilot, participants who were familiar with the basic functionality of the tablet were exposed to its settings features where they explored the accessibility features on their own and with some help from the students.

Email. During this workshop, we created personalized email addresses for participants that was needed to download applications from the Play Store and for future communication with us. Participants were not asked to create their own email addresses because the idea of logging in was still new and difficult for them. Participants were taught to send emails to each other from the email app where they were always logged in (unless they explicitly decided to log out). We provided a short overview of the benefits of using emails, in particular how it could help individuals keep in touch with friends and family members. We also wanted participants to learn how to send email attachments. Participants then chose to email each other pics from the last workshop. This activity invoked interesting dynamics among the participants since for them it was a new way to engage with one another. This workshop was repeated two more times to ensure everyone's email account had been set up. During the third edition of this workshop, participants were given the task of emailing us from home to let us know their impressions of the workshop. Learning the use of keyboard to type was also part of this workshop.

Applications Store. During this workshop, participants learned about apps and app stores. Using Facebook as an example, they learned how to use the Google Play Store to download applications of interests. We also created Facebook accounts for participants and briefly introduced the idea of social networking via Facebook to them. Some participants also took the initiative to find their family members online.

Internet, Pinterest and Pandora. During this workshop, participants were introduced to the Internet and web searching. They were also shown Pinterest and Pandora. The participants listened to the songs that they were familiar with such as gospel music. They also learned to create and manage theme-based image collections from the pictures they took such as events, interests, and hobbies.

Skype. This workshop was about teaching participants the basics of Skype. Skype accounts were created for participants who then got to experience video chatting with each other. Participants were explained the usefulness of Skype and its potential applications such as video-conferencing with their physicians and their friends and family.

Games. During this workshop, participants learned to play games that had been curated for them during the second pilot. In particular, they could play Bingo, Word Puzzles and Block Puzzles. The workshop facilitators spent 15 min giving a demo of features and mechanics of each game to participants. After each demo, participants tried to develop competency in the games by playing in front of the students and obtaining a real-time feedback. Help was provided whenever needed. In the words of students, *"I helped them start the puzzle and gave them hints that would help them."* Thus, this workshop was a combination of structured demo and free-playing session. Participants were assigned the homework to play these games on their own and come back with questions at the next workshop.

Calendar. This workshop was about teaching participants how to navigate the native Calendar app on the Samsung tablet. Participants learned to add personalized events and tasks to the calendar while learning how to set reminders for themselves. We described the usefulness of this feature and made suggestions on how might they use to improve the quality of their daily living.

Summary. Since the goal of this research was to teach tablet skills to seniors to help them improve their quality of life by paying attention to their health issues, the majority of conversations around explaining the application of various features of the tablet was related to management of health issues. For example, while explaining the Internet use we mentioned how seniors can search the Internet to read about any of their health conditions or how they can use the calendar to remind themselves of an upcoming doctor's appointment.

4 Challenges

4.1 Touch Screen

Using the touch screen was difficult for the majority of older adults. Using the pad of the finger to type with the keyboard and click icons was a struggle for many participants. We had to teach them how much pressure to apply and how long to apply it for. The touch screen was also overly sensitive to touch. This created some problems as explained by the students, *"I found it difficult to instruct the seniors on how to close out some of the windows they accidentally opened without seeing how they got there—Student"* The use of a stylus made touch screen interactions easier. One senior explained, *"My hand and touch function is limited. I needed stylus to increase ability to operate—Senior."*

Initially, the seniors also thought that the 7.0 inch tablet screen was too small. Since they were not as dexterous, small screens made it a bit difficult for them to use the key pads to type on. Several studies have reported similar challenges faced by older adults in using tablet touchscreens, including difficulties doing finger swipes and difficulties performing dragging actions due to reduced motor abilities [14,15].

4.2 Technology's Unexpected Nature

Initially, participants encountered a lot of difficulties with the tablet that ended up generating tremendous negativity among them. At times, the tablet applications ran slow or crashed unexpectedly. Sometimes the tablet generated system update messages such as "Android Keypad update required" that locked up the tablet and prevented participants from doing anything useful. The waiting time required to fix the issues at hand turned out to be a test of patience for several participants, and the unpredictable behavior of the technology frustrated many. There were a few participants who told us that they wanted to throw their tablet out of the window because they found the tablet too difficult to use. Even learning to power the tablet and keeping it charged to use was new to many participant. It increased stress when participants would find their tablets out of charge during the workshops.

4.3 Privacy and Security Concerns

Remembering their tablet passwords was an issue for participants. It was also common for participants to confuse (transpose) their usernames and passwords - not knowing where to enter which one - for various apps such as Facebook and Gmail. One participant wanted to quit the study because he continued to log himself out of the tablet and not remember his password for the application. Another participant lost all her photos when she forgot her password of her Dropbox account. We suggested participants to write down their login information on a piece of paper, which they kept enclosed in their tablet cases. Participants identified this as a security risk, and wanted a more secure way to protect their pictures, browsing history and medication information they had stored on their devices. In fact, several participants did not want to participate in the study from the beginning because they did not think it was safe to store their health issues and medication information (according to the requirement of the study [16]) on a tablet.

4.4 WIFI Access

Internet access was a major problem at the pilot sites. The WIFI signal was available in the building but it was not strong enough in most participants' apartments. The participants were advised to shut down their tablet and restart, turn WIFI off and back on or change locations for a stronger signal. This caused some discouragement and stress among many participants. One participant wanted to quit because this extra stress was exasperating her medical condition.

4.5 Independent Learners

Sometimes we learned that older adults were more interested in learning specific skills rather than what we had prepared to teach them during the workshop. For example, in one workshop one older adult wanted to learn how to generate a playlist in Pandora because he wanted to use that skill for activities in the church. While others specifically wanted to learn how to use Facebook, Internet searching or emailing. For the facilitators, managing different learning demands during a single workshop became challenging at times. However, one student thought it was not too challenging to manage independent learners. *"'They were very open to learning new things. They needed to be taught individually most of the time, but it was fine—Student"*. However, we realized that we need to be patient with older adults and teach them the skills they wanted to learn rather than worrying about teaching them what we thought was important for them.

4.6   Managing Distractions

We found participants to be extremely curious about the tablet. They wanted to master the use of their tablets and were curious to learn about every single detail. Sometimes, we were caught off guard because participants wanted to learn something that was too demanding on our time or we were not prepared for. Older adults were very curious and asked a lot of questions. It was common for participants to become disengaged and distracted during training. As a result, working with older adults required considerable patience. Sometimes, we ended up doing everything for the seniors such as entering their password or setting up their accounts, in order to show them what they wanted to learn and also to keep them engaged in the workshop.

5   Discussion

Based on our findings of workshop challenges, we recommend the following in planning and conducting tablet technology workshops for older adults.

5.1   Think Quality Versus Quantity

We learned that it is most important to let older adults become confident about one specific skill than to teach them a lot of different skills. They like to learn slowly. Giving them the time to re-do a certain skill over and over makes them learn it completely. We felt that older adults had to try at least four times to learn a new skill. *"The seniors do work slower but they are very attentive and want to learn—Student."* We noticed that whenever participants were able to master a skill, such as send an email with an attachment or create a theme-based image collection using the pictures they took, they were deeply pleased with themselves. It also boosted their moral and confidence. Especially one participant, who was still contemplating his decision to continue with the study, decided to stay enrolled after witnessing his own ability to master some technology skills.

We also found that not only participants' persistence with the technology helped them master it but we also had to provide continuous and need-based support. Repetition was the key—we reiterated workshop content until participants understood what needed to be done. Students reported, *"Sometimes it may take more than one time to explain something, but it is okay."* The reason for not understanding in the first time was that seniors could not understand what needed to be done or what should be the next logical step whenever they entered a new screen. Even with all the repetition, it is possible that seniors may not learn everything. *"We could not help them remember all the tips but they did very well—Student."* Each workshop was conducted two times with each participant group because repetition has been identified as the key in increasing computer knowledge and decreasing computer anxiety in older adults [17].

5.2 Personalize Instruction

It is safe to assume that in the beginning older adults are independent learners. Most participants in our workshops were self-directed, so it was important to provide one-on-one help in their journey towards learning a new skill. *"We split them up and worked with small groups at their own pace—Student."* Chunking participants into bigger groups meant losing some of them along the way. Therefore, providing individual help or small group help is important. *"I liked teaching them on a one-on-one basis because I felt that was the way they learned best—Student."* Sometimes, it may also mean preparing different handouts for different older adults. It is definitely worth the effort because this method helps older adults retain a learned skill for a longer time period. Moreover, older adults ultimately want to learn what they see their peers learning, so majority of the handouts will be reused with the rest of the group.

However, we have to be wary that sometimes it is better to split seniors according to their levels of familiarity with the tablet. During the second pilot study, seniors who had already mastered the basics of the tablet found themselves bored during tablet basic workshop. One senior explained, *"I already knew the simple things that were covered today. Unfortunately, they can't be skipped because people didn't know it. Maybe merge our class advanced w/other programs and beginners w/other beginners—Senior."*

5.3 Assign Homework

From the feedback sessions of the first pilot study, we learned that older adults wanted to be assigned homework tasks because they wanted to practice what they were learning on their own. Some participants suggested that we ask them to take a picture and allow them to email it to us with a story about it. Some wanted to research assigned topics on the Internet and then share their findings with the rest of the group at the next meeting. Therefore, it is important to encourage self-learning at home.

5.4 Step-by-Step Instructions

Generally, we found that the gulf of execution with the tablet is very high for older adults. *"Some of the seniors I was working with found it difficult to locate the button or words they needed to press to move on to the next screen—Student."* In the beginning, older adults needed to learn every little detail to gain mastery of the tablet, including how to charge their device, how to turn it on, how to connect to WIFI and what to do if they cannot.

5.5 Paper-Based Manuals

During the second pilot, we provided participants with manuals that reiterated skills taught during the workshops. We focused on creating simple and easy to follow handouts by including a screen shot of every single step that would lead to successful task completion. Participants appreciated receiving these manuals because they found screen shots on paper easier to read. Also, reviewing step-by-step breakdown along with detailed instructions of the demonstrated tasks gave older adults the opportunity to clarify many confusing concepts. Finally, participants thought that paper manuals were helpful in resolving technology troubles of other seniors, since many of them had taken it upon themselves to teach technology skills to those who were falling behind.

5.6   Encourage Often

We found that encouraging older adults was very important. Since using the tablet was unprecedented for many, their confidence in using the tablet was low. It was easy for them to get discouraged if they did not get something right the first time. We had to let participants know this process takes repetition (even for younger generation). Many challenges faced by participants were due to the fear of doing something wrong or of damaging the tablet. "I am really afraid that I will press a button and something will happen that I won't be able to recover from"—enior. Therefore, we had to provide assurances to older adults that it was really difficult to break the tablet, because of possible mistakes that they can make. Indeed, we found that encouraging participants often boosted their moral and confidence.

5.7   Collect Feedback

When we started the first pilot, our experience in working with the target population was minimal. Our main goal was to teach *seniorHealth* to our participants while teaching basic tablet skills along the way. However, after a first few weeks, we failed to see the required progress in participants who were still lacking confidence in using the *seniorHealth*. This prompted us to to conduct a feedback session to help us understand their difficulties. We learned that the lack of familiarity with the tablet was hurting participants' confidence with using the application. They were also more interested in learning other essential applications of the tablet such as camera, email client, Facebook, music, the Internet, etc. as opposed to *seniorHealth* to feel comfortable with the new technology. The workshop described in this paper were born out these feedback sessions.

Hence, we recommend conducting regular feedback sessions with older adults when teaching them technology skills. Understanding older adults' technology comfort levels, what other devices they use, what they are interested in learning and what is the value of what they are learning is important to know to determine the progress at the end of the study, as well as to see what opportunities exist to work effectively with them.

5.8   Create Peer Learning Communities

Participants, who were intimidated by the tablet and wanted to discontinue the study, found mentors among their peers who helped them resolve their tablet issues and regain motivation to stay in the study. Sometimes, we paired seniors who were experiencing problems with the tablet with other seniors. One technology facilitator while trying to address the issues of a frustrated participant decided to assign a technology mentor to him. *"During the workshops, I would hook him up with another participant who could walk him through the tablet, if he had questions. This participant happened to be his cousin, so he was already comfortable with it—Facilitator."* For those who emerged as mentors, it was an opportunity to demonstrate the skills they had learned in the workshops [18].

One high school student provides insight on this, *"Teaching them and their friends, I think, is the best way to do it. This is because they can learn with their friends and ask them questions when we are not there. Some of the seniors made it a competition to learn the most by the next time we came to visit—Student."*

5.9   Organize Self-learning Sessions

The general idea behind these sessions is conducting bi-weekly and weekly (regular) classes where learners come in with their own devices. Students can choose a topic of interest from a pre-assigned online learning source. They work their way through the tutorials and ask questions as they come up. It is ideal to run this class with multiple teachers such as high school mentors. The benefits of this type of class are many. It encourages self-learning that is suitable for older adults who usually have specific goals. It also allows a group-based teaching where more older adults can be served at one time with fewer instructors. The requirement, however, is that older adults who already have a little bit more familiarity with web and devices are involved.

5.10   Stay Positive

Finally, we found that older adults actually enjoyed interactions with technology assistants (students and staff) more than the actual technology. Therefore, it was very important for us to encourage students to enjoy their time with older adults and relax. And even though, sometimes we thought that older adults were complaining a lot, no one dropped out of the study due to their failure to learn to use a tablet. On the contrary, we witnessed participants learning and using the tablets in ways we did not anticipate. One student reported, *"I thought they learned a lot better than I expected, I was surprised—Student."* Therefore, it is very important to stay positive throughout the process and treat their negative comments as part of their learning process. The easier we can make it for them and less frustrating we can make it on them, we will have happier students.

6   Conclusion

Learning technology skills is a challenging endeavor for older adults. But, they have the capacity to build their skills when strategic and flexible teaching methods are employed. Many researchers have shared techniques they found useful in helping older adults overcome specific technology hurdles. Chaffin and Harlow developed a model that suggests that older adults learn best when their needs have been identified and the teacher is motivated to address those needs [10]. Fletcher-Watson and colleagues found that, in comparison to single or peer tutors, teams of tutors have a more positive impact on older adults' perceptions of self-efficacy of using a technology [11]. However, researchers have found that outcomes predicted by learning theories such as social interdependence theory and cognitive theory of multimedia learning are not always achieved. For example, Xie and colleagues found that learning outcomes did not significantly differ when older adults learn as a group or individually [19].

Overall, tablet workshops were interactive, provided new experiences and were appeared to be enjoyed by older adults. Apart for one or two seniors who stopped attending the technology workshops due to personal reasons, all other seniors improved their confidence in using the tablet. We found that technology learning helped strengthen relationships—participants helped each other and learned from their family members. We also found that repetition and one-on-one help were key to inculcating tablet skills in seniors. Homework assignment and paper-based tutorials were also very helpful in fulfilling self-learning needs of seniors. Our findings suggest that there is a threshold after which older adults feel confident about their technology abilities. As long as they are below that threshold, they will prefer collaborative learning over individualistic and vice versa. Moreover, older adults develop technology skills at different rates and hence, application of any learning theory should carefully consider older adults' skill levels.

7   Recommended Syllabus

We recommend teaching older adults following skills to help them master Android Samsung Galaxy Tab tablet.

Physical Components

- Home, Back and Recent App Buttons
- Volume Button on the Side
- The headphone Jack
- Power Button/Screen on and off Button (understanding power saving)

System Navigation

- Unlocking with a passcode
- Navigating between different pages
- Uninstalling apps
- Moving app icons from one page to the other
- Adding installed app icons to the home page
- Keyboard (understanding when it comes up, how to close it, how to use different modes)

– Accessing installed apps and widgets from the Home Page

Personalization Options

– Connections Settings
– Device Settings
– Controls Settings
– General Settings

Essential Applications

– Email/Gmail
– Facebook
– Skype
– Dropbox
– Camera
– Calendar
– Voice Recorder
– Gallery
– Clock
– Calculator
– Google Play
– Play Music
– S Voice
– Contacts

Acknowledgement. We thank everyone who participated in this research and gave us an opportunity to attain a deeper understanding of the issues pertaining to older adults. We also appreciate the organizational help of the independent living staff, especially Kimberly Green Reeves, for facilitating the workshops.

References

1. Report, C.F.: Aging in place in America (2007). http://www.clarityproducts.com/press-news. Retrieved 22 May 22 2018
2. Kathleen, M.M., Jennie, K.J., Verna, K.M.: Maintaining functional independence in elderly adults: the roles of health status and financial resources in predicting home modifications and use of mobility equipment. The Gerontol. **42**, 24–31 (2002)
3. Cotten, S.R., Anderson, W.A., McCullough, B.M.: Impact of internet use on loneliness and contact with others among older adults: cross-sectional analysis. J. Med. Internet Res. **15**(2), e39 (2013)
4. Waycott, J., et al.: Older adults as digital content producers. In: Proceedings of the SIGCHI Conference on Human Factors in Computing Systems, pp. 39–48 (2013)
5. Dasgupta, D., Chaudhry, B., Koh, E., Chawla, N.V.: A survey of tablet applications for promoting successful aging in older adults. IEEE Access **4**, 9005–9017 (2016)
6. Smith, A.: Older adults and technology use (2014). http://www.pewinternet.org/2014/04/03/older-adults-and-technology-use/. Retrieved 4 July 2018
7. Neter, E., Brainin, E.: ehealth literacy: extending the digital divide to the realm of health information. J. Med. Internet Res. **14**(1), e19 (2012)

8. Kutner, M., Greenberg, E., Jin, Y., Paulsen, C.: The health literacy of America's adults: Results from the 2003 national assessment of adult literacy. Online (2006). http://nces.ed.gov/pubs2006/2006483.pdf. Retrieved 4 July 2018
9. Mõttus, R., Johnson, W., Murray, C., Wolf, M.S., Starr, J.M., Deary, I.J.: Towards understanding the links between health literacy and physical health. Health Psychol. **33**(2), 164 (2014)
10. Chaffin, A.J., Harlow, S.D.: Cognitive learning applied to older adult learners and technology. Educ. Gerontol. **31**(4), 301–329 (2005)
11. Fletcher-Watson, B., Crompton, C., Hutchison, M., Hongjin, L.: Strategies for enhancing success in digital tablet use by older adults: apilot study. Geron **3**(3), 162–170 (2016)
12. Dasgupta, D., et al.: An integrated and digitized care framework for successful aging. In: 2014 IEEE-EMBS International Conference on Biomedical and Health Informatics (BHI), pp. 440–443. IEEE (2014)
13. Zahava, G., Ann, B.: Quality of life from the perspectives of older people. In: Aging and Society, pp. 675–691. Cambridge University Press (2004)
14. Lepicard, G., Vigouroux, N.: Comparison between single-touch and multi-touch interaction for older people. In: Miesenberger, K., Karshmer, A., Penaz, P., Zagler, W. (eds.) ICCHP 2012, Part I. LNCS, vol. 7382, pp. 658–665. Springer, Heidelberg (2012). https://doi.org/10.1007/978-3-642-31522-0_99
15. Yamagata, C., Coppola, J.F., Kowtko, M., Joyce, S.: Mobile app development and usability research to help dementia and Alzheimer patients. In: 2013 IEEE Long Island, Systems, Applications and Technology Conference (LISAT), pp. 1–6. IEEE (2013)
16. Dasgupta, D., Johnson, R.A., Chaudhry, B.M., Reeves, K.G., Willaert, P., Chawla, N.V.: Design and evaluation of a medication adherence application with communication for seniors in independent living communities. In: Proceedings of American Medical Informatics Association (2016)
17. Bean, C., Laven, M.: Adapting to seniors: Computer training for older adults. Florida Libraries (2003)
18. Chaudhry, B., Duarte, M., Chawla, N.V., Dasgupta, D.: Developing health technologies for older adults: methodological and ethical considerations. In: Proceedings of the 10th EAI International Conference on Pervasive Computing Technologies for Healthcare, ICST (Institute for Computer Sciences, Social-Informatics and Telecommunications Engineering), pp. 330–332 (2016)
19. Xie, B.: Older adults, e-health literacy, and collaborative learning: an experimental study. J. Am. Soc. Inf. Sci. Technol. **62**(5), 933–946 (2011)

A Qualitative Usability Evaluation of Tablets and Accessibility Settings by Older Adults

Dipanwita Dasgupta[1], Beenish Chaudhry[2(✉)], and Nitesh Chawla[1]

[1] University of Notre Dame, 384D Nieuwland Science Hall,
Notre Dame 46556, IN, USA
nchawla@nd.edu
[2] University of Louisiana, 301 E. Lewis Street, Lafayette 70503, LA, USA
beenish.chaudhry@louisiana.edu

Abstract. Tablet technology and its associated applications have the potential to improve the quality of life of older adults. Current tablet usability studies involving older adults have been performed using qualitative measures focused on older generations of tablets, limited by its weight, power, resolution and availability of appropriate applications. We adopt a qualitative approach involving 25 older adults in low-income independent living facilities for studying usability and accessibility settings. We discuss our findings and propose changes that could improve the tablet experience for older adults.

Keywords: Tablet · Older adult · Qualitative · Long-term · Accessibility settings · Usability

1 Introduction

Advances in technology are currently being exploited to overcome the following challenges: increasing healthcare costs [1,2], and decreasing number of care providers [3] including direct care-givers (nurses, physicians) [4] and family members. These technology-based solutions have proven to benefit the older adults residing in independent living facilities and assisted living facilities by improving their quality of life, and reducing their sense of loneliness [5] thereby enabling them to stay independent as long as they can. Tablet based applications have been developed for older adults aimed at managing medications [6–9], and improving physical exercise [10,11]. Playing tablet games can help maintain cognitive ability, an important factor for preventing dementia [12]. However, the majority of technological devices, including tablets and the applications, are not developed specifically for older adults as they are targeted towards technologically proficient individuals [13]. Hence, few research studies have been conducted to test the usability of tablets among older adults [14–17].

With the significant advances in tablet technology since 2012 (the time when these usability studies were conducted), some of the findings of these studies

© Springer Nature Switzerland AG 2021
C. Stephanidis et al. (Eds.): HCII 2021, LNCS 13096, pp. 183–204, 2021.
https://doi.org/10.1007/978-3-030-90328-2_12

could be outdated. For instance, the issues (heavy weight and cost), identified by recent studies [16], could be resolved by the current tablets available in varying specifications and cost.

Though the present technological advances can resolve the above issues, new questions arise: Does the increasing number of features available with the recent advances in technology pose new challenges to the older adults? Do the advances in technology affect the accessibility of the tablets? Research studies have shown that these accessibility features are very important for the older adults but are not very intuitive in nature [18]. However, these studies used predefined tasks (specifically designed for the study) or user-defined goals, and involved participants with little to no tablet experience. Little has been studied about the accessibility features available in the "Settings" options of the tablet and the older adults' interactions with these settings. The current tablets have introduced accessibility features for improving the tablet experience for older adults. However, only a small percentage of older adults use these tablets [19]. These further raise the following questions: Do these new features improve accessibility? What are the challenges faced in accessing these features for improving the overall tablet experience or for any specific application? Answering these questions are important for maintaining the overall tablet experience for older adults and keeping them engaged.

To this end, we conducted 25 semi-structured interviews and 2 focus groups, consisting of 7 and 9 older adults, for gathering information on the uses of the tablet, and settings for the tablet. We used a qualitative approach for answering the following research questions: (a.) What are the benefits of using a tablet for older adults? [RQ1]; (b.) What are the challenges faced in using a tablet? [RQ2]; (c.) How accessible are the accessibility settings? What are the challenges faced in using these settings? [RQ3]; and (d.) What are the possible design changes for improving the tablet experience? [RQ4].

Our study found that the participants preferred the entertainment applications over the information-based applications in the tablet. The tablet promoted a sense of purpose and helped in knowledge building. However, the participants were initially frustrated with the touchscreen but the use of stylus and extensive training helped them overcome these frustrations. The accessibility settings improved the tablet experience. A talking guide to accessing the tablet would further improve this experience.

2   Related Work

Since the introduction of iPads in 2010, few research studies have been conducted to study the usability of tablets for older adults. Werner et al. conducted a study with 11 participants (aged 60 years and older) to evaluate the general usability of the tablet and compare experience accessing the Internet using a tablet with that using a PC [14,15]. The study participants found the tablet easy to use and appreciated the non-intimidating look of the tablet. They also found the various actions (swiping, scrolling and pinching) to be easy and intuitive.

The magnification feature improved the readability on a tablet when compared to that using a conventional PC. However, the participants found typing to be difficult using the onscreen keyboard, though they felt that practice could improve typing.

Another qualitative usability evaluation study [16] with 77 participants (aged between 73–87 years) from eleven home-care settings in UK found findings similar to that in [14]. In addition, this study reaffirmed that the non-traditional form factor (the absence of keys and a mouse) promoted engagement with the tablet among the study participants. The tablet usage increased social connectedness, and, intra and inter generational communication. The study also found that the self-efficacy of the participants influenced their iPad experience. In contrast, the study participants found the tablet to be heavy and faced difficulties with the touchscreen technology. A study conducted with nine participants having less than two years of iPad experience found downloading applications easy [17]. However, this study highlighted some of the barriers to tablet adoption among older adults to be the complexity of the technology and the fear of losing the tablet. Other research studies have also identified that the swiping action on capacitive touchscreens pose challenges for the older adults [20–22].

In addition to these usability evaluation studies, research has been conducted to study the performance improvement gained for older adults from using a touchscreen (tablet/smartphone) in comparison to that using a desktop/laptop [23]. For instance, a study [24] comparing the performance of older adults (aged) using a touchscreen and a desktop with that of younger adults found that the performance gap between the two groups reduced considerably with a touchscreen when compared to that using a desktop, though the older adults were still slower than younger adults. Furthermore, there was no statistically significant difference in error rates using a touchscreen between younger and older adults. The older adults found dragging to be the most difficult task using the touchscreen.

Studies have been conducted for comparing the performance of older adults using a large touchscreen device and a small touchscreen device [25]. Though the participants preferred the larger screen size of a tablet, they found the smaller device to be more portable. The study participants found dragging and pinching to be easier than tapping. However, this contradicts with the findings of the above mentioned study which found dragging to be the most challenging task for the older adults. The study also found that the performance improved with time (a week's practice in this case).

2.1 Usability Challenges with Tablets

Based on focus group interviews with older adults, Vaportzis et al. [26] found that barriers associated with tablet technology use include lack of instructions and guidance, lack of knowledge and confidence, health-related barriers and cost. Some of the disadvantages and concerns expressed were: too much and too complex technology, feelings of inadequacy, and comparison with younger generations, lack of social interaction and communication, negative features of tablets.

In another study, Barnard et al. [27] identified three categories of problems that older adults experience while interacting with the tablet computer for the first time: problems with operating the touchscreen reliably, confusion about how to move the cursor to the desired location and conceptual problems, such as confusion between the concepts of backspace (delete to the left) and back (go to previous screen/back out of interface). The authors enumerate several deficiencies in the tablet interface designs that contribute these problems.

In another study, Chatrangsan found that low level design decisions such as text size, color contrasts are not sufficiently clear in default tablet modes. Moreover, zooming leads to loss of orientation when navigating web pages and tapping is difficult for most [28]. Zhou et al. found that tablet technologies currently do not employ metaphors that align with the mental models that depict the attempted digital technology understanding of older adults [29]. Therefore, it is important to employ analogies and metaphors based on systems that older adults are familiar with.

Based on their task analysis, Murad et al. [30] suggest that usability problems that older adults face with the tablet interfaces are a combination of age-related physical and cognitive declines and poorly designed interfaces. Other errors, particularly those related to deciphering iconography and textual labels can be attributed to a lack of prior experience with digital technology.

3   Methodology

We adopted a qualitative approach for answering our research questions. First, we conducted 25 individual interviews, gathering information on the benefits of and challenges in using a tablet. Second, we collected information on accessibility and "Settings" option by administering two focus groups (consisting of 9 and 7 individuals) and custom questionnaires, designed specifically for this study. We studied the following research questions:

- **Study 1**: What are the benefits of using a tablet for older adults? (RQ1) What are the challenges faced in using a tablet? (RQ2)
- **Study 2**: How accessible are the accessibility settings? What are the challenges faced in using these settings? (RQ3)

We combined our insights from these two studies for addressing our final research question: What are the possible design changes for improving the overall tablet experience for older adults? (RQ4).

We conducted both the studies in collaboration with Aging-in-Place (AiP) program, a community benefit program managed by Community Health Enhancement program of a local hospital. AiP, being operated in several independent living senior facilities, is aimed at maintaining health and well-being of its participating older adults so that they can stay independently as long as possible.

We organized an interest meeting at two independent living facilities for explaining the aims and objectives of our study. We selected those residents who met the following criteria: (a.) mild to no cognitive disability as identified by St. Louis University Mental Status Exam (SLUMS) [31], a 30-point screening questionnaire that tests for orientation, memory, attention, and executive functions; (b.) fluent in English; and (c.) Good vision.

We describe each of the above studies in detail in the following subsections.

3.1   Study 1: Tablet Benefits and Challenges

We conducted semi-structured interviews and administered questionnaires for gathering user perceptions of the tablet. 25 older adults, 15 females and 10 males, from two independent living facilities (part of AiP) were involved in this study. The age of these participants ranged from 56 years to 83 years, with mean 65 years ($SD = 7$). The age criterion for our participating locations were 55 years or more. Hence, our study included participants aged 56+ years. 22 participants had less than 16 years of formal education. They have used the tablet for at least 18 months and 23 participants were smartphone users. These participants were also part of a study, "ProjectH" (studying the impact of a custom application on the health and wellness of older adults) where they received a Android-based tablet. As a part of the study ["ProjectH"], the participants were taught the basic tablet functionalities and were allowed to keep the tablet upon successful completion of the tablet.

Each interview lasted approximately for 30 min and was voice recorded. The interview focused on different aspects of tablet use: (a.) the benefits of using the tablet i.e. why did the participant like the tablet?; (b.) the challenges faced/barriers to using the tablet; and (c.) any suggestions/improvements to the tablet for making it more usable and useful. We transcribed the recorded interview responses. Three members of our research team independently coded the responses using an open coding approach. Then, the similar codes were grouped together to a category by each researcher. Following the creation of code categories, the researchers compared the different categories. They agreed upon similar categories. The different categories were discussed until any consensus was reached. Finally, related categories were organized together to generate themes.

In addition to the interviews, each participant filled out the following questionnaire – Tablet Uses Questionnaire (TUQ). We conducted this questionnaire to gather information on various tablet uses. Based on our market research, we identified 18 different uses of tablet, listed in Table 1. For each use, the participants filled out the following information: (a.) a checkbox if they used the tablet to perform any task related to that category; (b.) if used, then the participants selected from a list of options the reasons for enjoying that task and from a separate list the challenges faced in performing that task; and (c.) if not used, then the participants selected from a list of options the reasons for not using it. In this paper, we do not report findings on the challenges faced and the reasons for not using the particular use.

3.2   Study 2: Settings and Accessibility

All the participants, who were part of Study 1, filled out the following questionnaire – Settings Questionnaire (SQ): A custom questionnaire for evaluating the
usefulness and ease of use for options listed in the "Settings" menu of a tablet. It
is important to study these options because they provide flexibility to the user
for making the tablet more usable and hence, increases their engagement.

Our insights from SQ led us to conduct 2 focus groups, one each at the
participating locations, for gathering their perceptions on the accessibility of the
tablet. 7 (2 males, 7 females, average age: 69 years [$SD = 7.77$]) and 9 (4 males,
3 females, average age: 66 years [$SD = 8.34$]) older adults attended the two focus
groups. These participants were part of Study 1 and their participation in this
study were completely voluntary.

The main aim for these focus groups was to understand the user's perception
about accessibility: the importance and challenges faced. We asked the following
questions: (a.) What do you mean by "accessibility"?; (b.) How usable will the
tablet be useful without "accessibility" features or the "Settings" option?; (c.)
What are the challenges faced while accessing the tablet from an "accessibility"
perspective?; (d.) How do you find solutions for these challenges? Do you face
any challenges in finding these solutions?; and (e.) How do you implement these
solutions? Any challenges faced?

Table 1. Usage for different tablet uses

Use*	Used[†]	Not Used[†]
Playing games	23(92)	2(8)
Clicking pictures	22(88)	3(12)
Looking for today's date and weather	18(72)	7(28)
Setting calendar reminders	16(64)	8(36)
Health Eduction	15(60)	10(40)
Internet surfing	14(56)	11(44)
Collecting information about or searching products or services	13(52)	12(48)
Reading	12(48)	13(52)
Social Networking	12(48)	13(52)
Listening music	11(44)	14(56)
Sending Emails	10(40)	15(60)
Receiving Emails	9(36)	16(64)
Searching information about jobs, education or business	6(24)	19(76)
Watching Movies	6(24)	19(76)
Video conferencing	4(16)	21(84)
Online Banking	3(12)	23(88)
Online Shopping	3(12)	22(88)
Participating in chats/forums	1(4)	24(96)

*Arranged in descending order of number of participants used a use
[†]Formatted as: number of participants (percentage of the total).

4 Results

In this section, we report the findings from the two studies conducted for answering our research questions.

4.1 Results: Study 1 [Tablet Benefits and Challenges]

Everyone in this study mentioned that he/she would continue using the tablet. Further, the majority of the participants ($n = 23$) would recommend the tablet to a friend. The participants used the tablet mostly in their apartments ($n = 11$). In addition, equal number of the participants ($n = 6$) used the tablet in the community room of the building and/or at doctor's office. Based on the thematic analysis of the interview transcripts, the following themes for benefits and challenges faced in using the tablet, emerged:

4.2 Tablet: Benefits

In the following sections, we describe the themes describing the advantages of using the tablet:

Communication. The tablet helped the participants to communicate in an effective way with their peers as well as with their grandchildren. The social networking applications (e.g. Facebook) helped them to connect with their friends and family members. *"I like Facebook. That's my connection with rest of the world."* Another participant remarked that *"I have a younger sister. I looked her up in Facebook and found her. We keep in touch now."* About 48% of the participants ($n = 12$) used Facebook on their tablet. Among these 12 participants, the majority used it to connect with their friends ($n = 8$) and with their family members ($n = 7$). The tablet became a medium of conversation among the participants. *"We get down together. We gather in the community room and use our tablets there. It's a good way of communication with people."* *"I like Facebook because I get to talk to people. When they send things, I can answer them. It's like keeping in touch with each other. I get to chat."* However, only 1 participant used the tablet/chat messenger to send messages.

Some participants emerged as mentors helping fellow participants maneuvering the tablet. *"I interact more because of the tablet. I do a lot of socializing with them now because of the tablet. I show people how to use it, show them different features that's there on it."* It also promoted inter-generational communication. *"Especially when I am with my greatgrandkid, we go to the park. I take this (the tablet) with us. We will do a puzzle or we will do a word game. They like it. We got something that we do together. It helps me to bond with them. I learn from them and they learn from me."* The grandchildren of the participants showed them and helped them to learn the different functionalities of the tablet. *"My 9-year old grandkid teaches me how to use the tablet."*

Benefits to Health. The tablet made the participants feel that they are a part of the modern/technological age. *"I feel I have taken a step forward with the tablet because I use the tablet now. I use it at church to record music, and use the computer to burn DvDs. I have seen how much fun people have with them and things they can do with tablets. The tablet makes me part of that fun group."* Another participant mentioned that *"I don't feel outdated. I don't worry about my old flip-flop phone."* The tablet gave some of the participants a sense of purpose and kept them motivated. *"I play around with it. It gives me a sense of purpose. It's very enlightening."* *"Something that gets me motivated. It keeps me going. I don't feel good when I don't have my tablet."* *"Its something new and different for me. I won't be bored."*

The tablet acted as a stress buster for the participants. *"It keeps me calm, especially when I am riding a bus. It's boring and there are crazy people in the bus. I am already crazy. I don't want any more craziness. So this keeps me calm."* It also helped them to relax and sleep well. *"I get up 2am in the morning. I can't go back to sleep. If I play a game or look at a Facebook page, I can sleep. It helps me to relax."*

Companion. The tablet acted as a companion for the participants. *"It's like a companion. It's always there."* *"It acts as my company. When I am on bus, it keeps me occupied. I don't get frustrated fast."* The tablet helped the participants to spend their time in an efficient manner. *"I enjoy. I have something to do without having to watch TV. You know what to do when you don't have anything to do."*

The tablet motivated the participants to remain active and perform tasks. *"At first, I wasn't talking and I wasn't doing things. I stayed in my apartment. I won't go out. Now I go out."* The tablet also kept the participants engaged. *"I have to go to the doctor and do something while waiting. They do have WiFi. I can take this."* *"If I have appointments somewhere, it keeps me busy."*

Knowledge/Learning. The participants improved their knowledge by using different applications on the tablet. *"I have gained a lot of knowledge out of this tablet. I never thought I would."* One of the participants became aware of new things that he/she did not have knowledge before using the tablet. *"I learn how to use my Gmail account. I receive some stuff there I did not know or I will qualify for. I got a coupon from Red Robin that I did not know off."* Further, the tablet helped the participants learn different things. *"I learned different things from the tablet. The tablet is a puzzle. I 'll keep doing stuff till I find out. They make me curious and keep me going."* *"My experience with the tablet is one I learnt a lot. I am still learning."*

The tablet makes information easily available to the participants. *"The information is accessible. It's just a click away. The tablet is absolutely marvelous."* Another participant felt that the tablet is a *"highway to information"* and *"a device for Internet".* 14 participants browsed the Internet using the tablet. Everyone would use the tablet again for accessing the Internet. The majority of these participants found the browser intuitive to use ($n = 11$), easy to search ($n = 7$) and easy to type ($n = 9$). 12 participants read articles on the tablet.

The participants used the Internet to look for information on health (medications and home remedies). 15 participants used the tablet to gather health-related information (Health Education). The majority of these participants ($n = 14$) found it convenient to access this information on the tablet. About 8 participants found the information trustworthy. *"I like looking up on the Internet. It's fascinating. Like some of medicines I look it up, I find the actions, and the positive and the negative part to the medicine." "Researching in health questions: how I feel, what bothers me." "When my grandchildren come with issues, I know there's gonna be a home remedy. I would go in and look for home remedies for different things, it opened a world of knowledge how to do this."* 18 participants used the tablet to find the current date and looked for current weather conditions. They ($n = 14$) found these features very convenient to use.

13 participants searched the Internet for looking up information on products and services. The participants felt that convenience ($n = 9$) and avoid going to the store ($n = 4$) were important factors for collecting information on products and services using the tablet. They ($n = 7$) also found the reviews for the products and services accessible. The participants also browsed the Internet for finding solutions for household issues. *"I look up recipes. I look up different things and I can't run from the kitchen to the bedroom all the time when I am looking at stuff." "I go in and look for things I can use to kill bugs for plants."* The participants enjoyed using the Internet. It provided a sense of purpose and kept them occupied. *"I love to google to find something. It's much easier than going to a telephone and looking up something." "I love going to google and have been playing with it lately. I find that it's right there." "I went here to look for how to do things on tablet. I search for things. I read the stuffs. It's frustrating sometimes. I do a lot of research for tablet."*

Reminder System. The participants ($n = 16$) used the calendar feature on the tablet for setting reminders. These reminders helped the participants to be organized and prevented them from forgetting important events (family occasions and doctor's appointment). *"I put my reminders in instead of having stick papers all around. I set the alarm and let's me know this is the day that you go to the doctor." "The dates, the reminders I have put: my kid's birthday. It 'll remind me because I 'll forget."*

Entertainment. The participants used the tablet as a source of entertainment. Playing games was the most popular source of engagement with the tablet. 23 participants enjoyed playing tablet games. However, some games were difficult to learn or to play. *"I do puzzles. I spent 2-3 h on it." "I like the mind games. I like to do things I think about."* Another participant remarked that *"Games keep me occupied for hours when I do decide to play."*

Another popular feature of the tablet (second most frequently used feature (Table 1: Clicking Pictures)) is the camera. The participants ($n = 22$) enjoyed clicking pictures. *"I like the pictures I take. It's lot better than a smartphone. I take that from time to time."* They ($n = 19$) appreciated the quality of the pictures. They also transferred the pictures from the storage card to the computer. *"I love to take the pictures. I love the way they come out and the sd card I can go and pull them off. It really takes beautiful pictures. I am in love with the pictures."* 5 out of 12 participants, who accessed Facebook using the tablet, even shared their pictures on Facebook. 1 participant remarked that he/she enjoyed commenting on his/her friends' posts and pictures.

The participants ($n = 11$) used the music applications (for instance Pandora, Spotify and YouTube) for listening music. They appreciated the ability to download music ($n = 3$) and enjoyed the music readily available through these applications ($n = 5$). A participant recorded his/her own music on the tablet. *"I have recorded some of my own music there. I can listen to that."*

The participants ($n = 6$) used the tablet applications (YouTube and Netflix) for watching movies. *"I like it (the tablet) because I can watch my movies. just entertain me."* *"I use YouTube to pull some videos."* Another participant expressed interest in learning how to watch movies on the tablet. *"I would like to watch a movie on there as I don't have cable."* One participant used the tablet to record videos and watched the recordings. *"Recording at church. I rewatch off it again."*

Portability. The participants found the tablet to be portable. *"I like it's portable. It's easy to carry around as long as it's charged. I put it in my pocket and walk around."* *"I carry my tablet wherever I go even to the hospital. When I was in the rehab, I used the tablet there too. I take it to the doctor. It's portable."* Further, the participants found the tablet to be light. *"The tablet is not heavy at all."* The participants felt the portability (the ability to carry around) made the tablet really convenient. *"It's very convenient. I can stick it in my purse and carry it around."* *"It's very convenient because its small."*

Screen Size. The screen size ($n = 13$) was an important factor for making clicking pictures popular among the participants. The screen size of the tablet ($n = 9$) made reading more enjoyable and convenient when compared to that using a smartphone. *"My phone is synced to my tablet. In that way, if something is too small on my phone, I can read it on here. It's easy for me to look up (on the tablet) something especially if I am gonna go somewhere."* *"I have my Bible in there. I can see it, the screen is big."* On further probing if the participant would revert to paper-based Bible, he/she remarked that *"No. I have gotten used to that. This is more convenient for me. I can find the chapters quicker."* The larger screen size of the tablet ($n = 4$), when compared to that of a smartphone, enhanced the movie experience. *"I use for movies, better for everything than a smartphone because of the bigger screen."*

The participants preferred using a tablet over a smartphone because of its larger screen. *"It has a larger screen."* *"With a IPhone, you can only make so much larger. Larger screen, lot more details than a smartphone."* *"I like it's larger than phone. The touchscreen is better than my phone. I would prefer the tablet of this size over phone."*

Ease of Learning. The participants initially faced difficulty in handling the touchscreen (sensitivity). However, it became easier with time and practice. *"The more I used it the easier it became. I don't type fast, but it still became easier to use." "Everything has become easier with time."* One of the participants felt that *"It's not really hard to learn. It's much easier than I expected." "It's not easy accessibility. Given the training, its easy." "You have to learn you can't punch too hard. It's a matter of training myself. I can't be so hard."* Now, the participants find the tablet intuitive to use. They can figure out things on the tablet on their own. *"It's right there. You just have to figure it out. I figured news myself." "I like going to different apps. I sit down and start messing with it."* One of the participants liked the tablet more than the desktop/laptop. *"I have not used my desktop since I got it."* However, one participant did not prefer to find things on the tablet himself/herself. *"I don't want to change, if it goes wrong, I don't like that."*

4.3   Tablet: Challenges

In the following sections, we describe the themes describing the challenges faced while using the tablet:

Privacy and Security. "Online banking" and "Online Shopping" are the least performed activities using the tablet (Table 1). The fear of private information being stolen discouraged the participants from using the tablet for banking ($n = 15$) and shopping ($n = 12$). Only 3 and 3 participants used the tablet for banking and shopping respectively. The participants who performed these activities found them very convenient. Further, they felt that they could get cheaper options (when compared to that in physical stores) while using the tablet for online shopping. The fear of private information breach prevented the participants from using the tablet for online shopping. *"I don't do shopping there. I don't use it for stuff like that."*

Fear of Losing. There was no direct consensus among the participants regarding the security of the tablet. Some participants had the fear of losing the tablet. This fear prevented them from taking the tablet outside their building. *"I don't carry it outside too much. I use it mostly in the building. I am scared somebody might steal it." "I don't carry the tablet wherever I go because I am afraid of losing it. Sometimes, I walk with many things in hand and I don't carry a purse. I use the tablet in the building."* However, a participant mentioned that he/she treats the tablet as a valuable just like his/her wallet/purse. *"I have no fear of losing it. I keep it like a wallet."*

Physical Limitations. Few participants found holding the tablet cumbersome. *"I use the cover on it to fold it and make it easy. The longer you hold it the more hurting, the worse it's gonna get."* They felt having a wrist band or having the tablet hung around their neck would increase the usability and portability of the tablet. *"We need a wrist strap that would actually hold it and I have my hands-free. So little bit easier to use." "It would really helpful if I have a case and an armstring. I can pop it open and close it. Even if I drop it, it won't hit the floor. If I can put it around my neck like my glasses, easy access. When I get to the doctor, I need to dig my bag to search my tablet and my stylus."* Disability or chronic conditions prevented some of the participants from using/holding the tablet using their hands. *"I don't hold it on my hands because of nerve damage. I put it on a table or on my lap." "Health issues - backache. I can't physically move. It prevents me from doing stuff and lot of pain."*

Frustration/Lack of Knowledge. The limited functionalities of the tablet frustrated the participants. *"When I got the tablet, I was upset because I couldn't find Microsoft Word. You 'll be able to do that on your tablet. That threw me for a loop. I want to write. I want to speak and text write. I don't know the keyboard mike option. That's not super accessible."* The absence of variations and challenges sometimes makes the participants bored. *"As I did for a while, I get bored with the games as I know everything and nothing curious."* Some of the participants found the tablet non-intuitive to use and felt that training helps to master the tablet applications and maneuvering skills. *"It is not intuitive to use, you require training to use it."*

Preference for Phone/Laptop. The participants found the smartphone to be more portable than the tablet. The primary reasons are the lack of Internet connectivity in absence of Wi-Fi (using Wi-Fi enabled tablets), the cost of data plan (4G enabled tablets), and the inability to call and message using a tablet. *"The tablet came the same time as my smartphone. I concentrated on learning the phone. The ability not to call limits the tablet." "I use my phone all the time as I have Internet there."* However, one participant mentioned that 4G enabled tablet would definitely boost the portability of a tablet over that of smartphone. *"Not having the Internet is frustrating for me. The Internet connectivity is an issue. If that's solved, I 'll use the tablet over my phone. 4g enabled tablet is better except to call and listen to music."*

Further, one of the participants expressed that he/she would prefer looking up information on his/her laptop/desktop because of the larger screen size when compared to that of the tablet. Another participant felt that the tablet had limited functionality when compared to that in a desktop/laptop. *"You cannot get as much done on a tablet as you would on a laptop. When I got the tablet, I was upset because I couldn't find Microsoft Word. You 'll be able to do that on your tablet. That threw me for a loop as I wanted to write."* Another participant could not perform certain tasks on certain websites using the tablet. *"You can't use it as a laptop/computer. It won't do. When I go online to att to change the password for Internet, I cannot use the tablet because it tells me there are things missing."*

Touchscreen/Accessibility. A participant with desktop/laptop experience found the touchscreen quite difficult to use. *"It's little bit touchy. I use my fingers. I kept punching the password to unlock missing all the time. But because of my fingers, I find it hard."* Another participant did not find uninstalling applications from the tablet intuitive. He/she would prefer having a button that could be pressed for uninstalling. *"I did try to play with it to take apps off because I thought I had too much stuff on it. I couldn't figure it out. It wasn't doing I thought it should do. I don't remember exactly what I didn't accomplish that I set out to do. It's just because there are no tutorials. Having a button that says uninstall would be super useful."*

4.4   Results: Study 2

In this section, we present our findings for Study 2 focusing on the usage of the various "Settings" options. The Table 2 provides the number of participants who have used the various options as well as the number of participants who found these options "easy to use" and "easy to find".

The "Settings" (accessibility) options are very important for enriching or enhancing the tablet experience. They help the participants to regulate the system and make the tablet user-friendly. *"Settings regulate the system. More user-friendly."* Without these settings, the participants would not use the tablet. *"I won't use them at all as you can't customize without settings."* Further, they felt that the tablet will lose its utility. *"You just shut it off and put it in the corner. Its pretty much useless."*

Few participants liked the challenge of figuring out things on their own, when they are faced with any challenge. *"Trying to figure where to go, just punch to get that result."* *"Sometimes in a situation like this, I just keep pushing buttons, and see where it takes me and where I need to go."* *"I like the challenge. It might not work for the first time but get in the second time."* Some other participants would seek help from the building staffs and their grandchildren. *"I would just to go my granddaughters, and say look what's going on here. She will tell me what I am doing wrong here."* They would also look up solutions on the Internet. *"I would go to search and ask how can I go about doing this. Go on the Internet."*

Some participants felt that it was easy to follow the instructions and implement the solutions. However, some participants faced difficulty in following the instructions. They would prefer if there was a human-emulator on the tablet that could walk them through the steps. This would provide them the flexibility to listen and pause the instructions at their convenience. *"You may not understand, you may leave a word off, or you may not understand the directions that they are telling you to do. They can say over and over and I can repeat, then I can follow the instructions little bit better, instead of going read it and go back try, then read it and try. I rather hear over and over and get the understanding*

Table 2. Usage for different Setting options

Use*	Used[†]	Not Used[†]	Easy to find[†]	Easy to use[†]
Sound Volume	24(96)	1(4)	23(96)	23(96)
Connect wifi	22(88)	3(12)	17(68)	22(88)
Screen lock using the power button	17(68)	8(32)	16(48)	16(48)
Wifi on/off	17(68)	8(32)	14(56)	14(56)
Font size	16(64)	9(36)	15(60)	15(60)
Font style	16(64)	9(36)	15(60)	15(60)
Magnification gestures	15(60)	10(40)	14(56)	13(52)
Screen lock time	14(56)	11(44)	12(48)	12(48)
Software update	14(56)	11(44)	11(44)	12(48)
Screen lock options	13(52)	12(48)	11(44)	11(44)
Color adjustment	12(48)	13(52)	12(48)	11(44)
Uninstall applications	12(48)	13(52)	8(32)	9(36)
Brightness	14(56)	11(44)	13(56)	13(56)
Text-to-speech	11(44)	14(56)	11(44)	10(40)
Audio recording while typing	10(40)	15(60)	8(32)	7(28)
Backup account	9(36)	16(64)	7(28)	7(28)
Storage tracking	9(36)	16(64)	8(32)	8(32)
Airplane mode	8(32)	17(68)	5(20)	6(24)
Clear Appln cache	7(28)	18(72)	7(28)	7(28)
Bluetooth	5(20)	20(80)	5(20)	5(20)
Speak passwords	6(24)	19(76)	5(20)	5(20)
Cloud (dropbox etc.)	4(12)	21(88)	3(12)	3(12)

*Arranged in descending order of number of participants used a use
[†]Formatted as: number of participants (percentage of the total).

better." One of the participants further added that it would be beneficial if the emulator also pointed out the errors committed while following the instructions and coaxed them when done correctly. These features would boost the user's confidence and increase engagement with the tablet. *"If I am doing something wrong, then it could pop up and say that you need to do abcd. It would tell me that I am making mistake, here's how you correct. Then I am right, its right there with me and coaxing me in the right direction."* Further, the participants felt that it would be helpful if there was a help menu where they can find solutions without asking anybody. *"I wish I could go to a simple place where I can go and explain to me how to get into it."*

"Sound Volume" ($n = 24$) and "Connect to Wi-Fi" ($n = 22$) were among top three options frequently used by the participants (Table 2). Of course, the sound is an important aspect of the tablet as playing games, and clicking pictures (the top two frequently used categories (Table 1)) utilize the sound feature for marking the completion of a task (could a level of a game, or subtask in a game, or a picture clicked). Even though the Wi-Fi networks available are listed, the tablet does not automatically connect to Wi-Fi and the user has to connect to the Wi-Fi network at least once. Wi-Fi connectivity is an important component for accessing the different features of the tablet. *"Go back to the Wi-Fi to see the different connections and go different places to pick up different Wi-Fi."* However, the majority of the participants did not have a backup account ($n = 16$) and/or cloud account ($n = 21$). The participants found these options difficult to use. Setting up these accounts involve numerous steps from creating to attaching the account to the tablet user. *"The hardest thing for me is email because so many steps that you have to do. Then you have a code. You have to write all that stuff down, if you don't write it down you will be lost." "Each time I did it, I got a whole tablet list of things."* In other words, these options are not a click away unlike the "Sound Volume" (accessible by a side button) and "Connect to Wi-Fi" (through the "Settings"). In fact, 21 participants controlled the volume using the side button. However, only 6 participants used the "Mute button" in the "Notification Bar" to put the tablet on mute. Usually, the participants used the side Volume button to perform this activity. 14 participants changed the "Brightness" of the tablet. Only 4 participants used the "Notification Bar" to change the brightness while 2 participants used both the "Settings" and "Notification Bar" for accessing this option. 10 participants mentioned that they used the Settings menu and not the slide bar in the "Notifications Bar".

Only 8 participants have used the "Airplane Mode" while 3 participants wish to use this feature in the future. The majority of these participants ($n = 5$) have used the "Settings" instead of the "Notification Bar" to access this feature. Only 1 participant used the "Notification Bar" while 3 participants used the side power button. 14 out of 17 participants, who turned the "Wi-Fi on/off", used the "Settings" instead of the "Notification Bar" button. Similarly, the majority of the participants ($n = 10$ out of 14) changed the "Brightness" using the "Settings" option. However, 5 participants have used "Bluetooth" to connect with other devices for sharing pictures using the "Notification Bar", instead of the "Settings" option. The participants preferred the "Notification Bar" over "Settings" button as it was quicker and provided easy access to the accessibility options. The majority of the participants have changed the screen lock time ($n = 14$) and other associated screen lock options ($n = 13$). *"I have problem with how long the tablet stays on. The light goes off too quick. I have tried to go into Settings, I couldn't do that. I didn't know where to go."* 17 participants knew how to lock the screen using the power button.

More than 50% of the participants changed the font style ($n = 16$) and font size ($n = 16$). The majority of the participants found these options easily ($n = 15$) and used them with ease ($n = 15$). *"How you can read it as far as the sizes of the writing it because I am blind. I make the font size larger. They are large enough for me."* However, not many participants were aware of voice-to-text ($n = 15$) and text-to-speech ($n = 14$) options available in the tablet. Among the participants who used these options, a limited number of participants found the "voice-to-text" ($n = 7$) and "text-to-speech" ($n = 10$) easy to use. Moreover, 6 and 3 participants expressed the desire to use these features respectively as these could assist them while typing on the tablet. *"I have used the voice search all the time. I want to find out where downearth, a health food store, is. I just ask for downearth and it gave me the address, the time it opens and closes."* Typing is reported to be cumbersome task for people especially with disability [14]. *"The people with paralyzed hands find it easier to use voice search there."* However, the inaccessibility to voice-to-speech option on a locked screen could pose challenges to people with disability. *"You got to get into it before you could use it. The font is too small on the locked screen."*

Further, the tablet of every participant in our study ran out of memory mainly because of the games installed and the pictures clicked. The participants were shown how to track the storage and even were provided with an external storage card. Even with the training, the majority ($n = 16$) of the participants did not use the "Storage Tracking" feature and found it difficult and non-intuitive to use/find. 12 participants were able to uninstall applications on their own. The majority of these 12 participants ($n = 9$) found this operation easy to use. One of the participants did not like the inability to uninstall the unused in-built applications. *"I don't need it because I don't read magazines here. I don't watch movies and none of the stuff."*

5   Discussions

We, in collaboration with an Aging-in-Place program at a local hospital, conducted usability studies with 25 older adults residing in two independent living facilities. We administered two custom questionnaires for gathering information on likes, dislikes and challenges faced in performing any task related to 18 possible tablet uses and the different settings options. In addition, we conducted 15-minute long interviews for gathering user perceptions about the tablet (benefits and disadvantages) and two focus groups for accessibility settings. Based on the analysis of the collected data, we found that all the participants enjoyed using the tablet and would continue using it. Our results regarding the portability of a tablet, when compared of that of a phone and a laptop/desktop, were similar to those published in literature [16,25].

The perceived usefulness of a tablet is a determining factor for initially engaging the older adults and thereby sustaining them as the use of technology is governed by its perceived usefulness (reasons for using the technology as determined by the end user) [32]. The main benefits of using a tablet are to promote interpersonal relationship and provide a sense of purpose. As identified by previous studies [16,17,33], our study found communicating with peers and with grandchildren to be one of the main benefits of using the tablet. The tablet helped to bridge the intergenerational gap by providing them a common platform of communication. In addition, the social networking applications helped the participants connect with their friends and family members. Moreover, the tablet became a companion for the participants, providing them a sense of purpose, and keeping them calm and motivated. This sense of purpose is particularly important as it plays an important role in health and well-being during old age [34] and has been linked with lower mortality and high levels of happiness in old age [35]. It usually declines with age and the older adults find it difficult to find a purpose [36]. Furthermore, active social engagement (communication), sense of purpose, motivation and relaxed mind reduce/control the risk for depression, that not only affects the individual physically and mentally [37], but also raises healthcare costs [38] and risk for mortality [37]. This effect is in agreement with existing research studies that have shown ICT uses to lower social isolation and risk for depression [39]. In addition, the study participants used the tablet for entertainment purposes and for finding information. Playing games and clicking pictures were the top two frequently used applications among the study participants (using the tablet for at least 1.5 years). However, research has shown that the entertainment-based applications are popular only during the initial learning phase and are slowly overtaken by the information applications with time [16,17]. The participants found information-based applications like date, time and searching on Google, easy and convenient to use. However, they found sending and receiving email to be a difficult task, which is in agreement with the findings from existing studies [5].

It should be noted that the excessive ICT use or the challenges faced in using the tablet or related applications could result in frustration and boredom. Our study participants faced difficulties with handling the tablet and interacting with the touchscreen. The participants found the basic functionalities (actions and basic handling including turning on/off, touch technology) of the tablet easy after considerable training. The touchscreen required considerable effort for learning as it was a new paradigm for the participants. The use of a stylus made the touchscreen handling a little less cumbersome, compared to that using with fingers. This is agreement with the studies performed for studying touchscreen interactions among older adults with disabilities [22]. Our study participants found the tablet to be light in weight. This contradicts the findings in recently published studies [16] where the participants found the study device to be heavy. However, it should be noted that these studies have used earlier versions of the tablet (year 2012) as the study device. Since 2012, drastic technological advances have made the tablets lighter. The participants with disabilities faced difficulties with holding the tablet in hand and maneuvering the touchscreen. They usually placed the tablet on a table with the case folded. In case of any challenges faced in using the tablet, the participants figured out the solutions on their own by simply punching the icons, looking up information on the Internet and/or asking their relatives (friends and grandchildren). However, few participants found it difficult to follow the instructions and felt that a human emulator (repeating the steps) would help them better understand and implement the instructions. They also felt that they would further benefit if this emulator pointed out their mistakes and applauded for their successes.

The accessibility settings in the tablet improved the overall tablet experience and kept the participants engaged. The majority of the participants ($n = 16$) changed the font style and font size to make the tablet suite their visibility needs. One participant (partially blind) found the large text option helped him/her better see things on the tablet. The participants with disabilities found the voice-to-text option to be convenient, when compared to typing, as found in [14]. However, the inability to use this option on a locked screen limited the use of the tablet as it involves typing in the password, usually in small font and encrypted style. The users, in this case, could use swiping option for unlocking the tablet. However, this could result in breach of privacy and security, that could further discourage the older adults from using the tablet as privacy and security is usually a major concern for older adults. Hence, using voice recognition or gesture to unlock the tablet could improve the experience for older adults especially with those having disabilities.

Our study participants used 8 GB tablet, where 4 GB (half of the storage) was dedicated to the tablet's internal applications and functioning of the tablet. Their tablets often ran out of memory due to incessant pictures clicked and games installed. For the same reason, the participants did not like the inability to uninstall the unnecessary, unused in-built applications. Further, they faced difficulties in setting up or using the back-up account and cloud storage for additional storage options as setting up these accounts required a lot of steps, which the older adults often found difficult and confusing to use. Thus, a minimal number of steps in setting up these accounts and having the flexibility to uninstall the unnecessary applications, can further encourage the older adults to use a tablet.

5.1   Design Recommendations

Based on our analysis of the data collected and our observations during the study, we suggest the following recommendations for the design community in making the tablet more accessible to older adults:

- Wrist Strap: Some of the participants found holding the tablet very cumbersome. As the aging process progresses, it would worsen because of the fragility of the bones. Having a strap around the wrist or the neck could resolve this issue. When designing these straps, caution should be taken regarding the weight of the equipment and the tablet; and their impact on the older adults. Further, they should also be concerned about the security and protection of the tablet, an important factor for tablet engagement among older adults upon successful completion of any task.
- Human Emulator: The participants found going back and forth for following instructions (from the Internet) and implementing these instructions difficult. A human emulator could resolve this problem by dictating the steps, identifying errors and appreciating their successful completion of steps. Older adults usually feel encouraged when they received incentives (stars, crowns or words of appreciation).
- Uninstalling applications: The study participants found uninstalling applications to be cumbersome. Having a button marked uninstall, instead of the hidden affordances (long click presently), could make this operation easier and a clearly visible affordance with a signifier. Further, the ability to uninstall

the in-built applications could improve the tablet experience as it could free storage and avoid the problem of running out of storage frequently, though storage cards can solve this problem.

– Voice-to-Text: The voice-to-text options promoted tablet engagement among the participants. However, inability to access this option for unlocking the tablet often poses an obstacle for the participants, especially with disabilities. Current tablets allow fingerprint recognition for unlocking the tablet (after enabling this feature in "Settings"). Although this feature can overcome the typing challenges, this could be a problem for older adults with arthritis or related condition as the finger recognition depends on the pressure applied through the fingers. Having a voice option for unlocking option can potentially overcome the pressure challenges, but caution should be taken in setting up this voice recognition as it could be easier to copy one's voice.

6   Limitations

While our small-sample study highlights important benefits and challenges of tablet usage and accessibility options, having a large sample size would make our findings more robust and generalizable. The participants were allowed to keep the tablet upon completion of a study. This could have served as an incentive and promoted tablet usage. Our study participants found the study device to be light weight. Since the tablet is available in a wide variety of varying specifications, a study with various tablets could better inform the user perceptions about the ergonomics of the tablet. Moreover, our study did not take into account how the cost of a tablet would impact the usage among low-income older adults.

7   Conclusions

In this paper, we present the results of a qualitative usability evaluation of a tablet among older adults. The main aim of this study was to explore how the older adults interacted with a tablet and the accessibility settings, and identify the challenges faced by older adults. Our findings revealed that the tablet served as a companion and a source of entertainment. They also helped the older adults to communicate effectively and made information easily available. The older adults found the tablet to be light, portable and convenient to use. Playing games and clicking pictures were the most popular applications among the older adults. However, Internet connectivity prevented the older adults from using the tablet. The accessibility options improved the overall tablet experience. Based on our analysis of the data collected and our observations, we provided a list of design recommendations that can make the tablet experience for older adults enriching and less cumbersome, and thus ensuring that the older adults are part of the digital era.

References

1. Hoffman, C., Rice, D., Sung, H.Y.: Persons with chronic conditions: their prevalence and costs. JAMA **276**(18), 1473–1479 (1996)
2. Koch, S.: Healthy ageing supported by technology-a cross-disciplinary research challenge. Inform. Health Soc. Care **35**(3–4), 81–91 (2010)
3. The 2007 Annual Report of the Board of Trustees of the Federal Old-Age and Survivors Insurance and Federal Disability Insurance Trust Funds: The 2014 annual report of the board of trustees of the federal oldage and survivors insurance and federal disability insurance trust funds (2014)
4. The Center for Technology and Aging: Technologies to help older adults maintain independence: Advancing technology adoption (2009)
5. Werner, J.M., Carlson, M., Jordan-Marsh, M., Clark, F.: Predictors of computer use in community-dwelling, ethnically diverse older adults. Hum. Factors: J. Hum. Factors Ergon. Soc. **53**(5), 431–447 (2011)
6. Mira, J.J., et al.: A Spanish pillbox app for elderly patients taking multiple medications: randomized controlled trial. J. Med. Internet Res. **16**(4), e99 (2014)
7. Pop-Eleches, C., et al.: Mobile phone technologies improve adherence to antiretroviral treatment in a resource-limited setting: a randomized controlled trial of text message reminders. AIDS (London, England) **25**(6), 825 (2011)
8. Silva, J.M., Mouttham, A., El Saddik, A.: Ubimeds: a mobile application to improve accessibility and support medication adherence. In: Proceedings of the 1st ACM SIGMM International Workshop on Media Studies and Implementations that Help Improving Access to Disabled Users, pp. 71–78. ACM (2009)
9. Dalgaard, L.G., Grönvall, E., Verdezoto, N.: Mediframe: a tablet application to plan, inform, remind and sustain older adults' medication intake. In: 2013 IEEE International Conference on Healthcare Informatics (ICHI), pp. 36–45. IEEE (2013)
10. Silveira, P., van het Reve, E., Daniel, F., Casati, F., de Bruin, E.D.: Motivating and assisting physical exercise in independently living older adults: a pilot study. Int. J. Med. Informatics **82**(5), 325–334 (2013)
11. Silveira, P., van de Langenberg, R., van het Reve, E., Daniel, F., Casati, F., de Bruin, E.D.: Tablet-based strength-balance training to motivate and improve adherence to exercise in independently living older people: a phase ii preclinical exploratory trial. J. Med. Internet Res. **15**(8), e159 (2013)
12. Chan, M., Haber, S., Drew, L.M., Park, D.C.: Training older adults to use tablet computers: does it enhance cognitive function? Gerontologist (2012)
13. Grindrod, K.A., Li, M., Gates, A.: Evaluating user perceptions of mobile medication management applications with older adults: a usability study. JMIR mHealth uHealth **2**(1), e3048 (2014)
14. Werner, F., Werner, K., Oberzaucher, J.: Tablets for seniors – an evaluation of a current model (iPad). In: Wichert, R., Eberhardt, B. (eds.) Ambient Assisted Living. ATSC, pp. 177–184. Springer, Heidelberg (2012). https://doi.org/10.1007/978-3-642-27491-6_13
15. Werner, F., Werner, K.: Enhancing the social inclusion of seniors by using tablets as a main gateway to the World Wide Web (2012)
16. Jones, T., Kay, D., Upton, P., Upton, D.: An evaluation of older adults use of iPads in eleven UK care-homes. Int. J. Mob. Hum. Comput. Interact. (IJMHCI) **5**(3), 62–76 (2013)

17. Israel, T.A.: Keeping in touch: tablets use by older adults. Int. J. Infonomics (IJI) **9**(1), 35–40 (2016)
18. Watkins, I., Kules, B., Yuan, X., Xie, B.: Heuristic evaluation of healthy eating apps for older adults. J. Consumer Health Internet **18**(2), 105–127 (2014)
19. Smith, A.: Pew internet survey (2014)
20. Lepicard, G., Vigouroux, N.: Comparison between single-touch and multi-touch interaction for older people. In: Miesenberger, K., Karshmer, A., Penaz, P., Zagler, W. (eds.) ICCHP 2012. LNCS, vol. 7382, pp. 658–665. Springer, Heidelberg (2012). https://doi.org/10.1007/978-3-642-31522-0_99
21. Williams, D., Alam, M.A.U., Ahamed, S.I., Chu, W.: Considerations in designing human-computer interfaces for elderly people. In: 2013 13th International Conference on Quality Software, pp. 372–377. IEEE (2013)
22. Yamagata, C., Coppola, J.F., Kowtko, M., Joyce, S.: Mobile app development and usability research to help dementia and alzheimer patients. In: 2013 IEEE Long Island Systems, Applications and Technology Conference (LISAT), pp. 1–6. IEEE (2013)
23. Motti, L.G., Vigouroux, N., Gorce, P.: Interaction techniques for older adults using touchscreen devices: a literature review. In: Proceedings of the 25th Conference on l'Interaction Homme-Machine, p. 125. ACM (2013)
24. Findlater, L., Froehlich, J.E., Fattal, K., Wobbrock, J.O., Dastyar, T.: Age-related differences in performance with touchscreens compared to traditional mouse input. In: Proceedings of the SIGCHI Conference on Human Factors in Computing Systems, pp. 343–346. ACM (2013)
25. Kobayashi, M., Hiyama, A., Miura, T., Asakawa, C., Hirose, M., Ifukube, T.: Elderly user evaluation of mobile touchscreen interactions. In: Campos, P., Graham, N., Jorge, J., Nunes, N., Palanque, P., Winckler, M. (eds.) INTERACT 2011. LNCS, vol. 6946, pp. 83–99. Springer, Heidelberg (2011). https://doi.org/10.1007/978-3-642-23774-4_9
26. Vaportzis, E., Giatsi Clausen, M., Gow, A.J.: Older adults perceptions of technology and barriers to interacting with tablet computers: a focus group study. Front. Psychol. **8**, 1687 (2017)
27. Barnard, Y., Bradley, M.D., Hodgson, F., Lloyd, A.D.: Learning to use new technologies by older adults: Perceived difficulties, experimentation behaviour and usability. Comput. Hum. Behav. **29**(4), 1715–1724 (2013)
28. Chatrangsan, M., Petrie, H.: The usability and acceptability of tablet computers for older people in Thailand and the United Kingdom. In: Antona, M., Stephanidis, C. (eds.) UAHCI 2017. LNCS, vol. 10277, pp. 156–170. Springer, Cham (2017). https://doi.org/10.1007/978-3-319-58706-6_13
29. Zhou, J., Chourasia, A., Vanderheiden, G.: Interface adaptation to novice older adults' mental models through concrete metaphors. Int. J. Hum.-Comput. Interact. **33**(7), 592–606 (2017)
30. Murad, S., Bradley, M.D., Kodagoda, N., Barnard, Y.F., Lloyd, A.D.: Using task analysis to explore older novice participants' experiences with a handheld touchscreen device. In: Contemporary Ergonomics and Human Factors 2012: Proceedings of the international conference on Ergonomics & Human Factors 2012, Blackpool, UK, 16–19 April 2012, p. 57. CRC Press (2012)
31. Tariq, S., Tumosa, N., Chibnall, J., Perry, H., III., Morley, J.: The saint louis university mental status (slums) examination for detecting mild cognitive impairment and dementia is more sensitive than the mini-mental status examination (mmse)-a pilot study. Am. J. Geriatr. Psychiatry **14**(11), 900–10 (2006)

32. Czaja, S.J., et al.: Factors predicting the use of technology: findings from the center for research and education on aging and technology enhancement (create). Psychol. Aging **21**(2), 333 (2006)

33. Neustaedter, C., Harrison, S., Sellen, A.: Connecting Families: The Impact of New Communication Technologies on Domestic Life. Springer, London (2012). https://doi.org/10.1007/978-1-4471-4192-1

34. Windsor, T.D., Curtis, R.G., Luszcz, M.A.: Sense of purpose as a psychological resource for aging well. Dev. Psychol. **51**(7), 975 (2015)

35. Boyle, P.A., Barnes, L.L., Buchman, A.S., Bennett, D.A.: Purpose in life is associated with mortality among community-dwelling older persons. Psychosom. Med. **71**(5), 574 (2009)

36. Riley, M.W.E., Kahn, R.L.E., Foner, A.E., Mack, K.A.: Age and Structural Lag: Society's Failure to Provide Meaningful Opportunities in Work, Family, and Leisure. Wiley, Hoboken (1994)

37. Frederick, J.T., et al.: Community-based treatment of late life depression: an expert panel-informed literature review. Am. J. Prev. Med. **33**(3), 222–249 (2007)

38. Olfson, M., Pincus, H.A.: Outpatient mental health care in nonhospital settings: distribution of patients across provider groups. Am. J. Psychiatry **153**(10), 1353 (1996)

39. Boz, H., Karatas, S.E.: A review on internet use and quality of life of the elderly. Cypriot J. Educ. Sci. **10**(3), 182–191 (2015)

Research on the Application of Role Theory in Active Aging Education Service System Design

Xiong Ding[✉] and Min Ran[✉]

Guangzhou Academy of Fine Arts, Guangzhou 510006, China

Abstract. The World Health Organization (WHO) put forward the framework of active aging in 2003, and China is also actively implementing this policy. This paper sorted the changes of the elder's role cognition and role expectation during retirement. At the same time, it combines the theory of "When Life Becomes Subject of Design" with the public service for the elderly, and puts forward the BEV-AAS framework of active aging service in the context of role theory. This framework includes three dimensions: social behavior based on role expectation, social environment aiming at role fulfillment and social values based on role cognition. With the design project about active aging public education service system which named LO-PAY & LO-GAIN as an example, this paper verifies the necessity, rationality and feasibility of the framework. Through interviews, the main stakeholders of the elderly are divided into elite and general elderly. On the one hand, the elite elderly will be encouraged to use their professional knowledge to become the providers of public education services, and then complete the productive aging. On the other hand, both elite and general elderly are encouraged and supported to realize their respective role expectations through personalized courses planning, customer journey optimization, online digital platform construction, offline teaching & learning space expansion, etc., so as to successfully realize the active aging.

Keywords: Role theory · Active aging · Public education for the elderly · Service system design

1 Introduction

In 1999, Chinese people who were over 60 years old accounted for 10% of the total population, indicting China has officially entering an aging society. As of the end of 2019, the proportion of the population over the age of 60 in China rose to 18.1%, and that was 12.6% for people over 65-year-old. Experts predict that during the 14th Five-Year Plan, the proportion of the population over the age of 60 in China will exceed 20%, and that of the population over the age of 65 will also exceed 14%, meaning China is entering a moderately aging society. According to relevant reports, China's aging will reach its peak in 2050, during which the population over 65 will account for 27.9% of the country's total population, and China will enter a severely aging society. Obviously,

© Springer Nature Switzerland AG 2021
C. Stephanidis et al. (Eds.): HCII 2021, LNCS 13096, pp. 205–222, 2021.
https://doi.org/10.1007/978-3-030-90328-2_13

China is a country that "gets old before getting rich". In response to the aging problem, the World Health Organization proposed active aging in 2003, and China is also actively enhancing this policy.

Active aging, proposed by the World Health Organization (WHO), refers to the process of obtaining the best possible opportunities for health, participation and security in order to improve the life quality in old age [1]. The three pillars of China's active aging policy framework are health, security and participation, of which social participation is its core and essence [2]. The basic research on the theoretical basis of the social participation of the elderly generally includes three types: (a) Disengagement theory, which believes that the elderly should play a secondary role in society due to the loss of vitality and role, voluntarily and gradually separate from society, and promote social and intergenerational replacement; (b) Activity theory which emphasizes social participation and social identification, denying the existence of old age as the elderly still keep the middle-aged lifestyle; (c) Continuity theory believes that activities in old age are the continuation of middle-aged life and extroverted people will actively participate in social activities, while introverted people will not [3]. Some scholars have proposed that the research on the social participation of the elderly can be analyzed from the four perspectives of intervention, role, activity and resources [4]. The author believes that retirement is the main reason for the major changes in the social roles and lifestyles of the elderly. After retirement, they will form a new lifestyle after role re-positioning, role expectation changing and role value realization. The elderly social participation has certain requirements for the environment provided by the society, and this is also the choice made by the elderly based on their own role cognition. Therefore, discussing the active aging service design framework from the perspective of role theory can provide a public service decision-making basis for relevant government agencies, and help designers design services suitable for the elderly.

2   The Design Framework for Active Aging Service Based on Role Theory and BEV-E Model

According to the statistics from *China Population and Employment Statistical Yearbook*, the proportions of young-old (60–69 years old), moderately old people (70–79 years old) and oldest-old (over 80 years old) of the total population in 2018 were 10.73%, 5.03%, 2.08%, respectively, and young-old took a much higher proportion than moderately old people and oldest-old. Compared with the elderly at other age groups, the young-old have the following characteristics: (a) they have better physical function, clear awareness and cognition; (b) they are economically independent, self-caring, and have few demands for caring from the people around them as well as the ability to recreate value; (c) their roles have been changed, but they are still eager to maintain socially connected and be re-employed [5]. After the elderly reach a certain age, their working ability declines and they quit their jobs in accordance with national requirements. In this process, the role and lifestyle of the elderly will change dramatically. Chen Bo has conducted in-depth research on the social adaptation of the retired elderly and found that such ability varies from person to person, and age is not a key factor. Most elderly people believe that external support can help them improve their adaptability, rather than relying solely on their own adjustment capabilities [6]. Ding Zhihong believes that the main reason for current urban retired elderly who are not well adapted to the social development was the elderly's health, educational, and economic resources, rather than their natural features (age, gender, etc.). Thus, he proposed the need for "improvement" on the social resources of the elderly [7]. Liu Susu's research found that after retirement, the elderly will adapt to the role changing through psychological adjustment and work continuation. Peer group is an important supporting factor to promote the role changing and role adaptation of the elderly [8]. The above studies indicted the importance of external support to the adaptability of retired elderly, and role adaptation is the core issue during the whole adaptation which requires proper intervention by the government and society, guiding guide them to adapt to their roles, develop an active and healthy retirement lifestyle, and achieve active aging.

2.1 Role Theory

The idea of role originated in drama. It does not refer to a specific character, but an abstract concept. Although the concept of role was born in drama, it has been widely studied and applied in sociology and social psychology. There are many definitions of roles, and scholars at home and abroad hold their own opinions, but it can be summarized into two categories: one is from sociological perspective, starting from social relations, social norms, social status, and social identity [9]; the other is from social psychology perspective, focusing on individual behavior and behavior patterns. Although scholars have different views on the definition of roles, they all regarded roles as a kind of "relationship", and discussed it around "social expectations" and "individual performance", which are the abstract roles based on sociology and psychology [9]. Therefore, we can think that a role is a certain social position in which an individual is in a social relationship, enjoying the corresponding role rights, and fulfilling his role obligations in accordance with social expectations and specific behavior patterns. Role expectation means that an individual plays a certain role, and his behavior conforms to the expectations and requirements of the world and himself [9]. Two things should be noticed here: (a) The expectations and requirements aligned with role identities and proposed by the world are practical and achievable; (b) Role players can perceive the role expectations put forward by the world, and should follow their willingness and successfully play their roles.

Retired elderly people usually need time to deal with role changing and social re-adaptation. During this period, the social adaptability of the elderly declines, and the duration of social discomfort varies with more than one year [10]. After retirement, the role of the elderly has undergone tremendous changes. From social perspective, they no longer need to work but to take a rest. At the family level, they have changed from a main role to a dependent role [11]. At this time, the elderly need to clearly recognize this change so as to achieve role's self-realization and adapt to new lifestyle through disrupting the definition of their own roles and acting with this new role.

2.2 BEV-E Model

Lifestyle has gone through stages of concept germination and formation. Many scholars in the fields of philosophy, sociology, economics and consumer behavior at home and abroad have discussed and defined lifestyle. Song Limin believed that design is the "dominant expression" of lifestyle, and lifestyle is the "invisible presence" structure behind design, which is the DNA of design [12]. At the same time, he proposed that "lifestyle design" should be established as soon as possible and scientific positivist methods should be introduced, for which still consider lifestyle as a context of design. Zhang Yue also held the "Lifestyle Design Discipline" and developed five major modules of the "Lifestyle Discipline" research: concept, scope, type, structure and research characteristics [13]. An Wa proposed that lifestyle has changed from context to design objects, and she emphasized that designers need to consider the user's past, current, ideal situations at the same time when lifestyle is the design object. The PCI model of life experience she has proposed aims to help designers get a better understanding of lifestyle design [14].

At present, the theory of lifestyle as a design object is still in the early stage, and there are few theoretical explorations in practice. Professor Xin Xiangyang proposed to take lifestyle as a design object, constructed a lifestyle "BEV-E" model and lifestyle design IDR method, and practiced and applied this concept and method in the corporate projects he presided over. The dimensions of lifestyle as the design object proposed by Professor Xin include behavior, environment and values. Behavior (interaction design): guide users to develop new behavior habits and behavior patterns to achieve life goals through five elements of interaction; Environment (service design): influence user behaviors by changing the user's behavior environment, and its design focuses on process, efficiency and users experience. Environment has two dimensions: physical environment (space, service contacts, etc.) and social environment (environmental system, system, etc.); Values (organizational innovation): create environment and atmosphere, guide and inspire users to understand life from a new perspective, discover new life goals, establish corresponding life principles, so as to adapt to a new environment, and develop a new life style [15].

2.3 The Construction of BEV-AAS Design Framework Based on Role Theory

Discuss active aging public service education from the context of role theory. Public education services provided by the government are obliged to guide and help the elderly build a sound lifestyle after retirement. The BEV-AAS theoretical framework for active aging service design can be constructed by referring to BEV-E model, which also includes three elements, namely, social behavior based on role expectations, social environment aiming at role realization, and social values based on role cognition. Through these three dimensions, public services can be designed to help young-old build their own retirement lifestyles (see Fig. 1). The specific presentation is as follows:

Social Action Based on Role Expectations. Elderly lifestyle will be affected by changing some of the behaviors and habits in their lives, such as the aging digital service platforms that constantly appear, and various health equipment designed for the elderly.

They are exploring likely connections through perspectives such as people and machines, people and people, as well as people and environment. These inextricable connections are the opportunities to help the elderly form new life behaviors and habits, so as to gradually realize their ideal retirement life. For example, since the outbreak of the coronavirus in 2020, the "Health Code" has isolated some elderly and disabled people from moving freely, which has aroused public debate and thinking. In November of the same year, the State Council issued the *Notice on the Implementation Plan for Practically Solving the Difficulties of the Elderly in Using Intelligent Technology*, which included many popular Apps in the list of the aging-friendly transformation. The Ministry of Industry and Information Technology also launched a "Special Action for the Aging and Accessibility of Internet Applications". All these measures enable a gradually-lowered threshold for using smart products, and special groups such as the elderly and the disabled can equally enjoy the convenience brought by the Internet. Another example is that, some elderly people need to take multiple drugs at the same time, and it is easy to forget or miss. Many smart medicine kits can provide regular reminders through sound, light, and electricity to help the elderly form medication habits. Whether it's the elder-friendly digital platforms or the smart medicine kits designed for the elderly, they are all designed to help them form behaviors and habits that fit their roles and get closer to their role expectations.

Social Environment Aiming at Role Fulfillment. Xin Xiangyang pointed out that by changing and shaping the environment, life habits will be affected, and the behavior and habits of service recipients and providers will also be influenced, until their living conditions and ways change. Today, when the number of elderly continues to grow, the space and product designs for them are not at the center of society. At this time, environmental construction, which includes physical and social environments, for the elderly has become particularly important. At present, aging public services are also being gradually implemented in China. The government has also put forward different ideas such as "community care for the elderly" and "home care for the elderly", which leads to explosively growing types of elderly care institutions. Some communities have also launched elderly activity centers and elderly canteens, providing a better life and physical environment for the elderly. What's more, different elderly people have different self-cognition and role expectations after retirement. Some want to enjoy their elderly life, and for some old people who are still passionate and healthy, platform and social environment should be developed to help them realize role fulfillment in an easier way.

Social Values Based on Role Cognition. Values are an important criterion for measuring lifestyles, including the value expectations that individuals can generate for themselves, groups and society, which profoundly affect the study of culture, society and personality, and are the key independent variables of researching attitudes and behaviors [16]. A person's value is formed by the interaction of family and society after birth, which is a mapping and result of his previous life experience. It will affect his future judgment and behavior, and will change with personal experience. Participants can develop new values, actively conceive and change their lifestyle through a series of behaviors and environment [15]. Public services for the elderly have the responsibility to help the elderly establish a positive outlook on aging and to inspire them so as to modify their own roles and discover new life goals. The role cognition here not only requires the role itself to recognize itself, but also requires other groups in the society to form a benign cognition of the role so as to create a harmonious and friendly social atmosphere for it. How to help the elderly and other groups correctly understand the role of the elderly is a question worth pondering.

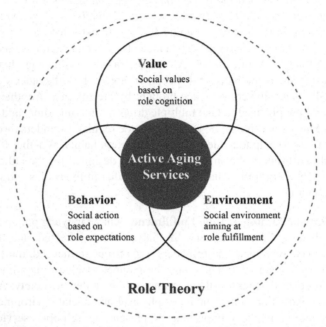

Fig. 1. BEV-AAS framework based on role theory (the author redraws on the basis of BEV-E model)

In summary, public education services for the elderly need to provide the elderly with certain activities and behavioral opportunities, which will depend on the corresponding social environment, including material support, so as to guide the elderly and the public to form a correct understanding of aging and develop a correct value on retirement lifestyle and positive aging values.

3   The Status Quo of Active Aging Education Service in China

Elderly education is a very important part of the retirement life, and it is also part of the role expectations of most Chinese elderly. Diversified, accessible, free or cost-effective public education can greatly enrich the retirement life and spiritual world of the elderly. Through the design of aging-friendly courses, teaching materials and teaching space, we can guide the elderly people's behaviors in group learning, or even the individual's participation in teaching.

3.1 The Particularity of Elderly Education

Elderly education and general education are very different in terms of educational purpose, form, content, and sponsoring institutions: (a) The particularity of investors. Educational services for the elderly require the government to intervene as the main body and invest continually, because market regulation cannot bring a stable, continuous and effective supply of resources to the elderly education services. (b) The particularity of the object. The elderly were once the main force in social construction and have made outstanding contributions. They have rich social and life experience. At the same time, they are facing the challenges of aging physically and psychologically, so their education needs are different from young people or children. (c) The particularity of the content. The current content of elderly education can be divided into leisure education, safety education, health education and role adaptation education, etc. It is a holistic education that focuses on the elderly adapting to retirement and achieving the active aging, so as to enhance the social adaptability of elderly and enrich their life. (d) The particularity of the form. At present, there are various forms of education for the elderly, such as leisure and tourism education, community education, family education, university education for the elderly, and online education.

3.2 The Present Situation of Elderly Education Supply

Through literature review and analysis, the main problems of China's elderly education include the lack of resources, uneven course quality, and one-sided understanding of elderly education. These problems can be exemplified by: (a) The short supply of education for the elderly. According to related surveys, 90% of the participants believe that education for the elderly is necessary, and 87% of the elderly have the idea of attending a senior-citizen college, but currently only 3% of the elderly have such opportunity. There is a huge gap between demand and supply. Among the people who have received elderly education, more than 50% of them had promising jobs before retirement, such as government officials, and technical personnel, and few of them were at the grassroots level. Besides, it is hard to acquire a seat in elderly university as there are no restrictions on admissions for elderly people, leading to the phenomenon of 'only enrollment but no graduate' [17]. (b) The quality of elderly education courses is low. The reasons are into two aspects: First, the curriculum format. The curriculum lacks flexibility or diversity, which ignore the differences in the learning needs and learning methods of the elder people's features such as gender, age, education level, residence, and economic conditions. Second, the courses content. The courses offered by most elderly education institutions are mainly for leisure and entertainment, and the content is unitary and of low quality, which ignores elderly people's needs for comprehensive and high-quality education so as to adapt to retirement. In fact, the education on safety, health, and role adaptation is also indispensable besides leisure education during the retirement. (c) One-sided understanding of elderly education. Educational institutions for the elderly should integrate the concept of 'live and learn' throughout the entire process of education planning. The teaching should go beyond entertainment courses. Considering that elderly education is a "passage" for the elderly to enter the society again, educational courses that allow the elderly to learn new knowledge and adapt to social development need to be developed accordingly. The elderly should also have a more open mind and maintain an open attitude towards education for the elderly.

China has gradually formed a four-level education system for the elderly from the perspective of education subject. At present, some cities in China have initially formed a four-level elderly education network of "city (university), district (college), street (school), and residence (teaching site)". Resources are tilted towards the street (town) in practices. In order to achieve a balanced elderly education in Guangzhou, it is very important to focus on the development on the street level, the effective incremental supply of educational resources and nearby supply.

From the perspective of learning methods, China's elderly education has become "online and offline integrated", and gradually forming a "three-dimensional" learning method. Take Guangzhou as an example. Based on the "Lifelong Learning Network" (www.gzlll.cn), the government has established online platforms such as the Open App, Official Account, and "Learning Map" Mini Program for the University for the Elderly; offline courses include lectures, course, study tours, exhibitions and performances. In addition to the public education services provided by the government, there are also some commercial learning Apps developed for the elderly on the market, such as Hongsong and online elderly colleges.

3.3 Survey on the Elderly Education Needs

In order to have a more in-depth and comprehensive understanding of the needs of public education services for the elderly, the research team conducted user interviews by telephone or face-to-face interviews. There were 10 interviewees, and the selection criteria were urban young-old retired elder people, had received college education, elderly center education or community elderly education. There are no gender restrictions, and the interview should be no less than 30 min. The interview includes 8 types of information or topics: demographic and sociological information, hobbies, current status of retirement, experience of elderly education activities, the purpose of attending elderly education, family members' attitudes and their participation, information acquisition channels, and expectations for elderly education. The focus of interviews was on the experience of elderly education activities, mainly to understand the types of education activities that the elderly have participated in (such as community lectures for the elderly, spontaneously-formed entertainment and learning group, self-learning, elderly university, elderly center, etc.), the courses and output of elderly universities, participation in online elderly education, etc.

After the interview, the research team used the "Empathy Map" to sort out the interviewees' observation, experiences and expectations, and summarized their pain points and goals, including: low efficiency for teaching in a large class of 70 people, inadequate learning space and unitary teaching content, long distance from teaching locations, lack of empathy for some young teachers with the elderly, lack of online elderly education service platform, small size of characters on corresponding App, complicated functions and unclear presentation of dance-like physical exercises. The above pain points can be further summarized as: (a) insufficient teaching space; (b) lack of small-class teaching; (c) generational differences between teachers and students; (d) vacancies in online education services for the elderly; (e) inadequate improvement in elderly-friendly for relevant websites and Apps.

4 The Service System Construction and Design Practice of Active Aging Public Education: With LO-PAY & LO-GAIN as an Example

The BEV-AAS public education service design framework was constructed on the basis of previous part, and the survey of the current situation of public education services for the elderly as well as their needs. The following part will take LO-PAY & LO-GAIN (hereinafter referred to as LP&LG), a system design project for active aging public education service as an example, and try to further verify the role theory's feasibility in the system design of public education service for elderly (role expectation, role realization, role cognition) through stakeholder's definition, service system construction, curriculum system design, and service touch point design.

4.1 The Stakeholder Definition of LP&LG

Clarkson divides stakeholders into primary stakeholders and secondary stakeholders according to their closeness to a company or organization [18]. In the LP&LG service system, the primary stakeholders include: the elderly, educational institutions for the elderly (elderly university, open university, community activity center for the elderly, etc.); secondary stakeholders include: children of the elderly, related academic research institutions, government offices on the elderly, suppliers of teaching materials, etc.

In order to better study the primary stakeholders, the research team carried out a more detailed classification of the elderly. Academia has gradually paid attention to the stratification within the elderly, and the standards of differentiation are varied. Chen Jing and Jiang Haixia divided the elderly into elite elderly and general elderly based on their education level, interpersonal resources, social participation, social influence, and dedication consciousness [19]. Retired elderly will also re-examine themselves, and their role expectations and role behaviors are also different after retirement. The author believes that, the classification of young-old should, on the one hand, base on their objective conditions, such as education level, social influence, economic status, and interpersonal resources; on the other hand, focus on their perception of their own roles, such as retirement lifestyle cognition, social participation, types of social activities involved, etc. Specifically, the elite elderly are professional and well-educated and their self-expectations for retirement include: continue to create value and obtain social recognition; create sustainable value (not a one-time activity). But the current situation is that they generally face a gap in the role of value creators and discontinuers, and their role expectations split. Therefore, they need to find a transitional lifestyle so as to balance the contradiction between creating value and enjoying retirement, and they have huge demands for creating social value. However, the education level and social influence of the general elderly are relatively low. Their self-expectations in retirement mainly include: maintaining social participation and connections, and a colorful retirement life.

This expectation also requires a transitional retirement lifestyle, but is more inclined to rich recreational retirement activities.

In the context of service production and service consumption, it is generally believed that the elderly are service recipients of elderly education. However, in some specific service systems, service providers are also the service receivers, and these two roles will integrate or transform [20]. The LP&LG service system encourage elite elderly people to use their professional knowledge and become providers of active aging public education services. Of course, they can also be service recipients. Two roles can complement each other and gradually complete a productive aging. After retirement, the general elderly pursue certain social participation and enjoy leisure and entertainment, becoming recipients of public education services for active aging.

Secondary stakeholders also provide support for the system operation. The children of the elderly can participate in the achievement exhibition of the elderly education and accompany to them during the retirement and the feel their happy life. Elderly education institutions, such as senior-citizen universities, open universities, and community activity centers for the elderly, support the operation of service system and provide space, materials and human resources required for teaching as secondary stakeholders. Relevant academic institutions provide references for the government to formulate policies through social surveys and academic research, and provide relevant teaching opinions and suggestions for elderly education institutions. Teaching aid suppliers provide corresponding teaching tools and materials according to the needs of educational institutions. These secondary stakeholders have formed a stakeholder system for active aging public education services with the elderly (including elite elderly and general elderly), and elderly education institutions.

4.2 The Service System Design of LP&LG

The system's name "LO-PAY & LO-GAIN" is derived from LOHAS (Lifestyles of Health and Sustainability), which implies happy "teaching" and happy "learning".

Service System Map. The active aging public education service system is basically constructed (see Fig. 2) after clarifying the system's stakeholder system and sorting out the relationships among multi-role stakeholders. It covers four types of elderly courses, and each will recruit elite elderly with relevant knowledge and abilities to provide senior education services. Constructing a multi-dimensional and multi-field public education service for active aging with the help of online digital platforms, senior education registration mechanisms, teaching aid products, curriculum planning and other touch points, is helpful for the elite and general elderly realize their own role expectations and successfully achieve active aging. The service system can be integrated into all levels of the senior education which is a beneficial and effective supplement to the fourth-level network, and introduce a new, flat and distributed service mode in the existing service structure of senior education.

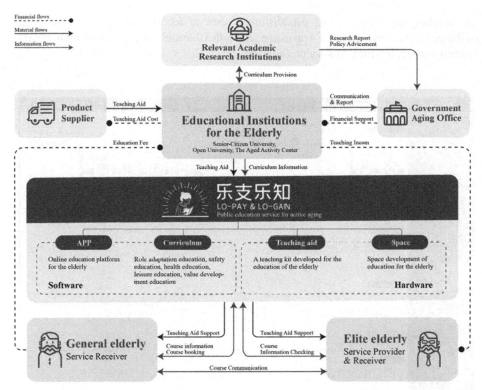

Fig. 2. Service system map of LO-PAY & LO-GAIN

Customer Journey Map. The customer journey map visually displays the user's experience in receiving a certain service, including the user's behavior, touch points, emotions, pain points and needs in the process. There are two main user types of LP&LG: elite elderly who provide senior education services and general elderly who receive senior education services. Their journey in the service system is shown in Fig. 3. The service stage includes course information, course registration/preparation, class and its presentation. The user's behavior in different service stages is visualized with icons, and the emotion curve is used to show the mood fluctuations at each stage. The user behavior and emotions here are based on the simulation of the user's real reaction, while the user's pain points and needs are obtained by mining and summarizing the user's reaction. The crests and troughs of the emotional curve are the key points to improve experience. For example, the elite elderly want to become teachers, but they do not understand the system operation mechanism and their own teaching ability, resulting in doubts and lack of confidence. This is reflected in the emotional curve as low points. At this time, designers can find the needs of the elite elderly, and alleviate or even eliminate the pain points of the elite elderly by setting up systemic mechanism illustration, teacher training and other services. The research team finally concluded the precise needs of two types of users. The needs of the elite elderly include: system operation mechanism illustration, App usage guide, teacher training, class-group communication, space for nearby teaching, and teaching history record for establishing a sense of accomplishment, etc. The needs of the general elderly include: App usage guide, flexible and editable curriculum, nearby learning space, learning history records, etc.

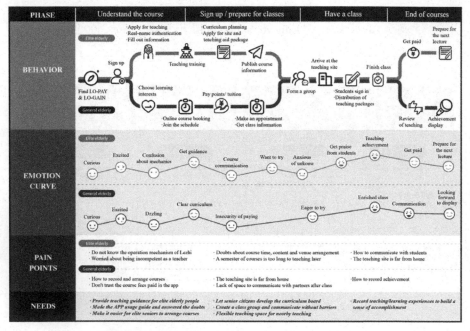

Fig. 3. Customer journey map of LO-PAY & LO-GAIN

4.3 The Curriculum System Design of LP&LG

The senior education curriculum of LP&LG includes 4 sections: role adaptation, safety education, health protection, and entertainment (see Table 1). In order to reflect the differences and characteristics of existing services, the curriculum needs to be developed at different levels such as breadth and depth, individualization and systematization. For example, courses which require highly on professional and repeated practice, such as vocal music, dance, etc., should be systemic and periodic, and it can be two classes a week for one semester. After completing the elementary courses, the elderly can take advanced courses following a step-by-step principle. The other type of courses are not consistent, but have distinct characteristics, such as first aid, self-help, etc., and one or two courses are sufficient based on the principle of spreading knowledge. In order to adapt to the development of the Internet and smart technology, as well as the post-epidemic lifestyle, the format of LP&LG course can take online, offline, or online-offline combined channel based on the course content and features. The forms of online courses include live courses in the App, or courses conducted on third-party online communication platforms (such as Ding Talk, Tencent Conference), which are suitable for less practical courses, such as health lectures; the venues of offline courses include senior-citizen colleges, community activity centers, LP&LG community teaching spaces, etc., which are suitable for courses with large proportion of communication and practices, such as photography.

In terms of course implementation and management, qualified elite elderly can be recruited through open recruitment and assessment based on the course content, such as retired lawyers, investment experts, psychologists, nutritionists, police, medical staff, teachers, etc. Elite elderly with dual identities as service providers and recipients can publish course arrangements through online platforms, utilize offline educational institutions or community teaching spaces flexibly, and provide senior citizens with online and offline courses.

Table 1. Course planning for LO-PAY & LO-GAIN.

Sections	Purposes	Courses (recruited elite elderly profession, class hours)	Course Format (Online / Offline)	
Role adaptation course	Improve the ability of the elderly to adapt to role changes	A1-Law education *(retired lawyers/judges, 12 hours)*	☑	☐
		A2-Financial management education *(retired bankers/investment experts, 6 hours)*	☑	☑
		A3-Psychological guidance *(Retired psychologist, 72 hours)*	☑	☑
Safety education course	Raise awareness of anti-fraud and safety at home and in travel for the elderly	S1-Nutrition knowledge education *(retired nutritionist, 8 hours)*	☑	☑
		S2-Anti-fraud education *(retired police, 10 hours)*	☑	☑
		S3-Emergency self-care *(retired medical staff, 6 hours)*	☑	☑
Health care course	Enhance the knowledge and health care ability of the elderly in physical and mental health	H1-Health care through TCM *(retired TCM doctors, 72 hours)*	☑	☑
		H2-Health yoga *(retired yoga teacher, 72 hours)*	☐	☑
		H3-Mental health lecture *(retired psychologist, 6 hours)*	☐	☑
		H4-Mental health consultation *(retired psychologist, 6 hours)*	☑	☑
Entertainment course	Enhance leisure skills and awareness of the elderly	E1-English/Japanese/Korean in tourism *(retired teacher/guide, 72 hours)*	☑	☑
		E2-Chinese painting/calligraphy *(retired calligraphy teacher, 72 hours)*	☐	☑
		E3-Vocal performance *(retired musician/singer, 72 hours)*	☐	☑
		E4-Poetry appreciation *(retired Chinese teacher, 72 hours)*	☑	☑
		E5-Digital Photography *(retired photographer, 72 hours)*	☐	☑
		E6-Chinese and foreign scenic spot culture *(retired teacher/guide, 72 hours)*	☑	☑
		E7-Chinese/World History *(retired teacher, 72 hours)*	☑	☑

4.4 The Digital Touch Point Design of LP&LG

The LP&LG App (see Fig. 4) is a platform that provides teaching services for the young-old. The main features are as follows: (a) You can add courses that you are interested. You can choose the course you are interested in when you log in to the APP for the first time, and you can edit it in "Me-Adjust Learning Interest" when you log in again. The home page will display information about the courses that the elderly care about, including live courses and online courses that can be booked, as well as offline courses that can be booked nearby. (b) Elite elderly can apply to become teachers. In "Me-Become a Teacher", elite elderly can apply to become a lecturer through real-name authentication and materials make-out. After the review is passed, they will be lecturers and can start to teach. The elderly can receive a letter of appointment from LP&LG elderly university, generous tuition compensation, and a professional operation team will provide them with online live broadcasting guidance and offline supporting equipment usage guidance; (c) Make an appointment for LP&LG learning space. You can search nearby LP&LG learning spaces in the map, or you can view and book the designated learning space by entering keywords; (d) An interest circle for the elderly to share learning experiences and hobbies. Here the elderly can share their learning experience with peers, and can browse other people's moments, so that they can have their own social circles and feel less lonely.

The aging-friendly adaptation of Internet applications and barrier-free reforms are being carried out on a large scale. Domestic and foreign scholars have proposed barrier-free design for the Internet applications of the elderly. The App design of this study mainly follows the following interface design principles and specifications. (a) Concise interface layout. The functional elements of the interface designed for the elderly should be distributed in a modular manner, and each module corresponds to a functional content, with a clear hierarchy and the same relationship between the content of the corresponding group [21]. The orderly, easy-to-index interface is more suitable for the elderly. The LP&LG App uses functional modules such as "My Class Schedule", "New Classes of the Week" and "Famous Teacher Hall" on the homepage to map the information that the elderly focus on. Under these function modules, some of the courses in progress will be sent to the elderly, including free live broadcasting courses and offline courses. (b) Easy-to-identify font. Chen Meiqi's research found that at a 50 cm equal viewing distance, the elderly can clearly read about 15pt words in print media such as magazines and newspapers [22]. In the LP&LG App interface, the title font is selected in bold, the maximum font size is 21pt, and the subtitles are adjusted according to the interface; the main body adopts Pingcube with the font size 14–16pt, and the annotation text 12–14pt. (c) Highlight color recognition. The color recognition ability of the elderly deteriorates due to the degeneration of the optic nerve and the decrease of retinal pyramidal cells when they grow old [23]. Practice has shown that apps that are dominated by elderly users need to avoid using low-brightness and low-contrast colors, and try to choose colors with large differences in brightness or strong contrast. The main color of the LP&LG App is dark red, and the function buttons use red, yellow, and blue as the background colors, with white icons to highlight functional information and reduce identification costs. (d) Highlight graphics applications. Internet two-dimensional graphics is a highly abstract and generalized image language. The elderly do not have high awareness of generalized two-dimensional graphics. They need to reinforce and associate to their memory many times, and they may not understand some of the simplified graphics, which has a certain cognitive cost. Therefore, the toolbar information such as "Favorite", "Join Class" and "Repost" in the LP&LG App is presented in a combination of graphics and text.

Fig. 4. Aging-friendly App interface design of LO-PAY & LO-GAIN (Color figure online)

4.5   The Physical Touch Point Design of LP&LG

The existing offline teaching venues are mostly senior-citizen universities, and it is generally difficult to make major changes due to conditions. The newly-added community teaching space in this study is a distributed supporting facility that can be highly customized, so it can be integrated into a better age-friendly design, and it can be adapted to the physical and psychological needs of the elderly and design a more humane space from barrier-free design point of view. The project selects modular building units developed by Coodo, a German company, and customizes classrooms based on individualization, differentiation and localization (see Fig. 5). In order to increase the diversity and flexibility of the teaching space for the elderly, two spatial scales of medium and small are customized. The medium-sized (M-type) classroom cover an area of 21 m², equipped with multimedia equipment, tables and chairs, drinking fountains, trash cans, curtains and other materials, which can accommodate 8–10 people and are suitable for small-class teaching. The small-sized (S-type) classroom covers an area of 12 m² and is only equipped with basic materials other than multimedia equipment. It can accommodate 3 to 5 people and is mainly used for extracurricular exchanges and exercises. Classrooms of two scales can be placed in parks, commercial blocks or complexes, outdoor spaces, clubs, and overhead floors of residential buildings according to a certain ratio, so as to serve as many surrounding residents as possible. With the growth of business and the maturity of technology, small classrooms can also be combined with driverless cars to become a mobile learning space.

Fig. 5. Community teaching and learning space of LO-PAY & LO-GAIN

The barrier-free design of the LP&LG community teaching space includes three aspects: (a) Emotional design. The elderly like quietness, comfort and cleanliness, so the interior design of the teaching space is based on the new Chinese style, and the color is mainly warm tones of raw wood, thus creating a warm, relaxed and comfortable atmosphere; (b) Easy-to-use design. Smart technology has been introduced into the using of teaching space. After the elderly make a reservation for the teaching space on the App, the teaching space can open the door for the elderly through face recognition. (c) Service design. Elderly people who use the teaching space for the first time will be afraid and anxious because they do not understand the process. Therefore, a small video can be made to illustrate the use methods and rules of the teaching space.

5 Conclusion

The design of the active aging service system should take into account the role changes of the young-old before and after retirement, and also pay attention to the changes in their self-cognition, role expectations, and role realization methods. Factors affecting the willingness and social participation of the elderly include the elder's own factors and how government protects their rights and interests. Active aging public education services in the context of role theory can better combine the self-cognition of the elderly and their rights, and make corresponding designs on social behaviors, social environment and social values. The research group hopes that the BEV-AAS framework's attempts and practice in the field of elderly education service design can inspire active aging services in other fields. What's more, a better aging environment can be developed through the efforts of the government, institutions, designers and the whole society, so that senior citizens can enjoy their elder life happily and gracefully.

Acknowledgment. This paper is supported by the 13th Five-Year Plan of Guangdong Education Science, which is "Research on the construction of knowledge system and teaching practice of service design under the interdisciplinary background (2020GXJK325)".

References

1. WHO: Active Ageing: A Policy Framework. Translated by China Association for the aged. Hualing Press, Beijing (2003)
2. Li, S., Zhou, Z.: An analysis of the change of elderly education in the perspective of active aging. China Adult Educ. (01), 12–15 (2011)
3. Wang, L.: A review of the theory, practice and policy research of social participation of the elderly in China. Popul. Dev. **17**(03), 35–43 (2011)
4. Duan, S., Zhang, H.: Basic research on the concept and theory of social participation of the elderly. J. Adult Educ. Coll. Hebei Univ. (03), 82–84 (2008)
5. Wu, Z.: Dictionary of Population Science. Southwest University of Finance and Economics Press, Chengdu (1997)
6. Chen, B.: Social adaptation of the urban elderly in aging era. J. Soc. Sci. (6), 89–94 (2008)
7. Ding, Z., Zhang, L.: Research on the status and influencing factors of social development adaptation of urban retired elderly. Lanzhou Acad. J. (1), 119–122+118 (2012)
8. Liu, S., Zhuang, M.: Post-retirement adaptation and productive aging: a qualitative study of community-dwelling older adults of Hong Kong. J. Soc. Work (4), 118–125 (2014)
9. Xi, C.: On Personal Roles: The Mutual Interaction Between an Individual and Society. Zhejiang University Press, Hangzhou (2010)
10. Zhang, X., Li, D.: Sociology of the Elderly in China. Social Sciences Academic Press, Beijing (2011)
11. Zhen, Y.: The Research of the Social Work Intervention on Social Role Adjustment of the Urban Retired Elderly: Based on Activity Theory Perspective. Hebei University, Shijiazhuang (2014)
12. Song, L.: Brief analysis on the relationship between lifestyle and design. Art Educ. (5), 37–40 (2018)
13. Zhang, Y., Wen, J.: Researching review and prospect of lifestyle and design. Design **32**(02), 113–117 (2019)

14. An, W.: Lifestyle from Context to Design Object. Packag. Eng. **40**(20), 15–21 (2019)
15. Xing, X.: Butterfly effect: when life becomes subject of design. Packag. Eng. **41**(06), 57–66 (2020)
16. Zhang, H.: Academic Research of Trends Persona Based on Lifestyle Transformation. Jiangnan University, Wuxi (2018)
17. Lu, Y.: Research on the supply and demand situation and countermeasures of elderly education under the background of aging: taking Zhenjiang City as an example. J. Jiangxi Rad. TV Univ. **21**(03), 7–13 (2019)
18. Mitchell, R., Agle, B., Wood, D.: Toward a theory of stakeholder identification and salience: defining the principle of who and what really counts. Acad. Manag. Rev. **22**(4), 853–886 (1997)
19. Chen, J., Jiang, H.: On the characteristics and value of the social participation of the elite elderly people from the perspective of role theory. J. Hebei Univ. Sci. Technol. (Soc. Sci.) **13**(01), 28–34 (2013)
20. Ding, X., Du, J.: The primary principle of service design: from user-centered to stakeholder-centered. Zhuangshi (3), 62–65 (2018)
21. Xiao, L.: A research on the old age's reading and web page layout design. Sci. Res. Aging **3**(12), 58–66 (2015)
22. Chen, M.: The effect of LCD text and background color combination on visual recognition of the elderly. Natl. Yunlin Univ. Sci. Technol. **115** (2002)
23. Li, F.: Study on the text recognition of the elderly in small TFT-LCD. Natl. Yunlin Univ. Sci. Technol. **6** (2004)

ACF: An Autistic Personas' Characteristics Source to Develop Empathy in Software Development Teams

Áurea Hiléia da Silva Melo[1,5], Ana Carolina Oran[2],
Jonathas Silva dos Santos[3], Luis Rivero[4(✉)], and Raimundo da Silva Barreto[5]

[1] EST, Universidade do Estado do Amazonas (UEA), Manaus, Brazil
asmelo@uea.edu.br
[2] USES, Universidade Federal do Amazonas (UFAM), Manaus, Brazil
ana.oran@icomp.ufam.edu.br
[3] Meliuz, Manaus, Brazil
[4] Programa de Pós-Graduação em Ciência da Computação,
Universidade Federal do Maranhão, São Luis, Brazil
luisrivero@nca.ufma.br
[5] PPGI, Universidade Federal do Amazonas (UFAM), Manaus, Brazil
rbarreto@icomp.ufam.edu.br

Abstract. Empathizing with the software's future users allows knowledge of their willingness and needs, enabling interfaces more attractive. Similarly, empathizing with autistic users is, above all, understanding their limitations and try to see things and people from their perspective. Despite the importance of the empathizing process, traditional requirements survey methods do not allow this for the autistic audience, mainly for those considered low-functioning. A low-functioning autistic users have a more significant impairment of their skills. Thereby, there is a need for methods that consider their difficulties and support the software requirements elicitation process for autistic users. Therefore, this paper proposes the ACF (Autistic's Characterization Form), composed of sections representing the four areas of impairment of an autistic person. With the ACF, we provide a set of characteristics representing enough information to support generating empathy between a designer and an autistic person during the requirements gathering phase. We also present a graph called AOG (Autistic's Overview Graph), which shows the disability rate of the autistic person in each area of limitation of the disorder. Through this work, we intend to support interface designers willing to build empathy during the user interfaces' requirements elicitation and creation processes.

Keywords: Interface design · Autism · ASD · Empathy · Software artifacts

© Springer Nature Switzerland AG 2021
C. Stephanidis et al. (Eds.): HCII 2021, LNCS 13096, pp. 223–236, 2021.
https://doi.org/10.1007/978-3-030-90328-2_14

1   Introduction

Companies in the field of software development are increasingly concerned with designing products to meet the target audience's real needs and human values [23]. It is important that interface designers have alternatives to better understand the end-user to develop more useful and pleasant software. This perception generates the development team's empathy with future users and thus a better understanding of their desires and needs, enabling creating more attractive interfaces.

In software development for the autistic public, this empathy becomes necessary, as the users have several limitations in communication, social interaction, behavior, and cognition [11]. Even when considering these aspects, few studies present techniques to support software designers when developing empathy with people with the Autism Spectrum Disorder (ASD), especially those with low functioning or severe degree of ASD.

In this paper, we present the Autism Characterization Form (ACF), which has specific characteristics about autism. With the help of specialists in different areas of autistic people care, such as educators, psychologists, and occupational therapists, we created the ACF in order to support the development of products for this audience. Furthermore, we present the Autism Characterization Form (ACF), which has a set of specific characteristics of autistic people capable of supporting interface designers in creating application interfaces aimed to autistic persons. To evaluate the use of the ACF, we carried out two experiments.

The remainder of this paper is organized as follows. Section 2 presents the background related to this research. Then, Sect. 3 presents our proposal of the ACF and the AOG. Furthermore, the evaluation and results are described in Sect. 4. Finally, the conclusions and future work regarding the proposal of these artifacts are presented in Sect. 5.

2   Background and Related Work

Autism or Autism Spectrum Disorder (ASD) is a widespread and lifelong neurodevelopmental disability in which early treatment reduces the symptoms and increases the functional capacity of an autistic person [14]. Autism belongs to the class Pervasive Developmental Disorder (PDD), and several functional areas of an individual.ASD can cause difficulties in communication, social interaction, and repetitive behavior patterns, interests, or activities [11].

In recent years, there has been an increase in the design and implementation of technologies to support autism [2]. Usually, autistic users like technologies that provide a wide variety of support, such as assistance on the management of their schedules, soften speech and language deficiencies, feedback on pronunciation, development of social skills practice, among many others [13]. For instance, Abdullah et al. [1], and Hourcade et al. [16] present applications for autistic people to facilitate the communication and social interaction of these users with the outside world.

The impact of these technologies allowed the creation of new software development approaches and artifacts to support the design of user interfaces of systems specific to the autistic public [4,5]. Therefore, it is essential to understand the needs, preferences, behaviors, and characteristics of autistic users for assisting the development of technologies [14]. To achieve this goal, for instance, Britto and Pizzolato [6] proposed a set of recommendations for designing accessible interfaces considering the main barriers of autistic people when interacting with computer system interfaces. However, this guide does not consider the need for the development team to empathize with autistic users.

Empathy is the ability to understand the reasons why individuals act the way they do [19]. Some techniques help development teams empathize with the end-users of their products, such as Personas and Empathy Map. Below, we present each of these techniques.

Persona is a technique that helps the development team to understand users, their characteristics, and what they expect from an application [12]. The creation of personas supports immersion in users' characteristics during the requirements engineering process [22]. Personas represent hypothetical archetypes of a real user or group of users, describing their goals, aptitudes, and interests [10]. Although there is no standard model or set of characteristics for determining a persona, their descriptions often contain information about personal lifestyle and important details for generating empathy [10].

Furthermore, Empathy Map (EM) is a technique used to create business models according to the client's perspectives. EM can be used to understand users' needs and services in general [15]. EM has six sections that serve as a guide for creating the customer/user profile [21]: (1) Sees - What the user sees in his environment; (2) Listens - How the environment influences the user; (3) Needs - What the user wants and what can be done to achieve their goals. (4) Speaks and Does - What the user says and how he behaves in public; (5) Thinks and Feels: What happens in the user's mind; Finally, (6) Pains/Challenges: Frustrations, challenges, and risks that the user faces.

The Personas and Empathy Map techniques provide support in building empathy towards any user. With the specific needs of autistic people, the use of these techniques can become ineffective. Because of this, we developed the PersonAut [20] and the EmpathyAut [19] artifacts based on the traditional Personas and Empathy Map models, respectively. However, we included sections more compatible with the reality of autistic people.

While applying these specific techniques, we noticed that we needed a way to collect autistic characteristics to help software engineers understand the autistic user. As a result, we develop the Autistic's Characterization Form and the Autistic's Overview Graph. The proposal of the ACF presented by this paper is the basis for fill in EmpathyAut. Precisely, the information contained in EmpathyAut is mapped directly from the ACF. PersonAut, on the other hand, uses only AOG to complete information about Persona. In the following sections, we present the development of these artifacts.

3 The Autistic Characterization Form

The following subsections present the motivation, design, adaptation, and definition of the ACF. In addition, we also offer case study results that have helped make improvements to the final version ACF.

3.1 Motivation

EmpathyAut is one of ProAut's artifacts and aims to create empathy maps specifically for autistic people. Since the focus of ProAut is low-functioning autistic people, we need a source of information about autistic people to populate EmpathyAut, because low-functioning autistic people are usually significantly compromised in the way they communicate. Therefore, the need arose to provide a set of characteristics of autistic people to support designers' empathy process while creating interfaces for this audience.

In the search for a way to collect autistic characteristics, we identified some instruments used to support the diagnosis of autism, [3–5,17,18] usually in the form of forms or questionnaires. Due to their purpose, these instruments represent a rich source of information about autism. Furthermore, these questionnaires do not allow subjective answers or misinterpretations. In addition, these questionnaires do not allow subjective answers or misinterpretations because their answers are limited to "yes or no." However, most of these questionnaires had the following disadvantages: (a) they describe specific characteristics for diagnosis, and (b) most characteristics refer to age groups between 0 to 30 months.

So we tried to find or compose a source of information about autistic people that was more generic and applicable to a broader age range. Thus, we tried to find or compose a source of information about autistic people that was more generic and applicable to a broader age range. Among the instruments, we found the ADT (Autism Descriptive Tool) [7,8], which addresses 3 of the main areas affected by autism and covers the age range from 2 to 6 years old.

3.2 ACF Conception

ADT presents the main areas that affect an autistic person: Socialization, communication, and Behavior. Each of these areas makes up sections of the ADT. And each of these sections has a set of information that represents specific characteristics of autism. The ADT also has an "OTHERS" section, which is inappropriate for our purpose because we feel that the name "OTHERS" would not allow for empathy. Therefore, we have chosen to remove it.

We conducted a survey by applying a questionnaire with specialists from different areas that cared for autistic people, such as educators, psychologists, and occupational therapists. The questionnaire had two groups of questions. The first group of questions characterized the participants, asking for name, e-mail, and the following questions: (a) *What is your area of expertise for assisting autistic children?*; (b) *What is your relationship with autism?*; (c) *How long have you worked in the current autistic caring area?*; and *What is your experience (in years) in this type of care?*. The second question group focused on identifying the characteristics of the "COGNITION" category and the reallocation of characteristics from the "OTHERS" category within the ADT form.

A total of 26 specialists signed an Informed Consent Form and agreed to answer the questionnaire. Among them, 29.2% were psychologists, 20.8% were pedagogues, and 20.8% were psycho-pedagogues; the remaining 29.2% were speech therapists. As for the time of experience in attending autistic patients, 28.6% had more than eight years of experience, 14.3% between 5 and 8 years of experience, 32.1% between 3 and 5 years, and 25% less than three years of experience. Regarding the respondents' location, 80.8% of the answers were residents of the Amazonas state in Brazil, and 19.2% were residents of other states in Brazil.

In the second part of the questionnaire, we focused on making changes to the ADT to make it more appropriate for data collection for EmpathyAut. to make it more suitable for EmpathyAut. The first change was to change the section's name from "Socialization" to "Social Interaction." The majority of respondents (92.3%) agreed with the change. This change was to draw attention to the word "Interaction" due to the context of the interface. The second change was to remove the "Others" section and reallocate its features to the other categories. So, we presented a matrix containing the rows that corresponded to each characteristic in the "Others" category, and the columns represented the new section. Table 1 shows the result of the main changes made in ACF concerning the category "Others".

Table 1. Redistribution of the characteristics of the Others Section

Characteristics in "OTHERS" Category	Interaction	Communication	Behavior
Reduced or absent imagination. Lack of variety in pretend play	35%	54%	12%
Overreaction or Hyporeaction to auditory stimuli	19%	27%	54%
Food Selectivity	19%	12%	69%
Emotional deregulation (Cry or laugh for not apparent reason; or cries in happy situations/ laughs in sad situations	19%	31%	50%
Atypical treatment of visual information such as peripheral vision and eyes squinting	69%	15%	15%

Finally, we asked the experts the following: (a) *In addition to Socialization, Communication, and Behavior, what other areas are affected by TEA?*; and (b) *What characteristic(s) is(are) affected in the area mentioned in the previous question?*. With regards to the first question, 42,3% of specialists proposed the Cognition category, 23,1% indicated the Sensory area, and 34,6% suggested various topics that did not allow grouping for summarizing, such as: emotion, auditory sensitivity, food selectivity, or still some already defined as interpersonal relationship, or simple interaction. With regards to the second question, we obtained the following suggested characteristics: interpretation of the environment, concentration, literacy, ability to make decisions, memory and ease of learning, lack of ability to undress and put on clothes or shoes, and memory.

The obtained answers were presented to two experts (a psychologist and a speech therapist) who were not part of the questionnaire group. They evaluated the experts' suggestions who answered the questionnaire and rewrote them to align with the characteristics of the other existing sections. Thus, we defined the new section called "Cognition." From the analysis of the two experts, we determined the following characteristics:

- Non-literate;
- Absence or reduction of Spatio-temporal interpretation;
- Absence or reduction of self-interpretation;
- Absence or reduction of perception of the environment;
- Inability to make decisions on their own;
- Absence or reduction of attention to perform tasks;
- Reduced long-term memory; and
- Reduced short-term memory (working memory)

After making all the changes, the final form was named the Autistic Characterization Form (ACF). The completed ACF has four columns: the first column refers to the category here called Area, the second column refers to the identification number of the characteristic, the third column contains the description of the characteristic, and the last one is called Response. Responses should have the value 1 for when the autistic person exhibits a characteristic and 0 otherwise. Table 2 shows an overview of the ACF.

We also needed an artifact to support the use of PersonAut. Therefore, the AOG is a graph that provides an overview of the rates of impairment of the autistic person in each area affected by the disorder. The higher the percentage, the higher the impairment level of the autistic person represented in the chart. The goal of the AOG is to help the designer generate empathy.

The answers entered in the ACF generate the AOG from a percentage calculation. For this calculation, we consider, in each section, only the responses marked with the value 1 for the characteristics. For example, the Communication category has nine items. Considering that seven of them have value 1, the autistic person will have a 78% impairment in this area.

Figure 1 shows an example of this graph. This graph refers to an autistic person with high levels of impairment in all areas (more than 50%), but communication is the most affected.

Table 2. Final version of the Autism Characterization Form

Area	ID	Characteristic	Ans
SOCIAL INTERACTION	01	Does Little or no eye contact (inability to keep look into another person's eyes while talking)	1
	02	Presents Stiffness or fixation in eye contact (keeps gaze fixed on a point, person, or object for a long time)	1
	03	Presents Reduction or lack of responses to social smile (if someone smiles, they rarely or never smile back)	1
	04	Has minimal or nonexistent vocabulary variations (rarely or never facially express feelings such as anger, pain, sadness, and surprise	1
	05	Presents Social isolation or tendency to loneliness (prefers to stay alone)	1
	06	Presents Little or no self-initiative to approach someone else of the same or different ages, known or not	1
	07	Does not feel comfortable when approached by someone else (for example, when someone tries an interaction, turns around, is indifferent, or dodges)	0
	08	Has inability to involving yourself in group activities	0
	09	Presents lack of spontaneous to share enjoyment, interests, or achievements with other people (e.g., do not show or point out objects of self-interest to other people)	0
COMMUNICATION	10	Has inability to point at objects of your interest and that be close	0
	11	Has inability to look at something pointed out by someone else	1
	12	Has little or no ability to imitate other people's behaviors (e.g., clapping, making faces, and dancing)	1
	13	Absence of verbal communication (speaks less than five words coherently)	1
	14	Little or no use of gestures to communicate with others	1
	15	Has echolalic language, meaning that hears words or phrases and repeats them outside the conversation context (a mere act of repeat)	1
	16	Presents voice tone that does not change and does not vary regardless of the feelings and situations experienced (e.g., a stronger voice in times of anger or a softer voice in tranquility moments)	1
	17	Has inability to use imagination and play make-believe. Not understands metaphors (e.g., Hit the books)	1
	18	Has inability to initiate or sustain a conversation with others	0

(*continued*)

Table 2. (*continued*)

Area	ID	Characteristic	Ans
BEHAVIOR	19	Tends to align or classify objects according to criteria that make sense just for own, or tends to line things following criteria such as colors, size, shapes, and texture	1
	20	Presents exaggerated interest in some objects or parts of them or even shows a preference for things unusual to own routine	0
	21	Presents mannerisms repetitive (e.g., hand or finger flapping or twisting, or complex whole-body movements or pacing around)	1
	22	Uses objects for things that are not their function (e.g., rub a rubber around the body or face)	0
	23	Beats or flapps hands	0
	24	Does repetitive body movements when standing or sitting	0
	25	Tiptoe walking	0
	26	Presents excessive attention to details (e.g., objects, situations, people, or places that usually go unnoticed)	0
	27	Presents hypersensitivity to auditory stimuli such as sirens, fireworks, barking, and car horns	1
	28	Stays indifferent to noise/sound often bothersome (e.g., sirens, fireworks, barking, and car horns)	0
	29	Presents interest in foods with flavors, texture, colors, and even brand specifics (e.g., takes juice only in yellow color, eats biscuit only of a particular brand, or eats only pasty food)	1
	30	Presents Emotional deregulation (Cries or laughs for no apparent reason. Cries in happy moments, or laughs in times of sadness)	1
	31	Demonstrates resistance in a routine change or when move one object to another place	1
COGNITION	32	Not literate	0
	33	Presents difficulty in perceiving the passage of time, notion of hours, present, past, future, yesterday, today, and tomorrow. Has also difficulty in understanding the geographic space (e.g., the notion of in what address, the city, state, and country lives)	1
	34	Has difficulty in reference about own yourself. Inability to use pronouns like I, mine, and me (e.g., many times, refers to oneself by his first name instead of using the I pronoun)	1
	35	Presents difficulty identifying the different environments according to their characteristics or behave according to the environment context (e.g., school as a place to study, church as a place to pray, and doctor's office for attendance)	1
	36	Has inability to make decisions alone	0
	37	Has concentrating difficulty and inability to maintain attention for a long time when performing tasks	0
	38	Presents difficulty in retrieving knowledge/information acquired days, months, or years ago (long-term memory)	1
	39	Presents difficulty in retrieving knowledge/information acquired in the last 30 min (short-term memory)	0

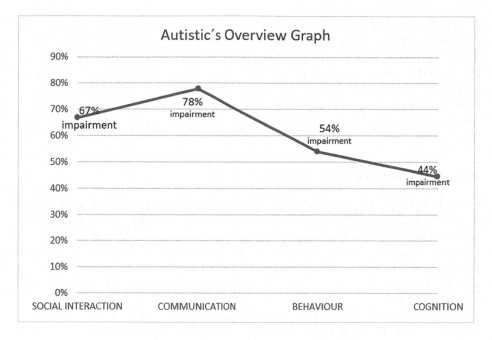

Fig. 1. Autistic's overview graph

4   Initial Evaluations and Refinements of the Proposals

4.1   Pilot Study

In order to evaluate the ACF, we conducted a pilot study with a development team. The team (T1) was composed of 7 members researching the characterization of autistic people to create Personas. The team was developing a prototype of an application to control the daily schedule of an autistic child. The participants agreed to use the ACF to help to map the characteristics of autistic users to improve empathy with the target audience.

Upon receiving the form, the team pointed out difficulties in understanding the listed characteristics. In a meeting with the team, we explained each characteristic contained in the form. However, even after the clarifications, the team reported that they still had difficulties in understanding the description of the characteristics in the ACF. The team also reported that their lack of understanding affected the development of empathy with the autistic users.

Based on the team's feedback, we conducted a new survey through an online questionnaire. This questionnaire was composed of a section containing information to contextualize autism, followed by a section to characterize the participants and a section presenting each characteristic belonging to the ACF. We asked if the participants were able to understand what the sentences meant. If not, the participants would state whether they understood the sentence entirely or partially, and in which part.

The survey had 78 participants. Regarding the level of experience with interface design, 40.5% of the participants had little experience, 36.7% had intermediate experience, and 21.5% had advanced experience. In the educational degree, 69.2% of the participants had an undergraduate degree, 15.4% a masters degree, and 15.4% a doctorate degree. The results indicated that 75% of the 39 characteristics listed in the ACF were not easily understood by the respondents, either totally or partially. Below, we explain how we used this information to refine the ACF to its final version.

4.2   Updating the ACF to Final Version

Considering that the majority (75%) of the respondents indicated that they could not understand the ACF characteristics easily, we decided to reformulate it. For that, we submitted the form to a new group of specialists in autism care. The group was formed by one psycho-pedagogue, one occupational therapist, and one psychologist. The mission group was to analyze each characteristic and rewrite it in a language more accessible to novice software developers in the field of autism.

The evaluations were carried out individually. The first to assess the ACF was the psycho-pedagogue (with 1 year of experience working with ASD users), followed by the occupational therapist (7 years of experience), and finally by the psychologist (over ten years of experience). For instance, Item 15 was changed from *"Repetitive verbal language"* to *"Has echolalic language, meaning that hears words or phrases and repeats them outside the conversation context (a mere act of repeat)."*. Table 2 shows the final version of the ACF after the refinement of the answers.

4.3   Evaluation of the Final Version of the ACF

After rewriting most of the ACF characteristics, another team of six members (team T2) evaluated the new version. The team had three developers, two designers, and one manager. Only the developers had less than two years of experience, but nobody had experience with autism. The team used an application to manage the routine and routine break of an autistic child. Through the application, the team intends to help parents and caregivers to prepare in advance for something that is out of their routine—for example, going to the dentist, hairdresser, visiting a relative, or even a trip.

To evaluate the ACF final version, we applied an online questionnaire. It was divided into three parts. The first was addressing the participants' characterization. The second included questions to evaluate the ACF using the Technology Acceptance Model (TAM). TAM is a model that evaluates to what extend a new technology could be accepted by the target audience base on the perceived usefulness and perceived ease of use of the technology from the point of view of users of such technology [9]. To evaluate these aspects we adapted the questionnaire from the TAM model, and evaluated the degree of agreement of the participants using the following scale: Strongly agree, Partially agree, Neither agree nor disagree, Partially disagree and Strongly disagree. Finally, we addressed the opinion of the participants.

Figures 2 and 3 show the quantitative results of the questionnaire in terms of perceived usefulness and perceived ease of use. In the quantitative evaluation, regarding perceived usefulness, two participants marked "partially agree" regarding the item "Using the ACF increased my performance for identifying autistic characteristics". While all the others marked "strongly agree" for all the items regarding perceived usefulness. With regards to perceived ease of use, one participant marked the "partially agree" option for item "I found it easy to fill out the ACF", and another gave the same answer for the question "Learning to use the ACF was easy for me". All the others marked "strongly agree" for all the ease-of-use questions. These results suggest that after the changes, a development team could use the ACF to better understand the characteristics of an autistic user, allowing them to build empathy with the target audience.

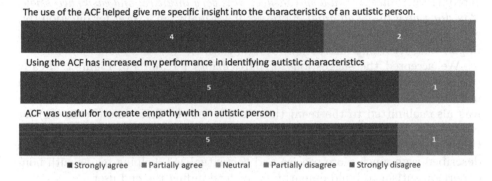

The use of the ACF helped give me specific insight into the characteristics of an autistic person.

Using the ACF has increased my performance in identifying autistic characteristics

ACF was useful for to create empathy with an autistic person

■ Strongly agree   ■ Partially agree   ■ Neutral   ■ Partially disagree   ■ Strongly disagree

Fig. 2. Quantitative results in terms of the perception of usefulness of the ACF

With regards to the qualitative evaluation, we asked the following questions: *(i) What are the ACF positive aspects? (ii) What are the ACF's negative aspects? (iii) Describe which aspects related to the ACF you found easier to fill (iv) Describe which aspects related to the ACF you found more difficult to fill (v) What improvements do you suggest for the ACF?* Some answers from the participants for question (i) were: (P1): *"For lay professionals in autism-related topics, the ACF provides excellent guidance for the questions that should be asked; and guide essential characteristics of the autistic individual. In addition, the automatic generation of the Autistic Overview Graph makes it very easy to compile and analyze the answers."*; (P3): *"As a layman on autism, I liked the tool very much because it directs the questions well, separating them by areas."*. Regarding difficulties, an answer for question (ii) according to P1 was: *"I had a little difficulty in answering the questions that were in the negative form, for example the'Does not participate in group activities.' phrase. The child in question did not usually participate in group activities. Moreover, I spent a little more time*

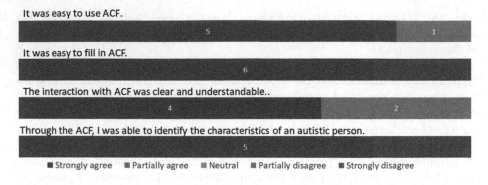

Fig. 3. Quantitative results in terms of the ACF perception of easy of use

choosing (no) or 1 (yes). I suggest that it be rewritten or include an example to better comprehension.". With regards to question (iii), some participants indicated: (P5): *"Since it is in a spreadsheet, it is very intuitive, and easily accessible. You don't need to install anything to use it.".* Finally, an answer for question (iv) was: (P6): *"I could indicate the interpretation of the generated chart. E.g., 22% impairment regarding interaction, 56% impairment regarding communication."*

We accepted the suggestions of participants P1 and P6. Figure 1 already presents the graph's modification. Also, the two characteristics that were in negative form (id 8 and 9) from the ACF were rewritten. The ACF's final version was also submitted to the team that used it for the first time (Team T1) for verification. In this new contact with the ACF, however, all team members agreed that the new version was much easier to understand; and that the characteristics described were much more precise and contextualized, helping teams with non-expert on autism to build empathy by understanding the end user.

5   Conclusion and Future Work

This paper presented the Autistic Characterization Form, which contemplates the four areas affected by Autistic Spectrum Disorder (ASD) as follows: Social Interaction, Communication, Behavior, and Cognition. The goal of the ACF was to present a set of characteristics specific to autistic individuals. As a result, the ACF represents a rich source to support the empathy process between the application designer and the autistic individual.

The ACF is part of a process called ProAut (process to support the design of interfaces for autistic applications), which is based on the Design Thinking and includes several artifacts that support part of the software development process, from requirements engineering to prototyping. EmpathyAut and PersonAut are examples of these artifacts that require the information from the ACF and AOG. Although the ACF is a source of information for EmpathyAut and PersonAut, it can be applied independently. Furthermore, the proposed graph allows the designer to overview the represented autistic person, showing his level of disabilities in the already mentioned areas. Therefore, along with the autistic overview chart, the ACF represents a significant and relevant tool for the empathy process.

We believe that the ACF represents a relevant contribution to the Human-Computer Interaction community since this research's partial results were satisfactory. That is why we still intend to carry out more ACF evaluations with others development teams in real software development scenarios. Also, as future work, we intend to develop a platform for filling out the ACF and generating the AOG in an automated way, including the choice of chart type (line, column, bar, line, and pie), without having to make use of spreadsheets, as it is being employed up until the publication of this paper. By making the ACF and AOG available and all other ProAut artifacts, we hope to improve the creation of interfaces for applications aimed at autistic people, helping them in their treatments, and improving their quality of life.

Acknowledgments. This research was partially funded by the brazilian Coordination for the Improvement of Higher Education Personnel (CAPES). The authors' thank the Universidade do Estado do Amazonas for their support. The results were published through the research and development activities of the project ACADEMIA STEM, sponsored by Samsung Electronics of Amazonia Ltda., with the support of SUFRAMA under the terms of Federal Law No. 8.387/1991.

References

1. Abdullah, M.H.L., Wilson, C., Brereton, M.: Mycalendar: supporting families to communicate with their child on the autism spectrum. In: Proceedings of the 28th Australian Conference on Computer-Human Interaction, pp. 613–617 (2016)
2. Alarcon-Licona, S., Loke, L.: Autistic children's use of technology and media: a fieldwork study. In: Proceedings of the 2017 Conference on Interaction Design and Children, pp. 651–658 (2017)
3. Alawami, A.H., Perrin, E.C., Sakai, C.: Implementation of M-CHAT screening for autism in primary care in Saudi Arabia. Global Pediatric Health **6**, 2333794X19852021 (2019)
4. Berument, S.K., Rutter, M., Lord, C., Pickles, A., Bailey, A.: Autism screening questionnaire: diagnostic validity. Br. J. Psychiatry **175**(5), 444–451 (1999)
5. Bölte, S., Holtmann, M., Poustka, F.: The social communication questionnaire (SCQ) as a screener for autism spectrum disorders: additional evidence and cross-cultural validity (2008)
6. Britto, T.C.P., Pizzolato, E.B.: Proposta de guidelines de interfaces com foco em aspectos do autismo. In: Companion Proceedings of the 13th Brazilian Symposium on Human Factors in Computing Systems, pp. 37–40 (2014)
7. Carlier, S., et al.: Improving autism screening in French-speaking countries: validation of the autism discriminative tool, a teacher-rated questionnaire for clinicians' use. Res. Autism Spectrum Disorders **61**, 33–44 (2019)
8. Carlier, S., Kurzeja, N., Ducenne, L., Pauwen, N., Leys, C., Delvenne, V.: Differential profiles of four groups of children referred to an autism diagnostic service in belgium: autism-specific hallmarks. J. Intell. Disabil. **22**(4), 346–360 (2018)

9. Chuttur, M.Y.: Overview of the technology acceptance model: origins, developments and future directions. Working Pap. Inf. Syst. **9**(37), 9–37 (2009)
10. Cooper, A., et al.: The inmates are running the asylum: why high-tech products drive us crazy and how to restore the sanity, vol. 2. Sams Indianapolis (2004)
11. Edition, F., et al.: Diagnostic and statistical manual of mental disorders. Am. Psychiatric Assoc. **21** (2013)
12. Ferreira, B., Santos, G., Conte, T.: Identifying possible requirements using personas-a qualitative study. In: International Conference on Enterprise Information Systems, vol. 2, pp. 64–75. SCITEPRESS (2017)
13. Frauenberger, C.: Rethinking autism and technology. Interactions **22**(2), 57–59 (2015)
14. Gong, Y., Yatawatte, H., Poellabauer, C., Schneider, S., Latham, S.: Automatic autism spectrum disorder detection using everyday vocalizations captured by smart devices. In: Proceedings of the 2018 ACM International Conference on Bioinformatics, Computational Biology, and Health Informatics, pp. 465–473 (2018)
15. Gray, D., Brown, S., Macanufo, J.: Gamestorming: A Playbook for Innovators, Rulebreakers, and Changemakers. O'Reilly Media, Inc., Sebastopol (2010)
16. Hourcade, J.P., Williams, S.R., Miller, E.A., Huebner, K.E., Liang, L.J.: Evaluation of tablet apps to encourage social interaction in children with autism spectrum disorders. In: Proceedings of the SIGCHI Conference on Human Factors in Computing Systems, pp. 3197–3206 (2013)
17. Johnson, C.P., Myers, S.M., et al.: Identification and evaluation of children with autism spectrum disorders. Pediatrics **120**(5), 1183–1215 (2007)
18. Marteleto, M.R.F., Pedromônico, M.R.M.: Validity of autism behavior checklist (ABC): preliminary study. Braz. J. Psychiatry **27**(4), 295–301 (2005)
19. Melo, Á.H.D.S., Rivero, L., Santos, J.S.D., Barreto, R.D.S.: Empathyaut: an empathy map for people with autism. In: Proceedings of the 19th Brazilian Symposium on Human Factors in Computing Systems, pp. 1–6 (2020)
20. Melo, Á.H.D.S., Rivero, L., Santos, J.S.D., Barreto, R.D.S.: Personaut: a personas model for people with autism spectrum disorder. In: XIX Brazilian Symposium on Human Factors in Computing Systems (IHC 2020), 26–30 October 2020, Diamantina, Brazil (2020)
21. Osterwalder, A., Pigneur, Y.: Business model generation: inovação em modelos de negócios. Alta Books (2020)
22. Schneidewind, L., Hörold, S., Mayas, C., Krömker, H., Falke, S., Pucklitsch, T.: How personas support requirements engineering. In: 2012 First International Workshop on Usability and Accessibility Focused Requirements Engineering (UsARE), pp. 1–5. IEEE (2012)
23. Väänänen-Vainio-Mattila, K., Roto, V., Hassenzahl, M.: Towards practical user experience evaluation methods. Meaningful Measures: Valid Useful User Experience Measurement (VUUM), pp. 19–22 (2008)

A Quantitative Study on Awareness, Usage and Reservations of Voice Control Interfaces by Elderly People

Dietmar Jakob[1]([✉]) [iD], Sebastian Wilhelm[1] [iD], Armin Gerl[2] [iD], and Diane Ahrens[1] [iD]

[1] Deggendorf Institute of Technology, Hauptstrasse 3, 94481 Grafenau, Germany
{dietmar.jakob,sebastian.wilhelm,diane.ahrens}@th-deg.de
[2] University of Passau, Innstraße 41, 94032 Passau, Germany
armin.gerl@uni-passau.de

Abstract. One third of Germans talk to *'Alexa'*, *'Siri'* and other voice-controlled devices. These devices become omnipresent and change the way how humans interact with digital technologies. We hypothesize, this Human-Computer-Interface can minimize barriers for elderly people in their usage of digital services. But, do elderly people even know about voice-controlled technologies? Are the systems used by elderly and what reservations do they have?

Based on a quantitative study in three municipalities in a rural area ($n = 747$), we found that 59% of people aged 55+ years know voice-controlled devices, 37% used them at least once and even 26% use them regularly. But, more than two thirds of respondents (69%) are concerned that their data are not safe. In contrast, only 35% express concerns to be unable to use the devices. The study concludes that there is a gap between the perceived usefulness and trust in the devices for the surveyed demographic.

Keywords: Empirical studies in HCI · Voice control · Voice user interface · Elderly · Quantitative study · Human Computer Interaction

1 Introduction

Digitization offers opportunities for enhanced social participation, quality of life and safety, and thus supports a self-determined life in old age. To enable such self-determined life of elderly people it is essential that on the one hand adequate devices and services are offered and on the other hand elderly people have

This work was funded by the *Bavarian State Ministry of Family Affairs, Labor and Social Affairs*.

Electronic supplementary material The online version of this chapter (https://doi.org/10.1007/978-3-030-90328-2_15) contains supplementary material, which is available to authorized users.

the ability to interact and operate them [1]. Nowadays, digital technologies are mostly operated via touch screens, keyboards or peripheral hardware. The complex feature and interface design often cause difficulties for elderly people [47]. There is a significant amount of elderly (36%) that refrain from using digital devices because the operation is too difficult. In addition a lack of knowledge prevents elderly from using such devices (46%) [49]. Thus, both knowledge of the devices and the ability to interact with the devices is essential.

Speech as a natural and familiar form of communication has advantages over gesture-based interfaces, because barriers for the users occur when motor, visual or cognitive impairments are present [21]. We hypothesize, Voice-Control as Human-Computer-Interface can minimize barriers for elderly people in their usage of digital services, since the operation of these devices is done by using spoken words.

So far, most of the previous work on Voice Controlled Devices (VCDs) related to the elderly focuses on the use and user experience of the systems. Only a few works consider the general awareness as well as reservations about VCDs by elderly people. However, these findings are of fundamental importance in order to understand how to reduce future barriers in human-machine interaction with VCDs by elderly people and to adapt these devices to their needs.

The main contribution of this work is to investigate to what extent the group of people aged 55+ is familiar with VCDs, what proportion of them own a VCD, for what purposes VCDs are used and what reservations do they have about VCDs. Thus, this work extends the focus of existing works, by not only focusing on the usage of VCDs for elderly people, but also including their general awareness from VCDs and reservations about VCDs. This serves as a basis for further qualitative research.

A quantitative study (n = 747) is conducted answering the following research questions (RQ) about people aged 55+:

RQ1 What proportion know a VCD?
RQ2 What proportion can name a VCD (specific product or brand)?
RQ3 What proportion knowingly own a VCD?
RQ4 What proportion claim to use a VCD frequently?
RQ5 What proportion claim to have used VCDs at least once?
RQ6 What reservations do they express about VCDs?

The remaining of the paper is structured as follows: Investigating literature relating to VCDs and media literacy by the elderly in Sect. 2 shows that there is a lack in empirical studies which consider awareness, usage and reservations of VCDs by the elderly. Section 3 details the methodology of the quantitative study carried out within this work, before the results of the study are presented in Sect. 4 and discussed in Sect. 5. Finally, the main findings of the paper are concluded and an outlook on future work is given in Sect. 6.

2   Related Work

VCDs and Voice Assistants (VAs) are investigated in various different scientific fields. Some of the work investigates the acceptability of VCDs using different methods of acceptance research [14,26,33,35,37]. *Hellwig et al.* [21], *Yamada et al.* [50] and *Bertoa et al.* [10] are concerned with the use of VCDs in home or residential care. How elderly people with dementia may interact with family members using VCDs through new forms of music therapy is explored by *Boumpa et al.* [13]. *Flores-Martin et al.* [20] recommends a system that improves the interoperability of smart devices in healthcare and smart-home through the use of semantic web and ontologies. Other application areas include forensics [16], the use of VCDs in smart-home environments [2,36,42], and in usability [3,31, 34,36,44]. *Reis et al.* [38] investigate the use of VCDs for maintaining social relationships of elderly people with their families and relatives. *Lopatovska et al.* [30] and *Jakob and Wilhelm* [25] deal with speech recognition issues. General privacy and security issues related to VCDs are considered in the work of *Hoy and Pomputius* [22] and *Lau et al.* [29].

This literature review focuses on studies that are primarily concerned with VCD awareness, ownership and usage, frequency of VCDs use, and reservations about VCDs. In particular, we consider studies that allow conclusions to be drawn about elderly people in this context.

VCDs, Awareness and Elderly. We could identify only two studies on the awareness of VCDs or VAs among the elderly, which is an indication that this topic is still studied quite poorly. First, the market research institute *Splendid Research GmbH* [45] conducted in 2019 an online survey among 1,006 people in Germany aged 18 to 69. Using an aided recall test they found, that 78% of all respondents know *'Alexa'*. However, the study was conducted online, which means that a certain affinity with technology must be assumed. The proportion of respondents aged 50–69 was 42%. Second, while developing an intelligent dialogue agent based on a voice assistant *Yamada et al.* [50] asked 25 participants which are older than 65 years about their experience with the *Amazon Echo Dot* speaker. None (100%) of the participants had experience with the devices and 12 (48%) were unaware of the device.

While *Splendid Research GmbH* [45] included elderly persons in the total population size up to an age of 69 years, *Yamada et al.* [50] exclusively investigated the group of persons over 65 years. Due to this fact, the authors also derive different results. A limitation of both studies is the definition of 'awareness'. Both studies use the aided-recall method and primarily measure brand awareness of VAs but less the general awareness of VCDs.

VCDs, Ownership, Usage and Elderly. In Germany *Arnold and Schneider* [41], *Bitkom* [28] and *Beyto* [11] already investigates the ownership and usage of VCDs and VAs. *Arnold and Schneider* report, that 85% of the people aged between 18 and 69 years own a VCD. More specific are the opinion polls by *Bitkom* [28] which shows that 28% of people over 16 in Germany even own a VA in the form of a smart-speaker. According to *Beyto* [11] the proportion of people aged 55+ owning a VA in form of a smart-speaker is only 18%. Among smart-speakers is *'Alexa'* the most intensively used by those over 45 years [41]. However, according to *Arnold and Schneider* [41], only 28% use a VCD in everyday life. Among owners of VAs, the proportion is significantly higher. Of those who own a VA in the form of a smart-speaker, 47% also use it daily [28]. *Arnold and Schneider* [41], *Bitkom* [28] and *Beyto* [11] also investigated which functions users favored. In this context, *Arnold and Schneider* [41] found that people 55+ use on average 3.2 different basic functions of VAs. The most frequently used functions are the search for information, setting alarms and reminders, listening to music and making calls. The VA-related studies by *Bitkom* [28] and *Beyto* [11] show that the functions listen to music/streaming services and the control of smart-home components are used more frequently on smart-speakers. It is particularly worth mentioning that 12% of the respondents over 65 years of age expressed the wish that a home emergency call system should be integrated into the VA [28].

The quantitative data collections on voice assistants in general or on voice assistants in the form of smart-speakers listed in this section do not allow many conclusions to be drawn as to whether people aged 55+ actually own and also use a voice assistant. Our present work closes precisely this gap by explicitly examining this population group. Further research by *Choi et al.* [15], *Schlögl et al.* [40], *Yamada et al.* [50] and Blocker et al. [12], is described below:

Choi et al. [15] conducted a field study with 19 participants in the age of 65+ to investigate the attitudes, needs, challenges, and preferences of elderly people to voice assistants in the form of smart-speakers. All participants were provided with a smart-speaker and their experiences and opinions were analyzed with semi-structured interviews before, after 1 month, and at the end of the 2-month trial period. In general, all participants expressed positive experiences. The most frequent questions were about the weather and reminders to take medications. Interestingly, participants discussed using the smart-speaker as a health management device to measure blood pressure or blood glucose. Unfortunately, this article lacks more detailed results on the use and operation of smart-speakers as well as detailed statements on the frequency of the services used.

Schlögl et al. [40] conducted how voice technology-controlled interfaces for elderly people should be designed and collected ideas for this in discussions with focus groups. They found that mobile and landline phones are the most preferred means of communication. Nevertheless, even older people with an affinity for technology have problems operating the touchscreens. The subjects felt that issuing commands via natural language was comfortable and they would prefer the language to a graphical user interface (GUI). The authors recommend research should be conducted in more detail on the use and utilization of voice assistants. Also, the relatively small sample of 18 participants should be increased for further studies.

Yamada et al. [50] conducted a field experiment to investigate the impressions of elderly people before and after using smart-speakers and which functions were expected and perceived as necessary. They used a combination of questionnaire and 30-minute test of the basic functions of the device, and finally an interview survey with evaluation. Interestingly, 12 of the 25 respondents were not familiar with the devices. However, 48% attested that using the devices was easy and 73% had a positive impression. The test persons criticized, between the devices and humans no natural interaction comes about, but were pleased, if they were addressed by the smart-speaker. They wished that these devices were equipped with a monitoring function to be able to recognize assistance situations in the household of elderly people. Before use, there was no interest in using a smart-speaker at home. However, the opinion changed after the experiment. The authors found that voice assistants have a low knowledge of awareness, if any at all, among the population of people aged 65+. Our work aims to shed more light on the extent to which people aged 55+ are aware of, owns, and uses or does not use the devices, thus contributing to a broader understanding.

Blocker et al. [12] deal with opinions of elderly people on the usefulness of the voice assistants Echo and Echo Show of the company Amazon. Their work aims at improving the understanding of elderly people on voice assistants. Using semi-structured interviews, they surveyed 18 people aged 65+. The respondents most liked the ability to manage shopping lists, play music, set alarms, timers and reminders, and control smart-home components. The respondents found the use of the smart-speaker with an integrated display most convincing, so that audio or weather data, personal photos and communication with relatives are also displayed visually. The authors' field study provides important insights into the design of smart-speakers as well as their use. The authors also highlighted the importance of further research within this population with larger samples.

VCDs, Reservations and Elderly. *Arnold and Schneider* [41] investigated reasons for not using voice assistants by surveying $n = 3184$ people across all age groups. 32% of respondents report stopping using voice assistants because commands were not understood. 23% feel uncomfortable talking to a device, 19% do not trust the technology or are afraid that data will be passed on to third parties, 16% are afraid of being wiretapped.

A study by the market research institute *Splendid Research GmbH* [45] shows that 35% of the respondents mention privacy concerns as the main reason for not using VCDs. Further reasons cited were that the devices would be too expensive (26%), it is scary to communicate with devices (15%), the technology is not yet mature (13%) and operation is too complicated (10%).

Similar results are shown in *Trajkova and Hammond*'s [48] field study. Respondents also indicated that they no longer use smart-speakers due to privacy concerns. Furthermore, respondents feel their privacy and confidentiality are no longer respected

Overall Assessment and Summary. *Sayago et al.* [39] already criticized in its suggestion paper, there are some published works on how people perceive voice assistants, interact with them and integrate them into everyday life. However, the authors go on to say, these works do not focus on the elderly population, although researchers have already noted that most digital technologies are designed by and for young people without considering the elderly population.

In summary, while the related work examined covers the topics addressed in our work, a closer look at these topics for people aged 55+ is largely lacking. We fill the gap by focusing exclusively on the 55+ group of people on awareness, usage and reservations about VCDs in our study.

3   Methodology

In order to fill the lack of empirical research described in Sect. 2 and providing an overview, we investigate the *Awareness*, the *Usage* and *Reservations* of VCDs by the elderly conducting an quantitative study using a standardized questionnaire for data collection. This ensures reliable, objective and valid data [18,19].

The written questionnaire method was chosen because online surveys can only be participated in with a certain affinity for technology. This cannot be generally assumed for the target group. A telephone survey could not be carried out due to the lack of contact data. A personal survey was not possible due to the lack of frequented places in rural areas (e.g., pedestrian zones, shopping centers). Using the questionnaire method all persons from the target group had the opportunity to participate.

Design of the Questionnaire Instrument. The fully standardized questionnaire developed within this work is structured according to elements of *Döring and Bortz* [19]. A short questionnaire title is used that roughly sketches the topic of the study, but does not provide a reminder, e.g., by specifically mentioning a brand or product. At the beginning of the survey, the participants are informed in a written way about the objective, the implementing institution, the underlying project as well as the duration and importance of participation. The specific object of research is not specified in detail in order to ensure an unbiased, neutral answer to the questions. We especially point out aspects of research ethics (e.g., voluntariness, anonymity).

The structure of the questionnaire is stringent and does not include filter questions, so that all questions can be answered by all participants. Open questions are avoided (with the exception of the semi-open question Q1) in order to prevent possible refusals to answer (*item non-response*).

Socio-demographic characteristics are limited to the technical affinity and age of the participants. In addition, conclusions can be drawn about the geographical location of the participants based on the distribution channels (see Sect. 3). The defined research questions do not require further differentiation of socio-demographic information. General information on media literacy among older people (e.g., with regard to gender or profession) is already surveyed in a previous study by *Wilhelm et al.* [49]. The questionnaire ends with a word of thanks.

The questionnaire includes a total of six questions, which are detailed below.

Q1 Do you know a device that you can control with your voice?
  Answer options: (i) Yes, namely <free text> (ii) No
  Explanation: The question serves to answer the research questions RQ1 and RQ2. This method of market research is used to obtain an unbiased picture of how well known a product is in the competitive environment ('folder tests'). The strictest form is the 'unaided recall test' (unsupported measurement of the memory effect of advertising media).

This is used to determine active brand awareness by asking the individuals to name a product or brand from memory, without any aid to memory [27,32].

Q2 Have you ever used the voice control function of devices for:
  (a) Search for information (e.g., weather forecast, traffic jam reports, news)
  (b) Entertainment (e.g., games, radio, movies, audio books)
  (c) Device control in the house (e.g., TV, lights, heating, shutters, smart-home)
  (d) Services and applications (e.g., reminders, alarm clocks, navigation, orders, garbage collection appointments)
  (e) Automated telephone hotlines (e.g., telecom[1] fault service, order hotline, customer services)

  Answer options: (i) never (ii) at least once (iii) frequently (more than once a week)

  Explanation: The question serves to answer the research questions RQ4 and RQ5. The selection of the application purposes to be investigated is based on a previous study by *Splendid Research GmbH* [45]. We limit ourselves to five application purposes (search for information, entertainment, device control in the house, services and application, automated telephone hotline), which are most frequently mentioned in the study. For a clear differentiation of terms, examples are provided for each purpose. To differentiate the intensity of use, three possible answers were given for each application. The differentiation of the intensity of use is intended to differentiate whether the individual is basically familiar with how the technology works (answer: *'at least once'*) or is familiar with its operation, uses it in everyday life (answer: *'more frequently'*) or has not yet come into contact with the technology (answer: *'never'*) which is an ordinal scale [19]).

Q3 Do you have any device that you can control with your voice?
  Answer options: (i) Yes (ii) No (iii) I don't know

  Explanation: The question serves to answer the research question RQ3. Individuals who answers this question with *'No'* at least believe that they do not own a VCD. However, due to the large number of integrated VCD (e.g., in smartphones or cars), we assume, that it can still occur that these individuals even own a VCD without knowing it. With the answer option *'Don't know'*, the individuals state that they are not aware of having or not having a VCD. We assume, that these individuals are the opinion not owning VCD, but are not sure that one of their devices does have this functionality.

Q4 How do you agree with the following statements about devices that respond to voice commands:
  (a) I see no benefit for me
  (b) I have concerns about being surveilled
  (c) I am not sure if I can operate these devices

---

[1] Well known telecommunications company in Germany and Europe.

(d) I am afraid of fraudsters

(e) I am concerned that my data is not safe

Answer options: (i) I agree (ii) I disagree

Explanation: The question serves to answer the research question RQ6. The selection of possible answers is based on a study by *Splendid Research GmbH* [45] in order to achieve the greatest possible comparability of the study results. A *'Likert Scale'* [18] was omitted from the selection options, because clear and unambiguous decisions should be made by the individuals.

Q5 Do you use digital technologies such as smartphones, tablets or PCs?

Answer options: (i) Yes (ii) No

Explanation: Informal question to find possible connections between interest in technology and affinity to VCDs.

Q6 How old are you?

Answer options: (i) 49 or younger (ii) 50–54 (iii) 55–59 (iv) 60–64 (v) 65–69 (vi) 70–74 (vii) 75–79 (viii) 80–84 (ix) 85–89 (x) 90 or older

Explanation: Statistical information for categorization by age groups. To ensure filtering of unwarranted completed questionnaires from persons outside the target population, the answer options *49 or younger* and *50–54* are also offered.

All questions were clearly arranged on one DIN-A4 page to avoid possible refusals (see supplementary materials).

Population. We choose three smaller municipalities (*Mauth*, *Philippsreut* and *Frauenau*) from the south-eastern part of the German state of Bavaria because of a previous project cooperation for performing our study. These three municipalities today already have an above-average proportion of elderly people. The average age of the population in Germany today is 43.9 [8]. In the selected municipalities, the average age is 46.6 in *Mauth* [6], 48.0 in *Philippsreut* [7] and 47.5 in *Frauenau* [5]. We obtained population data from the civil register of each municipality until July 2020 and identified a total of $N = 2569$ people aged 55+.

The three selected municipalities are located in an extensive rural area directly on the border with the Czech Republic. In the domain of VCDs, it should be mentioned that dialect language is predominantly used in these municipalities [51], which can my influence or limit the use of VCDs due limited dialect recognition [23]. Another restriction is that the individuals participating in the study must be at least 55 years old (55+). Thus, our target population consists of all people aged 55+ living in one of the three selected municipalities. We consider the age groups 55+ and older as relevant, since statistics show that the proportion of people in active jobs is already decreasing in the 55–59 age group. According to official data, 69% of people in the 50–54 age group in Germany are still in work, while the proportion in the 55–59 age group is only 62% and in the 60–65 age group only 45% [4,46]. The regular retirement age in Germany is 65+ years.

All individuals belonging to the target population were sent a questionnaire and thus had the opportunity to participate in the survey. Since not all individuals participate in the survey or are willing to provide information or were absent at the time of the survey, this corresponds to an *inference population* [19].

To ensure sufficient significance of the conducted study, the minimum required sample size is calculated according to *Israel* [24]. The calculation resulted in a required minimal sample size of $n_{req} = 529$.

Execution. After defining the type and form of the survey, the questionnaire was first subjected to a pre-test with ten individuals ($n = 10$) within the target population. The complete questionnaire (incl. introduction text and final layout) was submitted to the pre-test participants for filling out, with the request to discuss unclear questions with us.

We noted that several of the pre-test participants expressed a desire for examples of the individual categories in Q2, which we then supplemented. In Q4, we originally intended to ask the participants whether they consider VCDs to be too expensive ("The devices are too expensive for me"). The pre-test participants indicated that they can not answer this question objectively. We then decided to remove this answer option from the final questionnaire.

After the adjustments from the pre-test, the final questionnaire, including a stamped return label, was sent by mail to all persons belonging to the target population. The duration of the survey was set at six weeks and took place between July 15, 2020 and August 31, 2020. The returns were electronically recorded and evaluated.

All questionnaires are considered for evaluation, provided that at least the question about age (Q6) is answered.

For Q2, it should be noted that participants should only give one answer per category. For reasons of simplification, however, this is not mentioned in the questionnaire. In the case of multiple answers, however, only the highest valued frequency is recorded, since the term 'frequently' includes 'at least once'.

4 Survey Results

In this Section the results of the survey are presented. For reasons of simplification, all values have been rounded to the nearest integer. A total of 2569 questionnaires were sent out to individuals of the target population. Up to the deadline, 764 questionnaires were returned (gross response rate: 30%), whereby 2 questionnaires were incomplete (Q6 was not answered) and therefore not included in the evaluation. 15 persons stated that they are younger than 55 years and therefore do not belong to the defined target population. The net response rate is 29% (n = 747). The minimum required sample size of $n_{req} = 529$ calculated in Sect. 3 for sufficient significance is reached with the net response rate.

Section 4.1 first outlines demographic data and information on the participants general use of digital media. Subsequently, we present the evaluation results on awareness (Sect. 4.2), services used (Sect. 4.3) and reservations (Sect. 4.4) regarding the use of VCDs.

4.1 Demographic and Statistical Data

41% of all participants are between 55 and 64 years old. One third (33%) are between 65 and 74 years old, 24% are aged 75+. 1% of the respondents stated that they are in the 90+ age group. Figure 1 shows in detail the age structure of the survey participants who returned the questionnaire. In addition, the general use of digital media by age groups is shown (see Q5).

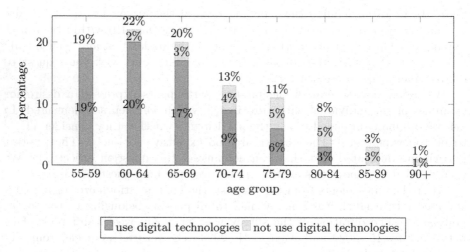

Fig. 1. Age structure and information on participants' general media usage (n = 740).

4.2 Awareness of VCDs

Using an 'unaided recall test' [27,32], the target population was asked if they knew any device they could control with their voice (see Sect. 3, Q1). We examines the proportions of participants who stated they (i) know a VCD (ii) know a VCD and can name at least one product or brand or (iii) did not know a VCD. The results by age group are shown in Table 1.

Table 1. Proportion of participants by age group who stated they (i) know a VCD (ii) know a VCD and can name at least one product or brand or (iii) did not know a VCD.

Option	55–59 (n = 146)	60–64 (n = 170)	65–69 (n = 149)	70–74 (n = 99)	75–79 (n = 80)	80–84 (n = 67)	85–89 (n = 27)	90+ (n = 9)	55+ (n = 747)
Yes	72%	71%	69%	56%	45%	23%	7%	0%	**59%**
Yes, namely	71%	68%	67%	53%	41%	0%	7%	0%	**55%**
No	28%	29%	31%	44%	55%	77%	93%	100%	**41%**

It can be observed that 59% of the participants stated they know a VCD and 55% could additionally name products or brands. By age group, the percentage of participants who stated they know a VCD was 71% in the 55–69 age group, 50% in the 70–79 age group and 16% in the 80+ age group.

The participants could enter multiple answers in the free text field of Q1. We standardized and clustered the answers (see supplementary materials). Only rarely mentioned answer options are grouped in the category 'other' (e.g., *Xbox, Bixby, Smartwatch, Fire TV-stick* see supplementary material). Due to the frequency of mentioning the brand name *'Alexa'* or *'Echo'*, these devices are not assigned to the 'smart-speaker' category and are considered separately. The clustered results are shown in Fig. 2. After 'smartphones' (46%) and *'Alexa'* (45%), navigation devices (13%) are named most often.

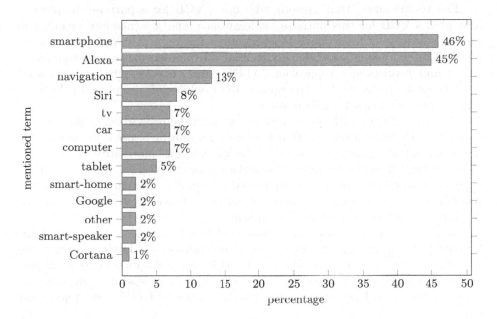

Fig. 2. Proportionate frequency of standardized and clustered product or brand names in Q1. Multiple answers were possible (n = 404)

4.3 Usage of VCDs

The target population was asked whether they have ever used the voice control functionality of devices for five predefined purposes. As options the respondents could answer 'never', 'at least once' or 'frequently' (i.e., at least once a week). Participants were able to provide information on the frequency of use for the predefined purposes 'search for information', 'entertainment', 'device control in the house', 'services and applications' and 'automated telephone hotlines' (see Sect. 3, Q2). The results are summarized in Table 2.

Table 2. Frequency of using VCDs for predefined purposes by people 55+.

Purpose	Never	At least once	Frequently
Search for information (n = 725)	72%	28%	18%
Entertainment (n = 723)	79%	21%	15%
Device control in the house (n = 720)	88%	13%	9%
Services and applications (n = 727)	75%	25%	14%
Automated telephone hotlines (n = 723)	78%	22%	8%

The results show, that persons who use a VCD for a purpose 'frequently' also used a VCD for this purpose 'at least once' and are therefore included in answer category 'at least once'. Most mentions for frequently used purposes are given to the purposes 'search for information' (18%) followed by 'entertainment' (15%) and 'services and applications' (14%). Fewer participants have ever used a VCD for device control in the house (13%), while 28% have used a VCD at least once to searched for information.

To answer RQ4 and RQ5 we further examine the proportion of people that stated that they had used a VCD at least once voluntarily or use it frequently. We define the term 'voluntary' as a use of the VCD despite alternative possibilities. When using telephone hotlines, the service provider decides whether a VCD is used or whether a request is processed personally. Therefore, no voluntary use can be assumed and the answers from the category 'automated telephone hotlines' are not considered in the following.

In Table 3, all participants are considered who answered at least one of the four purposes of 'search for information', 'entertainment', 'device control in the house', or 'services and applications'. The 'at least once' option includes all persons who have filled in 'at least once' or 'frequently' for at least one purpose. The category 'never' includes all persons which have answered all answered questions exclusively with 'never'.

Table 3. Frequency of voluntary use of VCDs by age group.

Option	55–59 (n = 145)	60–64 (n = 170)	65–69 (n = 143)	70–74 (n = 98)	75–79 (n = 78)	80–84 (n = 65)	85–89 (n = 27)	90+ (n = 9)	55+ (n = 735)
At least once	45%	39%	36%	31%	41%	32%	15%	0%	**37%**
Frequently	28%	27%	24%	26%	29%	28%	7%	0%	**26%**
Never	55%	61%	64%	69%	59%	68%	85%	100%	**63%**

In summary, we find that more than one-third (37%) of participants have used a VCD voluntarily at least once and more than one-quarter (26%) use VCD at least once a week.

We also investigate how many people already knowingly own a VCD to answer RQ3. The results are shown in Table 4.

Table 4. Proportion of participants who claim to knowingly own a VCD by age group.

Option	55–59 (n = 145)	60–64 (n = 168)	65–69 (n = 146)	70–74 (n = 99)	75–79 (n = 80)	80–84 (n = 67)	85–89 (n = 27)	90+ (n = 8)	55+ (n = 740)
Yes	61%	50%	45%	35%	38%	22%	11%	0%	43%
No	34%	45%	49%	57%	59%	69%	85%	100%	51%
I don't know	6%	5%	6%	8%	4%	9%	4%	0%	6%

With these results it is notable that although 43% state to own a VCD, but only 37% have used a VCD at least once (see Table 3). This leads to the observation that some of the participants know to own a VCD, but have never used it before. To specify this observation, Table 5 considers the frequency of voluntary use only of those participants who claim to knowingly own a VCD. This shows that 36%, although they own a VCD, do not use it. Possible reasons for this non-use are outlined in Sect. 4.4.

Table 5. Frequency of voluntary use of VCDs by participants who own a VCD by age group.

Option	55–59 (n = 88)	60–64 (n = 84)	65–69 (n = 65)	70–74 (n = 35)	75–79 (n = 30)	80–84 (n = 15)	85–89 (n = 23)	90+ (n = 0)	55+ (n = 320)
At least once	60%	65%	60%	69%	73%	60%	67%	n/a	64%
Frequently	40%	49%	38%	57%	50%	47%	33%	n/a	45%
Never	40%	35%	40%	31%	27%	40%	33%	n/a	36%

4.4 Reservations of VCDs

Based on a previous study by *Splendid Research GmbH* [45] we asked the target population about reservations on using a VCD (see Q4). Participants were able to agree or disagree with various predefined reservations to the use of VCDs. The results are summarized in Table 6.

Table 6. Reasons for reservations about VCD by age group.

Option	55–59	60–64	65–69	70–74	75–79	80–84	85–89	90+	55+
I see no benefit for me	52%	53%	51%	57%	50%	55%	73%	67%	54%
	(n = 141)	(n = 167)	(n = 136)	(n = 93)	(n = 72)	(n = 65)	(n = 26)	(n = 9)	(n = 709)
I have concerns about being surveilled	72%	66%	59%	56%	44%	51%	65%	50%	61%
	(n = 142)	(n = 163)	(n = 123)	(n = 88)	(n = 72)	(n = 59)	(n = 20)	(n = 8)	(n = 675)
I am not sure if I can operate these devices	22%	31%	35%	31%	41%	59%	68%	63%	35%
	(n = 134)	(n = 161)	(n = 124)	(n = 89)	(n = 73)	(n = 61)	(n = 22)	(n = 8)	(n = 672)
I am afraid of fraudsters	52%	54%	52%	51%	42%	58%	65%	63%	52%
	(n = 136)	(n = 160)	(n = 122)	(n = 85)	(n = 72)	(n = 59)	(n = 20)	(n = 8)	(n = 662)
I am concerned that my data is not safe	79%	72%	67%	68%	50%	63%	65%	75%	69%
	(n = 136)	(n = 160)	(n = 122)	(n = 85)	(n = 72)	(n = 59)	(n = 20)	(n = 8)	(n = 687)

It is significant that only 35% of participants believe they cannot operate VCDs. Most reservations about VCDs are related to data safety. 69% of all participants expresses concerns that their data are not safe. 61% are afraid of being surveilled.

In the following we analyze the reservations of two subgroups in more detail. On the one hand, we consider those participants who stated they know a VCD (Q1) but did not own one or were not sure about owning one (Q3) with Table 7. On the other hand, we investigates those participants who said they own a VCD (Q3) but do not use it according to Table 4 with Table 8.

We find that participants who already own a VCD have fewer reservations about the devices in all categories than those who only know a VCD. Both groups of participants, however, have the most reservations regarding data safety, analogous to all participants.

Table 7. Reservations of participants who claim to know but do not own a VCD or are not sure to own a VCD.

Option	55+
I see no benefit for me (n = 128)	68%
I have concerns about being surveilled (n = 122)	69%
I am not sure if I can operate these devices (n = 118)	37%
I am afraid of fraudsters (n = 117)	55%
I am concerned that my data is not safe (n = 123)	80%

Table 8. Reservations of participants who claim to own a VCD but do not use it.

Option	55+
I see no benefit for me (n = 114)	64%
I have concerns about being surveilled (n = 111)	63%
I am not sure if I can operate these devices (n = 110)	23%
I am afraid of fraudsters (n = 110)	47%
I am concerned that my data is not safe (n = 117)	74%

5   Discussion

In a written survey of elderly people aged 55+ in three rural municipalities, we found that 59% of the target population are familiar with VCDs (RQ1), 37% have used voice control devices at least once (RQ5) and 43% already knowingly own a VCD (RQ3). However, more than a third (36%) of those who knowingly own a VCD do not use it and 6% are not sure whether they even own a VCD. These results indicate some uncertainty among the elderly population and could be related to the finding that they do not see any benefit in it (54%). In order to achieve a higher acceptance of use, training measures could be suitable [43].

Analyzing the answers to question Q1 shows, 46% of participants mention smartphones and 45% mention the brand 'Alexa' when they are asked about a

VCD, suggesting that older people are as familiar with integrated voice control functions in devices as they are with stationary smart-speakers.

In the following the results of our study are compared with related work in Sect. 5.1, before the limitations are discussed in Sect. 5.2.

5.1   Comparison with Related Work

In the following we compare the results of our study with related literature from *Splendid Research GmbH* [45], *Wilhelm et al.* [49] and *Bitkom e. V.* [9,28], which are comparable, empirical studies dealing with similar issues.

In a study from 2019, the *Splendid Research GmbH* [45] is evaluating the use of VCDs and smart-speakers. 60% of the respondents states that they had already controlled a device with voice commands at least once. In our study, only 37% of the participants stated they had used a VCD at least once. The discrepancy can be explained by the different target groups of the two studies. In the study of the *Splendid Research GmbH* [45], persons aged between 18 and 69 years were considered, whereas the proportion of persons over 50 years was 42%, in contrast to our work, where only persons aged 55+ are examined.

In a study by *Bitkom 2019* [28], the interest and ownership of voice assistants is examined. The authors investigate how many smartphone users use the usually already integrated voice assistant. Only 29% stated not to use the voice control function, which is similar to our results from Table 8, where 36% of those who own a VCD state not to use it. The study also examines how often voice control is used by people who own a smart-speaker. It is shown that 75% of those who own a smart-speaker also use it several times a week. Our survey found that only 45% of those who own a VCD use it several times a week. This difference is on the one hand again due to the fact that in the study of *Bitkom 2019* [28] people of all age groups - also younger people - were surveyed and on the other hand our evaluation also includes people who have a voice assistance system only integrated in another device (e.g., smartphone).

Considering the purposes for using VCDs, we observe in this paper that most people state to use VCDs to search for information, followed by entertainment purposes. This conclusion is analogous to the study of *Splendid Research GmbH* [45], although the survey investigates people aged 18+.

More than one in two participants in our study stated that they do not see any benefit in using VCDs. This finding corresponds with numerous other studies both on media use by seniors in general and on the use of VCDs in all age groups. *Wilhelm et al.* [49] as well as *Bitkom 2020* [9] state that older people are generally reserved about the benefits of digital technologies. *Splendid Research GmbH* [45] concludes that 61% of German language assistants do not see practical uses for VCDs.

The fear of fraudsters, which is expressed by 52% of the participants in our study, also agrees with the work of *Wilhelm et al.* [49], which examined reservations about the use of digital technology by people aged 55+, in which 47% stated that they did not use digital technology because of this purpose.

A significant difference can be observed in the reservations that the data are not safe. In our study, most participants (69%) expressed concerns on this issue. In the total population, the proportion is only 35% [45].

Summarizing, it can be stated that the group of the elderly must be considered separately in the context of digital technologies, as there are sometimes significant differences in relation to awareness, usage and reservations compared to studies that consider the entire population (incl. younger generations).

5.2   Limitations

The empirical results in this study are furthermore critically assessed according to their limitations.

In the study we only consider people aged 55+ in three small municipalities in the southeastern part of the German state of Bavaria. The selection of the municipalities is not probabilistic but is based on previous project cooperation. Due to the composition of the target population, a feature-specific representativeness is not taken into account and therefore the sampling does not qualify as a quota sample [19]. Furthermore, we fully excluded residents of urban spaces in the study.

All people aged 55+ living in one of the three selected municipalities received a questionnaire by mail based on the address data from the residents' register. Due to legal restrictions (§51 BMG [17]), however, there is the possibility of an information block, which means that we are not able to obtain address data from this individuals and therefore cannot send a questionnaire to these persons. As a result, these individuals are not included in the study, although they belong to the defined target population.

Furthermore, persons who have reached the age of 55 during the survey period but were younger on the reference date for accessing the address data from the registration register are not taken into account.

Due to the fact that we only use written questionnaires, it is possible that physically handicapped people (e.g., the blind) or dyslexics cannot participate in the survey. In addition, it is possible that people who are absent for a longer period of time (e.g., on holiday or rehabilitation) may receive information about the data collection too late and thus not be taken into account in the evaluation of results.

Tables 1 and 3 to 6 show the results of the study broken down by individual age groups. Within the age groups, however, the number of answers usually does not correspond to the required minimum n according to *Israel* [24]. As a result, the individual results presented within the age groups are generally not sufficiently significant.

6   Conclusion and Future Work

We show by this quantitative study *(n = 747)* that 59% of the persons aged 55+ are familiar with VCDs and 55% can even name at least one product or brand.

The majority of participants recognize the 'smartphone' and *'Alexa'* as devices that can be controlled by voice. 43% of the participants already own a VCD, but of those who already own a VCD, only 45% use it regularly. 64% of those who own a VCD have tried it at least once. In the overall target population of the study, 26% use a VCD regularly and 37% have used it at least once.

As reservations against VCDs, most participants expressed concerns about the safety of the data. 69% are concerned that their data are not safe, 61% fear being surveilled by VCDs. In contrast, only one third (35%) of the participants think that they cannot control the devices.

In the study we ask about purposes for the use of VCDs. We observe that the participants regularly use VCDs primarily for searching for information, for entertainment or for services and applications. Only 9% of participants regularly use VCDs for the purpose of controlling devices in the home.

With this work, it was possible to fully answer the research questions introduced in Sect. 1 as shown in Table 9.

Based on the findings of this study new open questions arise. How can existing reservations about the use of VCDs can be reduced? Which mechanisms or interactions for VCDs are necessary to gain the trust of the users (security, safety and privacy)?

This study provides an overview of the status quo on awareness, usage and reservations of VCDs by the elderly. It is the basis for further work to investigate whether the use of VCDs enables the elderly to participate more in a digital society and simplify access to digital services. Qualitative studies should further investigate under which circumstances people 55+ are actually able to learn how to use VCDs and for which purposes they use them in their everyday life.

With the help of the results, manufacturers, developers and researchers will in future be able to give greater consideration to the needs of the elderly.

Table 9. Summarized answers to the research questions by people aged 55+.

Research Question	Answer
RQ1: What proportion know a VCD?	59%
RQ2: What proportion can name a VCD (specific product or brand)?	59%
RQ3: What proportion knowingly own a VCD?	43%
RQ4: What proportion claim to use a VCD frequently?	26 %
RQ5: What proportion claim to have used VCDs at least once?	37 %
RQ6:What reservations do they express about VCDs?	69% are concerned their data is not safe 61% are concerned about being surveilled 54% see no benefit 52% are afraid of fraudsters 35% are concerned about operating VCDs

References

1. Achter Altenbericht zur Lage der älteren Generation in der Bundesrepublik Deutschland: Ältere Menschen und Digitalisierung und Stellungnahme der Bundesregierung, Drucksache / Deutscher Bundestag, vol. 19/21650. Bundesministerium für Familie, Senioren, Frauen und Jugend, Berlin (2020)
2. Alexakis, G., Panagiotakis, S., Fragkakis, A., Markakis, E., Vassilakis, K.: Control of smart home operations using natural language processing, voice recognition and IoT technologies in a multi-tier architecture. Designs **3**(3), 32 (2019). https://doi.org/10.3390/designs3030032
3. Ammari, T., Kaye, J., Tsai, J.Y., Bentley, F.: Music, search, and IoT. ACM Trans. Comput. Hum. Interact. **26**(3), 1–28 (2019). https://doi.org/10.1145/3311956
4. Arbeitsagentur: Anzahl der sozialversicherungspflichtig beschäftigten in deutschland nach altersgruppen und geschlecht am 30.06.2019, July 2020. https://de.statista.com/statistik/daten/studie/1132916/umfrage/beschaeftigtenanzahl-nach-alter-und-geschlecht/
5. Bayerisches Landesamt für Statistik: Demographie-spiegel für bayern, gemeinde frauenau, berechnungen bis 2031. Beiträge zur Statistik Bayerns 550 (2019)
6. Bayerisches Landesamt für Statistik: Demographie-spiegel für bayern, gemeinde mauth, berechnungen bis 2031. Beiträge zur Statistik Bayerns 550 (2019)
7. Bayerisches Landesamt für Statistik: Demographie-spiegel für bayern, gemeinde philippsreut, berechnungen bis 2031. Beiträge zur Statistik Bayerns 550 (2019)
8. Bayerisches Landesamt für Statistik: Regionalisierte bevölkerungsvorausberechnung für bayern bis 2039. Beiträge zur Statistik Bayerns 553 (2020)
9. Berg, A.: Senioren in der digitalen Welt (2020). https://bitkom.org/sites/default/files/2020-08/bitkom-prasentation-senioren-in-der-digitalen-welt-18-08-2020.pdf
10. Bertoa, M.F., Moreno, N., Perez-Vereda, A., Bandera, D., Álvarez-Palomo, J.M., Canal, C.: Digital avatars for older people's care. In: García-Alonso, J., Fonseca, C. (eds.) IWoG 2019. CCIS, vol. 1185, pp. 59–70. Springer, Cham (2020). https://doi.org/10.1007/978-3-030-41494-8_6
11. Beyto GmbH: Beyto smart speaker studie 2020 — deutschland (2020). https://mcusercontent.com/cab8c0a7e9a3fef590fd49ce1/files/3cf2966b-5b46-4f79-a597-80fcdb04fcff/Beyto_Smart_Speaker_Studie_2020_Studienreport.pdf
12. Blocker, K.A., Kadylak, T., Koon, L.M., Kovac, C.E., Rogers, W.A.: Digital home assistants and aging: initial perspectives from novice older adult users. In: Proceedings of the Human Factors and Ergonomics Society Annual Meeting (2020). https://doi.org/10.1177/1071181320641327
13. Boumpa, E., Charalampou, I., Gkogkidis, A., Ntaliani, A., Kokkinou, E., Kakarountas, A.: Assistive system for elders suffering of dementia. In: 2018 IEEE 8th International Conference on Consumer Electronics - Berlin (ICCE-Berlin). IEEE, September 2018. https://doi.org/10.1109/icce-berlin.2018.8576216
14. Burbach, L., et al.: 'hey, siri', 'ok, google', 'alexa'. Acceptance-relevant factors of virtual voice-assistants. In: Laura, S.B. (ed.) 2019 IEEE International Professional Communication Conference (ProComm), pp. 101–111. IEEE (7/23/2019–7/26/2019). https://doi.org/10.1109/ProComm.2019.00025
15. Choi, Y., Demiris, G., Thompson, H.: Feasibility of smart speaker use to support aging in place. Innov. Aging **2**(suppl_1), 560 (2018). https://doi.org/10.1093/geroni/igy023.2073
16. Chung, H., Iorga, M., Voas, J.: Alexa, can i trust you (2017)

17. Deutscher Bundestag: Bundesmeldegesetz, June 2020. bundesmeldegesetz vom 3. Mai 2013 (BGBl. I S. 1084), das zuletzt durch Artikel 82 der Verordnung vom 19. Juni 2020 (BGBl. I S. 1328) geändert worden ist

18. Diekmann, A.: Empirische Sozialforschung: Grundlagen, Methoden. Anwendungen, Rowohlt-Taschenbuch-Verl (2004)

19. Döring, N., Bortz, J.: Forschungsmethoden und Evaluation in den Sozial- und Humanwissenschaften. S, Springer, Heidelberg (2016). https://doi.org/10.1007/978-3-642-41089-5

20. Flores-Martin, D., Laso, S., Berrocal, J., Canal, C., Murillo, J.M.: Allowing IoT devices collaboration to help elderly in their daily lives. In: García-Alonso, J., Fonseca, C. (eds.) IWoG 2019. CCIS, vol. 1185, pp. 111–122. Springer, Cham (2020). https://doi.org/10.1007/978-3-030-41494-8_11

21. Hellwig, A., Schneider, C., Meister, S., Deiters, W.: Sprachassistenten in der pflege - potentiale und voraussetzungen zur unterstützung von senioren (2018). https://doi.org/10.18420/MUC2018-MCI-0341. http://dl.gi.de/handle/20.500.12116/16665

22. Hoy, M.B.: Alexa, Siri, Cortana, and more: an introduction to voice assistants, January 2018. https://doi.org/10.1080/02763869.2018.1404391

23. Huang, C., Chen, T., Chang, E.: Accent issues in large vocabulary continuous speech recognition. Int. J. Speech Technol. **7**(2/3), 141–153 (2004). https://doi.org/10.1023/b:ijst.0000017014.52972.1d

24. Israel, G.D.: Determing Sample Size. University of Florida (1992)

25. Jakob, D., Wilhelm, S.: Amazon echo: a benchmarking model review (2020)

26. Kessler, K., Martin, M.: How do potential users perceive the adoption of new technologies within the field of Artificial Intelligence and Internet-of-Things? A revision of the UTAUT 2 model using Voice Assistants. Ph.D. thesis (2017)

27. Klaus Wübbenhorst, F.R.E.: Definition: Recalltest, February 2018. https://wirtschaftslexikon.gabler.de/definition/recalltest-45770/version-269058

28. Klööß, S., Tropf, T., Böhm, K., Esser, R.: Zukunft der consumer technology-2019, marktentwicklung, trends, mediennutzung, technologien, geschäftsmodelle. Bitkom, Berlin (2019)

29. Lau, J., Zimmerman, B., Schaub, F.: Alexa, are you listening? Proc. ACM Hum. Comput. Interact. **2**(CSCW), 1–31 (2018). https://doi.org/10.1145/3274371

30. Lopatovska, I., et al.: Talk to me: exploring user interactions with the amazon Alexa. J. Librarianship Inf. Sci. **51**(4), 984–997 (2018). https://doi.org/10.1177/0961000618759414

31. López, G., Quesada, L., Guerrero, L.A.: Alexa vs. siri vs. cortana vs. google assistant: A comparison of speech-based natural user interfaces. In: Nunes, I.L. (ed.) Advances in Human Factors and Systems Interaction, Advances in Intelligent Systems and Computing, vol. 592, pp. 241–250. Springer, Cham (2018). https://doi.org/10.1007/978-3-319-60366-7_23

32. Magerhans, A.: Marktforschung. Springer, Wiesbaden (2016). https://doi.org/10.1007/978-3-658-00891-8

33. Niehaves, B., Plattfaut, R.: Internet adoption by the elderly: employing IS technology acceptance theories for understanding the age-related digital divide. Eur. J. Inf. Syst. **23**(6), 708–726 (2014). https://doi.org/10.1057/ejis.2013.19

34. Nielsen Norman Group: Intelligent assistants have poor usability: a user study of Alexa, Google assistant, and Siri, 8 November 2020. https://www.nngroup.com/articles/intelligent-assistant-usability/

35. Peek, S.: PhDThesisSebastiaanPeek. Ph.D. thesis (2017)

36. Portet, F., Vacher, M., Golanski, C., Roux, C., Meillon, B.: Design and evaluation of a smart home voice interface for the elderly: acceptability and objection aspects. Pers. Ubiquitous Comput. **17**(1), 127–144 (2011). https://doi.org/10.1007/s00779-011-0470-5
37. Purington, A., Taft, J.G., Sannon, S., Bazarova, N.N., Taylor, S.H.: 'alexa is my new bff'. In: Mark, G., et al. (eds.) Proceedings of the 2017 CHI Conference Extended Abstracts on Human Factors in Computing Systems - CHI EA 2017, pp. 2853–2859. ACM Press, New York (2017). https://doi.org/10.1145/3027063.3053246
38. Reis, A., et al.: Using intelligent personal assistants to assist the elderlies an evaluation of Amazon Alexa, Google Assistant, Microsoft Cortana, and Apple Siri. In: Arsenio, S.R. (ed.) 2018 2nd International Conference on Technology and Innovation in Sports, Health and Wellbeing (TISHW), pp. 1–5. IEEE (6/20/2018–6/22/2018). https://doi.org/10.1109/TISHW.2018.8559503
39. Sayago, S., Neves, B.B., Cowan, B.R.: Voice assistants and older people. In: Cowan, B.R., Clark, L. (eds.) Proceedings of the 1st International Conference on Conversational User Interfaces - CUI 2019, pp. 1–3. ACM Press, New York (2019). https://doi.org/10.1145/3342775.3342803
40. Schlögl, S., Chollet, G., Garschall, M., Tscheligi, M., Legouverneur, G.: Exploring voice user interfaces for seniors. In: Makedon, F., Betke, M., El-Nasr, M.S., Maglogiannis, I. (eds.) Proceedings of the 6th International Conference on PErvasive Technologies Related to Assistive Environments - PETRA 2013, pp. 1–2. ACM Press, New York (2013). https://doi.org/10.1145/2504335.2504391
41. Schneider, A.: Intelligenz aus der konserve - sprachassistenten in deutschland: Kurzstudie, August 2019. https://www.hs-fresenius.de/wp-content/uploads/WIK_HSFresenius_Kurzstudie_Sprachassistenten_August_2019-1.pdf
42. Sciuto, A., Saini, A., Forlizzi, J., Hong, J.I.: 'hey alexa, what's up?'. In: Koskinen, I., Lim, Y.K., Cerratto-Pargman, T., Chow, K., Odom, W. (eds.) Proceedings of the 2018 on Designing Interactive Systems Conference 2018 - DIS 2018, pp. 857–868. ACM Press, New York (2018)
43. Sczogiel, S., et al.: Digital fit im alter handlungsempfehlung für gemeinden (2020). https://doi.org/10.13140/RG.2.2.23245.05609
44. Solano, L., Guerrero, Q.: User experience evaluation of voice interfaces: a preliminary study of games for seniors and the elderly. Proceedings **31**(1), 65 (2019). https://doi.org/10.3390/proceedings2019031065
45. Splendid Research GmbH: Digitale sprachassistenten eine repräsentative umfrage unter 1.006 deutschen zum thema digitale sprachassistenten und smartspeaker (2019). https://www.splendid-research.com/studie-digitale-sprachassistenten.html
46. Statistisches Bundesamt (Destatis: 14. koordinierte bevölkerungsvorausberechnung für deutschland (2019). https://service.destatis.de/bevoelkerungspyramide/
47. Sulaiman, S., Sohaimi, I.S.: An investigation to obtain a simple mobile phone interface for older adults. In: 2010 International Conference on Intelligent and Advanced Systems. IEEE, June 2010. https://doi.org/10.1109/icias.2010.5716254
48. Trajkova, M., Martin-Hammond, A.: 'alexa is a toy': exploring older adults' reasons for using, limiting, and abandoning echo. In: Proceedings of the 2020 CHI Conference on Human Factors in Computing Systems (2020). https://doi.org/10.1145/3313831.3376760
49. Wilhelm, S., Jakob, D., Dietmeier, M.: Development of a senior-friendly training concept for imparting media literacy (2019). https://doi.org/10.18420/INF2019_83

50. Yamada, S., Kitakoshi, D., Yamashita, A., Suzuki, K., Suzuki, M.: Development of an intelligent dialogue agent with smart devices for older adults: a preliminary study. In: Yamada, S. (ed.) 2018 Conference on Technologies and Applications of Artificial Intelligence (TAAI), pp. 50–53. IEEE (30-11-2018–02-12-2018). https://doi.org/10.1109/TAAI.2018.00020
51. Zehetner, L.: Der bayerische wald als dialektlandschaft (1985)

The Investigation into Design Elements of Auditory Pleasure Experience for the Elderly Based on a Testing Tools Development

Delai Men[(⊠)] and Lingfang Wu

School of Design, South China University of Technology, Guangzhou Higher Education Mega Centre, Panyu District, Guangzhou 510006, People's Republic of China
mendelai@scut.edu.cn

Abstract. The vision system of the elderly will undergo age-related changes. Hearing, as a sensory channel for processing external information second only to vision, will impair the use and perception of products or services. User experience is a hot topic in design research related to the elderly in recent years. Designers also pay more attention to thinking about the experience needs of the elderly from the perspective of multi-sensory channels. However, the research on auditory aging design has not been fully developed yet.

The purpose of this study was to investigate the design elements and characteristics of the elderly's auditory pleasure experience, so as to provide a reference basis for the auditory dimension of the aging design. The research methods include literature study, questionnaire, test, and interview. This study defined and extracted the elements that affect the pleasure auditory experience. A set of materials and tools was innovatively developed for the elderly auditory audio test. 40 elderly people took the hearing test. Through qualitative and quantitative analysis, the study had drawn the conclusion of the key features of the design elements of the elderly's auditory pleasure experience and proposed a suitable aging design strategy based on the elderly's auditory pleasure experience. In sum, the current study has guiding significance for aging design in different fields. The elderly's pleasant hearing experience test system developed and applied in this research is universal. The mapping relationship between the auditory design elements and the elderly's pleasant hearing experience revealed by it makes the sound more in line with the elderly's hearing experience preferences, which is helpful to enhance the interactive experience of products or services for the elderly.

Keywords: Elderly · Auditory experience · Aging design · Auditory preference · Hearing test for the elderly

1 Introduction

1.1 Research Background

Statistics show that the world's aging rate has accelerated significantly after entering the 21st century. The global aging trend is becoming severe and growing rapidly. By the end

© Springer Nature Switzerland AG 2021
C. Stephanidis et al. (Eds.): HCII 2021, LNCS 13096, pp. 258–276, 2021.
https://doi.org/10.1007/978-3-030-90328-2_16

of 2019, China's population over 60 years old was about 254 million, accounting for 18.1% of the total population. The speed and scale of aging in China are unprecedented (National Bureau of Statistics, 2020). The increasing trend of the elderly population means that the demand of the elderly will gradually increase in the future. China is the most populous country in the world with a large base of an aging population. Therefore, it is of typical significance to research the Chinese elderly. From the perspective of design research, sorting out the characteristics of the elderly's perception preferences will help to improve the elderly's pleasure experience and quality of their life.

The auditory system of the elderly will undergo age-related changes, which will impair the use and perception of products or services. 'The degenerative changes of the elderly's hearing are mainly manifested as pure-tone hearing loss, high-frequency hearing loss, and language comprehension. Difficulty in sound localization' [14]. 'Research shows that the rapid decline after the age of 55, it declines rapidly, especially for the pitch discrimination of high frequency sounds' [1]. 'Severity of hearing loss is associated with reduced quality of life in older adults' [2]. Therefore, it is particularly important for the quality of life of the elderly to adapt the sound to the changes of listening comprehension.

Hearing is a sensory channel for processing external information second only to vision, accounting for 15%–20% of the five senses. Hearing helps human to extract interesting or important sound content from the complex background noise environment quickly and accurately. In some aspects, hearing has advantages that vision doesn't have [3]. Compared with visual language, auditory language has five distinctive features: invisible, audible, subjective, open, and slow-acting [4]. However, compared with the visual research, the research on the relationship between human auditory phenomena and design has been neglected. In terms of product and interaction design, Donald Arthur Norman put forward 'pay attention to the natural signals provided by sound to realize the implicit communication between products and people' [5]. He analyzed how to achieve emotional design in the auditory dimension. 'Design can use sound to enhance sensory effects, break the unconscious state of hearing, and make sound become the source of aesthetic pleasure' [6]. At present, with the continuous improvement of living standards, the people-oriented concept exerts a subtle influence on various industries. And pleasure is the highest principle of humanized design. Therefore, only by clarifying the law of elderly's auditory preferences, revealing the relevance of design and the elderly's experience of auditory elements, and respecting the elderly's hearing habits, can we truly do a good job in the subtle and in-depth design and services suitable for the elderly.

The majority of previous research on the elderly's hearing has focused on the changes of auditory physiology and function of the elderly, as well as some aging designs. It is obviously lacking in fully understanding the elements and characteristics of the elderly's personal auditory pleasure experience, especially in reasonably developing the elderly's auditory materials. There is some literature related to the interactive design of the elderly's hearing products, the design of the audiovisual perception of the environment and space, and the aesthetic preferences of music. They put forward constructive suggestions on enhancing the pleasant experience, which laid a solid foundation for this research. Many results on the research hotspots of auditory interface and sound landscape, as well as the marketing value of sound communication, provide abundant cases for this research. However, there is currently no ready-made tool that can be directly used to obtain the hearing needs of the elderly. One work that supports the design progress of this research is the 'Study on the Aesthetic Preference of the Elderly for the Basic Elements of Music' [15], which takes pitch, rhythm, beat, interval, melody, and termination as examples from the perspective of music. In general, we know very little about the methods and tools of the research on the auditory preferences of the elderly.

1.2 Research Aim

Because the aging adaptation of auditory experience preference is rarely studied and there is scant tool for testing the auditory experience of the elderly. The research results are insufficient to meet the special needs of the elderly for high quality of life. The purpose of this exploratory study was to investigate the design elements and characteristics of the elderly's auditory pleasure experience, so as to provide a reference basis for the auditory dimension of the aging design.

This study defined and extracted the elements that affect the pleasure auditory experience. A set of materials and tools was innovatively developed for the elderly auditory test, which had been appropriately designed through preliminary tests. Through qualitative and quantitative analysis, we found the bias law of auditory preference of the elderly. The study had drawn the conclusion of the key elements of the design elements of the elderly's auditory pleasure experience and proposed a suitable aging design strategy based on the elderly's auditory pleasure experience. In sum up, this research has guiding significance for aging design in different fields.

2   Materials and Methods

We conducted our research through an auditory test conducted in a controlled environment. We let participants experience different audio materials and evaluate their preferences from the auditory dimension.

2.1 Participants

Participants were randomly recruited at local elderly care service centers and elderly activity centers. The effectiveness of participants is determined according to their age, physical and condition, and hearing status. Because this is an auditory test, the main selection criterion is the hearing health of the participants. The changes in hearing with age vary from person to person. Participants with normal listening, cognitive abilities and self-care ability can meet the basic requirements of the test.

We recruited 46 participants to participate in this auditory experiment, and 40 of them finally finished the test effectively and completely. They are between the ages of 60 and 87, come from two different regions of China. There were 30 women and 10 men among the participants. Their educational structure consists of 12 undergraduates, 8 junior colleges, 8 high schools (including high schools, technical secondary schools), 5 junior high schools, and 7 primary schools or below. Participants have the ability to take care of themselves, are in good physical and mental condition, and have normal hearing conditions, which meet the test requirements. As some items are related to music, the personal experience of music training will influence the evaluation results. Among the 40 participants, 1 had a professional background, 3 had music training experience, and the rest have non-professional background.

2.2 Definition of Auditory Elements and Development of Testing Tools

From a physical point of view, the sound is produced by the vibration of an object. In our life, we are always exposed to sound. According to their natural nature, they can be divided into: nature sounds, musical sounds and voice. (see Table 1) What is the auditory experience? Hearing experience is the feeling produced by a person after he perceives sound. People listen, then understand and then enter the perceptual experience of auditory aesthetics. Professor Meng [7] proposed that hearing be composed of six variables including pitch, sound quality, timbre, volume, duration, and sound source distance [7]. [15] concluded that the music industry believes that tempo, rhythm, pitch, melody, harmony, pitch, volume, timbre, theme, style, etc. Are some of the factors that affect music preferences? Yu [8] pointed out that auditory perception usually includes the experience and cognition of the loudness, timbre, tone, and predictability of sound. Their research provides an important reference for the research design of this article [8].

In this study, the volume, pitch, timbre, speed and other elements are extracted from the perspective of sound characteristics. According to the types of sounds that the elderly is frequently exposed to, they are divided into natural sounds, musical sounds, voices, and prompt sounds. From the perspective of music preference, music style also has a great influence on the listening pleasure of the elderly. According to these dimensions, we choose sound materials, or use the software 'FL studio' to make sound materials, as the main tool of hearing test. At the same time, we consult music professionals to ensure the professionalism of sound materials. In the volume test, sound materials are played on-site, and the volume that each participant feels comfortable with is determined. The test items of music genre, pitch, tempo and timbre were evaluated in five grades according to the experience preference of each participant.

Volume element. In the volume test items, we selected four sound types according to the living conditions of the elderly: music, natural sound, prompt sound, and voice. 'There is a high correlation between music familiarity and preference' [9]. In the music volume test items, songs familiar to the elderly are selected as test materials. Natural sound is concrete sounds from the real world. Natural sounds include sounds from nature and life. The violent storm and the singing of birds and water are also natural sounds, but people's psychological feelings are different. For example, the sound from the operation of the product and the sound from the movement of objects. Our experience of these sounds is not aesthetic and not pleasant. In the research of the pleasure experience of the elderly, pleasant natural sounds are mainly selected as the sound volume test materials, such as birdsong, the sound of running water, and the rustle of leaves blown by wind. The prompt music that is more accessible to the elderly is cell phone ringtones, so

Table 1. Auditory test items list

Test item type	Details
Volume	Music sound/natural sound/prompt sound/voice
Pitch	Bass/alto/treble
Speed	Voice/music
Timbre	Voice/music
Music genre	Pop music/jazz/electronic music/regional folk songs/Chinese national music/ballad/traditional opera/classical music/ancient Chinese style/rock and roll/R&B/Bossa Nova/American country

we use the mobile phone ringtone to measure the volume. In the voice test, a piece of voice broadcast material is used to test the volume. In the experiment, we recorded and calculated the corresponding decibel value according to the comfortable and pleasant volume of each participant.

Music genre element. understanding and inquiring about the elderly and considering the more common music genre in the market, the music genre test includes popular music, jazz, electronic music, folk songs, folk music, Beijing opera, classical music, ancient Chinese style, rock and roll, R&B, Bossa Nova, American country, etc. Repertoires familiar to the elderly were first selected as experimental materials. The tempo and the audio duration of the song should be kept as consistent as possible. Only by understanding the elderly's preference for music genre more realistically and objectively, can we better meet the elderly's leisure and entertainment needs, even for recuperation and rehabilitation.

Pitch element. The pitch is determined by the frequency. The higher the frequency, the higher the pitch, which will affect people's mood. 'The bass is deep and heavy, the **alto** is broad and gentle, and the treble is bright and brisk' [16]. In this pitch test item, the piano sound is used as the experimental material, and the 9 sound groups of the bass, alto, and treble registers of the piano in the arrangement software are used to play pure music with the same melody, tempo, and duration.

Speed Element. *Musical Beats Tempo.* Liu and Wei [10] clarified that the generation of individual musical emotions is not only related to the individual's musical experience but also affected by the tempo of music rhythm [10]. In the tempo element of this study, we understood the tempo acceptance and preference of the elderly from the aspects of voice speed and music tempo. In the music tempo test, the piano was used to play pure music with the same melody but different tempo. The tempo sound material was between 55 and 155 beats per minute, and each test tempo audio differs by 10 beats per minute.

Voice Speed Item. There are 5 voice speed types. Refering to the voice speed used in artificial intelligence, it can be divided into very slow (about 132 *words/min*), slow (about 191 *words/min*), normal (about 210 *words/min*), and fast (about 251 words/min), very fast (approximately 289 *words/min*). The tempo audio is played with the same text content.

Timbre Element. On the basis of repeated learning and experience accumulation, the human brain has complex and accurate judgments on the sound information of different timbre. The timbre items in this experiment were tested in two dimensions: voice timbre and musical instrument timbre.

Voice Timbre. Considering the common use of human voice timbre, the classification was based on age and gender. The older the age, the timbre of the sound tends to be rougher, and the pitch tends to be deeper. The boy's timbre is immature and vigorous, while the girl's timbre is immature and crisp. The timbre of young men is just and energetic, and the timbre of young women is soft and beautiful. The middle-aged male timbre is generous and calm, and the middle-aged female timbre is mature and peaceful. In the test, different timbres were used to play the same text content at the same tempo.

Instrument Tmbre. The classification of musical instruments timbre refers to the modern musical instrument classification, which divides musical instruments into chordophones, aerophone, membranophones and idiophones according to the way of sounding. There are too many types of instruments that it is impossible to test them all. Considering the relationship between the preferences of the elderly in China and their living backgrounds, 15 kinds of musical instruments were selected.

2.3 Preliminary Experiment

Before determining the final auditory experiment materials and experimental procedures, we conducted pre-tests on 5 participants using a preset standard operating procedure (SOP). According the pre-test results, the design of the experimental materials was optimized to make the experimental range closer to the range of the elderly's hearing pleasure. Meanwhile, the experiment time is limited, so useless measurement items should be reduced as far as possible to improve the efficiency of the experiment.

The results (see Table 2) of the pre-experiment led us to reduce the number of test items, and the difference between test items should be within the perceptible range of the elderly, so that the test results will be more accurate and useful. (1) In the music genre's preference test, the elderly often mentioned some popular Internet songs. After consideration, it was necessary to add popular Internet songs to the music genre preference test. (2) In the pitch preference test, it was reasonable to delete the test items of the sub-contra octave and 5-line octave, and retain the 7 complete sound groups of the piano (see Fig. 1). Because in the experiment, all participants showed dislike to the pitch. Moreover, the sound materials were further optimized. The originally pure music segment with no melody was changed to a pure music segment with a different pitch. The reason was that in the pre-experiment, it was found that it is difficult for the elderly to evaluate the pure pitch segments without melody during the test. (3) In the test of the music beat tempo, each tempo option was changed from 10 beats to 20 beats, so the original 12 options were changed to 6 options. The reason was that participants often ask, 'Is this different from the previous one?' When there are many and similar options, the elderly were prone to doubts and difficult to make accurate evaluations.

Table 2. List of optimized auditory test items.

Test item type	Details		
Volume	Music sound/natural sound/prompt sound/voice		
Pitch	Bass	Contra octave/Great octave	
	Alto	Small octave/one-lined/two-line	
	Treble	Three-line/four-line	
Speed	Voice	Very slow/slow/normal/very slow/very fast	
	Music	55 *beats/min*, 75 *beats/min*, 95 *beats/min*, 115 *beats/min*, 135 *beats/min*, 155 *beats/min*	
Timbre	Voice	Female	Child/young/middle-aged
		Male	
	Instrument	Chordophones	Piano/guitar/violin/Chinese dulcimer/the lute/erhu
		Aerophone	Flute/trumpet/tuba
		Membranophones	Side drum/snare drum/bass drum
		idiophone	Triangle/cymbals/chime bells
Music genre	Pop music/jazz/electronic music/regional folk songs/Chinese national music/ballad/traditional opera/classical music/ancient Chinese style/rock and roll/Internet pop music/R&B/Bossa Nova/American country		

Fig. 1. Selection range of piano register.

2.4 Data Collection and Analysis

In this study, self-made auditory test tools and questionnaires were used to investigate. The sound materials include the above-mentioned sound materials for testing preferences, such as volume, music genre, pitch, tempo, and timbre. The speaker was used to play the sound material, and the decibel tester was used to test the volume of the environment and the audio material. Mobile phones were used to collect questionnaire data and record the volume data of volume test items on site. Finally, the data were analyzed by SPSS.

Data were collected through auditory tests and oral interviews. The Likert scale was used to obtain the participants' evaluation data on sound materials. In the pre-experiment, the elderly often found it difficult to evaluate. Therefore, we made a reference table for auditory experience evaluation to provide the elderly with more evaluation-related words, which were showed and introduced to the elderly during the experiment (see Table 3). The higher the score, the higher the degree of preference. The purpose was to help the elderly to more quickly determine and evaluate the current listening experience more quickly. The observation method was also used to record participants' expressions, language, and physical reactions to collect data.

Table 3. Auditory experience evaluation reference.

Score	1	2	3	4	5
Experience evaluation	Very bad	Bad	Fair	Good	Particularly good
	Boring	Not satisfied	Just so so	Satisfied	Like it very much
	Hate	Dislike	Common	Prefer	Love it
	Very poor	Fail	Pass	Well	Excellent

2.5 Procedure

Every experiment follows the same SOP. In a quiet indoor space where the noise does not exceed 35 dB, the author tested participants one by one. The participants sat at the table, 60 cm away from the speaker. The experience evaluation reference table was placed in front of the participants. The author first ex-pressed gratitude to the participants and introduced the experimental process and evaluation criteria: their real experience of hearing every sound material. Do not introduce the purpose of the experiment to participants to avoid affecting the evaluation. The participants were asked about their ear health and hearing health in different conditions to confirm whether they are suitable for a complete test.

There were 6 groups of test items in the experiment. In the first group, each kind of sound material was played separately in the volume preference test. The button was adjusted from the smallest volume to the volume that the participant considers appropriate according to the participant's prompts, and then the current volume value of the speaker was recorded. After the experiment, the decibel tester was placed on the head of the subject, and the readings of the decibel tester were recorded. The acoustic calculation method was used to calculate the decibels of the sound material over a period of time. Finally, the decibel value of the volume deemed appropriate by each subject was obtained.

The 2nd to 5th groups were music genre, pitch, tempo, and timbre test groups. They were all tested by the same way: playing the audio materials separately, and evaluating the current experience according to the degree of preference after listening to the sound material. They scored values from 1 to 5 according to the Likert scale. Participants were interviewed after each test item. Group 6 mainly included basic personal information and auditory habits.

3   Results and Analysis

In order to verify the consistency and validity of the results of the questionnaire, this study used SPSS23.0 to analyze the reliability and validity of 57 items of the questionnaire except for demographic variables, as shown in Table 4. The reliability coefficient value in the table is 0.947, which is greater than 0.9, indicating that the reliability of the research data is high. KMO = 0.938 means the validity of the questionnaire is also very high. The analysis results show that the test items and results of this questionnaire are reliable and effective.

Table 4. Cronbach reliability analysis and Reliability statistics.

Number	Sample size	Cronbach α coefficient	Cloning Bach Alpha based on standardized terms	Clone Bach Alpha
57	40	0.937	0.938	0.928

3.1   Music Genre Preference

The data shows that the elderly's preference for pop music and regional folk songs is obviously higher than other types, followed by Internet pop music and Chinese national music (see Fig. 2). When the elderly listened to these songs, humming and laughing, and his bodies moved with rhythm. These behaviors also echoed the findings of the survey. 'Music preference is an individual's emotional response, which is related to the characteristics of music itself (such as pitch, tempo, rhythm, style, etc.). At the same time, music preference also reflects the listener's main music-related experience, emotional state, personality traits, values and social environment and other factors.' Besides, they showed a moderate to high preference for jazz, traditional opera, classical music, ancient Chinese style and Bossa Nova.

From the above, it can be found that pop music is the most popular music genre. Popular songs are industrialized and consumer cultural products that are easy to understand and accept. Internet pop music has a lower threshold of creation, which is widely spread and sung through the network. It is easier to understand and close to life. In general, there are several reasons why the elderly like it. (1) The pitch is appropriate and easy to sing. (2) It is brainwashed by deliberately repeating and undulating melody. (3) The lyrics are simple and straightforward which do not require deep thinking and insight. (4) The most important thing is that the melody is simple and the lyrics are easy to understand. The culture and living standards of the majority of the elderly are poor. These songs are within the scope of their understanding.

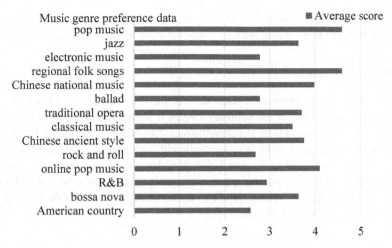

Fig. 2. Comparison of music genre preference evaluation.

Regional folk songs are traditional songs of laborers. The art of songs produced and developed by the people through extensive oral singing in daily life practice is full of rich life-breath. The preference for Chinese national music stems from experience. It sounds familiar and matches their life background and age. The preferences for traditional opera, classical music, and Bossa Nova is polarized. The elderly has strong subjective view on these three types of songs. Therefore, the application of these types of songs cannot meet the preferences of most elderly people, but it can be preferred by some elderly people [11].

Analyzing the relationship between music genre preference and background variables, pop music, regional folk songs, and Internet pop music has no difference in gender, age, and education level, showing greater universality. Men showed a higher degree of preference for Chinese national music, jazz, ancient Chinese style, and Bossa Nova. Women have higher preference for traditional opera and classical music. Older people who have received higher education and music training have a higher preference for classical music. Their past experience and the types of music they have listened to indirectly influence their familiarity and acceptance of classical music.

In the interview, they also expressed, 'Because I understand', 'because I can keep up with the tune', and thus prefer certain music.' There is a high correlation between music familiarity and preference. And it is the most obvious of the factors that affects preference' [9]. In the interview, they also mentioned that 'this kind of music is suitable for me to dance in public square dance', especially for women. They imply that they like dynamic music with a sense of rhythm. 'The music rhythm in Chinese square dance is obvious, which is well known to the masses. Its rhythm is usually brisk, clear and full of joy' [12]. Because of their daily music activities, they are more likely to come into contact with this kind of music genre. Its familiarity and usefulness affect the degree of preference for similar music. In addition, most elderly people mentioned that they are disgusted with loud, harsh, hard-sounding, and too intense music, such as rock and roll and electronic music. For music like ballad, the elderly pointed out that it is difficult to understand, as plain as speaking which should be liked by young people.

3.2 Volume Preference

As shown in the volume preference data Table 5, the volume results of the participants for the 4 sound types are that the volume of voice is higher than the prompt sound, and the volume of prompt sound is higher than the music and the natural sound. It can be seen that the volumes that need to be heard clearly and with specific information is higher than the volumes that need to be heard, followed by the sound types of appreciation, leisure and entertainment (such as music and nature sound, etc.). By calculation, the average variation range of several kinds of audio is 72.94 to 79.19 decibels, and the average perceived volume is 74.8 decibels.

Table 5. Volume preference evaluation data.

Sound type	Music sound	Natural sound	Prompt sound	Voice
Average equivalent decibel value (*dB*)	73.38	72.94	73.78	79.19
Median (*dB*)	72.98	74.70	69.86	79.86

3.3 Pitch Preference

The elderly's preference order for the pitch of the seven groups is: 1-lined, small octave, 2-line, 3-line, great octave, 4-line, contra-octave (see Fig. 3). The preference of the elderly for 1-lined octave is significantly higher than for other octaves, followed by the preference for small octave and 2-line, which are all above the middle. Comparing the pitches into bass, alto, and treble, the elderly like the alto register the most (see Fig. 4). According to the comparison table of piano pitch and frequency, the frequency ranges corresponding to small octave, line 1 and line 2 are (220.00 to 415.31 Hz), (440.00 to 830.61 Hz), (880.00 to 1661.22 Hz).

The treble register is crisp and bite. Alto register is soft and open, and the bass register is thick and heavy. In the interview, the elderly said that they 'like to listen to the pitch that they can keep up with'. Alto sound is bright and dexterous which is the most frequently used sound. The frequency range of speech and chat is usually in the alto register. Due to the extremely high frequency of use, alto has naturally become the most used and comfortable sound.

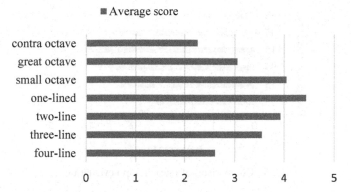

Fig. 3. Comparison of pitch preference evaluation.

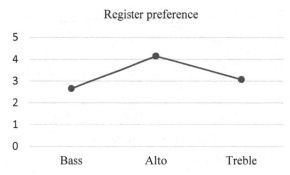

Fig. 4. Register preference.

3.4 Speed Preference

Music tempo preference. The average order of the elderly's preference for the 6 kinds of beats is: 115 beats/min, 95 beats/min, 135 beats/min, 155 beats/min, 75 beats/min, and 55 beats/min (see Fig. 5). Among them, the elderly's preference for tempo at around 115 beats/min is significantly higher than the others, followed by 95 beats/min and 135 beats/min, all of which are above the middle. There are significant differences in preference for 'slow', 'medium', and 'fast'. That is, the elderly prefers medium speed, followed by fast speed, and slow speed (see Fig. 6).

The tempo of music directly affects emotions and images. Generally speaking, the elderly prefers music with lively tempo and cheerfulness. The medium tempo is exciting which is close to our heart beat and breathing when we are excited [13]. Most of the square dances enjoyed by the elderly have a beat of around 100 beats per minute. The preference for music tempo is influenced by experience and listening habits.

By analyzing the relationship between music tempo preferences and background variables, it is found that gender shows significance at the 0.05 level for music tempo. The specific difference shows that the average value of men is obviously higher than that of women. Men may prefer fast music than women.

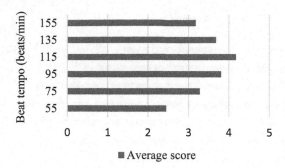

Fig. 5. Comparison of music tempo evaluation.

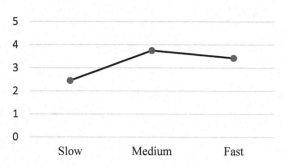

Fig. 6. Register preference

Voice speed preference. The elderly's preference for the 5 kinds of voice speed is in order: normal, slow, fast, very slow, and very fast (see Fig. 7). The corresponding voice seed quantization is about 210 words/min, about 191 words/min, about 251 words/min, about 132 words/min, about 289 words/min. The preference for normal and slow voice speed is obviously higher than the others, and the overall preference of the elderly is slow.

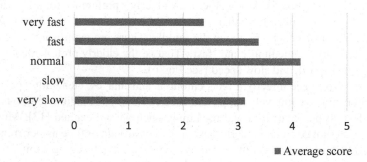

Fig. 7. Voice speed preference evaluation.

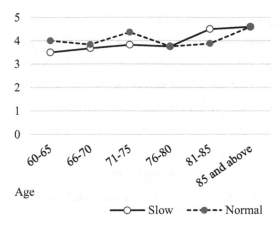

Fig. 8. Intersection analysis of voice speed and age.

Analyzing the relationship between voice speed preference and background variables, age is significant at the 0.05 level (F = 3.095, p = 0.013) for normal speaking rate (210 words/min). Figure 8 shows that the elderly under the age of 76 prefer normal speech speed (210 words/min). Elderly people over 76 prefer to more slowly speech speed (251 words/min). Therefore, the voice speed used by the elderly over 76 years old should be slowed down.

Analyzing the relationship between voice speed and music tempo, the results show that music tempo '55 beats/min' and voice speed 'very slow' (289 words/min) are significant, and the correlation coefficient values are 0.727, which is greater than 0. It means that there is a positive correlation between 55 beats/min and 'very slow' voice speed. Similarly, music tempo '155 beats/min' has a positive correlation with 'very fast' (289 words/min) and fast (251 words/min). People who prefer slower music tempo have a slower voice speed preference. The elderly's speed preferences for music and voice are habitually consistent.

3.5 Timbre Preference

Voice timbre preference. The average order of the elderly's preference for the six voice timbres is: middle-aged female, young female, young male, middle-aged male, girl, and boy. It is obvious that the timbre preference for middle-aged women is significantly higher than the others (see Fig. 9).

The timbre of voice will gradually change with age. Different voice timbre causes different subjective feelings. The children's voice timbre is crisp and immature. The young voice timbre is vigorous and energetic. The middle-aged vocal timbre sounds steady and heavy. The middle-aged female has mature and intelligent timbre, which is the favorite of the elderly. The elderly have rich life experience and accumulated more life experience, so they also prefer the mature and stable voice timbre.

The analysis of the relationship between voice speed preference and background variables shows that gender difference of middle-aged female's timbre is significant at the 0.05. The specific difference shows that male elderly prefer 'female middle-aged'

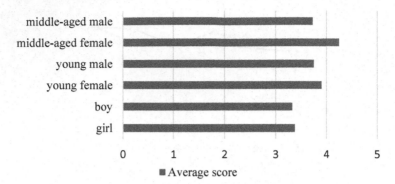

Fig. 9. Evaluation of voice timbre preference.

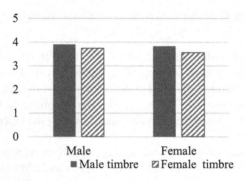

Fig. 10. Gender and voice timbre preference.

timber than females. Generally speaking, the elderly prefers the timbre of female (see Fig. 10). This is also consistent with the research conclusion of Professor Clifford Nass of Stanford University. Relatively speaking, people prefer female voices. The human brain also tends to prefer female voices.

Instrument timbre preference. The order of the elderly's preference for musical instruments timbre is: chime bells, guitar, piano, Chinese dulcimer, the lute, erhu, tuba, violin, bass drum, trumpet, flute, sidedrum, triangle, snare drum and cymbals (see Fig. 11). Among them, the preference of chime bells, guitar and piano is obviously higher than that of other musical instruments. The timbre of the chimes is ethereal and distant. The timbre of the guitar is warm and translucent. The register of the piano is regarded as be within the most comfortable range of human hearing. Its timbre conveys feeling of warmth and sincerity. By classifying and comparing the average values, it is found that the chordophones is the favorite of the elderly, followed by aerophone (see Fig. 11). Membranophones and idiophones are not good choices. The elderly also expressed their preferences in the interviews, such as 'clear voice', 'not too harsh', 'comfortable', and 'not muddy'. This means that the elderly like the pure and pleasant timbre (Fig. 12).

Analyzing the relationship between timbre preference and background variables shows that the satisfaction of 'life happiness' is significant at the 0.05 level for the bass drum (F = 2.723, p = 0.045). The specific difference shows that the higher the

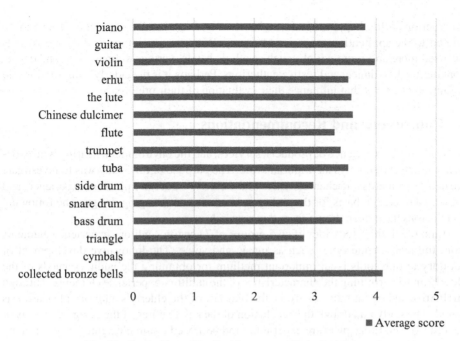

Fig. 11. Evaluation of musical instrument timbre preference

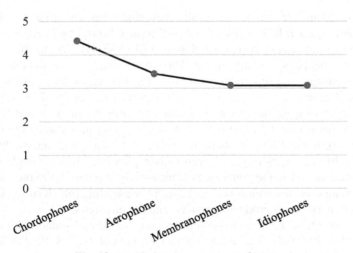

Fig. 12. Music instrument type preference.

satisfaction of 'life happiness', the higher the degree of love for bass drum. This may be related to the application scenarios of drums. With the development of society, drums are used more and more widely, such as ethnic bands, various dramas, song and dance, boat racing, lion dance, and festive gatherings. Perhaps it is the elderly's impression and cognition of drums that influence their evaluation of their preference.

4   Conclusions and Recommendations

In the elderly's experience of products, services, and the environment, hearing is an experience channel that plays an important role. The purpose of this study was to investigate the design elements and characteristics of the elderly's auditory pleasure experience, and provide a reference basis for the auditory dimension of the aging design. The following conclusions have been drawn from this research.

First of all, this study identified 5 groups of 7 specific auditory experience elements from the main sound types such as music and voice. The innovative development of auditory testing tools is an important medium for obtaining the auditory needs of the elderly and determining the characteristics of the auditory experience elements. Through qualitative and quantitative analysis, the bias law of the elderly's auditory pleasure was found. The study had drawn the conclusion of the key features of the design elements of the elderly's auditory pleasure experience and proposed a suitable aging design strategy based on the elderly's auditory pleasure experience. When others need to explore the auditory needs of the target elderly group through similar methods, this research can provide them with ready-made tools and targeted auditory aging design references, and enhance the pleasure experience of the elderly. At the same time, the research results are universal which can provide convenience and reference for the exploration of auditory needs of other ages. The following are the main results and key design strategies of this research.

The music genre preference test results show that when choosing a music genre, pop music and regional folk songs can be preferred, followed by Internet pop music, Chinese national music, and then jazz and ancient Chinese style. Try to choose one that matches the old people's life background. The lyrics should be easy to understand and the melody is simple and repeatable. If it is the familiar music they have heard, they may prefer it. The music genre is a complex. The preference results of music genre can provide references for music education, health care, music activities, and leisure and entertainment environment for the elderly. Music plays an important role in film and television, radio, nursing homes, shopping malls, restaurants, and other public places related to the life of the elderly, and even mobile phone ringtones. People who play music also want to cater to the preferences of the elderly. It can mobilize the emotions of the elderly, exaggerate the atmosphere and even play a healing role. It subtly influences the elderly's experience of products, services, and the environment.

In the volume test, the average perception range of several sound volumes by the elderly is 72.94–79.19 dB. The average perceived volume is 74.8 dB. For functional sounds that need to be heard clearly and with specific information (such as voice), it is suggested to choose a higher volume within the range for the elderly to hear clearly. The second is the prompt sound, which should be loud enough for the elderly to hear and avoid missing the prompt.

The results of the pitch preference test show that the elderly prefer the 1-lined pitch (440.00 Hz–830.609 Hz), followed by the small octave (220.000 Hz–415.305 Hz). When using or creating music for the elderly, it is suggested to give priority to the pitch of the 1-lined octave. Small octave and 2-line pitch are also good choices.

Although the physiology, psychology, and cognition of the elderly will undergo degenerative changes, it does not mean that the slower the music tempo and voice speed, the better. The music tempo preference test results show that the elderly prefer the cheerful and lively mid-beat tempo. The beats between 95 beats/min to 135 beats/min are preferred by the elderly. 115 beats per minute is a safe option. If there are more male users, you can choose the one with a faster rhythm within the range. Using or creating music with appropriate tempo can make the elderly happy.

The overall preference for voice speed of the elderly is relatively slow. Among the 5 types of voice speed, 191 words per minute is considered to be the most appropriate. 119–210 words/min is an appropriate range of speaking speed. When choosing the voice timbre, you can give priority to the mature and calm female middle-aged timbre. Generally speaking, the elderly prefers female timbre. You can choose female timbre first, especially in scenes with more male users. The suggestions on voice speed and timbre can provide voice reference for artificial intelligence and broadcasting for the elderly.

In terms of musical instrument timbre preference, the timbre of Chinese chime bells is the favorite of the elderly, followed by piano and guitar. Different musical instruments timbre conveys different emotional experiences. The elderly's preferences for chime bells, pianos, and guitars indicate that the emotions expressed by these musical instruments cater to the experience preferences of the elderly. In the timbre application that wants to arouse the pleasure of the elderly, such as the sound feedback design for the successful operation of the product, it is recommended to give priority to these three instruments. In the type of musical instrument, the elderly most like the timbre of chordophones. Therefore, chordophones can be selected first in the choice of instrument matching.

In short, through an in-depth understanding of each experience element and its characteristics, designers can refer to and apply them to hearing-related situations in the elderly market. For example, in the design of products for the elderly, familiar, simple and easy-to-understand music that meets the life background of the elderly can be used as the starting music or reminding bell, or for leisure and entertainment. It is reasonable to adjust a higher volume in the reference range, use the medium pitch and choose the cheerful tempo. At the same time, it is better to adjust the volume at different distances automatically. The female or middle-aged female voices used in voice interaction has the characteristics of calmness and peace of mind. The voice speed slows down slightly, but it is recommended not to be too slow. In the aspect of positive feedback, chime bells, pianos, guitars are preferred. Stringed instruments are a good match. Sound is an important design element of some products. The sound of aging products needs to adapt to the auditory characteristics of the elderly, meet the auditory needs of the elderly, enhance the auditory experience of the elderly, and ultimately enhance the quality and user experience of the product.

Acknowledgment. This project, Research on Elderly-Oriented Design Countermeasures based on the Elderly's Characteristics in Sensory Perception, is supported by Humanities and Social Sciences Research Planning Fund Program of the Ministry of Education of China (Grant No. 19YJA760043).

References

1. Shu-lian, X.: Changes in the visual, auditory and psychomotor responses of the elderly and their coping. Chin. Ment. Health J. **2**(3), 136–137 (1988)
2. Caballero, M., Franco, A., Navarrete, P., et al.: Impact of hearing loss on quality of life in older adults. Otolaryngol.-Head Neck Surg. **143**(Suppl. 2), P237 (2010)
3. Qing-shui, L., Zhigang, F., Mowei, S., Yuwei, C.: Sound use of auditory interface. Chin. J. Ergon. **7**(04), 41–44 (2001)
4. Pei-hong, X., Yu, D., Fang, G.: Research on sensory branding from sense of hearing preferences. J. Brand Res. (01), 50–55 (2016)
5. Norman, D.A.: Design Psychology: The Psychology of Everyday Things. Citic Press, Beijing, China (2015)
6. Ying, L.: Acoustic Experience: The Study on Sound Consciousness and Auditory Aesthetics in Design. Central Academy of Fine Arts, Beijing (2017)
7. Meng, L.: Mulimedia Cartographic Presentations-Animation and Anamorephosis. Institute of Surveying and Mapping. Information Engineering University, Zhengzhou (2007)
8. Yu, C.: The study on the space construction of community parks based on audiovisual perception of the elderly: taking Fuzhou city as an example. Fujian Agriculture and Forestry University (2017)
9. Hong, H., Li-man, C.: Research of relationship of familiarity, complexity, sensibility and favorite of music. Musicol. China (02), 131–140 (2007)
10. Liu, Y., Wei, D., Guang-yuan, L.: The neural effect of rhythm speed on different music experienced individuals' musical emotion. In: The 20th National Conference on Psychology: Psychology and National Mental Health. Chinese Psychological Society 2 (2017)
11. Xiao-wen, Z.: Research on the influence of internet songs in popular music. Natl. Music (04), 22–23 (2016)
12. Qiu-shuo, W.: Analysis of the characteristics of music use in square dance. Pop. Song (09), 215 (2016)
13. Qun-yi, W.: Dynamic, speed and emotional image: their essentiality, absoluteness and relativity in music. Hundred Sch. Arts **26**(S2), 366–368 (2010)
14. Cui-ying, Z.: Product operation feedback design based on the elderly people's sensory characteristics. J. Mach. Des. **31**(01), 116–119 (2014)
15. Xiang-nan, Huo.: A study on the aesthetic preferences of the elderly—taking the preferences of hearing dependence, sound type, volume, speed, and timbre as examples. J. Xinhai Conservatory of Music (03), 98–106 (2016)
16. Qian, Z.: Music Aesthetics Course. Shanghai music publishing house, Shanghai (2002)

A Research on the Correlation Between Tactile Perception Characteristics and Aging-Suitable Design in the Elderly Based on a Testing Tools Development

Delai Men[✉] and Yiya Li

School of Design, South China University of Technology, Guangzhou Higher Education Mega Centre, Panyu District, Guangzhou 510006, People's Republic of China
mendelai@scut.edu.cn

Abstract. "Aging" has become a common phenomenon in many countries. In order to allow the elderly to better integrate into this fast-developing society, and to provide more convenience for the elderly to travel and stay at home, aging-suitable design, which adheres to the design concept of "elderly-oriented" is being popularized. The most obvious feature of aging is five-sensation degeneration, of which tactile degeneration manifests in the decrease of sensitivity to the environment, temperature sensation, and pain. Tactile sensation is the most direct way for people to understand the external environment. The tactile sensation of different materials will affect people's evaluation of products. It has been found in the research articles that the number of experiments for measuring the tactile preference of the elderly for materials from the basic level is small, and most of them lack sufficient data. Therefore, in this study, we explored and developed a Material Tactile Preference Testing Tool for elderly. MTPTT is mainly used to test the elderly's tactile preference for different materials and their perception of material characteristics. The appropriate testing range and time length suitable for the elderly are reasonably set via the pilot studies. By means of random sampling, 42 elderly people aged between 60 and 89 were tested by experiments, questionnaires and in-depth interviews. The results showed that: (1) The elderly are more likely to feel smooth material, which is positively correlated with the evaluation of the material. (2) The environment and the temperature of the materials will greatly affect the evaluation of the materials by the elderly. (3) The elderly are more inclined to choose natural materials. The conclusion of this research and the design idea of material tactile evaluation scale can be widely used in product materials and architectural decoration, which has widespread guiding significance for aging-suitable design practice in different fields.

Keywords: Elderly tactile · Testing tool · Aging-suitable design

© Springer Nature Switzerland AG 2021
C. Stephanidis et al. (Eds.): HCII 2021, LNCS 13096, pp. 277–294, 2021.
https://doi.org/10.1007/978-3-030-90328-2_17

1 Background Introduction

1.1 Aging Trend

With the rapid development of science and technology, the living standard of human beings has been gradually improved and the average life span of human beings has increased. At the same time, the society is showing an "aging" trend. According to the criteria set out in the UN's "Population Aging and Its Socio-economic Consequences" in 1956, when a country or region's population aged 65 or older accounts for more than 7% of the total population, it means that the country or region is aging. So it seems that China has entered an aging society. Especially around 2050, the national aging population will reach its peak [1].

From the perspective of this trend, the market demand for the elderly in the future will be very large, and the negative impact of aging can be converted to a certain extent to promote economic development [2]. Facing the situation of "staying behind" and "empty nest" in the elderly group, how to create a suitable living environment for the elderly and provide products suitable for the elderly has become a problem discussed by many researchers. As a special group, the elderly will be more vulnerable and sensitive due to changes in social impression and status. Not only the psychological characteristics of the elderly are different from those of the young, but also the physiological functions of the elderly are affected due to the degeneration of sensation and perception.

1.2 Aging-Suitable Design

Aging-suitable design has gradually become a research hotspot in academia in recent ten years, which is closely related to the aging trend. Many scholars concluded that aging-suitable design refers to the design of creating a comfortable and friendly living environment for the elderly by comprehensively considering the physical size, living environment, behavior characteristics, psychological characteristics and functional requirements of the elderly [3]. Aging-suitable design is commonly found in the fields of home, daily necessities, travel aids, health care products, etc. It focuses on observing the physiological degeneration and psychological characteristics of the elderly and is gradually applied widely [4]. In our country, with the development of technology, there has been a part of more standardized guidance content for aging-suitable design, especially in the aspects of architecture and home. However, there is still a relative lack of normative and systematic basic design theory. In particular, the research on the perceptual characteristics of the elderly is relatively scarce.

1.3 Perception Characteristics of the Elderly

In terms of physiological characteristics, elderly people often show memory loss, decreased comprehension, and decreased ability to sense the five senses. In addition, changes will basically occur in human size, limb activity range, and flexibility, muscle strength, and multiple sensory perception ability. Moreover, the physiological characteristics of the elderly are basically degraded or weakened along with age [5, 6]. Therefore, the current product design for the elderly will try to make up for the physiological problems encountered by the elderly, and achieve aging-suitable design as much as possible.

Psychologically, the elderly easy to feel lonely, more vulnerable and sensitive, and their preferences are different from those of other groups, which may be related to the development of the country and the technological progress. Then before the relevant design, the preferences, habits and psychological characteristics of the elderly should be considered as much as possible, and the evaluation of different things by the elderly should be explored from the basic perspective, and the data should be combined with the design.

1.4 Characteristics of Tactile Degeneration in the Elderly

Five senses refer to the five sensory organs of human beings, including sight, hearing, smell, taste and tactile [7]. As the most commonly used abilities of human beings, vision and hearing have always been the focus of most researchers, and the research on seeing and hearing of the elderly is more mature. There are related reference materials for the use of colors and shapes, as well as the choice of tones and tunes. However, few people pay attention to the importance of touch in life. Tactile sensation is actually the most direct way for people to understand the external environment. The tactile sensation of different materials can directly affect people's evaluation on products [8].

Relevant studies have shown that, with the growth of age, the human tactile physiological degradation will manifest in the decrease of sensitivity to the environment, temperature sensation, pain, etc. In terms of tactile psychological characteristics, the elderly pay more attention to nostalgia and may not like modern products and materials. They pay more attention to safety and warmth, and hope to use more solid, safe materials. In terms of tactile behavior characteristics, the research mainly focuses on the elderly's feeling when touching, sitting, lying, walking and other behaviors are in contact with materials [9]. Their needs are not very similar to those of young people. The elderly will have higher requirements for the living environment and be more cautious in product selection. It can be seen that when product design is aimed at the elderly, it should also consider the difference between the elderly's tactile perception characteristics and other groups. When it comes to touch, it is often closely connected with materials. To study the characteristics of touch perception of the elderly, it is very important to obtain the touch data of the elderly.

Aging-suitable design also has some applications in tactile sense. For example, due to the rise of tactile threshold of the elderly, designers often consider appropriately increasing tactile stimulation to promote the interaction between the elderly and the environment when designing some buttons and handles; Some designs will refer to the perceptual language and characteristics of the materials themselves, and try to use the materials that the elderly are more satisfied with when producing [10]. Therefore, it is not difficult to find that the premise of aging-suitable design is to have a deep understanding of the basic data of the elderly and to observe the behavior of the elderly in a humanized and meticulous way. Some experiments also found that the elderly can use very few adjectives when describing tactile feelings, which makes it difficult to study tactile preferences [11]. On the whole, people generally pay less attention to the substantive effect brought by tactile sensation, which results in less related research. At the same time, the basic research on tactile preference becomes particularly important. The results of the research will provide certain reference value for the application of aging-suitable design.

The aim of this study is based on the basic experiment developed by independent testing tools, collecting the experimental data related to the subjective preferences of the elderly, analyzing their tactile preferences for different materials and their tactile evaluation of different materials, and obtaining the basic characteristics of their tactile perception of common materials. The objectives are (1) To develop a testing tool for collecting experimental data related to the subjective preferences of the elderly. (2) To analyze tactile evaluation of different materials by the elderly via the qualitative and quantitative analysis methods. (3) To define the basic characteristics of tactile perception of common materials among the elderly. (4) To propose the correlation factors of the aged tactile sensation characteristics and the aging-suitable design. These data can be used as reference for material selection in aging-suitable design of product orientation.

2   Research Methods

The main methods used in this study include literature review, questionnaire, in-depth interview, dark box experiment, and SPSS analysis.

- **Temperature Review:** (1) Multi-dimensional understanding of the physiological and psychological characteristics of the elderly and summarizing the tactile behavior characteristics of the elderly. (2) Further understanding of the relevant research methods and research values.
- **Material Tactile Preference Testing Tool (MTPTT) Development:** The process of basic tactile preference testing is improved, and the content of MTPTT as well as the required materials and tools are further improved.
- **Questionnaire:** The materials frequently contacted by the elderly in life were collected, as well as their perception characteristics of different materials.
- **Interview:** To understand why the elderly prefer a certain material and clarify the preference difference between the elderly and other groups.
- **Dark box experiment:** To avoid the visual impact on the experimental results, the subjects focused their feelings on the touch, and a five-level scoring method was used to obtain objective collection of tactile sensation data.
- **Analysis:** SPSS software was used for analysis. The experimental data were analyzed from multiple perspectives using descriptive analysis and analysis of variance.

3   Primary Studies

This research is mainly divided into several parts, including literature research, pre-experiment, material collection, testing material production, experimental testing, data collection and processing, result analysis, and strategy proposal. The research focuses on quantitative research, and the experimental test is carried out according to the content of the SOP (standard of process) experimental process.

3.1 Preliminary Experiment

Pilot Studies. First of all, through in-depth interviews and observation, the Pilot studies were conducted. Pilot studies were conducted to understand the materials frequently contacted by the elderly and provide reference for collection of materials. On the other hand, it was conducted to find out the missing and filling in the gaps, delete unnecessary questions unrelated to the experimental purpose, adjust the experimental process, and optimize the questionnaire content, so as to facilitate the reasonable setting of the appropriate scope and duration of the test for the elderly.

In the Pilot studies, five subjects were selected for the experimental test, and in-depth interviews were conducted according to the experimental content. Finally, the pre-experiment found that the elderly believed that the roughness of the material had a greater impact on the perception and evaluation of the tactile sensation. When the elderly described their tactile feelings, they had very few words. Therefore, this paper extracts the vocabulary with high repetition rate during the interview, and adjusts the structure of the questionnaire and the test content according to the participants' suggestions on the experiment. The research focuses on the test of the elderly's tactile preference for different materials and the test of the same material's tactile preference for different roughness, in order to explore the factors affecting the elderly's tactile preference and summarize the elderly's perception and evaluation of different materials.

Testing Material Collection and Treatment. Based on the results of pre-experiment and literature research, we found that the common product materials for the elderly were mainly divided into "hard" materials and "soft" materials. "Hard" materials include seven categories: wood, marble, plastic, metal, ceramic, glass and paper. According to pre-experiments, the elderly are known to be most concerned about the roughness of the materials, and the same material is divided into three levels: smooth, smoother and rougher. A total of 28 kinds of test materials of 10×10 cm are collected and manufactured. "Soft" materials are mainly cloth, including cotton, hemp, silk, chemical fiber and leather. Finally, the materials needed for this research are shown in the following table (Table 1).

Table 1. Table of material collection

'Hard' material	Wood	Stone	Plastic	Metal	Ceramic	Glass	Paper
'Soft' material	Cotton		Hemp	Silk	Chemical fibre		Leather

Unified treatment shall be carried out for the collected relevant material samples, including wrapping the edges of the material samples to avoid scratching the subjects.

Testing Box Development. According to the experimental content, we made relevant experimental dark box. The dark box includes two ports: an entrance and an experimenter observation port. In the dark box, the subjects could only feel the surface of the material with hand friction and pressing, and could not see the material, which avoided the visual effects (Fig. 1).

Fig. 1. A picture of material processing and a schematic diagram of the front and back of a black box.

Experimental Data Collection. Based on the preparation of the above experimental materials, this study adopts the method of random sampling, and carries out experimental tests, questionnaires and in-depth interviews on 42 elderly people aged between 60 and 89 who have the ability to take care of themselves and have no obvious tactile symptoms (they mainly live in Guangzhou City, Guangdong Province, Maoming City, Guangdong Province, and Xi'an City, Shaanxi Province, China).

During the experiment, the data were collected by electronic questionnaire and the interviews were recorded. The experiment is mainly divided into three parts (Fig. 2):

1. The first part is the collection of basic information of the elderly.
2. The second part is the experimental test, including the test of the elderly's tactile preference for materials, the test of the elderly's tactile perception characteristics of different materials and the test of the elderly's tactile preference for the same material with different roughness. There are 26 materials in total.
3. The test types are mainly based on Likert scale, multi-choice and ranking. The third part is in-depth interviews to explore the views of the elderly on different materials and market products.

The above picture mainly shows the details of the elderly when doing the experimental test. At the same time, in order to ensure the efficiency of the experiment and avoid the elderly feeling tired and decreased sensory ability caused by too long a time, in this study, the effective time was selected and the experimental time was strictly controlled to ensure that the time was within 15–35 min, so as to avoid the situation that too long a time would result in decreased concentration and insufficient patience among the elderly, which was not conducive to the experiment and the presentation of the results. The specific experimental process design is shown in the following figure (Fig. 3.).

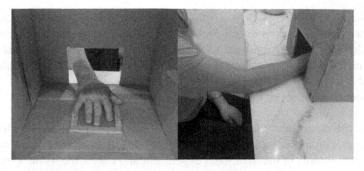

Fig. 2. The figures of older people doing experiments.

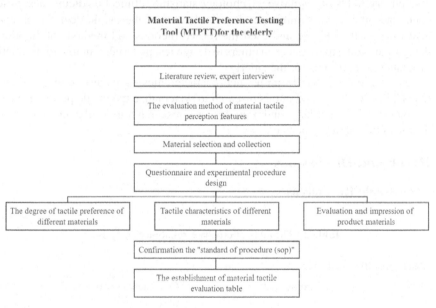

Fig. 3. Design of experimental process

Experimental Data Analysis. After the collection of experimental data, our research will use SPSS analysis tool to analyze the above data. Because SD semantic method and five-level Richter scale are mostly used in this questionnaire, descriptive analysis and variance analysis will be used to analyze the data and discuss whether there is correlation between tactile sensation characteristics and tactile preference of materials.

3.2 Research Significance

This research actually encountered many difficulties. Due to the lack of corresponding research results for the elderly in this field, there were no special methods that could be used for reference in the experiment. Including the choice of materials, is also one of the difficulties in this study. As a special group, the elderly need to consider more factors when conducting the experiment. However, after many group discussions and relevant information collection, a set of own method has been worked out in this research, including material selection and experimental process design. In this research, a set of tools suitable for tactile basis testing (MTPTT) was developed.

The innovative points of this research are mainly reflected in:

1. The synchronous online questionnaire and offline experiment are adopted for the first time, which breaks away from the constraint of carrying a large number of experimental tools in the traditional experiment and makes the whole experimental process more flexible and convenient.
2. Integrated Multiple Disciplines. In this research, based on the literature in the interdisciplinary fields of cognitive psychology, statistics, clinical medicine, design science, and others, we summarized the similarities of the tactile degradation characteristics of the elderly, and used the related theories and methods of emotional design, pleasant experience, and others to design test materials suitable for the tactile evaluation of materials for the elderly.
3. A test tool for the tactile preference characteristics of materials of the elderly (MTPTT) was developed in this research to systematize the tactile preference evaluation table for the elderly, and provide a user research tool for the age-appropriate design of the tactile dimension.

4   Result and Discussions

4.1   The Reliability Analysis

Table 2. The table of cronbach reliability analysis

Cronbach reliability analysis		
Number	Sample size	Cronbach α coefficient
12	42	0.754
Standardized Cronbach α coefficient: 0.755		

Before data analysis, in order to understand the accuracy of the questionnaire and the credibility of the choice of subjects, generally need to conduct reliability analysis, reliability analysis involves the consistency and stability of the questionnaire test results, its purpose is how to control and reduce random error. In this experiment, there were 12 kinds of "hard" materials and "soft" materials in total. In the test of the tactile preference of the elderly for different materials, a five-level Richter scale was used, which was divided into very disliked, disliked, average, liked and liked very much. As shown in the above table, the reliability coefficient value of the experimental data is 0.754, which is greater than 0.7, indicating that the reliability quality of the research data is very good. Detailed data analysis can be performed. The analysis results showed that the items and results of this questionnaire are reliable and effective (Table 2).

4.2 Demographic Analysis

In this experimental investigation, there are 42 subjects. Among them, the total number of male subjects is 15, which is 35.71% of the total number, and the total number of female subjects is 27, which is 64.29% of the total number, with relatively more females. Age distribution, mainly concentrated in the range of 60–74, accounting for more than 70%, they are also able to take care of themselves, in line with the expected survey of the main population. Their pre-retirement occupations were concentrated between teachers and farmers, which was in line with the national conditions of China at that time. Most people took farming as their main occupation, and the national policy strongly encouraged and supported young people at that time to engage in education. As part of the experimental population is concentrated in the university for the elderly, the educational level of the population in this research is higher, and the subjects understand the experimental content faster, which is more conducive to the experiment (Fig. 4).

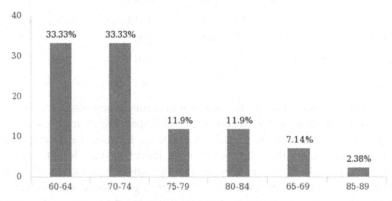

Fig. 4. The figure of age distribution

4.3 Material Score Analysis for Test One

In the first experiment (testing the tactile preference of the elderly for different materials), this paper tests 12 kinds of common products and clothing materials. The test questions are all set with five-level Richter scale, and the data are analyzed descriptively, mainly including minimum value, maximum value, average value, standard deviation and median value. The output results are sorted in descending order of average (see Table 3).

As shown in the above table, the highest average of the twelve materials was glass, followed by metal and ceramic. Among the "soft" materials, silk scored the highest while leather scored the lowest. Based on the average scores of the elderly on the above materials, the tactile preference order of the elderly on common materials was obtained in this paper (the higher the rank was, the higher the preference represented): glass, metal, ceramic, paper, wood, silk, stone, plastic, cotton, hemp, chemical fiber and leather.

Table 3. The descriptive analysis of tactile preference of the elderly for materials (n = 42)

The descriptive analysis

Name	Min	Max	Average	Standard deviation	Median
Glass	2	5	4.262	0.885	4.5
Metal	2	5	4.167	0.762	4
Ceramic	3	5	3.905	0.656	4
Paper	1	5	3.905	0.878	4
Wood	2	5	3.905	0.821	4
Silk	2	5	3.857	0.783	4
Stone	2	5	3.738	0.767	4
Plastic	1	5	3.667	0.902	4
Cotton	2	5	3.667	0.687	4
Hemp	1	5	3.548	0.889	4
Chemical fibre	2	5	3.429	0.77	3.5
Leather	1	5	3.19	1.018	3

Notably, the minimum value of the data for the ceramic group was 3, and the standard deviation was 0.656, showing the lowest degree of dispersion, indicating that although the average score of the ceramic material was not the highest, the overall evaluation of the ceramic material by the subjects was high. Based on the relevant literature and interviews with the elderly, it was believed that this might be related to the "natural" and "healthy" characteristics of ceramics. The elderly significantly preferred this type of material, believing that it was safety and natural to use. For "soft" materials, smooth and soft silk materials are preferred, which may be related to the preference of the elderly for smooth materials.

Based on the above results, we believe that the factors affecting the judgment of the elderly on the tactile preference for materials may be related to the social impression of materials, the perception and evaluation of different elderly on the characteristics of materials, the experimental environment, and the materials selected at that time, and there may be some errors.

4.4 Analysis of Tactile Perception Characteristics of Materials for Test Two

Combined with the literature and the results of pre-experiment, this paper found that it is difficult for the elderly to express their tactile feelings accurately. Therefore, the choice setting mainly uses words with opposite parts of speech for the elderly to choose, for example, the cold and warm feeling consists of two words, cold and warm. As the question type is multiple-choice, the data is analyzed through multiple responses, mainly looking at the response rate and penetration rate of different options, and judging which characteristic selects more subjects, so as to induce the tactile perception characteristics of a certain material.

In this paper, the option with a penetration rate of less than 50% (less than half of people choose this option) is deleted, and the higher the penetration rate, the more people choose this characteristic, the more representative it is. The tactile sensation characteristics of the above 12 materials are summarized in the following Table 4.

Table 4. Tactile characteristics of materials (n = 42)

Name	Tactile perception characteristics		
	Cold/warm	Hard/soft	Smooth/rough
Stone	Cold	Hard	Smooth
Plastic	Warm	Hard	Rough
Ceramic	Cold	Hard	Rough
Metal	Cold	Hard	Smooth
Paper	Warm	Soft	Smooth
Wood	Cold/warm	Hard	Smooth
Hemp	Warm	Soft	Rough
Silk	Warm	Soft	Smooth
Chemical fiber	Warm	Soft	Rough
Leather	Warm	Soft	Smooth
Cotton	Warm	Soft	Rough

Among them, it is noteworthy that a relatively large deviation occurs in describing the tactile sensation characteristics of wood. First, it shows that wood gives the elderly different feelings. Some people think that this kind of material is cold, and some people think that wood gives people a warm and steady psychological feeling. Second, it shows that the material may not be well selected, which leads to certain errors.

In addition, when the penetration rate exceeds 90%, it represents that the subjects have a high degree of unity on the perception characteristics, specifically including:

- The elderly generally believe that hemp has warm and rough perception characteristics;
- It is believed that silk is characterized by softness.
- It is considered that the rough property of chemical fiber is obvious;
- It is believed that metals have smooth characteristics.
- While 100% of the subjects indicated that the glass had smooth perception characteristics.

Based on the results of experiment 1, this paper surmises that glass and metal are favored by most of the subjects and may be related to the roughness of the materials themselves. Therefore, in order to verify this result, this paper conducted a correlation analysis to further explore the correlation between material tactile perception characteristics and material tactile preference.

4.5 Correlation Analysis

Correlation analysis is generally used to study the relationship between quantitative data, whether there is a relationship, the degree of close relationship, etc. In order to explore whether the tactile preference of the elderly for materials is related to the tactile perception characteristics of materials, Pearson correlation analysis was used in this research. Research has shown that the preference of the elderly for some materials is affected by the roughness of the materials, as follows (Table 5):

Table 5. Table of correlation between the degree of preference for cotton materials and perceived characteristics of cotton materials in the elderly

Pearson correlation-standard format		
	Cotton	p
Rough	−0.439**	0.004
Smooth	0.439**	0.004
*$p < 0.05$ **$p < 0.01$		

It shows that the correlation coefficient between the preference degree of the elderly for cotton and the roughness attribute is −0.439, and shows a significant level of 0.01, thus indicating that there is a significant negative correlation between the degree of preference for cotton and the roughness attribute of the elderly. That is to say, when the cotton material is smoother, it is more favored by the elderly, otherwise, it is not favored (Table 6).

Table 6. Table of correlation between the degree of preference for paper materials and perceived characteristics of paper materials in the elderly

Pearson correlation-standard format		
	Paper	p
Rough	−0.342*	0.027
Smooth	0.342*	0.027
*$p < 0.05$ **$p < 0.01$		

The same reason shows that when the paper material is smoother, it is more popular with the elderly. Therefore, when targeting products for the elderly, the packaging of rough paper materials should be reduced as much as possible. According to the interviews, the elderly felt that paper-based products were not durable or strong in use (Table 7).

Similarly, when the metal material is smoother, it is more popular with the elderly. It can be seen that the reason why metal materials are loved by the elderly is closely related to the roughness of the material itself.

Table 7. Table of correlation between the degree of preference for metal materials and perceived characteristics of metal materials in the elderly

Pearson correlation-standard format		
	Metal	p
Rough	−0.346*	0.025
Smooth	0.346*	0.025
*p < 0.05 **p < 0.01*		

More than that, the elderly's tactile preference for ceramic materials is also affected by its roughness, and the smoother the ceramic materials, the more they are favored by the elderly. The data shows a positive correlation of $p < 0.05$. Combined with the previous results, it is confirmed that the higher positive evaluation of ceramic materials is related to the smoothness of the test materials themselves.

In addition, the smoother the stone, the more popular it is among the elderly. Therefore, this research found that the elderly's tactile preference for materials is affected by the roughness of the materials.

Gender is not the Reason for the Difference. Through the analysis of variance, the research also found that elderly people of different genders have no difference in the tactile perception characteristics of different materials, indicating that when choosing different product materials, elderly people of different genders will not differ in their tactile perception of the materials. As a result of aging-suitable design, designers can adopt a more uniform method in material selection and product design.

4.6 Sorting Problem Analysis for Test Three

Experiment 3 continues to analyze the preferences of the elderly for different roughness of the same material. Because "soft" materials are difficult to distinguish in roughness, this paper focuses on the analysis of "hard" materials. Different roughness is mainly reflected in the texture and friction degree of the material, and the rest is consistent. The same material is specifically divided into three different roughness degrees, which are labeled as 1.2.3 in order to distinguish. The higher the score was, the higher the comprehensive ranking was, the more popular it was with the elderly. The calculation formula is as follows:

$$\begin{aligned} Option\ average\ comprehensive\ score\ = \\ (\Sigma\, frequency\ \times\ weight)/number\ of\ people\ filled\ in\ this\ question \end{aligned} \tag{1}$$

The experiment was still conducted in the dark box, and the order was randomly disrupted allowing the elderly to sort the touched three samples according to their personal preferences and touch feelings, so as to minimize the error.

Among the Same Materials, the Smoother is the More Popular. The average composite score of sample 1 was 2.38, the average composite score of sample 2 was 2.11, and the average score of sample 3 was only 1.50. The final result of the experiment shows that among the same material, the smoother the surface, the more popular the elderly.

Based on the above results, this research believes that among the materials commonly used in most products, whether they are the same material or different materials, the elderly are more inclined to choose smooth-touch materials.

From the perspective of consumer behavior, because the uses and prices of different products are different, when consumers choose certain products, their words and deeds may be inconsistent. For example, the elderly may prefer smooth materials, but if faced with crutches, they may choose to give up their favorite materials for functions and buy another product. Combined with aging-suitable design, perhaps designers should keep a balance between product functions and user needs.

4.7 Interview Information Analysis

In order to further explore the tactile preference of the elderly for different materials and the reasons that affect their preference evaluation, this paper summarized and sorted out the interview contents, and analyzed the frequency of keywords mentioned by different subjects many times. Among them, keywords include favorite materials, disliked materials, tactile perception characteristics, etc. For keywords that exceed a certain number of times, this paper sorted out the results in the following table (Tables 8 and 9):

Table 8. Table of reference frequency of positive evaluation

Reference frequency of positive evaluation	
Keywords	Frequency
Metal. stainless steel	11
Ceramic	10
Glass	9
Smooth	15
Soft	9

Table 9. Table of reference frequency of negative evaluation

Reference frequency of negative evaluation	
Keywords	Frequency
Plastic	10
Glass	8
Unsafety	8

First of all, it is not difficult to see that in subjective impression, the elderly have a high comprehensive evaluation of metal, and they think that the metal itself has smooth and solid characteristics. Secondly, the subjects have a good impression of ceramic materials with natural characteristics. As for the positive evaluation of material perception characteristics, the subjects all mentioned the keyword smoothness in a consistent way, which indicates that the elderly will have a higher evaluation of smooth materials.

Then the interview results were compared with the test results in Experiment 1. The results showed that metal, ceramic, and glass were all the materials with high positive evaluation, which indicated that the subjective impression of the subjects was consistent with the tactile sensation evaluation under the premise of excluding vision. However, in the reverse evaluation and frequency, it was found that some subjects did not give high evaluation to glass, which might be related to the fact that the subjects thought the glass material was unsafe, sharp, and hard, which made some subjects have a predetermined impression on glass.

According to the interview, it can be speculated that the roughness of the material accounted for an important part of the factors affecting the preference evaluation of the elderly on different materials. It is possible that the elderly are more inclined to choose the smooth material. Combining the results of Experiment 2 and Experiment 3, we found that the elderly did prefer smooth materials.

However, when using product materials, attention should still be paid to the evaluation of certain materials by the elderly and the properties of the materials themselves, so as to comprehensively apply the materials to an appropriate location. For example, for glass materials, the elderly prefer its smooth properties, but worried that it is easy to break, feel unsafe for it, then the designer should consider how to maintain the properties of the glass itself, to meet the needs of the elderly touch at the same time let the material more solid and hard-working, eliminating the concerns of the elderly.

The Elderly Believe that Good Product Materials Will Bring These Sensations. Combined with the answer of a multiple-choice question in the questionnaire, this research found that the elderly believed that a good product material would bring about the sensation of comfort, safety, easy-to-use, health, warmth, softness and smoothness, and they paid special attention to whether the material itself was safe and healthy. What is different from the contemporary young people is that they reject new materials such as plastics and prefer classic materials such as metals and ceramics. Therefore, most of them pay more attention to the factors such as the material itself, the shape and color of the products. They sometimes choose a product or not because of the material and touch.

4.8 Findings of Result

The above contents are the main findings of this research. In the research based on the physiological and psychological degradation characteristics of the elderly, as well as the haptic-related research, we mainly designed three experiments. The three experiments were logically connected with each other, which provided data support for subsequent result analysis and certain reference value for the tactile dimension thinking of aging-suitable design. The above research has found the following main contents:

The Order of Tactile Preference of the Elderly for Different Materials. The elderly have different tactile preferences for commonly used materials. The specific ranking (the higher the ranking, the higher the preference) is: glass, metal, ceramic, paper, wood, silk, stone, plastic, cotton, hemp, chemical fiber and leather. Among them, the evaluation of glass is polarized, and the touch shows a relatively unified preference. Some elderly people in the interview think that glass is unsafe; The comprehensive evaluation of ceramics is the highest, and the elderly are more inclined to choose pure natural materials.

The Elderly are More Likely to Feel Smooth Material, Which is Positively Correlated with the Evaluation of this Material. Combining the results of Experiment 2 and Experiment 3, this paper finds that the elderly prefer most smooth materials, saying that they feel better and don't like rough materials very much, which shows that although rough materials are commonly used in the market to increase friction, this product does not meet the tactile preference needs of the elderly. For the same kind of materials, the elderly also prefer smooth materials, but for wood, they seem to prefer wood with a little texture and not completely smooth surface.

The Tactile Preference of the Elderly is Different from the Actual Impression. According to the experimental data and interview results, this paper finds that there are some differences between the tactile preference of the elderly and the actual evaluation of the material. For example, glass gives them the highest evaluation on the tactile preference score, but some people say that the properties of glass itself give them unsafe psychological feelings. Although they also like smooth touch, they may not use glass products if they cannot eliminate the unsafe concerns.

5 Conclusion and Recommendations

When Designing the Products of the Elderly, Try to Follow the Table of Material Tactile Evaluation. Combined with the results of this experiment, this paper combs out a material tactile evaluation table for reference when people design for aging. See the following table (Table 10).

When Designing the Products, Try to Use the Materials that the Elderly Like. For the aging-suitable design, the materials mentioned above that meet the tactile preferences of the elderly, such as metal, ceramic, and so on, should be used as much as possible. Only if that tactile preference of the elderly are met will there be an opportunity to increase the frequency of use of the product. Whether it is a common living product such as a water cup, an electric cooker or a certain main button component, materials which are more in line with the tactile preference of the elderly can be used, so that the whole product is more humanized.

Table 10. Material tactile evaluation

Name	Score	Tips
Glass	4.26	Eliminate the established impression of glass and try to adopt new materials
Metal	4.16	The score is higher, and the material can be adopted more frequently
Ceramic	3.90	Highly rated, considering how to reduce weight while maintaining texture
Paper	3.90	The psychological impression of paper is not very good. It is considered that it is not durable and more water-proof and smoother paper materials should be used
Wood	3.90	Wood with texture and slightly higher friction coefficient can be adopted, which can further enhance the security of the elderly
Silk	3.86	Smooth silk seems to be preferred
Stone	3.73	The elderly people's preference for stone depends more on the environment, and the evaluation of stone in summer is slightly higher. Try to use insulation material technology
Plastic	3.67	Some elderly people think that plastics are not environmentally friendly and have a slightly higher evaluation of soft silica gel
Cotton	3.67	The elderly seem don't interested in cotton
Burlap	3.55	Because of the rough property of hemp, its score is not high
Chemical fiber	3.43	Unlike young people, they don't like the material of this imitation woven fabric
Leather	3.19	It is not recommended to use this material in elderly products

Material Properties Also Need to be Taken into Account When Using Smoother Materials. The elderly seem to prefer smooth materials. However, at present, in order to ensure the safety of products used by the elderly, the market often roughens the materials without considering the elderly's tactile preference and actual psychological feelings. This is a need to balance the focus, so designers in product design, need to combine the product's own function to choose materials. If it is necessary for the elderly to travel, support and other appliances, it may be necessary to sacrifice some tactile preference requirements and let the materials serve the products. However, if it is daily necessities, you can consider to use smooth materials, or even combine with the technology of the current new materials, so that the materials can keep or imitate a certain touch, and can ensure the safety.

Acknowledgment. This project, Research on Elderly-Oriented Design Countermeasures based on the Elderly's Characteristics in Sensory Perception, is supported by Humanities and Social Sciences Research Planning Fund Program of the Ministry of Education of China (Grant No. 19YJA760043).

References

1. Qian, Q.: Interaction Design Research of Elderly Home Health Monitoring Product. North China Electric Power University, Beijing, China (2017)
2. Zhenya, Z.: Research on the Barrier-Free Home Design Based on the Physiological and Behavioral Characteristics of the Elderly. Nanjing Forestry University, Nanjing, Jiangsu, China (2016)
3. Zheng, L., Zhang, S.: Research on the product design for the elderly based on physiological decline. Packag. Eng. **148**(10), 188–189, 210 (2007)
4. Ming, Z., Ya-jun, L.: Interactive service design for the aged in China. Hundred Sch. Arts **33**(01), 233–234 (2017)
5. Yangliu, Z.: Research on aging friendly design of products based on user requirements. Fujian Constr. Sci. Technol. (5), 13–15 (2019)
6. Xie, Q.: Research on residential environment for proper aging design based on perceptual perspective. J. Chongqing Technol. Bus. Univ. (Nat. Sci. Ed.) **36**(2), 96–103 (2019)
7. Zheng, C.: Product operation feedback design based on the elderly people's sensory characteristics. J. Mach. Des. **31**(1), 116–119 (2014)
8. Robert, J.-M.: Defining and structuring the dimensions of user experience with interactive products. In: Harris, D. (ed.) EPCE 2014. LNCS (LNAI), vol. 8532, pp. 272–283. Springer, Cham (2014). https://doi.org/10.1007/978-3-319-07515-0_28
9. Jia, H.: Study on the Evaluation of the Tactile Comfort of Old People's Living Space Decoration and Furniture Decoration Materials. Shenyang Jianzhu University, Shenyang, Liaoning, China (2017)
10. Vargiolu, R., Bergheau, J.M., Zahouani, H.: Aging effect on tactile perception: experimental and modelling studies. Wear **332**(333), 715–724 (2015)
11. Dagman, J., Karlsson, M., Wikström, L.: Investigating the haptic aspects of verbalised product experiences. Int. J. Des. **4**(3),15–27 (2010)

Use of a Video Game with Tangible Interfaces to Work Emotions in Children with Autism

J. Andrés Sandoval-Bringas(✉) ⓘ, Mónica A. Carreño-León ⓘ,
Teresita Álvarez-Robles ⓘ, Israel Durán-Encinas ⓘ, Alejandro Leyva-Carrillo,
and Italia Estrada-Cota

Universidad Autónoma de Baja California Sur, La Paz, B.C.S, México
{sandoval,mcarreno,tj.alvarez,iduran,aleyva,iestrada}@uabcs.mx

Abstract. Autism spectrum disorders (ASD) are characterized by difficulties in recognizing, identifying and understanding what others are feeling. Attention to people with disabilities has been a topic of interest for different areas of science and technology. The area of special education needs technological tools that allow teaching in an innovative way, helping to improve the education of its students according to their specific needs. This paper presents the design and development of a video game with tangible elements to support the teaching and learning process of emotional and social competencies of children with autism spectrum disorders. The proposal was first evaluated by teachers from the special education area, and in a second moment an educational intervention was designed for a child diagnosed as autistic using the developed video game. In both cases, the results obtained were favorable, confirming that the incorporation of technological means to the teaching of emotional and social competences supposes a support for children with autism spectrum disorders.

Keywords: Tangible UI · Video Games · Autism · Emotions

1 Introduction

Emotions play a very relevant role in our day-to-day life, as they help us to face situations that occur on a daily basis. However, children with Autism Spectrum Disorder (ASD) have difficulty recognizing, identifying and understanding what others are feeling. That is, autistic children present a great deficit in the perception of emotions, which constitutes an essential element to contribute to the affective and emotional development of the subject.

1.1 Emotions and Autism

According to Bisquerra [1], an emotion is a complex state of the organism characterized by an excitement or disturbance that predisposes to action.

Emotions can be classified as primary or secondary. Primary emotions would be linked to the maturation of the neural mechanisms and structures that are the bases

© Springer Nature Switzerland AG 2021
C. Stephanidis et al. (Eds.): HCII 2021, LNCS 13096, pp. 295–305, 2021.
https://doi.org/10.1007/978-3-030-90328-2_18

of the emotional process and that, throughout development, facilitate the formation of patterns of evaluation and response to emotions. Examples of them are joy, sadness and surprise. On the other hand, secondary emotions are the product of socialization and the development of cognitive abilities, such as guilt, shame, pride and jealousy. This type of emotions is influenced by the culture in which the person develops and their own personal history [2].

Emotional competencies must be accepted and understood as a main factor for life, essential to achieve a good integral development of the personality. These skills have a higher degree of difficulty than other skills.

Emotions are complex and are present in all individuals. These begin to appear in the newborn's first contacts with his parents, who will express his satisfaction or displeasure through his emotions. Children's understanding of emotions is closely related to their own experiences lived in their closest environment. According to [3] carrying out emotional education is a great advance to achieve greater personal and social development, which implies an improvement in the quality of life, mainly for children with autism.

Autism is a behaviorally defined disorder, but it is due to a variety of known and unknown disorders of biologically conditioned brain functions. The word autism comes from the Greek auto-de autos, "own, oneself". It is defined globally, as a constant and profound developmental disturbance that affects communication, imagination, programming and emotional reciprocity. Its stable and lasting clinical manifestations that are classically re-grouped in the so-called "Wing's triad" are difficulties in social interaction, in verbal and non-verbal communication and a restricted pattern of interests or behaviors.

People with autism have difficulties to perceive, recognize and understand emotions, as well as to understand the behavior of others [4]. Therefore, these difficulties negatively affect their capacities for social recognition. These skills need to be taught in people with autism to improve basic social skills and other skills not taught, and to understand emotions and beliefs [5].

Children with autism think and learn primarily visually. This aspect of their condition can be used to help them communicate, express themselves, and verbalize their feelings [6]. Visual communication is done mainly through images, drawings and colors.

1.2 Video Games and Tangible User Interfaces

The use of computer games and games in general for educational purposes offers a variety of presentations of knowledge and creates opportunities to apply them within a virtual world, which supports and facilitates the learning process [7].

According to the JISC (Joint Information Systems Committee), game-based learning refers to the different types of software applications that games use for learning or teaching [8].

In [9] seven characteristics are mentioned that make videogames a more attractive and effective learning medium:

1. They allow the exercise of fantasy, without limitations of space, time or danger.
2. They facilitate access to "other worlds" and the exchange of one another through graphics, clearly contrasting with conventional and static classrooms.

3. They favor instant replay in a safe environment.
4. They allow mastery of skills. Although difficult, players can repeat the actions, until they master them, gaining a sense of control.
5. They facilitate interrelation with other people.
6. There is a clarity of objectives. The player knows that there are clear and concrete tasks to achieve the objectives, which provides a high level of motivation.
7. It favors an increase in attention and self-control favoring individual success.

Some researchers suggest that through the use of virtual environments, users can practice skills safely, avoiding the consequences of the real world that can become dangerous, mainly for users with special needs. In [10] it is mentioned that Information and Communication Technologies (ICT) can decisively improve the quality of life of people with disabilities, in addition to being one of the few options to access the school curriculum, helping to communication and facilitating social and labor integration. For people with autism, the use of ICT can be considered a powerful tool to enhance and improve communication [11].

Tangible user interfaces (TUI) are user interfaces in which people interact with digital information through physical environments. Various studies show that tangible interfaces are useful because they promote active participation, which helps in the learning process. These interfaces do not intimidate the inexperienced user and encourage exploratory, expressive and experimental activities.

TUIs have been shown to enhance learning for children by enriching their experience, play and development [12, 13].

The use of tangible interaction in educational settings has been gaining importance, and has been the focus of study through different investigations [14–20].

Some authors address the need for TUIs for people with physical or cognitive disabilities [21, 22], other authors address them as necessary for older adults [23], early childhood [12, 24–26], in other words, these interfaces can have great potential for all people, which is why some authors also consider their use in general, independent of physical, cognitive and age capacities, among others, simply because of their practicality and improvement in the completion of certain tasks [27, 28].

This research presents the design of an experimental video game for children with autism based on the use of tangible elements, taking advantage of the child's psychomotor development process, allowing him to play with the computer just as he plays with the rest of his non-technological toys.

2 Methodology

For the construction of the video game, the life cycle model called evolutionary prototype was adopted. The evolutionary prototype is based on the idea of developing an initial implementation by exposing it to user comments and refining it through the different versions until a suitable system is developed, allowing a rapid response to changes that may arise.

During the design phase of the video game, working meetings were held with experts in the area of special education, as well as basic education teachers. Specific objectives were defined: to acquire knowledge of their own emotions and to identify the emotions of others and the reasons for them. The meetings also analyzed the strategies for learning emotions, as well as the fundamental requirements and characteristics of the elements of the video game.

On the other hand, taking into consideration the recommendations made by various authors [29, 30], regarding the characteristics that technological tools intended for children with autism should have, the following were defined:

- Configurable, that is, it adapts to the characteristics of the autistic child, their abilities and needs, their learning and processing pace, their interests, as well as their level of development.
- Friendly interface, that uses visual and auditory elements, in order to motivate its use.
- Gamified, which incorporates reinforcing elements for success and error, as well as levels of difficulty.

Figure 1 shows the schematic of the video game components: 1) The tangible user interface, 2) The RFID reader board and 3) The software that allows interaction with the RFID reader board and the tangible user interface.

2.1 Tangible User Interface

Historically, children have played with physical objects to learn a variety of skills, a tangible interface (TUI), therefore it would seem like a natural way for them.

TUIs were designed and created for each of the emotions considered by the experts to be incorporated into the video game. Figure 2 shows some of the images used. An RFID card associated with the emotion is inserted on the back of the object, which allows communication with the RFID reader board.

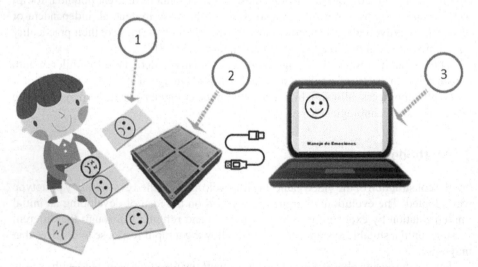

Fig. 1. Scheme of the video game components with tangible elements.

In [31] it is mentioned that people with autism may have difficulties in associating a meaning with a symbol and in recognizing real-world objects in a drawing. For this reason, the use of images with different levels of abstraction (real photographs, caricatured images and abstract representations) has been considered, to adapt to the particular needs that each user may present.

2.2 RFID Reader Board

RFID (Radio Frequency Identification) technology allows the use of real objects to interact with the computer, reducing the symbolic load of the interface, simplifying it by making it more natural and improving accessibility. Unlike other tags, RFID tags are immersed in objects without altering their attributes or interfering with user perception.

In Fig. 3 the design of the container that groups the electronic components used for the operation of the RFID reader board is physically observed.

Fig. 2. Examples of images used as TUI in the video game with tangible elements.

Fig. 3. Physical design of the electronic components container of the RFID reader board.

The basic components that were used for the construction of the RFID reader board are described below:

1) Arduino Mega Board. A Mega Arduino board was used, which consists of an electronic board that is based on an ATmega2560 microcontroller. It has 54 digital pins that function as input/output, 16 analog inputs, a 16 MHz oscillator crystal, a USB connection, a reset button and an input for the board power [32].

2) RFID-RC522 Chip Reader. Four chip readers were used. RFID readers are used mainly in identification systems. Its working principle is to pass a TAG near the RFID reader, and the TAG has the ability to send information to the reader. The information can be from a simple code or a whole package of information stored in the memory of the TAG.

2.3 Software

The software that allows the interaction of the TUI with the RFID reader board. Figure 4 shows the main interface of the video game, where the main options are shown: library, card registration and emotion management. The special education teacher is the user in charge of configuring the video game to be used as part of the autistic child's sessions.

1. The Library option, through this option, the set of previously registered tangible objects are preserved, which are available to be used in any session.
2. The TUI Registration option allows adding tangible objects that are recognized by the video game. An example of the interface that allows card registration can be seen in Fig. 5. The video game allows the registration of real, caricatured and abstract images, this in order to adapt to the needs and characteristics of the end user, and to the requirements that the expert considers convenient for the intervention with the autistic child.

3. The option that allows starting the child's interaction with the video game is: Emotions management, which can be seen in the main menu of Fig. 4. In order for the child to become familiar with the video game, it can be used in two modes: Test mode and Play mode.

Fig. 4. Initial video game interface with tangible user interfaces.

1) Test Mode. This mode allows you to recognize each of the emotions represented in the TUIs. The user can bring each of the TUIs to the RFID reader board, and once it identifies the code of the RFID card, it emits the corresponding audio through the loudspeaker at the same time that it displays the image on the computer screen. In this mode, no points are accumulated.

2) Play Mode. This mode allows the user to demonstrate that they know each of the emotions selected for the work session. The user is randomly requested to bring the corresponding TUI to the RFID reader board. During the game, a feedback is included, in order for the user to know if their selection was correct or incorrect. If the choice was incorrect, the user is asked to try again. In case it is correct, a point is accumulated for each hit.

Fig. 5. Interface to register tangible objects recognized by the video game.

3   Results and Conclusions

Two case studies made it possible to know the level of acceptance of the developed video game. The proposal was first evaluated by teachers from the special education area, and in a second moment an educational intervention was designed for a child diagnosed as autistic using the developed video game.

In the first case study, the video game was presented to four teachers from the special education area who reviewed each aspect of the video game. Additionally, they were given a questionnaire that was used to quantify the evaluation of the video game. The questions were based on functionality criteria and whose objective was to know if the tool met the requirements established by the experts. The results obtained were favorable, the experts agree that the tool meets the requirements, and that its use for autistic children is feasible.

For the second case study, in order to know the level of acceptance of the video game with tangible elements, an educational intervention was designed with activities related to the stimulation of emotional recognition and emotional comprehension skills. The tests were carried out in a preschool educational institution, where we worked with a 5-year-old autistic child diagnosed with autism, who presents social isolation and absence of language.

During the sessions that were carried out in which the child did not present problems when using the video game, on the contrary, he showed considerable interest. The results obtained in the evaluation of the video game with the user is considered favorable. Figure 6 shows a work session with the child interacting with the video game with tangible interfaces.

Finally, the autistic child, despite the difficulties he showed before the intervention process, has improved his ability to overcome tasks on emotional competencies.

Fig. 6. Video game test session with tangible interfaces.

The video game consists of tasks structured in levels, from low to high complexity, both for teaching the recognition of basic and complex emotions, and for teaching the prediction of people's actions based on their true beliefs or false. The results obtained confirm that the incorporation of technological means to the teaching of emotional and social competences supposes a support for students with autism spectrum disorders (ASD).

References

1. Bisquerra, R.: Educación emocional y bienestar. Educación emocional y en valores. Wolters Kluwer, Madrid, España (2011)
2. Fernández-Abascal, E., Rodríguez, B., Sánchez, M., Díaz, M., Sánchez, F.: Psicología de la emoción. Editorial Universitaria Ramón Areces (2010)
3. Martínez, J., Ruiz, S.: Utilización de las TIC's para desarrollar las habilidades emocionales en alumnado con TEA desde la colaboración escuela-familia-universidad: una experiencia en un aula abierta específica. Rev. DIM: Didáctica Innov. y Multimedia **3**, 1–16 (2015)
4. Lozano Martínez, J., Alcaraz García, S.: Personas con trastorno del espectro autista: Acceso a la comprensión de emociones a través de las TIC. Rev. ética net **10**, 1–17 (2011)
5. Lozano Martínez, J., Alcaraz García, S.: Enseñar emociones para beneficiar las habilidades sociales de alumnado con trastornos del espectro autista. Educatio siglo XXI: Rev. de la facultad de educación **28**(2), 261–288 (2010)
6. Terrazas Acedo, M., Sánchez Herrera, S.: Las TIC como herramienta de apoyo para personas con Trastorno del Espectro Autista (TEA). Rev. Int. Educ. inclusiva **9**(2), 102–136 (2016)
7. Pivec, M., Dziabenko, O., Schinnerl, L.: Aspects of game-based learning. In: 3rd International Conference on Knowledge Management, Graz, Austria (2003)

8. Joint Information System Committee: (2020). http://www.jisc.ac.uk/. [En línea]. http://www.jisc.ac.uk/
9. Gifford, B.R.: The learning society: Serious play. Chronicle of Higher Education, vol. 7, no. 7 (1991)
10. Tortosa, N.: Tecnologías de ayuda en personas con trastornos del espectro autista: guía para docentes, Murcia, España: CPR (2004).
11. Tecno-autismo, «Tecno-autismo. [En línea]. https://autismoytecnologia.webnode.es/investigando-/marco-teorico-autismo-y-nuevas-tecnologias/. (Último acceso: 18 noviembre 2020
12. Xie, L., Antle, A., Motamedi, N.: Are tangibles more fun? Comparing children´s enjoyment and engagement using physical, graphical and tangible user interfaces. In: 2nd International Conference on Tangible and Embedded Interaction, Bonn, Germany (2008)
13. Zaman, B., Abeele, V.: How to measure the likeability of tangible interaction with preschoolers, de CHI Nederland (2007)
14. O'Malley, C.: Literature Review in Learning with Tangible Technologies, NESTA Futurelab (2004)
15. Price, S.: A representation approach to conceptualizing tangible learning environments. In: TEI 2008, Bonn, Alemania (2008)
16. Marshall, P.: Do tangible interfaces enhance learning? In: TEI 2007, Baton Rouge, LA, USA (2007)
17. Manches, A., O'Malley, C., Benford, S.: The role of physical representations in solving number problems: a comparison of young children's use of physical and virtual materials. Comput. Educ. **54**, 622–640 (2009)
18. Zufferey, G., Jermann, P.L.A., Dillenbourg, P.: TinkerSheets: Using Paper Forms to Control and Visualize Tangible Simulations, de Third (2009)
19. Guisen, A., Baldasarri, S., Sanz, C., Marco, J., De Giusti, A., Cerezo, E.: Herramienta de apoyo basada en Interacción Tangible para el desarrollo de competencias comunicacionales en usuarios de CAA. In: VI Congreso Iberoamericano de Tecnologías de Apoyo a la Discapacidad (IBERDISCAP 2011), Palma de Mallorca, España (2011)
20. Sanz, C., Baldassarri, S., Guisen, A., Marco, J., Cerezo, E., De Giusti, A.: ACoTI: herramienta de interacción tangible para el desarrollo de competencias comunicacionales en usuarios de comunicación alternativa. Primeros resultados de su evaluación. In: VII Congreso de Tecnología en Educación y Educación en Tecnología. TE&ET, Buenos Aires, Argentina (2012)
21. Muro Haro, B.P., Santana Mancilla, P.C., García Ruiz, M.A.: Uso de interfaces tangibles en la enseñanza de lectura a niños con síndrome de Down. In: El hombre y la máquina, no. 39, pp. 19–25 (2012)
22. Avila-Soto, M., Valderrama-Bahamóndez, E., Schmidt, A.: TanMath: a tangible math application to support children with visual impairment to learn basic arithmetic. In: 10th International Conference on Pervasive Technologies Related to Assistive Environmentes (2017)
23. Galiev, R., Rupprecht, D., Bomsdorf, B.: Towards tangible and distributed UI for cognitively impaired people. In: Antona, M., Stephanidis, C. (eds.) UAHCI 2017. LNCS, vol. 10278, pp. 283–300. Springer, Cham (2017). https://doi.org/10.1007/978-3-319-58703-5_21
24. Gonzalez Gonzalez, C.S.: Revisión de la literatura sobre interfaces naturales para el aprendizaje en la etapa infantil (2017)
25. Devi, S., Deb, S.: Augmenting non-verbal communication using a tangible user interface. In: Satapathy, S., Bhateja, V., Das, S. (eds.) Smart Computing and Informatics: Proceedings of the First International Conference on SCI 2016, vol. 1, pp. 613–620. Springer, Singapore (2018). https://doi.org/10.1007/978-981-10-5544-7_60
26. Bouabid, A., Lepreux, S., Kolski, C.: Design and evaluation of distributed user interfaces between tangible tabletops. Univ. Access Inf. Soc. **18**(4), 801–819 (2017). https://doi.org/10.1007/s10209-017-0602-4

27. De Raffaele, C., Serengul, S., Orhan, G.: Explaining multi-threaded task scheduling using tangible user interfaces in higuer educational contexts. In: Global Engineering Education Conference (2017)
28. Dimitra, A., Ras, E.: A questionnaire-based case study on feedback by a tangible interface. In: Proceedings of the 2017 ACM Workshop on Intelligent Interfaces for Ubiquitous and Smart Learning (2017)
29. Hardy, C., Ogden, J., Newman, J., Cooper, S.: Autism and ICT. Routledge (2016). https://doi.org/10.4324/9781315069609
30. Martínez, J.L., Pagán, F.J.B., García, S.A., Márquez, M.C.C.: Las tecnologías de la información y comunicación (TIC) en el proceso de enseñanza y aprendizaje del alumnado con trastorno del espectro autista (TEA), Revista Fuentes, no. 14, pp. 193–208 (2014)
31. American Speech-Language-Hearing Association: Roles and responsibilities of speech-language pathologists with respect to alternative communication: position statement. ASHA Supplement, no. 25 (2005)
32. Arduino, Getting Started with Arduino MEGA2560 (2017). https://www.arduino.cc/en/Guide/ArduinoMega2560

Research on the Design of Smart Bracelets for the Elderly Based on Maslow's Hierarchy of Needs

Tianyu Shi and Wei Yu[✉]

School of Art Design and Media, East China University of Science and Technology, Xuhui District, No. 130, Meilong Road, Shanghai, People's Republic of China

Abstract. Under the dual trend of population aging and product intelligence, intelligent aging will become an important exploration direction in the future. This paper takes smart bracelets for the elderly as the research object, analyzes the shortcomings of existing products, and researches smart bracelet design strategies that truly meet the needs of the elderly and enhance user experience. This study is based on Maslow's hierarchy of needs theory and a methodological model of the hierarchy of needs mapping design strategy. Starting from the physiological and psychological characteristics of the elderly, we explore the multi-level needs and opportunity points of the elderly, and then study the design strategies of smart bracelets that take into account the needs of the elderly at all levels. The results of this paper provide strategic references for developing smart bracelets for the elderly that enhance user experience, and also provide new ideas for more smart product designs for the elderly.

Keywords: Elderly people · Smart bracelet · Maslow's hierarchy of needs · Design strategy · User experience

1 Introduction

Since mankind entered the 21st century, population aging has become an important social issue that countries around the world need to face together. According to the forecast of the United Nations, the global population of people aged 60 and above will reach 3.1 billion by 2030. From 2000 to 2050, the number of people aged 80 and above in the total global population is expected to increase from 70 million to 401 million respectively [1]. This shows that the global population aging problem will continue to intensify in the future. At the same time, the development of global information technology and intelligence has reached new heights. From 2010 to the present, smart hardware products represented by smart phones and smart bracelets have rapidly entered the consumer market. Smart hardware is a new type of intelligent terminal products and services based on platform-based underlying software and hardware, characterized by a new generation of information technology such as intelligent sensing and interconnection, human-computer interaction, new display and big data processing, and new design, new

© Springer Nature Switzerland AG 2021
C. Stephanidis et al. (Eds.): HCII 2021, LNCS 13096, pp. 306–317, 2021.
https://doi.org/10.1007/978-3-030-90328-2_19

materials and new process hardware. As the smart hardware industry continues to mature, different types of smart hardware will penetrate into all aspects of people's lives.

Under the dual trend of population aging and product intelligence, intelligent aging will become an important exploration direction in the future. As a kind of intelligent product emerging in recent years, smart bracelet has the characteristics of portability and immediacy, which can serve the elderly well and improve their lives. However, at present, smart bracelets are not yet widely accepted by the elderly, and the reason is that these products do not take into account the real needs of the elderly. Therefore, based on Maslow's hierarchy of needs theory, this paper will study the needs of the elderly at different levels and use them to guide the design strategy of smart bracelets for the elderly. Finally, the smart bracelet will become a new intelligent terminal product that is convenient, comfortable and humanized for the elderly.

2   The Current Situation of Smart Bracelets for the Elderly

Smart bracelet is a kind of wearable smart hardware, as shown in Fig. 1. Through the smart bracelet, users can record real-time data of the human body such as exercise, sleep and heart rate in daily life, and synchronize these data with cell phones, tablets and other terminal devices. Smart bracelets for the elderly are specially designed for the elderly to suit the living habits of the elderly.

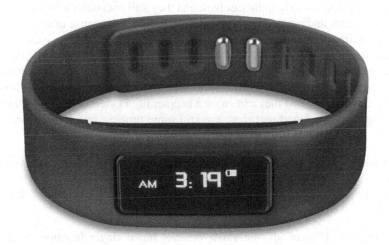

Fig. 1. Smart bracelets

2.1   Existing Functions of Smart Bracelets for the Elderly

Positioning Function. The GPS global positioning system is used to record the activity route of the elderly. Children can check the location of the elderly at any time through the APP bound to the bracelet on their smartphones. If the elderly accidentally get lost, wander off or have an accident, the children can locate the location of the elderly in time.

Help Function. There is an SOS button on the smart bracelet for seniors with a one-touch help function. If an elderly person has an accident, they can press and hold the button for 2 to 3 s and the bracelet will sound an alarm. At the same time, the bracelet will automatically notify the pre-set emergency helper.

Daily Health Monitoring Function. The smart bracelet is equipped with professional sensing devices that can not only monitor heart rate and measure blood pressure at any time, but also grasp the movement and sleep of the elderly. These data can be transmitted to the corresponding hospitals or the children of the elderly, which can track and understand the health status of the elderly.

Reminder Function. Smart bracelets can remind seniors to take their medication, exercise and other things by vibrating or making a sound.

2.2 Problems with Smart Bracelets for the Elderly

With the arrival of the Internet and the Internet of Things, smart devices are becoming more and more popular as they gain public recognition. Many traditional forms have become more efficient through online technology. People can make appointments, consult online, view examination reports, etc. through cell phones and computers. However, for the elderly, the operation is still relatively complicated. They don't know how to use these high-tech devices to help themselves, and they still encounter a lot of problems in medical treatment, and many elderly people lose their lives because of sudden illnesses that don't get timely treatment. The elderly smart bracelet is to change such a situation, through the mobile interconnection of smart devices, so that the children of the elderly, hospitals, communities and other common linkage to better help and care for the elderly. Not only that, the smart bracelet can also provide more functions to meet the high-level needs of the elderly, so that they can enjoy a happier life in their old age. However, after our investigation, we found that there are still some problems with the existing smart bracelets.

Low Quantity. At present, most of the smart bracelets on the market are for young people, and there are very few smart bracelets designed for the physiology and psychology of the elderly. The market of smart bracelets for the elderly is in a state of demand but little quantity.

Single Function. First of all, the smart bracelet has a single function. Some smart bracelets for the elderly only have GPS positioning function, or only have health detection function. Secondly, the level of demand satisfied by the function of smart bracelet is single. Most of the smart bracelets for the elderly only go to meet the physiological and security needs of the elderly, while ignoring the higher level of psychological needs of the elderly.

Poor Wearing Experience. The skin, muscles, bones and other physiological tissues of the elderly are more different from those of young people. The size, material and wearing style of some smart bracelets for the elderly do not match the elderly, making them uncomfortable to wear.

Poor Interaction Experience. The vast majority of smart bracelets are aimed at younger consumer groups. The product design is too technological, and the operation of the product is very complicated to use. Most of the elderly people are difficult to operate and use due to their weak learning and cognitive abilities.

3   The Theory and Method of Research

3.1   Maslow's Hierarchy of Needs

Abraham Maslow, an American social psychologist, introduced the Hierarchy of Needs theory in his *Theory of Human Motivation*. Maslow's Hierarchy of Needs theory classifies human needs from low to high: physiological needs, security needs, social needs, respect needs, and self-actualization needs, as shown in Fig. 2. Among them, physiological needs and security needs are the lower level needs, social needs and respect needs are the higher level needs, and self-actualization needs are the highest level needs. Needs are dynamic, and they are in a continuous process of change. Behavior is governed by the most urgent needs that are constantly changing. When a person's lower level needs are satisfied, they will rise to higher level needs. If a person's basic physiological needs are satisfied, the higher level needs will take the lead and act as the main motivation for the person's behavior. There are often several needs in the same period. However, there is always one dominant need in each period [2].

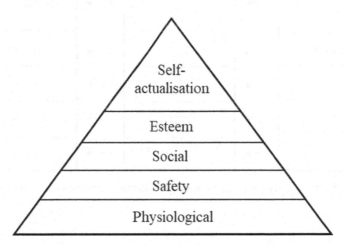

Fig. 2. Maslow's hierarchy of needs (Author's own drawing)

3.2   Modeling Methods Based on Theory

In traditional product design research, the research team would research and collect the needs of the target users and then filter them to arrive at the core needs of the users. However, in this process, the research team does not classify the users' needs in a hierarchical manner, resulting in the absence of some of the needs and the redundancy of some of the needs in the screening process. This is reflected in the fact that some products only satisfy users' low-level needs such as physiological needs and neglect high-level needs such as social and respect, or some products give too much consideration to high-level needs and neglect basic low-level needs. Therefore, this paper will build a methodological model of need hierarchy mapping design strategy based on the study of Maslow's hierarchy of needs theory, as shown in Fig. 3. In product design research, the research team classifies user needs by hierarchy after user research, and also maintains the hierarchy when further exploring opportunity points, and then gets the final design strategy by opportunity points. Such a research approach allows users' needs at each level to be mapped one by one to the final design strategy. These design strategies can cover the user's needs at each level, satisfying both the user's current dominant needs and the user's needs at other levels to further enhance the user's experience. Applying this method to the design of smart bracelets for the elderly will help remedy the existing defects of smart bracelets for the elderly mentioned above, and lead to more reasonable design strategies.

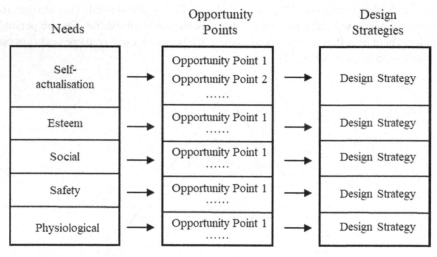

Fig. 3. Approach to requirements mapping strategy (Author's own drawing)

4   The Process of Research

4.1   User Research

In this phase, we researched the elderly population, studied the current situation of the elderly, collected their needs and classified them. The user research is conducted by both literature review as well as user interviews. First, this study reviewed a large amount of literature on the study of the elderly. The relevant knowledge points collected were studied, summarized and categorized as an important theoretical basis for the study. Then, face-to-face interviews were conducted by inviting older adults from three different communities, as shown in Fig. 4. A total of 50 older adults of different age groups were invited, namely 15 older adults aged 60–65, 15 older adults aged 66–70, 10 older adults aged 71–75, and 10 older adults aged 76–80. Finally, experts were invited to summarize and classify the current situation and needs of the elderly obtained from the research according to Maslow's hierarchy of needs.

Fig. 4. User interviews

Physiological Needs. Physiological needs are the most primitive and basic needs of people. Physiological needs include food, water, shelter, sleep, oxygen and sex, which is what we call food, clothing, shelter and transportation.

For the elderly, their physiological functions are beginning to decline. Their sensory abilities such as vision, hearing and touch are declining, their skin, muscles and bones are aging, and their cognitive abilities such as attention, imagination, memory and learning are declining to varying degrees. The decline of these physiological functions largely affects the clothing, food, housing and transportation of the elderly.

Therefore, in today's abundant material life, the elderly hope that the products and services in their life can adapt to or compensate for their physiological decline, so as to meet their most basic needs.

Security Needs. Safety needs include physical safety and psychological safety. Safety needs specifically refer to protection from external objects, protection from disease, and protection from psychological fear and anxiety.

For the elderly, aging reduces their immune system and mobility, and they are at higher risk of illness, injury or accident. In addition, some empty nesters live alone, and the use of fire and electricity, accidental diseases, etc. make their life safety situation worrying. In the COVID-19, the elderly are at high risk for infectious diseases due to their weakened immune function, poor resistance and the presence of chronic underlying diseases. Older people living alone away from their children after retirement, as well as fear of disease, are prone to tension and anxiety. Severe cases even have pessimism, depression, despair and other bad emotions.

Therefore, in real life, especially during epidemics and other emergencies, the physical and psychological safety of the elderly are not well met.

Social Needs. Social needs are also called belonging and love needs. It refers to the desire to establish and maintain an emotional relationship with others, to have a place in a group, and to give and receive love.

Social needs are difficult to meet on a daily basis. Nowadays, elderly people are often far away from their children and it is difficult for them to receive communication and care from their children. Some elderly people, especially those who are widowed and living alone, generally lack spiritual solace. They feel unprecedented loneliness and isolation, accompanied by complex emotions such as longing, self-pity and helplessness.

Therefore, the elderly need the care of their children, family members and society. They do not want to be isolated from life. They are eager to love and be loved, and to build harmonious and warm interpersonal relationships.

Esteem Needs. The need for respect includes two aspects: self-esteem; and respect from others.

For older people, respect is very important. However, in the impressions and perceptions of young people, older people represent senility, vulnerability, miserliness and are classified as "superfluous". This in effect constitutes ageism. Ageism is the stereotyping of older people as physically or socially weak, and the making of negative value judgments about older people. This can result in unfair treatment at the level of resource allocation and social participation. This is a great injustice and disrespect to older people.

However, in reality, as the literacy and cognitive adaptability of the elderly increase, more and more of them are trying to accept new things such as smart products to improve the quality of life in their old age. They gradually change from price-sensitive people to quality-sensitive people. The demand of the elderly for a healthy life is not only satisfied with extending their life span, but they start to change their lifestyle to meet their health needs. This is a very important point of transformation.

Therefore, society needs to be more open and inclusive of older people's self-esteem. We need to discard ageism and give respect to the elderly. At the same time, we should not let the elderly become "outsiders" to the development of the times and technology.

Self-actualization Needs. Self-actualization is the tendency of a person to make their potential come true, to become the most unique kind of individual they can be, to make themselves the kind of person they want to be.

For the elderly, even though they are vulnerable, they still have value and have the right to pursue their values. Nowadays, some seniors are shifting from family-centered to self-centered, more independent and more self-centered. At the same time, seniors are beginning to pursue goals and ideals that were not realized when they were younger.

Therefore, we need to open the channel for the elderly so that they can realize themselves and blossom in the last stage of their lives.

Through the analysis of the current situation and needs of the elderly, we further summarize the needs of the elderly according to the hierarchy, as shown in Fig. 5.

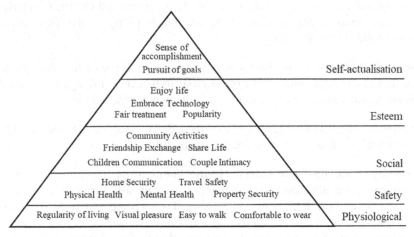

Fig. 5. Hierarchy of needs of the elderly (Author's own drawing)

4.2 Opportunity Points

After categorizing the needs of the elderly in layers, the needs of each layer further triggered the thinking of opportunity points. An opportunity point is the breakthrough between the problem and the solution. The process of uncovering opportunity points revolves around user needs, product pain points, and the creativity of the researchers. This study gets precise opportunity points without destroying the hierarchy of needs, which can satisfy both the expected needs and the potential needs of users.

Opportunity Points Based on Physiological Needs. Sleeping as well as eating regularly can make seniors healthier. Therefore, the elderly can be reminded by the outside world to maintain a regular rhythm of life.

Products for the elderly should not be old-fashioned in style and lacking in aesthetics, but should be as new, fashionable and aesthetically pleasing as products for the young. Beauty is the most basic visual pursuit.

Wearable products need to take into account the body size, skin, muscles, bones and other acceptable range of the elderly. The bracelet should maximize the convenience as well as comfort for the elderly to wear.

Opportunity Points Based on Security Needs. The product allows the physical condition of the elderly to be presented in real time in a visual format. This allows children or hospitals to keep track of the elderly's physical condition and safeguard their health. This can also make the elderly feel at ease.

The product has alarm and positioning functions to ensure the safety of the elderly out.

The time reminder function not only allows the elderly who need to take medicine regularly to miss the time of taking medicine, but also reminds the elderly of what they are doing or will do. Especially when it comes to home fire and electricity safety, it is necessary to remind the elderly to cut off the fire and electricity in time. This can ensure the safety of the elderly at home.

Opportunity Points Based on Social Needs. Young people socialize through smart phones, then older people can socialize through smart bracelets. Taking photos, sunshine friends circle and voice chat can also be the social way for the elderly.

Children's social circle should not block the elderly, but share with them at the first time, so that they can share the happiness of their children.

Opportunity Points Based on Esteem Needs. Young people can travel with just one smartphone to solve all problems, including payment, identity verification, health verification, etc. Smart bracelets for the elderly should also become smart assistants for the elderly to travel. This way the elderly can travel more autonomously and change the inherent impression of young people towards the elderly, thus gaining respect.

Opportunity points based on Self-actualization needs. There is something fulfilling about an older person being able to explore and use a smart product on their own. This often encourages seniors to try more new things, giving them hope for life and the confidence to take on new goals.

Finally we have summarized the opportunity points, as shown in Fig. 6.

4.3 Design Strategies

After studying the needs of the elderly at all levels and exploring the need-based opportunity points, we arrived at the final design strategy that relies on products and services to meet the needs of the elderly at all levels.

Design Strategies Based on Physiological Needs. Smart bracelets should have a form that meets the aesthetics of the user and will bring a better sensory experience to elderly users. For the elderly smart bracelet shape design should be simple and fashionable, to avoid the traditional elderly products that dull, boring feeling.

Smart bracelets need to meet the man-machine relationship, which will bring a better wearing experience to elderly users. The shape and size of the smart bracelet for the elderly should be in line with the ergonomics of the elderly wrist. The body of the

Needs	Opportunity Points

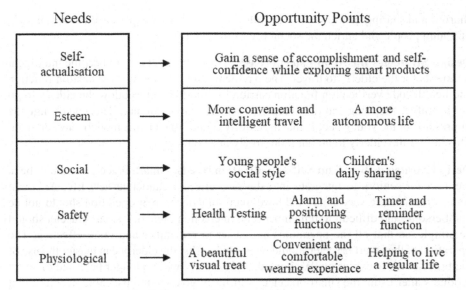

Fig. 6. Design opportunity points (Author's own drawing)

bracelet is rounded to protect the fragile bones of the elderly. The wristband is made of thermoplastic elastomer (TPE), which has a softer, skin-friendly feel and meets skin safety and non-allergenicity tests. The screen of the bracelet uses a large LED screen to facilitate visual interaction for the elderly.

The smart bracelets should be the recorder and supervisor of the elderly's life. By recording the sleep and diet of the elderly, it helps them to develop healthy and regular habits. The elderly can also record the things they need to accomplish in a short period of time and set up regular reminders, which can avoid the elderly from forgetting things.

Design Strategies Based on Security Needs. Smart bracelets should be the safety guardian of the elderly, with positioning and navigation and a key help function, to ensure the safety of the elderly out. The bracelet has GPS real-time positioning function, which can help the elderly to carry out real-time navigation. For the elderly with memory impairment, the location can be shared in real time to their children in case they encounter accidents such as getting lost. When an accident happens to the elderly, they can long press the screen to emergency contacts and send an alert.

The smart bracelet is to be a safety guardian for the elderly at home. It has timing and reminder functions to ensure the safety of the elderly at home with fire and electricity. Due to the memory loss of the elderly, they are likely to forget the electrical devices they are using. The elderly can set the reminder time before use, and the bracelet reminds the elderly to turn off the electrical equipment in time by vibration to prevent the danger.

Design Strategies Based on Social Needs. Smart bracelets are to become a new type of social tool for the elderly. Seniors can communicate frequently with their children and friends through the social software installed on their smart bracelets. Through the social software, the elderly can chat with their children and friends with voice, photo sharing and sharing of life news. This allows the elderly to experience the social style of young people and enrich the social life of the elderly.

Design Strategies Based on Esteem Needs. Smart bracelets are to become intelligent assistants for the elderly to travel. The payment function, identity verification function and health code verification function carried by smart bracelets allow the elderly to go out in traffic, shopping and play scenarios without any hindrance. This can change the impression of the young people that the elderly cannot adapt to the modern environment. This allows the elderly to go out more freely and confidently.

Design Strategies Based on Self-actualization Needs. Smart bracelets should be a medium for seniors to integrate into the new era and challenge new life. Although smart bracelets are very smart and have many functions, their operation should not be cumbersome and difficult to remember. The interaction logic of a smart bracelet should be simple, so that all the operations are easier to remember and more effective. The operation of the smart bracelet should be guided so that the elderly can master the use of the bracelet while exploring. We hope that the elderly will no longer be afraid of smart products after using the smart bracelet. And it can give them a psychological hint that they still have the ability to pursue new things and realize their self-worth.

I will briefly summarize the design strategy, as shown in Fig. 7.

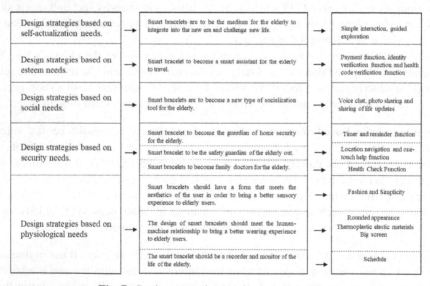

Fig. 7. Design strategies (Author's own drawing)

4.4   User Return Visit

This study derives a design strategy for smart bracelets for the elderly based on theory and methodology. In order to verify the rationality of the design strategy, we interviewed the elderly users again. We present the design strategy in a more generalized way to the elderly, who will score our strategies. After evaluation by 50 older adults, we found that the strategies derived from the study all generally met the expected needs of older adults while also meeting the potential needs of older adults. Therefore, the methodology of this study is feasible at the user level.

4.5 Shortcomings of the Study

Although this study is always based on users' needs to develop design strategies, the user base of our study needs to be increased. It is not enough to limit the user study to older people in one region and one country. Moreover, our strategy needs to be updated according to the development of the society. Finally, we need to further consider the actual development of the product to make the strategy fit the feasibility of the development.

5   Conclusions

This paper is based on Maslow's hierarchy of needs theory and constructs the method of mapping strategies to hierarchy of needs. The theory and method are applied to the strategy study of smart bracelets for the elderly. We visited those elderly users again after arriving at the design strategies and found that these strategies can effectively make the smart bracelet meet the needs of the elderly from low to high five levels. This is not only a perfection of the smart product itself for the elderly, but also a vivid manifestation of humanistic care. The findings of this paper provide strategy references for developing smart bracelets for the elderly that enhance user experience, and also provide new ideas for more smart product designs for the elderly. This paper hopes that the smart era can be more open and inclusive, so that the elderly can embrace technology and enjoy life.

References

1. United Nations: World Population Ageing 2017: Highlights, New York (2017)
2. Maslow, A.H.: Motivation and Personality. China Renmin University Press Co. Ltd, Beijing (2012)

Exploring Effectiveness of Absorbing Health Knowledge by the Middle-Aged and Elderly Using Chatbots

Wang-Chin Tsai[✉], Yu-Chen Hsieh, and Chang-Franw Lee

Department of Creative Design, National Yunlin University of Science and Technology,
Douliu, Yunlin 640, Taiwan
wangwang@yuntech.edu.tw

Abstract. World Health Organization (WHO) proposed the concept of "smart medical care". More and more middle-aged and elderly people use smart products. Under the shortage of the resources for medical care, if middle-aged and elderly people can maintain their physical health with excellent functions through the activities of self-health management, they can reduce the demands for medical care. This study focused on this for the discussion to explore the effectiveness of chatbots for middle-aged and elderly people's absorbing health knowledge via human-computer interaction, so as to facilitate the subsequent development and establishment of innovative service types and service experiences. From the results of the pre-test and post-test questionnaires, we can understand whether the use of chatbot for a week by the middle-aged and elderly people can help improve their health knowledge.

Keywords: Middle-aged · Elderly · Chatbot · Health knowledge

1 Introduction

1.1 Research Background and Motives

According to a survey conducted by Ministry of the Interior in 2015, there are no sufficient care resources to take care of the elderly in Taiwan, and this problem is more serious in remote areas. If the elderly can maintain healthy physical functions through self-health management, the need for care will be reduced. The percentage of Taiwanese mobile phone users access the Internet with their mobile phones continues to rise. According to research, the percentage of mobile phone users under 50 years old who accessed the Internet through information devices was higher than 98%, the percentage of mobile phone users of 50–59 years old accessing the Internet via mobile phones was 90.8% in 2019, and the percentage of mobile Internet users over 60 years old has also increased year by year with the current rate of 59.7%, which is close to 60%. With the advancement of communication technology, the demand for smartphones has increased. Due to the changes in lifestyles of the middle aged or senior citizens, their acceptance of science and technology has gradually increased, and it is necessary for them to use mobile phones

© Springer Nature Switzerland AG 2021
C. Stephanidis et al. (Eds.): HCII 2021, LNCS 13096, pp. 318–329, 2021.
https://doi.org/10.1007/978-3-030-90328-2_20

to assist in handling things in life. With the advent of the technological age, World Health Organization (WHO) proposed the concept of "smart medical care". More and more middle-aged and elderly people use smart products. Smart phone applications can provide various types of knowledge and applications for business, entertainment and life, but, these applications are mostly designed by young people with few content and systems specifically designed for the middle-aged and elderly people. Therefore, the service process of smartphones should make it easier and more convenient for patients to obtain relevant health information. This study focused on this for the discussion to explore the effectiveness of chatbots for middle-aged and elderly people's absorbing health knowledge via human-computer interaction, so as to facilitate the subsequent development and establishment of innovative service types and service experiences.

1.2 Research Purpose

There were 14 subjects in this experiment. The pre-test questionnaires on health knowledge and the description of the chatbot's experience mode and operation process were provided. Then the subjects were asked to use the chatbot randomly every day. After a week, the subjects were required to fill out the post-test questionnaire of health knowledge. Through the results of the pre-test and post-test questionnaires, we can understand whether the use of chatbot for a week by the middle-aged and elderly people can help improve their health knowledge.

2 Literature Review

2.1 Impact of Nutrition Education

American Dietetic Association pointed out that nutrition education is the process of adjusting intentions and attitudes, enhancing the cognition of food while meeting personal needs, implementing knowledge in daily life and guiding the correct dietary concept, and it can train the middle-aged and the elderly to follow the correct diet guidelines and choose the right food to facilitate the best nutritional status. According to the survey on the nutrition of the elderly, the risk of disease increases when the nutrition is insufficient, and long-term sitting and lack of regular exercise will lead to the decline in physical function. In order for the elderly to have good healthy behaviors, the first necessary thing to do is to start with dietetic education to enhance their nutritional knowledge, and to further improve their dietary behaviors through the improvement of dietary knowledge. Adjusting the appropriate ratio of calories and servings, selecting appropriate food and training good eating habits, combined with changes in exercise habits and drug control can help the elderly stabilize blood pressure, blood sugar and blood lipids, and prevent the occurrence of diseases. This shows the importance of nutrition education for disease prevention (Drewnowski and Shultz 2001).

2.2 Importance of Disease Prevention

The statistics from Health Promotion Administration indicate that one out of every 10 people over 20 years old in Taiwan suffer from chronic kidney disease. In addition, hypertension, high blood sugar and high blood lipids have always been the top ten risk factors for death in Taiwan. In order to reduce the incidence and mortality, it is important to promote and publicize disease prevention education (Liu 2012) so as to enable the public to its raise awareness and alertness of disease prevention as soon as possible, thereby enhancing self-health management. According to statistics, the median age of cancer in Taiwan in 2017 was 63 years old, it was 55 years old for breast cancer and 57 years old for oral cancer, so all the cancers occur in the middle-age to advanced-age stage. The top ten cancers are respectively in the order of colorectal cancer and lung cancer for men, and breast cancer, liver cancer and oral cancer for women. WHO pointed out that 30% to 50% of cancers are preventable. If long-term good habits are adopted with the five principles of life including quitting smoking and drinking, a balanced diet, regular exercise, weight control and regular screening, and the concept of cancer prevention is taken as a part of daily life, cancer can be prevented.

2.3   Middle-Aged and Elderly People's Demand for Mobile Phones

According to the statistics of Research, Development and Evaluation Commission, Executive Yuan in 2020, the percentage of Taiwanese mobile phone users who use their mobile phones to access the Internet continues to rise, with a significant rise from 35.3% in 2011 to 88.2% in 2018, and then slightly increased to 89.8% in 2019. At present, 90 out of every 100 people with mobile phones use mobile phones to connect to the Internet on average. Among them, the percentage of mobile phone users under 50 years old who have used information devices to access the Internet is higher than 98%. In 2018, the percentage of mobile phone users of 50–59 years old who have used a mobile phone to access the Internet was 90.8% with an average mobile surfing time of 2 h. The percentage of mobile Internet users over 60 years old who have used the mobile Internet has also increased year by year to a current rate of 59.7%, which is a usage rate close to 60%, and the average mobile Internet surfing time was also about 2 h. And the content that the middle-aged and elderly people need most are the provision of health information, the functional requirements of health applications, and the establishment of a medical system (Hsu 2013). The content that meet the needs of the middle-aged and senior citizens for health information when using smart phones is divided into health care knowledge, physiological value records and medical system services, which include food health, disease prevention, exercise fitness, weight control, chronic disease control, medical information, drug information and health lectures; and the functional requirements of health information by the middle-aged and elderly people using smart mobile phones are zooming in and zooming out of the screen, Chinese text and voice speaking, accurate search and clear data classification, the correctness of the information source, feedback and interaction, payment mechanism and no need to log in (Hsu 2013). The rapid development of science and technology has provided health information through mobile phones for middle-aged and elderly people to learn, and most middle-aged and elderly people are willing to learn health knowledge through mobile phones, and they hope to get help to improve their lives after learning it (Chan 2018).

2.4 Application of Medical Chatbot System

Smart phones are often used as the medium for mobile devices. The main reason is that smart phones are the items that people are used to carrying with them, and people are dependent on mobile phones. Mobile phones can also provide instant messaging functions, which can help patients or obtain health-related information in real time (Klasnja and Pratt 2012). Therefore, this study focused on smartphones to make chatbots on the LINE APP platform. Jiang (2019) pointed out that the design of chatbot service models should consider the ease of use, usefulness, trust, system characteristics, compatibility and production quality of the system as well as the explanatory results, which are all the factors that will affect the user's intention. When designing a chatbot, we must consider whether the system operation, information and screen meet the ease of use, and whether the use of it is effective, can shorten the time, improve the quality, and meet the principle of usefulness. Users will trust the medical robots developed due to the medical institutions or correct medical information that they trust, thereby increasing their use intention. However, there were too many types of mobile phone applications in the past, and it takes some time for middle-aged and elderly people to operate new programs and adapt to new interfaces. But, the LINE chatbot enables users to familiarize themselves with the interface operation, which can reduce the time to adapt to the interface and achieve the purpose more efficiently. Also, the degree of completion after the system is executed, and whether there is any positive help after using the chatbot need to be considered. The chatbot's system features are not confined by any time and place or personalized information. The above considerations are used as a reference for building a chatbot system.

3 Research Method

This study was mainly divided into two stages, the first stage was to explore the needs of chatbots for middle-aged and elderly people through the literature review, and understand the experience and needs of middle-aged and elderly people by interview. The main health information content included the exercise and diet for diabetes, hypertension and kidney disease, the prevention knowledge of the top five cancers in the country, colorectal cancer, lung cancer, female breast cancer, liver cancer and oral cancer, and six types of diets, which were used as health knowledge data stored in the database, and the content of graphics and texts suitable for middle-aged and elderly people were created as the information used by the chatbot for message reply. The prototype of the chatbot was developed with above rules and the health knowledge was pushed to all users at the time set through the back-end time setting, as shown in Fig. 1. In the second stage: (1) User tests were carried out to understand the learning effectiveness of middle-aged and senior users through questionnaire analysis. (2) The results of the questionnaire were analyzed and discussed.

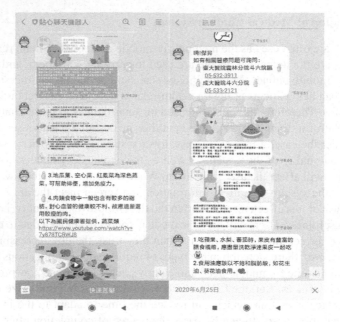

Fig. 1. Operation flow chart of push function

3.1 Research Subjects

1. Subjects: A total of 14 men and women.
2. Inclusion criteria for middle-aged and senior citizens: (a) 55 –80 years old. (b) Basic literacy skills. (c) Able to understand and follow instructions.
3. Questionnaire content: The manual provided by Ministry of Health and Welfare and the content recommended by doctors were adopted as the content of the questionnaire of the pre-test and post-test, such as regular exercise, diet control, disease prevention, etc., and considered as indicators of health care knowledge and health concept.

3.2 Research Tools

1. Purpose: A survey of health knowledge level as a standard for the improvement of diet knowledge, exercise knowledge, disease prevention, and health knowledge.
2. Process: The subjects got the first result after the pre-test, and the post-test was performed one week later.
3. Questionnaire design: There were 10 questions in this questionnaire including three multiple-choice questions and seven single-choice questions. 1 point was given for the correct answer to each question, and no point was given for one wrong answer for a multiple-choice question. The full score was 10, as shown in Table 1.

Table 1. Health knowledge content

Health knowledge			
Question type	Question	Options	Answer
Diabetes	Which of the following food can prevent diabetes? (multiple-choice)	Black beans, saury, salmon Spinach, milk, sweet potatoes Strawberries, whole wheat bread, oranges Beef, pork, lamb	1, 2, 3
Six categories of diet	Which of the following concepts is correct? (multiple-choice)	When eating apples, pears, tomatoes, you should wash them and eat them with the peels as the peels are rich in dietary fiber Edible oil with unsaturated fatty acids should be consumed, such as peanut oil and sunflower oil Sweet potato leaves, water spinach, and red phoenix are dark vegetables that can help defecation and increase immunity Meat foods generally also contain more fat, which is not good for cardiovascular health. Therefore, lean meat should be eaten in an appropriate amount	1, 2, 3, 4
Eggs, peas, fish and meat	Which food should I avoid? (multiple-choice)	Pork floss, dried pork, fried bean curd, fried chicken Beef and lamb chops, hot dogs, sirloin, ham Sausages, hot dogs, tribute balls, buns and minced meat Pork belly, pork butt, bacon, large intestine	1, 2, 3, 4
Diabetes	Which of the following is the best exercise time to prevent diabetes?	Exercise immediately after eating Start exercising 5 min after eating Start exercising 30 min after eating Start exercising 1 to 2 h after eating	3

(continued)

Table 1. (*continued*)

Health knowledge

Question type	Question	Options	Answer
Hypertension	Which of the following is the correct dietary recommendation to prevent hypertension?	Eat ham, sausage and kimchi Eat lard and butter Eat olive oil Add any seasonings (miso, pepper and salt)	3
Hypertension	How long should I exercise at least to prevent hypertension every week?	100 min 120 min 125 min 150 min	4
Kidney disease	What foods should be reduced to prevent kidney disease?	Brown rice, oats, whole wheat Canned food, minced pork balls, hot pot seasoning Green onion, Thai basil, lemon Chicken, duck, fish	2
Liver cancer	What kind of food can reduce the risk of liver cancer?	Eggs, peas, fish and meat Dairy products Vegetables Whole grains	4
Dairy products	When calcium intake is insufficient, how many glasses of milk should be consumed at least every day for calcium intake?	1 cup or 2 cups (1 cup of 240ml) 3 cups 4 cups 5 cups	1
Kidney disease	How many times at least you must exercise per week to prevent kidney disease? How long should it take each time?	1–2 times, 20 min each time 2–3 times, 20 min each time 3–4 times, 20 min each time 3–5 times, 30 min each time	4

4 Research Analysis

4.1 Questionnaire Analysis

In this study, 14 questionnaires were collected for reliability analysis to understand the accuracy of the Cronbach's α value of the questionnaire of the pre-test and post-test. The results showed that the reliability coefficient of the questionnaire was 0.745, and the Cronbach's α value greater than 0.7 indicates that the questionnaire has high reliability.

4.2 Introduction to the Subjects

The coding of the subjects in this study was based on the test order, represented with numbers 1–14, as shown in Table 2.

Table 2. Basic data of subjects

Subjects	Gender	Age	How long have you used the smartphone	How long do you use the line APP per day	Do you have any disease
1	Female	55	More than 3 years	1–4 h	No
2	Male	56	1–2 years	1–4 h	No
3	Female	55	More than 3 years	1–4 h	No
4	Female	58	More than 3 years	1–4 h	No
5	Female	60	More than 3 years	1–4 h	No
6	Male	62	More than 3 years	1–4 h	No
7	Female	65	1–2 years	More than 4 h	No
8	Female	65	More than 3 years	1–4 h	Hypertension
9	Female	70	1–2 years	Less than 1 h	High cholesterol
10	Female	66	More than 3 years	1–4 h	Diabetes
11	Female	66	More than 3 years	1–4 h	Heart disease
12	Female	72	1–2 years	1–4 h	Hypertension
13	Male	80	1–2 years	Less than 1 h	Hypertension
14	Male	77	More than 3 years	More than 4 h	Hypertension

4.3 Research Results

A total of 14 middle-aged and elderly people were surveyed in the pre-test of this study including 4 men and 10 women. 8 persons were 55–65 years old, and 6 persons were 65–80 years old. They had used smartphones for an average of more than 3 years, and the average daily time of using the line APP was 1 to 4 h. 4 people suffered from hypertension, 1 heart disease, 1 diabetic kidney disease, 1 high cholesterol, and the other 7 had no related diseases. The health knowledge and concepts were taken as questions in the questionnaire, and there were a total of 10 questions. 1 point was given for the correct answer for one question and the full score was 10 points based on the correct answer rate. After the test of the pre-test questionnaire, the chatbot intervened to allow the user to operate the chatbot, and a post-test questionnaire test was conducted one week later to explore whether the health knowledge and concepts of the middle-aged and elderly people improved after the chatbot intervention. The results of the pre-test questionnaire got an average score of 6.57 points, and the standard deviation of 1.34. After the chatbot was used for 1 week, the average score of the post-test result was 8.21, and the standard deviation was 1.37, as shown in Table 3.

Table 3. Effect analysis of middle-aged and elderly people after using Chatbots, paired sample t-Test

	Number	Average	Standard deviation	t	Significance
Pre-test	14	6.57	1.34	− 3.371	.005
Post-test	14	8.21	1.37		

** p < 0.01

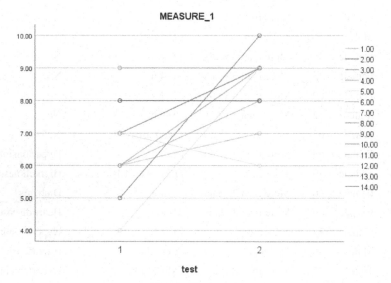

Fig. 2. Test results

5   Summary

The pre-test questions were based on health knowledge, and the middle-aged and elderly people were asked to take the test again after using the chatbot for a week. During the process, the chatbot sent messages at a fixed time every morning and evening in the form of push broadcast. The content was mainly based on the health knowledge and dietary knowledge in the chatbot database. Since the subjects usually had the habit of using the line APP, it was very convenient for them to receive and browse messages, and the messages will not disappear over time so that they can also browse the messages of the previous day. When the subjects were busy, they could wait to browse and watch when they were free without any stress or other burdens caused by not seeing the information. After a week, they absorbed and accumulated health knowledge to deepen the impression of health knowledge in daily life and the effectiveness was reflected in the post-test results. Regarding the test results (Table 3), there were significant differences between the pre-test and the post-test ($t = -3.371$, $df = 13$, $p < 0.01$), and the average of correct answers was 6.57 and 8.21 respectively in the pre-test and the post-test, which was significantly different (as shown in Fig. 2). The above results showed that after a week of using chatbots by the middle-aged and elderly people, the effect of improving health knowledge was significant. This has demonstrated that the use of chatbots can help the middle-aged and elderly people improve their knowledge of self-health management via nutrition education for intervention with diet, exercise and related health care knowledge. It is also verified that regardless of age restrictions and the presence or absence of diseases, these people can all learn new health knowledge through chatbots.

6 Conclusions

According to the statistics of the subjects, most of the subjects think that they can be familiar with the interface quickly and know clearly where the text is entered when they operated the chatbot for the first time by adding friends through the line APP, because the users themselves have had more than 3 years of experience in using the line APP, and they usually chatted with friends, which can reduce the operation steps and the burden of the operation process. Moreover, through the text and picture menus, the user can intuitively click, which is simple and clear and they can get started quickly. The information provided is mainly based on pictures plus short text descriptions. The pictures can be zoomed in and out, which can meet the needs of middle-aged and senior citizens. And through text assistance, they can understand the information content provided at the first time, which not only improves the practicality, but also clearly conveys the health information, so that users can simply and intuitively obtain the content they need. The line APP itself also has a recommendation function, which can promote this chatbot and share it with other friends in time. Compared with other apps that need to be downloaded, the line APP chatbot can be used by more people. And if you want the subjects to trust the chatbot, the conversation and the data presented in the chatbot must be marked with the source and made or provided by professional medical care personnel to establish the correctness of the information source. A stable and good operating system that makes it difficult to make mistakes in use is required to establish the trust of the user in the chatbot. And the user will also want to use chatbots to understand health-related knowledge. Regardless of whether they have related diseases or not, they will want to learn about related disease prevention knowledge through chatbots. Users can select the content they want to watch by clicking on it, or the system can push it regularly to users. The content is mainly provided with pictures, texts, and videos. The pictures and texts can accelerate the understanding of disease prevention in a short time, and the videos can clearly explain the content information. Users can choose according to their own needs, and this enhances their motivation to learn health knowledge.

Acknowledgements. The authors hereby extend sincere thanks to Ministry of Science and Technology (MOST) of the Republic of China (ROC) for their financial support of this research, whose project code is MOST 106-2410-H-431-017. It is thanks to the generous patronage of MOST that this study has been smoothly performed. The author also thanks to the Yang, Jieng-Sheng and all of the participants of the study.

References

Drewnowski, A., Shultz, J.M.: Impact of aging on eating behaviors, food choices, nutrition, and health status. J. Nutr. Health Aging **5**(2), 75–79 (2001)

Klasnja, P., Pratt, W.: Healthcare in the pocket: mapping the space of mobile-phone health interventions. J. Biomed. Inform. **45**(1), 184–198 (2012)

Liu, Y.C.: Hypertension, hyperglycemia, hyperlipidemia and the prevention of chronic kidney disease. Taipei City Med. J. **9**(3), 293–300 (2012)

Hsu, H.P.: A Research on the Requirements and the User Interface Design for the Elderly to Use Smartphone Apps – Take Health Information Apps as Example. Graduate School of Curriculum and Instructional Communications Technology (2013)

Jiang, Y.P.: A Study of Medical Chatbot Application. Department of Management Information Systems (2019)

Research, Development and Evaluation Commission, Executive Yuan. Survey report on digital opportunities (gap) over the years. https://www.ndc.gov.tw/cp.aspx?n=55C8164 714DFD9E9. Accessed on 20 Feb 2020

Annual Report of Health Promotion Administration. Accessed on 20 Feb 2020

Website: https://www.hpa.gov.tw/Pages/Detail.aspx?nodeid=4159&pid=1208. Accessed on 20 Feb 2020

Health Promotion Administration. Prevent hypertension. https://health99.hpa.gov.tw/educZone/edu_detail.aspx?CatId=12107. Accessed on 20 Feb 2020

Health Promotion Administration. Colorectal cancer has become a killer of many celebrities!? Tips for colorectal cancer prevention: starting with healthy diet, exercise and regular screening. https://www.mohw.gov.tw/cp-16-42808-1.html. Accessed on 21 Feb 2020

Health Promotion Administration. Say no to lung cancer! Tips to protect the lungs from Health Promotion Administration. https://www.hpa.gov.tw/Pages/Detail.aspx?nodeid=3804&pid=11256. Accessed on 21 Feb 2020

Health Promotion Administration. Lung protection, starting from your life (2019)

Health Promotion Administration. Handbook of Diabetes and Me (2015)

Health Promotion Administration. Study Manual for Hypertension Prevention and Treatment (2013)

Ministry of Health and Welfare. https://www.hpa.gov.tw/Pages/Detail.aspx?nodeid=127&pid=10478. Accessed 21 Feb 2020

Health Promotion Administration. Advocacy advertisement for colorectal cancer prevention and treatment (for farmers). https://health99.hpa.gov.tw/educZone/edu_detail.aspx?CatId=51062. Accessed on 22 Feb 2020

Ministry of Health and Welfare. Ministry of Health and Welfare publishes data on cancer occurrence. https://www.hpa.gov.tw/Pages/Detail.aspx?nodeid=4141&pid=12682. Accessed on 22 Feb 2020

Ministry of Health and Welfare. Two simple steps to prevent oral cancer. https://health99.hpa.gov.tw/educZone/edu_detail.aspx?CatId=30892. Accessed on 22 Feb 2020

Ministry of Health and Welfare. Prevention of liver cancer (5 minutes) (Mandarin version). https://health99.hpa.gov.tw/educZone/edu_detail.aspx?CatId=51341. Accessed on 22 Feb 2020

Ministry of Health and Welfare. Breast cancer prevention and treatment. https://www.hpa.gov.tw/Pages/Detail.aspx?nodeid=4141&pid=12682. Accessed on 23 Feb 2020

Cancer Prevention and Treatment Group of Health Promotion Administration. Advocacy for Breast Cancer Prevention and Treatment -I was screened, how about you? A 60-second advocacy video. https://health99.hpa.gov.tw/educZone/edu_detail.aspx?CatId=51048. Accessed on 23 Feb 2020

Ministry of Health and Welfare. Health Promotion. https://www.mohw.gov.tw/cp-4350-46712-1.
html. Accessed on 23 Feb 2020
Zhang, J., Oh, Y., Lange, P., Yu, Z., Fukuoka, Y.: Artificial intelligence chatbot behavior change
model for designing artificial intelligence chatbots to promote physical activity and a healthy
diet: viewpoint. J. Med. Internet Res. **22**(9), e22845 (2020)

A Study into Accessibility and Usability of Automated Teller Machines for Inclusiveness

Patrizia Willi, Leandro Soares Guedes[✉], and Monica Landoni

Università della Svizzera Italiana, TI 6900 Lugano, Switzerland
{patrizia.willi,leandro.soares.guedes,monica.landoni}@usi.ch

Abstract. At first glance, interaction with an Automated Teller Machine (ATM) tends to look limiting and prescriptive. Both hardware and interface do not seem to provide adaptability layers for vulnerable groups of users, particularly those with disabilities. This study considers users who have different requirements because of temporary or permanent disabilities and needs. After an overview of ATMs' functionality and principles of user interactions, we introduce the main topics of this study: accessibility and usability for inclusiveness. We then describe a heuristic evaluation exercise as well as the methods and criteria used in order to assess how ATM systems, even if sharing the same functionalities, differ substantially in providing a usable and accessible experience to users. Finally, we reflect on the emerging issues that affect the user experience with ATM and highlight how even for such a simple everyday use tool, we are still far from real inclusion. Therefore, with the support of the literature, we propose some recommendations for further studies.

Keywords: Accessibility · People with disabilities · ATM · Inclusiveness · Usability

1 Introduction

In recent years, substantial research and development efforts have been made to enhance Automated Teller Machines (ATM) functionality and usefulness, offering a remarkable body of expertise, demonstrations, and models of best practice [5]. ATMs are a particular category of devices that we need to study concerning accessibility and usability: the physical access to its hardware and the interaction with the graphical user interface (GUI), as both contribute to the overall user experience (UX). In general, ATMs are supporting a straightforward task that could be classified as of low complexity. Users need them to be simple, easy to learn and remember, resistant to errors, fast recovery from mistakes, efficient, and time-saving while providing an adequate safety level as expected when dealing with money. When it comes to users with temporary or permanent disabilities, it is essential to understand what kind of cognitive effort is required

© Springer Nature Switzerland AG 2021
C. Stephanidis et al. (Eds.): HCII 2021, LNCS 13096, pp. 330–342, 2021.
https://doi.org/10.1007/978-3-030-90328-2_21

during the interaction and what abilities are necessary to have an effective interaction with ATM, which ends with achieving the supported tasks. Given that users interact with a GUI, identifying, recognizing, and making sense of labels and icons is essential for successful interaction, as the only available alternative is the audio option. Besides, a limited number of ATM stations are made available where height is adapted to serve customers on a wheelchair. Thus, for instance, as a case study, we have Mary. During her evening walk with her dog Nero, she stops by an ATM to quickly withdraw some money and discovers to have left her glasses at home as well as her earphone. There is no way to accomplish her task, and she gets frustrated by the lack of available alternatives has to go back home to try again next time. Equally unsatisfied is John, who has never been able to read and has to guess the meaning of labels on the screen while hoping to remember his identification number (PIN) in order to get the sum he needs to pay for his daily expenses. These simple case scenarios show how while ATMs may bring substantial benefits in terms of 24/7 access to money deposits and withdrawing, accessibility is far from being attained. More needs to be done if such devices have to provide a genuinely inclusive UX. In the following sections of this paper, we will report on relevant literature covering the peculiarities of ATMs and describe the different needs these systems should serve to provide usability and accessibility to users with temporary or permanent disabilities. We will then discuss the approach and method used to assess the kind of UX currently provided when interacting with available ATMs and the findings of our analysis. Finally, we will show their implications on future study and design of more inclusive systems to support a broader range of different needs.

2   Automated Teller Machines (ATMs)

In the early 1970s and after the advent of credit cards, the next major technology was ATM's production, which began to fulfill much of the bank's teller duties. The ATM network has made a significant contribution to the quality of most financial transactions for consumers securely. ATMs give both banks and consumers valuable benefits. The machines encourage customers to withdraw and deposit cash at more convenient times and locations than during banking hours. Around the same time, ATMs reduce the cost of operation for some consumer needs by automating processes that have previously been completed manually. Such gains are compounded as banks exchange their ATMs with others, encouraging other banks' customers to access their accounts via a branch's ATM.

An ATM is an automated computerized telecommunications system that enables clients of financial institutions to enter their bank accounts through a straightforward and secure contact process. The ATM is a self-service banking terminal that collects cash and collects deposits. Most ATMs also allow users to carry out other banking transactions, such as balance checking or purchasing third-party services, link train tickets, or phone credit recharges. The ATM is enabled by inserting a bank card into the card reader slot and entering a valid PIN. For instance, ATM first connects the bank's machines to check the balance when a customer attempts to withdraw cash, then dispenses the money and finally transmits a completed transaction note.

While ATMs provide bank customers with a beneficial tool, they can often be challenging to use, and there is also much space for improvement in the design of the interface. For high usability standards, the successful design of the graphical user interface is, therefore, imperative. There are sometimes difficulties or inconveniences faced while using an ATM; some of the issues include: the inability to see well the ATM screen due to the sun reflection or other external factors, the incorrect insertion of the ATM card, especially for new users who are not familiar with their new card and the ATM, or the menu options on some ATMs may not be aligned with their corresponding menu key. Some more addressable usability-related issues of cash dispensers are understanding operations and the instructions on how to perform actions, which are pretty challenging to understand for some ATM users. Also, the banking jargon may be too complicated for inexpert users or specific users such as illiterates, semi-literates, or older people. Moreover, the ATM card is often returned to the user while further operations are required (e.g., once the user requests a sum of cash, the card is returned, and no additional operations are allowed). This will result in a very inefficient procedure, and time-consuming process since the client has to reinsert the card, increasing their time spent at the ATM further. Another inefficiency often happens while getting the necessary amount of money. Most ATM displays on the initial screen the available banknotes available to be withdrawn. Still, none will show the amounts after the customer has inserted the card and selected a custom amount to withdraw, leading the user to mistakes.

Different banks offer diverse ATM hardware architectures, depending on the machine's hardware producer, which results in distinct dispositions of the elements composing an ATM system. We can see some layout examples in Fig. 1. Although each ATM's architecture is different, they all contain the same essential components; a card reader who reads the information stored in the magnetic stripe on the back of an ATM card and relays the information to an internal device, connecting to the cardholder's register. A display screen that provides the interface between the internal device of the ATM and the cardholder, newer machines use touchscreen technologies while older ones still rely on buttons. The keypad allows choices and input details to be made by the cardholder, and all modern ATMs should have braille keyboards for the visually impaired. The number keys are used to input the PIN of the card or the amount to be withdrawn. Other external parts such as a cash dispenser, a receipt printer, seldom a deposit slot for banknotes or checks, cash dispensers, and speakers make it easier for the keys to beep. Sound feedback allows the user to recognize whether the button has been pressing hard enough to register with the machine, which is fundamental for older or visually impaired users. Different hardware architectures can cause usability issues for some users. Just imagine visually impaired or blind users reaching an ATM. They have to figure out where to plug in their headphones. This first step could result in a challenge since the hardware differs much from bank to bank. Moreover, the spot to plug in the headphones jack is very tiny, and there is no rule of thumb for the placement; usually, it is somewhere on the left side of the screen. In the pictures below are displayed three different architectures and dispositions of the hardware components.

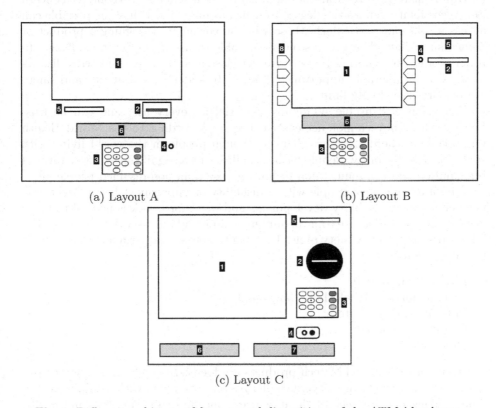

(a) Layout A   (b) Layout B

(c) Layout C

Fig. 1. Different architectural layouts and dispositions of the ATMs' hardware

The same heterogeneity holds for the machines' embedded software, which will produce different user interfaces and user experiences for the customer. Those different interfaces have been grouped into three categories and analyzed with several factors and criteria in the next section, focusing on usability concepts for users with temporary or permanent disabilities.

This paper aims to point out the most evident differences in user interfaces, design choices, hardware disposition and analyze each factor from an accessibility and usability point of view, focusing on particular need users.

3   Usability, Accessibility, and ATM Users

When interacting with ATMs, we consider all sorts of users, disabled and non-disabled users, with permanent or temporary conditions. To have software and hardware integrated with users' needs, we should consider Usability and Accessibility as key areas to enhance their experience. The term usability refers to the utility of a product or service and the simplicity with which individuals can use it. Unfortunately, in software development, it still remains a secondary concern [9]. Accessibility defines the degree to which as many individuals as possible can access a solution, particularly those with impairments. Designing a product or device such that all future customers are able to use it is often a challenge. In other words, not ignoring large consumer classes, such as persons with disabilities, is of considerable importance. Sauer [10] states that usability and safety studies are exceedingly limited.

Accessible and usable ATMs are essential for every user and can be frustrating when they cannot achieve their goal. According to the World Health Organization, there are more than one billion people in the world living with some form of disability. People with disabilities have significantly lower rates of information and communication technology use than non-disabled people [6].

The involvement of people with a disability or impairment has a direct positive effect on accessibility development, and way more work is needed to make accessibility indeed a core topic of our curriculum and industry development [12]. The users can have a variety of needs, being temporary or permanent disabilities and needs, such as:

- Physically impaired
- Visually impaired, colorblind and blind
- Illiterate and semi-literate
- Cognitive impaired
- Older adults

Many of the new ATM tech products are focused mainly on text communication and can thus cause severe challenges for consumers with disabilities [15]. The banking performance of these devices continues to be limited, and, sadly, assistive technologies are not necessarily adequate to enhance the accessibility of applications. Consequently, this ATM program provides low usability for most users, particularly for those with contrast sensitivity and visual acuity issues. Some of their challenges include: the height of the ATM screen and hardware for wheelchair users; button colors and not clear charts for visually impaired, colorblind, and blind users; illegible texts and numbers for illiterate and semi-literate users; hard-to-read textual information for cognitive impaired users; complex interfaces, be afraid to make mistakes, and the lack of feedback for older users [11]. In the next section, we are going to discuss our study and methodology.

4   Analysis and Discussion

We want to focus on new casual users as well as on expert users who interact with the same system or a different one. Users with temporary or permanent disabilities such as the visually impaired, color blind, and physically impaired are part of the user analysis, and older people who often can have physical and mental marks. We set realistic but straightforward tasks: withdrawing a standard and a non-standard amount of money, with or without a receipt, and interacted with locally available ATMs. Due to the COVID-19 pandemic situation, we could not involve directly vulnerable users in indoor spaces, such as ATM locations or evaluation labs. Therefore, we run an expert evaluation focusing on the interaction dimension of the UX. A standard user experience target table as proposed by Harton and Pyla [8] was adapted to this purpose. In order to proceed with feedback collection, we took photos and recorded videos from the main actions that can be performed in ATMs. In total, third-one videos were recorded from eleven different systems, with an average content length of three minutes per session. The number of videos varied because when one researcher was alone, there was a need to use both hands to interact with the ATM, and in other cases, the need to show extra explorations of the interface. The videos were analyzed and scored in a second moment by the authors, that are researchers and experts in the User Experience and User Interaction research area.

The adapted user experience target table is related to the most common services of an Automated Teller Machine. We list the actions to be performed chronologically, assuming that the user follows a standard sequence and no system error occurs. We measure the following usability aspects [14]:

- **Effectiveness:** Effectiveness is about whether users can complete their goals with a high degree of accuracy.
- **Efficiency:** Users can perform tasks quickly through the most straightforward process.
- **Engagement:** The users find it pleasant to use and suitable for its industry.
- **Error tolerance:** It supports a range of user operations and only exhibits an error in real erroneous conditions. Error tolerance is achieved by finding out the type, number, and severity of typical errors users perform and how easily users can recover from those errors.

After the analysis of the interactions with the different ATMs when performing the set tasks, we grouped ATMs by similarity, as presented in Fig. 1. Group A is composed of four Swiss banks, Group B by three and Group C by one. The experts analyzed the four usability aspects of each task. Table 1 reports the results ranging from 1 (very unsatisfied) to 10 (very satisfied). Likewise, the discussion about the findings are presented as follow:

1. Insertion of the card: The three groups, A, B, and C, are getting the same scores across the four usability aspects. In terms of Effectiveness, all of them could do slightly better if adopting more innovative solutions in the banking industry, such as card-less withdrawals. They are all faring very well under Efficiency since users can complete their goals with a high degree of accuracy. Engagement is just above sufficient as users may not engage with the system as they could be concerned about security, have to wait in long queues, and therefore feel time pressure, or simply have forgotten the correct card. Finally, across the three groups, all ATMs are highly error-tolerant; if the user inserts a wrong card or the correct card in the wrong way, the machine ejects the card immediately.

Table 1. Adapted User Experience target tables for different ATM tasks and groups

User task	Effectiveness			Efficiency			Engagement			Error tollerance		
	Group A	Group B	Group C	Group A	Group B	Group C	Group A	Group B	Group C	Group A	Group B	Group C
1. Insertion of the card	9	9	9	10	10	10	7	7	7	10	10	10
2. Enter PIN	9	9	9	9	9	9	6	8	8	5	5	5
3. Homepage/Menu	9	9	10	10	10	10	7	9	7	10	10	10
4. Select withdrawal from menu	10	10	10	9	9	10	8	8	8	5	5	10
5.1. Select amount	10	10	10	5	5	5	6	6	6	5	5	10
5.2. Select other amount	10	10	10	5	5	5	6	8	8	5	5	5
6. Receipt? (yes/no)	10	10	10	9	9	5	8	6	5	5	5	5
7. Withdraw card	10	10	10	5	5	5	10	7	10	10	10	10
8. Withdraw cash and receipt	10	10	10	10	10	10	10	8	10	10	10	10

2. Enter PIN: The three groups have similar scores on all factors but Engagement. Effectiveness and Efficiency across all groups get very high scores since the process is straightforward and can be completed with a high degree of accuracy (as long as the users remember their PIN). Engagement for group A is rated just sufficient because nowadays, technology proposes much more attractive and secure ways to authenticate users using bio-metrics. Engagement for group B has a good grade because of the interactive PIN-input fields, the same score for group C thanks to the immersive PIN-input areas. Still, there is a margin of improvement for both by looking at innovative technology to provide far more enticing and safer forms to authenticate users. All three groups get a low score for the system's error tolerance because if a customer types in the wrong PIN, the machine keeps the card after the third attempt. In order to get back the banking card, the user has to face a time-consuming procedure with the bank.

3. Homepage/Menu: The three groups have the same Efficiency and Error Tolerance scores, with different Engagement results and very similar for Effectiveness. In Group A and C, the lack of icons in the menu makes the GUI less engaging for the user, while in Group B, the presence of icons makes the GUI more engaging. If a user clicks the wrong button in the group A and B, it is no longer possible to go back to the main menu. The banking jargon may be hard to understand for some novice users of the industry. In group C, it is tough to understand which buttons or keys have to be used to input a command; the system provides no touchscreen but lateral buttons and keypad buttons.

4. Select withdrawal from menu: The three groups have the same Effectiveness and Engagement scores, with different Error Tolerance results and very similar for Efficiency. In the group A and B, if the users press the wrong button in the menu (e.g., withdraw Euro), they can not go back and correct the selection. Also, the banking jargon may be too complicated for some inexpert users (e.g., sometimes called PIN, sometimes NIP), which will face problems in understanding the various options. Likewise, icons and any graphical support are missing.

5.1 Select amount: Effectiveness is very high for all groups as all machines support the task across all groups. Efficiency is insufficient as the system does not smoothly support the withdrawal of amounts that do not match those preset. Moreover, the last withdrawn amount is only saved by the used machine; if the customer changes ATM within the same bank, the amount will not be displayed. Lastly, the user cannot save a favorite amount from being held. Engagement is just sufficient in all three groups. In group B also, unfortunately, the default amount list is very short in this ATM. The error rate for groups A and B is rated relatively low because of the impossibility of going back to the main menu. In group B, the inclusion of an "Other amount" button icon is an exciting improvement. Nevertheless, the buttons and text size are tiny and, therefore, offer very poor legibility. For group C, Error-tolerance has a very high score because of the possibility of going back to the main menu if the current session has been initiated by mistake.

5.2 Select other amount: If the users cannot find the desired amount in the standard list referred to above, they have to insert the amount manually. Across the three groups, scores for Effectiveness and Efficiency are the same as for the "Select amount" with the same rationale. For group A, Engagement is barely sufficient; other systems offer a keypad's visual support to make the action more straightforward. Moreover, the system does not show the user the possible amounts and banknote sizes available to be withdrawn (it is only offered on the very first screen of the ATM - before inserting the card). Users also have to know their daily or monthly limits on their own since the bank gives no information at all. Instead, Engagement gets a higher score for groups B and C as they provide tactile support for a keyboard to make the operation more transparent. The error tolerance score is insufficient for all three groups as the customer cannot go back to the previous interface.

6. Receipt? (yes/no): For all three groups, once the users have inserted the desired amount, they have to confirm it and select if they would like to have a receipt or not. Unfortunately, if the users approved a wrong amount in the previous action, they cannot correct it; instead, they have to abort the entire procedure and start over. This is why they all get a very high score for Effectiveness and a low one for Error rate. Group A has good Efficiency, while Engagement could be improved for this particular task; the whole screen is left entirely blank. Group B has a high grade for Efficiency, but Engagement should be enhanced; even if icons are applied to the action buttons, the color elements are absent. The text, in comparison, is incredibly tiny and difficult to read. For group C, both Efficiency and Engagement are low as users cannot see the amount as a confirmation of the withdrawal. The system only gives the possibility to choose whether or not they would like to have a receipt.

7. Withdraw card: For all three groups, once the amount is confirmed, the customer is required to remove the card; this may be rather inefficient since no further operation may be taken (e.g., verifying the balance or making another withdrawal), which decreases the Efficiency score to 5. Effectiveness instead is very high for all. Group A has high Engagement and Error tolerance scores as the activity is supported by an animated icon that alerts the customer to collect their card once removed. Engagement is scored seven for group B instead because the icons are small and the text too, even though the operation is accompanied by an icon that invites the customer to remove their card. Finally, for group C, Engagement is scored higher than for the previous task because the icon is animated and more understandable.

8. Withdraw cash and receipt: Groups A, B and C get the maximum scores for all factors except for group B where Engagement is lowered due to the small icon compared to those used in the previous task.

We applied the adapted User Experience target tables for the different groups that present similar interface layouts. In Fig. 2 we can see the difference between groups. Group A, available in the Fig. 2a, has an uncomplicated menu with alternatives for withdrawing money (button 6) or changing the PIN that the interface presents as NIP. In group B, Fig. 2b, we have an alternative to withdrawing money in two different currencies and the possibility of changing the PIN. The options have icons, which can help illiterate, semi-literate, and older users. In Fig. 2c we can see Group C's interface. The menu has more alternatives for the user, but no icons or numbers are available. Also, the contrast with the yellow color can be challenging for some users.

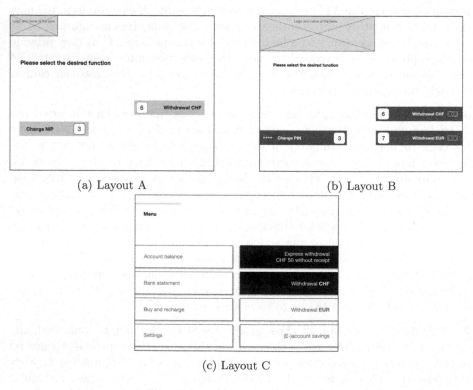

(a) Layout A   (b) Layout B

(c) Layout C

Fig. 2. Different interfaces of ATMs from different groups

Overall, all considered ATMs performed well in terms of effectiveness while we detected some issues with efficiency, and even more so with engagement and error tolerance. The work by Curran and King [2] specifically addresses efficiency and error tolerance by proposing a "best-of-breed" ATM menu system: the OptiATM. The OptiATM menu design proved to be a more usable and efficient system than existing ATMs, as it solved the problem of users having to reinsert their ATM cards to perform another transaction. An issue we reported across all ATM systems in our study and summarised in Table 2, under "Execute two distinct actions" that is also closely related to another entry in the same table: "Go back to previous screen". Therefore, few years after that work was published, current ATMs are not taking advantage of what back then was innovative research. Moving on to consider ways to improve engagement, we start by focusing on improving security, a problematic issue with all ATMs in our study, as reported in Table 2 under "Additional security". Moncur et al. [4] report how multiple graphical passwords are noticeably more effective than multiple PINs, even more so by using mnemonics to aid their recall. On a related note, De Luca et al. [3] explore how the increased use and popularity of ATM needs new authentication mechanisms to be developed to overcome PINs' security problems. The results from a field study and two smaller follow-up studies on real-world ATM use, show that there is a number of contextual factors having an impact on security and performance in PIN-based ATM use. All to be accounted for when designing alternative ATM authentication systems as means to increase accessibility and engagement while protecting security.

Still looking at ways to increase engagement via innovative, more accessible, and usable approaches to security, Coventry et al. [1] describe how usable are leading-edge biometrics techniques based on iris verification technology when integrated with the Automated Teller Machine (ATM) user interface. The paper also mentions future work in the area.

When considering alternatives to text and graphics based interfaces, audio support is a highly desirable feature for users, such as the visually impaired who struggle in reading small texts, illiterate people who face barriers in reading or cannot read at all, or blind users who have to rely entirely on audio support if they want to use the service autonomously. Most of the systems analyzed in our study had an insufficient audio quality because of different factors (surrounding noise, inability to adjust the volume, unclear sound). In contrast, other machines had no support at all. Moreover, none of the analyzed machines are equipped to offer remote assistance; users who face issues in handling the systems, especially users with physical and/or cognitive impairment, have to find an alternative way to withdraw money, often visiting their local bank branch during opening times. Oswal [7] describes a user study to understand better the impact on accessibility and usability of voice directions for operating ATMs. Their findings confirm there is still much work to be done in order to make such support systems accessible, usable, and useful, as observed in our study and reported in Table 2, under "Audio quality" as well as "Assistance or help button". Therefore, they strongly encourage the active involvement of people with disabilities in the design team.

Table 2. Summary table of usability and accessibility for different ATM systems

UI and UX elements	Group A	Group B	Group C
Text size and style	8	6	6
Button size	8	7	10
Background vs buttons and text	9	9	9
Amount of text and options to select	9	9	9
Screen space optimization	8	7	8
Special buttons	7	9	1
Icons on screen	1	8	1
User action icons	10	8	10
Screen to keypad matching numbers	10	10	1
Language settings	6	6	6
Assistance or help button	1	1	1
Select amounts to withdraw	6	6	1
Pressing CORR or STOP abort the process	5	5	9
Go back to previous screen	1	1	9
Execute two distinct actions	1	1	1
Additional security	1	1	1
Sound feedback	10	8	10
Audio quality (headphones)	7	5	7

A similar co-design approach is proposed by Thatcher et al. [13] when describing an attempt to design more inclusive and usable icons for ATM interfaces, to address the problematic issue we reported in Table 2, "Icons on-screen". Their study engaged a group of functionally illiterate bank account holders in developing icons to provide guidance to customers and take them through the various stages of the ATM withdrawal transaction.

Together with our findings, this brief overview confirms that while ATM interfaces are still lagging behind in terms of usability and accessibility, researchers in this area are actively exploring and proposing valid solutions for more inclusive systems. The hope is that banks will take notice of their efforts and rank accessibility and inclusiveness higher in their busy agenda.

5   Conclusions

We set out to explore the accessibility and usability of a very popular system providing an essential service to users. At first glance, ATM systems seem to share the same structure and a simple, straightforward interaction style. In this exploration, we examined and analyzed eleven different systems in a detailed way by considering tailor-made UX target tables focusing on accessibility and usability for users with temporary or permanent disabilities and needs. Using expert evaluation to compare different ATMs brought to light differences from a hardware perspective and from the user interface point of view, usability problems, and an overall poor user experience in terms of quality of interaction. Especially when considering users with temporary or permanent disabilities and needs when it comes to reading and making sense of icons and text used to provide on-screen instructions to guide them in the withdrawing process. This is a significant concern as it could mean that a substantial share of the population, temporarily or permanently affected by cognitive and/or sight impairment, would be excluded from taking advantage of a modern commodity such as having access to banking services 24/7. Even if our findings have to be tested with real users in order to confirm this assumption, we feel that the issue per se should be further explored as it had profound implications on the quality of life and inclusion of vulnerable users. The main limitation of this study is that, due to the COVID-19 pandemic, it was not possible to conduct a user-based evaluation and collect feedback, assessments, opinions, and suggestions directly from users as much as to run direct observations. Instead, we had to resort to expert evaluation. Nonetheless, we feel we have managed to highlight a number of crucial issues regarding the UX of such a simple system.

The developed target tables have been derived from literature, expanded and adapted to be used with ATMs, and analyze the main steps of the withdrawal process. Therefore, enabling us to assess usability and accessibility for users with temporary or permanent disabilities and needs. These tables can be used in future work to address research involving different users' communities and expanded to address specific needs. It is also important to notice how when designing for users with limited eyesight and/or cognitive abilities, legibility, as well as the availability of graphical and audio support, are important aspects to consider in order to provide inclusion via accessibility and usability. None of the analyzed systems are adaptive; they are all standard and not personalizable. The only customization, if available, is the setting of a "quick withdrawal" amount, which will be displayed in the menu. Offering users the possibility to adjust text and icon sizes to their needs as well as providing the option of automatically detecting if a user is color blind and in that case use the appropriate combination of colors would all together improve legibility and make the system more inclusive.

We believe ATMs are still far from being inclusive and that a joint effort from researchers in academia and industry is necessary if we want to get there. Adopting a solution that suits the majority, like the current one, can be financially and pragmatically the right thing to do. Still, people are not statistics, and it should be a priority for banks to offer basic services more inclusively, as that is the right thing to do.

References

1. Coventry, L., De Angeli, A., Johnson, G.: Usability and biometric verification at the ATM interface. In: Proceedings of the SIGCHI Conference on Human Factors in Computing Systems, CHI 2003, pp. 153–160. Association for Computing Machinery, New York (2003). https://doi.org/10.1145/642611.642639
2. Curran, K., King, D.: Investigating the human computer interaction problems with automated teller machine navigation menus. Interact. Technol. Smart Educ. (2008)
3. De Luca, A., Langheinrich, M., Hussmann, H.: Towards understanding ATM security: a field study of real world ATM use. In: Proceedings of the Sixth Symposium on Usable Privacy and Security, SOUPS 2010. Association for Computing Machinery, New York (2010). https://doi.org/10.1145/1837110.1837131
4. Moncur, W., Leplâtre, G.: Pictures at the ATM: exploring the usability of multiple graphical passwords. In: Proceedings of the SIGCHI Conference on Human Factors in Computing Systems, CHI 2007, pp. 887–894. Association for Computing Machinery, New York (2007). https://doi.org/10.1145/1240624.1240758
5. Moquillaza, A., et al.: Developing an ATM interface using user-centered design techniques. In: Marcus, A., Wang, W. (eds.) DUXU 2017. LNCS, vol. 10290, pp. 690–701. Springer, Cham (2017). https://doi.org/10.1007/978-3-319-58640-3_49
6. World Health Organization: World report on disability 2011. World Health Organization (2011)
7. Oswal, S.K.: How accessible are the voice-guided automatic teller machines for the visually impaired? In: Proceedings of the 30th ACM International Conference on Design of Communication, SIGDOC 2012, pp. 65–70. Association for Computing Machinery, New York (2012). https://doi.org/10.1145/2379057.2379071
8. R. Hartson, P.S.P.: The UX Book. Process and Guidelines for Ensuring a Quality User Experience. Morgan Kaufmann, Elsevier (2012)
9. Singh, S., Kotzé, P.: An overview of systems design and development methodology with regard to the involvement of users and other stakeholders (2003)
10. Sauer, G., Holman, J., Lazar, J., Hochheiser, H., Feng, J.: Accessible privacy and security: a universally usable human-interaction proof tool. Univers. Access Inf. Soc. 9(3), 239–248 (2010)
11. Soares Guedes, L., C.A. Ribeiro, C., Ounkhir, S.: How can we improve the interaction of older users with devices? In: 9th International Conference on Software Development and Technologies for Enhancing Accessibility and Fighting Info-Exclusion, DSAI 2020, pp. 158–162. Association for Computing Machinery, New York (2020). https://doi.org/10.1145/3439231.3440611
12. Soares Guedes, L., Landoni, M.: How are we teaching and dealing with accessibility? A survey from Switzerland. In: 9th International Conference on Software Development and Technologies for Enhancing Accessibility and Fighting Info-Exclusion, DSAI 2020, pp. 141–146. Association for Computing Machinery, New York (2020). https://doi.org/10.1145/3439231.3440610
13. Thatcher, A., Mahlangu, S., Zimmerman, C.: Accessibility of ATMs for the functionally illiterate through icon-based interfaces. Behav. Inf. Technol. 25(1), 65–81 (2006)
14. Whitney, W.: Dimensions of usability: defining the conversation, driving the process (2003)
15. Z. Omariba, O.K.J.: Investigating ATM system accessibility for people with visual impairments (2013). https://www.researchgate.net/publication/325323200

Learning Experiences

The Annual BUILD Snapshot: Tracking Alumni Outcomes

Nancy Carrada Zuniga$^{(\boxtimes)}$ and Ashley Colbern

California State University Long Beach, Long Beach, CA 90804, USA
{Nancy.CarradaZuniga,Ashley.Colbern}@csulb.edu

Abstract. As the number of alumni of the CSULB BUILD Student Training Program continues to grow, it has become vital to develop a systematic way to track each trainee's graduate school enrollment and persistence. Developing a system that tracks post-graduate outcomes is not only important for determining the success of the program, but it also creates opportunities for the program to continue supporting its former trainees. A major challenge to tracking is that alumni are not very engaged in the process. To address this challenge, we developed the Annual BUILD Snapshot, a personalized unique Excel file designed to collect information on student activities during their time in the BUILD Program and after graduation. In this paper, we describe the development and implementation of the Annual BUILD Snapshot. We also discuss the strategies we used to launch the Snapshot, the administration process, and the outcomes and lessons learned from the process. Our findings have implications for similar training programs that need to track the short-term and long-term outcomes of their students and aim to remain connected to their alumni in unique and creative ways.

Keywords: Alumni tracking · Data management · Undergraduate research outcomes · Training programs

1 The BUILD Program

1.1 Goal of the BUILD Program

The CSULB BUilding Infrastructure Leading to Diversity (BUILD) initiative, funded by the National Institutes of Health (NIH), provides an intensive research training program for undergraduate students pursuing a biomedical or behavioral graduate degree [1]. One of the primary goals of the BUILD Program is to introduce students to research and help them enter graduate school, ultimately increasing the diversity of the biomedical workforce. The CSULB BUILD Program is implemented in two distinct funding phases, with BUILD I (2014–2019) which focused on the ramp up and implementation of various institutional, faculty and student programs, and BUILD II (2019–2024) which aims to refine, institutionalize, and disseminate activities developed during BUILD I that are identified to be effective and sustainable beyond the NIH funding period. For student training, this means that we need to determine how successful the program is in providing enriched research training to undergraduate students, especially those

© Springer Nature Switzerland AG 2021
C. Stephanidis et al. (Eds.): HCII 2021, LNCS 13096, pp. 345–360, 2021.
https://doi.org/10.1007/978-3-030-90328-2_22

from historically underrepresented minority groups, and in making them competitive for Ph.D. programs in biomedical and behavioral science disciplines. Thus, CSULB BUILD tracks its trainees' undergraduate and post-undergraduate research activities and outcomes. This paper describes the creation and implementation of a personalized unique Excel file designed to collect data on student outcomes during and after BUILD, known as the Annual BUILD Snapshot.

1.2 Importance of Tracking BUILD Alumni

The NIH Diversity Program Consortium includes all ten BUILD Programs across the U.S., which are evaluated at the consortium level to unveil the interventions necessary to help increase the diversity of the biomedical workforce [2]. In addition, each BUILD institution conducts its own local evaluation. This program assessment is based on data from active and former student trainees. Various types of data are gathered from active trainees including indicators of personal background (e.g., gender, race/ethnicity, first-generation status), academic performance (e.g., GPA, GRE scores), research interests and discipline(s), research productivity (e.g., conference presentations and publications), off-campus summer research experience participation, and graduate school outcomes (e.g., application and acceptance).

Alumni are also an important resource as they can provide valuable feedback about how the BUILD Program impacted their postgraduate progress as well as other insights regarding the effectiveness of program components. In fact, undergraduate research training programs are known to miscalculate the time it takes for underrepresented students to be fully prepared for graduate programs; after all, graduation does not equate preparedness [3]. With this in mind, BUILD's efforts began to focus on its alumni. Maintaining a relationship with alumni comes with major benefits for both parties. The program benefits by obtaining updates on alumni's post-graduation experiences such as matriculation, research experiences, and career progress. Research experiences may include awards, recognitions, and publications. Career progress can include the completion of milestones in graduate school and beyond. These updates allow programs to update their data for program evaluation and for dissemination efforts. Other lesser known nuances critical to the program's success may be obtained from alumni such as the time it takes to complete graduate degrees and graduate attrition [4]. Finally, obtaining continued feedback from alumni may help the program make changes to its curriculum [5] and may foster a community for alumni support [6]. Benefits to alumni may include the opportunity to mentor active trainees in the program [7] and participate in networking events such as conferences [6].

Efforts to strengthen a better relationship with alumni were developed (e.g., BUILD Fall Virtual Reunion, BUILD Summer Virtual Reunion). In terms of data collection, BUILD focused on data that could answer important questions related to the success of the program, such as: How many of its trainees entered a graduate program? How many graduated with their Master's or Ph.D. degrees? What career paths did they pursue? Although data about graduate school admissions were obtained from students upon completion of the program, long-term tracking is key to determining graduate school matriculation and attrition rates as well as late graduate school entry and other matriculation updates (e.g., going from a Master's to Ph.D.). Another marker of success for BUILD is trainees' entrance into the biomedical research workforce. Finally, professional achievements such as research publications and awards (e.g., scholarships, fellowships, grants) are evidence that speaks to the program and trainee success.

1.3 Previous Approaches to Alumni Tracking Methods

Obtaining data from active trainees is straightforward because they are in regular communication and contact with the program faculty and staff while they are in the program. In contrast, it is challenging to obtain data from alumni who typically move away from their undergraduate institution and are busy with adjusting to graduate school or other post-baccalaureate work. By the beginning of Phase II, the BUILD trainees' composition shifted to having more alumni than active trainees. In anticipation of the increasing complexity of data management, due to the growing number of BUILD alumni, a Program Data Management (PDM) team was created at the start of Phase II that would manage all aspects of data collection. As such, the BUILD leadership and the PDM team evaluated the strategies that were previously used to collect data from active trainees and alumni. It is important to note that the PDM team may be unique to the CSULB BUILD Program. Not all research training programs have the resources to form a PDM team. We hope that by describing our previous data collection and how it influenced the development of the Snapshot, other training programs can leverage the lessons learned from our efforts.

Prior to the Snapshot, BUILD staff relied on several informal methods to gather alumni data, such as obtaining updates from faculty mentors who maintained a relationship with their trainees or periodically checking social media (e.g., LinkedIn). However, as the number of alumni began to grow, these methods were too time-consuming to perform and not sustainable to capture alumni outcomes over the long run. By the end of BUILD I, an online survey was designed to have alumni directly fill out the information being tracked. This survey was used to streamline the alumni data collection during BUILD II. In May 2019, the Alumni Qualtrics Survey was administered to 176 BUILD I alumni (i.e., students who completed BUILD as of spring of 2019). Our initial plan was to administer the survey over a two-week window and provide one reminder e-mail a few days before the survey closed. However, we only received 12 responses by the survey closing date. Due to the low response rates, we followed up with each alumnus with the survey link using a personalized e-mail invitation. Although this additional step was time-consuming, 98 alumni (56%) eventually completed the online survey.

While we had a fair response rate, we discovered several limitations with this data collection method. First, we realized that collecting longitudinal data from our BUILD alumni in future years would be far more time-consuming if we continue to send individual e-mails to each alumnus. Second, we realized that our BUILD I alumni were not a homogeneous group, meaning they were completing our program at various points in their undergraduate schooling (see Table 1). Because the BUILD Program consists of a variety of training programs (lower-division vs. upper-division programs), we needed to devise a method that could capture our alumni's unique post-undergraduate experiences without overwhelming them. For example, the 2019 Alumni Qualtrics Survey included all post-CSULB outcomes (e.g., graduate school items, industry items, career plans, etc.,) and the survey became lengthy because alumni were required to complete all sections of the survey. It was necessary to display all possible outcomes because not all alumni entered graduate school after completing BUILD (e.g., entered multiple graduate programs; took time off school and then entered a graduate program; went straight into industry). With a survey, we also could not communicate to the alumni which sections we needed updates for, so we requested for the alumni to complete all the sections which led to a great deal of redundancy. For that reason, many alumni who participated in this survey reported having had a very frustrating experience. Lastly, the items in this survey were too general (e.g., How many Masters programs did you apply to and get accepted into?) and we ended up with responses that lacked context such as "Applied to zero master programs," and "Accepted into one master program." In this example, the BUILD staff was left wondering whether the trainee erroneously entered zero master applications or was rejected from a Ph.D. program but offered admissions to a master's program instead. These types of data discrepancies led the program staff needing to further communicate with the alumni and/or their mentors via e-mail to fill in the gaps.

Table 1. Students enter the CSULB BUILD program at different class standings: scholars and fellows divisions are upper divisions. The associates program is a lower division program.

BUILD I & II components/Programs	Entry class standing	Length of division	May transition to an upper division
Associates	Sophomores & Juniors	1-year	Yes
Scholars I & II	Juniors	2-years	No
Fellows	Seniors	1-year	No

Given all the limitations mentioned above, the PDM team identified several factors that can aid the planning of future alumni data collection: (1) Establish or re-establish rapport and transparency with the alumni in regards to what data the program is required to collect for NIH and program evaluation purposes; (2) Reduce survey burden by decreasing the number of repeated inquiries with each data collection attempt and shortening the time that it would take to update trainee data or enter new data into the database; and (3) Introduce the new data collection method to the active trainees so they could become familiar with the process while they are in the program. With these factors in mind, the PDM team developed a unique Excel file for each BUILD trainee (active trainee or alumnus) that included their information (i.e., BUILD Program data and outcomes) pre-populated. The purpose of the individualized Excel file is to serve as a unique data collection tool for active trainees and alumni, allowing them to easily provide new updates, changes, and milestones every year.

The Annual BUILD Snapshot. The PDM team titled this new data collection method "The Annual BUILD Snapshot." The Snapshots included specific outcome sections that covered all possible unique paths. This would give our students their own 'Snapshot' of their undergraduate experiences and post-BUILD trajectories. With this method of collecting data, our trainees would simply fill in the sections specific to their career paths at the time of Snapshot administration. These personalized Excel files would be stored in a secure data encrypted CSULB Microsoft One-Drive folder. With the Snapshots, the PDM would simply e-mail the active trainees and alumni a link to their individualized Excel file that is pre-populated with their data. We hoped this new data collection method would also help create transparency since students would be able to see the data that is collected and maintained. Furthermore, the use of this shared file may reduce the response burden for alumni because they would be able to update pre-populated data, add new data, and add comments to further clarify any section.

2 Method

2.1 Developing the BUILD Snapshot

BUILD Snapshot Design. The design of the Snapshot began in the summer of 2020 and lasted a total of two months. This process can be summed up in three steps: (1) identifying the data to be collected; (2) designing and formatting the Snapshot for readability and usability; and (3) piloting and incorporating alumni feedback into the Snapshot template and instructions (discussed in Sect. 2.2).

Identifying Data to be Collected. The PDM team first identified the program and outcome data needed for the Snapshot. For both phases of the program, the type of data collected was largely guided by the NIH requirements which included two categories: active trainee data and alumni data. The following data elements and outcomes were collected for active trainees and alumni. Refer to Table 2 for an outline of the data collected.

Table 2. Data elements of the snapshot.

Data elements	Data collection/Verification method
CSULB E-mail & Personal E-mail	E-mails are the main contact source
LinkedIn URL	Alumni are contacted via LinkedIn if their e-mails are no longer active
Standardized Test Scores & CV Link	GRE scores (or official reports) and CVs are obtained via a Qualtrics Survey link
Estimated CSULB Graduation	CSULB graduation estimation is obtained at the application phase
Major while in BUILD	Majors are verified with transcripts
Official CSULB Graduation Date	Official graduation dates are verified with transcripts
Degree-Major and Minor at CSULB Graduation	CSULB degree, major(s), minor(s) are verified with transcripts
List of Undergraduate Research Experiences (URE)	URE Program/location (e.g., OURS, HRPG, BUILD Fellow) and participation date range are collected

(continued)

Table 2. (*continued*)

Data elements	Data collection/Verification method
List of Post-Bacc/Graduate Programs & Admission Statuses	Information on the first round of post-undergraduate program applications and admission status is obtained. (Subsequent application rounds are not obtained) If no applications are provided, we ask: "Are you planning to apply?" and "If yes, what year?" If trainees are not applying, we ask: "What is the reason?"
Postbaccalaureate/Graduate Program Matriculation and Program Status	All programs students matriculated into are obtained. This includes the name of institution, the field of study, the type of degree/certificate, start date, current status, and graduation date
Academic and Non-Academic Employment	Title, employer, date range are obtained after graduating
Conference Presentations	Presentations (title, type, authors, conference name, and dates) are obtained during BUILD
Publications	Publications (title, published date, authors, publication type, publisher, status) are obtained during BUILD and post-BUILD
Honors/Awards	Awards are obtained during BUILD and post-BUILD
Milestones & Accomplishments	Students are asked to share any milestones and accomplishments that could not be captured by the previous outcomes

In addition to the data needed for the annual reports to the funding agency, the Snapshot gathered data needed for internal evaluation purposes. For example, capturing the reasons trainees did not matriculate to graduate school could help the program improve resources and support. Additionally, the BUILD Program was interested in learning which graduate schools trainees applied to and whether they were accepted during their first application cycle. To capture this, the PDM team created a section in the Snapshot that included the universities and programs the trainees applied to and their application/admission status (e.g., not accepted, accepted and declined, accepted and enrolled). With these data, we will be able to identify trends and examine the acceptance and enrollment rates within our partner institutions (i.e., University of California, Irvine, and University of Southern California).

Designing and Formatting the Snapshot for Readability and Usability. Using an Excel file that has been designed as a data collection tool is different from using a general spreadsheet. Thus, we developed Snapshot instructions to help the alumni and active trainees understand the layout and functions of the Snapshot. Two challenges that surfaced during the development of the instructions had to do with (1) figuring out whether new or updated data was entered by a participant and (2) telling apart participants who viewed their Snapshots but had no updates from those who have not had a chance to update their Snapshots. To address these concerns, we instructed participants to highlight new data entries or updates. We also instructed them to provide their initials and date of completion at the bottom of the Professional Scholar Activities sheet.

The instructions also helped trainees navigate the Snapshot. An example was the drop-down menu options in some of the Snapshot sections that were denoted with an asterisk in the header cell. The drop-down menus prevented trainees from entering data in their own words and instead forced them to choose an option from the drop-down menu. This was helpful in sections that focused on data that would be updated repeatedly over the years (e.g., graduate school application or matriculation status). A second Excel feature we used was the embedded messages. These messages allowed the PDM team to add specific directions to a particular cell or section. For instance, we embedded a message that read "Please enable pop-ups so you can click on the survey hyperlink." The survey link would then direct participants to a Qualtrics survey that collected GRE/MCAT scores and CVs. This survey was designed to avoid displaying tests scores in the Snapshot and thereby ensure privacy.

As mentioned above, GRE/MCAT scores were not displayed in the Snapshots because tests scores are protected under FERPA. Program assistants were part of the data entry process which is another reason why the GRE/MCAT scores were obtained via a Qualtrics survey. Lastly, the PDM team incorporated BUILD colors and the Annual BUILD Snapshot logo (see Fig. 2) to make it aesthetically appealing.

2.2 Snapshot Pilot Test

Once a template of the Snapshot was fully developed, the PDM team pilot tested the Snapshot in mid-September 2020. Four BUILD I alumni were invited to pilot the Snapshot because of their uniquely complex post-graduate experience:

- *Person A*: Scholar I, Scholar II, and Scholar III Participant

  - Career path: accepted into a Ph.D. program but declined, pursued industry

- *Person B*: Associate, Scholar I, and Scholar II Participant

  - Career path: entered 2 master programs but left both, pursued industry

- *Person C*: Scholar I, Scholar II, and Scholar III Participant

  - Career path: entered Ph.D. program and transferred to a different Ph.D. program to continue research with mentor

- *Person D*: Scholar I and Scholar II Participant

  - Career path: completed master's program and entered Doctor of Medicine program

To help structure the participants feedback, the PDM team designed a short 9-item Qualtrics survey that inquired about their experiences with navigating the Snapshot sections, usefulness of the examples provided, effectiveness of the guidance provided by the instructions, and likelihood that the alumni would complete the Snapshot annually. Two open-ended items asked for feedback on the specific sheets, Graduate Employment and Professional Scholar Activities. Lastly, one open-ended item asked about the parts of the Snapshot the alumni found challenging to complete. In addition to the survey, the PDM team scheduled a 30-min Zoom feedback meeting with each of the participants. The alumni provided in-depth feedback about the instructions, the organization and formatting of the template, and the template data fields.

Populating the Snapshots. By early October 2020, the Snapshot template (see Fig. 1) and the instructions were finalized. The next step was to populate the Snapshots for all active trainees and alumni, meaning enter each individual's data into the Snapshots.

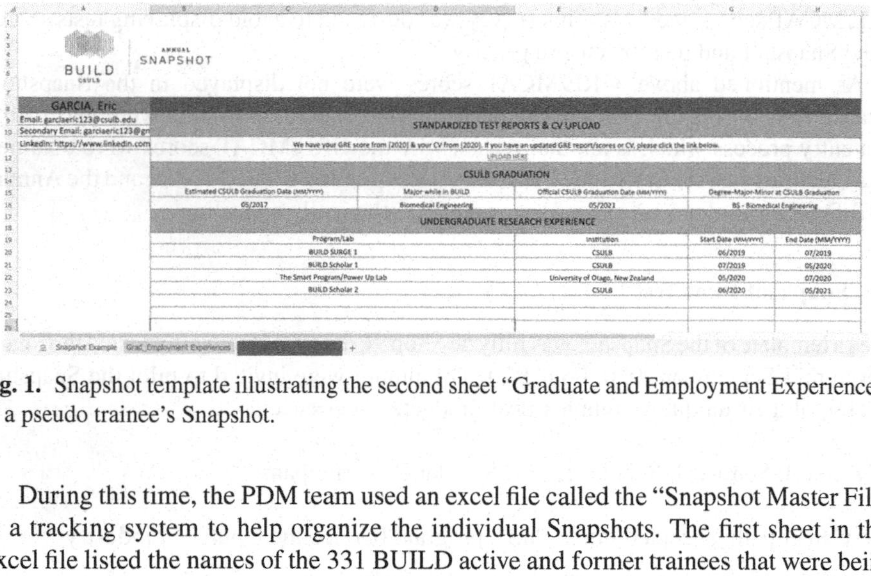

Fig. 1. Snapshot template illustrating the second sheet "Graduate and Employment Experiences" of a pseudo trainee's Snapshot.

During this time, the PDM team used an excel file called the "Snapshot Master File" as a tracking system to help organize the individual Snapshots. The first sheet in this Excel file listed the names of the 331 BUILD active and former trainees that were being tracked at the time of the launch and their start date in terms of the BUILD award year. Two columns were created to help organize the trainees in terms of BUILD Phase (1 or 2) and Batches (smaller subset of data for management purposes). The BUILD Phase column consisted of BUILD I Alumni (award years 1–5), BUILD II Alumni (award years 6–10), and whether the student is an active trainee. Each trainee was assigned to their appropriate category. The Batches column assigned a number to trainees from 1–6 to divide them into smaller groups. Note that Award year 6 was a unique grant year as some trainees overlapped between BUILD Phases I and II.

Once this tracking system was set up, the PDM team obtained the existing program data from a database system that the BUILD Program was using called FileMaker® Pro. This database includes BUILD active trainee and alumni outcome data. Please see Table 2 for all the outcome data that were exported to the Snapshots. Upkeeping the existing data in FileMaker® Pro is an important task for the PDM team in order to provide the most updated data files to BUILD leaders and partners who plan on presenting or publishing. With this in mind, it is important to note that all data stored in FileMaker® Pro came from various sources such as the CSULB BUILD application, 2019 Alumni Qualtrics Survey, social media updates, and updates from BUILD faculty members. The Snapshot would be an additional source of data collection that would further update BUILD's database. The existing data from FileMaker® Pro was used to pre-populated the Snapshots, a process that took about three weeks.

2.3 Snapshot Launch

By early November 2020, all Snapshots were pre-populated and ready for launch. Next, an e-mail was designed to help plan the mass e-mails for all active trainees and alumni. We first e-mailed the Snapshot links to the active trainees because this would allow the PDM team to test and adjust the e-mails before sending the e-mails to the alumni. We used the LISTSERV® Maestro E-mail Marketing Software to send out our e-mails. With this software, the PDM team was able to design an e-mail template with a header, structure the content, attached several attachments, specify students by their names, and include unique Snapshot Excel links. Another important feature of this software was the ability to send out e-mails on behalf of a specific CSULB BUILD Program leader that the students know.

A schedule was set with dates of when the e-mails would be sent. The BUILD Training Directors who had the most contact with the student trainees during their time in the program served as the "influencers" for the alumni e-mail launch. For the active trainees, an announcement was made during their Learning Community class. The Snapshots were scheduled to launch in early November and close in early December. The active trainees would be the first to receive their Snapshots followed by the alumni three days later. The schedule also included three e-mail reminders.

Once the schedule was set, the PDM team worked with the faculty and staff in the BUILD Student Training Program to obtain their insight on the e-mail content. First, they advised the PDM team regarding how to word the introduction in the e-mail launch to make it more sensitive to the students during the period of the COVID-19 pandemic and the Black Lives Matter Movement. The leadership recognized this sensitivity was necessary since some of the alumni just completed the BUILD Program in May of 2019 and there had been minimal alumni contact before this Snapshot launch. The Student Training faculty and staff also suggested emphasizing the purpose of this new data collection method and why BUILD was no longer using its Qualtrics survey. In addition, they indicated that reinforcing the purpose of alumni data collection was essential to include in the e-mail launch. As a result, the following phrase was added: "Keeping track of your progress in graduate school, career, and/or future career plans allows BUILD to modify student training and share your success with BUILD's current trainees, program faculty and staff, as well as BUILD's funder the National Institutes of Health (NIH)." During the discussion, the faculty and staff of the Student Training Program also suggested the need for a marketing plan. They believed there needed to be more awareness about the Annual BUILD Snapshot among the trainees since the PDM team was relying on the students' personal e-mails on file as the only source of communication.

Marketing Campaign. The BUILD leadership and PDM team decided that the Snapshot would be part of the annual data collection that takes place for active trainees in spring. Introducing the active trainees to the Snapshot before they leave the BUILD Program will help build familiarity with this data collection process. After they complete the program, they can easily update their personalized Snapshot. Considering that we were implementing a new program requirement and that the Annual BUILD Snapshot would serve as the catalyst to engage and re-build the connection and rapport among the CSULB BUILD alumni, we developed a marketing campaign to raise trainees' awareness of the Snapshot and to reconnect with our alumni.

As part of this marketing campaign, the alumni would be provided with incentives if they participated in the Snapshot. Two incentive plans were implemented to thank the alumni for taking the time to update their Snapshot and increase response rates. For the first incentive, the first 40 alumni who completed their Snapshot received a $5 Amazon e-card. The second incentive was a raffle to win one of four $25 Amazon e-cards for alumni who completed the Snapshot by the deadline of December 9.

The marketing of the Snapshot also involved the creation of an Annual BUILD Snapshot logo (see Fig. 2). We embedded this logo in the Snapshot and all advertisements and promotional marketing tools, including flyers, infographics, a 6-min video, and social media posts.

Fig. 2. Annual BUILD snapshot logo

Flyers and an infographic (see Fig. 3) were created using Canva (a free online infographic template). The flyers introduced the Annual BUILD Snapshot and its launch and deadline dates, and described the two types of incentives to encourage alumni participation. The infographic provided active trainees and alumni with 3 main steps to help them fill out the Snapshot. Within each step, important sub-instructions were included. The first step focused on the resources (e.g., PDF instructions) we included in the e-mails that would guide participants when updating their Snapshots. The second step highlighted specific Snapshot sections that the PDM team expected to be overlooked by the alumni such as their updated contact information, standardized test scores and CV survey link. One of the sub-instructions directed their attention to the second sheet where additional outcomes could be updated. The third step reminded participants to initial and date at the bottom of the second sheet for the PDM team to recognize that they completed the Snapshot.

Social media announcements helped reach out to alumni who were active on such platforms. During late October to early December flyers were posted on the program's social media platforms (e.g., Instagram, Facebook, and LinkedIn) along with video clips (refer to the Snapshot Video section). We posted twice a week for the first month

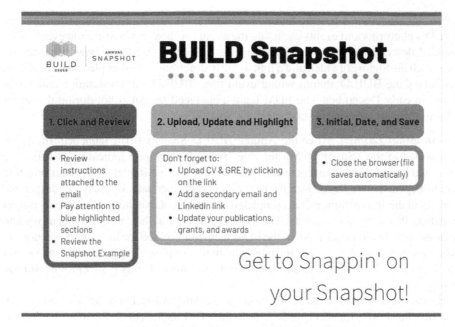

Fig. 3. Annual BUILD snapshot infographic

and reduced the number of posts to once a week for the final two weeks. Lastly, we posted a description that covered the purpose of the Snapshot in our LinkedIn account. In total, we made 17 social media posts (eight on Facebook, eight on Instagram, and one in LinkedIn) and a total of 14 short video clips, seven for each of the program's Facebook and Instagram accounts, providing an overview and instructions for filling out the Snapshot.

Snapshot Video. To simplify the Snapshot completion process, a video was created that described the Snapshot with tips to show how to properly complete the main sections. Training Directors of the Student Training Program narrated the video. The content of the video included:

- Introductions of the Training Directors
- Acknowledgment of the current events at that time: COVID-19 Pandemic and outcome of the presidential election
- BUILD's support of the Black Lives Matter Movement
- Purpose of tracking data during and after completion of the BUILD Program
- Acknowledgement of previous collection of alumni data
- Introduction of the Annual BUILD Snapshot
- Heads-up of the Snapshot e-mail invitation
- Tips for filling out the Snapshot sections

The video was uploaded to the BUILD YouTube channel in mid-October. A link of the video was included within the influencer e-mails to our alumni.

Additional Snapshot Advertisements. The PDM team advertised the Snapshot in other BUILD's platforms and events including the alumni webpage where alumni events were posted. A description of the Snapshot with the title "Keep Us Updated!" was also included along with the Snapshot video and a link to the instructions. Another place we advertised was during the BUILD alumni winter event title "BUILD Virtual Reunion and Trivia Night" in early December. The PDM team announced the Snapshot during this event and reminded all attendees to complete the Snapshot.

Post-Snapshot Launch. After the Annual BUILD Snapshot was launched, the PDM team added to the "Snapshot Master File" two columns, one indicating whether the individual Snapshot was complete and the other if it was incomplete. The Snapshots that were not opened were flagged for the next e-mail reminder date. By early December, the majority of the active trainees had completed the Snapshot, but there were several alumni Snapshots that were not accessed. The PDM team sent out the early bird incentives and the raffle incentive reminder. Next, the PDM team highlighted the incomplete sections in green and then e-mail these alumni asking them to complete the green sections. Alumni who had active LinkedIn accounts were contacted through this platform with similar messages.

By early February, the data collection for the Annual BUILD Snapshot was closed. To thank the alumni for their participation, the PDM team sent all the alumni who had completed or partially completed their Snapshot a short survey asking for their home address in order to receive a reusable BUILD face mask. Finally, the PDM team and one student assistant entered the data obtained from the Snapshots into FileMaker® Pro. An expiration date was added to all the Snapshot links to prevent the Snapshots from being accessed. The Snapshots were cleaned and saved in a new folder for the next administration.

3 Results

3.1 Overall Snapshot Participation

A total of 319 Snapshots were e-mailed to the CSULB BUILD active trainees ($N = 58$) and alumni ($N = 261$) in November of 2021 (see Table 3 for a breakdown of participation).

Table 3. Snapshot participation for CSULB BUILD trainees

BUILD trainees	Did not participated		Participated		Total
	n	%	n	%	
BUILD alumni	126	48.28%	135	51.72%	261
Active trainees	6	10.34%	52	89.66%	58
Total	132	41.38%	187	58.62%	319*

Note: * Total includes the 4 alumni who participated in the pilot phase

Of the total of 135 alumni who participated in the Snapshot, 52 (38%) had minor incomplete Snapshot sections. Active trainees were required to participate in the Snapshot as part of their Learning Community activities.

3.2 Comparison of Alumni Qualtrics Survey and Snapshot Response Rates

The response rates of the Alumni Qualtrics Survey and the Annual BUILD Snapshot were compared by using the sample of alumni ($n = 176$) who were previously invited to participate in the Qualtrics survey. This sample only includes BUILD alumni who completed the BUILD Program as of spring of 2019.

Both data collection methods had unique labor-intensive processes. For the Alumni Qualtrics Survey, it was the process of emailing every alumnus a personalized e-mail asking them to complete the survey. As described earlier, the Annual BUILD Snapshot included a targeted campaign that included incentives, e-mail reminders, and social media posts. Both methods produced fairly similar results (see Table 3), and each method required about a 4-month data collection window (see Fig. 4).

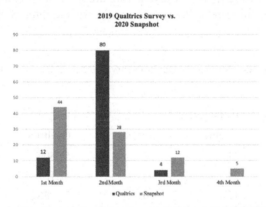

Fig. 4. Participation in the Alumni Qualtrics Survey and the Annual BUILD Snapshot within a four-month period (excluding alumni who participated in the Snapshot pilot phase)

One unique component of the Snapshot campaign is the use of incentives. As seen in Fig. 4, the Snapshot received more than triple the number of responses compared to the Qualtrics survey in the first month. It appears that the incentives may have helped increase the alumni participation in the early weeks, compared to the Qualtrics survey where we had very low participation during the first month.

In Table 4 we provide the response rates for each data collection method with the sample of alumni ($n = 176$). The Alumni Qualtrics Survey (56%, $n = 98$) had a higher response rate than the Snapshot (53%, $n = 93$), but it is important to note that both data collection methods are quite different. A Qualtrics survey may be an easier process compared to the Snapshot as it requires reading instructions and understanding what can be added or updated in each of the sections.

Table 4. Response rates by participation in the Alumni Qualtrics Survey and/or Annual BUILD Snapshot

2019 Qualtrics vs. 2020 Snapshot Participation		
	n	%
2019 Qualtrics only	46	26.14%
2020 Snapshot only	41	23.30%
Both	52	29.55%
Neither	37	21.02%
Total	176	100%

Observing the response rates for the Scholars and Fellows cohorts is important because these upper-division programs provide students with intensive research training. Since the Fellows program started in the fourth year of the BUILD I phase with a small number of students during its first two years, we are not able to compare participation rates by cohorts for this group. Participation rates for the three Scholars cohorts are outlined in Table 5.

Table 5. Comparing participation in the Qualtrics survey and the Snapshot by the BUILD Scholars Cohort

Scholar cohorts	Participation		Response rate	
	Qualtrics	Snapshot	Qualtrics	Snapshot
Cohort 1 ($n = 40$)	21	22	52.50%	55.00%
Cohort 2 ($n = 38$)	24	22	63.15%	57.89%
Cohort 3 ($n = 35$)	12	30	34.28%	85.71%
Total ($n = 113$)	57	74	50.44%	65.48%

Obtaining data from older alumni cohorts is relatively challenging, however the two data collection methods provided similar response rates for the first and second Scholars cohorts. For the last cohort, the Snapshot response rate of 85.71% is much higher than the 34.28% of the Qualtrics survey. This low response rate for the Qualtrics survey may be explained by timing. The Qualtrics survey was administered right after the third Scholars cohort had completed BUILD. The timing of the Qualtrics survey was probably too soon for this group of alumni since the BUILD Program collects active student data during the spring. Among the Scholars cohorts, the Snapshot has a higher response rate compared to the Qualtrics survey, 65.48% and 50.44% respectively.

3.3   Benefits of Snapshot

Unfortunately, a limitation in our process of comparing the Qualtrics survey to the Snapshot is not being able to quantify or provide the unique quality of data obtained by the Snapshot. Despite this limitation, the response rates suggest that the Snapshot is as successful as a Qualtrics survey when reaching out to alumni. Because of this promising finding, we believe it is important to highlight several potential benefits when using Snapshots as a data collection tool. First, using Snapshots to collect data from both alumni and active trainees does create transparency between the program and trainees. Participants of the Snapshots were able to review the data that was populated in their own Snapshot which included BUILD data and post-BUILD data. We did not receive e-mails from alumni asking us to clarify why we were requesting such data or ensuring we had previously obtained such data from them in the past. These types of inquiries were prominent during the Qualtrics survey administration. We believe this transparency led to better communication between the program and alumni, our second benefit. Communication between the PDM team and the alumni was smooth because the Snapshot allowed participants to include comments in several key outcome sections (e.g., matriculation, honor/awards, publications, etc.,). Lastly, the Snapshot allowed us to capture dynamic data, meaning the unique career paths of our alumni. Because alumni data is nonlinear, having a data collection tool that allows participants to enter new data and update old entries is essential as this may help programs obtain better quality data.

4   Lessons Learned & Recommendations

As other programs have discovered, collecting data from alumni is a challenging task and regardless of the data collection method, it requires a lot of work and planning. With the Qualtrics survey, it was apparent that e-mail reminders alone were not sufficient to connect with the alumni. The alumni were more responsive to personal requests from their faculty mentors and we had to contact the trainees' mentor to solicit their help with data collection. Going forward with the Snapshot, we knew that the first administration of this new data collection method would require significant effort. We also knew that in order to jumpstart this process, we would have to incentivize completion of the Snapshot and bring awareness by launching a social media campaign. This also took a lot of work, but we were fortunate that the BUILD Program already had a social media presence and platform to post Snapshot information and details. Additionally, reminder e-mails were strategically scheduled.

One discovery that was made during the Snapshot administration was that the BUILD Program was contacting many of the alumni via an old e-mail or a mailbox that the alum did not check often. We suspect that we may not be connecting with many of the alumni because of this problem. Going forward for the next administration of the Snapshot, it would be worth the effort to inquire about any e-mail address changes at alumni events to update our contact list.

Additionally, to increase participation in the Snapshot from all programs in the upcoming years, we may have to be more strategic with our data collection procedures. It would be beneficial to directly e-mail the alumni who have not been in contact with BUILD to help increase participation, instead of including them in the mass e-mail list.

We believe that over time the Snapshot may reduce redundancy in reporting and increase transparency between the program and alumni. We will continue to use the Snapshots for the remaining BUILD II years to evaluate the effectiveness of our program. We believe that programs like CSULB BUILD can benefit from implementing the Snapshot if their trainees enter the program at various undergraduate stages (e.g., Juniors, Seniors, etc.,) because it will streamline the data collection process. An important consideration is the timing needed to develop a template of the Snapshot and an efficient Snapshot tracking system. Once this is set up, the maintenance of the Snapshot is fairly simple. Another time-consuming aspect of the Snapshot is entering the data from the Snapshot into a database system for data storage. Our PDM team entered the data manually from the Snapshots to the database, but this process may be simplified if an Excel code is applied to help generate reports. Lastly, to collect alumni data, program leadership should introduce the alumni data collection methods to active trainees and continue a relationship once trainees become alumni. These efforts will lessen the burden of creating an intensive marketing campaign. The next steps for our program are to continue our long-term alumni tracking efforts and establish engaging alumni events. Over time, we believe the BUILD Program will benefit from the quality of data obtained from the Snapshot. The accuracy and completeness of the Snapshot data will be examined in a future paper.

Acknowledgments. This work was supported by the National Institute of General Medical Sciences of the National Institutes of Health under Award Numbers UL1GM118979, TL4GM118980, and RL5GM118978. The content is solely the responsibility of the authors and does not necessarily represent the official views of the National Institutes of Health.

References

1. Urizar, G. G., et al.: Advancing research opportunities and promoting pathways in graduate education: a systemic approach to BUILD training at California State University, Long Beach (CSULB). BioMed Central (BMC) Proc. **11**(12), 27–40 (2017)
2. Davidson, P.L., et al.: A participatory approach to evaluating a national training and institutional change initiative: the BUILD longitudinal evaluation. BioMed Central (BMC) Proc. **11**(12), 157–169 (2017)
3. McGee, R., Jr., Saran, S., Krulwich, T.A.: Diversity in the biomedical research workforce: developing talent. Mount Sinai J. Med. A J. Trans. Pers. Med. **79**(3), 397–411 (2012)
4. Lightfoot, R.C., Doerner, W.G.: Student success and failure in a graduate criminology/criminal justice program. Am. J. Crim. Justice **33**(1), 113–129 (2008)
5. Younis, N.: Impact of alumni feedback on the curriculum. In: Proceedings of the 2002 American Society for Engineering Education Annual Conference & Exposition, pp. 1–9 (2002)
6. Ingram, K.W., Haynes, L.L., Davidson-Shivers, G.V., Irvin, R.: Building an instructional design alumni support community: tracking alumni for program evaluation and added value. In: Association for Educational Communications and Technology (2004)
7. Skrzypek, C., Diebold, J., Kim, W., Krause, D.: Formalizing alumni mentoring in social work education: lessons learned from a three-year program evaluation. J. Soc. Work Educ. 1–14 (2020)

Using Self-developed Mobile APP and Arduino to Provide Integrated Multimedia for Lower Graders' English Vocabulary Learning

Pei-Yin Chen[1], Yaming Tai[2], Teng-Hui Tseng[3], and Yu-Liang Ting[4(✉)]

[1] Lu Jiang Elementary School, Luzhou, New Taipei City, Taiwan
[2] Department of Children English Education, National Taipei University of Education, Taipei City, Taiwan
[3] Department of Communication Engineering, Oriental University of Science and Technology, New Taipei City, Taiwan
[4] Department of Technology Application and Human Resource Development, National Taiwan Normal University, Taipei City, Taiwan
yting@ntnu.edu.tw

Abstract. This study investigated the effects of using self-developed mobile APP and Arduino in English vocabulary learning, to find out the impact on students' vocabulary learning ability, to understand students' perception of such learning patterns, and to evaluate the feasibility of lower graders using APP in English vocabulary learning. Arduino was adopted to be associated with APP to provide integrated multimedia support. The study adopted Single Subject Research Design. Five first graders from New Taipei City Taiwan were selected and the experiment was conducted for 10 times in 8 weeks. Data were collected through testing, observation, interviews and questionnaires. The results showed that self-developed English learning APP has a positive impact on students' vocabulary learning ability. Students gave positive response and held positive attitude toward English learning through APP. Students were willing to learn with English learning APP and enjoy learning. The integration of English learning and APP and Arduino was addressed and hoped to broaden the spectrum of English learning design in mobile devices.

Keywords: English vocabulary learning · First grade · Mobile learning · Mobile APP

1 Introduction

With the rapid development of information and communication technology, the widespread use of versatile technology for language learning has led to the emergence of various applications, which are diverse and rich in types and functions [1]. Related researches and studies emerged [2]. Learning through mobile apps has become a new kind of learning. Personalization, convenience and autonomy, coupled with the mechanism of immediate feedback, bring many advantages to mobile learning, so that learning

© Springer Nature Switzerland AG 2021
C. Stephanidis et al. (Eds.): HCII 2021, LNCS 13096, pp. 361–372, 2021.
https://doi.org/10.1007/978-3-030-90328-2_23

is no longer restricted by time and space. The development of hardware technology for novel mobile devices such as smartphones and tablet computers has strengthened the convenience of learners in classroom learning and self-study after class, and has also promoted the prosperity of mobile learning research. Song [3] used short message service (SMS) for vocabulary learning research and pointed out that through mobile technology, learning becomes a kind of portable learning, and the use and combination can improve learners' English learning effectiveness and attitudes. Milrad and Spikol [4] argued in their research that mobile vehicles have unique characteristics that allow students to learn on their own and replace computers in classrooms, and through the combination of related software and mobile equipment, learners can not only learn by themselves, but also cooperate and learn with peers. Li [5] also put forward the concept of mobile learning in his research, and believed that this intelligent user interface learning mode can effectively enhance students' learning interest and learning motivation. Due to the lightness and portability of mobile technology, the proportion of students holding smartphones or tablet computers is increasing, and their age is gradually decreasing. As mobile vehicles have gradually become an indispensable learning tool in students' daily lives, mobile learning strategies have also been widely used. Related learning software (APP) have emerged one after another and have sprung up like mushrooms, and the direction of development is gradually becoming adaptable. The integration of APP learning programs and language learning is getting closer and closer. The integration of technology and language learning should not only learn language content and structure accurately and accurately, but also can effectively use language to communicate in life [6].

Vocabulary learning is the basis of English learning. Vocabulary is one of the important elements of language composition and the key to building language knowledge and skills [7]. Linking newly learned language information with old concepts and knowledge through meaningful visual images and sounds can help vocabulary learning and enhance memory. Researchers have also discovered through their own teaching experience that in addition to repeated reading, in the vocabulary teaching of the lower grades, collocation of actions and pictures can indeed enhance students' learning connection and memory. In addition, children in the lower grades love games and animations, and immediate positive enhancement is of great help to the learning of the lower grades. Therefore, through interesting and vivid textbooks, the motivation and interest of the lower grades in vocabulary learning can be enhanced, thereby enhancing their learning effectiveness.

Although there are many English vocabulary learning apps in the market, the content is with varying degrees of difficulty. Therefore, this research will use the mobile phone's authoring tool and digital technologies, which are the ability to process voice messages, and integrate the learning content of elementary schools into the training process of listening, speaking, reading, and writing skills in English. This study will use the game interface that students love to design their vocabulary learning. In addition to exploring students' acceptance and perception of vocabulary learning activities, it also studies how APP can improve students' learning effectiveness. At the same time, the self-made APP combined with the sensor device of the Arduino monitor can solve the traditional teaching problem that teachers cannot take into account and understand the learning situation of all students at the same time. The APP application used in this research is self-designed, using the voice recognition system in the mobile device to train students to recognize and read English words, within which designing two layers of pictures and voice prompts, in order to achieve multimedia learning. The purpose of this research is to explore the influence of self-developed English learning APP on the English vocabulary learning ability of first-year students in elementary school, and the feasibility of developing self-made English learning apps.

2 The Literatures Review

Vocabulary Teaching
Vocabulary teaching is a very important part of English teaching and the key to language learning. Many scholars have also pointed out the importance of vocabulary knowledge in the first or second language [8]. Research on vocabulary learning indicates that students with more vocabulary their vocabulary learning ability are relatively better in listening, speaking, reading, and writing. In addition, some scholars have also pointed out that learners' vocabulary ability will affect their reading comprehension. Vocabulary teaching is a crucial teaching focus in any language learning method. In elementary school English teaching, vocabulary teaching is one of the main curriculum activities. Teachers spend a lot of effort on vocabulary teaching. Different exercises are adopted to help students improve vocabulary proficiency, and they are combined with sentence structure activities and integrated into reading comprehension and writing.

Since the 1980s, vocabulary teaching began to receive attention, and many vocabulary teaching methods, strategies and techniques have been proposed in the field of language learning [9]. Vocabulary is not easy to sort out general rules, because most of the language research focuses on grammar and phonetics. Vocabulary teaching should not only teach the meaning of vocabulary itself, but must be able to help learners expand their vocabulary knowledge. Jalongo and Sobolak [10] believed that high-quality vocabulary teaching can not only help students improve their vocabulary learning ability, but also provide them with a positive learning experience. They further proposed that teachers should provide a wealth of vocabulary instruction, including: thinking, questioning, clarifying, repeating, pointing to words, and supplying examples. And provide appropriate definitions of words. Learners' learning attitude and motivation also affect their vocabulary learning performance. Researchers have observed from their own teaching experience that active learners will have relatively high vocabulary learning performance. Younger learners must be active and engaged in order to remember new vocabulary or learn different meanings in vocabulary [10].

Teaching methods and skills will change with many factors, such as teaching content, teaching time, and value to students. Teachers will not use a specific teaching method for all vocabulary teaching. In the APP vocabulary learning activity designed in this research, the research object is considered as the first grade. Therefore, the above-mentioned repetitive and visual principles are used as the basis for the research, and vocabulary learning is focused on the learning effect achieved after repetition and reading. And the aid of visual images can bring closer and stronger connections to vocabulary learning and help memorize and learn. As mentioned above, the use of pictures is to give students hints and links, through visualization assisted vocabulary learning.

Multimedia Learning Design

Mayer and Moreno [11], based on dual code theory of imagery and verbal processes, proposed a dual processing theory for the integration of text, visual and auditory media information in the learning process. The theory is that visual and auditory information will first enter the visual and auditory sensory and working memory, and then be transformed into long term memory. For example, the language information presented in text will first enter the visual sensory memory, and then it will be converted into speech and enter the auditory working memory. According to the above-mentioned theory, the prompts designed in the self-developed APP are divided into pictures and voice prompts, which are in line with the principle of dual processing theory, meaning that learners can use images and voice to help generate information connections. When the first-level picture prompts to answer, the second-level voice and pictures appear synchronously, helping learners achieve the joint operation of visual and auditory memory, generating effective links, and getting the correct answers.

In the design of the self-developed mobile learning APP, this research adopts not only the signal principle and the coherence principle for the design of the game description interface, but also the principle of space proximity and time proximity [11]. In addition, the prompt design arrangements at different levels in the APP also conform to the formal principles and multimedia principles in the multimedia learning theory. In addition, the self-made APP uses the mobile game theme that students are familiar with (Pokémon), which conforms to the principle of pre-training, so that the learner can understand the clearance game mechanism before using it, and it is easier to put the APP into use and use in practicing English.

Mobile English Learning Applications

The mobile English app combines the advantages of text, voice and images, and through proper design and use, learning can achieve multiplier results with half the effort. Messages in words, images or sounds can help people repetitively encode messages into long-term memory in different ways. Among the English textbooks for elementary schools, English vocabulary is the most basic and easier to understand. Students can use multiple memory methods such as voice, text, and images to assist their learning. The APP game software in this research is presented as a task-based game, which provides students with group activities for operation and use, emphasizes customized learning, and matches the teaching content. The choice and arrangement of words are set according to the student's level and learning status. This APP was put forward by teachers, under the guidance of instructors and relevant experts, through professional research teams to make and modify the APP. Its architecture is presented in the form of Android platform games. The purpose of choosing the Android platform is the universality and openness of the platform. The research result can be promoted to assist more English teachers in relevant teaching applications without much technical difficulty.

3   Experiment and Proposed Learning Design

This research adopts a single-subject research method to explore the primary school students' learning English vocabulary through a self-made APP, and understand and analyze the students' English vocabulary learning effectiveness, learning perception and acceptance of the self-made APP. The research framework consists of three parts, namely independent variables, dependent variables and control variables (Fig. 1).

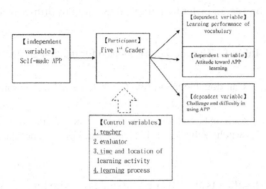

Fig. 1. The structure of research and variables.

The independent variable is a self-developed mobile APP, which allows the research objects to self-learn through the self-edited APP and to recognize and read English vocabulary, so as to understand the effect of this experiment on the English vocabulary learning of lower grade students. The dependent variables refer to the maintenance effect and immediate effect of the research object's English vocabulary recognition and reading ability after receiving the intervention of the self-edited APP experiment. This effectiveness is measured by the research object's response performance on the "English Vocabulary Recognition and Reading Ability Test" compiled by the researcher. The control variables of this study are the teacher, the assessment, the teaching time and place, and the teaching process. The experimental teaching performed twice a week, each time about 30 min, a total of 5 weeks, and a total of 10 experiments.

Development of English Learning APP
The experiment uses self-made APP as a tool for students' vocabulary practice (Table 1). This APP is an application program developed by researchers in cooperation with the students of the engineering department after the researchers put forward their needs from the perspective of the English teacher. The design concept is to use the voice recognition system in mobile devices to train first graders to recognize and read single words. Through the immediateness of voice feedback, students can understand whether they are reading correctly. If first graders encounter difficulties, they can use pictures and voice prompts to reach the goal of learning. At present APP market, the English vocabulary learning APP suitable for elementary school students is mostly scant in terms of the thematic in content and question bank. Commerical APP cannot be matched with the specific school curriculum progress, and this research aims to establish a new

question bank. In addition, if information can be incorporated into long-term memory in both visual and language forms, the effectiveness of subsequent recall can be greatly improved. Mayer and Moreno [11] combined double code theory and derivative learning theory to put forward the "Multimedia Learning Cognitive Theory". They also believes that in multimedia learning, the information processing process should include "voice and image", the related theory of the dual channel. Therefore, the design of this self-made APP focuses on using pictures to assist English learning, allowing students to recognize and read English words through text, and provide picture prompts as assistance, and finally give voice prompts, in order to achieve integrated multimedia learning assistance.

Table 1. The vocabulary adopted for the first grader

Target (13)	Cat, dog, elephant, fox, girl, hat, ink, jam, lion, monkey, net, queen, sun
Supplementary (24)	Cup, fish, goat, hen, insect, kite, lake, nose, ox, pink, rabbit, toy, up, watch,, zebra, bird, jet, bag, cake, king, up, pot, fan, bag

Since the research subjects are lower grade students, who love stories, animations and games. The packaging of animations or stories can effectively arouse students' learning motivation. Studies have pointed out that simple stories can establish the background of the game and help learners learn in the game and experience the meaning of learning. Therefore, this self-developed APP uses the *Pokemon* mobile phone grabbing game, which is currently popular among students, as the interface design and packaging. The concept of sliding the screen in the original game to grab treasure is modified to allow students to read specific words on their mobile phones. In order to catch the treasure, and then successfully enter into the higher level, this study adapted and redesigned current mobile games that students are familiar. Such attempt can not only increase students' motivation, but also reduce the burden on the teacher in describing the rules. Figure 2 shows the procedure of operating the self-developed mobile English learning APP.

The test question bank set by the APP is 5 questions at a time, including 2 questions for the applied vocabulary that have been learned and 3 supplementary vocabulary questions that have not been learned. The questions for each test are not repeated in order to avoid sequential memory of students, and the questions are random arrangement, not in alphabetical order. In addition, the self-developed APP emphasizes personal learning progress and adaptive learning. Therefore, the topics of the last two tests will be customized based on the overall learning performance of the research subjects in the first eight times, to help them review less familiar words again and pursue personal progress.

1.Mobile phone connects through blue tooth to the ArduinoMonitor。

2.Click on the screen and speak out the word on screen。

3.If the answer is correct, "Exceller show up on the screen。

4.It the answer is wrong，student can have 'hint'，the picture then the pronunciation of that word，

5.After "hint"，student provide correct

Fig. 2. The procedure of operating the self-developed Mobile English learning app

In order to solve the problem that teachers cannot take into account and review and guide students' learning progress one by one in large-class teaching, the vocabulary learning APP combines Arduino driving technology and uses the light bulb mechanism to expand the learning from independent learning to group collaborative learning. And teachers can also use this tool to view the learning status of all students, and then provide immediate assistance and guidance. The Arduino monitor board designed by this study is shown in the Fig. 3. Through the Bluetooth connection function of the mobile phone, the performance results of the individual students can be presented through the LED light bulb on the board in Taiwan shape. There are a total of 5 students in this experiment. Each student's mobile phone is connected to some of the light bulbs of the Arduino monitor board. One person represents one color, with 2 light bulbs. If the student give the correct answers at the first time, the Arduino board will light up two LED Light; if the answer is correct after being prompted, one light is lited.

Fig. 3. Arduino monitor board in Taiwan shape shows students' progress

The above discussion illustrated the importance of Technological Pedagogical Content Knowledge, a teacher knowledge construct in relation to integrating technology into teaching [12, 13]. However, due to limited knowledge and resources, English teacher in this study needed engineers' help to tailor the mobile APP and Arduino technology. Engineers used authoring tools of mobile app to design an English-learning app, in which English teachers provide feedbacks for revision, and a preliminary cross-disciplinary collaboration is asserted [14]. This collaboration among English teacher and engineer is one example of how participants have only partial knowledge and control over the interpretation of an English mobile app, but by interacting with, reacting to, and negotiating with each other, they can build new ideas regarding authoring English-learning apps [14]. Both English teacher and engineer focused on improving the mobile app from their own perspectives.

Figure 4 shows English teacher (first author) guiding students to recognize the interactional relationship between the mobile APP and the Arduino board. The detailed use of mobile APP and Arduino board is that students take turns to practice the APP vocabulary. Every time the students read a word, the Arduino monitor board will sense and light up. The light mechanism is that when student gives the right answer at the first try, he will get two points (two LEDs light up). Failing the first try, student will get the mobile APP's assistance of picture prompt, and he will have one LED light up if give the right word. Finally, the light will not be lited if student read it right after the voice prompt. On the mobile phone screen, the text encouragement that students get will also be different. The text encouragement that is right for student's first try is "Excellent"; after that, the text encouragement is "Good Job".

Fig. 4. Teacher (first author) guided students to recognize the interactional relationship between the mobile APP and the Arduino board

In each round, each student must answer 5 questions, one question at a time. The student can enter the next question after he give correct answer justified by the Mobile APP. For each correct answer, the Arduino monitor board will light up according to the correct answer. Each student has the same 5 questions. The researcher will design the order of the words according to the student's level. Through this design mechanism, it will also provide students with opportunity to observe and learn from each other. If the learning history recorded on the APP shows that students need to use the assistance of the prompt more than half of the vocabulary, they would continue with the second round of activities. The estimated time for each experiment is 20 min.

4 Results

The data collected in this study included quantitative data of performance test (Table 2), attitude survey questionnaire (Table 3), and qualitative data of classroom video and interview. Figure 5 showed that students used mobile APP to practice English and the Arduino board showed their learning progress. Among the 5 students, four students had higher post-test scores than the pre-test. Among them, the low-achieving student's post-test score reached 30 points, which was a significant improvement of 18 points compared with the previous test score of 12 points. Another low-achieving student's pre- and post-test scores varies from 19 points to 26 points, an improvement of 7 points. The third middle achievement student also made significant improvement, from 23 points to 36 points, an improvement of 13 points. High-achieving students also showed a slight improvement in the pre- and post-performance tests, from 33 points to 37 points. It shows that for the above four research subjects, the self-made English learning App can indeed improve their English vocabulary recognition and reading ability. The fifth best student's performance in the pre-test reached the full mark, and the performance in the post-test is also the same, although it means that there is no obvious difference in the vocabulary recognition performance of high-achieving students before and after the APP experiment.

Fig. 5. Students used APP to practice English

Table 2. Self-developed English vocabulary test for 1st grader

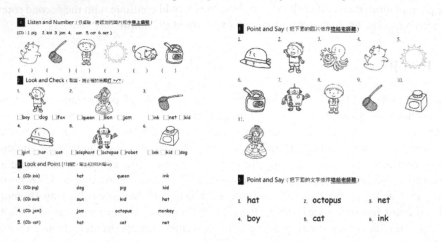

In order to understand the research subjects' perception of using the self-developed English learning APP (Table 3), the researcher conducted data analysis upon recorded video data and individual in-depth interviews to understand the students' experience of using APP to learn English.

Table 3. Attitude toward using APP for English learning (5: very agree; 1 very dis-agree)

	Question	☺ ⟶ ☹					Ave.
		5	4	3	2	1	
1.	I like to use this APP for learning English	5	0	0	0	0	5
2.	Using this APP to learn English makes my English better	5	0	0	0	0	5
3.	I was willing to speak out during the use of this APP	3	1	0	0	1	4
4.	I know how to use the APP to learn English	2	1	1	0	1	3.6
5.	The App helps me know whether I am right or wrong	5	0	0	0	0	5
6.	I can keep practicing English with the APP	5	0	0	0	0	5
7.	Compared with English class, I like using APP for English learning	5	0	0	0	0	5
	Average						4.66

Overall, students are quite satisfied with the using the self-developed APP for English vocabulary learning. During the interview, the student said that using a mobile phone to learn English would make him more daring to speak, because "less nervous, and no need to speak to the class", and the student even said "mobile phone will give me courage". It indicates that the personal use of the mobile phone APP can reduce students' learning anxiety and encourage students to dare to practice English. For the research subjects, using the self-made APP to learn English vocabulary is also positive and quite favorite. The students have a positive learning attitude towards using the APP to learn English vocabulary. This was echoed with the result of Table 3, showing very positive attitude toward the use of this study's APP with average of 4.66 over the 5-point Likert's scale. Figure 6 shows a student enjoying playing the APP to practice English; he happily raised their hands after he learned that he got the correct answers, showing his excitement and enjoyment for the English mobile APP.

Fig. 6. Student enjoyed playing the APP to practice English (From left to right: speak out the word, check the answer, answer is correct)

5 Conclusions

This study investigated the effects of using self-developed mobile APP and Arduino in English vocabulary learning. Arduino was adopted to be associated with APP to provide integrated multimedia support, and the App also utilized students' favorite mobile game theme to make students enjoy learning. The first-grade students had no difficulty in using the proposed self-developed mobile APP and were willing to practice and learn English vocabulary. The research results showed that students were quite satisfied with the self-made APP and had a high acceptance. The proposed mobile APP brought students an alternative learning surprise and excitement, making them more willing to learn English vocabulary. In addition, English teacher in this study needed engineers' help to tailor the mobile APP and Arduino technology. A preliminary cross-disciplinary collaboration was held, through which English teacher and engineer respectively have only partial knowledge and control over the English mobile app. By interacting with, reacting to, and negotiating with each other, they can build new ideas regarding authoring English-learning apps [14]. Under such collaborative work, the self-developed mobile APP's potential of teaching will become greater and greater in the future. Therefore, it is suggested that future research can focus on the design of self-developed APP and Arduino, combining different domain fields and learning skills to increase its richness and diversification.

Acknowledgments. Note: This study was part of the first author's Master thesis at National Taipei University of Education, Taipei, Taiwan, and was financially supported by Ministry of Science and Technology in Taiwan under the contract of MOST 105-2511-S-003-007.

References

1. Lan, Y.-J.: Guest editorial: pan-pacific technology-enhanced language learning. Comput. Assist. Lang. Learn. **34**(1–2), 1–5 (2021). https://doi.org/10.1080/09588221.2021.1883927
2. Reinders, H., Lan, Y.J.: Big data in language education and research. Lang. Learn. Technol. **25**(1), 1–3 (2021). http://hdl.handle.net/10125/44746
3. Song, Y.: SMS enhanced vocabulary learning for mobile audiences. Int. J. Mob. Learn. Organ. **2**(1), 81–98 (2008)
4. Milrad, M., Spikol, D.: Anytime, anywhere learning supported by smart phones: experiences and results from the MUSIS project. J. Educ. Technol. Soc. **10**(4), 62–70 (2007)
5. Li, C.: SMS-based vocabulary learning for ESL students (Unpublished master's thesis). Auckland University of Technology, New Zealand (2009)
6. Kern, R.: Perspectives on technology in learning and teaching languages. TESOL Q. **40**(1), 183–210 (2006)
7. Cameron, L.: Teaching Languages to Young Learners. Cambridge, Cambridge (2001)
8. Hargrave, A.C., Sénéchal, M.: A book reading intervention with preschool children who have limited vocabularies: the benefits of regular reading and dialogic reading. Early Child. Res. Q. **15**(1), 75–90 (2000)
9. Hatch, E., Brown, C.: Vocabulary, Semantics, and Language Education. Cambridge University Press, 40 West 20th Street, New York, NY 10011-4211 (1995)
10. Jalongo, M.R., Sobolak, M.J.: Supporting young children's vocabulary growth: the challenges, the benefits, and evidence-based strategies. Early Childhood Educ. J. **38**(6), 421–429 (2011)
11. Mayer, R.E., Moreno, R.: A split attention effect in multimedia learning: evidence for dual processing system in working memory. J. Educ. Psychol. **90**(2), 312–320 (1998)
12. Tseng, J.J., Cheng, Y.S., Yeh, H.N.: How pre-service English teachers enact TPACK in the context of web-conferencing teaching: a design thinking approach. Comput. Educ. **128**, 171–182 (2019)
13. Tseng, J.J., Chai, C.S., Tan, L., Park, M.: A critical review of research on technological pedagogical and content knowledge (TPACK) in language teaching. Comput. Assist. Lang. Learn. 1–24 (2020). https://doi.org/10.1080/09588221.2020.1868531
14. Tai, Y., Ting, Y.-L.: English-learning mobile app designing for engineering students' cross-disciplinary learning and collaboration: a sample practice and preliminary evaluation. Australas. J. Educ. Technol. **36**(2), 120–136 (2020). https://doi.org/10.14742/ajet.4999

Using Cobots, Virtual Worlds, and Edge Intelligence to Support On-line Learning

Ana Djuric, Meina Zhu, Weisong Shi, Thomas Palazzolo, and Robert G. Reynolds(⊠)

Wayne State University, Detroit, MI 48202, USA
robert.reynolds@wayne.edu

Abstract. In this project the use of Virtual World technology and Artificial Intelligence to produce a shared social landscape for the society of learners. The idea is to create a Virtual World in which learners can participate and interact. One that is parallel to the learning environment or classroom. This can be viewed as an online multi-user environment such as "Second-Life" where on-line learners can interact and construct their own spaces. Their ability to work in that space is governed by input from their robot mentor. Skills in the Virtual World are provided as a result of a student's behavior in the learning environment. The Virtual World can persist after the learning session is concluded so it provided an incentive for learners to do well in the learning session so that they can acquire points that translate into skills in the corresponding Virtual World. That Virtual World can be shared by several learning sessions or classes to provide a more comprehensive learning environment.

The overall approach is two-tiered in that each Robot mentor can acquire knowledge about the learner's behavior within a given learning environment or class. The learner's behavior is then translated into focus scores that can be applied to the Virtual World by a Supervisor, the Instructor Robot Learning Unit (IRLU). The Supervisor is in charge of updating the world based upon learner performances and compiling an ethnography of the social activities that take place within the environment. This ethnography of online users will describe in general terms how the environment is utilized by the group of learners. This information can be used by the Supervisor to adjust the Robots interaction with the learners and th cycle begins again. Such an approach with a singl learner has been studied previously by the authors [1].

Keywords: Cobots · Human-robet learning units · Edge computing · Artificial ethnographies · Virtual world · Learner focus

1 Motivation and Vision

A Cobot is a robot intended for direct human interaction within a shared space. Unlike traditional industrial robots that whose actions are isolated from their human counterparts [1]. Cobots were invented in 1994 by J. Edward Colgate and Michael [8]. Cobots can be used in variety of situations including public spaces Plishkin providing informational services [5]. This is the context in which we view them here. The International Federation of Robotics [4] has identified 4 different categories of Cobots [7]:

© Springer Nature Switzerland AG 2021
C. Stephanidis et al. (Eds.): HCII 2021, LNCS 13096, pp. 373–386, 2021.
https://doi.org/10.1007/978-3-030-90328-2_24

- Coexistence: The human and the robot work along each other with a partition but have no shared workspace.
- Sequential collaboration: The human and the robot are both active within a shared workspace but their actions are sequential and they don't work at the same time.
- Cooperation: The human and robot work on the same task at the same and are both in motion.
- Responsive collaboration: The robot responds in real-time to the actions of its human counterpart.

It is this latter category that is of concern here. This project is concerned with the development of a Human Robot team (Human Robot Learning Unit) that is able to participate in a society of online learners. The motivation behind this that one way to maintain a learner's attention is to have a "paraprofessional" monitor their activity online. However, it is difficult for a single human to closely monitor a large group of learners especially since individuals have different learning styles and learning rates. In addition, a learner can simply turn off their audio and visual and fly under the radar. The classic case is where a student thought that they had switched off their audio and video so the observer was able to see them playing video games in the background the entire session.

In this project the use of Virtual World technology and Artificial Intelligence to produce a shared social landscape for the society of learners. The idea is to create a Virtual World in which learners can participate and interact. One that is parallel to the learning environment or classroom. This can be viewed as an online multi-user environment such as "Second-Life" where on-line learners can interact and construct their own spaces. Their ability to work in that space is governed by input from their robot mentor. Skills in the Virtual World are provided as a result of a student's behavior in the learning environment. The Virtual World can persist after the learning session is concluded so it provided an incentive for learners to do well in the learning session so that they can acquire points that translate into skills in the corresponding Virtual World. That Virtual World can be shared by several learning sessions or classes to provide a more comprehensive learning environment.

The overall approach is two-tiered in that each Robot mentor can acquire knowledge about the learner's behavior within a given learning environment or class. The learner's behavior is then translated into focus scores that can be applied to the Virtual World by a Supervisor, the Instructor Robot Learning Unit (IRLU). The Supervisor is in charge of updating the world based upon learner performances and compiling an ethnography of the social activities that take place within the environment. This ethnography of online users will describe in general terms how the environment is utilized by the group of learners. This information can be used by the Supervisor to adjust the Robots interaction with the learners and the cycle begins again. Such an approach with a single learner has been studied previously by the authors [1].

Although there are many dimensions to the learning activity that can be studied the system described here addresses the most fundamental aspect of learning, how a learner maintains focus in their environment. Other qualities can be added in down the road. The challenges that online learners face in terms of focus will be discussed in the next section.

2   Challenges to the Focus of Online Learners

The loss of online students' attention to learning is a common and severe problem. Due to the COVID-19 pandemic, more than 200 million students, consisting of 12.5% of total enrolled students worldwide, were influenced by the university and school closures in December 2020 [2]. It is clear that the Pandemic has accelerated the process of shifting courses from a traditional face-to-face format to an online one [3, 4]. Online learning offers students more choices and flexibility in necessary coursework, which requires increased skills to plan, monitor, and manage learning [5, 6]. However, online education is challenging for both students and teachers. The loss of focus of attention and engagement in online learning is one of the primary challenges of online education [7]. Given that attention comes prior to cognitive learning, staying focused and engaged is vital to cognitive learning activities [8]. Losing focus affects lectures, labs, tests, quizzes, group activities, and projects in online education (see Fig. 1).

Fig. 1. Losing focus affects online learning activities

The factors that can possibly lead to losing focus of attention can be categorized into the external state (see Fig. 2) and internal state (see Fig. 3). The students' external state reflects the impact that their learning environment has on their cognition. Engagement, tiredness, overload, loneliness, and lack of communication with classmates and instructors [9] (see Fig. 3).

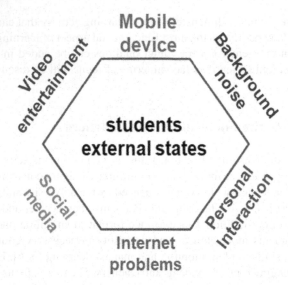

Fig. 2. External state

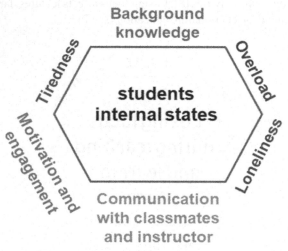

Fig. 3. Internal state

Robotic technologies have played a significant role in education. Research has indicated that online pedagogical agents can promote effective instruction [10, 11]. For example, robots have taken diverse roles in education, such as addressing absenteeism [12], enhancing motivation [13], supporting students' emotions [14], triggering productive conversation in language education [15], promoting collaboration [16, 17], fostering computational thinking [18, 19], and enhancing creative thinking and problem-solving skills [20]. However, a majority of the agents were virtual robotics or physical robotics for classroom teaching. Little research has focused on the use of physical robots as participants in an online students' learning environment. In other words, each student would have a robot mentor that will help monitor the student's progress and provide feedback to the instructor. The instructor can then use that information at a meta-level to make strategic decisions about class trajectories.

The vision of this project is to exploit the synergistic potential of the robot student team. That is, humans can perform certain tasks better than robots and vice versa. The goal is to exploit the complementarity nature of their relationship in order to produce a true marriage of minds. This Human-Robot-Learning-Unit (HRLU) is the fundamental building block upon which to scaffold a new framework for online learning. In the next section the basic structure of the HRLU will be discussed along with the information that can be passed to the Supervisor. The Supervisor will then use that information to update the Virtual World based on learner's performances and update their ethnography. The updated ethnography will be the basis for adjusting the HRLU components for the next learning session.

3   HRLU Methodology

Robots are used as teaching and learning tools to be manipulated and operated by students in many schools. For online teaching, the robot assistants will be located at online learner's homes. Because of that, we made a comparison between different teaching robots based on their suitability for such an application. The factors that are compared include their functionality, price, weight, software, hardware, etc. Therefore, this research uses a robot, like Misty (https://www.mistyrobotics.com/), to facilitate students' self-regulation in the online learning environment (see Fig. 4).

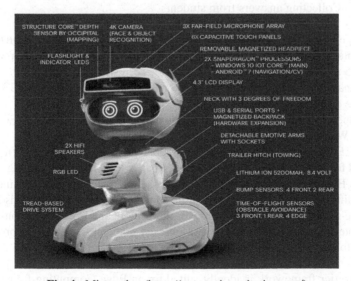

Fig. 4. Misty robot (https://www.mistyrobotics.com/)

The Robots contribution to the HRLU can be as follows:

1. First, robots can provide pre-scheduled learning activities during the entire semester in order to support students' time-management.
2. Second, the robots can monitor the students' learning behavior through eye-tracking and monitoring facial expressions and gestures during synchronous classroom and related meeting sessions. Based upon learned patterns in the students' behavioral data, the robot can track students' learning progress and provide interventions to facilitate students' cognition and meta-cognition.
3. Third, robots can facilitate formative assessment and provide immediate feedback to students in online learning.
4. Fourth, robots can communicate not only with students but also with the Supervisor. The Superviso Unit (ILRU) will facilitate communication between the HRLUs and with the Virtual World.

The HRLUs communicate in the virtual classroom with other HRLUs. See Fig. 5. The communication will be arranged such that each student is communicating with a personalized robot, while all robots are communicating in the network, and the instructor (IRLU) is communicating with all robots in the network. It is possible that the Instructor will have their own intelligent agent learning unit.

In order to control the online HRLU classroom, instructor(s) (IRLU) will be using provide scripts for interactions (e.g., questions) prepared using their previous teaching experience. See Fig. 5. The control flow can be as following:

1. Input - scripted interactions that are designed to get information about the students' internal state)
2. Output - Collecting answers from students
3. Output - Analysis of students answers
4. The Supervisor (IRLU) updates the Virtual World parameters based upon the student robot interactions. The Virtual World is referred to as the Virtual Classroom Matrix in Fig. 5 as a reference to the "Matrix" in the corresponding films
5. Data Analytics of the updated VCM in order are performed by the IRLU to adjust the state of the Virtual World.
6. The Supervisor ILRU updates the Ethnography Classroom Matrix (ECM) of the Virtual World using the adjusted VR parameters from 5 above.
7. Express ECM and VCM parameters in a graphical update using a GUI. This GUI will be used for generating a virtual classroom map using Machine Learning techniques such as Evolutionary and Deep Learning. The interface represents an indicator for controlling students' focus of attention. The instructor(s) will use this display to improve students' self-regulation skills, motivation, and learning outcomes.
8. Calculate the error between expectations and outcomes in order to produce new scripts for the HRLUs and repeat the cycle.

This two tier framework is ideally suited for an Edge Computing framework how the framework can be used to support the workflow above will be the subject of the next section.

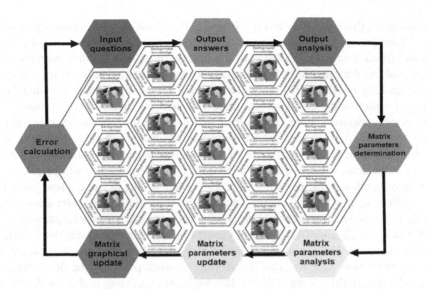

Fig. 5. Graphical representation of the dynamic virtual classroom matrix (VCM).

4   Using Edge Intelligence to Support the HRLU and IRLU Cycle

Capturing students' real-time learning status is vital to effective online learning. Sensor technology can objectively gather students' learning behaviors. Prior research and educators [21, 22, 23, 24, 25]) have utilized sensor technology to capture students' behavior, including eye movement, facial expressions, and body movement. Through students' learning behavior, we can detect and indicate to what extent students stay focused on online learning scenarios. Prior research was primarily focused on traditional face-to-face education settings or capture the video data only. For intelligent agent-based approaches, prior studies used to train one single model and deploy it for all users without considering the personalized factors. In the early detection phrase in our system, we move forward to include two factors that are usually neglected by the community: one is environmental noise, which is a passive factor that can affect the concentration; another is personalized behavior, as different students will demonstrate different distraction behavior and expression. To this end, we propose a cloud-edge collaborative system to provide personalized detection based on multi-dimensional data. We jointly combine video and audio data for Focus Index (FI) detection. Our pro system encapsulates detection objects in module units and provides APIs for third-party integration. Beyond that, we propose the idea to leverage edge intelligence for personalized model training and serving.

Edge computing [26] has become the most popular computing paradigm with the development of the Internet of Things and other devices located at the edge of the network. Statistics show that these devices will generate 60% of the data in the future, reaching PB level data volume. One typical data generation scenario is HRLU, where cameras are highly used to help detect the distraction degree of one student. Each camera generates a considerable volume of video data every day (in GB level). In cloud computing, all the video data has to be sent to the cloud for processing, which poses considerable pressure on the bandwidth and workload of the data center. Edge computing can offload data from the cloud to the process units near the data source or even offload tasks to the camera itself. There are two main factors that ignite us to leverage edge computing in HRLU: (a) Large data volume. Uploading all the generated data to the cloud is impossible and is also a waste of bandwidth, transmission resources, and cloud storage resources. Edge computing can help to pre-process and filter the valuable data before sending it to the cloud for centralized control or offload the whole task. (b) Reliable performance. The distraction of students is expected to be detected in a timely fashion. If the detection relies on cloud processing, its performance will be affected by many uncertainties: network connection, data center status, to name a few. Especially when online learning already takes a considerable bandwidth, edge computing is more reliable to guarantee near-real-time processing with capable hardware equipped.

Artificial Intelligence (AI) has been greatly developed in this decade thanks to hardware development. The convolutional neural network (CNN) promotes the development of Computer vision [27], and the Transformer network promotes the development of Natural Language Processing [28]. Spoken language processing is also accelerating its momentum with deep neural networks [29]. AI-related services usually rely on the computation resources on the cloud to provide service. Recently, with the development of lightweight AI models, edge-oriented hardware and software, edge devices, and platforms gain the capability to execute AI algorithms, i.e., Edge Intelligence [30]. Edge intelligence not only inherits the advantages from edge computing, where offloading the processing from the cloud; it also brings intelligence to the edge devices and demonstrates a huge potentiality to serve the real world. In the HRLU, we propose an edge intelligence system for the robot, which is designed to detect the student's state and intervene when necessary for online learning. Considering the functionality of the robot, which is equipped with a microphone array, 4K camera, HIFI speakers, it is capable of capturing input data in different dimensions and deploying different types of AI models to make decisions jointly.

The following section describes how the Focus detection HRLU prototype can be expressed in terms of the Edge Computation Environment.

5   HRLU System Design on the Edge

To quantify the distraction degree of the students, we use Focus Index (FI) to represent the focus degree of a student. FI ranges from 0 to 100. In a course evaluation, this score is translated into points that can be used by the learners in order to participate in the Virtual World simulation. The points can be exchanged for traits and objects that allow them to interact with others and create individual and social structures in the Virtual World.

The early detection system is presented in Fig. 6. It is a cloud-edge collaborative system for FI prediction based on personalized multi-dimensional data. To provide a reliable and solid detection for a valid intervention, the cloud is responsible for training a general detection model with a large amount of labeled data. The cloud collects the video and audio data in order to obtain the students' focus information and predict FI

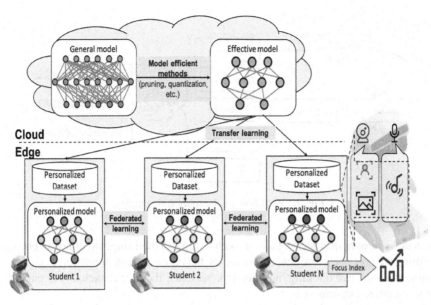

Fig. 6. Cloud-edge collaborated early detection system.

based on the trained detection model. Considering the scale of the dataset, the intelligent model generated by the cloud will be expensive for edges to compute and store. To fit the developed intelligent model to resource-constraint edge nodes, some model efficiency methods will be taken [31]. For example, model pruning [32], quantization [33], knowledge distillation [34], and network architecture search [35] can all contribute to effective pruning of the model. The processed efficient FI evaluation model is then deployed on each robot through transfer learning. With the built-in camera and microphone array, each robot can capture video and audio as the input of the efficient model to compute the FI for the students and assessed. Every so often the models performance in FI detection can be assessed and the data used to update the model in the cloud.

Figure 7 details the workflow designed for the HRLU robotic component (edge node). In the detection design, each function is modularized; thus, the detection results can be reused if necessary to save the computation resources and improve responsiveness. For example, emotion analysis, eye tracking, and head movement are three face-based detection tasks. By modularizing the face recognition, these three modules can retrieve the input from the same interface. Modulation also enables customized usage. If one function is disabled by the user (for example, emotion analysis), the system can still compute the FI based on other available detection results as they work in a parallel manner.

In previous work, we developed the edge-based personalized model to detect abnormal driving behavior based on structured data [30]. In focus analysis activity, we detect FI with unstructured data (e.g., video and audio) captured by the robot. CNN has shown significant promise to extract data features at different scales on both audio [36] and video recognition [27], and it provides an ideal framework for feature representation and classification for our collected data. We propose an audio detection model that

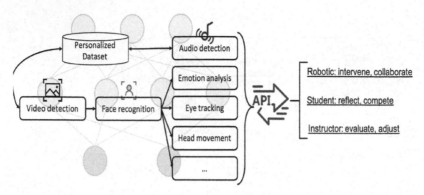

Fig. 7. Workflow on the robot (edge node).

detects environment distraction factors, such as the doorbell ring, street noise. For video streaming, we propose a few detection models that can cooperate for different tasks (e.g., emotion analysis, eye tracking, and head movement); they are detachable to each other for a modularized design.

The proposed detection system has an integrated design. Besides the detected FI, it also provides APIs that can be easily integrated to benefit the online-learning. The robot can fetch the FI from the API and take intervention when necessary. The students can reflect on their reactions and get motivated by comparing with anonymous peers' FI. The instructors can evaluate the FI of the course, assess students' performance, and adjust the syllabus accordingly. Leveraging edge intelligence, our proposed system enables FI detection in both personalized and collaborative ways. Edge intelligence enables the robots to train the personalized model based on a personalized dataset. With the efficient model transferred from the cloud, each robot can run the model for inference, i.e., compute the FI with newly collected data. With more rounds of inference, the robotic collects more personalized data and is allowed to generate a personalized model with labels given by the user. With a well-trained general model, the data volume required for a personalized model is small.

HRLUs can potentially collaborate with each other as a group in the same class. Viewed as an effective way to engage students, peer competition is also helpful for robotics to calculate the FI. For example, in a complex and difficult course (e.g., Introduction to Partial Differential Equations), the reaction from peers can be leveraged as a criterion to evaluate FI. If one student is quite relaxed, while the average reaction is focused and confused, he/she has a higher chance of distraction. In contrast, if the average reaction is relaxed, the robot-agent can learn from the collaboration and avoid false detection. To achieve privacy-preserved collaborative FI, federated learning is a potential solution [37]. Usually, federated learning shares the same AI model among multiple decentralized edge nodes. In our proposed design, instead of sharing the parameters of the personalized model, collaborative robots share the prediction results and average with others to update personalized models.

6   The Virtual World (VCM) and Digital Ethnography (ECN) Components as Supported by the IRLU

In the previous section the basic structure of the HRLU and its support in the cloud was detailed. The key component was the F1 detection model that was trained in the cloud and distributed to the FRLU for use in assessing the learners focus. Every so often the cloud based detection model was update based upon its performance. In this section the second tier of the system is presented. Those components are supported via the IRLU. The design of the IRLU here will be similar to work previously done for a specialized Virtual World designed to collect the experience of modern day hunters in an ancient Virtual World, the Land Bridge [1]. The approach was based upon the work of McCarthy and Wright [38]. The proposed a four part framework for constructing a digital ethnography. Their approach was applied to the construction of a portion of the multiuser world Second Life by Bardzell and Odum [39].

The IRLU design for this project is similar to that one. The design consisted of a Virtual World model of an ancient environment. Participants were asked to utilize the model and an ethnography of their behaviors was extracted. That ethnography was then used by a Supervisor program to reconfigure and adjust the model based upon the extracted results. Figure 8 gives a screenshot of a GUI used by the Supervisor to configure the Virtual World and to collect the Ethnographic information. More details can be found in [1]. The Supervisor can then adjust the Virtual World to reflect hypotheses produced through the examination of the collection ethnographic information. Figure 9 gives an example of the Virtual World that was made available to participants.

Fig. 8.   The Ancient Land Bridge Virtual World with a Caribou herd migrating in the background.

The Supervisor was able to adjust the physical and biological aspects of the environment to reflect different challenges for the participants. Data from participants' activities is collected and incorporated in the collective ethnography. The system has been tested with Alaskan hunters and has been used to successfully predict the location of ancient structures. The Artificial Intelligence software that underlies the systems performance such as Cultural Algorithms is used to support the development of the IRLU here.

Fig. 9. The Supervisor GUI for the LandBridge System.

7 Conclusion

In this paper the use of Virtual World technology and Artificial Intelligence are employed to produce a shared social landscape for the society of learners. The idea is to create a Virtual World in which learners can participate and interact. One that is parallel to the learning environment or classroom. This can be viewed as an online multi-user environment such as "Second-Life" where on-line learners can interact and construct their own spaces. Their ability to work in that space is governed by input from their robot mentor. Skills in the Virtual World are provided as a result of a student's behavior in the learning environment. The Virtual World can persist after the learning session is concluded so it provided an incentive for learners to do well in the learning session so that they can acquire points that translate into skills in the corresponding Virtual World. That Virtual World can be shared by several learning sessions or classes to provide a more comprehensive learning environment.

The framework consists of a network Human-Robot Learning Units (HRLUs) and a Supervisor Learning Unit (IRLU). This framework is well suited to an Edge Intelligence approach. The design of an edge-based system to support a network of HRLUs and the development of an adaptive cloud-based approach to assess learner focus is provided. The ILRU will then take that assessment and translate into points for users in a parallel social world. A description of efforts along those lines is provided as well.

References

1. Palazzolo, T., Lemke, A., Zhang, C., Saad, S., Reynolds, R.G., O'Shea, J.: DeepDive: The use of virtual worlds to create an ethnography of an ancient civilization. HCI International (2021)
2. UNESCO, COVID-19 Educational Disruption and Response. 22 Dec 2020. https://en.unesco.org/themes/education-emergencies/coronavirus-school-closures
3. Gardener, L.: COVID-19 Has Forced Higher Edu to Pivot to Online Learning. Here Are 7 Takeaways So Far. The Chronicles of Higher Education (2020)
4. Kelly, R.: 4,000-Plus U.S. Higher Ed Institutions Impacted by COVID-19; More Than 25 Million Students Affected. Campus Technology (2020)
5. Ally, M.: Foundations of educational theory for online learning. In: Theory and Practice of Online Learning, Athabasca University, Athabasca (2004)

6. Sun, J.C.Y., Rueda, R.: Situational interest, computer self-efficacy and self-regulation: their impact on student engagement in distance education. Br. J. Educ. Technol. **43**(2), 191–204 (2021)
7. Wu, J.Y.: The indirect relationship of media multitasking self-efficacy on learning performance within the personal learning environment: implications from the mechanisms of perceived attention problems and self-regulation strategies. Comput. Educ. **106**, 56–72 (2017)
8. Petersen, S.E., Posner, M.I.: The attention system of the human brain: 20 Years After. Ann. Rev. Neurosci. **13**(1), 73–89 (2012)
9. Kuo, Y.C., Walker, A.E., Schroder, K.E., Belland, B.R.: Interaction, internet self-efficacy, and self-regulated learning as predictors of student satisfaction in online education courses. Internet High. Educ. **20**, 35–50 (2014)
10. Heller, B., Procter, M.: Embodied and embedded intelligence: actor agents on virtual stages. Intelligent and Adaptive Learning Systems: Technology Enchanged Support for Students and Teachers, pp. 280–292 (2012)
11. Pereira, A., Martinho, C., Leite, I., Paiva, A.: iCat, the chess player: the influence of embodiment in the enjoyment of a game. In: Proceedings of the 7th International Joint Conference on Autonomous Agents and Multiagent Systems, pp. 1253–1256 (2008)
12. Mac Iver, M.A., Mac Iver, D.J.: STEMming the swell of absenteeism in urban middle grade schools: impacts of a summer robotics program. Society for Research on Educational Effectiveness (2014)
13. Gomoll, A., Hmelo-Silver, C.E., Sabanovic, S., Francisco, M.: Dragons, Ladybugs, and Softballs: Girls' STEM engagement with human-centered robotics. J. Sci. Educ. Technol. **25**(6), 899–914 (2016)
14. Dennins, M., Masthoff, J., Mellish, C.: Adapting progress feedback and emotional support to student personality. Int. J. Artif. Intell. Educ. **26**(3), 877–931 (2016)
15. Tegos, S., Demetriadis, S., Tsiatsos, T.: A configurable conversational agent to trigger students' productive dialogue: a pilot student in the CALL Domain. Int. J. Aritif. Intell. Educ. **24**(1), 62–91 (2014)
16. Hwang, W.Y., Wu, S.Y.: A case studet of collaboration with multi-robots and its effect on children's interaction. Interact. Learn. Environ. **22**(4), 429–443 (2014)
17. Menekse, M., Higashi, R., Schunn, C.D., Baehr, E.: The role of robotics teams' collaboration quality on team performance in a robotics tournament. J. Eng. Educ. **106**(4), 564–584 (2017)
18. Chen, G., Shen, J., Barth-Cohen, L., Jiang, S., Huang, X., Eltoukhy, M.: Assessing elementary students' computational thinking in everyday reasoning and robotics programming. Comput. Educ. **109**, 162–175 (2017)
19. Leonard, J., et al.: Using robotics and game design to enhance children's self-efficacy, STEM attitudes, and computational thinking skills. J. Sci. Educ. Technol. **25**(6), 860–876 (2016)
20. Liu, E.Z.F., Lin, C.H., Liou, P.Y., Feng, H.C., Hou, H.T.: An analysis of teacher-student interaction patterns in a robotics course for kindergarten children: a pilot student. Turkish Online J. Educ. Technol.-TOJET **12**(1), 9–18 (2013)
21. Daniel, K., Kamioka, E.: Detection of learner's concentration in distance learning system with multiple biological information. J. Comput. Commun. **5**(4), 1 (2017)
22. Hwang, G., Chang, H.: A formative assessment-based mobile learning approachto improving the learning attitudes and achievements of students. Comput. Educ. **56**(4), 1023–1031 (2011)
23. Krithika, L., Lakshmi Priya, G.G.: Student Emotion Recognition System (SERES) for e-learning improvement based on learner concentration metric. Procedia Comput. Sci. **85**, 767–776 (2016)
24. Su, Y., Hsu, C., Chen, H., Huang, K., Huang, Y.: Developing a sensor-based learning concentration detection system. Engineering Computations (2014)

25. Sharma, P., Joshi, S., Gautam, S., Maharjan, S., Filipe, V., Reis, M.J.: Student engagement detection using emotion analysis, eye tracking, and head movement with machine learning. arXiv (2019)
26. Shi, W., Cao, J., Zhang, Q., Li, Y., Xu, L.: Edge computing: vision and challenges. IEEE Internet Things J. **3**(5), 637–646 (2016)
27. Krizhevsky, A., Sutskever, I., Hinton, G.E.: Imagenet classification with deep convolutional neural networks. Commun. ACM **60**(6), 84–90 (2017)
28. Vaswani, A., et al.: Attention is All You Need. In: Advances in neural Information Processing Systems, pp. 5998–6008 (2017)
29. Amodei, D., et al.: Deep speech 2: end-to-end speech recognition in english and mandarin. In: International Conference on Machine Learning, pp. 173–182 (2016)
30. Zhang, X., Qiao, M., Liu, L., Xu, Y., Shi, W.: Collaborative cloud-edge computation for personalized driving behavior modeling. In: Proceedings of the 4th ACM/IEEE Symposium on Edge Computing, pp. 209–221 (2019)
31. Han, S., Pool, J., Tran, J., Dally, W.: Learning both weights and connections for efficient neural network. In: Advances in Neural Information Processing Systems, pp. 1135–1143 (2015)
32. Han, S., Mao, H.D.W.J.: Deep Compression: Compressing Deep Neural Networks with Pruning, Trained Quantization and Huffman Coding (2014). https://papers.nips.cc/paper/2015/hash/ae0eb3eed39d2bcef4622b2499a05fe6-Abstract.html
33. Gong, Y., Liu, L., Yang, M., Bourdev, L.: Compressing Deep Convolutional Networks Using Vector Quantization (2014). [Online]
34. Hinton, G., Vinyals, O., Dean, J.: Distilling the Knowledge in a Neural Network (2015). [Online]
35. Cai, H., Zhu, L., Han, S.: Proxylessnas: Direct Neural Architecture Search on Target Task and Hardware (2018). [Online]
36. Cao, J., Cao, M., Wang, J., Yin, C., Wang, D., Vidal, P.P.: Urban noise recognition with convolutional neural network. Multimedia Tools Appl. **78**(20), 29021–29041 (2019)
37. McMahan, B., Moore, E., Ramage, D., Hampson, S., Arcas, B.A.: Communication-efficient learning of deep networks from decentralized data. Artif. Intell. Stat. **54**, 1273–1282 (2017)
38. McCarthy, J., Wright, P.: Technology as experience. Interactions **11**(5), 42–43 (2004)
39. Bardzell, S., Odom, W.: The experience of embodied space in virtual worlds: an ethnography of a second life community. Space Cult. **11**(3), 239–259 (2008)
40. Zhang, X., Wang, Y., Lu, S., Liu, L., Shi, W.: OpenEI: an open framework for edge intelligence. In: 2019 IEEE 39th International Conference on Distributed Computing Systems, pp. 1840–1851 (2019)

Developing Academic Engagement Through a Virtual Week of Research, Scholarly, and Creative Activity: Rethinking Collaboration

Enri'que Flores$^{(\boxtimes)}$, Kim-Phuong L. Vu, and Simon Kim

California State University Long Beach, Long Beach, CA 90804, USA
{Enrique.Flores,Kim.Vu,Simon.Kim}@csulb.edu

Abstract. The goal of having a Week of Research, Scholarly, and Creative Activity (RSCA) virtual event was to highlight and acknowledge the valuable array of research, scholarly, and creative activities that are currently being done across the entire campus at California State University Long Beach (CSULB). There's no doubt that in 2020 and 2021, our lives have been impacted in a multitude of ways. The COVID-19 global pandemic placed restrictions on in-person gatherings that forced many to rely on virtual meetings. Even with 'zoom' fatigue taking over, we felt that it was essential to hold the Week of RSCA event virtually in the 2020–2021 academic year. Students, faculty, and staff on campus are a community that supports one another, and CSULB seeks to enhance its local/national/global communities with the research, scholarly and creative activities that we conduct on our campus. This paper describes the development of the Week of RSCA event, its transition from an in-person to virtual event, the challenges for delivering a virtual event, and the lessons learned when we have to rethink collaboration during a pandemic.

Keywords: Research · Collaboration · Education · Virtual events

1 Engaging Students in Research, Scholarly, and Creative Activities (RSCA)

1.1 The Role of Research, Scholarly, and Creative Activities in Undergraduate and Graduate Education at CSULB

Engaging students in research is a high impact practice that has been shown to improve student retention and persistence in disciplines relating to science, technology, engineering and mathematics (STEM) [1]. In addition to the hands-on research experience that students gain working with their faculty mentors in research labs or with professionals in the field/industrial settings, professional development opportunities, such as professional presentations, often enrich the student learning experience. California State University Long Beach (CSULB) is a diverse comprehensive university that engages faculty and students in research, scholarly and creative activities. Traditionally, undergraduate

© Springer Nature Switzerland AG 2021
C. Stephanidis et al. (Eds.): HCII 2021, LNCS 13096, pp. 387–405, 2021.
https://doi.org/10.1007/978-3-030-90328-2_25

research training at CSULB was specific to a particular department and supervising faculty member. That is, students will solicit and engage in research in their departments and department-affiliated programs under the supervision of a faculty member. The type of training that students receive often followed an apprentice model and was tailored to the needs of the faculty member's research, scholarly, and creative activities.

In 2016, CSULB established an Office of Undergraduate Research Services (OURS). The major goal of OURS was to expand undergraduate research opportunities to the general CSULB student body by coordinating research programs and centralizing where students can learn about research opportunities available on campus. The OURS staff work in collaboration with all CSULB colleges, departments, divisions and programs to cultivate strong relationships in support of undergraduate research. In short, OURS serves as a "single-stop shopping" venue for CSULB student research. Although OURS developed and maintained its own undergraduate research training programs, an expansion of research opportunities and formalized research training across different colleges and departments at CSULB was made possible when CSULB received one of 10 BUilding Infrastructure Leading to Diversity Phase 1 (BUILD I, 2014–2019) awards from the National Institutes of Health (NIH). One aim of the CSULB BUILD I award was to develop a student-centered program that would provide intensive research training experience to undergraduate students from a variety of departments conducting health-related research in the colleges of Engineering, Health and Human Services, Liberal Arts, and Natural Sciences (for more information about CSULB BUILD I, see [2]). In 2019, CSULB received a second phase of the BUILD (i.e., BUILD II, 2019–2024) award to institutionalize program components developed in the first phase of the award within designated offices and centers at CSULB.

One aim of BUILD II was to establish a campus-wide research event that fosters a research culture to recognize and support student research across the university. The intent of this event was to help remove research silos between departments and colleges at CSULB, and promote the appreciation of discipline-specific as well as interdisciplinary approaches to research in general, and health related-research in particular. This Week of Research, Scholarly, and Creative Activity (RSCA) event was also intended to be the venue for outreach of research training programs on campus to our diverse student population. The BUILD II award provided the impetus and resources to initiate, develop, and implement this university-wide event for promoting research on campus.

1.2 The Week of RSCA as a Campus-Wide Event

The Week of RSCA was originally planned to focus on the research that was being conducted on campus, and was simply called the Week of Research. It was proposed to be a unified event that promotes and celebrates the contribution of student research on our campus. The need for the Week of Research was a result of the fact that many colleges, departments, and programs celebrate their student research experiences and achievements within their own, local events. Some of these events are publicized outside of the discipline and others are not. This siloed approach does not allow all members of the university to learn about the research being conducted by students on our campus. Thus, the Week of Research was intended to be impactful to the campus in the sense that it would bring together all campus groups to celebrate student research. This event would change the research culture by:

Recognizing research conducted by students on campus
Engaging in discussions about research
Supporting faculty and students conducting research on specific topics
Exploring research opportunities available in different departments and colleges, and at the university
Advocating diversity in research
Reaching out to the local community and regional partner institutions
Communicating the impact of research
Helping families and potential donors understand how integral research is to our students' education.

Because students at CSULB are largely from underrepresented groups, the campus-wide event was also intended to allow students the opportunity to see themselves as researchers and be inspired by other students with whom they can relate. Further, students would be able to see how research can mitigate and ameliorate psychosocial and health problems disproportionately affecting their own communities.

Initial plans for the Week of Research event began in the fall of 2019. CSULB's University Research Advisory Committee (URAC) was utilized as a focus group to gather feedback on the premise of the event's scope and intent. This group was selected as it is comprised of high-level administrative representatives (e.g., associate deans and directors) from all of the university's colleges that have more insight regarding the types of RSCA activities that their students and faculty engage in and program needs. Once talks were completed surrounding the event's goals, URAC members were asked to go back to their respective colleges and talk with their respective Dean and faculty to suggest 1–3 events that would be representative of the RSCA work from their college.

In addition to consulting with the URAC members, the organizers of the Week of Research met with representatives from different colleges, departments and programs on campus. In these meetings, it was clear that the focus solely on traditional research will exclude many disciplines that conduct important scholarly and creative activities with their students. Thus, the title of this event was changed from the proposed Week of Research to the Week of RSCA to highlight *R*esearch, *S*cholarly, and *C*reative *A*ctivity. In terms of marketing the Week of RSCA to the campus leadership and community, we developed two main goals for the event:

1. Highlight work currently being done by CSULB students, faculty, and staff, within the sciences, humanities, arts, engineering, and business.
2. Create engagement across the campus environment by encouraging individuals to attend events outside of their disciplines.

With the development of the 2021 event, the Week of RSCA is intended to become an annual event on campus that will grow with each subsequent year; placing spotlights on all of the research, scholarly, and creative works produced at CSULB. To encourage support by the campus community, the proposers of the Week of RSCA made presentations to the CSULB leadership, which included the President, Provost, Associated Vice Presidents, and Deans. In addition, they met with the Chair of the Academic Senate and other campus leaders to present the event and solicit additional feedback. Based on the discussion and feedback received from the various stakeholders, it was decided that the proposer of the event put out a general call for the Week of RSCA Program Chair. The duties of the Program Chair included:

- Working with the proposers to finalize the schedule of events (at that time a preliminary list of College-sponsored in-person events had already been compiled).
- Meeting with campus-wide stakeholders (e.g. college representatives, event services, parking, university marketing, University Research Advisory Committee, Academic Senate, Associated Students Incorporated, etc.) to promote and market the event.
- Working with each College event organizer to finalize timelines for each event being held during the week.
- Constructing the final program for the event.
- Organizing for opening and closing remarks by university leadership.
- Writing a report on the event outcomes, which would be provided to CSULB's AVP of Research and Sponsored Programs.

Applications for the Week of RSCA Program Chair were to be submitted and processed by the Academic Senate to show the University's support of this event. The program chair would receive a stipend and some professional development (i.e., professional travel) support. Unfortunately, due to the time commitment that the position involved, no applications were submitted for the Program Chair position. As a result, CSULB's AVP of Research and Sponsored Programs became the Chair and a staff member the Co-Chair.

Once the Chair and Co-Chair were in place, the call for session ideas went out towards the end of 2019 and was announced through the university's URAC members. The initial call for sessions indicated that every college could sponsor up to three events with departments and programs within their college. An event application was setup for colleges to submit their event proposals. The submissions were reviewed by the Week of RSCA organizers. All events that fit within the scope of the Week of RSCA were accepted. There were 13 events that were accepted as in-person sessions from this initial call for proposals.

The departments/programs selected for leading a session were in charge or creating the session, deciding what topic(s) to discuss, coming up with the format, and gathering speakers or presenters. With the small team organizing the Week of RSCA, the initial launch of the event was to have already established events be a part of RSCA. This would minimize the additional workload a department would have to burden if they created a new event altogether. However, colleges would have the opportunity to decide on moving forward with one of their established events or to create a new one. For each session, a college lead was designated to oversee its production. The Week of RSCA co-chair met with each event lead to discuss the premise of their event and flesh-out the logistics of the in-person format.

1.3   Response to the COVID-19 Pandemic Restrictions

Originally, the Week of RSCA was to coincide with CSULB's hosting of the National Conference on Undergraduate Research (NCUR) in April, 2021. However, due to the move to remote instruction and restrictions to travel and in-person events in response to COVID-19, the Council on Undergraduate Research (CUR) decided to transform NCUR 2021 to a virtual conference that would not be hosted by CSULB. The COVID-19 restrictions on public gathering also meant that the 2021 Week of RSCA had to be either postponed or transformed into a virtual event. It was decided by the Week of RSCA proposers to transform the event to a virtual platform because many students were isolated from campus due to the COVID-19 closures, and the Week of RSCA could play an important role serving students by providing them with a venue to not only present their work, but to learn about other research and creative activities being conducted at CSULB.

The goal of this paper is to describe the process of transforming the Week of RSCA from an in-person to virtual event. In the subsequent sections, we describe how the virtual platform for hosting the event was selected, the process for working with the individual event organizers to transform their in-person event to a virtual one, and how we worked with the University to brand and market the event. We end the paper with lessons learned and recommendations for organizers of future events who want to move from an in-person to virtual format.

2   Method: Transforming an In-Person Event to a Virtual Event

2.1   Selection of Platform

As noted earlier, the initial idea for the Week of RSCA was to have the event held on the CSULB campus with the intent of in-person interactions. However, COVID-19 restrictions led to a decision to produce the event through a virtual environment. With a variety of university departments already selected to participate, the event required a platform that would allow for a mixture of presentations to be showcased (e.g. live stream, pre-recorded video, poster presentations). While the university already used the Zoom video conferencing software that can accommodate different types of presentations and group meetings, this event required a centralized hub for organization of materials and showcasing of content.

A search was conducted to locate a video conferencing platform that would allow for all of the features that were being asked for by the individual event organizers participating in the Week of RSCA. During the month of May 2020, emails were sent out to event planners that were coordinating scientific conferences through virtual platforms to determine which platforms are currently being used by different organizations. A list of potential virtual platforms was compiled, and the event co-chair researched the capabilities and features of each. The search was then narrowed down to a top three list of companies that conference organizers were using: Socio, Eventfinity, and Cvent.

Each of the platforms came with some similar applications for the event developer: centralized registration, event database access, social media feed, event email templates, video conferencing, exhibitor halls, and appointment settings with session presenters.

However, since many of these virtual conferencing platforms worked primarily with large corporations, the needs of a university-based conferences were still fairly new to them. Due to COVID-19, many organizations were also looking at virtual platforms to host their events, and at the time, Socio, Eventfinity, and Cvent were still working on adding new features to their platforms in order to meet the needs of this new market.

This adaptation to a new sales market opened the creation of new features that were previously not considered by these companies. While the adaptation to these needs were being created, it then played a major role in deciding which platform to use for the Week of RSCA. Both Socio and Eventfinity were adding new features each month that allowed for a better user experience, such as gamification, and would appeal to tech-saavy undergraduate students. The result of this; however, meant that their product fees also increased with every new feature that was added. Although the cost of the features would be easily accommodated by adding a participant registration fee, this was not an option for our event since it is being made freely available to CSULB students. An estimate cost of one single event using Socio and Eventfinity exceeded our event budget for the Week of RSCA. With the increase in purchase price for a platform, the selection for which one to use came down to cost effectiveness.

Cvent retained its lower price point while it was generating new conference capabilities through the virtual setting. These features include an event website, registration page, customizable emails for registrants, attendee hub, appointment settings, personalized session spaces with video, and a mobile application to name a few. It also allowed for a developer platform that allowed for quick learning and a range of free courses to learn new techniques for developing online conferences. These features were sufficient for the Week of RSCA, so the organizers selected Cvent as the virtual platform.

2.2 Working with Campus Leadership on Transitions of Events from Face-To-Face to Virtual Formats

During the month of March 2020, CSULB closed the campus for regular day-to-day operation of in-person classes and in-office work due to COVID-19 stay-at-home orders issued from the State of California. This situation moved a majority of staff to work from home, with very limited access to the campus. The uncertainty of the global pandemic caused for plans for the Week of RSCA to come to a halt, as the planning of how to situate campus staff to work from home and administrators looking for answers as to how to keep the campus secure and safe for everyone became the priority. As the months proceeded into summer 2020, there was uncertainty regarding when the campus would re-open for in-person instruction or how on-campus events would be allowed to proceed.

To keep things moving forward, the event chairs decided to produce the Week of RSCA through a virtual platform in August 2020. While many other webinars and events started being produced through online platforms, such as Zoom, the event chairs needed to figure out the best solution for incorporating a multitude of sessions with a range of presentation options. Considering the many players involved with organizing all of the sessions, having a system that could centralize the registration and presentation productions was the best option for follow.

Once the decision was made to purchase the Cvent platform (see Sect. 2.1), the next step was to contact each of the session leads, update them with the information regarding the online platform, and discuss whether they were planning on continuing with their session. Of the initial 13 sessions, only 7 of the event organizers indicated that they would move forward with the sessions and modify their event to fit the virtual platform. A targeted call for additional events was sent out to several department administrators. From this search, 5 new sessions were added to the Week of RSCA event. However, as the fall 2020 and spring 2021 semesters progressed, some of the planned events were canceled due to a variety of reasons and new sessions were added to the schedule.

Moreover, the event team was small (2 individuals, plus limited support from other university staff and graduate students), it was important to have department administrators assist with the collection of their session information. Their department team would be collecting all of their required content, review it for approval, and then submit to the event co-chair for final review. This would allow for thorough review of content, while managing a small production team.

3 Implementation

3.1 Setting up the Virtual Platform

CSULB's Week of RSCA event was held Aril 4–9, 2021 using the Cvent virtual platform. However, prior to the event, all sessions had to be created in the Cvent platform. Within the platform, the event organizers were allowed to create features to enhance the online virtual experience. Features provided through the system enabled for university logos, images, wording and color palettes to be placed throughout the environment. These details allow for any organization's or company's event streamlined with the rest of their products they release for marketing.

The following figures (see Figs. 1–3) are some of the examples of the customization allowed through the virtual environment:

Fig. 1. Cvent customizable website for the week of RSCA

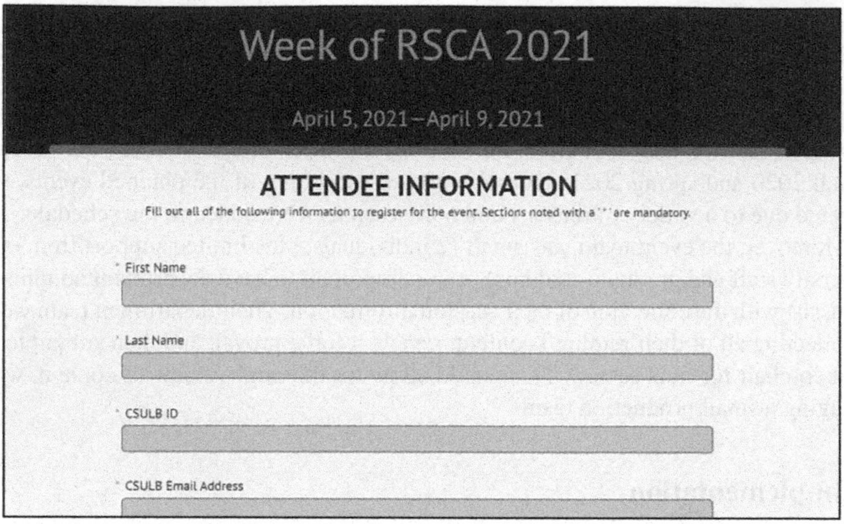

Fig. 2. Cvent customizable event registration page for the week of RSCA

Fig. 3. Cvent App illustrating the up-coming week of RSCA event (A), a speaker profile (B) and session attendee profiles (C).

Central to CSULB's Week of RSCA event is the customization capability of the platform to accommodate the formats of the various session types. This allowed for easier transitions from in-person to virtual formats.

3.2 Marketing

To begin the efforts of promoting the event across the university, content needed to be created. To assist with the marketing efforts of the event, the CSULB Strategic Communications Department was asked to join the event collaboration by creating a logo

(Fig. 4), banners for the CSULB event website (Fig. 5) and virtual platform, mobile app, and access to the campus photographic repository.

Fig. 4. Week of RSCA logo

Fig. 5. Week of RSCA webpage on the CSULB website (www.csulb.edu/rsca) highlighting the event and a schedule "at a glance"

As the intent of the Week of RSCA is to bring all sections of the university together, it is important to utilize CSULB resources that are established for creating marketing content. The Strategic Communications Department consisted of web designers and visual artists that are responsible for keeping the university's image streamlined. Having access to these individuals was valuable in that you were privy to their knowledge of what is currently allowed at the university with respect to marketing materials. This prevented going back and forth with concepts and ideas for logos, color palettes, and other details associated with branding. The utilization of the university's marketing team was also a strategic move to allow for more buy-in with the university.

To reach other communities within the university, student communication groups and administrators were asked to join the efforts with promoting the event. The student led DigMag magazine would take on the efforts of writing articles on the different sessions taking place within the event. University administrators (e.g. president, provost, deans) were also informed of the latest updates with the events and asked to promote the event within their regular communication with their departments. The university's student body, ASI (Associated Student, Inc), also joined the efforts of promoting the event across the campus.

3.3   Working with the Department Leads to Populate the Events Within Cvent

Originally, each session lead would then be responsible for putting out a call for participants, based on the in-person session format they chose to go with. However, when the event moved to the virtual platform, this allowed for an increase in opportunities for individuals to participate within sessions. Departments that were planning on holding research presentations, now were able to allow more students and faculty to take part as presenters. The option to have pre-recorded, live, or a mixture of both within a session or multiple session, paved the way for a wider range of participation. The online event also allowed the expansion of the inaugural Week of RSCA from a 3-day event following CSULB's hosting of the NCUR conference (which, as noted earlier, was no longer being hosted by CSULB due to COVID-19 restrictions) to a full week event. The Week of RSCA co-Chair reached out to other organizations, programs, and departments on campus to obtain additional events for the week of RSCA. Also, as some events were canceled as time came closer to the event, the co-Chair added additional events up to the week prior to the event. For the final program, there were 28 sponsored events, held over 40 individual sessions for the Week of RSCA.

Because the event was new to campus, and the move to the online platform resulted in the Week of RSCA organizers having to set up the initial sessions in Cvent and populate it, this increased the workload drastically for the organizers. Moreover, at the time of the event's production, the Cvent platform did not allow for pre-recorded video presentations to be individual links that were grouped together in a single session. Therefore, each student presentation needed its own session to be created within the platform. This particular activity required the creation of over 60 individual presentation sessions within the platform. While the system allowed for sessions to be cloned, the additional steps added more time to the production.

With the timing of the event being right after the university's spring break session, this caused for many delays related to session content submissions. Students were also preparing for midterms and faculty were administering and grading those exams, all prior to the break. As a result, deadline submissions kept getting pushed back and content that was submitted was not complete. Since late submissions became an obstacle with a majority of the departments involved in the program, having a strict deadline to omit content would not have worked. If a strict cut-off date was used, the program itself would have consisted of a very thin line-up. Each event lead kept in contact with the co-Chair to submit content as soon as it was sent to them. While this was not the optimal procedure for the production, flexibility needed to be a component in order to have a complete program. Event leads were appreciative with the consideration of the situation.

In preparation for the start of the event, the co-Chair scheduled a training appointment with every individual that was going to moderate a live session. Each of these sessions lasted between 60–90 min. Within the training, the co-Chair went through a step-by-step process of how to engage with the Cvent platform and what duties the moderator was in charge of. Moderators were able to test out the system by completing a 'dry-run' session through the platform. This allowed them to go through the log-in process for the Attendee Hub, learn how to locate their session, how to make their session go live, and monitor the question and answer feature within their session.

The Cvent Attendee Hub utilized Zoom for its virtual meeting room that was a familiar setting for each of the session leads who had used the system for over a year during the country's quarantine phase. However, as this was a live event, this did add some nervousness to each of the sessions. Considering that wi-fi played a role with everyone's connection to Zoom, a backup plan needed to be put in place. Thus, during the entire week of the event, the co-Chair was on call throughout the day via mobile phone. If individuals were having issues with the platform (i.e. logging in, unable to view specific settings), then they would call or text the co-Chair. The co-Chair would then immediately jump into the Zoom session and assist with the situation. Additionally, the set of speakers and moderators for each of the sessions would also join the Zoom sessions 15 min prior to the start of their session. This would allow time for presenters to organize themselves and review any last-minute changes to their session. At this point, the co-Chair would also join the team and make sure that everyone was fine with their virtual settings and knew how to navigate the session.

4 Results of 2021 Implementation

4.1 Registration

Registration for the Week of RSCA was kept free of charge for all CSULB students, staff, and faculty. As there was a limitation on how many individuals could attend, attendees were kept to only current CSULB community members when registration opened on February 1, 2021 until a week prior to the event. During the last week of the event, registration was open to everyone. The registration trend is captured in Fig. 6.

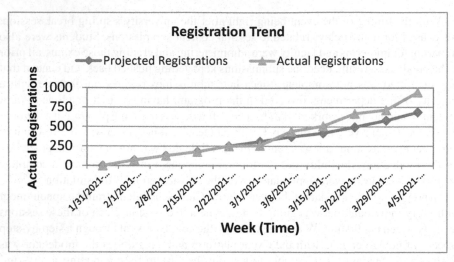

Fig. 6. Registration trend over time.

The event had a total of 942 registered participants (see Tables 1a and 1b), with about 25% of participants registering during the week of the event. The registered attendees were from mostly from CSULB, with many of the colleges and programs on campus being represented.

Table 1a. Number of registered participants by college/program

College/Program of registrants	Number of registrants
Liberal arts	239
Natural sciences and mathematics	194
Health and human services	150
Arts	75
University research opportunity program	67
Education	58
Engineering	37
Business	17
BUILD	8
Office of undergraduate research services	6
University library	5
Office of research and sponsored programs	3
Did not specify or listed N/A (e.g., guests)	74
Other: academic affairs, office of research and sponsored programs, president's office, graduate studies, etc	9
Total	**942**

Table 1b. Number of registered participants by role

Registrants' self-identified role	Number of registrants
Student (Undergraduate)	437
Student (Graduate)	153
Faculty	246
Guest (Non-CSULB Attendee)	47
Staff	37
Administrator	10
CSULB (Alumni)	12
Total	**942**

4.2 Final Program

The final program consisted on 40 sessions from different disciplines across the CSULB campus, plus the welcoming remarks from the President of the University, see Table 2. In addition, there were over 300 speakers/presenters/moderators/judges. All sessions were attended by attendees from different disciplines.

4.3 Feedback from Evaluation Surveys

The response rates for the session and general surveys were low, with 66 attendees providing feedback about the individual sessions (see Table 3) and 87 about the general event (see Table 4).

Session Surveys. Because the response rate for the individual sessions were low, we report the average ratings across sessions. Overall, those who provided feedback on the session indicated that they agreed that the sessions were informative/useful and engaging, and that they would recommend the session to others who would be interested in the topic.

General, End-of-Event Survey. The general survey was designed to assess whether the Week of RSCA achieved its goals. Attendees were asked to indicate the extent to which they agree or disagree with the statements listed in Table 4 about the *Week of RSCA* event using a scale of 1 (Strongly Disagree) to 6 (Strongly Agree). The mean rating for each of the questions are listed in Table 4. For all questions, except for Question 5, attendees' ratings were significantly higher than a test-value of 4, indicating that their level of agreement was higher than somewhat agree and not different from agree.

Table 2. Week of RSCA sessions and number of speakers and moderators/judges

Session Name (40 sessions+ Welcome Remarks)	# of Speakers	# of Moderators/ Judges
55th Annual Comparative Literature Conference: Outcasts & Outliers in Literature, Music & Visual Arts	4	1
Beach Mentor, Building an Inclusive Partnership Between Science and Filmmaking	6	1
Biochemistry: Poster/Pre-Recorded Presentations	5	
Biology: Poster/Pre-Recorded Presentations	15	
Chemistry: Poster/Pre-Recorded Presentations	7	
College of Natural Sciences and Mathematics (CNSM) Virtual Student Research Symposium - Department of Biological Sciences	6	1
CNSM Virtual Student Research Symposium - Department of Chemistry & Biochemistry (Session A)	6	1
CNSM Virtual Student Research Symposium - Department of Chemistry & Biochemistry (Session B)	5	1
CNSM Virtual Student Research Symposium - Department of Chemistry & Biochemistry (Session C)	12	1
CNSM Virtual Student Research Symposium - Department of Mathematics & Statistics	4	1
CNSM Virtual Student Research Symposium - Department of Physics & Astronomy	9	1
College of Education Graduate Research Colloquium (Session A)	6	1
College of Education Graduate Research Colloquium (Session B)	6	1
College of Education Graduate Research Colloquium (Session C)	6	1
College of Education Graduate Research Colloquium (Session D)	6	1
College of Education Graduate Research Colloquium (Session E)	4	1
College of Education Graduate Research Colloquium (Welcome Session)	1	1
College of Engineering	1	
CSULB BUILD: Poster/Pre-Recorded Presentations	11	
Dance, Design, and Music Research and Performance Fair (Session A)	5	1
Dance, Design, and Music Research and Performance Fair (Session B)	5	1

(*continued*)

Table 2. (*continued*)

Dance, Design, and Music Research and Performance Fair (Session C)	3	1
Fiction Reading with MFA Creative Writing Students	5	1
Mobilizing for Health and Social Justice - Research, Teaching, and Practice: (Aging)	5	1
Mobilizing for Health and Social Justice - Research, Teaching, and Practice: (Clinical Practice)	5	1
Mobilizing for Health and Social Justice - Research, Teaching, and Practice: (Health & Wellness I)	7	1
Mobilizing for Health and Social Justice - Research, Teaching, and Practice: (Health & Wellness II)	7	1
Mobilizing for Health and Social Justice - Research, Teaching, and Practice: (Health Equity)	7	1
Mobilizing for Health and Social Justice - Research, Teaching, and Practice: (Social Justice)	6	1
Perspectives On Voting	5	1
Playwrights, Trans Rights, and LGBTQ Fights for Justice: Engaging LGBTQIA Research	5	1
Psych Day Research Competition (Session A)	7	3
Psych Day Research Competition (Session B)	4	3
Psych Day Research Competition (Session C)	10	3
Psych Day Research Competition (Session D)	7	3
UROP: Poster/Pre-Recorded Presentations	65	
Undergraduate Research Opportunity Program Symposium (Session A)	5	1
Undergraduate Research Opportunity Program Symposium (Session B)	10	1
Using Your University Library for the "R" in RSCA	3	
Using Your University Library for the "R" in RSCA (2)	3	
Welcome Remarks - CSULB President Jane Close Conoley	1	
TOTAL	**300**	**40**
Note: Shaded sessions represent parallel sessions		

Table 3. Session ratings. Participants were asked to rate their level of agreement with the following statements using a scale of 1 (Strongly Disagree) to 5 (Strongly Agree).

Question	Range of individual session ratings	Mean rating n = 66
This session was informative and/or useful	4.2–5.0	4.82
I would recommend this session to a friend/colleague interested in this session's topic	4.2–5.0	4.78
This session was engaging	3.6–5.0	4.53

Table 4. General *feedback for the week of RSCA*. (1 = Strongly Disagree, 2 = Disagree, 3 = Somewhat Disagree, 4 = Somewhat Agree, 5 = Agree, 6 = Strongly Agree, or Don't Know).

Question	N	Mean rating	Standard deviation	Largest test value
1. After attending the *Week of RSCA* event, I am more knowledgeable about research, scholarly and creative activities (RSCA) at CSULB	85	5.15	0.98	Test value = 4 $t(84)$ = 10.82, p < .001
2. After attending the *Week of RSCA* event, I am more knowledgeable about RSCA opportunities *available to me* at CSULB	79	4.52	1.33	Test value = 4 $t(78)$ = 3.47, p < .001
3. Because of the *Week of RSCA* event, I am interested in learning more about RSCA at CSULB	81	4.83	1.02	Test value = 4 (80) = 7.28, p < .001
4. During the *Week of RSCA* event, I learned about important RSCA conducted at CSULB that can lead to improving the lives of people in our community	81	5.20	1.04	Test value = 4 t(80) = 10.35, p < .001
5. During the *Week of RSCA* event, I learned about RSCA that CSULB faculty and students conduct in partnership with *other universities*	70	4.10	1.40	Test value = 3 $t(69)$ = 6.60, p < .001
6. During the *Week of RSCA* event, I learned about RSCA conducted by CSULB investigators in partnership with community collaborators (e.g., health agencies, non-profit organizations, community partners)	75	4.56	1.31	Test value = 4 $t(74)$ = 3.71, p < .001
7. Research, scholarly, and creative activities are important at CSULB	84	5.52	1.05	Test value = 5 (83) = 4.59, p < .001
8. Research, scholarly, and creative activities are major components of campus culture at CSULB	84	5.10	1.16	Test value = 4 t(83) = 8.67, p < .001

In addition, attendees were asked, "Prior to attending the Week of RSCA event, were you involved in research, scholarly and/or creative activities at CSULB?" 80.5% (n = 70) indicated "yes", 17.2% (n = 15) indicated "no", and 2.3% (n = 2) indicated "not sure". For those who responded "yes", 55.7% (n = 39/70) indicated that they attended any sessions outside of their discipline at the *Week of RSCA* event. For those who responded "no", 73.3% (n = 11/15) indicated that they planned to get involved with research, scholarly and/or creative activities because of attending this event.

The final question asked, "What recommendations do you have for future annual Week of RSCA events?" Forty two (42) comments were provided.

- Eighteen percent of the comments (n = 8) were related to the Cvent platform. Specifically, participants indicated that the Cvent platform was either hard to navigate through or that they did not like the login process.
- Sixteen percent of the comments (n = 7) recommended making the session more interactive (e.g., live Q&A sessions; use of zoom features for interactions; allow more time for discussion).
- Eleven percent of the comments (n = 5) indicated that the event should be made an in-person event.
- Nine percent of the comments (n = 4) were related to the notification of the event and event program. These attendees wanted more advertising of the event and to be provide with the full program schedule earlier.
- The following comments were each provided by two (2) attendees:
- provide on demand videos for all sessions
- avoid scheduling conflicts or scheduling during busy time of the semester
- provide a central portal for submission of presentations; clear instructions for presenters
- The following comments were each provided by one (1) attendee:

  - include more joint faculty-student events
  - provide more information about who to contact to get more information about research or to become involved in research
  - have better audio quality
  - mix up the disciplines in a specific session
  - have more industrial presentations/opportunities

- Seven (7) attendees provided no additional recommendations or indicated that they were content with the event as delivered.

5 Discussion

5.1 Lessons Learned

University Collaborations: Creating a large campus event to engage community members is a great feature to include within a yearly academic calendar. With the event being held on a regular basis, all stakeholders and participants will know what to expect. Because this event was new to campus this year along with the COVID-19 restrictions on in-person events, there was some confusion about what the Week of RSCA event was, who was organizing it, and how it will be delivered. When deciding to create an event for the university that comprises of all departments, it is very important to have high-level administrators in the meetings that are deciding these items. The importance of having the buy-in from administrators (e.g. president, provost, deans) from the start of the planning is crucial. These individuals have the ability to start the promotion across campus and can place your event in the forefront of the university's news. In addition, it is critical to have funding for the event, and BUILD was able to cover the costs associated with the online platform and individual sessions, as well as some of the personnel costs for administering the event. For campuses that may not have a specific funding source for the event, plans need to be made regarding how to cost-share and distribute the personnel workload by leveraging existing campus events, personnel, and resources.

Technology: With the new technology for virtual meetings and presentations evolving rapidly, it is valuable for universities to access these resources to engage wider audiences. Since the current market for virtual conferencing is quickly expanding, the pricing for utilizing these resources is quite high. However, with more companies creating new products to create video conferencing environments, the high spike in pricing may not be a hindrance in the coming years. Also, it is important to think about the "must haves" versus the "wants". For our event, we went with the standard package recommended from Cvent. We ended up not using some of the features we paid for (mainly due to a lack of time to launch those features and train speakers/attendees) and did not have access to other features that were available at an additional cost. Unfortunately, some of the features that we would have liked to have implemented were not launched by the company until after our event ended. The event organizers should also keep in mind accessibility requirements such as the ability to have closed captions or interpreter videos.

Unforeseen Events: With the pandemic hitting the global community extremely hard, it managed to halt all planning for the Week of RSCA. Many session leads had to manage organizing their departments transition from in-person teaching to virtual classrooms. With a large learning curve to deal with, many months of planning were lost. However, as there was a shift in everyone learning how to use a new software, it played as an advantage when the decision was made to move the event to a virtual platform. As the months progressed, the campus community had already become accustomed to the new virtual classroom and office settings. This made it easier to propose new ideas to them, have them consider new ways of rethinking how to present virtually, and how they could engage more students to participate. However, we still had to spend a lot of time to train the speakers and moderators on how to use the Cvent platform, which was novel to them.

5.2 Recommendations for Transforming In-Person Events to Virtual Ones

The 2021 Week of RSCA was produced virtually due to the global pandemic that commenced in 2020. This was undoubtably a scenario that could not be avoided, but that did not mean that continuing with the planning of an event was not possible.

Here are some recommendations for transitioning to a virtual event:

- Get the buy-in from the campus leadership;
- Plan out a draft of what the requirements are for your event (e.g. live presentations, concurrent sessions). Make sure you consider what your event's 'must have' and 'would like' features would be.
- Prepare a budget for what you are able to spend on producing your virtual event.
- Research available virtual conference platforms. Compare your list of event requirements with the available functions that each platform guarantees to have. This process can assist you with narrowing down your options of products. You can then setup meetings with a company representative to go over pricing and features. Make sure to ask what each price package encompasses and if any new features will be included.
- Create your deadline schedule that every party involved with the event needs to follow. While obstacles due occur and dates may need to get pushed back, it is still important that everyone involved knows when the initial deadline dates are.
- Ensure that you train session moderators how to utilize the software interface. While most functionalities for live streaming are common practice, do not assume that every individual is comfortable in using them. Doing a walkthrough of how to use the system benefits the user and the production team.
- Set up a team to assist moderators on the day of the event. As everyone will have varying degrees of wi-fi access, you should plan on having someone from your team available to assist with any issues that may occur. Keeping in contact with the moderator and speakers of a session will ease some of the stress that occur when there are technical issues.

Overall, keeping in communication with all the parties involved with the event is crucial. This will allow for understanding of what is expected from each party and will build a relationship between them. That relationship will assist with the production of the event as each individual knows that someone is relying on them to complete their task.

Acknowledgments. This work was supported by the National Institute of General Medical Sciences of the National Institutes of Health under Award Numbers UL1GM118979. The content is solely the responsibility of the authors and does not necessarily represent the official views of the National Institutes of Health.

References

1. Nagda, B.A., Gregerman, S.R., Jonides, J., von Hippel, W., Lerner, J.S.: Undergraduate student-faculty research partnerships affect studen retention. Rev. High. Educ. **22**(1), 55–72 (1998)
2. Urizar, G.G., et al.: Advancing research opportunities and promoting pathways in graduate education: a systemic approach to build training at California State University, Long Beach (CSULB). BioMed Central (BMC) Proc. **11**(12), 26–40 (2017)

Heightmap Examiner. A Descriptive Tool for Education in Digital Cartography

Luis A. Hernández-Ibáñez(✉) ⓘD and Viviana Barneche-Naya ⓘD

Advanced Visualization and Cartography Group (VAC/videaLAB), Universidade da Coruña,
15071 A Coruña, Spain
{luis.hernandez,viviana.barneche}@udc.es

Abstract. This paper describes a graphic application named *Heighmap Examiner* designed to help educate students on the computer graphics techniques that constitute the core of visualisation modules in GIS software. It applies various pixel-based algorithms over elevation datasets or heightmaps to obtain topographic and cartographic representations such as those made in professional software. The code is open and organised following this educational standpoint to let students understand and modify it if needed, even including new features to the application. This way, they can learn how modern topographical applications deal with terrain data under a computer graphics perspective to obtain contour maps, hypsometric maps, sunlight simulation, rain watersheds, etc., and also any combination of those. This paper describes the software's overall organisation and the different algorithms applied to enhance performance and visual quality.

The application has been used as part of the MSc curriculum in Civil Engineering being taught at our university.

Keywords: Heighmap · Cartography · GIS education · Topographical visualization

1 Introduction

1.1 Traditional Education in Topography and Cartography

Topography and Cartography are essential subjects in education in those studies related to construction and land management such as civil engineering, architecture and land planning. Traditionally, students in these fields were instructed to use the classic representation systems and drawing techniques to manage the territory and plan the earthworks required to construct the wide variety of projects involved in their profession. They also get a deep knowledge of topographical mapping, which is crucial in urban design studies, land management, road and railway design, etc. Most of this work was carried out using drawing techniques only.

The popularisation of CAD technology in the '80s fostered digitising the map collections and topographical graphic data hosted by the national mapping services worldwide. Some years later, Geographical Information System (GIS) technology changed

© Springer Nature Switzerland AG 2021
C. Stephanidis et al. (Eds.): HCII 2021, LNCS 13096, pp. 406–416, 2021.
https://doi.org/10.1007/978-3-030-90328-2_26

this paradigm from vectorisation of existing charts to the generation of new representations of the terrain as a graphic outcome from a database of elevations and other features instead of as a set of existing linear drawings. [1, 2].

Nowadays, students have many computer tools at their disposal to deal with any terrain-related problem, no matter how complex, but on the other side, they still learn the underlying theory of terrain representation based on classical topographical drawing. This way, students can solve terrain-related problems such as earthmoving, sunlighting, or obtention of watersheds using the traditional graphical tools provided by Descriptive Geometry.

Nowadays, GIS tools as ArcGIS [3], QGIS [4] or gvSIG [5] use computational approaches to generate such representations, and students use them without any knowledge of the diverse computer algorithms and procedures involved. The authors firmly believe that understanding how a technology works is crucial to use it properly. They have already applied the same approach to other related disciplines, such as Computer Aided Drawing, making graphical applications to illustrate how computer geometrical operators are used to obtain 3D views of objects.

This paper presents an educational tool used to acquire competencies related to cartographical mapping and terrain representation. Specifically, it has focused on knowledge, use, and application of processing techniques used in computer graphics in this field.

The application takes any existing heightmap as input. Heightmaps are a common form of Digital Elevation Model (DEM) used to store topographical data. These maps consist of a one-channel raster image representing an extension of terrain in the form of a discrete grid where each pixel in the image represents a squared-shaped piece of the terrain. The value of the pixel's luminance is related to the height of the terrain in this area, with black representing minimum height and white representing maximum elevation. This kind of topographical data is easy to obtain on the Internet for educational purposes. There are websites such as *Tangram Heighmapper* that provide free heightmap information for any place on the planet [6].

The application uses this data format to provide different terrain representations, from contour lines to hypsometric maps or shaded relief. The application's output can consist of any combination of graphical layers containing some of these feature representations (i.e. hypsometric, shaded relief with contour lines). The students had full access to the code to analyze the program's structure, modify it and include new features.

2 Methodology

2.1 Objectives

The main objective of this work was to create an educational tool to help students understand how to use computer graphics to represent the following features of a terrain:

- Contour lines. Obtainment, representation and algorithms for real-time display.
- Hypsometric map. Palettes. Height colour assignation.
- Shaded relief. Calculation of terrain illumination based on Sun position.
- Shadows. Obtainment of terrain self-shadowing.
- Variable sea level. Illustrating the effect of climatic change on coastal areas.

– Rain emulation. Displaying water impoundment and flood hazard.

We chose the heightmap DEM format because this kind of images is very easy to find in the internet for any part in the world, so we can easily use examples of well-known landscapes and famous terrains.

Since the code is open, students are taught the process involved in the calculations mentioned above under a programmer's perspective and are also encouraged to modify the code to obtain different variations of the graphic results.

2.2 Application Design

The authors developed the application using the Processing 3 graphical library and programming environment developed by researchers at MIT [7]. Processing is a flexible software sketchbook and a Java-based language for coding within the context of the visual arts, promoting software literacy within the visual arts and visual literacy within technology. [8].

The application is designed to be as simple as possible yet covering all aspects needed. Its main structure follows the standard Processing scheme consisting of a setup function, executed when the program starts, and a draw function that is executed every frame and contains all the code needed to display the graphic layers while managing user's interaction.

The setup function performs the operations needed to initialize the graphical output, prepares the graphical interface, sets the layer masks and loads a default terrain, extracting the height values corresponding to each pixel. Every time a new file is loaded, the height matrix is reset and filled with new values.

Since heightmaps can be of any size, the input file is resampled to a fixed size (i.e. the maximum display size) for the analysis, and the results are resized again to match the current application window size, which is also resizable and changes its proportions according to the aspect ratio of the heightmap image.

The draw function executes a sequence of other functions that calculate the data related to every display mode. Those calculations are performed to every pixel of the image and stored in a 32-bit raster image with an 8 bits alpha channel that gives them the partial transparency needed to combine them as overlapping layers. The user can switch on and the visibility of every layer. The visible ones are displayed one over the other in the following order (from top to bottom) (Figs. 1 and 2):

1. Heightmap
2. Shaded relief
3. Shadows
4. Hypsometric
5. Sea

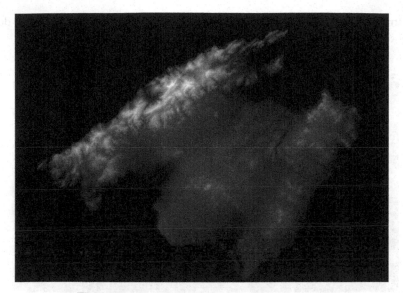

Fig. 1. Heightmap representing the Majorca Island.

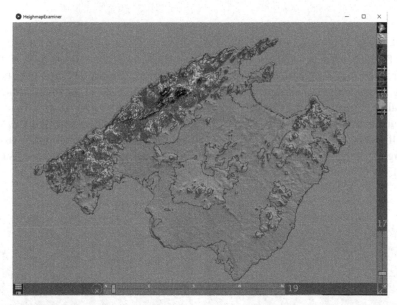

Fig. 2. Heightmap examiner user interface and viewport displaying a combination of topographical features based on the Majorca heightmap.

The individual layers that display the terrain cartographical representation are calculated as follows.

Heightmap Layer. This layer just displays the heightmap raster image. It is the default display configuration when the program starts (Fig. 3).

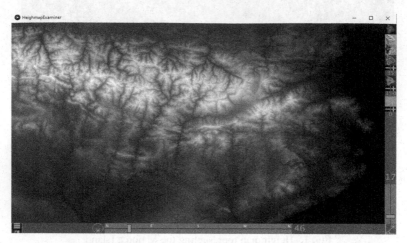

Fig. 3. Heightmap layer corresponding to the East pirenees

Shaded Relief. This kind of representation, also known as hill-shading, displays the shape of the terrain more realistically by showing how its surface would look if illuminated from a point light source. Typically, the cartographic representation uses top-left lighting in which the light source lies near the upper-left corner of the map. Although it is unrealistic lighting in the northern hemisphere, it is usually placed this way to avoid multistable perception illusions, in which the topography appears inverted [9], which is a well-known effect in map-making. Since the user can change the lighting azimuth and height interactively, this tool is ideal for explaining and demonstrating this effect. (Fig. 4).

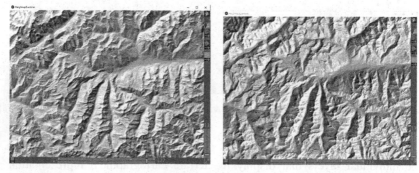

Fig. 4. Shaded relief representation of an area of the Italian Alps with NW lighting (left) and SE lighting (right) Note the alternating perception of valleys and mountain ranges.

In order to display the shaded relief, we used a simplification of the Lambertian reflectance shading model [10], commonly used for real-time visualization of 3D objects. (Fig. 5). This model obtains the diffuse reflection I_d on a point on a surface depending on the angle of incidence θ of light to the surface. Using this model, light reflection is calculated by taking the dot product of the suface's normal vector N, and a normalized light-direction vector L pointing from the surface to the light source. This number is then multiplied by the colour of the surface K_d and the intensity of the light L hitting the surface.

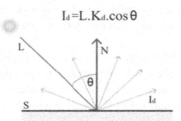

$$I_d = L.K_d.\cos\theta$$

Fig. 5. Lambertian reflectance shading model

For this kind of cartographical representation, the absolute value of the incident light is not relevant for the shading as long as it is displayed ranging from 0 (black) to 1 (white), and the colour of the relief is homogeneous. Hence, both L and K_d can be removed from the equation, and the value of the cosine of θ can then be used to represent the lighting of the pixel in the range [0,1].

To obtain the normal to the surface in every pixel, we take the height of the pixel considered and the height of the nearest pixels to the right and below and consider a constant horizontal distance between two consecutive pixels. Hence the normal vector N can be obtained as the cross product of the resultant vectors. Although it is just a coarse approximation of the surface variation, the accuracy of this simplification is enough for a good representation of the behaviour of the terrain under the light. This way, lighting is extremely fast to calculate to achieve the required immediate visual response to changes in the lighting angles. (Fig. 6).

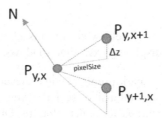

Fig. 6. Obtainment of surface normal at pixel $P_{y,x}$

Shadows. Hill-shade routines colour the terrain according to exposition towards the sun (white for directly exposed and black for unexposed areas), but they do not model the light path. There are no shadows in hillshades. As a result, a canyon floor will be rendered the same way as a wide valley, which impedes the correct perception of depth.

GIS software commonly calculates shadows for vector data over the terrain (i.e. buildings), but the representation of the self-shadows cast by the elevation surface is rarely present. Since it is important to better understand the terrain, especially in mountainous areas, *Heightmap Examiner* incorporates a shadow layer.

Shadow calculations are among the most time-consuming tasks in Computer Graphics. In order to implement them for real-time display and variation with the light angle, we took advantage of the particularities of a terrain surface to implement an algorithm for fast shadow rendering.

The methods used in CGI to obtain cast shadows require checking the interference of light rays by the objects present in the scene. The position of every shadow-casting object in the scene has to be analyzed to obtain their nature as occluder or non-occluder for every given point in the surface of the visible geometry. All these calculations are performed in a 3D space.

A heightmap presents several particularities that can simplify this process enormously. On the one hand, we know that only the pixels that lie in the horizontal projection of the light vector **R** that reaches a given pixel $\mathbf{P_{y,x}}$ (shadow sensor) can be candidates to cast a shadow on this pixel. On the other hand, we only have to compare the height value of the terrain at every pixel that the sensor hits and the height value of the shadow sensor for this point. If the terrain elevation is higher than the sensor line in this pixel, $\mathbf{P_{y,x}}$ will definitely lie inside the shadow. Once this condition is reached, there is no need to continue calculating in this direction, and the pixel is marked as shadowed. (Fig. 7).

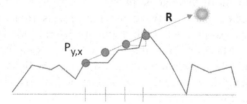

Fig. 7. Obtainment of cast shadows for a given pixel using a shadow sensor.

This algorithm performs extremely well in terms of speed and permits to change interactively the light angles displaying real-time shadows. (Fig. 8).

Contour Lines. Contour lines mark points of equal elevation on a terrain map. Topographical maps traditionally make intensive use of this kind of representation in the form of curves indicating equal elevations at regular intervals. DEM contouring is commonly obtained by calculating the intersection of all facets of the associated polygonal mesh with horizontal planes situated at the required elevations, hence obtaining consecutive straight line segments that approximate the control curves. Since those lines lie in a 3D space, they follow any perspective changes applied to the model.

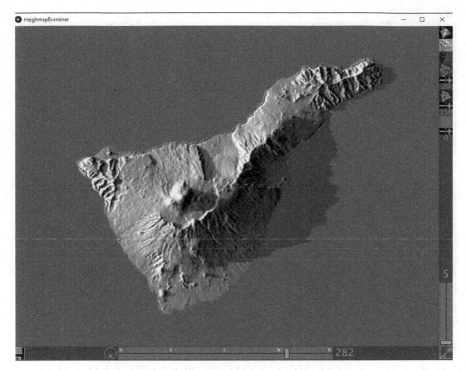

Fig. 8. Shadows cast by Teide volcano on Tenerife Island.

Our application presents only a top view of the terrain. This condition allows simplifying the contour calculation by just checking if a pixel is over or under a specific height of a given contour line compared to their three neighbouring pixels in the raster direction (right and below). The procedure marks the pixel as belonging to a contour line if it lies in a different elevation interval than the others. This way, we can obtain a plan view of the contouring of the terrain defined by all marked pixels very quickly, hence permitting changing intervals and see the results in real-time. (Fig. 9).

Hypsometric Tints. Also called layer tinting are colours placed at regular elevation ranges. Their limits always follow a contour line that may or may not be represented. The colours are appear as bands in a graduated schema. This application uses a discrete banding palette that can be customized to meet different cartographic criteria.

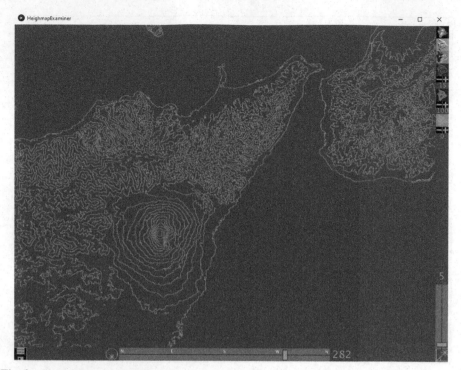

Fig. 9. Contours representation of the Strait of Messina. Sicily is on the left. Note the concentric contour lines around Mount Etna.

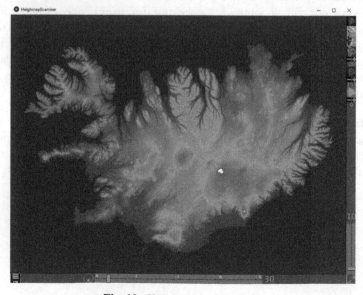

Fig. 10. Hypsometric tints alone.

According to their elevation, the hypsometric tint layer assigns a colour of the hypsometric palette to each pixel in the image. (Fig. 10). This layer has an alpha channel to make it transparent at will so that it can be displayed alone or combined with other map features (Fig. 11).

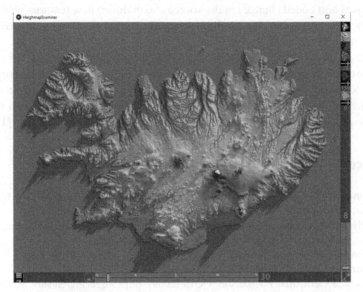

Fig. 11. Hypsometric tints combined with shaded relief and shadows.

Sea Level. The effect of climatic change on the oceans' level can be easily described by raising the elevation of the base plane height. The user can change the elevation of this transparent plane, and the application reflects the changes instantly. (Fig. 12).

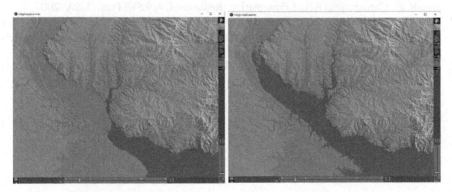

Fig. 12. Effect of raising the sea level in a heightmap of the Rio de la Plata estuary.

3 Results

Heightmap Examiner was used as part of the course "Territorial Representation Systems", a part of the curriculum of the MSc in Civil Engineering at the University of A Coruña. Not only did the students use the executable version of the software, but they also suggested and coded changes in the source and included new features such as painting over the heightmap itself to modify the terrain in real-time and simulate different kinds of earthworks.

Further develop of the application were carried by the authors, together with PhD students, to take advantage of the simplicity and speed of the software and incorporate an option for Kinect real-time depthmap data input. As a result, we fabricated a museum-like installation both for educational and research purposes. [11]. *Heightmap Examiner* is available on the internet for educational purposes at the authors' website. [12].

References

1. Hutchinson, M.F., Gallant, J.C.: Representation of terrain. In: Geographical Information Systems, vol. 1, pp. 105–124. John Wiley & Sons, Inc., New York, NY (1999)
2. Kennelly, P.: The Geographic Information Science & Technology Body of Knowledge (2017). https://doi.org/10.22224/gistbok/2017.4.9. Accessed June 2021
3. Environmental Systems Research Institute, ESRI (1999). https://www.esri.com/en-us/arcgis/about-arcgis/overview. Accessed June 2021
4. Open Source Geospatial Foundation, QGIS (2009). https://qgis.org/en/site/. Accessed June 2021
5. gvSIG Association, gvSIG (2004). http://www.gvsig.org/en/web/guest/home. Accessed June 2021
6. Mapzen, Tangrams Heightmapper (2014). https://tangrams.github.io/heightmapper/. Accessed June 2021
7. Reas, C., Fry, B.: Processing: A Programming Handbook for Visual Designers and Artists. The MIT 412 Press, Cambridge, MA, USA (2014)
8. Fry, B., Reas, C.: Processing.org (2001). https://processing.org/. Accessed May 2021
9. Imhof, E.: Cartographic Relief Presentation, Redlands, CA. ESRI Press, USA (2007)
10. Ikeuchi, K.: Lambertian Reflectance, de Encyclopedia of Computer Vision, Springer, (2014)
11. Puertas, J., et al.: An augmented reality facility to run hybridphysical-numerical flood models. Water **12**(3290) (2020)
12. Advanced Visualization and Cartography Group (VAC/videaLAB). https://videalab.udc.es. Accessed June 2021

Virtual Classrooms for the Development of Practical Laboratories in a Colombian Higher Education Institution

Henry Herrera[1](✉), Alonso Barrera[1], Marlene Ballestas[2], Ingrid Ballestas[3], and Carlos Schnorr[1]

[1] Universidad de la Costa, 58 street #55 66, Barranquilla, Colombia
hherrera8@cuc.edu.co
[2] ITSA, 18 street # ##39-100, Soledad, Colombia
[3] Universidad del Atlántico, 43 street #50-53, Puerto Colombia, Colombia

Abstract. This research was developed with the aim of determining the effect of conducting virtual laboratories with respect to the subjective evaluation of professors and the standardized tests of a Colombian higher education institution. To achieve this objective, an explanatory descriptive study with a quasi-experimental, field, and longitudinal design was proposed to execute a comparative analysis between the conduct of face-to-face and virtual laboratories in the selected higher education institution. The research was developed between the periods 2019–1 and 2020–1, being the first period when face-to-face laboratories were taught, meanwhile the second period when the students were assisting classes through virtual platforms. The results of the research process indicate that there is a dependency between grades corresponding to 10% and 20% in each of the three periods for the 2019–1 semester and the 2020–1 semester, and it is evidenced that the number of students in the insufficient category in the 20% test decreased. Another representative finding is that the scores of professors' subjective evaluations are consistent with the results within the standardized tests of the university under study. It is then concluded that the implementation of various virtual spaces for teaching allows knowledge development process to be better, where the opportunity is provided to a large number of resources or processes that could be expensive for universities in low-income countries. Similarly, virtual classrooms open the opportunity for more students, especially the ones from the most remote locations to be able to participate in the classes.

Keywords: Virtual laboratories · Technologies towards teaching · Higher education institutions

1 Introduction

Educational institutions play an important role within society because these have a duty to educate people from the earliest stages in life, in order to ensure that they are fully formed within the various competences areas that give them the tools to develop in their environment [1, 2]. In this way, higher education plays an extremely key role because it is

© Springer Nature Switzerland AG 2021
C. Stephanidis et al. (Eds.): HCII 2021, LNCS 13096, pp. 417–425, 2021.
https://doi.org/10.1007/978-3-030-90328-2_27

responsible for the professionals learning, equipping them with the skills and knowledge necessary to carry out these activities in compliance with quality and ethics standards that all professionals must comply with [3].

In this sense, it should be noted that the entry of new technologies has represented a significant change within the paradigms of all organizations, where new ways of establishing lines of communication and transmitting knowledge [4]. This reality certainly does not exclude the educational environment because important dynamics have been created, aimed at using new technologies towards learning processes [5], reaching the point where the strengthening of the civic behavior in these spaces has been achieved in some contexts [6].

In this way, significant progress has now been made when using virtual spaces for the development of educative processes [5], carrying out various practical laboratories for learning strengthening, recognizing how in various academic programs, these laboratories are crucial for students, within a controlled space accompanied by a professor, to be able to fully function within the working field [7].

In this regard, it should be mentioned that the emergence of the new reality, because of the COVID 19 pandemic, has resulted in significant changes in how students are provided with educational services [8]. This has led to the assumption of virtuality processes to continue providing education to students, which has also had a big impact on the implementation of virtual learning spaces, which have become the main space for student learning and experimentation [9]; being an example the practical laboratories.

It is clear that important unknowns arise as to whether these spaces do not represent a degrade of the necessary conditions to provide a true quality education [10]. That is the reason why this research was developed with the aim of determining the effect of conducting virtual laboratories with respect to the subjective evaluation of professors and the standardized tests of a Colombian higher education institution.

1.1 Research Experiences on the Application of Technologies on the Education Field

The implementation of new technologies has represented a milestone for the education system, because it has allowed the creation of a new paradigm which recognizes technology as a tool for the development of knowledge; taking advantage of its functionalities for the implementation of the educational processes that are carried out in both outside and inside the classroom [11].

However, there are two important points to be mentioned in the implementation of educational resources within the educational processes [12]:

- First, technology should not only be used as a tool to facilitate the work developed by institutions and teachers, or for cost reduction, because this would imply improvisation in the implementation of the technology itself.
- On the other hand, the implementation of this requires a review of the organizational and training elements of the institutions, so that they adapt to new trends and go in unison towards strengthening quality education.

In this way, the application of technology in the educational field shows the following benefits [13]:

- Becoming better efficiency and effectiveness in the classroom.
- The implementation of ICT in education increases the motivation of young people in academic fields, as it makes the learning stage more profitable.
- They supply accessibility and adaptability, allowing students to manage their own pace of learning.
- It makes it more understandable. The use of ICT more easily captures and keeps the attention of students. As a result, content is assimilated faster.
- Provide autonomy. They are in charge of developing self-learning, with the aim of forming self-sufficient people capable of solving any real problem. The use of new technologies in education promotes the administration and management of content. Thanks to this methodology, students are taught to learn how to learn, building their own knowledge. Furthermore, the Internet allows countless sources of information and promotes the ability to select and manage the most appropriate.
- Encourage teamwork. Technology generates interaction between students and promotes teamwork. In the professional field most of the projects that are developed are in teams and require the collaboration of different professionals, so developing the ability to work in a team as children is essential.
- Enhances critical thinking. Both in the case of the Internet and in the case of social media, its use translates into sharing points of view and opinions. To debate is very important when teenagers' abilities are developing. In addition, the enormous possibilities of technology to break the space-time paradigm, allows to interconnect infinite sources of knowledge worldwide, to connect with people from other countries and cultures and exchange information.
- It encourages creativity, since ICTs provide tools that facilitate interaction and content generation for students.

From an empirical approach, it is possible to locate that one of the first studies developed on the subject is the one carried out by Medina, Saba, Silva & de Guevara (2011) titled "Virtual labs and remote labs in engineering teaching" where a study of a bibliographic nature is exposed where the different types of virtual laboratories and the various applications and benefits that they can have for the educational environment are analyzed. This research is presented as a precedent of the first formal steps that are taken around the implementation of these laboratories for the use of higher education institutions, in the specific case of Mexico in the Veracruzana University [14].

Similarly, García & Ortega present the scientific article "ICT in the teaching of Biology in secondary education: virtual laboratories"; which is formulated from the premise of studying the faculties of the application of virtual laboratories in ICT-based classes within the subject of biology at the level of secondary education. The results allowed to show an effect on the quality of the classes developed based on virtual laboratories [15].

2   Method

To achieve this objective, an explanatory descriptive study with a quasi-experimental, field, and longitudinal design was proposed to execute a comparative analysis between the conduct of face-to-face and virtual laboratories in the selected higher education institution.

The sample of the study consisted of 1846 students from the laboratories of:

- Physics
- Chemistry
- Field physics
- mechanical physics
- physics, heat, and bands

Then, from the inclusion criteria that they had to be studying these laboratories for the first time. In addition, virtual laboratories for these classes are developed through PHET software, which has obtained a high level of recognition in recent years. Below are screenshots of the software about some types of labs (Figs. 1 and 2):

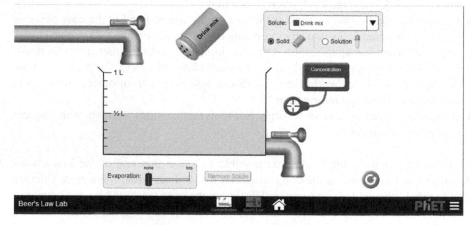

Fig. 1. Phet software screenshot 1

The research was developed between the periods 2019–1 and 2020–1, being the first period when face-to-face laboratories were taught, meanwhile the second period when the students were assisting classes through virtual platforms. Data collection tools were standardized tests consisting of 20 questions from the university under study and the subjective evaluation of laboratory professors.

The valuation scale considered was a Likert scale and consisted of the following items:

- Insufficient [<3.0]
- Minimum [3.0–3.5]

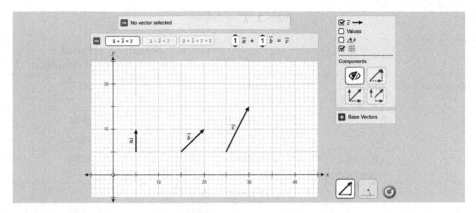

Fig. 2. Phet software screenshot 2

- Sufficient [3.5–4.0]
- Advanced [4.0–5.0]

Finally, data processing was developed with normality tests that determined that the data was non-parametric, so a simple correlation was not performed.

3   Results

The results of the study are presented in the following explanatory tables corresponding to the non-parametric correlations considered for the development of the research, regarding the subjective and standardized tests within the institution (Tables 1, 2 and 3):

Table 1. Correlations period 1

			Period 1 subjective	Period 1 standardized
Spearman's ρ	Period 1 subjective	Correlation coefficient	1,000	,142**
		Sig. (2 tailed)		,000
		N	1624	1624
	Period 1 standardized	Correlation coefficient	,142**	1,000
		Sig. (2 tailed)	,000	
		N	1624	1624

**. Correlation is significant at level 0.01 (2 tailed).

The tables above indicate that there is a dependency between the grades corresponding to subjective tests and standardized tests in each of the three periods of the 2020–1

Table 2. Correlations

			Period 2 subjective	Period 2 standardized
Spearman's ρ	Period 2 subjective	Correlation coefficient	1,000	,115[**]
		Sig. (2 tailed)		,000
		N	1624	1624
	Period 2 standardized	Correlation coefficient	,115[**]	1,000
		Sig. (2 tailed)	,000	
		N	1624	1624

**. Correlation is significant at level 0.01 (2 tailed).

Table 3. Correlations

			Period 3 subjective	Period 3 standardized
Spearman's ρ	Period 3 subjective	Correlation coefficient	1,000	,099[**]
		Sig. (2 tailed)		,000
		N	1624	1624
	Period 3 standardized	Correlation coefficient	,099[**]	1,000
		Sig. (2 tailed)	,000	
		N	1624	1624

**. Correlation is significant at level 0.01 (2 tailed).

semester. Below is the grade obtained (subjective and standardized) students in each of the first semester 2020 periods and in which it is evident that the number of students placed in the insufficient category in the standardized test decreased (Tables 4, 5 and 6).

When reviewing the table above it is possible to recognize how within the tests carried out by the professors, there is a significant decrease of the students who obtained the qualification of insufficient, from 58 in the first period (face-to-face modality) to 15 and 21 (virtuality modality). Meanwhile, in the sufficient category there is a significant improvement, from 14 in the first period to 39 in the Second and 28 in the third.

Table 4. Correspondence table period 1

Correspondence table

Period 1 subjective	Period 1 standardized				
	Insufficient	Minimum	Sufficient	Advanced	Total
Insufficient	58	26	14	12	110
Minimum	63	27	25	21	136
Sufficient	144	87	59	35	325
Advanced	355	254	251	193	1053
Total	620	394	349	261	1624

Table 5. Correspondence table period 2

Period 2 subjective	Period 2 standardized				
	Insufficient	Minimum	Sufficient	Advanced	Total
Insufficient	15	42	39	49	145
Minimum	3	47	26	22	98
Sufficient	1	64	37	62	164
Avanced	1	415	257	544	1217
Total	20	568	359	677	1624

Table 6. Correspondence table period 3

Period 3 subjective	Period 3 standardized				
	Insufficient	Minimum	Sufficient	Advanced	Total
Insufficient	21	71	28	22	142
Minimum	3	75	25	25	128
Sufficient	1	87	51	28	167
Advanced	6	623	277	281	1187
Total	31	856	381	356	1624

4   Discussion and Conclusions

The results of the research process indicate that there is a dependency between grades corresponding to subjective and standardized in each of the three periods for the 2019–1 semester and the 2020–1 semester, and it is evidenced that the number of students in the insufficient category in the standardized test decreased.

Another representative finding is that the scores of the professors' subjective evaluations are consistent with the results within the standardized tests of the university under study. It is then concluded that the implementation of various virtual spaces for teaching allows knowledge development to be better, where the opportunity is provided to a large number of resources or processes that could be expensive for universities in low-income countries. Similarly, virtual classrooms open the opportunity for more students, especially the ones from the most remote locations, to be able to participate in the classes.

The findings of the present research are contrastable with other cases, where the great impact that linking virtual contexts within educational processes has been demonstrated, showing extremely positive results in student outcomes, as long as this is complemented by a model where it is understood that this modality is not the result of a contingency need or a second-hand product [16].

Certainly, the experience presented in this studio reflects how the education system has evolved significantly in order to be able to respond effectively to the contingency of the Covid 19 pandemic [8], demonstrating great results and allowing a new generation of educational institutions to articulate with technology as the basis of their entire action. However, it should be emphasized that achieving this requires clear methodological lines of action towards virtual education and that it does not imply a significant increase in existing training gaps [10].

It is important that future studies be developed aimed at measuring the real impacts of the implementation of virtual laboratories within higher education institutions; even if the contingency of the current pandemic is overcome as the progress achieved so far has shown an important potential to increase the installed capacity of educational materials of educational institutions with lower costs of materials and equipment and greater security; as long as the quality of education does not deteriorate.

It is recommended to continue developing studies within the area and that they have a special emphasis on the implementation and quality of the human resource trained under this paradigm within the labor market.

References

1. Lay, N., Ramírez, J., Parra, M.: Desarrollo de conductas ciudadanas en estudiantes del octavo grado de una institución educativa de Barranquilla. In: Memorias del I congreso internacional en educación e innovación en educación superior. Caracas, Venezuela (2019).
2. Niebles, W., Martínez-Bustos, P., Niebles-Núñez, L.: Competencias matemáticas como factor de éxito en la prueba pro en universidades de Barranquilla. Colomb. Educ. y Humanismo **22**(38), 1–16 (2020)
3. Parra, M., Duran, S: Desarrollo organizacional y tecnoformación en instituciones de educación superior colombianas. In: Cambios e innovación: una visión estratégica, p. 278. Mexico, Universidad autonoma del Estaso de Hidalgo (2015)
4. Lay, N., et al.: Uso de las herramientas de comunicación asincrónicas y sincrónicas en la banca privada del municipio Maracaibo (Venezuela). Revista Espacios **40**(4) (2019).
5. Crisol-Moya, E., Herrera-Nieves, L., Montes-Soldado, R.: Educación virtual para todos: una revisión sistemática. Educ. Knowl. Soc. **21** (2020)

6. Parra, M., Marambio, C., Ramírez, J., Suárez, D., Herrera, H.: Educational convergence with digital technology: integrating a global society. In: Stephanidis, C., Antona, M., Ntoa, S. (eds.) HCII 2020. CCIS, vol. 1294, pp. 303–310. Springer, Cham (2020). https://doi.org/10. 1007/978-3-030-60703-6_39

7. Ima, N., Viegas, C., García-Peñalvo, F.J.: Different didactical approaches using a remote lab: identification of impact factors. IEEE Revista Iberoamericana de Tecnologías del Aprendizaje (IEEE RITA) 14, 76–86 (2019)

8. García-Peñalvo, F.J., Corell, A., Abella-García, V., Grande-de-Prado, M.: Online assessment in higher education in the time of COVID-19. Educ. Knowl. Soc. 21 (2020)

9. Fardoun, H., González-González, C.S., Collazos, C.A., Yousef, M.: Estudio exploratorio en Iberoamérica sobre procesos de enseñanza-aprendizaje y propuesta de evaluación en tiempos de pandemia. Educ. Knowl. Soc. 21, 1–9 (2020)

10. García-Peñalvo, F.J., Corell, A.: La COVID-19: ¿enzima de la transformación digital de la docencia o reflejo de una crisis metodológica y competencial en la educación superior? Campus Virtuales 9, 83–98 (2020)

11. Núñez-Barriopedro, E., Sanz-Gómez, Y., Ravina-Ripoll, R.: Los videojuegos en la educación: Beneficios y perjuicios. Revista Electrón. EDUCARE 24, 240–257 (2020)

12. Ocampo, J., Pulupa, J., Knezevich, A.: Beneficios y limitaciones del empleo de TIC en la orientación vocacional de estudiantes de educación secundaria de Guayaquil. Ecuador. Maskana 8, 333–342 (2017)

13. Certinet, https://certificacionestic.net/ventajas-uso-de-las-nuevas-tecnologias-en-la-educac ion/. Accessed 21 July 2021

14. Medina, A.P., Saba, G.H., Silva, J.H., de Guevara Durán, E.L.: Los laboratorios virtuales y laboratorios remotos en la enseñanza de la ingeniería. Rev. Educación en Ing. 4, 24–31 (2011)

15. García, M.L., Ortega, J.G.M.: Las TIC en la enseñanza de la Biología en la educación secundaria: los laboratorios virtuales. Revista Electrónica de enseñanza de las ciencias 6, 562–576 (2007)

16. García-Peñalvo, F.J.: Modelo de referencia para la enseñanza no presencial en universidades presenciales. Campus Virtuales 9, 41–56 (2020)

Towards a Computerized Approach to Identify Attentional States of Online Learners

Indika Karunaratne[1(✉)] and Ajantha S. Atukorale[2]

[1] Faculty of Inforamtion Technology, University of Moratuwa, Katubedda, Moratuwa, Sri Lanka
indikak@uom.lk
[2] University of Colombo School of Computing, Colombo, Sri Lanka
aja@ucsc.cmb.ac.lk

Abstract. In this study we investigated how digital leaners' behavior could be used to identify their attentional state at the time. It was expected to map attentional states with the level of challenge presented and the level of engagement achieved by an activity related to learning. To identify the main attentional considerations and related behavior, we have administered a questionnaire among 43 participants and requested them to self-report on attentional states, the measures of motivation, and the required effort. The questionnaire was adapted from Everyday Life attentional Scale (ELAS), and tested on 6 activities related to learning, directly or indirectly. The average level of focus the participants reported on these activities ranged from 50%–65%. They also declared to feel restless (53.5%) and stressed (41.9%) when motivated to do a task. Interestingly, 67.4% of the participants attributed to social media use when distracted from the learning activity. This study opens several avenues to use behavioral data of digital learners to identify the attentional state shifts of digital learners. Relationships among the cognitive load, the behavioral interactions, and level of attention can be observed. However, the nature and the magnitude of such relationships are yet to be explored.

Keywords: Online learning · Attention · Learners' behavior

1 Introduction

Online Learning has become 'de facto' in education at all levels today. Even though, Internet and digital technologies have been an integral part of the college students for over a decade now [28], we at the current time witness an unprecedented embracing of online learning technologies by the communities around the world [9]. Online learning, in the simplest definition is the learning through digital devices. It can further be illustrated as the learning facilitated using digital devices and communication [6]. However, keeping the students engaged with the

© Springer Nature Switzerland AG 2021
C. Stephanidis et al. (Eds.): HCII 2021, LNCS 13096, pp. 426–438, 2021.
https://doi.org/10.1007/978-3-030-90328-2_28

learning activity, and maintaining their attention throughout online teaching sessions are still considered challenging. Thus, to ensure better learning experience to the learners, effective integration of learning and technology becomes a necessity [9].

At the outset, We aim to develop a computerized model which can identify the attentional state of the online learners real-time. Considering the current hype in online learning, automatic recognition of online learners' attentional states will be advantageous in facilitating and engaging in online learning. This information can then be used effectively both by the learner and the facilitator to ensure quality and effective learning. In this research, we will explore how interactive technologies can be used to identify the learners' attentional state at the time. Learners' attention is known to be associated with the challenge imposed on the learner by the learning activity, and the level of engagement of the user with the learning task [24]. Thus, we take initiatives to identify the level of attention of the learner at a time, and map it with (1) the level of engagement of the learner with the activity, (2) and the challenge imposed by the activity on the learner.

Current computational approaches of measuring human attention vastly involve physiological signals collected using devices such as EEG headsets, GSR monitors etc. [5]. However, majority of these devices are intrusive and costly, and therefore, are not practically suitable to measure and monitor attentional state of learners in the real-time, in regular basis. Some researchers use eye-tracking which is relatively cheaper, and less intrusive. These methods mainly focus on the visual attention of learners [29]. We could not find ample amount of work taking hybrid approaches to recognize attentional states of online learners in the real-time. Also, little research was done to recognize the attentional shifts caused by both the internal and external divided attention.

Our research has two spotlight objectives; (1) to recognize how interactive technologies be utilized to capture both internal and external divided attenion of online learners, (2) to harmonize both the physiological aspects and behavioural aspects of online learners, and propose a cost effective hybrid model to identify online learners' attentional state in the real-time.

Accordingly, we first investigated how technology can be used to identify the learners' attentional state while engaged with an online learning activity. We, plan to examine the relationships of physiological signals and behavioral changes of online learners in varying attentional states. For that, we have conducted a questionnaire survey to investigate the learners' susceptibility to distractions causing divided attention; both internal and external. We also examined how distractions are reflected in online learners' behaviour, and their opinion on the usefulness of a computational model to alert the about their attentional shifts, while engaging in an online learning activity.

This paper presents the findings of the preliminary survey administered among 43 undergraduates experienced in online learning. Section 2 presents the related literature, reviewed, while Sect. 3, and Sect. 4 are dedicated to present the process of data collection, from the planing stage to the administration stage, and discussion of results respectively.

2   Others' Work

Recently, a lot of scholarly work has been carried out considering and revealing the effect of interruptions and multitasking in peoples' lives. Relevant studies were conducted in many areas including work and college [7,14,23,24]. It has also noted that more exposure to media implies high amount of multitasking [14], task switching is common in computing-related work [14], and information work is highly fragmented [7,13]. When the peripheral tasks interrupt the primary task it requires more time to complete the primary task [4], more often they take significantly more time to return to and resume work [14]. Based on an empirical study conducted focusing college students, Mark, Wang, and Niiya state that the amount of multitasking is positively associated with stress [24]. The stress is also identified as a cause for sleeping deficiencies, declining of positive affect, conversation and activity [33]. Negative moods cause reduced attention [23], while students with less sleep could become more distracting, both internally and externally. Smartphone overuse is another significant reason for attention deficits and sleep deprivations among college students [20]. Smartphone notifications are known to be a great contributor to increasing inattention. It elicits and increases hyperactivity symptoms even in those who do not have Attention Deficit Hyperactivity Disorder (ADHD) [16]. The excessive use of modern communication technologies, stress, sleeping deficiencies and attention-related problems seem to be interlinked, and impactful of one another. Constant switching is said to be habitual, and millennials are known to be multitasking more than adults. Specifically, multitasking frequency of college students is double compared to an information worker [30]. Higher multi-taskers are said to have shorter focus durations [23,24], providing further implications of the declining of attentional capacities, and learning performance of individuals. Even though some amount of multi-tasking does not have adverse effects on performance [8], an intensive amount of multitasking causes poor performance [2,3].

2.1   Effects and Impact of Interruptions and Multitasking

Jo, Kim, and Seo have considered the effect of interruptions on a text reader highlighting the fact that the reader might find it difficult to resume the reading immediately after returning from the distraction. Scanning through the document and identifying where to start re-reading from costs time, effort, and interest. They presented the concept of gaze-based bookmarking to assist the reader to resume reading after being interrupted from a text reading task [15]. Besides, the effect of chronic multitasking on analytical writing has also been identified as negative. The writing suffered from the increasing number of switching between tasks, both when multitasked to access relevant information and irrelevant information [22]. Email checking habits of a person are also identified as influential on their productivity based on the nature and the intensity of interruption the email checking process induces on the task being attended at the time. If one decides to check emails based on the email notification as and when it arrives or check emails according to his liking. The former is an external interruption, and the latter is an internal interruption [25], causing external divided attention and internally divided attention respectively.

2.2 Technological Interventions in Capturing and Maintaining Attention

Xiao and Wang proposed OneMind to detect the presence, type, and intensity of into attention of learners in MOOC learning environments. OneMind adopts a tangible video control interface to manipulate video lessons, using the back camera of a mobile phone as the play button of the learning video. Covering the camera using the finger elicits 'play' command whereas uncovering elicits the pause 'command'. Commodity camera-based PPG sensing was used to monitor the pulse rate of the user, as a physiological measure related to the situation. Xiao and Wang reveal that internally divided attention has a significant negative impact on learning in MOOC learning environments, and it is reflected in students' learning outcomes. They propose to switch to less-attention-demanding activities when the consistent divided attention is detected [34].

2.3 The Task: Load, Challenge, Engagement, and Attention

The attentional state of an information worker may change due to various reasons such as the task at hand, Interactions, and affective state of the user. It may also get affected by interruptions and other contextual conditions. Those who are engaged in digital activities may multitask frequently, and these digital activities may cause fragmented attention, and thereby the negatively affect the engagement in the work [23]. The theoretical framework (shown in Fig. 1) proposed by Mark et.al. presents four different attentional states based on the challenge of work and engagement with work. This could be used to assess engagement and challenge in work activities. The quadrants of the framework give an insight into the expected changes in attention when the level of engagement and the challenge of task changes. For the worker to focus on the task, it needs to present him with enough challenge, while providing ample opportunities to get engaged with it. The tasks which solicit engagement but do not have a sufficient amount of challenge fail to capture attention [24] and therefore the worker becomes more susceptible to distractions.

The load theory of attention and perception provides a complimentary insight but goes deeper into the attention capacity of an individual. According to load theory, the attention capacity of an individual is fixed, and when multitasking occurs the attention is divided between the tasks. Its key argument is that if the task at hand presents enough perceptual load to fill the attention capacity, the receptiveness for distraction is reduced [11,19]. Distractor can be internal or external, and also task-relevant or task-irrelevant. The current task's perceptual load determines whether to accept or reject the task-irrelevant distractor [12]. This emphasizes the importance of task-load assessment if required to capture and keep attention. NASA- Task Load Index (NASA-TLX) assesses the overall workload [27], and has been tested in many disciplines including health and students in schools and colleges [17,32].

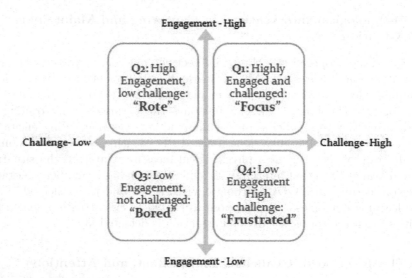

Fig. 1. A theoretical framework of quadrants representing different attentional states in the workplace [24].

3   The Process

This section will discuss in detail the instruments used, the selection of participants, and the method of data collection.

A questionnaire was developed by adapting the Everyday Life Attention Scale (ELAS), and sectioned out [1,35] with the objectives of (1) forming an overall idea about how levels of attention of digital learners in their everyday activities including learning; (2) mapping of how motivation and effort on an activity correspond with the attentional state at the time; (3) identifying how attention shifts/distractions are reflected in learners' behavior; (4) assessing the requirement/ willingness to accept a computerize model monitor them in the background, and support managing attentional shifts better.

Section 1 of the questionnaire contained a few questions for collecting of demographic data of the participants. The Sect. 2 consisted of the quesitons adapted from the ELAS questionnaire. It originally assess 9 situations in everyday life; reading a book, watching a movie/documentary, attending a lecture, having a conversation, preforming an indoor activity, doing an assignment, preparing a meal, cleaning up, and driving [1,35]. Three out of these nine situations were chosen as imprudent after considering the applicability in online learning contexts, and therefore eliminated from the instrument, These situations were namely, preparing a meal, cleaning up, and driving a car. The other six situations were selected with the consideration of its relevance to learning, or the potential to use for learning activity development in online learning environments. The situations, watching a movie/documentary, performing an indoor activity, and having a conversation were selected with the assumption that these activities can be used in designing and developing learning activities in online learning environments to keep the learners motivated and engaged.

Under each situation in Sect. 2 of the questionnaire, 6 questions were asked. These questions become instrumental in assessment of attentional state in each of these situations, and they could subsequently useful in the development of computerized model based on learners' behavior. Question 1 investigates how long a person could engage with activity without getting distracted. This duration was checked against 120 min set as the timeline to engage in an activity. The second question collects information about the level of focus (as a percentage) one can maintain when doing an activity. The first two questions are more generic and therefore can be used to identify the person's learning activity preferences and his ability to focus on an ongoing task. Question 3 is used to gain an idea about the external divided attention, as it examines how well a person could focus when there are external disturbances. Question 4 gathers information about the susceptibility to internally divided attention examining how well a person could concentrate when he needs to do things simultaneously. Questions 5 and 6 exhibit a closer link with the Engagement and challenge discussed under the theoretical framework of quadrants [24]. Motivation can be synonymous with engagement, while effort is synonymous with the challenge.

The developed questionnaire was subjected to two forms of validation before administering among subjects; first through face validation; and then by Experts' review based on Delphi Technique. It has also been reviewed and approved by the Ethics Review Committee of University of Moratuwa, Sri Lanka.

The questionnaire was administered online, distributing it among computer literate the undergraduates who are also familiar with online learning. Information sheet was made available to each participant electronically, and consent for participation has also been obtained. The participation was voluntary, and also anonymous. Data collection, storage, and reporting strictly follow the anonymity.

4   Results and Discussion

The results of the questionnaire will be presented and discussed under 4 main sections; (1) Implications of attention in everyday activities; (2) Reflection of Distractions, (3) Views on a computerized model to assist maintaining learners' attention, (4) Limitations.

4.1   Implications of Attention in Everyday Activities

The first question under each situation in Sect. 2 was to collect the duration a person could carry out a task without mind-wandering in a 120 min time slot. As all the other questions soliciting responses as a percentage, the responses for the question 1 were also converted as a percentage values based on original 120 min time span. The summary of responses is shown in Table 1.

Table 1. Attention, Motivation, and Effort on Every day (Learning) Activities (N=43).

Activity	Duration	Focus			Motivation	Effort
		No distractions	With distractions	Mind wandering		
Reading	20	54	28	23	49	50
Movie	57	65	50	40	60	40
Indoor activity	32	59	43	38	52	42
Lecture	33	50	34	26	49	55
Conversation	38	61	45	32	53	45
Assignment	31	58	36	31	55	59

Focus on when is significantly low in all six activities compared to the expected attention span of 120 min. The maximum mean duration percentage indicated is 54% under the activity of watching a video. 'Reading a book' activity has the lowest mean percentage, 20% of the allocated time spent without mind wandering. Alarmingly, situations, 'doing an assignment', and 'performing an indoor activity' have the second and third lowest mean percentages, 31% and 32%, in utilizing the time allocated effectively. The highest mean duration percentages among the listed activities were recorded (57%, and 38%) against the activities, 'watching a movie', and 'having a conversation'. The study, in overall reveals comparatively low attention spans among the undergraduates when engaged with the most widespread learning activities reading books, attending lectures, and doing assignments.

In general, the subjects recorded a minimum of 50% of the focus on any activity engaged under normal circumstances. Watching a movie is the most focused activity (65%), and attending a lecture is the least focused (50%). Three activities, namely, 'watching a movie', 'performing an indoor activity', and 'having a conversation' recorded the highest mode focus percentages, 100% each.

When there are external distractions, the focus percentages become significantly lower compared to the values recorded under the normal setting. A significant negative impact on the focus and attention can be observed with external distractions causing external divided attention. For example, a 54% mean focus which could be maintained when reading a book in a normal situation has been reduced to 28% when external distractions are present. Ability to focus when reading a book significantly reduced when there are external disturbances, recording a drop of 26%. Compared to the other activities reading a book has the highest drop in mean focus (48.14%) caused by external divided attention.

The drops in focus gets steeper when there are internal distractions. The ability to focus has been reduced in all the six situations concerned when there is a tendency for mind-wandering. It reveals that in situations of reading a book mean focus drops to 23% when you have something else to do simultaneously. Multitasking brings in internal distractions casing internally divided attention. In many of the activities concerned, the multitasking is expected to reduce the mean focus by nearly 50%. These results showcase that internally divided attention has a great negative impact on an individual's focus and attention spans.

Highest mean motivation (60%) is observed for the activity 'watching a movie', while the lowest mean motivation (49%) is recorded against the activities; 'reading a book' and 'attending a lecture'. The attention-drop with distractions, both internal and external are relatively low (23% and 38% respectively) in the 'watching a movie' activity. There is a positive relationship between the motivation and focus of the cases concerned under this study (higher the motivation, higher the focus, e.g.: in 'watching a movie' activity), however, this needs to be further investigated before making strong claims.

It is also interesting to observe that even though the time spent without mind-wandering was relatively low with the activities attending a lecture' and 'doing an assignment', the mean effort put on these are the highest among the rest, 55% and 59% respectively. Reading a book records the third highest mean effort (50%). Interestingly, these three situations directly related to learning, has been designated as the most demanding in terms of effort. It would also be reasonable to consider the effort as an indication of the challenge presented by the activity.

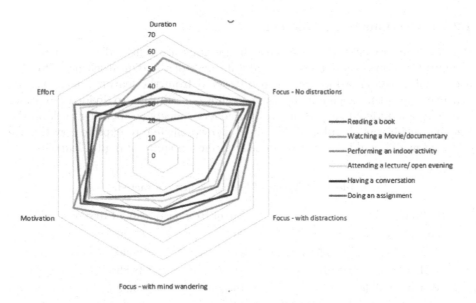

Fig. 2. The degrees of attention, motivation, effort, and duration of engagement in different situations.

The Table 2 summarizes how motivation is recognized and reported by learners. Most of the respondents voted for 'restlessness' as an effect of motivation to perform some activity. 53.5% of the participants feel restless, while 41.9% mentioned they become stressed when highly motivated towards something. Therefore, we can assume that any automated measure of restlessness or stress of an individual could also be taken as proportionate with the level of motivation he is experiencing at the time.

Table 2. Recognition of motivations.

Feeling	No. of Responses	No. of Responses %
Restless	23	53.50%
Stressed	18	41.90%
Anxious	9	20.90%
Rise in the heart rate	7	16.30%

As illustrated in Fig. 2, there is a clear indication of the lowest focus level while engaging with an activity with causes for mind wandering, and internal divided attention, emphasise the need for developing tools to assist overcoming such situations in online learning. The research needs to anchor on the objective of identifying internal divided attention.

4.2   Reflections of Distraction

It is also important to identify how distractions are reflected in the behavior of digital learners. As depicted in Table 3, most of the digital learners (67.4%) use social media as a hideout when distracted from the learning activity. The concern here is that social media usage itself is contributing to divided attention. The learners' hideout may bring further adverse effects on focusing back on the activity which was abandoned. Yet, it is also worthwhile to explore how the use of social media could be used to identify attention shifts of digital learners.

Table 3. Behavior of learners when distracted.

Reflection	No. of Responses	No. of Responses %
Log into social media	29	67.40%
Talk to a friend/Family member	21	48.80%
Walk out of the room	21	48.80%
Watch tv/Video	19	44.20%
Play a game (on computer/phone)	13	30.20%
Try to resume work	11	25.60%
Change the place	10	23.30%
Read a book/Newspaper	3	7.00%
Check email	2	4.70%
Read an online article	1	2.30%

4.3 Views on a Computerized Model to Assist Maintaining Learners' Attention

Also, in exploring the digital learners' readiness in accepting 'digital assistance' to enhance their awareness of attention shifts, 88.6% of participants considered it useful (54.5% - very useful, 25% - moderately useful, 9.1% - slightly useful) The concept of this study is based on the load theory of attention [19], and the theoretical framework of quadrants representing different attentional states in the workplace [24]. We can observe some relationship between the perceptual load presented by an activity, and the effort taken by the participant on the activity. Thus, we can expect that the effort associated with each activity will reveal some measure of the perceptual load presented by that activity. Also, in the attempt to complement the theoretical framework of the attentional state quadrant, we can consider the level of motivation, and the level of effort subjected to a given activity, as indicators of engagement and challenge respectively. However, to reveal the nature of the relationship it is required to explore these further.

4.4 Limitations

Main limitation of this study is the less number of participants. However, as this study mainly aims at conducting a within-subject analysis, where the prescribed minimum subjects is 30, the 43 subjects was considered adequate. We emphasis the need of employing significantly higher numbers of subjects when collecting data in the subsequent stages of the research, as it requires between subject analysis in model generation and testing. Also, this study used homogeneous sample, and therefore the results cannot be widely generalized.

5 Conclusion and Further Works

The results of the study are in compliance with the Mark et al.'s theoretical framework of quadrants representing different attentional states in the workplace [24] and the Lavie's load theory of attention [19]. It is also identified that the perceptual load presented by a task is synonymous with the challenge imposed by it. The study provides justifications to use learners' interactions to gauge the level of engagement. Accordingly, the further work in this research is to explore how to map the perceptual load with the effort and motivation and bring the perceptual load into the equation.

Acknowledgements. We would like to acknowledge the participants of this questionnaire-based survey who contributed voluntarily. We thank the administration of Faculty of Information Technology, University of Moratuwa, Sri Lanka for granting us permissions to administer the questionnaire, and the academics who got involved in questionnaire validation. I would also acknowledge the Senate Research Committee (SRC) of University of Moratuwa, Sri Lanka for the financial assistance (Grant number: SRC/ST/2021/20) for this project.

References

1. Fuermaier, A.B.M., Groen, Y., Tucha, L., Weisbrod, M., Aschenbrenner, S.F., Tucha, O.: Everyday Life Attention Scale (ELAS): normative data of n = 1,874 dutch participants. Applied Neuropsychology: Adult (2019). https://doi.org/10.1080/23279095.2019.1605994

2. Adler, R.F., Benbunan-Fich, R.: Juggling on a high wire: multitasking effects on performance. Int. J. Hum.-Comput. Stud. **70**, 156–168 (2012). https://doi.org/10.1016/j.ijhcs.2011.10.003

3. Adler, R.F., Benbunan-Fich, R.: The effects of task difficulty and multitasking on performance. Interact. Comput. **27**, 430–439 (2015). https://doi.org/10.1093/iwc/iwu005

4. Bailey, B.P., Konstan, J.A.: On the need for attention-aware systems: measuring effects of interruption on task performance, error rate, and affective state. Comput. Hum. Behav. **22**, 685–708 (2006). https://doi.org/10.1016/j.chb.2005.12.009

5. Chen, C.-M., Wang, J.Y., Yu, C.M.: Assessing the attention levels of students by using a novel attention aware system based on brainwave signals. Br. J. Educ. Technol. **48**(2), 348–369 (2017). https://doi.org/10.1111/bjet.12359

6. Clark, R.C., Mayer, R.E.: E-Learning and the Science of Instruction, 4th edn. Wiley, Hoboken (2016)

7. Czerwinski, M., Horvitz, E., Wilhite, S.: A diary study of task switching and interruptions. ACM Press, pp. 175–182 (2016). https://doi.org/10.1145/985692.985715

8. Davidson, C.N.: Now you see it: how the brain science of attention will transform the way we live, work, and learn. Viking, New York (2011)

9. Ferri, F., Grifoni, P., Guzzo, T.: Online learning and emergency remote teaching: opportunities and challenges in emergency situations. Societies **10**(4), 86 (2020). https://doi.org/10.3390/soc10040086

10. Foehr, U.G.: Media Multitasking among American Youth: Prevalence, Predictors and Pairings (Unpublished PhD Thesis). Stanford, CA, USA (2003)

11. Forster, S., Lavie, N.: Harnessing the wandering mind: the role of perceptual load. Cognition **111**, 345–355 (2009). https://doi.org/10.1016/j.cognition.2009.02.006

12. Forster, S.: Distraction and mind-wandering under load. Front. Psychol. **4**, 283(2013). https://doi.org/10.3389/fpsyg.2013.00283

13. Gonázlez, V.M., Mark, G.: Constant, constant, multi-tasking craziness: managing multiple working spheres. ACM Press, pp. 113–120 (2004). https://doi.org/10.1145/985692.985707

14. Iqbal, S.T., Horvitz, E.: Disruption and recovery of computing tasks: field study, analysis, and directions. In: Proceedings of the SIGCHI Conference on Human Factors in Computing Systems, p. 677. ACM Press, New York City (2007). https://doi.org/10.1145/1240624.1240730

15. Jo, J., Kim, B., Seo, J.: EyeBookmark: assisting recovery from interruption during reading. In: Proceedings of the 33rd Annual ACM Conference on Human Factors in Computing Systems, pp. 2963–2966. ACM Press, New York City (2015). https://doi.org/10.1145/2702123.2702340

16. Kushlev, K., Proulx, J., Dunn, E.W.: Silence your phones : smartphone notifications increase inattention and hyperactivity symptoms. In: Proceedings of the 2016 CHI Conference on Human Factors in Computing Systems, pp. 1011–1020. ACM Press, New York City (2016). https://doi.org/10.1145/2858036.2858359

17. Laurie-Rose, C., Frey, M., Ennis, A., Zamary, A.: Measuring perceived mental workload in children. Am. J. Psychol. **127**, 107–125 (2014)
18. Lavie, N., Beck, D.M., Konstantinou, N.: Blinded by the load: attention, awareness and the role of perceptual load. Philos. Trans. R. Soc. B Biol. Sci. **369**, 20130205–20130205 (2014). https://doi.org/10.1098/rstb.2013.0205
19. Lavie, N., Hirst, A., de Fockert, J.W., Viding, E.: Load theory of selective attention and cognitive control. J. Exp. Psychol. Gen. **133**(3), 339–354 (2004). https://doi.org/10.1037/0096-3445.133.3.339
20. Lee, U., et al.: Hooked on smartphones: an exploratory study on smartphone overuse among college students. ACM Press, pp. 2327–2336 (2014). https://doi.org/10.1145/2556288.2557366
21. LNCS Homepage. http://www.springer.com/lncs. Accessed 4 Oct 2017
22. Lottridge, D.M., et al.: The effects of chronic multitasking on analytical writing. In: Proceedings of the 33rd Annual ACM Conference on Human Factors in Computing Systems, pp. 2967–2970. ACM Press, New York City (2015). https://doi.org/10.1145/2702123.2702367
23. Mark, G., Iqbal, S.T., Czerwinski, M., Johns, P., Sano, A.: Neurotics can't focus: an in situ study of online multitasking in the workplace. In: Presented at the CHI 2016, pp. 1739–1744. ACM Press, New York City (2016). https://doi.org/10.1145/2858036.2858202
24. Mark, G., Iqbal, S.T., Czerwinski, M., Johns, P.: Bored mondays and focused afternoons: the rhythm of attention and online activity in the workplace. In: Proceedings of the SIGCHI Conference on Human Factors in Computing Systems, pp. 3025–3034. ACM Press, New York City (2014) https://doi.org/10.1145/2556288.2557204
25. Mark, G., Iqbal, S.T., Czerwinski, M., Johns, P., Sano, A., Lutchyn, Y.: Email duration, batching and self-interruption: patterns of email use on productivity and stress. In: Proceedings of the 2016 CHI Conference on Human Factors in Computing Systems, pp. 1717–1728. ACM Press, New York City (2016).https://doi.org/10.1145/2858036.2858262
26. Monk, T.H., Buysse, D.J., Potts, J.M., DeGrazia, J.M., Kupfer, D.J.: Morningness-eveningness and lifestyle regularity. Chronobiol. Int. **21**, 435–443 (2004). https://doi.org/10.1081/CBI-120038614
27. NASA Task Load Index (TLX), n.d
28. Chen, P.S.D., Lambert, A.D., Guidry, K.R.: Engaging online learners: the impact of Web-based learning technology on college student engagement. Comput. Educ. **54**(4), 1222–1232 (2010). ISSN 0360–1315, https://doi.org/10.1016/j.compedu.2009.11.008
29. Deng, Q., Wu, Z.: Students' attention assessment in elearning based on machine learning. In: proceedings Earth and Environmental Science, vol. 199 (2018). https://doi.org/10.1088/1755-1315/199/3/032042
30. Rodgers, S., Maloney, B., Ploderer, B., Brereton, M.: Managing Stress, Sleep and Technologies: An Exploratory Study of Australian University Students. Presented at the ozCHI, Launceton, TAS, Australia (2016)
31. Sharma, K., Jermann, P., Dillenbourg, P.: With-me-ness: A gaze-measure for students' attention in MOOCs. In: ICLS (2014)
32. Tubbs-Cooley, H.L., Mara, C.A., Carle, A.C., Gurses, A.P.: The NASA Task Load Index as a measure of overall workload among neonatal, paediatric and adult intensive care nurses. Care Nurs, Intensive Crit (2018). https://doi.org/10.1016/j.iccn.2018.01.004

33. Wang, R., et al.: StudentLife: assessing mental health, academic performance and behavioral trends of college students using smartphones. In: Proceedings of the 2014 ACM International Joint Conference on Pervasive and Ubiquitous Computing, pp. 3–14. ACM Press, New York City (2014). https://doi.org/10.1145/2632048.2632054
34. Xiao, X., Wang, J.: Undertanding and detecting divided attention in mobile MOOC learning. ACM Press, pp. 2411–2415 (2017). https://doi.org/10.1145/3025453.3025552
35. Groen, Y., Fuermaier, A.B.M., Tucha, L., Weisbrod, M., Aschenbrenne, S., Tucha, O.: A situation-specific approach to measure attention in adults with ADHD: the everyday life attention scale (ELAS). Appl. Neuropsychol. Adult **26**(5), 411–440 (2019). https://doi.org/10.1080/23279095.2018.1437730

Accompanying Reflection Processes by an AI-Based StudiCoachBot: A Study on Rapport Building in Human-Machine Coaching Using Self Disclosure

Vanessa Mai[✉], Annika Wolff, Anja Richert, and Ivonne Preusser

TH Köln/University of Applied Sciences, Cologne, Germany
{vanessa.mai,anja.richert,ivonne.preusser}@th-koeln.de,
annika.wolff@unitybox.de

Abstract. The establishment of a working alliance, which in human-machine interaction is comparable to the establishment of rapport, is considered a central factor for successful coaching. The goal of this study is to gain insights into how such a relationship can be established between a coaching chatbot and students. One factor considered to establish rapport is the concept of self disclosure. To this end, the self disclosure of a coaching chatbot is examined as a factor influencing student self disclosure and perceived rapport. An interaction script for coaching via chatbot on the topic of exam anxiety was developed and tested with students of the TH Köln/University of Applied Sciences in a Wizard-of-Oz experiment. Following the coaching, a survey and an interview took place. The results show that students disclosed themselves to the chatbot and built a relationship with it. However, contrary to the assumption, more self disclosure and rapport was found on average in the control group (information disclosure by the chatbot) than in the experimental group (self disclosure by the chatbot). This suggests that general information disclosure seems to be sufficient and tends to generate even more self disclosure and rapport among students than chatbot self disclosure. The results also suggest that chatbot coaching in its current form is already well received by students and helps them reflect on their exam anxiety. By having the coaching done by a machine, students find it easy to open up. There is a great willingness to use it.

Keywords: Coaching · Chatbot · Self disclosure · Rapport · Reflection

1 Introduction

Coaching has become an important didactic tool for reflecting learning processes in higher education. It is used as a curricularly integrated element for the promotion of reflection skills in the context of experience-based learning settings (for engineering education see [1]). A particular challenge is to make reflection processes scalable for a large number of students, such as in mechanical engineering. AI-based technologies can

© Springer Nature Switzerland AG 2021
C. Stephanidis et al. (Eds.): HCII 2021, LNCS 13096, pp. 439–457, 2021.
https://doi.org/10.1007/978-3-030-90328-2_29

help to make feedback more individual, systematic and process-oriented. They enable low-threshold, automated feedback and stimulate self-coaching processes in preparation for personal reflection sessions [2, 3].

In this context, AI-based dialogue systems are increasingly used in higher education to provide expert guidance to students [4, 5]. Outside of academia, there are a variety of (social) chatbots that act as empathic conversation partners [6] or stimulate self-reflection on psychological well-being.[1] In corporate contexts, they are used to reflect on work and team processes[2] or as a self-coaching tool in human resource development.[3] Building on existing coaching formats at the Faculty of Process Engineering, Energy and Mechanical Systems at TH Köln/University of Applied Sciences, reflection conversations are made scalable by implementing a coaching chatbot.

As part of a PhD project at Cologne Cobots Lab, a text-based StudiCoachBot is currently being developed and implemented to deepen students' self-reflection on learning strategies in a coaching process. In such a process, goals are defined (e.g. dealing with exam anxiety) in order to implement interventions based on these. These consist of a structured coaching conversation that uses open-ended questions to deepen students' self-reflections, as well as materials in the form of summaries, videos, reflection tools such as self-assessment tests and scales.

Interaction with a coachbot cannot replace real-world reflection and feedback conversations between students and teachers, but it offers advantages: In AI-based interactions, the willingness to disclose something about oneself may be higher – especially for sensitive topics – because the systems are perceived as unbiased by users [7]. This may lead to earlier self-awareness of counseling concerns by students. In addition, AI-based offerings are good preparation for more in-depth conversations with teachers, where students can then formulate specific concerns. At the end of a coaching session via coachbot, next steps are therefore agreed with the students, which may include (counseling) conversations with teachers. In the future, the StudiCoachBot will be made available university-wide. A curricular anchoring in modules of the BA Mechanical Engineering program – e.g. to prepare for reflection discussions with teachers – is planned.

The coaching processes between StudiCoachBot and students are researched. The focus is on investigating effectiveness factors in the working alliance between coachbot and human coachee [8]. From the current research discourse, key factors for an effective working alliance in AI-based coaching were operationalized into intervention strategies in the first step. In particular, the concept of self disclosure as an effectiveness factor for buidling a relationship between coachbot and human coachee (e.g. [9]) is explored in more detail. Based on a developed dialog concept, the effects of a coachbot avatar's self disclosure of information, feelings, and strategies on the coachee's self disclosure and perceived rapport are investigated and conclusions about relationship quality are drawn. In the following, the results of a validation study are presented in which the dialogue concept was tested in a Wizard-of-Oz setting [10].

---

[1] Z.B. Woebot Health: https://woebothealth.com/ (10.06.2021).

[2] Z.B. Coachbot von Saberr: https://www.saberr.com/ (10.06.2021).

[3] Z.B. Coach Sally von Sklls: https://sklls.de/sally_personalentwicklung (10.06.2021).

2 Definitions and Related Work

Workplace and Learning Coaching. Coaching is defined as a professional consulting process in professional contexts in the area of conflict between person, role and institution [11]. The overarching goal is to support coachees in developing professional competence and clarity about roles, tasks, and goals. Coaching is intended to promote self-reflection and perception in contexts characterized by high complexity [12]. Learning coaching is a form of counseling that focuses on optimizing learning processes. Specific goals include identifying learning difficulties, developing and optimizing learning processes and strategies, resolving learning blocks, and increasing learners' self-design potential and motivation [13], as well as providing supportive management of learners' own emotions and moods [14]. In order to achieve the goals, coaching interventions start with the resources and solution potentials of the learners.

Digital Coaching via Chatbots. Coaching via chatbots can be classified as digital self-coaching [15]. In coaching, on the one hand, chatbots perform simple tasks, e.g., by suggesting internet resources relevant to the coachee or feedback and tips on specific topics. On the other hand, there are chatbots that enable coaching interactions based on coaching methods and models to promote coachee reflection. While the machines cannot implement all the skills of a human coach in a conversation, they are helpful for certain coaching aspects, e.g., questions about reflecting on strengths, approaches, and decision-making processes [15]. The majority of coaching chatbots can be classified into three application domains: the work context, well-being/mental health, and the university context (although chatbots only partially perform a coaching function in the university context).

Effectiveness Factors in (Human-Machine) Coaching: Working Alliance and Rapport Building. One of the basic attitudes in coaching is the importance of relationship building between coach and coachee. The basis for change processes in coaching is a trusting working alliance [12]. The coach should have certain qualities that can be described by terms such as empathy, openness, credibility, and confidentiality, which enable the coachee to experience self-efficacy. The concept of working alliance from coaching has its origin in the concept of the same name by Bordin [16] from psychotherapy. It is based on the therapeutic alliance approach. This refers to the quality of therapeutic collaboration and includes elements such as the emotional cohesion of patient and therapist and agreement on the therapeutic procedure.

To operationalize Bordin's working alliance, Horvath and Greenberg [17] developed the Working Alliance Inventory (WAI). Using these and other measurement tools to examine the therapeutic relationship or alliance, correlations between the therapeutic alliance and the success of therapy have been found many times. There are also studies specifically in coaching that demonstrate the relationship or working alliance between coach and coachee as an effective factor [e.g., 18, 19].

Rapport is a concept that originated in psychotherapy and is understood as a "warm, relaxed relationship of mutual understanding, acceptance, and benevolent compatibility between or among individuals" (APA Dictionary of Psychology, n.d.). The concept shows similarities to the working alliance between therapist and patient or coach and coachee. Sharpley [20] sees rapport as comparable to the bonding aspect of the working alliance model.

The term has been adopted by researchers from the field of human-machine interaction, where it stands for the feeling of harmony, ease, synchronicity, and connectedness in a good conversation, similar to psychotherapy [21, 22]. This research area investigates how dialogue systems should be designed or what methods are appropriate for people to feel rapport when interacting with a machine, and whether and how people exhibit rapport-building behaviors when interacting with a machine [23].

Reciprocal Self Disclosure, Information Disclosure and Rapport Building in Human-Machine Interaction. Rapport can be established through a variety of nonverbal [24], paraverbal [20, 25, 26], and verbal influencing factors. One verbal rapport-building factor is sharing information. Gremler and Gwinner [40] identified that imparting knowledge, giving advice, and asking questions are strategies that retail employees use to build rapport with customers. Although this study refers to retail, it seems that this influencing factor is also effective in coaching and is therfore described as information disclosure in this study. Another verbal factor ties in with the sharing of information: (reciprocal) self disclosure is considered promising for establishing rapport between a coaching chatbot and a coachee – a factor that is on the one hand an influencing factor of rapport in human-machine interaction and on the other hand considered a success factor in digital coaching [27].

Reciprocal self disclosure means that a person discloses information and as a result the interlocutor also discloses information at a similar level of intimacy [28]. Reciprocity of self disclosure has already been demonstrated by studies in human-human interaction [e.g., 29] and theories have been developed to explain the phenomenon [e.g., 28, 29]. Studies in human-machine interaction demonstrate reciprocal self disclosure [7, 9, 30, 31]. Reciprocal self disclosure is also believed to occur in a learning coaching scenario with a chatbot and a student.

That reciprocal self disclosure leads to rapport has been argued several times in the literature [e.g., 25, 26]. Studies in human-machine interaction have shown an influence of reciprocal self disclosure on constructs that have similarity to rapport and also indicate a good human-machine relationship, for example, social attraction, copresence, and attachment [7, 9, 32].

Research Question and Hypotheses. Through the research gaps uncovered, the following research question emerges: What is the impact of a coaching chatbot's self disclosure on a student's self disclosure and perception of rapport? Hypothesis 1 is: If a coaching chatbot exhibits self disclosure, then a student will exhibit higher self disclosure than if a coaching chatbot does not exhibit self disclosure. Hypothesis 2 is: If a coaching chatbot shows self disclosure, then a student will perceive stronger rapport than if a coaching chatbot shows no self disclosure.

3   Method

3.1   Development of an Interaction Script

Chatbot Concept. The chatbot in this study is intended to coach students on the topic of exam anxiety. This coaching topic was chosen for two reasons. First, it contributes to exam preparation, one of the areas where students see a high need for support according to Traus et al. [33]. Second, exam anxiety is a rather intimate topic within learning coaching, which several authors consider necessary to explore self disclosure. They argue that too little intimacy in topics or questions limits the variance in depth of disclosure in responses [e.g., 32].

According to the coaching topic, the target group for the chatbot coaching is students of the TH Köln/University of Applied Sciences who suffer from exam anxiety, whereby in this case, in order to reach more people, the term exam anxiety is defined very broadly and also includes nervousness before or during exams.

The goal of chatbot coaching is to encourage students to reflect on their own experiences with the topic by asking them questions about their exam anxiety, so that they can expand their options for action and find their own strategies for reducing or overcoming their exam anxiety. In the long run, such coaching should contribute to a more successful coping with studies and improve the students' self-reflection skills and solution-oriented thinking. The goal of chatbot coaching, on the other hand, is not to provide students with as much knowledge as possible on the topic of exam anxiety or to give advice or instructions.

The bot persona was designed as follows: The chatbot is intended to appear as a machine and not as a human, as handled in other self disclosure studies [e.g., 9, 30]. It also does not specify gender. However, despite appearing as a machine, it is also supposed to exhibit some human characteristics, such as expressing emotions. This has the background that the chatbot is meant to serve for the exploration of self disclosure and thus has to reveal things about itself. With the expression of emotions, its disclosure becomes deeper than when it reveals purely factual information about itself. In addition, it is to be a peer agent, i.e., seen as an equal colleague with slightly more experience and knowledge. This is to be achieved by the familiar form of address and a casual tone, which leads to a higher acceptance by the students. Since the chatbot only coaches on the topic of exam anxiety and does not offer any other coaching topics, it can be seen as a specialist in the field of exam anxiety coaching.

Interaction Script. First, the coaching session was subdivided into the process steps onboarding, situation description, goal identification, solution search, selection of measures, farewell & evaluation (see Fig. 1, left). This subdivision is roughly based on the coaching process according to Berninger-Schäfer [27]. The clarification of the concern was deliberately omitted, since in the case of the topic of exam anxiety the concern was already determined in advance. Instead, it was replaced by onboarding, which is an integral part of a chatbot concept. Subsequently, suitable coaching questions were developed for the individual phases from the coaching literature on the topic of exam anxiety.

After the coaching questions were developed, self disclosure statements from the chatbot were inserted into the script for the experimental group. These were placed

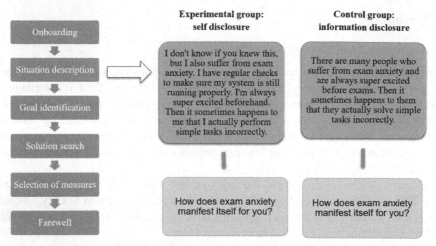

Fig. 1. Coaching process steps of interaction script (left), example of self disclosure statement followed by coaching question (experimental group, middle) and example of information disclosure followed by coaching question (control group, right).

before each of the coaching questions. It was decided that the chatbot should talk about its own experience with exam anxiety, for example, "I don't know if you knew this, but I also suffer from exam anxiety. I have regular checks to make sure my system is still running properly. I'm always super excited beforehand. Then it sometimes happens to me that I actually perform simple tasks incorrectly" (see Fig. 1, middle).

Since the study of the influence of self disclosure also requires a control group in which the chatbot does not disclose itself, the script for the control group was slightly modified. The coaching questions remained the same, as did the onboarding, farewell, and evaluation. What changed, however, was the self disclosure. To make self disclosure the only difference between the experimental groups, the control group did not just ask and answer the questions or reveal information about the next question, but revealed the same or similar information as the experimental group, just not from the chatbot's perspective. Instead of the 1st person self disclosure statement above, the chatbot in the second script said, for example, "There are many people who suffer from exam anxiety and are always super excited before exams. Then it sometimes happens to them that they actually solve simple tasks incorrectly" (see Fig. 1, right).

3.2 Experimental Design: Test Procedure, Survey and Interview

The developed interaction script was embedded next in an experimental design that included a combination of experiment, survey, and guided interview methods.

The questionnaire was programmed with the survey software EFS Survey and was mainly used to capture the student's perceived rapport in chatbot coaching. This was followed by the measurement of the rapport. The four-item subscale bonding of the German short form of the Working Alliance Inventory, WAI-SR [34], was used to measure rapport. However, in order to make the WAI-SR subscale bonding suitable for this study, minor adjustments were made. In addition to rapport, the questionnaire also asked about the subjects' openness to disclose information and their talkativeness. The reason for this is that not only the self disclosure of the chatbot, but also openness and willingness to talk could be variables that influence the subjects' self disclosure. Thus, openness and talkativeness are surveyed as additional explanatory variables for low or high self disclosure of the subjects. Three items were created for this purpose. The first item "I am a talkative and communicative person" was taken from the extraversion scale of the Big Five personality test [35]. The other two items were self-developed and asked to what extent one discloses a lot of personal information to familiar people and to what extent one discloses personal information quickly to strangers.

The interview was intended to gather deeper insights into the subjects' experiences of chatbot coaching, their impressions of the chatbot's self disclosure or information disclosure, their own self disclosure, and their relationship with the chatbot and perceived rapport. For this purpose, a guided interview was chosen [36].

The chatbot coaching was conducted as a Wizard-of-Oz experiment in Microsoft Teams under two different experimental conditions. Wizard-of-Oz in this case means that subjects assume they are interacting with a chatbot, but the chat is controlled by a human. The Wizard-of-Oz method is used to study human-machine interactions in systems that are in the developmental stage [10]. The messages that the subjects received during the coaching were not generated by a programmed chatbot, but were sent to the subject by the experimenter via copy & paste from the interaction script. In the further course, the interlocutor of the test subjects will continue to be referred to as chatbot. Half of the subjects interacted with a chatbot that revealed personal information about itself before asking the participants questions (interaction script with self disclosure; experimental group), while the other half interacted with a chatbot that disclosed only general information (interaction script without self disclosure; control group). Following the chatbot coaching, subjects completed the online questionnaire and participated in the online interview with the experimenter.

Before the actual study, a pretest was conducted with two subjects. The purpose of the pretest was to estimate the time required to conduct the experiment and to identify potential problems with the execution and comprehension difficulties on the part of the subjects.

3.3 Data Evaluation

The subjects' self disclosure shown in coaching was considered in terms of breadth and depth. As in other self disclosure studies [7, 30, 32], the breadth of self disclosure was measured by the subjects' word counts. To compare the self disclosure breadth of the experimental group and the control group, the word counts of the subjects were transferred to the SPSS statistical software and the average word counts of the two experimental groups were calculated.

Participants' depth of self disclosure was captured by coding subjects' responses given in the coaching session using Barak and Gluck-Ofri's [37] categories and levels. Barak and Gluck-Ofri consider self disclosure statements at the level of information, thoughts, and feelings and rated within each of the three categories whether they were no self disclosure (level 1), low self disclosure (level 2), or high self disclosure (level 3).

The definitions were based on those of Barak and Gluck-Ofri, but had to be adapted for this study to provide clarity about the allocation of levels to statements and to differentiate the depth of the subjects' self disclosure.

The self disclosure depths of the subjects' information, thoughts, and feelings were entered into SPSS for each question included in the analysis. Subsequently, the variables self disclosure depth of information, self disclosure depth of thoughts, and self disclosure depth of feelings were formed by calculating the mean values of all depths within a category. From this in turn, the variable self disclosure depth total could be formed (mean value of the depth of information, thoughts, feelings). After forming the necessary variables, the average self disclosure depth of the experimental group and the control group could be calculated.

To evaluate the participants' perceived rapport, the questionnaire results were transferred into SPSS and the four items that captured rapport were combined into one variable (mean of the four items). The mean values of the two experimental groups were then calculated for the variable.

The interviews were transcribed and analyzed on the basis of content-structuring qualitative analysis according to Kuckartz [38], in which the material is structured by forming categories and coding the interview statements.

4   Results

4.1   Sample Description

Twelve students participated in the experiment, six of whom interacted with a coaching chatbot that disclosed personal information about themselves and six of whom interacted with a coaching chatbot that disclosed only general information. Nine trial participants (75%) were male and three (25%) were female. The age of the subjects ranged from 21 to 39 years, with 11 subjects (91.7%) between 21 and 29 years old, which is a typical age range for students in Germany [39]. Half of the subjects were in the bachelor's program, while the other half were in the master's program. Mechanical Engineering students were the most common (five subjects, 41.7%). Two subjects were studying Renewable Energy and the remaining subjects were studying Educational Science, Digital Games, Integrated Design, Media Technology and Rescue Engineering.

The talkativeness of the subjects had a mean of 3.75 (SD = 1.36), and there were more talkative subjects in the group without self disclosure of the chatbot (M = 4.17, SD = 0.98) than in the group with self disclosure (M = 3.33, SD = 1.63). Openness to strangers had a mean of 2.50 (SD = 1.24) and this variable was also higher in the control group (M = 2.83, SD = 1.47) than in the experimental group (M = 2.17, SD = 0.98). Towards familiar people the sample described themselves as more open than towards strangers (M = 4.25, SD = 0.97). For this item, the group with self disclosure showed higher values (M = 4.33, SD = 0.82) than the group without self-disclosure (M = 4.17, SD = 1.17).

In addition, the sample can be described according to the strength of the students' exam anxiety. On a scale from 1 = very low to 10 = very high, the average exam anxiety of the subjects was 5.79 (SD = 1.72). The minimum of test anxiety was 3 and the maximum was 8. In the control group, the subjects had a slightly higher exam anxiety (M = 5.83, SD = 2.14) than in the experimental group (M = 5.75, SD = 1.41).

4.2 Hypothesis Testing

Self Disclosure. The first hypothesis was that students will show higher self disclosure when a coaching chatbot shows self disclosure than when a coaching chatbot does not show self disclosure. To test this hypothesis, students' self disclosure in chatbot coaching was analyzed in breadth and depth.

Students' word count in chatbot coaching, representing the breadth of self disclosure, was higher in the group without self disclosure ($M = 220.33$, $SD = 55.50$) than in the group with self disclosure ($M = 170$, $SD = 85.13$). The minimum and maximum number of words in coaching was achieved in the group with self disclosure and was 72 and 302 words, respectively. An overview of the breadth of self disclosure in the two groups is provided in Table 1.

Table 1. Breadth of self disclosure by group affiliation

Group	n	M	SD	Min	Max
With self disclosure	6	170	85.13	72	302
Information disclosure	6	220.33	55.50	139	293

The depth of self disclosure, as determined by coding the students' statements made during coaching according to Barak and Gluck-Ofri, was also higher in the group without self disclosure ($M = 2.02$, $SD = 0.16$) than in the group with self disclosure ($M = 1.89$, $SD = 0.10$). Thus, hypothesis one must be rejected with respect to both self disclosure breadth and self disclosure depth.

The same result is obtained when analyzing the depth of self disclosure separately for the categories information, thoughts and feelings. The depth of information had a mean of 2.71 ($SD = 0.26$) in the control group and 2.63 ($SD = 0.19$) in the experimental group. For depth of thoughts, the control group had a mean of 1.75 ($SD = 0.16$) and the experimental group had a mean of 1.71 ($SD = 0.10$), and depth of feelings was also higher in the group without self disclosure ($M = 1.60$, $SD = 0.12$) than in the group with self disclosure ($M = 1.33$, $SD = 0.13$). All results related to self disclosure depth are summarized in Table 2.

Rapport. Hypothesis 2 hypothesized that students would perceive stronger rapport when a coaching chatbot exhibited self disclosure than when it did not. The analysis showed that students in the group without self disclosure perceived a higher rapport with a mean of 3.71 ($SD = 1.38$) than students in the group with self disclosure, for whom the rapport was 3.42 ($SD = 1.46$) on average. Thus, hypothesis 2 must be rejected.

The higher mean in the control group is due to higher scores on items two "The coachbot and I respect each other" and four "I feel that coachbot stands by me even when I say something it does not approve of." For item two, the mean score in the control group was 4.00 ($SD = 1.55$), while in the experimental group it was 3.17 ($SD = 1.47$). For item four, the control group had a mean of 4.33 ($SD = 1.03$) and the experimental group had a mean of 3.67 ($SD = 1.51$). The results of items one, "I think

Table 2. Depth of self disclosure by group affiliation

Group		Self disclosure depth information	Self disclosure deep thoughts	Self disclosure deep feelings	Self disclosure depth Total
With self disclosure	M	2.63	1.71	1.33	1.89
	SD	0.19	0.10	0.13	0.10
	n	6	6	6	6
Information disclosure	M	2.71	1.75	1.60	2.02
	SD	0.26	0.16	0.12	0.16
	n	6	6	6	6

the coachbot likes me", and three, "I feel the coachbot appreciates me", look different. No group differences can be found for item three (M = 3.17, SD = 1.84). Item one is rated higher in the group with self disclosure of the chatbot (M = 3.67, SD = 1.51) than in the group without self disclosure (M = 3.33, SD = 1.97). Table 3 provides an overview of the results.

Table 3. Rapport by group affiliation

Group		Item 1	Item 2	Item 3	Item 4	Total rapport
With self disclosure	M	3.67	3.17	3.17	3.67	3.42
	SD	1.51	1.47	1.84	1.51	1.46
	n	6	6	6	6	6
Information disclosure	M	3.33	4.00	3.17	4.33	3.71
	SD	1.68	1.55	1.84	1.03	1.38
	n	6	6	6	6	6

4.3 Findings from the Interviews

In the interviews, it was mentioned particularly frequently that the coaching had helped the study participants to reflect: "[…] that also helped a bit to reflect what the actual problems are and what you can do" or: "It encouraged you, I thought the questions from the bot were very good, […] to just write and question yourself […], the, yes, strategies you have to deal with exam anxiety. It teased that out of you quite well." The coaching was also effective in that the problem was brought closer and solutions were worked out together. In addition, the students liked that the chatbot gave them suggestions for solutions, but these were only formulated as an offer: "That above all nothing is shown to you in the sense of, okay, do it this way, but that impulses are given, examples, possibilities, and that you then have to reflect on yourself through the question to which you then have to answer, and that you have to work out a solution for yourself, with this assistance."

In addition, the way the conversation was conducted was positively highlighted. The students stated that the chatbot set up a genuine conversation, which was characterized, for example, by the initial introduction of oneself or the giving of impulses.

The most frequently mentioned criticism of the coaching was that the chatbot was not responsive enough to the subjects' answers: "What I didn't like so much is that I felt that my problem was not really captured, there were very interesting suggestions or impulses given, but I kind of felt that it didn't quite go in the direction that, yeah, that my problem just, yeah, involved."

In addition, concrete suggestions for improvement were mentioned. The greatest wish is for more individualized answers and tips from the chatbot, which can be implemented, for example, by the chatbot picking up on certain words that the student uses and responding to them: "So for example, I wrote that [...] the biggest problem, for example, is that [...] I'm kind of nervous and then maybe the answer is, yes, I know nervousness too, I've experienced it before, instead of which, I think the answer was something like very interesting, [...]." Suggestions were also made to make the chatbot's questions dependent on the users' answers and to target the coaching specifically to certain topics or different forms of exam anxiety. In addition to suggestions for improving the content of the coaching, students also mentioned formal aspects that could be improved, such as the order of questions and information or the division of larger blocks of text into individual messages.

Finally, all but one student concluded that they would use the chatbot again if they had a need for coaching. They cited curiosity, the reflection that takes place in the coaching process, and that they want to learn something new from it as reasons for continued use.

4.4   Consolidation of the Results of Coaching, Survey and Interview

The rating given at the end of the coaching session on a scale of one (not at all helpful) to ten (very helpful) reached an average value of 5.58 (SD = 2.19). The smallest value given was a 2 and the largest value was a 10. Scale values of 6 and 7 were given most often (3 times each). On average, the experimental group rated coaching better (M = 6.50, SD = 2.59) than the control group (M = 4.67, SD = 1.37). In most cases, this evaluation given in the coaching also matched the evaluation given in the interview.

The coaching rating did not appear to be related to breadth of self disclosure, depth of self disclosure, or rapport. Nor did the strength of exam anxiety appear to be related to how much or how deeply subjects disclosed. Similarly, talkativeness and openness to strangers and familiar people did not appear to be directly related to subjects' self disclosure.

Although the breadth and depth of self disclosure in coaching varied between subjects, all subjects in the interview indicated that they found it easy to talk to the chatbot about their exam anxiety. Also, the rapport reported in the questionnaire did not match the rapport described in the interview in all cases.

There seems to be a correlation between self disclosure breadth and perceived rapport. Low self disclosure breadth was often associated with low perceived rapport. In contrast, there was no correlation between self disclosure depth and rapport. Furthermore, a high self disclosure breadth was not always accompanied by a high self disclosure depth.

5 Discussion

5.1 Self Disclosure and Rapport Building

Analysis of the coaching chats revealed that students in both experimental groups disclosed themselves. In terms of depth of disclosure, the mean of both groups was closest to Barak and Gluck-Ofris level 2, which corresponds to a low depth of self-disclosure. The deepest disclosures occurred at the level of information in both groups, and the least depth occurred in students' feelings.

Contrary to the assumption that students show higher self disclosure when a coaching chatbot shows self disclosure than when a coaching chatbot does not show self disclosure (Hypothesis 1), however, higher mean values in self disclosure breadth and depth were found in the control group than in the experimental group. Regarding self disclosure depth, this was true for total depth as well as for information depth, thought depth, and feeling depth. The results suggest that general information disclosure by a coaching chatbot leads to more and deeper disclosure by students than when a coaching chatbot shows self disclosure. Hypothesis 1 must therefore be rejected.

Thus, the study could not confirm the results of Kang and Gratch [9], Lee et al. [7], Moon [30], and Ravichander and Black [31], who found a positive influence of a machine's self disclosure on a human's self disclosure. The reason for this discrepancy is believed to be in the methodology, more specifically in the design of the experimental condition without self disclosure of the chatbot. In the studies listed, only questions were asked in the group without self disclosure or the conversation part in which the machine's self disclosure took place was skipped. In contrast, in the study of this paper, general information was disclosed in the group without self disclosure of the chatbot. The fact that disclosing general information and information about the next question leads to more self disclosure than not disclosing information before the questions is supported by the study of von der Pütten et al. [32]. Although there was also a talkative condition in Moon's study [30], and less self disclosure by the human was found in this condition than in the condition with self disclosure by the machine, only information about the next question was revealed in the talkative condition. Thus, the results of this study should not be seen as contradicting previous research on self disclosure in human-machine interaction, but rather as complementing it. Not only was reciprocal self disclosure investigated in a new application domain, learning coaching, but the study also sheds light on whether it is really self disclosure that leads to self disclosure, or whether general information about the conversational topic is sufficient to generate self disclosure.

The evaluation of the questionnaire showed that rapport, i.e. a bond between the students and the chatbot, could be established in both experimental groups. The mean values of the two groups were between three and four, which means that the students in both groups agreed with the rapport items on average rather to very often.

Hypothesis 2 was that students would perceive higher rapport when a coaching chatbot exhibited self disclosure than when a coaching chatbot did not exhibit self disclosure. However, contrary to this assumption, the control group perceived higher rapport on average than the experimental group. A general information disclosure of a coaching chatbot seems to generate a higher rapport among the students than the self disclosure of a coaching chatbot. Hypothesis 2 must thus be rejected. The result suggests that general information disclosure builds a stronger working alliance according to Bordin [16] than self disclosure of a coaching chatbot, since a higher level of attachment is generated by the disclosure of general information.

The result contrasts with the findings of previous research in which a machine's self disclosure had a positive effect on the rapport-like constructs of copresence [9, 32], social attraction [9, 30], and enjoyment, intimacy, and trust [7]. The cause, as already stated above, is seen in the different construction of the control condition. General information disclosure, as in the control group of this study, seems to build a better relationship than not disclosing any information at all, as was handled in the control groups in Kang and Gratch [9], von der Pütten et al. [32], and Lee et al. [7], or giving information about the next question, as in Moon [30]. This is also supported by a study by Gremler and Gwinner [40], in which sharing information, consisting of knowledge transfer, advice, and questions, was found to build rapport. Although this study refers to retail, it seems that this influencing factor is also effective in coaching. This would mean that in the study of this paper, not only was self disclosure compared to no self disclosure, but self disclosure was compared to another rapport-building factor.

In summary, based on the results of this study, the self disclosure of a coaching chatbot has no effect on a student's self disclosure and perception of rapport. In both the group with self disclosure and the group without self disclosure of the chatbot, students disclosed themselves and perceived rapport. Thus, the disclosure of general information seems to be sufficient and even tends to generate more self disclosure and rapport among students than the self disclosure of a chatbot.

5.2 Evaluation of the Chatbot Coaching

Overall Evaluation. The interview showed that the coaching chatbot was well accepted by the students of both experimental groups. With the exception of one person, all would use the chatbot again if they needed coaching, but partly on the condition that the coaching was more subject-specific, that the problem exactly matched the coaching, or that the chatbot was only used for an initial conversation. Subjects found the chatbot helpful primarily because it prompted them to reflect. Stimulating reflection is seen as a goal in coaching [e.g., 12, 15] and was accordingly formulated as a goal in the briefing for the chatbot of this study. Therefore, this goal can be considered as achieved. In addition, the dialogic approach of coaching and the personality of the chatbot were positively emphasized. The main criticism was that the chatbot did not respond enough to the students' messages and their type and severity of exam anxiety. Accordingly, more individualized answers from the chatbot were mentioned as the biggest wish for improvement.

Perception of Self Disclosure vs. Information Disclosure. Both the chatbot's self disclosure and information disclosure were predominantly positively evaluated, but in different ways. Self disclosure influenced the perception of the chatbot and the coaching experience. The chatbot seemed more human through self disclosure and the disclosure was described as cute, funny, and uplifting. In part, the chatbot's self disclosure also helped students open up more. The latter statement is consistent with other relevant research [7, 9, 30, 31] that found a correlation between a machine's self-disclosure and users' self-disclosure. However, in the coaching chats of this work, the effect of chatbot self disclosure described in the interview could not be found.

In contrast to self disclosure, information disclosure was more likely to be described as interesting and mentioned as helpful tips. Thus, it is clear that the general information, even if it strongly matches the content of the chatbot's self disclosure, is more likely to be identified as advice than the self disclosure. Furthermore, the information partly led the students to think and answer in a certain direction when asking the questions. On the one hand, this can be interpreted positively as the information helps students understand what the question is aiming at and gives them food for thought, but at the same time it can also limit their reflection as they are already given answers to follow without considering many other possibilities.

Self Disclosure by Subjects. All subjects found it easy to talk to the chatbot about their exam anxiety. The main reason for this was that they thought they were merely interacting with a machine and assumed that the chats were anonymous. This aspect is consistent with the interview results of Lee et al. [7]. In their interviews, it was found that the subjects were able to speak openly with the chatbot because it was not a person and they did not have to worry about their own words or the other person's reactions.

Furthermore, some characteristics and behaviors were mentioned that a chatbot should have in order to disclose much to it. First, these were aspects that the chatbot in the study exhibited, namely self disclosure, giving answers, and a polite, witty, social personality. Second, they would disclose a lot to a coaching chatbot if it gave individualized answers. The above aspects of self disclosure, giving answers, politeness, and humor represent influencing factors of rapport. It can be concluded that the influence of self disclosure on rapport investigated in this study can also have a reverse effect, namely that people who sense rapport open up more.

Relationship Building with the Coaching Chatbot. Regarding relationship building with the chatbot, no differences were found between the group with and without self disclosure of the chatbot. When subjects indicated that they were able to build a relationship with the chatbot, it was predominantly described in both groups using terms with positive connotations such as appreciative, good, open, friendly, and amicable. In addition, trust could be established. As an explanation for the fact that in the study of this paper, in contrast to other studies such as [7], no differences were shown in the description of the relationship in the interview, reference is made to the different design of the control group. Due to the general information disclosure of the chatbot in the control group, the chatbot of this work was more interactive in the control group than the chatbot in the control groups of other studies [e.g., 7], in which the complete interview part that included self disclosure was skipped.

What the students lacked, or what they would have found helpful for relationship building, would be more individual engagement with them and a face and voice for the chatbot. The fact that a face and a voice would be helpful for relationship building can be explained by the fact that additional nonverbal factors [24] can be used for relationship building through a face and paraverbal factors [20, 25, 26] through a voice.

Humanity, Personality and Language Style of the Coaching Chatbot. Furthermore, the interviews showed that the chatbot was perceived as human by subjects of both groups, which they found positive. Comments were also made about its personality. This was mainly described as courteous and polite, which was expressed in the bot's nice phrases and responses. Thus, not only the rapport-building factor of self disclosure but also the influencing factor of politeness was present in the study [40]. However, since politeness was found in both experimental groups, this did not affect the study of the self disclosure factor.

In addition to nice and courteous, the chatbot's language style was also described as appropriate and fitting for the addressee. One subject mentioned that the language style was like a conversation among students. Thus, the student's perception coincides with the intention formulated in the concept (see Sect. 3.1) to have the chatbot act as a peer agent.

5.3   Design Implications

For the design of a coaching chatbot at a university, both self disclosure statements and general information about the coaching topic should be programmed to enable a good working alliance between chatbot and students, and thus for successful coaching. Since in some cases the general information influenced the students' answers, one option would be to provide the general information only after the subjects' answers.

In addition, the chatbot's responses should be more customized to the user's messages and their level and type of exam anxiety. This can be realized by programming different branches for the chatbot that are played when the subject gives certain answers or uses keywords. If a branch is based on a keyword, it should also appear in the chatbot's message. In addition, the user should be notified in the chat that their message is being processed, for example by displaying three dots at the bottom of the chat. This not only informs the user about the status of the processing, but also enables the chatbot to send the currently quite long text blocks in several messages, since the user sees that there is another message to follow.

5.4   Limitations and Future Research

The study is accompanied by some limitations. First, the sample is very small with 12 subjects. For this reason, the results on self disclosure and the perceived rapport of the students, represented by mean values, only show initial tendencies. Whether statistically significant differences exist between the groups with and without self disclosure of the chatbot could not be determined from the data. It can therefore be stated that no conclusions can be drawn about the overall population from the results of the study.

Second, it should be noted that the interviews and coaching chats were coded by only one person, the experimenter. In order to check the quality of the coding, qualitative research often uses two persons who code the texts independently and discuss the coding afterwards [38]. Especially in the coding according to Barak and Gluck-Ofri [37], a second coder would have been useful, as it was not always easy to classify whether a statement had no, low, or high self disclosure within the different categories. Another coder might have classified some statements into other levels. However, since all statements were coded by the same person using the same principle, the differences between the groups can still be considered reliable.

Finally, the Wizard-of-Oz design used brings limitations. It remains open whether the subjects would have had the same experience with a real chatbot and whether the same results would have been obtained. A real rule-based chatbot would have a different response time than the human-played chatbot.

Future research can build on the limitations of the study mentioned above. The next step should be to program a chatbot using the interaction script developed in this paper and then conduct the coaching with a real chatbot with a larger sample. In this way, the results of this study can be verified. Furthermore, it is advisable to collect additional characteristics of the subjects in the post coaching survey besides the openness and talkativeness of the person in order to obtain further explanations for group differences or to be able to exclude aspects as causes. For example, it is possible that attitudes toward chatbots, willingness or openness to coaching, motivation to type texts, or belief in the extent to which a relationship can be established with machines have an impact on students' self disclosure or perceived rapport.

In addition, further experimental groups could be formed, e.g., an experimental group in which no information is revealed at all, as in [7], an experimental group in which information about the next question is revealed, as in [30], or mixed forms, such as a combination of general information and self disclosure by the chatbot. This would allow to verify whether the results of the listed studies can be applied to a coaching scenario, and to identify a more accurate cause of self disclosure and rapport. It would also be interesting to investigate whether differences in self disclosure and rapport occur when the chatbot discloses from the perspective of a machine, as in this study, or from the perspective of a human.

Furthermore, future research should address other influencing factors of a good working alliance between coaching chatbot and students besides self disclosure. For this, reference is made to the verbal influencing factors of rapport presented in this study. Another possibility would be to use a voice-based chatbot or an embodied conversational agent for the study. This would also allow testing paraverbal and nonverbal influencing factors in a coaching scenario.

6   Conclusion

In the present study, reciprocal self disclosure was investigated in a new field of application, learning coaching. The study also provides insight into whether it is really self disclosure that leads to self disclosure or whether general information about the topic of conversation is sufficient to generate self disclosure. The results indicate that the disclosure of general information seems to be sufficient and tends to generate even more self disclosure and rapport among students than the self disclosure of a chatbot. Moreover, the results indicate that in the study of this paper, not only was self disclosure compared to no self disclosure, but self disclosure was contrasted with another rapport-building factor (sharing information/information disclosure). In follow-up studies, therefore, the research design presented here should be conducted with a larger sample and expanded to include a third experimental group in which no information is revealed at all to better understand effect sizes.

The results also suggest that chatbot coaching, as it is, is already well received by students and helps them reflect on their exam anxiety. By having the coaching done by a machine, students find it easy to open up. There is a great willingness to use it. The script with self disclosure proved to be as good as the script with general information.

In a next step, the interaction script on the topic of exam anxiety is to be further differentiated and, in addition to the self disclosure questions, answer pools for dealing with exam anxiety are to be developed (e.g., inputs in the form of methods). The selection and testing of a suitable system architecture for programming the interaction script is being planned.

In addition, other fields of application for the StudiCoachBot are conceivable, such as coaching on learning and work strategies or on project management and communication in teams. It could also be interesting to use the StudiCoachBot in the context of study counseling/ student advisory service and/or for the preparation and follow-up of seminars for students on relevant topics such as exam anxiety, learning and work strategies, project management and communication. This also opens up possibilities for the use of the CoachBot beyond university contexts, e.g. in the context of accompanying coaching in corporate contexts.

References

1. Mai, V.: Projektcoaching und Leadership-Coaching als integrative Elemente in der Ingenieurausbildung. Eine Wirksamkeitsstudie zur Entwicklung von Metakompetenzen. In: Heuchemer, S., Hochmuth, R., Schaper, N., Szczyrba, B. (eds.): Forschung und Innovation in der Hochschulbildung, vol. 8, research paper (2020). https://cos.bibl.th-koeln.de/frontdoor/index/index/docId/926. Accessed 10 June 2021
2. Terblanche, N.: A design framework to create artificial intelligence coaches. Int. J. Evid. Based Coach. Mentoring 18(2), 152–165 (2020). https://doi.org/10.24384/B7GS-3H05
3. Graßmann, C., Schermuly, C.: Coaching with artificial intelligence: concepts and capabilities. Hum. Res. Dev. Rev. 1–21 (2020). https://doi.org/10.1177/1534484320982891
4. Giebermann, K., Friese, N.: MathWeb – interaktives Lernen in Mathematikmodulen. die hochschullehre. Beiträge zu Praxis, Praxisforschung und Forschung 4, 361–376 (2018)
5. Goel, A.K., Polepeddi, L.: Jill watson: a virtual teaching assistant for online education. In: Dede, C, Richards, J., Saxberg, B. (eds.): Learning Engineering for Online Education. Theoretical Contexts and Design-Based Examples, chapter. 7. Routledge, New York (2018)
6. Zhou, L., Gao, J., Li, D., Shum, H.-Y.: The Design and implementation of xiaoice, an empathetic social chatbot. Comput. Linguist. 46(1), 53–93 (2019). https://doi.org/10.1162/COLI_a_00368
7. Lee, Y., Yamashita, N., Huang, Y., Fu, W.: I hear you, i feel you: encouraging deep self-disclosure through a chatbot. In: Proceedings of the 2020 CHI Conference on Human Factors in Computing Systems (CHI 2020). Association for Computing Machinery, New York, pp. 1–12 (2020). https://doi.org/10.1145/3313831.3376175.

8. Mai, V., Richert, A.: AI coaching: effectiveness factors of the working alliance in the coaching process between coachbot and human coachee – an explorative study. In: Proceedings of 2020, EDULEARN20, pp. 1239–1248 (2020). https://library.iated.org/view/MAI2020AIC.

9. Kang, S., Gratch, J.: People like virtual counselors that highly disclose about themselves. Stud. Health Technol. Inform. **167** (2011)

10. Dahlbäck, N., Jönsson, A., Ahrenberg, L.: Wizard of Oz studies-why and how. Knowl.-Based Syst. **6**, 258–256 (1993)

11. International Organization for Business Coaching (IOBC), Standards for the Coaching Process (2020). https://www.iobc.org/en/standards/coaching. Accessed 10 June 2021

12. Lippmann, E.: Coaching – Angewandte Psychologie für die Beratungspraxis. Springer, Berlin/Heidelberg (2013)

13. Nicolaisen, T.: Lerncoaching-Praxis – Coaching in pädagogischen Arbeitsfeldern. 2nd edn. Juventa (2017)

14. Nicolaisen, T.: Einführung in das systemische Lerncoaching. Carl-Auer (2017)

15. Kanatouri, S.: The Digital Coach. Routledge (2020)

16. Bordin, E.S.: The generalizability of the psychoanalytic concept of the working alliance. Psychother. Theor. Res. Pract. **16**, 252–260 (1979)

17. Horvath, A.O., Greenberg, L.S.: Development and validation of the working alliance inventory. J. Couns. Psychol. **36**(2), 223–233 (1989). https://doi.org/10.1037/0022-0167.36.2.223

18. de Haan, E., Grant, A.M., Burger, Y., Eriksson, P.-O.: A large-scale study of executive and workplace coaching: the relative contributions of relationship, personality match, and self-efficacy. Consult. Psychol. J Pract. Res. **68**(3), 189–207 (2016). https://doi.org/10.1037/cpb0000058

19. Lindart, M.: Was Coaching wirksam macht: Wirkfaktoren von Coachingprozessen im Fokus. Springer (2016)https://doi.org/10.1007/978-3-658-11761-0

20. Sharpley, C.F.: The influence of silence upon clinet-perceived rapport. Couns. Psychol. Q. **10**(3), 237–246 (1997). https://doi.org/10.1080/09515079708254176

21. Gratch, J., Wang, N., Gerten, J., Fast, E., Duffy, R.: Creating rapport with virtual agents. In: Pelachaud, C., Martin, J.-C., André, E., Chollet, G., Karpouzis, K., Pelé, D. (eds.) IVA 2007. LNCS (LNAI), vol. 4722, pp. 125–138. Springer, Heidelberg (2007). https://doi.org/10.1007/978-3-540-74997-4_12

22. Huang, L., Morency, L.-P., Gratch, J.: Virtual rapport 2.0. In: Vilhjálmsson, H.H., Kopp, S., Marsella, S., Thórisson, K.R. (eds.) IVA 2011. LNCS (LNAI), vol. 6895, pp. 68–79. Springer, Heidelberg (2011). https://doi.org/10.1007/978-3-642-23974-8_8

23. Seo, S.H., Griffin, K., Young, J.E., Bunt, A., Prentice, S., Loureiro-Rodríguez, V.: Investigating people's rapport building and hindering behaviors when working with a collaborative robot. Int. J. Soc. Robot. **10**(1), 147–161 (2017). https://doi.org/10.1007/s12369-017-0441-8

24. Tickle-Degnen, L., Rosenthal, R.: The nature of rapport and its nonverbal correlates. Psychol. Inq. **1**(4), 285–293 (1990)

25. Argyle, M.: The biological basis of rapport. Psychol. Inq. **1**(4), 297–300 (1990). https://doi.org/10.1207/s15327965pli0104_3

26. Zhao, R., Papangelis, A., Cassell, J.: Towards a dyadic computational model of rapport management for human-virtual agent interaction. In: Bickmore, T., Marsella, S., Sidner, C. (eds.) IVA 2014. LNCS (LNAI), vol. 8637, pp. 514–527. Springer, Cham (2014). https://doi.org/10.1007/978-3-319-09767-1_62

27. Berninger-Schäfer, E.: Online-Coaching. Springer (2018).

28. Guerrero, L.K., Anderson, P.A., Afifi, W.A.: Close Encounters: Communication in Relationships. Sage (2007)

29. Altman, I.: Reciprocity of interpersonal exchange. J. Theory Soc. Behav. **3**(2), 249–261 (1973). https://doi.org/10.1111/j.1468-5914.1973.tb00325.x

30. Moon, Y.: Intimate exchanges: using computers to elicit self-disclosure from consumers. J. Cons. Res. **26**(4), 323–339 (2000). https://doi.org/10.1086/209566
31. Ravichander, A., Black, A.W.: An empirical study of self-disclosure in spoken dialogue systems. In: Proceedings of the 19th Annual SIGdial Meeting on Discourse and Dialogue, pp. 253–263 (2018). https://doi.org/10.18653/v1/W18-5030
32. von der Pütten, A.M., Hoffmann, L., Klatt, J., Krämer, N.C.: Quid Pro Quo? reciprocal self-disclosure and communicative accomodation towards a virtual interviewer. In: Vilhjálmsson, H.H., Kopp, S., Marsella, S., Thórisson, K.R. (eds.) IVA 2011. LNCS (LNAI), vol. 6895, pp. 183–194. Springer, Heidelberg (2011). https://doi.org/10.1007/978-3-642-23974-8_20
33. Traus, A., Höffken, K., Thomas, S., Mangold, K., Schröer, W.: Stu.diCo. – Studieren digital in Zeiten von Corona. Universitätsverlag Hildesheim (2020). https://hildok.bsz-bw.de/frontd oor/index/index/docId/1157. Accessed 10 June 2021
34. Wilmers, F., et al.: Die deutschsprachige Version des working alliance inventory – short revised (WAI-SR) – Ein schulenübergreifendes, ökonomisches und empirisch validiertes Instrument zur Erfassung der therapeutischen Allianz. Klinische Diagnostik & Evaluation **1**(3), 343–358 (2008)
35. Satow, L.: B5T® Big-Five-Persönlichkeitstest: Test- und Skalendokumentation. Leibniz Institute for Psychology (2020). https://doi.org/10.23668/psycharchives.4611
36. Döring, N., Bortz, J.: Forschungsmethoden und Evaluation in den Sozial- und Humanwissenschaften. Springer, Berlin Heidelberg (2016). DOI: https://doi.org/10.1007/978-3-642-41089-5.
37. Barak, A., Gluck-Ofri, O.: Degree and reciprocity of self-disclosure in online forums. CyberPsychol. Behav. **10**(3), 407–417 (2007). https://doi.org/10.1089/cpb.2006.9938
38. Kuckartz, U.: Qualitative Inhaltsanalyse. Methoden, Praxis, Computerunterstützung. 4nd edn. Beltz (2018)
39. VuMA, VuMA Touchpoints Monitor (2021). https://touchpoints.vuma.de/#/zielgruppen/. Accessed 10 June 2021
40. Gremler, D., Gwinner, K.: Rapport-building behaviors used by retail employees. J. Retail. **84**, 308–324 (2008). https://touchpoints.vuma.de/#/zielgruppen/

A Feasible Design of Ballet Learning Support System with Automated Feedback

Mondheera Pituxcoosuvarn[(✉)] and Yohei Murakami

Faculty of Information Science and Engineering, Ritsumeikan University,
Shiga, Japan
mond-p@fc.ritsumei.ac.jp

Abstract. Online courses have become increasingly common in recent years. Many people have also begun to exercise and learn new activities, including dancing, at home by watching online videos and lessons, particularly during the COVID-19 epidemic. Classical ballet is one of those physical activities that conventionally requires visits to a studio, not only to dance but to receive feedback to improve poses. Since guidance is needed, it is difficult for the at-home learner to learn new dance poses and movements simply by watching videos. As a result of this problem, this late-breaking paper propose a support system that can assist at-home ballet learners in providing feedback of their dance poses.

Keywords: Computer-supported learning · Computer vision application · Ballet

1 Introduction

During the COVID-19 epidemic, many people have begun to exercise and learn new activities. Since, online courses have grown in popularity, there are courses available online and allow people to acquire new skills at home by watching online videos and lessons.

Ballet dancing is one of those physical activities that traditionally necessitate studio visits, not only to practice but also to receive feedback on poses. Lately, free and paid videos have become available on the internet. It is not difficult to watch the pose on the video but what is lacking from a real face-to-face class is the feedback and the position correction by the teacher.

We solve this problem by designing a system that can provide at-home beginner ballet learners with feedback to help them learn new poses correctly.

Human body parts can now be detected using modern technology without the use of a special RGB-D camera. Computer vision software can estimate body position and poses using a standard camera, phone camera, or webcam. This technology can be used to detect dance students' poses and provide feedback to students or anyone else trying to learn a new dance position or move at home.

© Springer Nature Switzerland AG 2021
C. Stephanidis et al. (Eds.): HCII 2021, LNCS 13096, pp. 458–466, 2021.
https://doi.org/10.1007/978-3-030-90328-2_30

2   Related Work

2.1   Ballet Learner Support

A number of researchers have proposed technological methods to support ballet learners.

In 2014, Hallam et al. [6] proposed a wearable technology garment with LED and microcontrollers to be worn by the instructor. This garment acts as a communication device that holds the student's attention on the teacher. In 2017, the concept called Relevé was introduced [10]. The researchers put pressure sensors and bending sensors on a soft-sole ballet shoe and connect them to a microcontroller board; the data from these sensors is used to realize real-time feedback. Some of the limitations of previous proposals include the high cost of the hardware and the movement space needed.

Even with the advances made, it remains a design challenge to provide a support system that is feasible enough to provide at-home dancers with useful and effective feedback.

2.2   Pose Recognition Using Computer Vision

A more recent study [4] used computer vision technology instead of sensors. They identified the features important for ballet pose recognition by ranking the important pose features using several classifiers with OpenPose [3].

There are several groups of researchers who applied OpenPose to similar types of activities for example, sports biomechanics [2], yoga [11], basketball [8], etc.

3   Ballet Positions

For this research, we are focusing on giving feedback on the most basic ballet positions, at this moment.

3.1   Feet Positions

We began with the five fundamental foot positions in classical ballet. These positions are the first technical challenge involving the lower limbs that the novice must master [1].

As shown in Fig. 1, for the first position, the feet should be turned out with the toes pointing away from each other with the heels touching. The second position is similar to the first position but with the heels apart, around 10 in. to 12 in.. The third position requires that the feet to be turned out, parallel, and partly overlapped with one foot in front of the other and heels touching the middle of the other foot. For the fourth position, feet are turned out and parallel with one foot about 8 in. in front of the other. The fifth position is similar to the fourth position, but the feet are brought together till they touch [5].

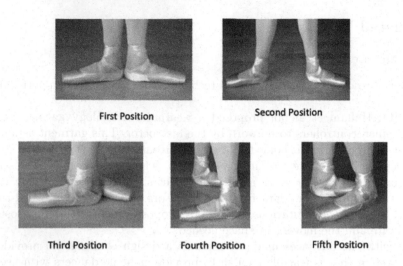

Source: Wikipedia (Creative Commons license)

Fig. 1. Five basic feet positions of ballet

3.2 Arm Positions

In classical ballet, there are five basic arm positions that are numbered similarly to the foot positions [7]. Based on Royal Academy of Dance(RAD) [9], for the first position, the arms stretch in front of the body and form an oval shape. The tips of the fingers should be in line with the navel or no higher than the sternum. The second position requires the arms to be stretched to the sides with the elbows slightly lower than the shoulders. For the third position, one arm should be in the first position and the other arm should be in the second position. For the fourth position, one arm is rounded and raised over the head, while the other is in the second position(*ordinary position*) or first position(*crossed position*). Fifth position requires the arms to maintain the same oval shape but both arms are raised over the head.

However, there are variations of the arm positions depending on the ballet method. Aside from the five positions and their variations, there is a preparatory position called *Bras Bas*. In this position, the arms are rounded and stretched out in front of the body, almost touching.

4 Automated Feedback System Overview

We designed a system that can use simple input from web cameras; the position of the dancer's body is determined using OpenPose [3]. Then, proper feedback is generated to improve the dancers' pose by following the procedures shown in Fig. 3.

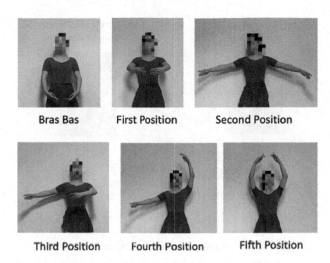

Fig. 2. Basic arms positions of ballet

4.1 Creating Model

First, the training data or the images of each pose are processed to extract the coordinates using OpenPose [3], which is a system from Carnegie Mellon University that can jointly detect human body parts as shown in Fig. 4. The version we used can detect 25 body keypoints described in Table 1. Since the initial coordinates are based on pixel position in the image, we adjust the coordinates by shifting the origin to the middle of the body. At this moment we use the middle of the hip point.

Second, human evaluator(ballet teacher) critiqued training data poses. We fed the shifted coordinates and the feedback from the human evaluator into the random forest algorithm to create a model. This algorithm was chosen because a previous study showed that random forest algorithm offered the best performance for ballet pose recognition [4].

4.2 Using Model to Create Feedback

To use the model, the system receives videos or images from the learner; OpenPose is used to generate body part coordinates. Then, the coordinates are adjusted, the same as for the training data. The translated coordinates are sent into the model, which then generates feedback. Following that, the feedback is sent to the learner.

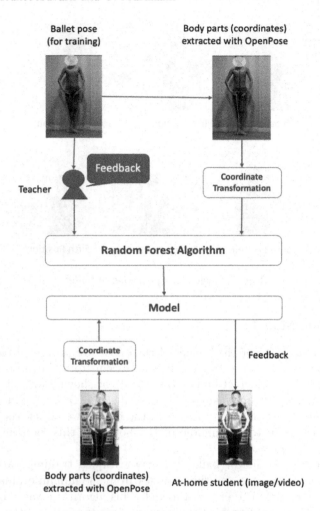

Fig. 3. Design of a ballet learner support system with automated feedback.

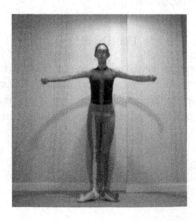

Fig. 4. Skeleton created using Openpose

Table 1. OpenPose keypoint list for body parts

Part number	Body part	Part number	Body part	Part number	Body part
0	Nose	9	Right hip	18	Left ear
1	Neck	10	Right knee	19	Left big toe
2	Right shoulder	11	Right ankle	20	Left small toe
3	Right elbow	12	Left Hip	21	Left heel
4	Right wrist	13	Left knee	22	Right big toe
5	Left shoulder	14	Left ankle	23	Right small toe
6	Left elbow	15	Right eye	24	Right heel
7	Left wrist	16	Left eye		
8	Middle of hip	17	Right ear		

5 Prototyping

5.1 Data Collection

To construct the prototype, we gathered example photographs and videos of volunteer people performing various foot and arm positions. The comments was then created by a qualified ballet teacher for each image. Figure 6 depicts some examples of feedback that was translated from Thai, the mother tongue of the evaluator, to English.

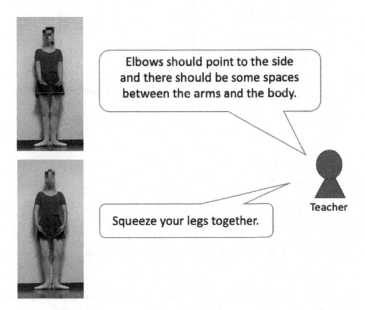

Fig. 5. Examples of feedback from human evaluator (ballet teacher)

Using the previously mentioned procedure, we prepared the data and extracted the positions of the body parts. We utilized this dataset to train the model after matching the coordinate sets with the feedback from teacher.

5.2   Prototype Design

We are currently attempting to create a prototype of the system based on the created model.

To clarify how the prototype is designed, the system processes are shown in the swimlane flowchart in Fig. 6.

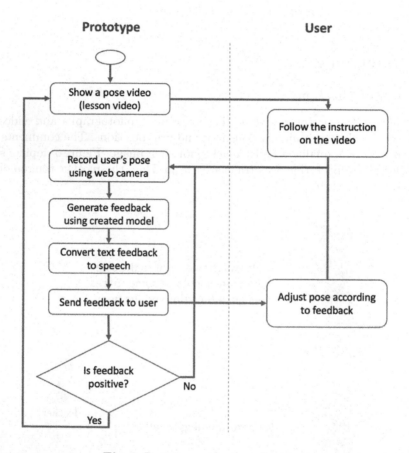

Fig. 6. Prototype swim lane diagram

First, the user is offered a tutorial video that teaches a new dance posture. The user should next follow the instructions in the video. The system will use a web camera to record the user's pose while the user is performing. The model that was previously built will then be used to generate feedback.

To mimic human teachers, the prototype will convert text feedback to speech, allowing the user to adjust her/his pose in response to the feedback.

If the feedback is deemed positive, the system will display the next lesson video. Otherwise, the prototype will record the modified pose and continue the feedback loop.

6 Discussion

6.1 Combination with Other Modalities

During conventional ballet practice, the students try to check themselves by looking at the mirror and compare their poses with the teacher's. Sometimes students do not know how to correct the position and the feedback is needed. Even though our proposed system does not require any dance mirror, it would be more beneficial if the student could receive both feedback from the proposed system and direct visual feedback from a regular mirror.

6.2 Other Applications

This system is designed for online learning at home. However, it would also benefit the students who learn at ballet studios and practice at home.

Even though this proposed design is aimed at supporting novice ballet dancers at home, it can be applied to other kinds of dances, sports, and exercises. It will benefit activities that involve the control of muscles and body position where feedback from teachers or trainers is needed.

7 Limitations and Future Work

There are several points in the proposal that need further study. Even though classical ballet is a well-known traditional artistic dance, it has evolved differently in different places around the world. It is possible that a model trained using data from one style or one region might not work well for a different style or different region for some movements.

This late-breaking work still needs further study and the model is needed to be evaluated. We plan to test prototypes with actual learners so we can investigate the results in more detail. We are now designing an experiment to study the reaction of the learner after having received the system's feedback.

Another limitation of this work includes the hardware requirement for the computational load. Even though this system is designed to be feasible and can be used at home without any special equipment, the computer should have medium to high hardware specifications. Therefore, further work is needed to clarify this point.

Using this proposal, it is possible to create models for different dancer poses and thus generate feedback that is style-specific. In the future, we plan to expand the variety of dance poses and cover a full repertoire of dance movements. We are also planning to examine the use of different machine learning methods.

8   Conclusion

This late-breaking paper proposed a automated system to support at-home ballet learners. We applied computer vision to extract body part coordinates from photos and videos. The photos and videos are input to a model developed by the Random Forest algorithm trained using feedback from dance teachers. The model generates feedback to help the dance student at home. Our proposal focuses on feasibility so it can be used by average users at home. It can be also applied to support learning in similar activities such as Yoga and different types of dances.

However, future studies on user interaction are required to compare how the learner reacts to the model's feedback and conventional learning without the feedback.

Acknowledgements. This research is partially supported by Ritsumeikan University's Individual Research Allowance. We also want to thank Ms. Patcharawalai Tiplamai for her ballet advice and assistance with data collection.

References

1. Agrippina, I., Vaganova, A.: Basic principles of classical ballet: Russian ballet technique. Courier Corporation (1969)
2. Albaili, Y.: Vision-based human pose estimation for sports biomechanics. B.S. thesis, University of Malta (2020)
3. Cao, Z., Hidalgo Martinez, G., Simon, T., Wei, S., Sheikh, Y.A.: Openpose: Real-time multi-person 2d pose estimation using part affinity fields. IEEE Transactions on Pattern Analysis and Machine Intelligence (2019)
4. Fourie, M., van der Haar, D.: A feature importance study in ballet pose recognition with openpose. In: Degen, H., Reinerman-Jones, L. (eds.) HCII 2020. LNCS, vol. 12217, pp. 243–254. Springer, Cham (2020). https://doi.org/10.1007/978-3-030-50334-5_16
5. Grosser, J.: ABC of Ballet. Dover Publications (1999)
6. Hallam, J., Keen, E., Lee, C., McKenna, A., Gupta, M.: Ballet hero: building a garment for memetic embodiment in dance learning. In: Proceedings of the 2014 ACM International Symposium on Wearable Computers: Adjunct Program, pp. 49–54 (2014)
7. Miller, G.: Beginning Ballet. Human Kinetics (2013)
8. Nakai, M., Tsunoda, Y., Hayashi, H., Murakoshi, H.: Prediction of basketball free throw shooting by openpose. In: Kojima, K., Sakamoto, M., Mineshima, K., Satoh, K. (eds.) JSAI-isAI 2018. LNCS (LNAI), vol. 11717, pp. 435–446. Springer, Cham (2019). https://doi.org/10.1007/978-3-030-31605-1_31
9. Ryman, R.: Dictionary of classical ballet terminology. Royal Academy of Dancing (1997)
10. Wang, C., Wang, S.J.: Relevé: an at-home ballet self-learning interactive system. KnE Engineering, pp. 242–248 (2017)
11. Yadav, S.K., Singh, A., Gupta, A., Raheja, J.L.: Real-time yoga recognition using deep learning. Neural Comput. Appl. **31**(12), 9349–9361 (2019)

Facebook Interface in External Communication. Case: Educational Peruvian School, 2020

Moisés David Reyes Pérez[1]([⊠]) [iD], Jhoselit Lisset Facho Cornejo[2] [iD],
Alberto Gómez Fuertes[1] [iD], and Enrique Roberto Azpeitia Torres[3] [iD]

[1] Cesar Vallejo University, Pimentel Km 3.5, Peru, Mexico
[2] San Martin de Porres, University, Pimentel Km 2, Peru, Mexico
[3] Guadalajara University, 976 Juárez Col Americana, Mexico

Abstract. Currently it is a priori need for companies to use optimal communication with their different audiences, so that they can interact and attract potential customers for their benefit. Facebook, being one of the most recognized and used social networks worldwide, has become an indispensable medium for people and companies; which allows, within the framework of external communication, an exclusive approach with its audiences (Barrio 2017). The general objective of this research was to analyze the influence of the social network Facebook as the main communication tool. The design was non-experimental, descriptive and qualitative in focus. The population consisted of 500 high school students, parents, and school workers. The sample consisted of 24 students, divided into 3 groups of 8 students from the third, fourth and fifth grade of secondary school, a group of 6 parents and the head of the Public Relations area, being chosen with the type of non-probability sampling for convenience. After analyzing the data collected in the focus groups, 3 factors were identified that make the social network facebook a main external communication tool: digital competence as the first factor (digital platform with the largest number of users, virtual traffic and easy to use), the second factor is the prestige (image and reputation that the social network has managed to consolidate through the influence it generates in its users) and the third factor is the impact (efficiency and effectiveness of the information and interaction that the users).

Keywords: Facebook interface · External communication · Public relations

1 Introduction

Currently, it is a priori need for companies to use optimal communication with their different audiences, so that they can interact and attract potential customers for their benefit. A fact that shows that external communication plays an important role in this process, since it aims to communicate and inform its different audiences about the product or service they offer, to then satisfy them and create a favorable image of the company itself. Esteban (2008) define external communication as the transmission of information outside the company, aimed at external audiences of the organization (consumers, distributors, prescribers, press, interest groups, among others). In this context, it is defined

© Springer Nature Switzerland AG 2021
C. Stephanidis et al. (Eds.): HCII 2021, LNCS 13096, pp. 467–479, 2021.
https://doi.org/10.1007/978-3-030-90328-2_31

as a tool that allows the dissemination of messages to the different audiences of the company, where it not only covers consumers or potential clients, but also all those who are outside of it, as well as the interest groups and the different means of communication that they may use.

The techniques and activities in organizational communication are aimed at facilitating and speeding up the flow of messages that are given inside and outside the organization, in such a way that the opinions, attitudes and behaviors of the internal and external public could be influenced. external to meet the objectives. (Anonymous, p. 11). In this way, it seeks to provoke a reaction from these, through concepts, opinions and changes in behaviors that help or aim to meet the organizational objectives of the company. However, for the organization to comply with them, it must first land and know exactly what types of external communication they should use, being these: strategic, operational and notorious.

Thus, focusing more on the commercial sector and placing it in the field of education, the strategy that is most used is that of notoriety, because it makes the company known, the products or services it offers and improves its image.

Likewise, it is the one in charge of almost all areas of communication: public relations, marketing, advertising, sponsorships and other activities that make the company known to its different audiences.

Botto (2011) states: In Argentina, most middle-level educational establishments, except the larger ones, still do not give the importance it deserves to institutional communication as a strategic planning instrument for the implementation of policies. medium and long-term communication programs aimed at working with internal and external audiences. (p.1).

In Peru, the situation regarding the importance of external communication in middle-level educational establishments does not occur in the same way as in Argentina, since educational centers at the national level do value communication not only as a tool but also as a business factor where advertising and public relations prevail.

In Lambayeque, there is an average of 8 private high-school education centers that do use organizational communication as the main tool to inform and attract potential students as well as to retain them with their service. Among them, the schools: San Agustín, Innova School and Santa María Reina stand out, due to the fact that they have greater interaction in their main communication platforms such as social networks and website.

In this line, the Educational Institution evaluated is found, with regard to organizational communication, and within this framework, it is observed that the school maintains constant communication with its public through the Facebook social network, which is their main interaction platform, allowing them to know the impact and effectiveness of their publications thanks to the actions of the institutional image area.

However, this area is managed by a single worker, who, despite being a professional in the area, is unable to supply all the important functions of the new communication model, which is based on defining policies and strategies that are in accordance with the organizational objectives to be achieved.

Facebook, being one of the most recognized and used social networks worldwide, has become an indispensable tool for people and companies; which allows, within the framework of external communication, an exclusive approach with its audiences. From this, the need arose to study the influence of the social network Facebook as the main external communication tool in the Educational Institution.Now, we ask ourselves: how does the Facebook social network influence as the main external communication tool in the Institution Educa-tiva? What are the main factors that make the Facebook social network a main external communication tool in the Educational Institution? What is the level of importance of the social network Facebook as the main external communication tool? And what types of public relations strategies do they employ through the social network Facebook?

The present research work would benefit the area of Institutional Image of the Educational Institution that allocate the management of external communication through the social network Facebook as an important channel to achieve greater prestige and recognition in Lambayeque These would have full access to the research results, managing to recognize and adapt them for efficient work in the area. The study will serve as a guide for researchers in the subjects of Communication Sciences, especially in Public Relations, Middle Level Educational Institutions, Public Relations and Advertising Agencies, among others interested in the subject.

1.1   Theoretical Framework

Communication Theory. Communication Theory defines this as the action of transmitting ideas and thoughts with the aim of putting them in common with another. This supposes the use of a shared communication code, that is, a set of symbols and signs which must be understood by the protagonists of the process. Thanks to this it is that the messages are transmitted from person to person.

This is where the importance of considering theory starts because it makes it clear that the media do directly influence the minds of audiences; Therefore, as the social network Facebook has become one of the most widely used communication channels worldwide, it is considered the most effective tool for mass dissemination of messages that incite the public to change their behavior.

External Communication. External communication is, as its name indicates, that which the organization establishes with external audiences, that is, it is about the interrelation of the constituent elements of the internal environment, with those that exist abroad, in a way that nera particular, or in a general way, as the representation of a whole. According to Hilda Saladrigas (2006).

Therefore, external communication is considered as the process in which the company interacts with the external public in order to achieve greater efficiency in its management that positively influences its corporate image.

External Communication Channels
Relations with the media and press. Cabrera and Villalobos (2014) point out that it is essential to maintain humane, cordial, close, personalized, agile, transparent, professional, effective and permanent relationships with the journalists who make up each and every one of the news media with which the company deals and / or institution, in order

to transmit the messages that they want to convey to their various external audiences. He mentions that the most important functions of relations with the media could be summarized in 5 aspects, in which the company must provide information to the media in order to cover a need regarding a specific topic of interest.

Salinas (2017) stresses that:

Emotions can be generated in person, via telephone communication, letter, but the important thing is how I am receiving it and what is the impact on me and who receives it, in order to channel it through the Media. In other words, the way it is interpreted will be a consequence of both advertising and public relations of the media. (s / n).

On the other hand, there is the Press, which according to Lombardi (2006) its service is a valid way of making a business known, but for a press campaign to be effective it is imperative to know what to communicate; who to communicate it to and how to direct that information to the media.

In other words, the company must strategically analyze the contents of the message and the identification of its audience in order to turn this information into news that is accepted by public opinion and clearly differentiates itself from advertising.

In conclusion, it is a priori need for companies to have a direct relationship with the media and the press, since they allow their information to be directed in an ideal way to the different audiences they are directed to.

Institutional Advertising. Communication aimed at changing, maintaining or increasing the image of the business or institutional organization, but paying the media for the dissemination of such messages". Thus, this type of advertising is "made and bought in a common way. However, its objective is not to directly sell the products or services of the company, but to improve the public's conception of a company or defend its policy (Herreros, 2004).

That is to say, it is a technique of cultivation or positioning of the image of the company that, in addition, is aimed at both the public and internal, in the long term, because it does not have a specific date.

For Gruning and Hunt (2008), the primary goals of Corporate Advertising are to improve relationships with consumers, business relationships, with the community, with employees, and improve image and reputation. Palencia (2011) indicates that the main objectives of corporate communication with advertising forms could be considered to be: achieving credibility and trust, modifying a negative attitude arising from a conflict and making known little-known aspects of the relationship between the organization and its audiences, retain the audiences to which the campaign is directed and solve problems that have derived from the social context of the organization.

From this, institutional advertising becomes an indispensable channel in every organization, because it achieves full knowledge not only of the product or service itself it offers, but also of the company, thus generating an identification and loyalty of the user and / or consumer.

Graphic and Audiovisual Material. They denote that within the external communication channels we present graphic and audiovisual material as support tools, because at present the trends in design and the cinematographic world have impacted, and, at the same time, influenced companies to generate content interactive, creative and brief to communicate your different types of communicational messages. (Cabrera and Villalobos 2014) Then, we can understand as graphic material the brochures, flyers, brochures, cards, communications and institutional memories as strategic pieces for the planned and necessary external communication for each type of public that the company carries out with the purpose to provide more information.

Likewise, Xifra (2005) points out that:

The transversal techniques are the speeches; the documents of the organization (brochures, company magazine, annual reports (social and activity reports); the corporate book; the framework of the organization as a public relations technique (geographical framework, architectural framework and information provided to the visitor; as well as the edition of corporate videos or other audiovisual materials.

In this way, it is understood that the set of graphic and audiovisual material is essential for the company, because Pulido (2007) highlights that the communication objectives that these pursue can be diverse: or to be displayed on the Corporate Website or to be broadcast on radio or TV, and thus present the organization's position to public opinion.

As detailed above, the graphic and audiovisual technique are tools that currently allow companies to achieve greater interactivity, dynamism and presence among their audiences, seeking to improve market segmentation, allowing them to selectively identify content towards every niche.

Website and Social Networks. The internet is a network that contains a world full of advantages and opportunities, a communicative world without borders, still undeveloped". A Corporati-va Web page is a portal on the Internet that "presents the basic information and resources of a company or institution, aimed at all publics on the planet. In this portal, all the basic contents of the organization are displayed in an orderly fashion - through a logical design". In this way, the public of the organization - internal and external - can have the information available on the web with great speed and solve all the doubts they have in relation to the organization. (Cabrera and Villalobos 2014).

Regarding Social Networks, Paul Venturino del Canto (2011), points out that they are the most visible element in the online world. They are the digital expression of the networks that people have traditionally formed based on their interests, tastes, fears or needs. Internet-based social networks have achieved global reach, are immediate, and allow people to share information and interact on a scale never before achieved. Thanks to the development of the internet, Social Networks can interact without borders and deliver a wealth of information and involvement that was previously only given by face-to-face and long-term interactions.

Social networks, such as Facebook or Twitter, mark the communication strategy of companies, which must now have a digital identity and take care of their reputation on the web. Adán (2016) points out that "the rise of social networks has incorporated new paradigms in the communication management of companies and their brands". The digital identity of a company "ceased to be something as simple as having a page on the web and keeping its content updated, but it goes further, which means considering the presence on social networks with a strategy and plan that are aligned with the objectives and goals of the business, and that they attend, consider, take into account and respond to the signals of their followers on social networks, which - it should be noted - are no longer a boom, they are emerging media that have no return behind".

Therefore, the Website and Social Networks allow a digital identity, where users are kept updated on the different actions carried out by the company so that they can be informed and interact with it.

Facebook Social Network. The most popular Web 2.0 service is social networking, online meeting places where people can meet up with their friends and friends of their friends. Social networking sites link people through mutual business or personal connections, allowing them to poll their friends (and their friends) for sales initiatives, job search suggestions, new friends. (Laudon and Laudon, 2012).

Corporations establish their own Facebook and Myspace profiles to interact with potential customers. Fernández indicates that business firms can also "listen" to what social media users say about their products, as well as obtain valuable feedback from consumers.

Facebook has become one of the most recognized names on social media. These networks allow people to find friends, colleagues with similar tastes or to find business opportunities, all based on a continuous exchange of information. Networking has always been an important marketing tool that has evolved over time in different channels and situations, but whose essence continues to remain firm (Merodio 2010).

Characteristics of E - Marketing on Facebook +. Gonzáles (2017) defines e-marketing as something more than merely having awebsite, which can help the company achieve a number of key objectives, namely: attract new customers, strengthen ties with existing customers, strengthen brands and improve loyalty.

Casado and Sellers (2008) add that it can also serve to generate a fundamental change in business and in interaction with clients/consumers similar to the one that occurred with the incorporation of the car and the telephone; that is, the one that transformed the way in which products and services are presented in the market.

Undoubtedly, more and more companies consider social networks as a place to advertise aimed at a certain audience, because, with hundreds of those sites and millions of users around the planet, the growth of social networks is phenomenal and represents an effective method of targeting and communicating with the online community.

Facebook and Consumer Behavior. Social networks influence the purchasing decisions of users and consumers, although there are great differences depending on each country. Consumers use social networks more and more frequently in order to obtain information on which to base their purchasing decisions.

In this way, in social networks, consumers can participate in conversations to inform, and even influence other consumers about various products and services. (Molina 2015).

These influence in a very effective way their purchasing decisions, including in a special way multiscreen users, this refers to the consumers who use it. (Martínez 2017). In addition, Loli (2017) concludes by mentioning that "the user gives more importance to the opinions of others about a product or service than to the messages of traditional marketing", alluding that their favorite places to listen to the recommendations of others are the social networks, especially Facebook. mobile, tablet, laptop, personal computer, tv and cinema in whole or in part and make inter-action.

1.2 General Objecives

Analyze the influence of the social network Facebook as the main communication tool.

Specific Objectives. Determine the main factors that make the Facebook social network a main external communication tool.

Study the level of importance of the social network facebook as the main external communication tool.

1.3 Variables

(See Tables 1 and 2).

Table 1. Operationalization of the external communication variable

Variable	Pre category	Trait
External communication	Planning	Contents Bells Advertising Design elements Curricular and extracurricular activities
	Strategies	Communication skills Digital skills Positioning strategy
	Perception	Image Influence Prestige Reputation
	Efficiency and effectiveness	Impact level Service level Results level
	Feedback	Impact level Service level Results level

Table 2. Operationalization of the Facebook social network variable

Variable	Pre category	Trait
Facebook social network	Current situation	Information Efficiency and effectiveness Communication and information technologies
	Strategies	Content strategy Commercial strategy Social media strategy
	Planning	Good practice manual Compliance with schedules
	Technological trend	International trend National trend Local trend
	Effectiveness	Scope Sectorization Innovation

2 Methodology

The design was non-experimental, descriptive and qualitative in focus. The population consisted of 500 high school students, parents and school workers. The sample consisted of 24 students, divided into 3 groups of 8 students from the third, fourth and fifth grades of secondary school, a group of 6 parents and the head of the Public Relations area, being chosen with the type of non-probability sampling for convenience, It was considered the main requirement that they be users of the social network Facebook and followers of the School's fan page. The following techniques and instruments were used to collect the information: observation, focus groups, in-depth interview, and how instruments were developed a questionnaire, question guide and registration form.

The validity of the instrument was determined through the technique of the validation judgment of three experts who evidenced the relationship between the proposed objectives, the dimensions, the indicators, the items and the response options, considering coherence, relevance and writing. of these. Expert judgment is a useful validation method to verify the reliability of an investigation that is defined as "an informed opinion of people with experience in the subject, who are recognized by others as qualified experts in it, and who can provide information, evidence, judgments and evaluations"(Escobar-Pérez and Cuervo-Martínez, 2008: 29).

Consistency as the level of cohesion of the different items or aspects of the instrument that can be verified through different statistical methods such as, for example, Cronbach's Alpha coefficient, used more frequently (Arribas 2004). Regarding temporal stability, it refers to the scarce variability of the measurements of the object when the measurement process is repeated in different situations.

For this reason, being a qualitative research it does not require reliability.

3 Results

Main Factors that Make the Facebook Social Network a Main External Communication Tool.
According to the answers given by the subjects proposed in this research, it is evident that the main factors that make the social network Facebook a main external communication tool in the Educational Institution, is that it is a digital competence that both as children, adolescents, young people and adults know and know how to use, and that this not only ends there, but also has an image and reputation of its great capacity for influence, managing to impact its audiences.

Our interviewees show that this network is not only used by different audiences, but also has a high degree of reputation, where its efficiency and effectiveness is guaranteed. Added to this is the immediacy of the information it provides and the benefits of using it for the growth of companies, whether to offer or promote a product or service. All these factors make reference to the fact that the social network Facebook at present and at the national and international level is a main communication tool, because everything mentioned above does exist and is evidenced in the results of the subjects proposed for the analysis of its influence.

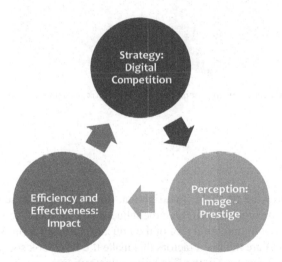

Fig. 1. Main factors that make the social network Facebook a main external communication tool

Level of Importance of the Social Network Facebook as the Main Tool External Communication.
Based on the analyzed responses of the interviewees, the level of importance of the social network Facebook as the main external communication tool of the Educational Institution, lies, in a great significance of both groups, in that the current situation of this network at the Worldwide has an impact on all its audiences and that the level of

results, together with the immediacy of information and quality of service due to its applications and innovations, makes this network have a high level of importance to use as the main communication tool external, showing that it provides not only influence, but effectiveness.

It should be noted that in most of the responses, in terms of their gestures and expressions, it was noted that they responded with confidence, almost without hesitation; and giving importance to this network, since as they said, it not only provides entertainment but also allows them to be informed in real time.

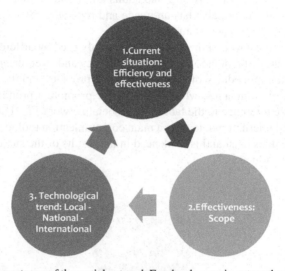

Fig. 2. Level of importance of the social network Facebook, a main external communication tool

4   Discussion

After having conducted the field investigation, the results are presented below. Their order depends on the logic of analyzing the influence of the social network Facebook as the main external communication tool in the Educational Institution. Where, first of all, it is addressed: what are the main factors that make the Facebook social network a main external communication tool in the Educational Institution.

4.1   Influential Factors

Communication Strategy. According to the research, the interviewees, both as students, parents family and area manager, frequently responded that the main factors that make the social network Facebook one of the main external communication tools, is that it is a digital competence that most people know and know how to use, and followed by this is the degree of knowledge and / or prestige that this platform obtains on the level of impact and effectiveness that it generates without exception in the different audiences, in such In this sense, at a significant level what was found by Madero is verified (2009) who, in a study in Madrid, also obtained the importance of internal and exte nal communication media in organizations; where It mainly evokes social networks, framing Facebook. In other words, the cases analyzed reveal that the main factors make the social network Facebook one of the main tools for external communication is for its level of influence, backed with the prestige that you get by reaching all audiences. In this sense, it is evident that it is a main digital strategic tool, which has influence and its level of impact it is for all audiences; without any distinction.

This is justified according to Lasswell (1927), the mass media have a capacity to influence audiences, but of course, the way of receiving the message varies according to opinions, intelligence, culture, etc. Also, Venturino del Canto (2011), points out that social networks have achieved global reach, they are immediate and allow people to share information and interact in a magnitude that had never been achieved. In this second section, and based on the previous results, together with other questions designed to answer: how is the level of importance of the social network Facebook as the main external communication tool in the Educational Institution was found:

Level of Importance of the Social Network Facebook as the Main Tool. Through planned questions for students, parents, and in charge of the area to answer this second objective, it was obtained as result, in a greater significance, the pre categories, Current situation; where efficiency and effectiveness are involved, together with Technological Trend and Feedback, evidencing that its level of importance lies in which the social network Facebook is one of the main tools of communication due to its level of impact at national and international level, level of results, immediacy of information and quality of service; based on scope and sectorization of the different audiences destined to influence, through this supports what was found by Flores Salinas (2016) who in a study in Trujillo also demonstrated the positive impact of promotions on networks social networks, focusing again on the social network Facebook for its ability to influence and effectiveness.

For this reason, through these two evidences of investigative works where there is great similarity in the search for results, it is stated that the level of importance of the social network Facebook as one of the main tools external communication, relies on its efficiency, effectiveness, tendency technology and feedback that it provides, in a significant greater, both in the present investigation, as in the one cited above.

Fact that directly supports the great capacity and effectiveness of this tool today, predicting that this happens in most of the organizations.

From this, this result is supported according to Gonzáles (2017), who defines to e-marketing on Facebook, as more than just having a website that can help the company achieve a number of key objectives, but namely: attract new customers, strengthen brands and improve loyalty.

5   Conclusions

The influence that occurs in the social network Facebook as the main external comunication tool in the Educational Institution, inbased on the participants analyzed (students, parents and manager) it was evidenced that not only does it exist, but that it is at a high, since most frequently answered that it is a very used by different audiences, and has a massive reach, which is fast and immediate, as well as, as corroborated by the contributions of the theory on the subject as found by other field studies previous, and it is demonstrated and supported that the social network Facebook does influence directly on your users.

The main factors that make the social network Facebook a main one communication tool in a great significance of groups analyzed, fall on the fact that it is not only used by different audiences, but also has a high degree of reputation, where it is guarantees its efficiency and effectiveness, thus verifying what than other studies in their results, reflected that the effectiveness of social networks -which within them evokes Facebook-are due to their great capacity for impact, immediacy and quality of service.

The level of importance of the social network Facebook as main external communication tool is given at a very high level in the participants analyzed, because it is efficient and effective by the impact it has on all its audiences, and the immediacy of information and quality of service in the applications it offers, guaranteeing that it currently provides not only influence, but effectiveness. social networks -which within them evokes Facebook- are due to their great capacity for impact, immediacy and quality of service.

The level of importance of the social network Facebook as the main external communication tool occurs at a very high level in the participants analyzed, because it is efficient and effective due to the impact it has on all its audiences, and the immediacy of information and quality of service in the applications it offers, guaranteeing that it currently provides not only influence, but effectiveness.

5.1 Recommendations

The Institutional Image area of the Educational Institution must consider and re-plan strategies and / or tactics to improve its feedback, where it basically makes the user feel a satisfaction in their questions and answers that it grants, in order to improve the influence and effectiveness this network Facebook; as has been evidenced throughout the investigation process.

The Institutional Image area must improve or apply new design strategies that go beyond corporate colors, shapes and content (concept), in a way that generates more impact and participation of users who are more in contact with the Institution page.

For researchers interested in this matter, they could focus and land more research focusing on the variable Facebook social network, since this is the platform that is currently marking a century of this technological era, and it is not known if it will continue to mark history and keep companies holding on to it to achieve their goals, and reach out to their diverse audiences.

References

Bernays, E.L.: Public Relations Idea Book. Printers IN Pub. Co, USA (1958)
Botto, M.: La Comunicación en las instituciones educativas de nivel (2011)
Medio. Buenos Aires, Argentina. Recuperado de http://www.quadernsdigitals.net/datos/hemero teca/r_1/nr_502/a_6870/6870.pdf

Cabrera, D.A., Villalobos, E.C.: Características de la comunicación (2014) interna y externa del Instituto de Educación Superior Tecnológico Privado Stendhal. Arequipa, Perú

Chiavenato, I.: Administración de Recursos Humanos. 8° ed., p. 500. Colombia, McGraw-Hill (2012)

Comunicación Idoneos. (s/f). Teoría de la Comunicación [Mensaje en un blog]. Recuperado de https://comunicacion.idoneos.com / teoria_de_la_comunicacion/

Curras, R.: Identidad e imagen corporativas: revisión conceptual e interrelación. Valencia, España (2010)

Esteban, R.: La comunicación externa en universidades privadas con estudios a distancia en pregrado. Razón y Palabra **01**(1), 5–15 (2008)

Gonzales, D.T.: Las redes sociales Facebook y Twitter y el comportamiento de co sumo de las mujeres jóvenes en las Boutiques de la ciudad de Huaraz. Huaraz, Perú (2017)

Fernández, k. (s/F): Teorías de la comunicación [Mensaje en un blog]. https://karinafernandez.es.tl/Teor%EDas-de-la-Comunicaci%F3n.ht

Flores, F.E.: Impacto de la promoción realizada a través de la red social Facebook en los socios de la cooperativa de ahorro y crédito León XII. Trujillo, Perú (2016)

Hernández, R. Fernández, C., Bautista, P.: Metodología de la investigación (5 ed.) México: McGraw-Hill (2014)

Maldonado, M.: Qué es la comunicación estratégica [Mensaje en un blog]. Recuperado de https://maridaliamaldonado.blogspot.com/2012/02/que-es-la-comunicacion-estrategica.html (2012)

Moragas, M.: Sociología de la Comunicación de masas. España, Barcelona (1985)

Osorio, S.: La función de la comunicación interna y externa como instrumento estratégico para mejorar el servicio al cliente en Madero y Maldonado, Corredores de Seguros S.A. Bogotá, Colombia (2009)

Rodríguez, I.: Teorías de la comunicación organizacional. Gestiopolis. Recuperado de (2005). https://www.gestiopolis.com/teorias-comunicacion-organizacional/

Riquelme, M.: La Ventaja Competitiva según Michael Porter[Mensaje en un blog]. Recuperado de (2014). https://www.webyempresas.com/la-ventaja-competitiva-segun-michael-prer/#Plan_para_lograr_una_ventaja_competitiva%20https://www.gestiopolis.com/teorias-comunicacion-organizacional/

Riquelme, M.: Teoría de la ventaja competitiva [Mensaje en un blog] (23 de junio del 2017). http://www.emprendices.co/teoria-la-ventaja-competitiva/

Seitel, F.: Teoría práctica de las Relaciones Públicas. Málaga, España (2013).

Universidad de Palermo. (s/f). Informe sobre las Relaciones Públicas. http://fido.palermo.edu/servicios_dyc/blog/alumnostrabajos/8245_7642.pdf

Villavicencio, E.: Implementación de medidas de comunicación externa de la Dirección de Comunicación e Imagen de la Policía Nacional del Perú durante el 2014. (Tesis de pregrado). Pontificia Universidad Católica del Perú. Perú (2016).

Viñarás, M., Cabezuelo, F.: (s/f). Publicidad Corporativa y de la RSC: ¿Oportunidad o alternativa en tiempos de crisis para ganar confianza? http://www.aeic2012tarragona.org/comunicacions_cd/ok/278.pdf

Xifrá, J.: Planificación estratégica de las relaciones públicas. Paidós Papeles de Comunicación, Barcelona (2005)

Gender Differences in Psychosocial Experiences with Humanoid Robots, Programming, and Mathematics Course

Solveig Tilden[1], Ricardo G. Lugo[2,3(✉)], Karen Parish[3,4], Deepti Mishra[5], and Benjamin J. Knox[2,3]

[1] Department of Psychology, Inland Norway University of Applied Sciences, Lillehammer, Norway
[2] Østfold University College, Fredrikstad, Norway
[3] Department of Information Security and Communication Technology (IIK), Norwegian University of Science and Technology, Gjøvik, Norway
Ricardo.g.Lugo@ntnu.no
[4] Department of Education, Inland Norway University of Applied Sciences, Hamar, Norway
[5] Department of Computer Science (IDI), Norwegian University of Science and Technology, Gjøvik, Norway

Abstract. Introduction: There is a gender imbalance in Computer science (CS) and STEM education and careers where males are more represented. With evolving technologies arising and the need for a more diverse workforce, it is important to identify factors that may cause females to be more prone to not persist in CS careers.

This study investigated gender differences and psychosocial perceptions of experiences in a CS education class.

Method: Twelve students were recruited to the study. Data on judgements of performance and psychosocial aspects of the course was collected (learning, difficulty, enjoyment).

Results: There were no significant differences between boys' and girls' perceptions of performance and experiences in the course. Females, however, reported small to medium effect sizes in experiencing more learning, more enjoyment and experienced more difficulties than boys in the course.

Conclusion: Future studies should control for gender differences in CS and STEM education. Same sex role models might influence experience and perceptions of performance, which can influence persistence of females in CS careers.

Keywords: Gender differences · Computer science · Human-robot interaction · Psychosocial perception · Metacognitive assessment · Preadolescent students

1 Introduction

There is a gender imbalance within computer science (CS). For instance, within major companies such as Google, Facebook and Twitter females comprise less than 20% of

© Springer Nature Switzerland AG 2021
C. Stephanidis et al. (Eds.): HCII 2021, LNCS 13096, pp. 480–490, 2021.
https://doi.org/10.1007/978-3-030-90328-2_32

the workforce [1] and this is usually attributed to labor supply and demands. Despite this imbalance, recent research shows that females in CS education are similar to males in their cognitive styles and abilities [2] but their self-perception of their abilities may lead to different career choices. Females in CS education report better verbal fluency and artistic abilities than males, however with poorer self-assessment in academic achievement and leadership abilities [3]. Research has identified several cultural aspects that can explain the low representation. For instance, gender-role-modelling, community acceptance, and institutional support moderated participation and performance of females in CS [2, 4]. Further, females studying CS who had access to female role models in the field, and had instructors and institutions that encouraged and supported female representation, reported less negative stereotypical perceptions of themselves [4], showed greater adherence and completion of their studies, and outperformed their male counterparts [2]. Due to the gender imbalance in CS, female students are encouraged to choose educational programs within science, technology, engineering and mathematics (STEM) (see for instance https://www.sheffield.ac.uk/dcs/about-department/women-computer-science). This gender imbalance gives reason to assume that early influence, as in educational institutions, play a gender-specific role for later career choice. For this reason, the current project addresses preadolescent boys' and girls' experience on STEM – specifically programming, mathematics, and human-robot interactions – in education, including the experienced difficulty, enjoyment, and gains in learning.

1.1 Psychological Factors in Programming, Mathematics and Human-Robot Interactions

Being part of CS, a rapidly growing branch in technology is within robotics, which is gaining ever-expanding functions in society [5]. For example, robots have been implemented in school in functions as independent teachers, teaching assistants [6], classmates, peers, entertainers [7], support for children with special needs [8] and as a mediators for increased experience of presence in school for homebound children [9]. When the function of such robots is to interact with humans, they are designed to resemble and behave more like humans, so that a human-robot interaction (HRI) is possible [6]. Research shows that such robots can support development within areas including language, argumentation and discussion skills, problem solving, self-regulation, and building of relationships [6, 7, 10]. Unlike interactions with the teacher, the student may experience a more balanced dialogue when interacting with a robot, which to some students may involve less anxiety and embarrassment. This in turn may result in students daring to take chances in their thinking, coming up with ideas, and solving problems [6].

Robots can assist the teacher in following up individual students [7] which may provide several benefits, including development of self-regulated learning skills such as self-assessment, goal-setting, and the execution of strategies within a metacognitive process, which correlates highly with academic achievement [11]. Metacognition is understood as a representation of cognition, with the functions of monitoring and control, for instance planning, evaluation, and knowledge of what one knows and does not know [12]. According to Zimmerman [13] such self-regulated learning is associated with active participation in one's own learning process, involving the use of strategies within metacognition, motivational processes (e.g., self-efficacy), and behavior (e.g., optimizing one's learning environments). Jones and Castellano [11] suggest that social robots can be used to support the development of such skills which furthermore have the potential to be transferred to long-term behavior change, with a generalizing effect to contexts outside the classroom. However, such social robots may also have a distracting effect, thus influencing the students' attention and cognitive performance negatively [14]. Robots may nevertheless enable new ways of learning and teaching, and the presence of such social robots in teaching can prepare children for an everyday life which, independent of robots, is characterized by advanced technology [6].

1.2 Social Aspects in Programming, Mathematics and Human-Robot Interactions

When implementing a social robot into an educational setting, the students' social interaction (e.g., smiles, eye contact) with the robot have been found to vary. This may be due to variations in the robot's 'wow-factor' with a possible distracting effect [15], or due to variations in the students' level of internalized self-regulation and thus reliance on the robot to master the task [11]. For technology to have a supportive function in the child's development the child should be involved and engaged and the technology should promote a strong language model [16]. Varied and tailored feedback from social robots in education has been found to support and increase children's self-confidence and mastery. For example, Ahmad and colleagues [15] found that emotionally tailored feedback from the robot maintained the students' social engagement when positive, but not when feedback was negative or neutral. However, the researchers also found a preference for negative feedback compared to neutral feedback, possibly meaning that in some situations, criticism may increase motivation and focus, which in turn may contribute to learning.

Lishinski and colleagues [17] found a reciprocal relationship between self-efficacy and performance in programming, however this relationship was additionally found to be influenced by goal orientation and metacognitive strategies. This process also revealed gender differences, by females being influenced by the feedback earlier in the process compared to males. This suggests an increased risk of lowered self-efficacy among females due to early failures being internalized – which then influences further performance, enjoyment, and persistence within this field.

1.3 Importance of Diversity Inclusion in Programming, Mathematics and HRI

Organizations within technology have been shown to be more innovative and increase their market growth when having diversity and inclusion in their workforce. Females have been shown to be an underrepresented group within STEM fields, and interventions focusing on gender diversity within STEM fields are advised to promote potential career choices to young students through role models [18]. Experience with, exposure to, and high academic performance within CS, in addition to social support and encouragement to pursue CS in future endeavors have all been found to be factors influencing persistence within CS. Additionally, females tend to rely on self-confidence and self-efficacy – and not so much on objective skills and abilities alone. Programming involvement and having the intent to continue learning CS while in high school have been found to be the most prominent predicting factors for persistence in CS among females [19].

1.4 Previous Findings

Gender has been identified as a moderating factor of accurate judgment of learning, where females are better at both self-assessment and performance assessment than males [20]. Although girls perform as competently as boys in various academic domains, they are inclined to report lower self-efficacy, especially in mathematics [21], and similar trends are reported in the field of programming. Although there is no significant difference between programming performances of students and gender [22, 23], there are differences in the perception of programming for girls and boys [24, 25]. Studies have shown that girls' attitudes towards programming are significantly lower than boys' [25–27].

Girls have been found to underperform within STEM if they were presented stereotypes of females performing worse than men on mathematics tasks, compared to when no such information was given [28]. However, it is suggested that such stereotype threat is of greatest influence on performance within mathematics when identification with mathematics (e.g., motivation) is high and the level of difficulty is neither too high nor low, but at the boundary of their abilities [28]. Having a female teacher has been shown to be associated with fewer gender differences on programming tasks, while boys were found to outperform girls when having male teachers [29].

Recent findings have shown that females perform no worse than males [2, 30]. Situational factors such as mentoring, female role-models and peer-support were identified [2] as contributing to retention and enhanced performance among female students at a cyber-defence academy. Accounting for gender difference in learning environments and introducing approaches that minimize risks associated with for example low self-efficacy and anxiety may directly support metacognitive development.

There have been found gender differences in attitudes towards robots, in that females reported higher social and physical attraction towards more human-like robots compared to males who reported better liking of the robot with the least human likeness [31].

Within mathematics, girls have been found to show lower self-efficacy compared to boys, and additionally boys reported a greater liking towards learning mathematics compared to girls, however with small cross-cultural effect size on the latter [32]. Girls and boys have been found to be equivalent in mathematic solving abilities, although they have been shown to use different strategies: boys tended to use covert strategies, such as retrieval, while girls tended to use overt strategies, such as counting on fingers [33].

Females exhibit lower mathematics and computer self-efficacy than males with significant gender differences emerge in late adolescence for mathematics self-efficacy [34] as well as decline in girl's interest in learning computer-related skills [35]. Other studies report mixed gender results in computer self-efficacy [36], and no significant gender differences in mathematics [37], STEM [38] self-efficacy and CS performance [39]. Hence it can be concluded that findings have been inconsistent regarding gender differences in academic self-efficacy [34], and therefore, further investigation is required.

1.5 Aims of Study

This research aims to identify gender differences and psychosocial perceptions of experiences (difficulty, enjoyment and learning) in a CS education class where students participate in human-robot interaction, programming, and mathematics tasks.

2 Methods

2.1 Participants

The participants were Grade 6 students attending a primary school in a medium sized town in Norway ($N = 17$; $n_{female} = 6$).

2.2 Measurements

Independent Variable
Metacognitive assessment (JOP): Participants were asked for a metacognitive judgment concerning how they expected to perform working with the mathematics, human-robot interaction, and programming. All judgements were measured on a 5 point visual analogue scale. Before the task, participants were asked 'How well do you think you will be able to do on the task?' and after the task was completed, they were then asked 'How well do you think you did on the task?'. The judgment of performance accuracy was defined as ratio between self-assessed performance expectation (JoP_{pre}) and their actual perceived performance after task completion (JoP_{POST}) given by the formula:

$$JoP = (\frac{(JoPpost - JoPpre)}{JoPpost})$$

Scores closer to 0 correspond to more accurate performance judgements, scores less than zero indicate overestimation performance, and scores greater than zero indicate underestimation of performance.

Dependent Variables:
The dependent variables were defined as learning, fun, and difficulty in each category (human-robot interaction, mathematics, programming). Learning, fun, and difficulty perceptions were measured on single 5-point likert scales (not-very) for each of the categories. A total score for fun was also computed by summing the individual fun scores (Cronbach's $a = .762$).

2.3 Procedure

The data was collected during a 3-day workshop which involved the following activities:

- Activity 1 - Introduction to humanoid robots - presentation and class discussion led by the researchers.

- Activity 2: The participants completed a structured online pre-test questionnaire on a secure platform. The information gathered was completely anonymous.
- Activity 3 – The class teachers divided the participants into gendered groups of four or five. The researchers conducted each group through an hour-long session. The robot was used to do basic programming and mathematics tasks during the lesson. The mathematics exercises were created in consultation with class teachers to ensure that they were appropriate in difficulty and curriculum-related.
- Activity 4 - After the tasks, the participants completed a secure online post-test structured questionnaire. The information gathered was completely anonymous.

2.4 Ethical Approval

The study conformed to the ethical guidelines for experimental studies set by the Norwegian Social Science Data Services (NSD). After the initial NSD online application was filled in, formal application was not required since only non-identifiable and non-health-related data were used in this research. Written informed consent was obtained from parents/guardians of the participating students. In addition, the students were informed about the aims of the project, their role in it, planned use of the data, and their right to withdraw. Participants were informed that they could withdraw from participation at any time and without any consequences throughout and after the session. However, it was made clear to them that the pre-test and post-test data was anonymous and therefore their survey data could not be withdrawn. The secure online provider used for the pre and post-test surveys is authorized by the author´s research institutions.

2.5 Data Reduction and Analysis

JASP version .14.1 was used for statistical analysis. Due to the number of participants, non-parametric mean comparisons were used to test the hypothesis for gender differences. Alpha levels were set to .05.

3 Results

Descriptives for each gender are given in Table 1. To test for gender differences, non-parametric means comparison (Mann-Whitney U) analysis was done. While there were no significant differences between genders, there were differences with small to medium effect sizes ($RBC = .278 -.389$; see Table 1).

Girls were more accurate in their performance judgements in human-robot interactions ($RBC = .278$), but even though they were less accurate in their mathematics ($RBC = .028$) and programming ($RBC = .000$) judgements compared to boys, these differences were negligible.

Girls reported equal or more fun on all three tasks than the males (HRI: $RBC = .000$; mathematics: $RBC = .389$; Programming: $RBC = .333$).

Girls did have divergent reports on their perceived difficulty. While girls reported less difficulty in the interactions with the robot ($RBC = .500$) they also reported more difficulty than boys in the mathematics tasks ($RBC = .389$). Due to a technical error during data collection difficulty scores for programming were not recorded.

Overall, females reported that they learned less ($RBC = .167$) but had more fun ($RBC = .278$) than the males. Both males and females rated the CS course equally as difficult ($RBC = .000$).

Table 1. Gender differences ($N = 12$)

	Mean		U	p	ES
	Males	Females			
JOP HRI accuracy	.17 ± .20	.07 ± .19	23.00	.451	.278
JOP Math accuracy	.06 ± .23	.08 ± .20	17.50	1	.028
JOP programmng accuracy	.08 ± .39	.11 ± .28	18.00	1	.000
Fun with HRI	4.83 ± .41	4.83 ± .41	18.00	1.00	.000
Fun with math	3.83 ± 1.42	4.33 ± .51	16.00	.247	.389
Fun with programming	4.33 ± .52	4.67 ± .52	12.00	.311	.333
Difficulty with HRI	2.50 ± .55	1.83 ± .75	27.00	.137	.500
Difficulty with math	2.17 ± .75	2.67 ± .52	11.00	.247	.389
Total learning	1.67 ± .1.03	1.33 ± .82	21.00	.595	.167
Total fun	9.17 ± .75	9.50 ± .84	13.00	.432	.278
Total difficulty	4.67 ± 1.03	4.50 ± .1.05	20.00	.801	.000

ES: effect size given by Rank Biserial Correlation; JOP: Judgement of Performance; HRI Human-Robot Interaction

4   Discussion

This study set out to investigate gender differences in performance judgements and in psychosocial experiences (difficulty, enjoyment and learning) in a classroom course focused on human-robot interaction, mathematics, and programming.

Previous research showed that gender was a predictive factor in perceived judgments of performance where females are better at self-assessing their skills [20]. While there were no significant gender differences found in our study, some tendencies (small to medium effect sizes; RBC = .278—.389; see Table 1) did emerge that support previous findings. While there were no significant gender effects, there were differences with small effect sizes. Girls did have divergent reports on their perceived difficulty as reported in previous research. While girls reported less difficulty with interactions with the robots (RBC = .500), they did report the mathematics as being more difficult (RBC = .389) to work with. Girls reported better accuracy in their robot interaction perceptions (RBC = .278), more fun with programming (RBC = .333), and less learning (RBC = .167). In the mathematics condition, girls also reported more difficulty (RBC = .389) but also reported that mathematics was more fun (.389). This gives support to the Schripsema et al. [20] findings that females may be better at self-assessment, especially at school ages where girls are generally better at self-regulated learning [13], and to findings that females perform as good as males in programming when situational factors are accounted for [19].

The associations found in this study, that females reported better outcomes than males, supports more recent findings that females who receive programming experience increased their interest in technology and programming [30]. This may lead to more persistence in pursuing and continuing STEM education in females [2, 19, 29]. This may be moderated by situational factors such as same sex peer support and instructor gender [2, 29].

One aspect that might have influenced the results of this study was that the course the students completed was delivered by two female teachers, one with expertise in CS and one with expertise in pedagogy development. The girl's performance on the different tasks can be moderated by the teachers. Previous research has shown that same gender role models can increase self-efficacy which also influences performance [2, 4, 29]. This may have contributed to the more positive results for females in enjoying human robot interaction while experiencing less difficulties in the interactions. While both teachers have competencies in education ad CS, this may also explain the results for the mathematics tasks. The girls reported more difficulty with the mathematics, similar to previous findings [21] but that they enjoyed the mathematics task more than the boys may be due to access to the same sex role model [29].

The students participating in the study are preadolescent and this may also explain the non-significant findings. Previous studies show mixed results where late adolescent males report higher self-efficacy in mathematics but primary and middle school children do not show any differences [35, 37, 38].

While this study did not find any significant differences, it does highlight the importance of other psychological factors that may influence female participation in CS and STEM education. Females who are exposed to CS and STEM subjects early in their educational development, and who have access to same gender role models, are more likely to persist in the field and develop careers within CS [18, 19].

4.1 Limitations of Study

This study only included twelve participants, and this may explain the non-significant findings. Also, the measurements used in this study are self-reports. Alongside the age of the participants, the self-evaluation of their performance and experiences may be subject to wide variance of understanding. The course was delivered by female teachers, and as with the benefits of same gender role-models, the boys in this study may have been negatively influenced due to the lack of a male role-model. The gender of the teacher has been shown to influence student performance [24, 25].

5   Conclusion

The study showed that preadolescent boys and girls report similar experiences with a CS course that included human-robot interaction, mathematics, and programming. This study included students' perceptions of their performance, an aspect future studies should incorporate into their designs and that situational factors, such as teacher gender, might impact student experiences. CS research and instruction should include both male and female teachers as this could be an influencing factor on student performance and future career choices.

Funding. This project was not funded. The authors thank the students and teachers for their participation in the research.

References

1. Murciano-Goroff, R.: Missing women in tech: The labor market for highly skilled software engineers. Work in progress. http://stanford.edu/~ravivmg/papers/JMP.Pdf (2018)
2. Lugo, R.G., Firth-Clark, A., Knox, B.J., Jøsok, Ø., Helkala, K., Sütterlin, S.: Cognitive profiles and education of female cyber defence operators. In: Schmorrow, D.D., Fidopiastis, C.M. (eds.) HCII 2019. LNCS (LNAI), vol. 11580, pp. 563–572. Springer, Cham (2019). https://doi.org/10.1007/978-3-030-22419-6_40
3. Lehman, K.J., Sax, L.J., Zimmerman, H.B.: Women planning to major in computer science: who are they and what makes them unique? Comput. Sci. Educ. 26(4), 277–298 (2016)
4. Karlin, M.: Strategies for Recruiting and Retaining Female Students in Secondary Computer Science, in School of Education. Indiana University, p. 223 (2019)
5. Lin, P., Abney, K., Bekey, G.A.: Robot Ethics: the Ethical and Social Implications of Robotics. Intelligent Robotics and Autonomous Agents series (2012)
6. Newton, D.P., Newton, L.D.: Humanoid robots as teachers and a proposed code of practice. In: Frontiers in Education, vol. 4, p. 125 (2019)
7. Pandey, A.K., Gelin, R.: Humanoid robots in education: a short review. Hum. Robot. Ref. 1–16 (2017)
8. Alcorn, A.M., et al.: Educators' views on using humanoid robots with autistic learners in special education settings in England. Front. Robot. AI 6, 107 (2019)
9. Ahumada-Newhart, V., Eccles, J.S.: A theoretical and qualitative approach to evaluating children's robot-mediated levels of presence. Technol. Mind Behav. 1(1) (2020)
10. Crompton, H., Gregory, K., Burke, D.: Humanoid robots supporting children's learning in an early childhood setting. Br. J. Edu. Technol. 49(5), 911–927 (2018)
11. Jones, A., Castellano, G.: Adaptive robotic tutors that support self-regulated learning: a longer-term investigation with primary school children. Int. J. Soc. Robot. 10(3), 357–370 (2018)
12. Efklides, A.: Metacognition: defining its facets and levels of functioning in relation to self-regulation and co-regulation. Eur. Psychol. 13(4), 277–287 (2008)
13. Zimmerman, B.J., Schunk, D.H.: Handbook of Self-Regulation of Learning and Performance. Routledge/Taylor & Francis Group (2011)
14. André, V., et al.: Ethorobotics applied to human behaviour: can animated objects influence children's behaviour in cognitive tasks? Anim. Behav. 96, 69–77 (2014)
15. Ahmad, M.I., et al.: Robot's adaptive emotional feedback sustains children's social engagement and promotes their vocabulary learning: a long-term child–robot interaction study. Adapt. Behav. 27(4), 243–266 (2019)

16. Bavelier, D., Green, C.S., Dye, M.W.: Children, wired: for better and for worse. Neuron **67**(5), 692–701 (2010)
17. Lishinski, A., et al.: Learning to program: gender differences and interactive effects of students' motivation, goals, and self-efficacy on performance. In: Proceedings of the 2016 ACM Conference on International Computing Education Research (2016)
18. Peixoto, A., et al.: Diversity and inclusion in engineering education: looking through the gender question. In: 2018 IEEE Global Engineering Education Conference (EDUCON). IEEE (2018)
19. Weston, T.J., Dubow, W.M., Kaminsky, A.: Predicting women's persistence in computer sciencecomputer science-and technology-related majors from high school to college. ACM Trans. Comput. Educ. (TOCE) **20**(1), 1–16 (2019)
20. Schripsema, N.R., et al.: Impact of vocational interests, previous academic experience, gender and age on situational judgement test performance. Adv. Health Sci. Educ. **22**(2), 521–532 (2017)
21. Schunk, D.H., Meece, J.R., Pintrich, P.R.: Motivation in Education: Theory, Research, and Applications. Pearson Higher Ed. (2012)
22. Lau, W.W., Yuen, A.H.: Modelling programming performance: beyond the influence of learner characteristics. Comput. Educ. **57**(1), 1202–1213 (2011)
23. Su, A.Y., et al.: Investigating the role of computer-supported annotation in problem-solving-based teaching: an empirical study of a S cratch programming pedagogy. Br. J. Edu. Technol. **45**(4), 647–665 (2014)
24. Gunbatar, M.S., Karalar, H.: Gender differences in middle school students' attitudes and self-efficacy perceptions towards mblock programming. Euro. J. Educ. Res. **7**(4), 925–933 (2018)
25. Rubio, M.A., et al.: Closing the gender gap in an introductory programming course. Comput. Educ. **82**, 409–420 (2015)
26. Baser, M.: Attitude, gender and achievement in computer programming. Middle-East J. Sci. Res. **14**(2), 248–255 (2013)
27. Korkmaz, Ö., Altun, H.: Engineering and ceit student's attitude towards learning computer programming. J. Acad. Soc. Sci. Stud. Int. J. Soc. Sci. **6**(2), 1169–1185 (2013)
28. Spencer, S.J., Steele, C.M., Quinn, D.M.: Stereotype threat and women's math performance. J. Exp. Soc. Psychol. **35**(1), 4–28 (1999)
29. Sullivan, A., Bers, M.: The impact of teacher gender on girls' performance on programming tasks in early elementary school. J. Inf. Technol. Educ. Innov. Pract. **17**(1), 153–162 (2018)
30. Master, A., et al.: Programming experience promotes higher STEM motivation among first-grade girls. J. Exp. Child Psychol. **160**, 92–106 (2017)
31. Tung, F.-W.: Influence of gender and age on the attitudes of children towards humanoid robots. In: Jacko, J.A. (ed.) HCI 2011. LNCS, vol. 6764, pp. 637–646. Springer, Heidelberg (2011). https://doi.org/10.1007/978-3-642-21619-0_76
32. Reilly, D., Neumann, D.L., Andrews, G.: Investigating gender differences in mathematics and science: results from the 2011 trends in mathematics and science survey. Res. Sci. Educ. **49**(1), 25–50 (2019)
33. Carr, M., Jessup, D.L.: Gender differences in first-grade mathematics strategy use: social and metacognitive influences. J. Educ. Psychol. **89**(2), 318 (1997)
34. Huang, C.: Gender differences in academic self-efficacy: a meta-analysis. Eur. J. Psychol. Educ. **28**(1), 1–35 (2013)
35. Blackhurst, A.E., Auger, R.W.: Precursors to the gender gap in college enrollment: children's aspirations and expectations for their futures. Prof. Sch. Counsel. **11**(3), 2156759X0801100301 (2008)
36. Peng, H., Tsai, C.C., Wu, Y.T.: University students' self-efficacy and their attitudes toward the Internet: the role of students' perceptions of the Internet. Educ. Stud. **32**(1), 73–86 (2006)

37. Friedel, J.M., et al.: Achievement goals, efficacy beliefs and coping strategies in mathematics: The roles of perceived parent and teacher goal emphases. Contemp. Educ. Psychol. **32**(3), 434–458 (2007)
38. Brown, P.L., et al.: An examination of middle school students' STEM self-efficacy, interests and perceptions. J. STEM Educ. Innov. Res. **17**(3) (2016)
39. Qian, Y., Lehman, J.D.: Correlates of success in introductory programming: a study with middle school students. J. Educ. Learn. **5**(2), 73–83 (2016)

Using Synthetic Datasets to Hone Intuitions Within an Adaptive Learning Environment

Walter Warwick[1]([✉]), Rod Ford[2], and Matt Funke[1]

[1] TiER1 Performance, Covington, KY, USA
{w.warwick,m.funke}@tier1performance.com
[2] Azimuth Corporation, Fairborn, OH, USA
rford@azimuth-corp.com

Abstract. Adaptive learning typically focuses on the challenge of adjusting the presentation of instructional material based on an automated assessment of real-time student performance. The goal is to move away from a one-size-fits-all approach to learning toward a more personalized experience. While we support this goal, in this paper we focus on a related but logically prior challenge, namely, the development of an adaptive environment that helps the instructional designer build better learning materials in the first place. Rather than focus on the automated assessment of student performance, we have instead focused on mining data generated by the instructional designers as they developed new course materials. Working on the assumption that the discovery of patterns in past design decisions will inform better future design decisions, we have applied an off-the-shelf machine learning technique to explore associations between learning contexts and the selection of specific learning activities. Although machine learning techniques have become commodities, practical guidance regarding their expected performance is harder to come by. We have filled this gap by systematically generating our own synthetic data sets that represent notional histories of user interactions to hone our own intuitions about the performance of the Bayesian network that underpins our adaptive environment. Our intent is not to add yet one more benchmark data set to promote Bayesian approaches but, rather, to describe by way of example a method for generating such data sets that will help the practitioner understand what an otherwise black box is doing.

Keywords: Instructional design · Adaptive learning · Bayesian networks

1 Introduction

Adaptive learning typically focuses on the challenge of adjusting the presentation of instructional material based on an automated assessment of real-time student performance. The goal is to move away from a one-size-fits-all approach to learning toward a more personalized experience. While we support this goal, in this paper we focus on a related but logically prior challenge, namely, the development of an adaptive environment that helps the instructional designer build better learning materials in the first place. Rather than focus on the automated assessment of student performance, we have instead

© Springer Nature Switzerland AG 2021
C. Stephanidis et al. (Eds.): HCII 2021, LNCS 13096, pp. 491–500, 2021.
https://doi.org/10.1007/978-3-030-90328-2_33

focused on mining data generated by the instructional designers as they developed new course materials.

We have prototyped an instructional design environment that includes a "recommendation engine" to provide instructional designers with suggestions for course content given the job task being trained, the desired level of proficiency (e.g., low, high) and the instructional goal of the training (e.g., the introduction of a new topic, remediation). The recommendation engine is intended to help instructional designers manage the complexity of course design that follows when even just a handful of learning activities is available by providing context sensitive suggestions. Rather than hard-code these suggestions into the system, the recommendation engine records and subsequently mines interaction data generated by instructional designers as they develop new courses. This functionality provides both the potential to adapt content recommendations over time as well as a mechanism to explore patterns of use.

Among the literally dozens of machine learning (ML) techniques used for pattern discovery and adaptation, we used an off-the-shelf Bayesian network package to implement the recommendation engine. While Bayesian networks stand out among ML techniques for their intuitive knowledge representation, there is still a need to demonstrate what and how a Bayesian network will learn when applied to this domain. In the remainder of this paper, we describe in detail how we verified the performance of the recommendation engine in using a variety of synthetic data sets. These included: a "null" data set; data sets with varying degrees of "noise"; data sets to explore the discoverability of different rules (i.e., sets of rules relating content choice to instructional context); and data sets to explore the discoverability of complexity within a rule (i.e., Boolean combinations of antecedent conditions that define a how a single rule relates content choice to instructional context). In addition to helping us verify the function of our recommendation engine, these data sets have been designed with an eye to interpretability for the practitioner; the "rules" of these data sets are intended to represent different choices an instructional designer would make.

We begin with a brief introduction to Bayesian networks and how we have applied them to the problem of content recommendation for the instructional designer. Next, we describe what it means in general to verify the performance of the recommendation engine. Finally, we review the specific data sets we generated and the results we obtained when those data were mined by the recommendation engine.

2   Bayesian Networks

Bayesian networks have long been used to support both knowledge representation and discovery [1]. These networks provide the analyst an intuitive graph-based representation of the probabilistic relationships that exist among various factors. More precisely, nodes represent variables (either continuous or discrete), and the edges between nodes represent probabilistic dependencies among those factors. A variety of interesting inferential relationships can be captured in these dependencies—predictive, diagnostic, even causal. Moreover, there is a wealth of open-source routines that implement efficient reasoning with and learning for these networks [2].

The construction of a Bayesian network begins with the identification of the relevant factors. In our case, the relevant factors are the inputs the instructional designer provides to the system (e.g., Instructional Goal, Job Task, Target Proficiency) and the different types of learning activities the recommendation engine can suggest (e.g., instructor-led lecture, group activity, e-learning module etc.).

The next step is to identify the structure of the graph that relates these factors and to specify the probabilistic dependencies between linked factors (i.e., nodes directly connected by an edge). While it is possible to ask a subject matter expert to describe the graphical relations and dependencies, it is often easier to learn this structure directly from data. In this case, the data are the records of previous associations between input factors and learning activities. As previously mentioned, there is a variety of open-source routines that implement efficient structure learning. Once learned, this network structure encodes the joint probability distribution of a feature space (in this case, the input factors and learning activities). In addition to providing a more compact encoding of the joint probability distribution (via local conditional probabilities between directly connected factors), a Bayesian network supports the efficient calculation of conditional probabilities which can be used to implement different patterns of inference. In short, by partitioning the network into a set of nodes that represent input features and those that represent output, we can use a conditional probability query as the basis for recommendations. Specifically, given a combination of input factors, the recommendation engine will return the probability of a particular learning activity being selected based on previous user interactions with the system.

This ability to learn graphical structure makes the Bayesian approach powerful. While the feature space for our current prototype is relatively small, the addition of even a few more input factors would significantly increase the size of the feature space, making the direct inspection of the joint distribution needed for recommendation inscrutable to the instructional designer.[1] The graphical structure at the heart of the Bayesian network allows the instructional designer to manage the complexity of the feature space by revealing only the significant relationships among the features and, further, by allowing the instructional designer to consider the most direct local relationships among learning activities and the various inputs. The Bayesian approach is more than just a tool for managing complexity; it is a way to refine the instructional designer's understanding of a domain. While the user interface to any support system is intended to capture only the most relevant inputs, the relationships among those inputs might only be faintly understood by the interface designer. Likewise, actual practice with a support system might evolve significantly from the original intent captured by the designer, reflecting any number of changes, for example, in best practices, content, or shifts in user needs. By recording actual use within the system and continually updating the Bayesian network given new data, we provide the instructional designer the opportunity to refine her understanding of the domain.

---

[1] In earlier prototypes, we considered using 11 different multi-valued inputs which resulted in 8,398,080 unique combinations of input values and learning activities. While this number is manageable from the perspective of data base limitations, it far outstrips human comprehensibility.

3   Verifying the Performance of the Recommendation Engine

Given the significant role of learning in the recommendation engine, it is important to understand what can be learned and how quickly learning occurs. The instructional designer is unlikely to be an expert in Bayesian structure learning or parameter estimation, so verifying the performance of the recommendation engine should be couched in terms familiar to the instructional designer rather than, say, analytical demonstrations of algorithmic convergence. For this reason, we have taken an "empirical" approach to verification in which we have generated a variety of data sets, each of which represents a notional history of user interactions with the system. Because we build these data sets from scratch, we have complete control over what kinds of interactions we build into the history. Specifically, we can build different patterns of user interactions into the data where each pattern represents a "rule" that the notional user applies when assigning a learning activity to a given input.

For example, whenever the Instructional Goal is "Adding Complexity," the Job Task is "Customer Support," and the Target Level of Proficiency is "High" our notional instructional designer might assign "Decision Tree" as the learning activity. The instructional designer might have several such rules in mind when assigning learning activities to different combinations of Instructional Goal, Job Task, and Target Level of Proficiency. In fact, given the current set of learning activities and input factors in our prototype system, there are 384 unique combinations, each of which could, potentially serve as a rule the instructional designer might apply in developing a lesson plan. This is a worst case bound on the number of rules; not every combination of input factor and learning activity will be plausible, and some activities might be suitable for several different combinations of input factors, and vice versa.

Given this variety of possible mappings between input factors and learning activities, verification of the recommendation engine is a matter of determining how well it detects patterns in user interactions, where a pattern consists of a particular set of rules.[2] More precisely, we are interested in how performance of the recommendation engine varies with changes in both the relative frequency with which a particular pattern appears (with respect to the total number of recorded user interactions) and the complexity of the pattern itself (with respect to the number and structure of the rules that constitute the pattern). Intuitively, changes in relative frequency allow us to explore how often specific associations between learning activities and inputs must appear before a pattern is detected. Likewise, changes in in complexity allow us to explore whether subtle changes in a pattern can be discriminated. Because recommendations are given as conditional probabilities, we measure changes in performance as changes in the conditional probabilities associated the rules that constitute a pattern. We can then summarize overall performance of the recommendation as a "learning curve" in which changes in conditional probabilities are graphed as a function of both the relative frequency of that pattern and the complexity of the pattern itself.

---

[2] For present purposes, it does not matter which of the 384 possible rules we use to verify performance. We leave the question of whether particular set of rules represents best practice to domain experts. We are only interested in determining how well the recommendation engine is able to pick out *any* pattern of use.

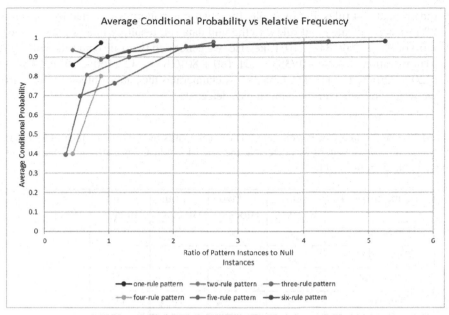

Fig. 1. Preliminary verification of the recommendation engine. Each data point represents an average conditional probability (taken over the conditional probabilities of the individual rules that constitute that pattern) at a given relative frequency of that pattern to the 384 "null" instances included in each data set (as further described in the next section). We varied relative frequency by adding rules in fixed blocks of 20 instances to a pattern. For this reason, this graph should not be used for interpolation (we used a line graph only to support better legibility in grouping patterns).

4   The Synthetic Data

Before we created 24 data sets to generate the results depicted in Fig. 1, we created a "null rule" data set. That data set contains one instance of each of the 384 possible combinations of input factors and learning activities. Given the probabilistic underpinnings of the Bayesian network, we expected (and verified) that this null data set would not reveal any patterns; indeed, because every combination of input factors is associated with each learning activity exactly once, there can be no difference in the relative frequency of association between any one combination of input factors and a particular learning activity. Intuitively, this null data set represents "white noise" that we can use to determine the various circumstances in which the recommendation engine can pick out the "signal" of different patterns when they are appended to that data set.

With this conceptual model in mind, we generated additional data sets as follow:

1) We randomly selected six rows from the null data set. Each of these rows represents a rule a user might apply; we refer to these as "rule j", "rule k" etc.
2) We created blocks of twenty instances for each selected rule. We chose block size of twenty to facilitate efficient exploration of the performance space.
3) For each pattern (e.g., one-rule, three-rule), we systematically appended blocks of selected rules to the null data set to vary the frequency of the selected rules relative to

the original 384 rules. For example, for a two-rule pattern, we started by appending 20 instances of rule j and rule k to the null data set, resulting in a "signal to noise" ratio of $(20 + 20)/384 = .10$. Likewise, we generated two-rule data sets with signal to noise ratios of $(40 + 40)/384 = .21$, $(80 + 80)/384 = .42$, $(160 + 160)/384 = .83$, $(320 + 320)/384 = 1.7$. The table below enumerates the pattern-block combinations we tested and whether the pattern was detected.

Table 1. Initial Summary of Performance. The check marks indicate the number of blocks that was required before a pattern was detected; the asterisks indicate that the pattern was detected using a reduced set of input factors.

Pattern/Blocks	One Block	Two Blocks	Four Blocks	Eight Blocks	Sixteen Blocks
One-rule	✗	✗	✗	✓*	✓
Two-rule	✗	✗	✓	✓	✓
Three-rule	✗	✓*	✓	✓	✓
Four-rule	✗	✓*	✓*	TBD	TBD
Five-rule	✗	✓*	✓*	✓	✓
Six-rule	✗	✓	✓	✓	✓
Eight-rule	TBD	TBD	TBD	TBD	TBD

4) We presented the data to the recommendation engine to determine: 1) whether any pattern had been detected and 2) if detected, the conditional probability associated with each rule constituting that pattern. We then averaged the conditional probabilities to arrive at an overall probability for the pattern.

5 Additional Considerations

As we previously described, this approach allows us to determine how frequently a pattern must appear before it is detected by the recommendation engine. In addition, this approach allows us to explore how detection varies with the complexity of the pattern (with respect to both the number of rules that constitute the pattern and the mapping between non-disjoint input factors and learning activities). It is clear that the recommendation engine begins to detect patterns (i.e., average conditional probability > 50%) relatively quickly (i.e., often requiring just 40 instances of the rules of more complex patterns before detection occurs). This provides some assurance that, in practice, the recommendation engine could be adapting to users after dozens or hundreds of interactions rather than thousands and thousands of interactions. There is also some evidence that the recommendation engine is capable of reducing the complexity of the input factors. In several instances (noted in the table above with the asterisks), patterns were recognized using only a subset of the three input factors.

Having verified the basic function of the recommendation engine, we next considered the performance of recommendation engine given less straightforward user interactions. For example, rather than generate data representing the use of distinct rules, we turned to cases where a single learning activity might be associated with several different combinations of input factors. Intuitively, such a many-to-one mapping represents a case where different users each have their own heuristic for picking out a learning activity. Conversely, we also considered the case where a single set of input factors was associated with multiple learning activities. This one-to-many mapping can be thought of as a case where users disagree about the appropriate learning activity.

5.1 Many-to-One Mappings

Like Table 1, Table 2 summarizes the performance of the recommendation engine given different patterns of many-to-one rules. The single asterisk (*) indicates that the pattern detected depended on only two input factors and the double asterisks (**) indicate that the pattern detected depended on only one input factor (Fig. 2).

Table 2. Many-to-one summary of performance

Pattern/Blocks	Two Blocks	Four Blocks	Eight Blocks	Sixteen Blocks
Two-Rule	✗	✓*	✓*	✓
Four-Rule	✗	✗	✓**	✓*
Eight-Rule	✗	✗	✓**	✓**

Learning many-to-one patterns requires a greater ratio of rule patterns to null instances. Intuitively, learning these patterns is "slower." Moreover, by the time the recommendation engine learns to detect the Eight-rule pattern, it can only discriminate three distinct rules, individuated by a single input factor.

5.2 One-to-Many Mappings

Following the same procedure we used to verify performance in the multi-rule and many-to-one pattern, we started by searching for the ratio of pattern instances to null instances at which detection occurs. Using a two-rule pattern in which the same input factors mapped to different activities, detection occurred with four blocks of the pattern instances. But unlike the multi-rule and many-to-one rule patterns, the conditional probability of the recognized pattern did not increase with additional blocks. In fact, the conditional probability associated with the two-rule pattern varies, unsurprisingly, at roughly 50–50. At this point, we decide to see how the conditional probabilities vary as the ratio of the two rules varies with respect to each other. The intuition here is to see how many more instances of one rule ("Rule 1") is necessary to "un-learn" the other rule ("Rule 2"). Figure 3 summarizes these results.

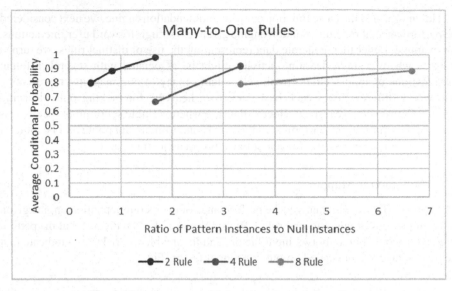

Fig. 2. Learning curves for the many-to-one rule patterns.

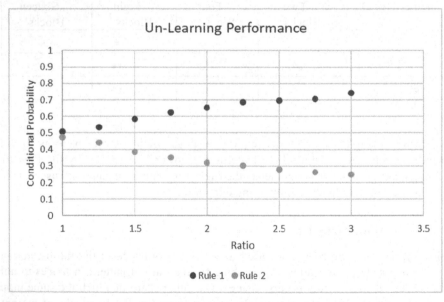

Fig. 3. "Un-learning" performance

In general, the relative conditional probability between two instances of a one-to-many rule varies with the ratio of their frequency. In this case, the performance of the recommendation engine is quite democratic.

6 Discussion

These synthetic data sets serve two purposes. First, they can be used as "unit tests" to verify that new instances of system produce the consistent recommendations. The goal here is to ensure that a known set of user inputs will produce a known recommendation under identical initial condition; a failed unit test should prompt the system administrator to verify that the system has been properly installed and configured. Second, the synthetic data sets can be used to establish the basic functionality of the recommendation engine to detect patterns in instructional design choices. Although the patterns we baked into the data sets are entirely notional, they do cover a range of situations we expect instructional designers to encounter in actual practice. That is, we expect that instructional designers will vary in the choices they make when developing lesson plans. We expect that with a rich collection of learning activities there will be a variety in the assignment of specific activities given different combinations of input factors (i.e., learning contexts). The ability of the recommendation engine to detect patterns comprising such variety is promising as is the time scale at which such learning occurs. Likewise, a given learning activity might be appropriate under several different learning contexts. Again, the fact that the recommendation engine is able to detect these cases, albeit more slowly, is promising. Finally, instructional designers might disagree about the choice of learning activity for a given learning context. In this case, pattern detection is more difficult (not surprisingly) but still possible. Moreover, the fact that detection is predicated on a reduced set of input factors tells us that that the current set of input factors might not be sufficiently granular to distinguish the different choices instructional designers are making in a single learning context; either the current factors need to take on more values or new factors need to be added. Alternatively, the presence of such patterns could also point to a shift in the instructional designers thinking; an activity that was once considered appropriate for a given learning context has been replaced by another activity. This ability to "unlearn" previous patterns ensures that the recommendation engine can adapt to at least some systematic changes in user interactions.

As we previously mentioned, the synthetic data sets we used for verification are not intended to represent best practices in instructional design or course development in a specific domain; rather, the notional rules cover general patterns of use when different instructional designers interact with the system. We expect that instructional designers will rely on a variety of rules when developing course content and that these rules will comprise different mappings between learning contexts and activities. Further, we expect that such rules could change over time. The synthetic data sets allow us to verify, in a piecewise manner, that the recommendation engine can detect these different use patterns. Even if actual use results in a blend of different patterns, the synthetic data sets provide a framework for exploring how different combinations of patterns might impact the recommendation engine's ability to detect. Specifically, by combining exemplars from the different data sets in different ratios (e.g., a new data set containing a 50–50 blend of a multi-rule pattern and a many-to-one rule pattern), the analyst can determine whether at and what point blended pattern becomes detectable. In addition, the synthetic data sets provide the analyst clues for understanding actual use patterns. For example, whenever a pattern is detectable using a reduced set of input factors, the analyst will know that a one learning activity has been associated with many learning contexts. In sum, the synthetic data sets provide the user a tool for both verifying the function of the recommendation engine as well as a method for honing intuitions about user interactions.

As important as it is to benchmark the performance of any AI or ML technique, we see a deeper utility in the development of these data sets when it comes to applying such techniques to the challenge of adaptive learning. Indeed, unlike so many other domains where "prediction products" are in vogue, advancing the state of the art in adaptive learning requires more than just verifying the performance of an algorithmic black box. Likewise, rather than just replace the human instructor, there is significant benefit if the AI or ML we use to support adaptive learning can also be used to explore the learning contexts in which it is applied. It is in this spirit that we developed our synthetic data sets; not only do they provide some assurance that our recommendation engine will work as intended, they also allow us to develop intuitions about the scope and limits of the underlying Bayesian network *in terms that are familiar to the practitioner.* The data sets we developed represent notional but plausible examples of user interactions—examples where instructional designers have more or less complex rules of thumb guiding their choice of activity. The data sets allow us to hone our intuitions "empirically" about how different patterns of use will impact performance of the recommendation engine and, conversely, how different kinds of use patterns can be diagnosed from the observed performance of recommendation engine. While it is certainly possible to understand the performance of the recommendation engine in purely mathematical terms, it is more immediately useful to see how, for example, conflicting rules might impact the performance of the recommendation engine. More generally, we hope the approach we described here provides a method for bridging what is otherwise a yawning gap between theoretical discussions of AI and ML and the practical considerations that are needed to apply these techniques to the challenge of adaptive learning.

References

1. Pearl, J.: Probabilistic Reasoning in Intelligent Systems: Networks of Plausible Inference. Morgan Kauffman Publishers Inc., San Francisco (1988)
2. Scutari, M., Denis, J.-B.: Bayesian Networks with Examples in R. CRC Press, Boca Raton (2015)

Metasynthesis of EU-Based Initiatives to 'Open Language' to Individuals and Groups with Migrant Biographies

Elena Xeni[✉], Panagiotis Kosmas[✉], and Charalambos Vrasidas[✉]

CARDET – Centre for the Advancement of Research and Development in Educational Technology, University of Nicosia, Nicosia, Cyprus
{elena.xeni,panagiotis.kosmas}@cardet.org, vrasidas.c@unic.ac.cy

Abstract. Metasynthesis is the systematic review of qualitative data for the purposes of analyzing data across qualitative studies. Within the process of this qualitative-based research approach, the researcher identifies a specific research question and then addresses this within the realm of searching, selecting, evaluating, summarizing and combining existing evidence.

Metasynthesis does the opposite of meta-analysis, i.e. it focuses on qualitative data and evidence – instead of qualitative – in constructing meaning and interpreting the issue in question. It is a contemporary approach in qualitative-oriented research and a 'new kid on the block' in the realm of educational studies and social studies research, with research practices linking to critical review, meta-ethnography, and process-oriented research. It generates avenues for in-depth research, analysis and interpretation, with results targeting quality management and change, policy making and sustainability.

This metasynthesis-targeted contribution, reports on decisions made in the framework of EU-based funded initiatives focusing directly or indirectly on individuals' or groups' with migrant biographies (additional) language learning skills. Evidence that are being investigated under a metasynthesis lens, involve a variety of existing texts and contexts reporting the process and the products of the selected (additional) language learning and migration initiatives engaged in 'opening the additional language' to individuals and groups with migrant biographies. In the context of this contribution, project proposals, policy papers, language e-learning platforms, (open) educational resources, language learning training programmes and courses, agendas, minutes and reports are all considered to be metasynthesis data, mirroring the *'whats'*, *'hows'* and *'whys'* of attempts 'to open the language' of the host community to individuals and groups with migrant biographies. Serving as a meta-review, this metasynthesis-grounded contribution systematically and critically reviews priorities, decisions and actions made in providing an 'open' space for individuals and groups with migrant biographies to learn a language, so as for possibilities in vital sectors of their new life and integration, from their well-being to education, profession, and so forth, to 'open' and gain meaning, perspective and hope.

The study being ongoing, results presented hereby focus on digital storytelling as a good practice in opening pathways and possibilities to migrant populations for language learning in engaging, meaningful and beneficial ways.

© Springer Nature Switzerland AG 2021
C. Stephanidis et al. (Eds.): HCII 2021, LNCS 13096, pp. 501–512, 2021.
https://doi.org/10.1007/978-3-030-90328-2_34

Keywords: Metasynthesis · Language learning and migrants · EU funded initiatives · Digital storytelling

1 Introduction

EU funded-based initiatives to support migrant populations in the process of language learning in the context of the new community are highly prioritized. Actions providing 'open spaces' and 'open access' to the language of the community are being included on the agendas and implementations of the host community, struggling to address language learning as a major migration integration need.

Aiming at examining the 'whats', 'hows', and 'whys' of additional language learning initiatives in better understanding good practices targeting effective migration integration in the EU and beyond, this methasynthesis contribution, attempts to investigate decisions, choices and actions taken in addressing migrant target groups for learning the language of the host community (the 'whats'), the ways they were implemented (the 'hows', and the reasons behind the decision-making and implementations (the 'whys'). Based on metasynthesis conducted so far, good practices revealed involve needs-based and interests-based actions and multimodal (con)texts that provide opportunities to learn and interact with knowledge, the self and others in meaningful and engaging ways.

The present contribution tackles digital storytelling as a prevalent good practice in learning an additional language. Data gathered from a number of official documents of the five (5) projects under review (e.g. project proposals, policy papers, language e-learning platforms, (open) educational resources, language learning training programmes and courses, agendas, minutes and reports) revealed that a predominant trend in the design and implementation of the selected projects is digital storytelling, serving as a good practice in attempts to successfully make the host community language accessible to migrant populations, opening new pathways to education, well-being and other opportunities.

In the following lines digital storytelling is tackled as a language learning good practice in the framework of an ongoing metasynthesis attempt to better understand and support the processes and results of EU funded-based projects targeting migrant individuals' and groups' needs in the host community.

2 Digital Storytelling as a Prevalent (Additional) Language Learning Opportunity

Digital storytelling is primarily a short form of digital multimedia production that allows the presentation of a story (Jakes and Brennan 2006; Lambert 2002). It is a multimodal text, as it includes and combines text, photos, videos, animation, sound and music (Miller and McVee 2012). At the same time, it is a multimedia text, as it includes and combines movies, cartoons, superheroes and digital books, as well as narrative games, thus providing multiple options for presenting a story (Gee 2003; Robin 2008).

Digital storytelling is a result of the development and advancement of technology in recent decades (Mills 2010; Robin et al. 2011). With deep roots in storytelling, it evolves and provides multiple opportunities to a variety of recipients and environments, performing multiple roles and purposes (Tsilimeni 2007; Benmayor 2008; Ohler 2006). Its multiple roles and purposes are widely acknowledged, with the didactic (Ohler 2006; Robin, 2008; Yuksel-Arslan et al. 2016) entertainment (Murray 1997; Sawhney 2009), and cognitive (Green 2002) being widely acknowledged. As a cognitive tool, digital storytelling supports meaning, organizing children's experiences in the form of storytelling, to support information retention and concentration, in order to enhance understanding (Burmark 2004; Robin 2008; Sadik 2008; Sarica and Usluel 2016). As a pedagogical tool, digital storytelling is recognized for enhancing comprehension. It thus fosters active learning (Smeda et al. 2014), supporting learners' active participation in the learning experiences, processes and outcomes; learning motivation (Robin 2008; Sawhney 2009); and learning outcomes (Sarica and Usluel 2016; Sawhney 2009; Smeda et al. 2014, etc.). Digital storytelling also provides opportunities to cultivate a variety of literacy skills, such as writing and comprehension. Critical literacy skills may be cultivated and fostered in the context of digital storytelling, such as reflection, revision, negotiation of meanings and choices, decision making, transformations, etc. (Sadik 2008; Sarica and Usluel 2016). At the same time, digital literacy skills are cultivated, such as search, analysis, comprehension, evaluation, organization, etc. (Mills 2010). As a recreational tool, digital storytelling provides opportunities for learners to engage systematically in learning experiences that are enjoyable (Benmayor 2008). The complex, diverse and dynamic role of digital storytelling is emerging as a result of the significant range of possibilities that it provides as a tool that enhances education processes and outcomes. It also successfully contributes to practicing traditional and contemporary skills (e.g. storytelling, writing, comprehension, communication, revision, transformation, decision making, creativity, imagination, critical literacy, digital literacy, etc.), contributing to the promotion of traditional and contemporary literacy in in-school practices and beyond.

3   Digital Storytelling and Target Groups with a Migrant Biography

Digital storytelling is a multi-tool in the school environment and beyond (Mileer et al. 2012; Ohler 2008, 2006; Robin 2008; Suwardy et al. 2013; etc.). It can be used at all levels, sectors and types of education; official and unofficial education; school and adult education; lifelong learning programmes; school years learners; adult learners; learners with special needs; migrant learners, etc. (Heo 2009; Mills 2010; Fokidis, et al. 2016; Tsilimeni 2007). It can also be combined with numerous learning methodologies, approaches and strategies, including collaborative learning, problem-solving, object-based learning, role play, brainstorming, etc. (Goutsiukosta 2015; Karamitropoulos 2017; Meliadou et al. 2011, Serafeim and Fesakis 2010; Tsilimeni 2007; Robin and Pierson 2005; etc.).

For the case of individuals and groups with a migrant biography, digital storytelling is a multimodal text and a multimodal tool that encourages – amongst other things – learning the language of the host country (Bull and Kajder 2005; Lathem 2005; Matthews-DeNatale 2008; Meadows 2003), in a meaningful, engaging, motivating and joyful environment. In this context, individuals and groups with a migrant biography are invited to participate in the learning processes and to be actively engaged in the various experiences concerning the additional language, e.g. to watch, to observe, to locate, to hear, to perceive, to repeat, to express, to feel, to create, etc. (Fokidis et al. 2016; Robin et al. 2011).

4 Digital Storytelling Initiatives Targeting Individuals and Groups with a Migrant Biography

In the course of the metasynthesis that is being conducted for the purposes of the present study, digital storytelling emerges as prevalent practice in decisions taken regarding the design and implementation of initiatives targeting migrant learners. In the course of the methasynthesis, where qualitative data went through a thematic analysis from a metasynthesis lens (Barnett-Page and Thomas 2009; Finfgeld 2003; Finlayson and Dixon 2008; Sandelowski and Barroso 2007; Thomas and Harden 2008; Walsh and Downe 2005, etc.), digital storytelling has either a primary or a secondary role to play in (the additional) language learning environments. Data collection included the five (5) projects' interim and final reports (totaling 10 reports) which referred to negotiations, discussions, choices and decision-making on the procedures followed for the implementation of the actions/activities of the projects, as well as the material produced (e.g. detailed programs, guides, training platforms, activities, etc.).

The selected projects, where digital storytelling emerges as good practice for (additional) language learning, are briefly introduced below. The role of digital storytelling is explained, with the skills practices or fostered, in each case, being noted:

i.   *i.e.-EVALINTO –Evaluation environment for fostering intercultural mentoring tools and practices at school* [Project number: 2016-1-ES01-KA201-025145] – https://evalinto.eu

e-EVALINTO aims at intercultural education and good practices on inclusion and it targets populations with migrant biography. Digital storytelling is presented as an option and it used for better comprehension, expression, decision-making as well as enjoyment.

ii. *MEDIS – Mediterranean Inclusive Schools* [Project number: 592206-EPP-1-2017-1-ES-EPPKA3-IPI-SOC-IN] – https://medisinclusiveschools.eu/

MEDIS project aims to collect best practices for the inclusion of populations with a migrant biography in the school context and beyond. Digital storytelling is prevalent in several activities for the purposes of enhancing comprehension, motivation and active participation.

iii. *ODISSEU – Online gaming and Digital tools to promote the asylum seekers Integration and increase awareneSS amongst schools of the refugees' crisis in Europe* [Project number: 2018-1-IT02-KA201-048187] – https://odisseu-project.eu/en/

ODISSEU project focuses on digital literacy and digital storytelling as a tool for cultivating and promoting inclusive and equality attitudes and behaviors, targeting populations with migrant biographies.

iv. *SOFIE –Support for Empowerment and Integration of Refugee Families* [Project number: 2017-1-AT01-KA204-035083] – https://support-refugees.eu/

SOFIE project encouraged mothers and children to learn the host community language in meaningful, motivating and joyful ways. Mothers and children were invited to interact and co-learn an additional language in environments where digital storytelling played a key role in comprehension, active participation and having fun.

v.   *VALUE – Valuing all Languages to Unlock Europe* [Project number: 2015-1-IT02-KA201-015407] – http://www.valuemultilingualism.org/index.php/en/

VALUE project focused on good practices for learning European languages. Digital storytelling was amongst other choices a good teaching practice selected to foster the learning of the additional language to speakers of other languages with migrant backgrounds.

5 Methodology

For the purposes of the present study, meta-synthesis was used as a method of qualitative research. Metasynthesis is the systematic review of qualitative data for the purposes of analysis and interpretation. It is a secondary research, as it focuses on the analysis of data that has been collected in advance, since it is qualitative-oriented research data deriving from previous research or surveys. In the framework of this qualitative research approach, the researcher identifies a specific research question (or questions) and then examines it by searching, selecting, evaluating, summarizing and combining existing data (Barnett-Page and Thomas 2009; Finfgeld 2003; Finlayson and Dixon 2008; Sandelowski and Barroso 2007; Thomas and Harden 2008; Walsh and Downe 2005; etc.).

In the context of meta-synthesis what takes place is the opposite of what happens in meta-analysis. The researcher focuses on qualitative data and evidence, rather than quantitative, in order to answer the research question (or questions) set and make sense of the issue (or issues) under investigation. It is a contemporary approach to qualitative-oriented research, which first appeared in the eighties (1980s) in the medical science literature (Khan et al. 2007; Knowles 2014; Lachal et al. 2017; etc.) and an innovation in educational research (Au 2007; Camilli-Trujilio and Romer-Pieretti 2017; Cobb 2009; Erwin 2011; Forness 2001; Miller 2013; etc.) and research in the social sciences (Achterbergh et al. 2020; Altree 2005; Lachal et al. 2015; McKenna-Plumley et al. 2020). Basic research processes and practices of meta-synthesis refer to critical review (Dixon-Woods 2007; France et al. 2014; Hannes and Macaitis 2012; Stansfield 2014; etc.), to meta-ethnography (Atkins et al. 2008; Lee et al. 2014; Noblit and Hare 1988; etc.) and to process-oriented research (e.g. Vandenbussche 2018) Metasynthesis paves the way for in-depth research and in-depth analysis and interpretation, and for results aimed at quality management and change, policy-making and sustainability (Finfgeld-Connett 2010; Tong et al. 2012, 2016; etc.).

In the context of this ongoing research, decisions taken in the context of EU-funded language learning-related initiatives that target directly or indirectly individuals or groups with a migrant biography are examined from a metasynthesis perspective. The data investigated, e.g. the interim and final reports on the work done, provide information on a variety of existing (con)texts focusing on good practices in (additional) language teaching and learning, from curricula, guides and training platforms designed and revised, to training resources designed, developed, implemented, updated and evaluated, and many more. These (con)texts reflect the 'whats', 'hows' and 'whys' of the decisions made regarding the selection, the design and the implementations of initiatives that promote opening the language of the host community to migrant target groups. To be more specific, for the purposes of this contribution, where emphasis is given to digital storytelling being a prevalent language teaching and learning good practice revealed, three key research questions linking to the 'whats' the 'hows' and 'whys' are addressed:

1. What is digital storytelling about?
2. How are issues approached?
3. What are the reasons behind the choices regarding digital storytelling?

In this contribution, attempting a meta-critique based on meta-synthesis, the priorities, decisions and actions designed and implemented, with a focus on digital storytelling as a good practice in (additional) language learning-related EU funded projects targeting individuals and groups of a migrant biography, are systematically and critically examined. In what follows, a better understanding on digital storytelling as a practice that enhances effective (additional) language learning will be attempted.

6   Results

During the metasynthesis, the interim and final reports of the five (5) projects under consideration (totaling 10 reference reports) were examined. The metasynthesis-based examination resulted – amongst others – in a variety of examples of digital storytelling activities targeting the language learning of individuals and groups with a migrant biography. During the thematic analysis, data investigated addressed the key research questions and revealed interesting insights into what is selected for design and implementation, how is it designed and implemented and why. To be more specific, the thematic analysis, in the course of metasynthesis, provided a better understanding of the topics (what) that are selected for the digital storytelling, aiming at fostering the individuals' and groups' with a migrant biography language learning, they ways they are approached in the context of digital storytelling (how) and the reasons that lie behind the choices, decisions and implementations (why). In what follows, the results of the metasynthesis conducted addressing primarily digital storytelling are tackled.

6.1   What is Digital Storytelling About?

It goes without saying that digital storytelling addresses the priority and the topic for which each project has been funded, i.e. to foster the migrant target groups' learning of the host community language. Therefore, digital storytelling addresses, to begin with, the basic needs of this target group that include their smooth and effective integration in the host community, language learning, self-confidence, safety and health, etc., which at the same time serves the project and funding agency general and specific priorities. Besides opening pathways for language learning, digital storytelling makes topics and (con)texts (e.g. 'myself', 'my hobbies', 'my family', 'my favourite place'/ 'food'/ 'colour'/ 'star'/ etc.) accessible, easy to approach, to understand and to work with, fostering motivation and engagement.

6.2   How Are Issues Approached in Digital Storytelling?

The strategies of *authenticity* and *familiarity* are used in an attempt to open the language of the host community to individuals and groups of a migrant biography. In the context of digital storytelling, authentic heroes and realia, a background and scenes that resemble the real context as much as possible, and content that does not link to fake situations are chosen. Along with *the authentic, the familiar* is also promoted in an attempt to make the additional language approachable to the target group. Familiar hero figures in terms of appearance, clothing, attitudes, interests, etc., as well as known contexts and situations that the target group may easily understand, identify and engage with, are preferable in the context of digital storytelling for promoting (additional) language learning. These choices serve specific reasons that will be tackled below.

6.3   What are the Reasons for the Choices Concenring Digital Storytelling?

As derives from the metasynthesis carried out in the context of the present research, what lies behind the choices made, in terms of the design and implementation of projects focusing on migrant target groups' host community language learning, is an attempt to create authentic and familiar contexts and situations that are mainly provided in the contexts of digital storytelling. From data collected and analysed, digital storytelling serves the purposes of authenticity and familiarity that are the main reasons that lie behind the choices made for the effective language learning for migrant target groups. Resources and (con)texts promoting the authentic and the familiar emerge as strategies that may foster language learning skills, engagement, motivation, learning in joyful environments, etc. Supporting the real and the known and opposing to what is fake and unknown, emerges as a practice that enhances language learning for migrant target groups, paving the way for meeting their language and other needs (e.g. safety, self-confidence, connectedness, etc.) in the early days (and/ or later) in a host community.

From the metasynthesis conducted for the purposes of the present ongoing research, it is made obvious that choices that concern language learning good practices targeting individuals and groups of a migrant biography are not unjustified. In focusing on digital storytelling as a good practice in the learning of an additional language it emerges that design and implementation choices made are for authenticity and familiarity to be served as key strategies and contexts to foster language learning (and other critical needs), opening new avenues to migrant populations lives in the host community. The key strategies are tackled below.

7   Discussion of Results

According to the findings of the meta-synthesis carried out for the purposes of the present ongoing research, digital storytelling targeting the language learning for individuals and groups with a migrant biography serves pedagogical, cognitive and recreational purposes. Digital storytelling aims to actively involve the target group in question in a variety of learning and entertainment experiences. Digital storytelling takes place in a framework of choices based on strategies of authenticity and familiarity. Though the strategy of authenticity creates avenues for understanding the host community as key to a successful integration, the strategy of familiarity generates some discussions on how authenticity may be fully achieved, since only what is familiar is fostered and what is unfamiliar is left behind.

Examining the reasons behind the choices sheds light to the origins of decision making, where, though attempt is made to mirror the reality in the choices made in the design and implementation of good language learning practices, through practices serving familiarity, parts of the reality, especially those that familiarity will not serve, seem to remain 'blocked', displaying only one part (or some parts) of the real. Besides serving authenticity partly and not fully, familiarity, though fostering engagement and motivation, may also limit the pedagogical, cognitive and recreational functions of digital storytelling and "imprison" its potential as a multi-tool, since its full potentials to serve the authentic will not be made used of. Interestingly, this is also the case with developing materials for children, where the tendency of adults, who feel responsible to always make things clear, easy and enjoyable to children, tend to "underestimate" the abilities of child learners by making choices that protect children from cognitive load and other potential challenges. This tendency links back to the classical times and the Middle Ages, as well as the 13th and 14th century AD with adults, who had the predominant societal power to protect the children from 'the unknown', 'the difficult', 'the impossible' and 'the dangerous' to provide limited choices to children. This limitation links back to the ongoing discussion of power relations in societies and how these influence the making and flow of society and its phenomena. At the same time, it demonstrates the need for an in depth study of the profile of individuals and groups of a migrant biography in order to better understand their potentials. This, along with making use of the full potentials of good practices in addressing their needs (such as digital storytelling in additional language learning, for the case of the present study) will ensure the effectiveness of our support to migrant target groups, paving the way for sustainable migration integration, sustainable communities and sustainable (additional language) teaching and learning practices.

8 Final Thoughts

Undeniably, digital storytelling is a pedagogical, cognitive and entertaining tool in modern educational environments (and beyond), which due to its dynamic role, can improve and meet educational needs and challenges. In this ongoing methasynthesis-oriented qualitative research, an examination of digital storytelling was attempted as a prevalent good practice in learning an additional language. More specifically, the 'whats', 'hows' and 'whys' of digital storytelling choices for the language learning of individuals and groups with a migrant biography were studied in the context of EU-funded educational projects.

This research confirms the timeless contribution of storytelling to acquiring basic learning skills and meeting basic needs, as well as digital storytelling, as a contemporary form of storytelling, resulting from the technological development, in the cultivation of both traditional and contemporary learning skills and in meeting the emerging needs of migrant target groups. Apart from its pedagogical value, both the cognitive and the recreational value came to be visible and the need for making use of digital storytelling at its full potentials emerged.

At times when modern societies are faced with a multitude of economic, pedagogical, social, etc. challenges, it is interesting how digital tools in funded initiatives that are located in cyberspace and are, therefore, universally accessible, turn to provide solutions, answers and perspectives and to serve as an additional literacy good practice option fostering understanding, engagement and joy. Creating spaces for such good practices to be accessible and for methodologies to support their detection and deconstruction for better understanding and implementing these, emerges as critical in planning for sustainable actions.

References

Achterbergh, L., Pitman, A., Birken, M., Pearce, E., Sno, H., Johnson, S.: The experience of loneliness among young people with depression: a qualitative meta-synthesis of the literature. BMC Psychiatry **20**(415), 1–23 (2020). https://doi.org/10.1186/s12888-020-02818-3

Altree, P.: Parenting support in the context of poverty: a meta-synthesis of the qualitative evidence. Health Soc. Care Community **13**(4), 330–337 (2005)

Atkins, S., Lewin, S., Smith, H., Engel, M., Fretheim, A., Volmink, J.: Conducting a meta-ethnography of qualitative literature: lessons learnt. BMC Med. Res. Methodol. **8**(1), 1–10 (2008)

Au, W.: High-stakes testing and curricular control: a qualitative meta-synthesis. Educ. Res. **36**, 258–267 (2007)

Barnett-Page, E., Thomas, J.: Methods for the synthesis of qualitative research: a critical review. BMC Med. Res. Methodol. **9**(59) (2009). https://bmcmedresmethodol.biomedcentral.com/art icles/. Accessed 30 Dec 2009

Benmayor, R.: Digital storytelling as a signature pedagogy for the new humanities. Arts Humanit. High. Educ. **7**(2), 188–204 (2008)

Bull, G., Kajder, S.: Digital storytelling in the language arts classroom. Int. Soc. Technol. Educ. **32**(4), 46–49 (2005)

Burmark, L.: Visual presentations that prompt, flash transform. Media Methods **40**(6), 4–5 (2004)

Camilli-Trujilio, C., Romer-Pieretti, M.: Meta-synthesis of literacy for the empowerment of vulnerable groups. Media Educ. Res. J. **25**(53), 9–18 (2017)

Cobb, B., Lehmann, J., Newman-Gonchar, R., Alwell, M.: Self-determination for students with disabilities: a narrative meta-synthesis. Career Dev. Except. Individ. **32**, 108–114 (2009)

Dixon-Woods, M., Booth, A., Sutton, A.J.: Synthesizing qualitative research: a review of published reports. Qual. Res. **7**, 375–422 (2007)

Erwin, E.J., Brotherson, M.J., Summers, J. A.: Understanding qualitative metasynthesis: issues and opportunities in early childhood intervention research. J. Early Interv. **33**(186) (2011). https://doi.org/10.1177/1053815111425493

Finfgeld-Connett, D.: Generalizability and transferability of meta-synthesis research findings. J. Adv. Nurs. **66**, 246–254 (2010)

Finfgeld, D.: Metasynthesis: the state of art – so far. Qual. Health Res. **13**(7), 893–904 (2003)

Finlayson, K.W., Dixon, A.: Qualitative meta-synthesis: a guide for the novice. Nurse Res. **15**(2), 59–71 (2008)

France, E.F., Ring, N., Thomasm, R., Noyes, J., Maxwell, M., Jepson, R.: A methodological systematic review of what's wrong with meta-ethnography reporting. BMC Med. Res. Methodol. **14**(119), 2–16 (2014)

Forness, S.R.: Special education and related services: what have we learned from meta-analysis? Exceptionality **9**, 185–197 (2001)

Gee, J.P.: What Video Games Have to Teach as About Learning and Literacy?, 1st edn. Palgrave Macmillan, New York (2003)

Green, B.: A literacy project of our own. Engl. Aust. **134**, 25–32 (2002)

Hannes, K., Macaitis, K.: A move to more systematic and transparent approaches in qualitative evidence synthesis: update on a review of published papers. Qual. Res. **12**(4), 402–442 (2012)

Heo, M.: Digital storytelling: an empirical study of the impact of digital storytelling on pre-service teachers' self-efficacy and dispositions towards educational technology. J. Educ. Multimed. Hypermedia **18**(4), 405–428 (2009)

Jakes, D., Brennan, J.: Capturing Stories, capturing lives: an introduction to digital storytelling. Illinois School Library Media Association: Arlington Heights, Illinois (2006). http://www.jak esonline.org/dst_techforum.pdf. Accessed 30 Dec 2020

Khan, N., Bower, P., Rogers, A.: Guided self-help in primary care mental health: meta-synthesis of qualitative studies of patient experience. Br. J. Psychiatry **191**, 206–211 (2007)

Knowles, S.E., et al.: Qualitative meta-synthesis of user experience of computerised therapy for depression and anxiety. PLoS One **9**(1) (2014). https://jour-nals.plos.org/plosone/article?id= 10.1371/journal.pone.0084323. Accessed 30 Dec 2020

Lachal, J., Orri, M., Sibeoni, J., Moro, M.R., Revah-Levy, A.: Metasynthesis of youth suicidal behaviours: perspectives of youth, parents, and health care professionals. PLoS One **10**(5) (2015). https://jour-nals.plos.org/plosone/article?id=10.1371/journal.pone.0127359. Accessed 30 Dec 2020

Lachal, J., Revah-Levy, A., Orri, M., Moro, M.R.: Metasynthesis: an original method to synthesize qualitative literature in psychiatry **8**(269) (2017). https://www.frontiersin.org/articles/10.3389/ fpsyt.2017.00269/full. Accessed 30 Dec 2020

Lambert, J.: Digital Storytelling: Capturing Lives, Creating Community. Digital Diner, Berkeley (2002)

Lathem, S.: Learning communities and digital storytelling: new media for ancient tradition. In: Crawford, C., et al. (eds.), Proceedings of Society for Information Technology Teacher Education International Conference, pp. 2286–2291. AACE, Chesapeake (2005)

Lee, R.P., Hart, R.I., Watson, R.M., Rapley, T.: Qualitative synthesis in practice: some pragmatics of meta-ethnography. Qual. Res. **15**, 334–350 (2014)

Matthews-DeNatale, G.: Digital Storytelling: Tips and Resources. Simmons College, Boston (2008)

McKenna-Plumley, P.E., Groarke, J.M., Turner, R.N., Yang, K.: Experiences of loneliness: a study protocol for a systematic review and thematic synthesis of qualitative literature. Syst. Rev. **9**(1), 1–8 (2020). https://sys-tematicreviewsjournal.biomedcentral.com/articles/10.1186/ s13643-020-01544-x. Accessed 30 Dec 2020

Meadows, D.: Digital storytelling: research-based practice in new media. Vis. Commun. **2**, 189–193 (2003)

Miller, S.M.: A research metasynthesis on digital video composing in classrooms: an evidence-based framework toward a pedagogy for embodied learning. J. Lit. Res. **45**(4), 386–430 (2013)

Miller, S.M., McVee, M. (eds.): Multimodal Composing in Classrooms: Learning and Teaching in the Digital World. Routledge, New York (2012)

Mills, K.A.: A review of the "digital turn" in the new literacy studies. Rev. Educ. Res. **80**, 246–271 (2010)

Murray, J.H.: Hamlet on the Holodeck: The Future of Narrative in Cyberspace. The Free Press, New York (1997)

Noblit, G.W., Hare R.D.: Meta-Ethnography: Synthesizing Qualitative Studies. SAGE, Newbury Park (1988)

Ohler, J.: Digital Storytelling in the Classroom. Corwin Press, Thousand Oaks (2008)

Ohler, J.: The world of digital storytelling. Educ. Leadersh. **63**(4), 44–47 (2006)

Robin, B.: The effective uses of digital storytelling as a teaching and learning tool. In: Flood, J., Heath, S., Lapp, D. (eds.) Handbook of Research on Teaching Literacy through the Communicative and Visual Arts, vol. 2, pp. 429–440. Lawrence Erlbaum Associates, New York (2008)

Robin, B., McNeil, S. Yuksel, P.: Educational uses of digital storytelling around the world. In: Koehler, M., Mishra, P. (eds.) Proceedings of Society for Information Technology & Teacher Education International Conference – SITE 2011, pp. 1264–1271. Nashville, Tennessee, USA: Association for the Advancement of Computing in Education (AACE) (2011)

Robin, B., Pierson, M.: A multilevel approach to using digital storytelling in the classroom. In: Crawford, C., et al. (eds.) Proceedings of Society for Information Technology & Teacher Education International Conference – SITE 2005 (pp. 708–716). Association for the Advancement of Computing in Education (AACE), Chesapeake (2005)

Sadik, A.: Digital storytelling: a meaningful integrated approach for engaged student learning. Educ.Technol. Res. **56**, 487–506 (2008)

Sandelowski, M., Barroso, J.: Handbook for Synthesizing Qualitative Research. Springer, New York (2007)

Sandelowski, M., Docherty, S., Emden, C.: Qualitative meta-synthesis: Issues and techniques. Res. Nurs. Health **20**(4), 365–371 (1997)

Sarica, H.Ç., Usluel, Y.K.: The effect of digital storytelling on visual memory and writing skills. Comput. Educ. **94**, 298–309 (2016)

Sawhney, N.: Voices beyond walls: the role of digital storytelling for empowering marginalized youth in refugee camps. In: ACM Proceedings of the 8th International Conference on Interaction Design and Children, pp. 302–305. Association for Computing Machinery, New York (2009)

Smeda, N., Dakich, E., Sharda, N.: The effectiveness of digital storytelling in the classrooms: a comprehensive study. Smart Learn. Environ. **1**(1), 1–21 (2014). https://doi.org/10.1186/s40 561-014-0006-3

Stansfield, C., Brunton, G., Rees, R.: Search wide, dig deep: literature searching for qualitative research. An analysis of the publication formats and information sources used for four systematic reviews in public health. Res. Synth. Methods **5**(2), 142–151 (2014)

Suwardy, S., Pan, G., Seow, P.-S.: Using digital storytelling to engage student learning. Acc. Educ. **22**(2), 109–124 (2013)

Thomas, J., Harden, A.: Methods for the thematic synthesis of qualitative research in systematic reviews. BMC Med. Res. Methodol. **8**(45), 1–10 (2008). https://bmcmedresmethodol.biomed central.com/articles/https://bmcmedresmethodol.biomedcentral.com/arti-cles/10.1186/1471-2288-8-45. Accessed 30 Dec 2020

Tong., A., Flemming, K., McInnes, E., Oliver, S., Craig, J.: Enhancing transparency in reporting the synthesis of qualitative research: ENTREQ. BMC Med. Res. Methodol. **12**(181) (2012). https://bmcmedresmeth-odol.biomedcentral.com/articles/10.1186/1471-2288-12-181. Accessed 30 Dec 2020

Tong, A., Palmer, S., Craig, J.C., Strippoli, G.F.M.: A guide to reading and using systematic reviews of qualitative research. Nephrol. Dial. Transplant. **31**(6), 897–903 (2016)

Vandenbussche, L., Edelenbos, J., Eshuis, J.: Plunging into the process: methodological reflections on a process-oriented study of stakeholders' relating dynamics. Crit. Policy Stud. **14**(1), 1–20 (2018). https://www.tandfonline.com/doi/full/10.1080/19460171.2018.1488596. Accessed 30 Dec 2020

Walsh, D., Downe, S.: Meta-synthesis method for qualitative research: a literature review. J. Adv. Nurs. **50**(2), 204–211 (2005)

Yuksel-Arslan, P., Yildirim, S., Robin, R.B.: A phenomenological study: teachers' experiences of using digital storytelling in early childhood education. Educ. Stud. **42**(5), 427–445 (2016). http://digitalstorytelling.coe.uh.edu/survey/SITE_DigitalStorytelling.pdf. Accessed 30 Dec 2020

e-EVALINTO – Evaluation environment for fostering intercultural mentoring tools and practices at school, Project number: 2016-1-ES01-KA201-025145. https://evalinto.eu/. Accessed 30 Dec 2020

MEDIS – Mediterranean Inclusive Schools, Project number: 592206-EPP-1-2017-1-ES-EPPKA3-IPI-SOC-IN. https://medisinclusiveschools.eu/. Accessed 30 Dec 2020

ODISSEU – Online gaming and Digital tools to promote the asylum seekers Integration and increase awareneSS amongst schools of the refugees' crisis in Europe, Project number: 2018-1-IT02-KA201-048187. https://odisseu-project.eu/en/. Accessed 30 Dec 2020

SOFIE – Support for Empowerment and Integration of Refugee Families, Project number: 2017-1-AT01-KA204-035083. https://support-refugees.eu/. Accessed 30 Dec 2020

VALUE – Valuing all Languages to Unlock Europe, Project number: 2015-1-IT02-KA201-015407. http://www.valuemultilingualism.org/index.php/en/. Accessed 30 Dec 2020

SketchMeHow: Interactive Projection Guided Task Instruction with User Sketches

Haoran Xie$^{(\boxtimes)}$ (ID), Yichen Peng (ID), Hange Wang, and Kazunori Miyata (ID)

Japan Advanced Institute of Science and Technology, Ishikawa 9231292, Japan
xie@jaist.ac.jp

Abstract. In this work, we propose an interactive general instruction framework SketchMeHow to guidance the common users to complete the daily tasks in real-time. In contrast to the conventional augmented reality-based instruction systems, the proposed framework utilizes the user sketches as system inputs to acquire the users' production intentions from the drawing interfaces. Given the user sketches, the designated task instruction can be analyzed based on the subtask division and spatial localization for each task. The projector-camera system is adopted in the projection guidance to the end-users with the spatial augmented reality technology. To verify the proposed framework, we conducted two case studies of domino arrangement and bento production. From our user studies, the proposed systems can help novice users complete the tasks efficiently with user satisfaction. We believe the proposed SketchMeHow can broaden the research topics in sketch-based real-world applications in human-computer interaction.

Keywords: User sketch · Spatial augmented reality · Projector camera system · User guidance · Task instruction

1 Introduction

In our daily lives, numerous tasks required special skills or adequate experience, which usually frustrate the common and amateur users to make any attempt. In addition, the daily tasks may be tedious and complex procedures, and it is difficult and challenging to conduct creative activities. In the research fields of creativity support in human-computer interaction, the previous works mainly focused on the graphical user interface in the computer environment. In this work, we aim to help the common user to complete the designated tasks under the computed guidance in real-world applications.

To solve this issue, the common approaches are spatial computing techniques of instruction systems in a workspace, such as augmented reality approaches with head-mounted display and projection, see-through displays such as tablet [2, 12]. Considering the system stability and cognitive loads of the instruction systems, we adopt the spatial augmented reality technology with projector-camera system

© Springer Nature Switzerland AG 2021
C. Stephanidis et al. (Eds.): HCII 2021, LNCS 13096, pp. 513–527, 2021.
https://doi.org/10.1007/978-3-030-90328-2_35

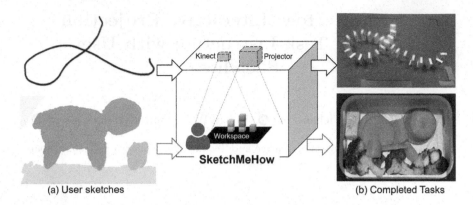

(a) User sketches   (b) Completed Tasks

Fig. 1. The proposed interaction framework of SketchMeHow.

[5]. Especially, the depth camera was used for sensing the depth information for instruction generation rather than the standard web cameras. In the previous instruction works [5,23], the users are asked to complete the designated task with the given target where the requirement of satisfying the users' design intention is absent. In this work, we combine the creativity support and instruction systems to help users to conduct tasks with their own designs. To achieve this research purpose, we utilized the freehand user sketches as system input which are difficult to be handled due to the ambiguous and abstract visual representations.

Therefore, we propose an interactive instruction system, SketchMeHow that can provide the users with projection-based guidance in real-time with spatial augmented reality technique. As shown in Fig. 1, the system input of SketchMe-How may include freehand line drawing or color illustration. With the help of user guidance in projector-camera systems, the completed tasks can be achieved at low time costs and high success rates.

To verify the proposed SketchMeHow framework, we conducted two usage applications for task instruction from user sketches: domino block arrangement and bento production. In the block arrangement system, the stroke input is analyzed with the individual block, and the gradient colors are projected on the blocks for guiding the correct positions. Finally, the domino blocks can be collapsed successfully. In the bento production system, we adopt both stroke and color of user sketches as input. The food ingredients are recommended based on user input and arranged with the projected color guidance. The accomplished bento is in compliance with the user sketches well. From our user study and subjective questionnaires, we verified that the proposed framework of Sketch-MeHow can provide the interactive projection guidance to help non-skilled users to complete theirs desired target in specific tasks. The proposed systems are effective and useful compared with the conventional approaches without guidance. We believe SketchMeHow can facilitate sketch-based systems for real-world applications.

2   Related Work

2.1   Sketch-Based Interface

Freehand sketches can present the users' design intention and have been adopted intensively in two-dimensional content design. Teddy proposed the sketch-based interface to construct 3D polygonal models from freehand drawn sketches [11]. A sketch-based interface was usually adopted in the image and shape retrieval [3] and drawing guidance [26]. Recently, the deep learning algorithms were widely developed in the sketch user interface, such as facial image editing [19] and drawing [10], anime image editing [15], image translation [6] and normal map estimation [7]. Besides static applications of image editing, the physical dynamics were controlled with user sketches such as hair [27] and fluid [9]. In this work, we especially focus on the sketch interfaces for task instructions with augmented reality approaches.

2.2   Sketch-Based Guidance

It is challenging and useful to adopt the sketch-based design for real-world applications with interactive user guidance. Sketch and run used the sketch-based interface for robot control based on a top-down camera view [21]. Lighty proposed the guidance system of room lights by sketching a target illumination area on tablet devices [16]. However, these proposed systems were designed for automatic machine control where the user guidance was absent such task instruction. To solve this issue, Sketch2Domino proposed a sketch-based guidance system for domino toppling production [17]. Sketch2Bento proposed the guide system for ingredient arrangement of designing lunch boxes [24]. In this work, we aim to propose a general instruction framework for sketch-based user guidance in real-world applications.

2.3   Projection-Based Guidance

The spatial augmented reality adopts interactive projection for various real-world applications. Illuminating clay was proposed as a tangible interface for landscape design [18], Flagg et al. worked on the implementation to guide oil painting using the projection techniques [4]. There are several works to adopt projection-based guidance in fabrication purposes, such as sculpting [20]. For large-scale fabrication, BalloonFab guided the user to create the large-scale balloon art [25]. A similar approach was used in newspaper sculpture [14]. For daily activities, the projection guidance can also be helpful in solving the puzzle of Rubik's cubes [1], calligraphy practice [8], and sports training [22]. For room-scale projection, Roomalive was proposed for multiple projector-camera systems [13]. In contrast to these projection-based guidance approaches, we first adapt user sketches as system control to meet user design intentions.

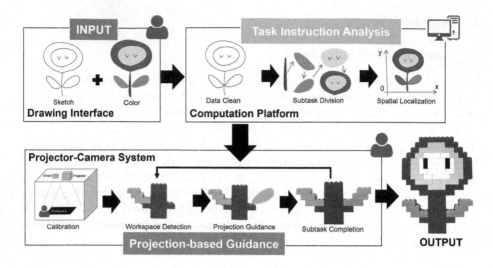

Fig. 2. The proposed interaction framework of SketchMeHow.

3   Framework Overview

Figure 2 shows the proposed framework of SketchMeHow which is composed of three modules on the separated platforms: system input, task instruction analysis, and projection-based guidance. For the input module, a drawing user interface is developed with the stoke and coloring function with pen-based interaction on a tablet or real workspace. For the task instruction analysis module, the input hand-drawn sketches are cleaned with stroke smoothing to exclude the infeasible instructions. According to the requirements of specific works, we divide the whole sketch instruction into separated sub-tasks with the elemental objects, such as individual blocks in element construction. Finally, the locations of each task object are calculated based on the subtasks. For the projection-based guidance module, we adopt the projector-camera system with the depth camera. The system calibration is conducted based on multi-pin correction to adjust the projector and camera coordinates. Then, the current workspace is detected with depth differences from the captured depth maps. With the calculated task instruction, the guidance information is projected onto the workspace overlapped with the calculated operations. After the iterative processes of subtasks, the desired productions can be achieved with guidance.

3.1   Drawing Interface

The sketching interface can be developed based on the graphical user interface or tangible physical interface. The examples of user interfaces are shown in Fig. 3. For the graphical drawing interface, the canvas is used for stroke-based interaction as Fig. 3(a). Besides the canvas, the user can select tools from the toolbars includes pencil, eraser, line, and different shapes. In addition, the user can select

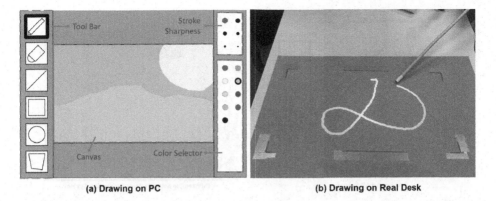

(a) Drawing on PC   (b) Drawing on Real Desk

Fig. 3. Drawing interface can be implemented as graphical user interface on computer (a) or the 3D spatial interface on real desk (b).

the stroke sharpness and stroke color. For the physical drawing interface, it is convenient for the user to draw with a pen-type input device. A simple solution is to use the retro-reflective marker on the pen tip in a depth camera-projector system as Figure Fig. 3(b). In our case studies, we implemented both graphical and physical drawing interfaces in the SketchMeHow framework.

3.2   Spatial Augmented Reality

Due to the absence of head-mounted devices, it is more convenient in instruction guidance systems using interactive projection [5]. As shown in Fig. 4(a), a projector-Camera System is usually adopted in the setup of spatial augmented reality system. The analyzed results from the drawing interface are projected on the workspace. In the prototype systems in our case study, we used a depth camera to capture the depth map or image recognition in infrared frames. An example setup of the proposed system is shown in Fig. 4(b). We used the pinpoints tool to ensure the appropriate calibration of projector-camera system.

3.3   User Guidance

In our prototype systems, the depth data of captured depth map is used to guide the arrangement of instruction elements. For the projector calibration, the guidance image projected onto the workspace is distorted to match the coordinates of the depth view. In addition, we stored the pixel positions for each color in the scaled guidance image to provide guidance for each sub-tasks. The guidance image is projected onto the workspace with different colors to help complete tasks as shown in Fig. 5(a). We map the stored color list to the depth data to obtain the areas, and the user can place the objects under the corresponding tasks. For example, a black color denotes the area where the object should not be placed. In addition, the green color refers to the correct placement, and the red color

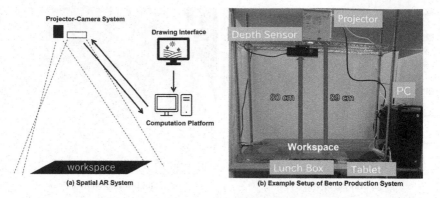

Fig. 4. Spatial augmented reality system (a); an example setup for bento design (b).

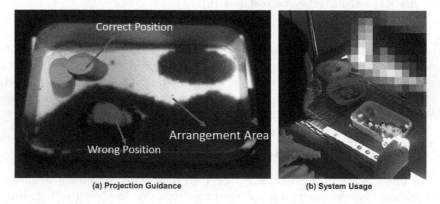

Fig. 5. Projection guidance for task instruction (a) and the system usage of the proposed SketchMeHow framework with bento production (b). (Color figure online)

for incorrect placement. An example of the usage of the proposed instruction system is shown in Fig. 5(b).

4   Case Study

To verify the proposed SketchMeHow framework, we conducted two case studies of domino arrangement and bento production.

4.1   Domino Arrangement

To support designing a complex chain reaction such as domino blocks, we implemented a sketch-based instruction system for the domino placement according to the user customized sketch in this case study [17]. The prototype system applied interactive projection-mapping technology to guide users to places the domino blocks. Users were allowed to design the blueprint of the arrangement

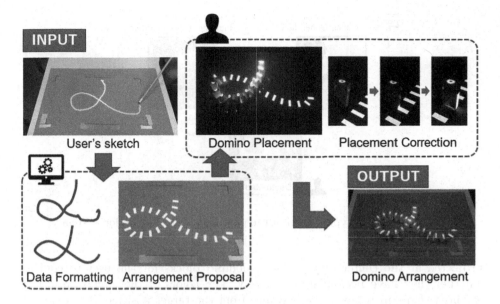

Fig. 6. The prototype system of the proposed domino arrangement system.

by the freehand sketches without considering the physical limitations of domino placement following the rules of chain reaction.

System Overview. As shown in Fig. 6, users can draw the sketch for the intention design of the domino arrangement. The proposed system analyzed the stroke data of input sketches to make the domino blocks collapse successfully in a valid arrangement where the vertices are excessively dense or the angles are quite acute. After that, the users can locate the domino blocks following the projection guidance to confirm the target positions.

System Environment. Similar to the example setup in Fig. 4, we set the working space (70 cm-high desk) with a laser projector (LG HF80JG, 2000 lumen), and a depth camera (Microsoft Kinect V2, the resolution of depth image is 512 × 424). The projector and camera were set vertically 85.1 cm and 77.8 cm above the desk. The size of the projection area was 57.2 cm × 32.1 cm. In this study, standard domino blocks (23 mm wide, 46 mm high and 8 mm thick) were used which was certified by the Japan Domino Association.

Projection Guidance. The users can use a pen stick with the marker to draw a sketch directly on the projection area. The arrangement proposal according to the drawn target is projected as visual guidance of the valid domino's positions, so that the user can arrange the domino blocks in the order following the design. For the correction of the valid domino's position, a gradient-colored circle is

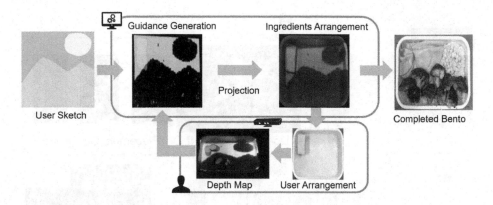

Fig. 7. The prototype system of the proposed bento production system.

projected at the center of the placed domino blocks for the user to confirm whether they have been placed correctly. The colors of the circles are set in gradient colors in terms of the distance from the target position. The circle on the top of the block is in red color if the distance is larger than 2.0 cm from the target position. The circle turns yellow about 1 cm away. The circle turns green when is correctly placed. Note that the target positions of domino are shown by white rectangles from the beginning.

User Study. We conducted a comparison study to verify the effectiveness of the proposed system. We compared the domino arrangement with and without the proposed system. In conventional approach without the systems, the participants were asked to place the domino blocks following the hand-drawn sketches on a printed paper without explicit guidance on the intervals between the domino blocks. The criterion for a successful design was that all the domino blocks could collapsed with one simple push. 12 graduate student participants (11 males, 1 female) joined the comparison study.

For our prototype system, the participants were asked to arrange the domino blocks with the help of the visual guidance. The user can start the arrangement from any location, because the arrangement order is non-trivial. Note that we adopted the same blueprint design used in the conventional approach. Both operational time costs and the results were recorded. In addition, we conducted a questionnaire for the subjective evaluations of the prototype system. The questionnaire had four questions: a) Which approach is easier for arranging domino blocks? b) Which perfection do you have confidence in? c) Which result gave you a sense of accomplishment? d) Which approach was more interesting?

4.2   Bento Production

In this case study, we implemented an ingredient placement support system for bento (lunch box) production based on the user hand-drawn sketches [24]. The prototype system allows users to make the bento following creative intentions without relying on existing recipes.

System Overview. As illustrated in Fig. 7, the user first sketches the desired arrangement image with the drawing interface. Then, the system provides the projection guidance to lunch box from the sketch input. Under the help of the production guidance, the user can complete the ingredient arrangement for desired bento. Finally, the real-time guidance is achieved based on the current working progress.

System Environment. As shown in Fig. 4, we set the similar setup for domino arrangement where the desk height is 77 cm, a projector (EPSON dreamio EF-100, 2000 lumen), a Kinect V2 depth camera, and a pen tablet (Wacom Intous CTL-6100WL). The projector was placed 89 cm above the desk, while the height of camera was 80cm. The size of the lunch box was 20 cm × 13.5 cm × 4 cm. Because the light reflection may influence the captured infrared image, we placed a kitchen paper inside the box. We adjusted the canvas size of drawing interface to match the size ratio of the lunch box to be used. We set the canvas size to be 600px × 405px as shown in Fig. 3.

Projection Guidance. The color selection is decided according to the colors of the prepared food ingredients. We investigated the common food ingredients which are often used in character bento production and determined the color of the ingredients correlated to the sketch. The ingredients used in the prototype system were broccoli, fried egg, crab stick, and sausage. Therefore, the drawing interface allows the use of green, yellow, orange, and pink colors according to the above ingredients.

We use the depth sensor to detect the positions of food ingredients placed by the user. The depth map of the workspace without any ingredients is used as the environment map. In the comparison with the depth map with food ingredients, the environment map is excluded for noisy data. In our implementation, we decided the depth difference of 8.0 mm as the threshold value to detect the placement of food ingredients. If 70% of the projected color area has been filled with food ingredients, the arrangement is considered to be correct with the projected green color. On the contrary, the red color will be projected when the ingredients are placed outside of the target area. The arrangement is considered to be completed if the area of red color is less than 20% of the non-target area. The arrangement area then switches to the next step with a different color. If the subtasks of all colors are completed, a white color is projected.

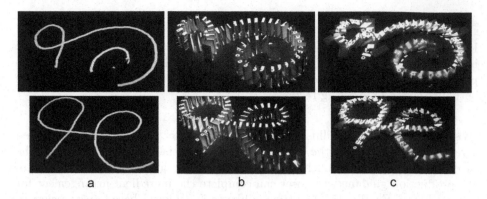

Fig. 8. The collapsed results (c) of domino arrangement (b) under user sketches (a).

User Study. We conducted a comparison study to verify the effectiveness of the arrangement support with the prototype system. 12 participants were recruited in two groups: Group A with the proposed system; Group B without the proposed system. All the participants were asked to arrange a lunch box. We evaluated the time costs and the levels of completion with a questionnaire in five-point scale ("did you complete your lunch box the way you wanted?"). For Group B, the participants created bento by drawing the blueprint on paper as a reference. For Group A, the participants used the guidance of the proposed system. All the participants were asked to fill a questionnaire about the sketching interface and the arrangement support system after the task. In our questionnaire survey, we designed three questions items with 5-Point Likert scale (1 for strongly disagree, 5 for strongly agree). The questions include: Q1: Did you follow the guidance?; Q2: Easy to observe the guidance; Q3: Easy to understand the guidance.

5   Results

In this section, the task instruction and evaluation results of two case studies developed in SketchMeHow framework are discussed, and we explore the further potential application with the proposed framework.

5.1   Domino Arrangement

Figure 8 shows the final arrangements of the domino matched the participants' sketches well. The operational time cost of with/without the domino arrangement system is shown in Fig. 9(a). The average time cost using our system was 140 s (min 109 s, max 185 s). The average time cost without the system was 155 s (min 88 s, max 231 s). The variation and average of the processing time costs were reduced using the proposed system. We counted the number of participants who accidentally knocked down the domino blocks during arrangement which had 4 using the proposed system, and 8 without the system. Therefore, it is verified that SketchMeHow can not only shorten the arrangement time cost but also provide stability.

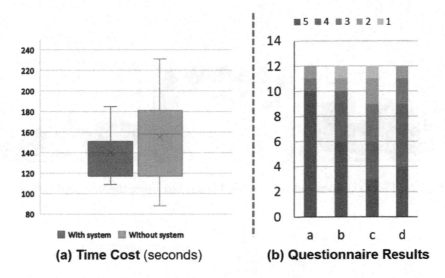

(a) Time Cost (seconds)   **(b) Questionnaire Results**

Fig. 9. Arrangement time cost (a) and the results of questionnaire (b).

Figure 9(b) shows the results of the questionnaire in 5-Point Likert scale with the prototype system. It is verified that the proposed system has higher evaluation than without the system except for question c). In the case of the sense of accomplishment, the visual guidance that asked the participants to follow the projected positions may make participants feel boring. This issue can be improved by providing users more freedom of the modification in stroke drawing and domino blocks arrangement.

5.2   Bento Production

Figure 10 shows examples of bento produced in the proposed SketchMeHow framework. Figure 11 shows the comparison results of production time cost of with/without the proposed system and level of completion (5 for the highest degree of completion). The average production time cost of Group B is 280.2 s, while that of Group A with the proposed system was 250.6 s. We found that the production time cost decreased with the proposed system. For the level of completion, the average score for Group B was 2.4, while Group A was 3.3. Group B achieved lower scores because the participants had difficulty to arrange ingredients without any guidance. The participant spent more time in production because the participants may hesitate to adjust the positions of ingredients to match the sketch.

Figure 10(c) shows The results of questionnaire that the scores of Q2 (4.1) and Q3 (4.3) were relatively higher than Q1 (3.6), which confirmed most of the

Fig. 10. Users sketches and the arranged bento box using the proposed system.

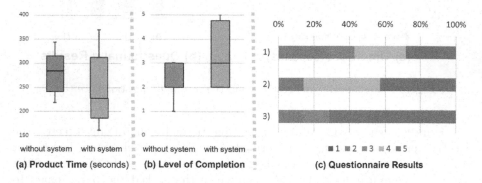

Fig. 11. From left to right: the production time costs (a), level of completion (b), and the questionnaire results (c).

participants were satisfied with the system guidance and the prototype system. Scores for Q1 was above 3.0, so the participants can follow the guidance well. Meanwhile, we found that the size of the lunch box is small and lack of ingredient choice in the study. The user may fail to fit the ingredients to the prompted position due to the inaccuracy between the food size and the prompted area.

5.3   Discussion

Cooperative Instruction System. In contrast to the instruction systems with head-mounted displays and tablets [5,12], SketchMeHow can support not only individual use and also cooperative working styles. It is possible for multiple users to collaborate in sketch drawing and task completion.

Real World Applications. Not limited to the prototype systems developed in this work, we believe various real world applications may benefit from the proposed SketchMeHow framework, such as assembly tasks of hand craft and furniture construction, and fabrication work of hand-made objects and arts.

Large Scale System. In our case study, the desk-based tasks were adopted for framework verification. However, it is also feasible to support large scale instruction system, such as architecture-scale fabrication. For large-scale systems, the volumetric projection calibration may be required for accurate visual guidance, such as layered projection mapping technique [25].

6   Conclusion

In this work, we proposed an general sketch-based task instruction framework, SketchMeHow with the users' hand-drawn sketches as system inputs. The framework consists of the drawing interfaces in graphical and physical styles, the computation platform for task analysis, and the projection guidance with a projector-camera systems. To verify the proposed SketchMeHow framework, we conducted two case studies of domino arrangement and bento production. In terms of the user studies in two prototype systems, it is verified that SketchMeHow framework can help novice users in task instruction in low computation cost and high completion levels. The participants were satisfied with the usage and visual guidance provided by the prototype systems.

Based on the free comments in our case studies, the participants reported that the accuracy of recognition should be improved. In future, we plan to adopt depth sensor with higher resolution of depth images than the Kinect, such as the RealSense D455 depth camera. We believe that a higher resolution depth sensor can also reduce the noise data in prototype implementation. Under the SketchMeHow framework, the instruction system with user sketches can improve both the work efficiency and user satisfaction of our daily activities.

Acknowledgement. The authors thank the anonymous reviewers for their valuable comments. We greatly thank Yuki Mishima, Yamato Igarashi, Ryoma Miyauchi, Masahiro Okawa, Haruka Kanayama, Shogo Yoshida, Shogo Okada for idea discussion and experiment design. We would thank Ze Wang for sharing the codes of drawer interface. This project has been partially funded by JAIST Research Grant, Hayao Nakayama Foundation for Science & Technology and Culture Grant A and JSPS KAKENHI grant JP20K19845, Japan.

References

1. Ajisaka, S., et al.: Learning Rubik's cube through user operation history. In: 2020 Nicograph International (NicoInt), pp. 43–46. IEEE (2020). https://doi.org/10.1109/NicoInt50878.2020.00015
2. Blattgerste, J., Renner, P., Strenge, B., Pfeiffer, T.: In-situ instructions exceed side-by-side instructions in augmented reality assisted assembly. In: Proceedings of the 11th PErvasive Technologies Related to Assistive Environments Conference, PETRA 2018, pp. 133–140. Association for Computing Machinery, New York (2018). https://doi.org/10.1145/3197768.3197778

3. Eitz, M., Richter, R., Boubekeur, T., Hildebrand, K., Alexa, M.: Sketch-based shape retrieval. ACM Trans. Graph. (TOG) **31**(4), 31:1–31:10 (2012). https://doi.org/10.1145/2185520.2185527
4. Flagg, M., Rehg, J.M.: Projector-guided painting. In: Proceedings of the 19th Annual ACM Symposium on User Interface Software and Technology, pp. 235–244 (2006). https://doi.org/10.1145/1166253.1166290
5. Funk, M., Kosch, T., Schmidt, A.: Interactive worker assistance: comparing the effects of in-situ projection, head-mounted displays, tablet, and paper instructions, UbiComp 2016, pp. 934–939. Association for Computing Machinery, New York (2016). https://doi.org/10.1145/2971648.2971706
6. Ghosh, A., et al.: Interactive sketch & fill: multiclass sketch-to-image translation. In: Proceedings of the IEEE International Conference on Computer Vision (ICCV), pp. 1171–1180. IEEE, Long Beach (2019). https://doi.org/10.1109/ICCV.2019.00126
7. He, Y., Xie, H., Zhang, C., Yang, X., Miyata, K.: Sketch-based normal map generation with geometric sampling. In: Nakajima, M., Kim, J.G., Lie, W.N., Kemao, Q. (eds.) International Workshop on Advanced Imaging Technology (IWAIT) 2021, vol. 11766, pp. 261–266. International Society for Optics and Photonics, SPIE (2021). https://doi.org/10.1117/12.2590760
8. He, Z., Xie, H., Miyata, K.: Interactive projection system for calligraphy practice. In: 2020 Nicograph International (NicoInt), pp. 55–61 (2020).https://doi.org/10.1109/NicoInt50878.2020.00018
9. Hu, Z., Xie, H., Fukusato, T., Sato, T., Igarashi, T.: Sketch2VF: sketch-based flow design with conditional generative adversarial network. Comput. Anim. Virtual Worlds **30**(3–4), e1889 (2019). https://doi.org/10.1002/cav.1889
10. Huang, Z., et al.: dualFace: two-stage drawing guidance for freehand portrait sketching. Comput. Vis. Media (2021). https://doi.org/10.1007/s41095-021-0227-7
11. Igarashi, T., Matsuoka, S., Tanaka, H.: Teddy: a sketching interface for 3D freeform design. In: Proceedings of the 26th Annual Conference on Computer Graphics and Interactive Techniques (SIGGRAPH), pp. 409–416. ACM, New York (1999). https://doi.org/10.1145/311535.311602
12. Jasche, F., Hoffmann, S., Ludwig, T., Wulf, V.: Comparison of different types of augmented reality visualizations for instructions. In: Proceedings of the 2021 CHI Conference on Human Factors in Computing Systems, CHI 2021. Association for Computing Machinery, New York (2021). https://doi.org/10.1145/3411764.3445724
13. Jones, B., et al.: RoomAlive: magical experiences enabled by scalable, adaptive projector-camera units. In: Proceedings of the 27th Annual ACM Symposium on User Interface Software and Technology, UIST 2014, pp. 637–644. Association for Computing Machinery, New York (2014). https://doi.org/10.1145/2642918.2647383
14. Li, S., et al.: Skeleton-based interactive fabrication for large-scale newspaper sculpture. In: 2021 Nicograph International (NicoInt). IEEE (2021). https://doi.org/10.1109/NICOINT52941.2021.00021
15. Luo, S., Xie, H., Miyata, K.: Sketch-based anime hairstyle editing with generative inpainting. In: 2021 Nicograph International (NicoInt). IEEE (2021). https://doi.org/10.1109/NICOINT52941.2021.00009
16. Noh, S., Hashimoto, S., Yamanaka, D., Kamiyama, Y., Inami, M., Igarashi, T.: Design and enhancement of painting interface for room lights. Vis. Comput. **30**(5), 467–478 (2013). https://doi.org/10.1007/s00371-013-0872-7

17. Peng, Y., et al.: Sketch2Domino: interactive chain reaction design and guidance. In: 2020 Nicograph International (NicoInt), pp. 32–38. IEEE (2020). https://doi.org/10.1109/NicoInt50878.2020.00013

18. Piper, B., Ratti, C., Ishii, H.: Illuminating clay: a 3-D tangible interface for landscape analysis. In: Proceedings of the SIGCHI Conference on Human Factors in Computing Systems, CHI 2002, pp. 355–362. Association for Computing Machinery, New York (2002). https://doi.org/10.1145/503376.503439

19. Portenier, T., Hu, Q., Szabó, A., Bigdeli, S.A., Favaro, P., Zwicker, M.: FaceShop: deep sketch-based face image editing. ACM Trans. Graph. (TOG) **37**(4) (2018). https://doi.org/10.1145/3197517.3201393

20. Rivers, A., Adams, A., Durand, F.: Sculpting by numbers. ACM Trans. Graph. **31**(6) (2012). https://doi.org/10.1145/2366145.2366176

21. Sakamoto, D., Honda, K., Inami, M., Igarashi, T.: Sketch and run: a stroke-based interface for home robots. In: Proceedings of the SIGCHI Conference on Human Factors in Computing Systems, CHI 2009, pp. 197–200. Association for Computing Machinery, New York (2009). https://doi.org/10.1145/1518701.1518733

22. Sano, Y., Sato, K., Shiraishi, R., Otsuki, M.: Sports support system: augmented ball game for filling gap between player skill levels. In: Proceedings of the 2016 ACM International Conference on Interactive Surfaces and Spaces, pp. 361–366 (2016). https://doi.org/10.1145/2992154.2996781

23. Smith, E., Semple, G., Evans, D., McRae, K., Blackwell, P.: Augmented instructions: analysis of performance and efficiency of assembly tasks. In: Chen, J.Y.C., Fragomeni, G. (eds.) HCII 2020. LNCS, vol. 12191, pp. 166–177. Springer, Cham (2020). https://doi.org/10.1007/978-3-030-49698-2_12

24. Wang, H., Kanayama, H., Peng, Y., Xie, H., Okada, S., Miyata, K.: Sketch2bento: Sketch-based arrangement guidance for lunch boxes. In: 2021 Nicograph International (NicoInt). IEEE (2021). https://doi.org/10.1109/NICOINT52941.2021.00032

25. Xie, H., Peng, Y., Chen, N., Xie, D., Chang, C.M., Miyata, K.: BalloonFAB: digital fabrication of large-scale balloon art. In: Extended Abstracts of the 2019 CHI Conference on Human Factors in Computing Systems, pp. 1–6 (2019). https://doi.org/10.1145/3290607.3312947

26. Xie, J., Hertzmann, A., Li, W., Winnemöller, H.: PortraitSketch: face sketching assistance for novices. In: Proceedings of the 27th Annual ACM Symposium on User Interface Software and Technology (UIST), pp. 407–417. ACM, New York (2014). https://doi.org/10.1145/2642918.2647399

27. Xing, J., Kazi, R.H., Grossman, T., Wei, L.Y., Stam, J., Fitzmaurice, G.: Energybrushes: interactive tools for illustrating stylized elemental dynamics. In: Proceedings of the 29th Annual Symposium on User Interface Software and Technology, UIST 2016, pp. 755–766. Association for Computing Machinery, New York (2016). https://doi.org/10.1145/2984511.2984585

Cultural Experiences

An Indoor Location-Based AR Framework for Large-Scale Museum Exhibitions

Sumin Ahn and Dongsoo Han[(⊠)]

School of Science, Korea Advanced Institute of Science and Technology, Daejeon, Korea
{smahn,ddsshhan}@kaist.ac.kr

Abstract. New exhibitions using AR technology are emerging in exhibition venues such as museums. As most people carry smartphones, museum visitors can easily enjoy AR exhibitions by using their smartphone cameras. However, most current AR exhibitions operate in an auxiliary form by recognizing the image of the actual exhibit. In this paper, we propose a new AR framework that works with an indoor positioning technique for large-scale museum exhibitions. The proposed system estimates the user's location and guides the AR exhibits available at the location. The results of high accuracy were obtained through the experiment, which shows that it can provide convenient and attractive AR exhibitions to visitors.

Keywords: Indoor positioning · Hidden Markov model · Location-based AR

1 Introduction

As new IT technologies are applied to the exhibition, the convenience of touring the museum is increasing. In particular, a lot of AR contents are exhibited with physical exhibits. The AR contents are mainly provided through applications in smartphones that almost all visitors are holding. Visitors can easily enjoy those contents by just installing an application and looking at exhibits through a smartphone camera. Most of them create an AR object that matches the surrounding exhibits by operating with QR code recognition or image recognition. Because of their mechanism, there have been many problems with practical use in the field. For a seamless AR experience, it is required to have a target image continuously. However, Image recognition is often impossible due to the light reflection of showcases, or an exhibition hall is too dark. There are cases where visitors cannot capture the target image because it is crowded with many people. Another problem is the safety issue. There is a possibility that users will be injured or damage exhibits while focusing on AR contents and walking around carelessly [1].

Meanwhile, indoor location-based services are provided in many exhibition places through applications in smartphones. Indoor positioning technology has been studied to estimate indoor location accurately and quickly by combining various information, such as measurements from sensors mounted on smartphones. Among indoor location-based services, indoor navigation is widely used in many spacious indoor places. However,

C. Stephanidis et al. (Eds.): HCII 2021, LNCS 13096, pp. 531–541, 2021.
https://doi.org/10.1007/978-3-030-90328-2_36

utilization as an exhibition technology for museum contents other than navigation is still insufficient.

In this paper, we propose a new AR exhibition method based on indoor location. The proposed system automatically recognizes the exhibition hall where a user is located, creates an AR object prepared in the exhibition hall, and displays it to the viewers. For indoor positioning, we used Wi-Fi fingerprinting and sensor fusion framework [2]. Figure 1 shows the system architecture. The system consists of three components: Area classification module, AR list extraction module, and an application on a smartphone. Unlike existing AR applications based on image recognition, the user first needs to request indoor location estimation. In this system, we use Wi-Fi fingerprinting to estimate the location. The application then collects Wi-Fi fingerprints for a second and sends them to the location-based AR server. The area classification module classifies which exhibition hall the received Wi-Fi fingerprint belongs to at room-level. The resulting place information is sent to the AR list extraction module. This module queries the database with the exhibition hall and extracts the AR objects information that can be used in the exhibition hall. When the user's smartphone receives the information and selects an AR object to be viewed by the user, the application is switched to the viewing mode, the camera of the smartphone is activated, and tracking of the corresponding AR object is started.

The proposed system presents high-accuracy indoor positioning capability and convenient AR exhibition environment by incorporating various sensors in smartphones. In our experiment, the initial position estimation right after the positioning request showed sufficient room-level estimation accuracy. When an image corresponding to an AR object is recognized, the error block distribution converges quicker, and the system produces more accurate indoor positioning results.

2 Related Works

AR techniques are used in various exhibition venues. The most widely used form is recognizing the position of a real material and creating AR objects prepared according to it. The form includes a method of assisting physical exhibits, such as highlighting them with markers on the exhibits or delivering digital information with interactive buttons [6]. Narumi et al. presented an MR digital diorama system by preparing background images or videos that harmonize with the real exhibit [5]. In addition, there are studies where AR contents are used to increase the educational effect by emphasizing the aspect of visual experience rather than printed texts [7, 8]. On the other hand, there are also studies of AR exhibitions based on the location of user devices such as smartphones rather than exhibited materials. Most of them recognize the user's location with GPS and let the user search for the AR objects at specified locations around the user [8, 9]. However, since only GPS is used for location estimation, it is unsuitable for indoor exhibition environments.

In indoor positioning, GPS is not used as the primary signal because GPS signals do not reach indoors well due to the walls of buildings. As most people use smartphones, many indoor positioning studies utilize signals that smartphones can collect. The most widely used method for indoor positioning is Wi-Fi fingerprinting. In addition to this, sensor fusion utilizes smartphone sensors for more accurate indoor location estimation. HMM is one of the frameworks for the sensor fusion process. Lee et al. proposed an HMM-based adaptive sensor fusion framework working in dynamic environments [2]. They used the aggregate result, the final product of one unit-process of HMM, as feedback to the error block distribution storing accumulated errors. Zhou et al. combined an HMM framework and a particle filter to reduce the location estimation error [10].

3 Method

The proposed system automatically recognizes the exhibition hall where a user is located, creates an AR object prepared in the exhibition hall, and displays it to the viewers. Figure 1 shows the system architecture. The system consists of three components: Area classification module, AR list extraction module, and an application on a smartphone. Unlike existing AR applications based on image recognition, the user first needs to request indoor location estimation. In this system, we use Wi-Fi fingerprinting to estimate the location. The application collects Wi-Fi fingerprints for a second and sends them to the location-based AR server. The area classification module classifies which exhibition hall the received Wi-Fi fingerprint belongs to in room-level. The resulting place information is sent to the AR list extraction module. This module queries the database with the exhibition hall and extracts the AR objects information that can be used in the exhibition hall. When the user's smartphone receives the information and selects an AR object to be viewed by the user, the application is switched to the viewing mode, the camera of the smartphone is activated, and tracking of the corresponding AR object is started.

Table 1. Wi-Fi fingerprint structure

| MAC Address | AP_{1MAC} | AP_{2MAC} | AP_{3MAC} | ... |
| RSSI | AP_{1RSSI} | AP_{2RSSI} | AP_{3RSSI} | ... |

3.1 Location Estimation Request

There is no special operation in the smartphone application before the request. The first step of the proposed system is for the user to start a location estimation request. This process is initiated by the user pressing the Start Location Estimation button. A Wi-Fi fingerprint is then collected and sent to the server. The structure of the Wi-Fi fingerprint is depicted in Table 1, a list of MAC address and Received Signal Strength Indication(RSSI) pairs. Each pair represents a Wi-Fi signal collected from one AP during the fingerprint collection.

When there are exterior exhibition spaces, GPS signals are also used for location estimation. If a GPS signal is available, it is also sent with the fingerprint for fast indoor positioning. GPS signals do not reach indoors well, and even if reached, it usually has poor accuracy. Nevertheless, when performing area classification indoors, the search space can be significantly reduced. The details are described below.

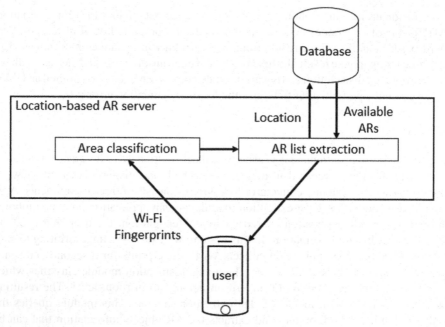

Fig. 1. System architecture

3.2 Area Classification

Fingerprints of the entire museum site are mapped in advance based on which exhibition hall they collected from. Upon receiving a location estimation request from the user, the area classification module starts searching where the fingerprint received belongs.

It is checked first whether a GPS signal is included. If there is a GPS signal, the fingerprint search space can be drastically reduced. Figure 2 shows an example of the process limiting the indoor positioning area. The exhibition halls within a certain preset distance from the GPS coordinates are selected as candidates. In the example, Hall A, B, and C are the candidates. Among the fingerprints belong to the three places, the area classification module checks that there are fingerprints with one or more MAC addresses included in the received fingerprint. If such fingerprints exist, the place whose fingerprint with the highest similarity to the received fingerprint is the area classification result. Otherwise, if there is no same MAC address, increase the search radius from the GPS coordinate and repeat until the module finds fingerprints that meet the conditions described above.

When GPS information is not included, all the exhibition halls in the museum are iterated. However, it is inefficient to find the similarity for all fingerprints. We set about 2-3 representative fingerprints for each hall and calculate the Wi-Fi similarity with them first. They are the fingerprints that have received the most AP signals or are the finger-prints collected at the center of the exhibition hall. These fingerprints are first iterated to check that there is an intersection in MAC addresses. When a fingerprint with overlap-ping MAC address is found, the exhibition hall containing the fingerprint with the highest similarity among them is derived as the final estimated location. Entire fingerprints are iterated if no MAC address intersection is found.

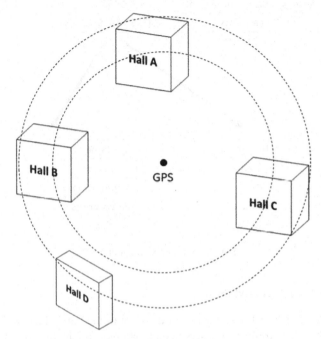

Fig. 2. Example of limiting the target area for indoor positioning using GPS

3.3 AR List Extraction

After specifying the exhibition hall where the user is located, the AR list extraction module extracts AR objects information from the database. Figure 3 shows the structure of the database. The most outer objects are exhibition hall areas. Each exhibition hall object includes essential information such as an identification number of its representative fingerprint, a list of fingerprints belong to the exhibition hall and a list of available AR objects.

An AR object in the database contains its position information and miscellaneous information. The position information indicates the indoor location where the AR exhibit is displayed when viewed through a smartphone application. In an AR object data, the Location field has a 2D coordinate on the indoor floor plan of an exhibition hall that the AR object belongs to. The Orientation field indicates the ideal direction for generating AR exhibits. Figure 4 shows an example of the position of the AR exhibit, "Rotating Gears" in Fig. 3. A red rectangular in the example is the designated location, and direction where "Rotating Gears" will be created. Its 2D coordinate is (75,8, 13.7) and direction is 300 degree in Science Hall.

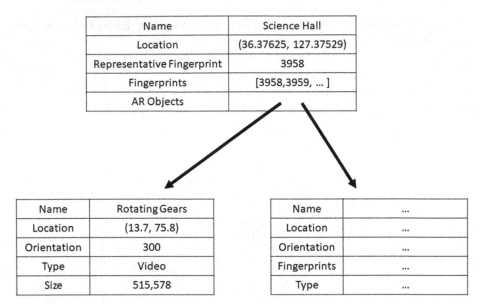

Name	Science Hall
Location	(36.37625, 127.37529)
Representative Fingerprint	3958
Fingerprints	[3958,3959, ...]
AR Objects	

Name	Rotating Gears
Location	(13.7, 75.8)
Orientation	300
Type	Video
Size	515,578

Name	...
Location	...
Orientation	...
Fingerprints	...
Type	...

Fig. 3. AR database structure

3.4 Location-Based AR Exhibition

Receiving an AR object list from the server does not immediately lead to the generation of an AR exhibit. AR Application users need to choose which AR exhibit they want to watch. When one of the exhibits is chosen, the distance between the user and the position of the exhibit is calculated, and the orientation of the user's smartphone is measured.

If the direction of the front camera of the smartphone deviates a lot from the default orientation value of the AR exhibit, the application displays a direction indicator so that the user can point the smartphone camera in the right direction. There are two kinds of direction indicators, left and right. A Direction indicator is generated according to the difference between the direction of the user's smartphone and that of the AR exhibit's. It can be represented by the following equation.

$$\textbf{Generate Right Indicator } \textit{if } 180 > (O_e - O_u) \textit{ mod } 360 > 30$$
$$\textbf{Generate Right Indicator } \textit{if } 180 > (O_e - O_u) \textit{ mod } 360 > 210 \tag{1}$$

In Eq. (1), O_e is the default orientation of the AR exhibit, and O_u is in degree. When the angle difference is less than 30°, the indicator disappears, and the application displays a message prompting the user to look for a physical exhibit corresponding to the selected AR exhibits. If the distance to the exhibit is too far, the user is guided to reach the proper distance.

During the AR viewing phase, the continuous estimation of indoor position and orientation is performed through the sensor fusion algorithm devised by Lee et al. [2]. The indoor positioning sensor fusion framework is based on Hidden Markov Model(HMM), where each state corresponds to the indoor position with 1 m². By dynamically correcting errors occurring in real time, stable AR experience can be provided through accurate

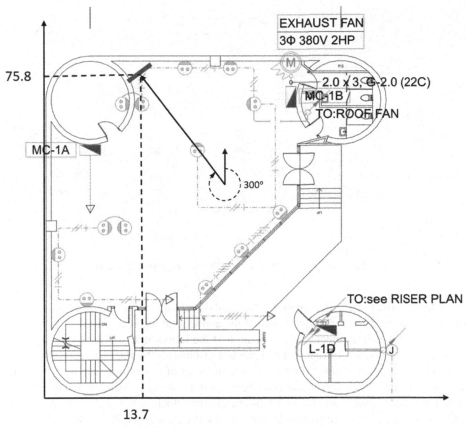

Fig. 4. Example of AR object position

position and direction estimation. Figure 5 shows how the error correction process works. The process uses a probability distribution called error block distribution to correct sensor errors in an adaptive manner. The figure depicts the situation in which the user's movement from the time t0 to t3 is tracked. At t0, the starting time of tracking, the initial error block distribution is a uniform distribution $u(-2\sigma, 2\sigma)$, where σ is the standard deviation of measured values. For example, the standard deviation of heading orientation is set to $15°$, and its initial error block distribution is $u(30°, 30°)$ in the proposed system. At the next time point, t1, the user made a move, and a transition has occurred to an adjacent location. The transition result, the blue arrow in the figure, is derived by the aggregate result, which is a summation of sensor measurements. However, the orientation arrow colored in red has a different angle from the tracking result. The difference value is regarded as an error, and an error block of a predefined size is accumulated in the error block distribution. The distribution is then no longer uniform but skewed toward the opposite direction of the error. The orientation value obtained at the next time point is modified by the value extracted from the error block distribution. Errors showing a constant value such as bias error are canceled out after several transitions.

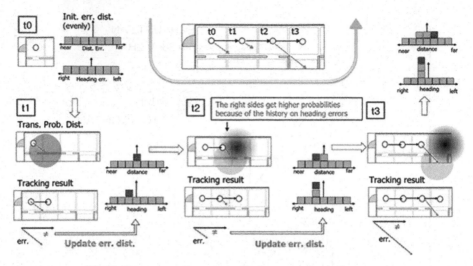

Fig. 5. Error correction process in the sensor fusion framework

Additionally, the user's current position and direction are also corrected through the known position of the real exhibit, which the application has recognized. As shown in Fig. 3, all AR exhibit objects have a location of the indoor map 2D coordinate system. Their known location is exact and reliable unless changed by the exhibition hall manager. Therefore, they show higher reliability in terms of positioning accuracy than the aggregate result. When there is an error between the AR object location and the current sensor measurements from the smartphone, an error block of twice the height is accumulated. By accumulating large size error blocks, the error block distribution converges faster.

4 Evaluation

Our goal is to provide a convenient location-based AR exhibition service system with low computational cost. In order to evaluate the proposed system, the server system and the application are implemented and experimented. The server consists of MongoDB [4] for the AR objects database and request processing unit written in JavaScript. The application is written in Kotlin and works on Android smartphones. To examine the device heterogeneity effect in location estimation accuracy, the following smartphone models are tested: Samsung Galaxy S9, Samsung Galaxy Note 10, Samsung Galaxy Note 20 Ultra, LG V50 ThinQ, HUAWEI Mate 20, and HUAWEI Mate 20 Pro. The application is packed with Google ARCore [3] to recognize images of real exhibits and manage AR objects.

The experiment is done on the 7th floor of N1 building, Korea Advanced Institute of Science, Daejeon, Korea, to test places with narrow passageways. Test for the open spaces is done on the first floor of the same building. Floor plans of the two testbeds and experiment scenarios are depicted in Fig. 6. In the figure, the red dot represents the default position of an AR object to be generated, and the blue directional path is the movement line that the user moves after selecting the AR exhibit pointed by the path. The test was conducted with three scenarios where the user moves to look for an AR object from a distance. For indoor positioning based on Wi-Fi signals, a radio map for each floor was constructed by HMM offline phase learning. Each Wi-Fi fingerprint constituting the radio maps fills the space that people can travel at intervals of 1 meter. When collecting fingerprints, Wi-Fi scan throttling was disabled, and five fingerprints were collected for about 15 s in one position. Their average RSSI is used to construct the radio maps.

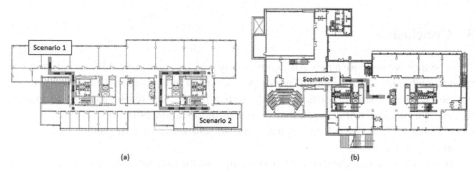

Fig. 6. Experiment scenarios

The indoor positioning accuracy and AR object generation location accuracy of the proposed system for each scenario are tested. Test data were collected at a constant speed with a constant stride. Figure 7 shows the experiment results in two situations. In the graph, each step refers to the state after a transition on the HMM. The step proceeds every 3 s, which is the Wi-Fi fingerprint collection interval. The error distance is the average of the error distances of 6 different devices.

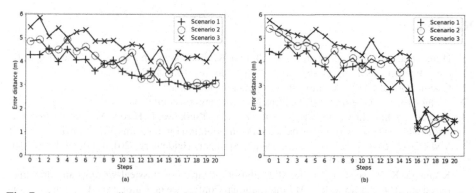

Fig. 7. Average error distance by scenarios. (a) No image detection. (b) Image detection at the 15th step.

Figure 7 (a) shows the result of moving along the scenario path without AR image detection. In all three scenarios, the error distance tends to decrease gradually over time due to the error correction from the error block accumulation. Scenario 3 showed large error distances of about 5 m, whereas, in the other two scenarios, the error distance converges to around 3 m. This is because the indoor environment of scenario 3 is an open space. In open spaces, the influence of the RSS value error of the Wi-Fi fingerprint is greater than the bias error of the sensor. On the other hand, Fig. 7 (b) shows the case where the image is detected, and the indoor position was corrected through its position. The detection occurs in the 15th step for three scenarios. All scenarios similarly showed an average distance error of about 1 m due to the correction effect.

(Orientation Error and Wrong indicator)

5   Conclusion

In this paper, we propose a new AR exhibition system by combining AR and indoor positioning techniques. For accurate indoor positioning, the proposed system incorporates various sensors in smartphones via HMM sensor fusion. The online learning technique using error block distribution further increases the location estimation accuracy as the user moves around. Based on accurate user location, the system guides users to the location of AR exhibits.

In our experiment, the distance error of the indoor location estimation request was not bigger than 6 m, which leads to accurate area classification. Additionally, the distance error converges to about 3 m when the user moves around while using the application. Future work will be a study of mutual location error correction between a user and AR objects created, even when the recognized image is no longer detected.

Acknowledgments. This research was supported by Capacity Enhancement Program for Scientific and Cultural Exhibition Services through the National Research Foundation of Korea(NRF) funded by **Ministry of Science and ICT (2018X1A3A106860321)**.

References

1. Hunsucker, A.J., Baumgartner, E., McClinton, K.: Evaluating an AR-based museum experience. Interactions **25**(4), 66–68 (2018). https://doi.org/10.1145/3215844
2. Google: Google ARCore. https://developers.google.com/ar
3. MongoDB, I.: MongoDB (2021). https://www.mongodb.com/
4. Narumi, T., Hayashi, O., Kasada, K., Yamazaki, M., Tanikawa, T., Hirose, M.: Digital diorama: AR exhibition system to convey background information for museums. In: Shumaker, R. (ed.) VMR 2011. LNCS, vol. 6773, pp. 76–86. Springer, Heidelberg (2011). https://doi.org/10.1007/978-3-642-22021-0_10
5. Kitamura, K.: Case study of digital exhibition of Japanese classical writings and drawings based on AR technology. In: 2017 International Conference on Culture and Computing (Culture and Computing), pp. 125–126 (2017). https://doi.org/10.1109/Culture.and.Computing.2017.43
6. Dunleavy, M., Simmons, B.: Assessing Learning and Identity in Augmented Reality Science Games. Brill, Leiden, The Netherlands (2011)

7. Sommerauer, P., Müller, O.: Augmented reality in informal learning environments: a field experiment in a mathematics exhibition. Comput. Educ. **79**, 59–68 (2014). https://doi.org/10.1016/j.compedu.2014.07.013
8. Georgiou, Y., Kyza, E.A.: A design-based approach to augmented reality location-based activities: investigating immersion in relation to student learning. In: Proceedings of the 16th World Conference on Mobile and Contextual Learning. Association for Computing Machinery, New York (2017). https://doi.org/10.1145/3136907.3136926
9. Li, R., Zhang, B., Sundar, S.S., Duh, H.-L.: Interacting with augmented reality: how does location-based AR enhance learning? In: Kotzé, P., Marsden, G., Lindgaard, G., Wesson, J., Winckler, M. (eds.) INTERACT 2013. LNCS, vol. 8118, pp. 616–623. Springer, Heidelberg (2013). https://doi.org/10.1007/978-3-642-40480-1_43
10. Zhou, D., Zhang, K., Ravey, A., Gao, F., Miraoui, A.: Online estimation of lithium polymer batteries state-of-charge using particle filter-based data fusion with multimodels approach. IEEE Trans. Ind. Appl. **52**(3), 2582–2595 (2016). https://doi.org/10.1109/TIA.2016.2524438

Environmental Analysis and Design Directions for Non-contact Exhibition Spaces

Choi Jung Ai[✉] and Da Young Ju

Kookmin University, Seongbuk-gu, Seoul 02707, Korea
{cho-e,dyju}@kookmin.ac.kr

Abstract. Entering 2020, COVID-19 spread around the world. As a result, a non-contact, non-face-to-face culture established itself in everyday life. In addition, exhibition spaces, convention centers, museums, and other cultural arts fields are also looking for ways in which the public can safely view works, without coming into contact with other people and, potentially, viruses. Therefore, social distancing, closed, crowded, and close contact should not be used. This will increase the likelihood of contagion. However, due to its nature, the exhibition-culture industry is maintained through meetings of people [1]. Due to the nature of the exhibition space, many people are forced to gather in a specific place. So, in 2020, most exhibition-culture industry events and museums were not held. Accordingly, this study aims to grasp the current status of the exhibition-culture industry by way of a survey about its condition. Second, this paper analyzes the impact of social distancing and the changes brought by non-contact culture on the exhibition space. Third, we propose the direction in which the exhibition space should change in a non-contact environment. The purpose of this study is to provide a safe and comfortable exhibition for visitors in a non-contact environment. In addition, we intend to propose a safe and comfortable exhibition space to prevent the spread of infectious diseases such as COVID-19 in the future. And it is meaningful to establish a non-face-to-face, safe interior architectural design strategy in the exhibition space. Furthermore, we intend to establish a non-face-to-face safe interior architecture design strategy in the exhibition space.

Keywords: Non-contact · Exhibition space · COVID-19

1 Introduction

1.1 Research Background and Purpose

In March 2020, the World Health Organization (WHO) declared a "global pandemic" [2]. A pandemic is a state in which infectious diseases are prevalent around the world. With COVID-19, the world entered into a pandemic, the highest warning rating for infectious diseases. So, new terms to describe society before and after COVID-19 emerged, such as "BC (Before Corona)" and "AC (After Corona)" [3]. As a result, the world is facing an unprecedented era of crisis. WHO emphasized that the fundamental end of COVID-19 may be difficult, and in order to overcome the virus completely, all human lifestyles

C. Stephanidis et al. (Eds.): HCII 2021, LNCS 13096, pp. 542–557, 2021.
https://doi.org/10.1007/978-3-030-90328-2_37

must be completely changed [4]. One of these changes—intended specifically to prevent transmission by airborne viruses—emphasizes maintaining a social distance of 2 m or more. It also calls for openness and dispersal to prevent contagions from becoming serious in dense cities and spaces [5].

As the non-contact environment is prolonged, the exhibition-culture industry has been temporarily reduced and postponed, resulting in a rapid stagnation. However, research on spatial methods and spatial activation methods according to these problems is relatively insufficient. Therefore, the purpose of this study is to plan a method for revitalizing the exhibition-culture industry even in a non-contact environment. In addition, this study suggests ways for visitors to enjoy a pleasant exhibition that is safe from infectious viruses. In so doing, this study aims to contribute to the continuous growth and vitalization of the exhibition-culture industry.

1.2 Research Background and Purpose

COVID-19 has destroyed traditional ways of living and damaged the global economy. This study describes an approach that can implement strategies to improve resilience by coping with, adapting to, and recovering from the adversity caused by the COVID-19 pandemic, targeting exhibition spaces [6].

The scope and method of this study are as follows.

First, focusing on what will happen after COVID-19, we examine the literature and websites on the social impact of the non-contact environment on the exhibition industry and exhibition space. In addition, we understand the actual situation through the UFI (The Global Association of the Exhibition Industry).

Second, we investigate the problems of the exhibition space in a non-contact environment and present a direction by which the exhibition space can improve upon the virus environment.

Third, the architectural elements and designs for exhibition viewing in a safe and comfortable non-contact environment are drawn and summarized as a conclusion.

2 Change to a Non-contact Environment

2.1 Social Change

With the rapid spread of COVID-19, the world has completely controlled movement between all countries. In addition, movement between regions and within regions has been controlled to prevent the spread of infection. In addition, direct contact with people has been blocked, with governments issuing orders prohibiting gatherings for all facilities and areas where large numbers of people gather. Many scholars and experts have predicted various changes, defining new routines and standards after COVID-19 as the "New Normal" [7].

As a result, the world has proposed social distancing, and many changes have occurred in people's living environments and patterns. Social distancing was implemented to reduce the risk of infection by maintaining enough of a physical space between people so as to prevent the transmission of the virus. The exact meaning of social distancing is the practice of keeping away from other people as much as possible. This eventually changed the form of social relations between people because of the need to secure a safe space [8].

As a result of social distancing, the radius of activity to the outside was narrowed in order to minimize face-to-face contact. In addition, as we entered a non-contact society in which people can engage in activities without meeting other people, many changes have taken place in the national economy and industry. In today's pandemic era, a non-contact environment is a necessity, not merely an option. Furthermore, the creation of a non-contact environment has begun to contribute greatly to preventing the spread of the virus as an alternative that can minimize confrontation with people.

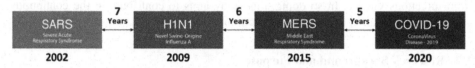

Fig. 1. The incidence cycle of new infectious diseases

However, from the outbreak of SARS (Severe Acute Respiratory Syndrome) in 2002, H1N1 (Novel Swine-Origin Influenza A) in 2009, MERS (Middle East Respiratory Syndrome) in 2015, and COVID-19 (Corona Virus Disease-2019) in 2020, new viral infectious diseases continue to develop, and the cycle between them is getting shorter (Fig. 1) [9]. The world after COVID-19 will no longer be free from the pandemic. It is expected that the current pandemic could continue over the next few years. This means that even if the vaccine for COVID-19 is developed or terminated, the threat from the new virus will continue into the post-COVID-19era. Therefore, it is necessary to overcome the current problem situation facing the exhibition-culture industry and re-analyze the space according to the crisis period. Therefore, in the post-corona era, planning for exhibition spaces for preemptive responses to the exhibition-culture industry is needed above all else.

2.2   Changes in the Exhibition Industry

As a result of the non-contact spread of the pandemic environment, gatherings were prohibited and movement was controlled. Due to the risk of infection and transmission of the virus, furthermore, people have been extremely concerned about the behavior of gathering in one space, and their movement to the outside has been minimized. So, it directly had a huge impact on the exhibition-culture industry. The exhibition-culture industry is an industry that has created various values through direct encounters and exchanges between people. However, due to the psychological burden of the participants of the exhibition event, would be exhibition spectators have been banned from gathering and viewing exhibitions. As a result, various exhibition and cultural events have been postponed or canceled. The exhibition and cultural event spaces in which people from all over the world gather are highly likely to become a hotbed for the spread of infectious diseases due to the uncertain nature of the crowd. Thus, many conferences and exhibitions around the world that were scheduled to take place in 2020 were canceled (Fig. 2) [10].

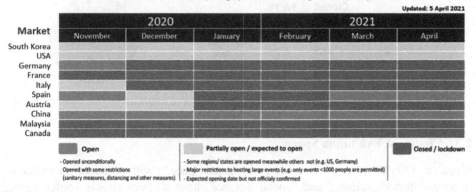

Fig. 2. ufi (The Global Association of the Exhibition Industry) Exhibitions & events reopening by market, following the COVID-19 pandemic

According to the BBC (British Broadcasting Corporation), in March 2020, SXSW (South by Southwest), a global film, music, and convergence content festival held in Austin, Texas, was canceled for the first time in 34 years due to the spread of COVID-19 [11]. The CES (Consumer Electronics Show), an electronics, IT, and home appliance exhibition, with thousands of companies exhibiting every year and more than 100,000 visitors, was held online in 2021, focusing on presentations and discussions rather than exhibitions. In 2021, the MWC (Mobile World Congress) in Barcelona, Spain and the IFA (Internationale Funkausstellung) in Berlin, Germany were also held offline and digitally. As such, the exhibition-culture industry is responding to COVID-19 in digital form. The pandemic situation resulting from COVID-19 has brought greater visibility to contactless interactions with consumer IoT devices [12]. However, it is difficult to expect the intrinsic value of the exhibition cultural events provided by the face-to-face event.

In the exhibition-culture industry, securing a market through face-to-face consultations and meetings between the buyer, organizer, and customer, is an important factor. The most important factor, however, is the direct exchange and communication between the exhibition planner and the viewers. In this vein, the experiential element that comes from the sense of space is absolutely necessary. Therefore, the online exhibition form has a limitation to solve the experiential needs of visitors. In addition, small and medium-sized companies and small-scale exhibitors have relative difficulty preparing for online exhibitions.

The status of museums in 2020 was surveyed by the ICOM (International Council of Museums), considering museums from 107 countries. It was observed that 94.7% of museums worldwide were closed as of April 2020 (Fig. 3) [13]. A survey by UNESCO's related report also found about 90% of the world's museums to be closed in 2020, of which 13% reported that they would be permanently shut down [14]. As such, the non-contact environment caused by the pandemic has had a great influence on the exhibition-culture industry.

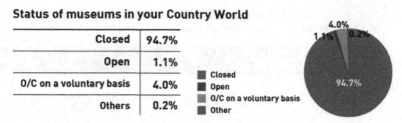

Status of museums in your Country World

Closed	94.7%
Open	1.1%
O/C on a voluntary basis	4.0%
Others	0.2%

Fig. 3. ICOM (International Council of Museums) Status of museums in your country world

2.3 Change of Exhibition Space

Since the COVID-19 era, terms such as "spread space," "self-isolation," "movement of virus-infected patients," and "social distance" have all been closely related to the relationship of "space" [8]. The COVID-19 virus spreads through human droplets or airborne viral contact. Therefore, confined, dense, and tightly confined spaces have become a problem. To prevent airborne transmission, then, social distances of at least 2 m must be kept, and openness and dispersion are required in dense spaces.

As such, the exhibition space should not be "Closed," "Crowded," or "Close-Contact," and contagion-prevention rules and social distance must be maintained to prevent transmission. In the exhibition space in which the public gathers, the number of visitors is uncertain, so it is basically in the form of a group. As it relates to an exhibition space, a group is defined as "a large number of people who temporarily gather together and do not have a certain organization." By planning such a group, it becomes possible to secure smooth circulation and create a pleasant and safe exhibition space.

The method of configuring a non-contact space to avoid and induce congestion and confusion of visitors in the exhibition space is as follows. Groups in the exhibition space should not loiter, and in order to maintain a comfortable walking space, it is necessary to induce the flow at all times while leaving a 2 m distance. The path should not change the flow in a hurry, and the space should be able to respond flexibly to the situation [5] (Table 1).

As such, there is a need for a safe alternative method by which to cope with highly infectious viruses in the exhibition space. Directions must be presented from the planning stage of the exhibition space to the architectural space. The exhibition space basically grasps the group's scale and behavior. Unlike the situation before the pandemic, the standard must be newly expanded and defined in accordance with the 2 m distance principle. Therefore, the exhibition space should apply "Open," "Dispersed," and "Segmentation" in applying the concept of non-contact. As such, non-contact changes in the exhibition space and countermeasure research are necessary.

As such, the exhibition space should not be "Closed," "Crowded," or "Close-Contact," and contagion-prevention rules and social distance must be maintained to prevent transmission. In the exhibition space in which the public gathers, the number of visitors is uncertain, so it is basically in the form of a group. As it relates to an exhibition space, a group is defined as "a large number of people who temporarily gather together and do not have a certain organization." By planning such a group, it becomes possible to secure smooth circulation and create a pleasant and safe exhibition space.

Table 1. Components of smooth circulation of the exhibition space

Division	Contents
Flexible flow of exhibition visitors	· To prevent the flow rate from dropping, the entrances, gates, and stairs are widened
Use of slope rather than stairs	· Ramps need distance. Less anxiety in gait by creating time
Simplification of separation	· Establish a one-way passage for visitors who are in a hurry to proceed · Separate visitors who are familiar with movement from those who are not familiar with them · Distinguishing the difference in behavior: Young, old, child, man, woman, etc
Maintain straight queues	· Do not process or bend movement for circulation of movement
Adjust movement length	· Shortening the moving line considering the fatigue of exhibition visitors· Depending on the nature of the exhibition, visitors should avoid moving lines · Creating a flow using routes

The method of configuring a non-contact space to avoid and induce congestion and confusion of visitors in the exhibition space is as follows. Groups in the exhibition space should not loiter, and in order to maintain a comfortable walking space, it is necessary to induce the flow at all times while leaving a 2 m distance. The path should not change the flow in a hurry, and the space should be able to respond flexibly to the situation [5].

As such, there is a need for a safe alternative method by which to cope with highly infectious viruses in the exhibition space. Directions must be presented from the planning stage of the exhibition space to the architectural space. The exhibition space basically grasps the group's scale and behavior. Unlike the situation before the pandemic, the standard must be newly expanded and defined in accordance with the 2 m distance principle. Therefore, the exhibition space should apply "Open," "Dispersed," and "Segmentation" in applying the concept of non-contact. As such, non-contact changes in the exhibition space and countermeasure research are necessary.

3   Proposal of Non-contact Exhibition Space

3.1   Non-contact Suggestion of Communication Method

Before the pandemic, the exhibition space did not just have one-way communication between the exhibition visitors and the exhibits but two-way communication. Moreover, such communication between the exhibition planner and exhibition visitors was not contactless but took place through "Contact Communication." However, the current exhibition space should provide a pleasant and safe exhibition hall, and it is necessary to present a new direction by finding ways to cope with new environments such as that of a pandemic. Therefore, we identify the problems with the communication method in the current exhibition space and propose a non-contact communication method to communicate in a safe environment.

In the pandemic environment, the problem of the existing exhibition space was the "Contact Communication" method [15]. "Contact Communication" is a method by which people can contact and communicate with each other by narrowing the physical distance between exhibition visitors. This was an important factor in establishing relationships and communicating with participants in the exhibition. However, in a pandemic environment, the "Contact Communication" method has a problem due to its distance within the space.

Therefore, it is necessary to develop the exhibition through "Direct Communication" as an alternative method [15]. In the "Direct Communication" method, the exhibition planner organizes and plans the exhibition situation in advance. This offers a way for spectators to systematically approach the exhibits according to the planner's intention. To minimize the contact between exhibition visitors, planners pre-set plans, concepts, storytelling, and routes. In addition, this is a method of meeting and communicating with exhibition visitors directly according to the planner's intention. Therefore, it is possible to create a non-contact exhibition space between exhibition visitors according to the exhibition planner's intention.

3.2 Presenting Problems in Exhibition Space

In the current pandemic environment, the "Three Cs (3C: Closed, Crowded, Close-contact)," which means "close contact between humans," has emerged as a problem.

The WHO stated that the risk factors were higher where the three overlaps "Close-contact settings," "Crowded Places," and "Confined and enclosed spaces." Therefore, it was recommended to avoid the "Three Cs" and pay attention to safety [16]. Accordingly, the Japanese MHLW (Ministry of Health, Labor and Welfare, Japan) aimed at a "Zero C (Closed spaces, Crowded places, Close-contact settings)" policy to reduce the spread of COVID-19 [17]. Given the need to reestablish to existing exhibition space, the biggest problem was face-to-face contact due to crowds of visitors congregating in a closed space. Therefore, exhibition spaces should also avoid the "Three Cs." Furthermore, it is necessary to realize the distance between visitors and develop "Direct Communication" with the exhibits as an exhibition method.

As a way to prevent the spread of COVID-19, it is necessary to reestablish the basic direction as an exhibition space that allows the viewing of an exhibition while maintaining social distance (Fig. 4).

The closed space is opened so that the indoor and outdoor areas are connected. Exhibition visitors should avoid "Closed," and "Close-Contact" areas and have a space plan with "Dispersed" and "Segmentation." To do this, first of all, the "Three Cs" should be limited, and the opposite concept of "Open," "Dispersed," and "Segmentation" should be applied. In addition, the concept of the non-contact exhibition space must be reorganized.

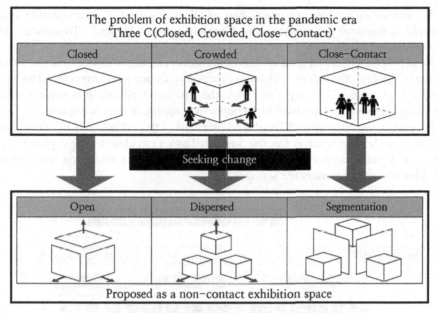

Fig. 4. Seeking change into a non-contact exhibition space

3.3   Proposal for the Direction of Exhibition Space

In order to create an exhibition space in a non-contact environment, "Direct Communication" with the exhibits must be developed as an exhibition component. In addition, it is possible to maintain distance between visitors only when "Closed," "Crowded," and "Close Contact" are set. Moreover, it was found that the opposite concept should be reorganized into "Open," "Dispersed," and "Segmentation" [18].

Table 2. Direction of non-contact exhibition space

From closed to open	From crowded to dispersed	From close contact to segmentation
· Openness of the exhibition space · Combination and creation with external space · Connection and communication between indoor and outdoor exhibitions · Concentration and aggregation of outdoor spaces	· Small-scale multiple nucleation due to dispersion · Distributed exhibition space · Dividing the mass · Various changes in the exhibition space using units · Forced separation of route nodules	· Layering using the stacking of exhibition spaces · Building the boundaries of segmental points · Movement using aisles

To achieve such a reorganization, first of all, the concept of the exhibition space is newly reorganized by applying the three concepts of "Open," "Dispersed," and "Segmentation" (Table 2).

First, the concept of "Openness" makes the unit of exhibition indoors open by selecting them indoors. So, indoor and outdoor exhibitions are interconnected. The main exhibition space should be separated from the auxiliary facilities. It is suggested that exhibition visitors circulate smoothly without overlapping in the open space.

Second, in the concept of "Distributed," the unit of the exhibition is multinucleated on a small scale. The space is forcibly separated and a circulation-type copper wire is applied as a forced copper wire. Accordingly, the place where exhibition visitors meet is divided so that the visitors are separated.

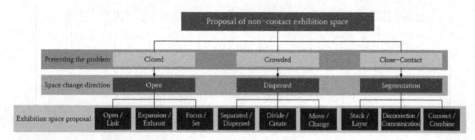

Fig. 5. Non-contact exhibition space proposal

Third, in terms of the concept of "Segmentation," the unit of exhibition is layering. Spaces should be stacked and mounted. The segmented spaces are connected and linked with each other by being adjusted in accordance with the intended movement of the exhibition planner through passages (Fig. 5).

In this way, the three concepts of non-contact environment were applied. Therefore, the direction of creating a safe exhibition space as an architectural, spatial, and path factor is presented to the exhibition visitors.

4   Non-contact Exhibition Space Proposal

4.1   Proposal of Open Exhibition Space

The closed exhibition space has an architectural character that attracts visitors to the exhibition. The central-square type with strong central aggregation, as well as the corridor type that arranges exhibitions by subject, increases the risk of close contact with exhibition visitors. Therefore, the structure of the non-contact exhibition space should have a flexible form. The structure of the closed space should be freely installed and dismantled without any restrictions. Accordingly, it is necessary to be able to respond to problems caused by direct contact with architectural elements.

The open-type exhibition space enhances the openness of indoor exhibitions and opens them to the outside so that indoor and outdoor exhibitions are interconnected. In addition, when the space is open and connected, the routes do not overlap for visitors. Therefore, the circulation of exhibition viewing can be smooth.

Table 3. Open unit characteristics

Unit type	Characteristic	Layout
Open Type	· Servant Type · Indoor/outdoor interconnection · The main exhibition space and the auxiliary exhibition space are clearly separated · Separated space can be connected as a linking space · Spaces are separated and open according to the concept and purpose of the exhibition	Main exhibition space Joint space Secondary exhibition space Joint space Main exhibition space

The open-space configuration secures the physical distance between the building structure and the exterior, enabling the distribution of the density of exhibition visitors. The island-type main structure is dispersed and opened from the central exhibition space to the space for each section by using several passages. It can be connected so that the connection between the outside and the inside is flexible according to specific exhibition requirements (Table 3).

By placing the central hall in an open space, it is possible to organize an intensive participatory exhibition as needed. Communication between the inside and outside areas is also convenient. In addition, the exhibits are open to the outside, allowing free viewing in an open space without distinction between indoors and outdoors (Table 4).

Table 4. Proposal of open exhibition space

Proposal of open exhibition space			
Configuration	Open / Link	Expansion / Exhaust	Focus / Set
Unit Configuration			
Space Configuration			
Configuration Element	· Open Type · Indoor/outdoor interconnection · Clear division of exhibition space and sub space · Provide open space	· Detachable type · Optional exhibition viewing possible in the discharged space · Advantageous to independent exhibition	· Focus on the outside space · The external central hall is located in an open space to gather exhibition visitors to the outside · Creating a participatory exhibition hall where the inside and outside communicate

As such, the open exhibition space can go beyond the limitations of the existing enclosed exhibition space.

4.2 Presenting Dispersed-Type Exhibition Space

A "dispersed-type" exhibition space is proposed in order to remove the elements that cause visitors to crowd in one place. In a dispersed-type exhibition space, each object is basically divided into a unit type. In addition, it is a type that can be distributed and constructed sequentially by separating several groups into a kind of multi-nucleated unit structure and module structure.

Table 5. Dispersed unit characteristics

Unit type	Characteristic	Layout
Dispersed Type	· Pavilion Type with different personality for each group · Distributed arrangement into several groups by forcibly separating the space · Can be expanded sequentially according to the concept · Selectively viewing the distributed space	Exhibition space Court Exhibition space

Furthermore, such a space can be maintained and operated independently and individually depending on the size and situation of the exhibition. The distributed exhibition space is a Pavilion type, in which the separation of the exhibition area and the sub-exhibition space is strict (Table 5).

By strictly separating the space for each function, it is possible to prevent exhibition visitors' routes from overlapping. Depending on the purpose and necessity of each exhibition, a certain portion of the space is restricted or repurposed to enable non-contact exhibition. By forcibly separating the routes in the enclosed space and distributing them into several groups, the space can be forcibly zoned (Table 6).

Table 6. Proposal of dispersed exhibition space

Proposal of dispersed exhibition space			
Configuration	Separated / Dispersed	Divide / Create	Move / Change
Unit Configuration			
Space Configuration			
Configuration Element	· Pavilion Type · Distributed placement into several groups · Non-contact display availa-ble for each group	· Dispersed Type · Creation of a new space · Variety of newly created spaces	· Move the space to another place · Various shapes can be changed according to move-ment · Maintaining physical dis-tance for each group · Can be expanded sequen-tially

This will minimize the contact of exhibition visitors and provide a safe exhibition space in the era of non-contact.

4.3 Presenting Segmentation-Type Exhibition Space

The segmentation-type exhibition space can be used by separating the open and dispersed-type exhibition spaces into both upper and lower sides. In the segmentation-type exhibition space, structures can be stacked. Therefore, it is possible to secure the circulation path along with the openness of each floor.

The exhibition room can be separated from the top to the bottom based on the central exhibition hall on the first floor. By deriving in detail all the movement lines leading to the exhibition spaces on each floor, the audience's dispersion can be ensured. Then, the zoning is cut off by distributing the space between the top and bottom sides. Therefore, the exhibition space can be moved individually up and down through the planned story line and various structures. The relationship between exhibits and exhibition visitors in the exhibition space is formed by visual, perceptual, and experiential elements. In general, then, exhibition visitors spend a lot of time and concentrate on the spaces that contain the exhibits in which they are interested.

The space of the pandemic era should exclude the commonly used free-moving lines. In order to manage a pleasant exhibition space, "Planar circulation route," "Corridor access route," and "Forced route" should be applied.

Table 7. Segmentation unit characteristics

Unit type	Characteristic	Layout
Segmentation Type	· Separating the space up and down · Securing circulation routes for each floor · Distribute routes to each floor · Use of planar circulation path route to access each floor sequentially · Use of corridor space by using corridor as circulation · Force intended path	Main exhibition space Joint space Secondary exhibition space

The "Planar circulation route" is a form of sequentially connected exhibition rooms. The exhibition operator plans a route so that each floor can be viewed sequentially, ensuring that the routes of the viewers do not overlap each other and thereby constructing a safer exhibition (Table 7).

"Corridor access route" can extend a route using a corridor. Corridors and zoning on each floor can be extended and disconnected. It is easy to close the exhibition space on each floor if necessary. In addition, a part of the corridor can be used as an exhibition space.

"Forced Route" removes the confusion elements of the route in advance by thoroughly calculating the movement, view, flow, intersection, and course of each floor.

Table 8. Proposal of segmentation exhibition space

Proposal of segmentation exhibition space			
Configuration	Stack / Layer	Disconnection / Communication	Connect / Combine
Unit Configuration			
Space Configuration			
Configuration Element	· Arrange structures up, down, bi-directionally, sideways · Prevention of overlapping of the movement lines of each floor	· Separation of copper wires for each floor · Possible to sequentially close each floor · Flexibility of communication by connecting the upper and lower parts using passages	· Possible to increase sequentially by floor · Connection can be combined according to the use of each floor · Secure circulation through corridor

"Forced route" moves the route according to the intention of the exhibition organizer. Therefore, it is possible to make the exhibition space safe from viruses by systematically circulating the path according to the planning intention of the exhibition operator (Table 8).

The exhibition space in the non-contact era can be designed in a variety of ways for each floor according to the content, concept, and situation, so that the dense space can be operated more safely. Therefore, exhibition space planners can actively respond to the demand and expansion of the exhibition industry.

5   Conclusion

New terms for the post-COVID-19 society have emerged, such as "BC (Before Corona)" and "AC (After Corona)" (3). And the world is facing an era of unprecedented crisis. However, proper vaccination could end COVID-19. However, in the upcoming post-corona era, moments of uncertain and unpredictable crisis will occur frequently. Therefore, the exhibition-space environment will require a specific method to prepare for this.

This study specifically grasped the impact of changing into a non-contact environment in terms of social, cultural, and exhibition culture. In order to create a safe and comfortable exhibition space in a non-contact environment, an appropriate communication method was studied. Through research on "Contact Communication" and "Direct Communication," a communication method was suggested to minimize contact between visitors. Through this study, it was found that maintaining social distance is necessary as a living rule to prevent the spread of the virus in the exhibition space.

In addition, for a pleasant and safe exhibition space, we studied the composition and character of the "Three Cs (Closed, Crowded, Close-Contact)," which has emerged as an existing problem, and proposed a modification intended.

As a result of the study, it was found that the exhibition spaces connected indoors and outdoors should be open to provide an open space. Therefore, the crowded and close-contact areas of the exhibition were avoided, and dispersed and segmented spaces were suggested. In addition, a concrete method was proposed with unit structure, spatial structure, and components.

The results of the proposal are as follows.

First, the closed exhibition space was changed to an open exhibition space. By connecting the openness from the indoor to the outdoor area, the route of exhibition visitors in the open space was prevented from overlapping. The open space secured the physical distance between the inside and outside areas, enabling the distribution of the density of exhibition visitors. The island-type main structure was connected by several passages to freely separate the space for each section both inside and outside. Therefore, it is possible to view exhibitions freely without distinction between the outside and the inside, beyond the limits of the existing closed exhibition space.

Second, the dense exhibition space was proposed as a dispersed-type exhibition space. For the same time period and viewing, exhibition visitors are concentrated in the same place. This was divided into groups of spaces and distributed in each group. By strictly separating the space for each function, exhibition visitors can be prevented from being exposed to overlapping routes. In addition, it is possible to divide and recreate a certain part of the space according to each exhibition's concept and purpose, enabling non-contact exhibitions.

Third, a close-contact exhibition space was proposed as a segmentation exhibition space. This space is segmented by organizing the exhibition space for each floor. Therefore, by creating a flat circulation path using corridors and zoning on each floor, visitors to the exhibition are suggested to be distributed without staying in one place. As each floor can be viewed sequentially, the routes of visitors do not overlap, making the exhibition safer and more comfortable. The corridor connecting each floor can be used as an exhibition space depending on the exhibition concept. Above all, according to the planned intentions of the exhibition planner, floor-by-floor movement, viewing, flow, crossing, and paths are provided in a planned manner, enabling safe viewing.

Through this study, it was found that the establishment of absolute change is necessary for the sustainable development of the exhibition-culture industry, and the implications are as follows.

Until now, in a pandemic environment, the exhibition-culture industry has lacked research on architectural buildings and space design. In this study, the area of the exhibition-culture industry in the non-contact environment that was used in other industries was expanded and applied in terms of architecture and spatial design. This study theoretically established the crisis situation in the wartime-culture industry.

Therefore, this study is expected to serve as a cornerstone for revitalization of follow-up research in order to construct a safe exhibition space and achieve sustainable development in both the domestic and international exhibition industries in the future.

References

1. Park, P.W., Lim, T.: Changes in exhibition and convention in the era of un-tact and online exhibition case study. Korea Assoc. Trade Exhib. Stud. **15**(5), 57–82 (2020)
2. WHO Homepage. Director-General's opening remarks at the media briefing on COVID-19. https://www.who.int/. Accessed 11 Mar 2020
3. The New York Times Homepage: Our New Historical Divide, BC and AC the World Before Corona and the World After. https://www.nytimes.com. Accessed 17 Mar 2020
4. WHO Homepage. Director-General's opening remarks at the media briefing on COVID-19. https://www.who.int/. Accessed 21 Aug 2020
5. Oh, S.A.: A study on the impact of the COVID-19 pandemic on museums' exhibitions. Korea Assoc. Art Des. **23**(4), 155–169 (2020)
6. Nah, F., Keng, N.: COVID-19 pandemic – role of technology in transforming business to the new normal. In: HCI International 2020 – Late Breaking Papers: Interaction, Knowledge and Social Media, pp. 585–600 (2020)
7. Buheji, M., Ahmed, D.: Planning for 'The New Normal': foresight and management of the possibilities of socio-economic spillovers due to COVID-19 pandemic. Bus. Manag. Strategy **11**(1), 160–179 (2020)
8. Roggeveen, A.L., Sethuraman, R.: How the COVID pandemic may change the world of retailing. J. Retail. **96**(2), 169–171 (2020)
9. McKinsey & Company Homepage: Beyond coronavirus: The path to the next normal", McKinsey & Company. https://www.mckinsey.com. Accessed 23 Mar 2020

10. Na, H.S.: Securing of a space safe from disease and social history of social rights in space. Korea Assoc. World Hist. Cult. **56**(1), 39–69 (2020)
11. No, H.J., Kim, J.Y.: A study on food & beverage space alteration of COVID-19. Korean Inst. Spat. Des. **15**(8), 69, 573–582 (2020)
12. UFI (The Global Association of the Exhibition Industry) Homepage. Reopening of the Exhibition Industry Exhibitions & events reopening by market, following the COVID-19 pandemic. https://www.ufi.org. Accessed 01 May 2021
13. BBC Homepage: South by Southwest festival cancelled over coronavirus. https://www.bbc.com. Accessed 07 Mar 2020
14. Kathuria, R., Wadehra, A., Kathuria, V.: Human-centered artificial intelligence: antecedents of trust for the usage of voice biometrics for driving contactless interactions. In: Stephanidis, C., Antona, M., Ntoa, S. (eds.) HCII 2020. CCIS, vol. 1293, pp. 325–334. Springer, Cham (2020). https://doi.org/10.1007/978-3-030-60700-5_42
15. ICOM: Museums, museum professionals and COVID-19. Survey results, pp. 3–5 (2020)
16. UNESCO Homepage: Museums around the World in the face of COVID-19. https://en.unesco.org. Accessed 27 May 2020
17. An, Y.S.: Exhibition Studies Dictionary. Japan Exhibition Society, p. 77. Chaegbo Publisher (2009)
18. WHO Homepage: Avoid the Three Cs. https://www.who.int/brunei/news/infographics-english. Accessed 01 May 2021
19. MHLP (Ministry of Health, Labor and Welfare) Homepage: Important notice for preventing COVID-19 outbreaks, Avoid the 'Three Cs!. https://www.mhlw.go.jp/stf/covid-19/kenkou-iryousoudan_00006.html. Accessed 01 May 2021
20. Yoo, D.H.: A Study on New Experiences of Spatial Contents that Accommodates Unchanging Human Desires in Corona Coexistence Age. The Research Institute for Global Management of Technology for Catching Up, pp. 51–88 (2020)

Critical Art with Brain-Computer Interfaces: Philosophical Reflections from Neuromatic Game Art Project

Anna Dobrosovestnova[1](✉), Mark Coeckelbergh[2], and Margarete Jahrmann[3]

[1] TU Wien, Vienna, Austria
anna.dobrosovestnova@tuwien.ac.at
[2] University of Vienna, Vienna, Austria
[3] University of Applied Arts, Vienna, Austria

Abstract. Commercial brain-computer interfaces raise interesting critical political-philosophical and artistic questions. Drawing on our research and experiences with the "Neuromatic Game Art" project, and using critical theory from philosophy of technology (Feenberg), among other theories, this paper examines the power relations involved in the use of commercial BCI and argues that BCI artworks simultaneously subvert and engage the hegemony narratives offered by the technological tools and their commercial environment.

Keywords: Brain-computer interfaces · Critical theory · Art

1 Introduction

Commercial EEG wearables are sold with the bold promises of helping users to discover, understand and regulate the inner workings of their brains to become better learners [37], workers [33], meditators [1]. While at first glance exciting and promising of new possibilities to gain control over one's life, these technologies raise important questions about how they reshape our corporeal experiences on an individual level, and about the ideologies and ideas about self-improvement, self-knowledge and well-being they promote, on the societal level.

In this paper, we present preliminary outcomes of our research and experience of interacting with commercial BCI in the context of the "Neuromatic Game Art" project[1]. The project was conceived as an interdisciplinary arts-based research exploration into brain-computer interfaces (BCI). Through the reflective lenses of philosophy of technology, game design, neuroscience and arts-based research, we critically examine the questions around the societal and ethical implications of BCI, and explore possibilities to artistically (re-)interpret technologies outside of their commercial environments and promoted use scripts.

---

[1] https://neuromatic.uni-ak.ac.at/ Apart from the authors of this paper, the project team includes Stefan Glasauer, Charlotta Ruth, Georg Luif, Zarko Aleksic and Thomas Wagensommerer.

© Springer Nature Switzerland AG 2021
C. Stephanidis et al. (Eds.): HCII 2021, LNCS 13096, pp. 558–574, 2021.
https://doi.org/10.1007/978-3-030-90328-2_38

In this paper, we focus on the presentation of the philosophical strand of the research conducted within the project thus far. More precisely, the paper pursues two objectives: (i) by drawing on critical perspectives on EEG-based technologies and critical constructivism as presented primarily by philosopher of technology Andrew Feenberg, coupled with our first-hand experience of interacting with EEG-based devices, we critically analyse one of the most popular commercial headbands Muse and its supporting environments (i.e. Muse meditation app). Our focus in this analysis is to identify the main assumptions about self-knowledge, well-being that are ingrained in the seemingly neutral technical codes [11] of the said technological device; (ii) to discuss how artistic practices with devices such as Muse engage with, challenge, subvert - but also, in some ways, reinstate - the biases and implicit assumptions imprinted in the design of commercial BCI, as identified in the analysis section of the paper. For this discussion, we engage, among other, with the concept of *critical art*, and its role for democratic process, proposed by Belgian political theorist Chantal Mouffe.

The rest of the paper is structured as follows. In the Sect. 2, we briefly sketch out the key premises of the critical constructivism framework put forward by Feenberg and outline the core principles that stem from his framework and inform our techno-philosophical investigations. In the same section, we proceed to overview some of the existing work in philosophy of technology and Science, Technology and Society (STS) studies that has critically addressed biofeedback and body wearable technologies. In Sect. 3, we rely on the critical perspectives outlined in Sect. 2 to ground our analysis of commercial EEG-based headband Muse based on our experience of participation in a 7 days meditation challenge with this device. As pointed out above, the goal in this section is to lay out - through the analysis of Muse for meditation, some of the assumptions (about well-being, self-knowing, emotions etc.) and biases that are hidden behind the technical features and commercial environments of Muse. In Sect. 4, we bridge the critical perspectives on EEG wearables with a conversation on how these are engaged in artistic practices with BCI. We preface this section with a brief general discussion on the role of art for democracy and technology democratization respectively. Then, by case studies of selected BCI artworks, including our ongoing artistic work in the project, we show how artists can make visible and challenge the assumptions built into designs. The paper concludes with a short discussion section where we reflect on the relationship between art and technology and make suggestions for future work.

2 Related Work

2.1 Key Lessons of Critical Constructivism

The techno-philosophical background of the "Neuromatic Game Art" project is critical theory in philosophy of technology [5], more precisely, the critical constructivism framework developed by philosopher Andrew Feenberg. Building on the traditions of the Frankfurt Critical School [14], on the one hand,

and hermeneutics and STS studies on the other hand, Feenberg's critical constructivism positions technological evolution at the intersection of "technical rationality" and the lifeworld (experience) [12]. According to Feenberg, in modern societies technical know-how tends toward differentiation: that is, towards a gradual formalization in technical disciplines and specialised institutions, such as research institutes and labs, and subsequent concentration of decision-making about technology designs within the hands of selected few. This process of differentiation may give an impression that technology is just as autonomous from socio-cultural domain as is science; this in turn may further legitimize technology as "rational" and "objective".

Against views of technology development as rational and deterministic, Feenberg draws on constructivist approaches in philosophy and case studies in STS to argue that the idea of the autonomy and supposed rationality of technology is an illusion. The praxis of technology design is deeply marked by culture and the socio-economic structures wherein the research, development and production are situated. From this perspective, technical designs are not neutral nor objective. To the contrary, they are biased and reflect selected values, norms and assumptions while excluding or marginalizing others. This means that technology research, production and implementation in society are inherently political: technical designs function as a cite of struggle where different ideas, perspectives, interests and values compete for representation.

Culture also plays a crucial role in how technology is used and interpreted by different people once it leaves the environments of research institutions and laboratories. The meaning that is assigned to technical objects through their everyday use in society goes beyond what was intended and built-in by designers. In STS and technology studies, this process is commonly referred to as interpretative flexibility (see e.g. [25]). Importantly, through the reinterpretation and discovery of new use cases and ways of engaging with technology, society can push back and ultimately reshape original designs [12].

The dialectics between the process of technology differentiation, on the one hand, and the reinstatement of the individual and collective agency of people in decision-making about technology, on the other, is recognized as an important contribution of Feenberg to philosophy of technology. However, the proposed framework is not immune to criticisms. To briefly outline some of them here: from an STS perspective, critical constructivism still presupposes a kind of neat, organized and transparent decision-making in place of the situated, messy and improvised practice that is science and technology research as shown in STS case studies (e.g. [20]). Further, Feenberg's political aspirations about democratization of technology are considered by some overly optimistic due to the implicit assumption of the possibility of counter-hegemonic consensus that can be achieved if only technology design process were open to more people. In response to this consensus-oriented view of democracy, political philosophers such as Laclau and Mouffe, argue that democratic consensus is an ontological impossibility [19,27]. Finally, Feenberg leaves open the exact mechanisms of the political counter-action to hegemonic practices of technology designs - the process that he refers to under the term of *subversive rationalization* [11]. Despite these and other criticisms (see e.g. [4, 16, 17]), we abide by the critical constructivist as a framework that offers a strong theoretical backing to the studies of technologies in society such that they are both critical and, at the same time, leave space for human subjectivity and agency as a part of political force that can participate in (re-)shaping of the socio-cultural horizon of technical objects and in decision-making about technology designs. The key implications of critical constructivism that we rely on in our work in the Neuromatic GameArt Project are:

- Technology research and design are not neutral: (selected) values and socio-cultural norms are imprinted in technical features and intended use cases of technical artifacts.
- Individual and collective human agency have a place in technology design, among other, by means of: (a) (re-)defining of a problem space that a given technical artifact is designed to address; (b) Interpretations that technical objects receive through use in everyday life; (c) (Political) acts of resistance. We argue that art has an important role to play in all three processes. We return to this discussion in Sect. 4.
- Technology research and design are inherently political: more often than not, values and norms that are ingrained in technology designs are representative of the (rationality) hegemony [11]. Technical objects reinforce forms of hegemony through promotion of specific types of social activities/practices and exclusion or marginalization of others.

2.2   Critical Perspectives on BCI and Other Brain Wearables

How do wearable technologies shape, and how are they shaped by, the socio-cultural milieu? What are some of the assumptions and biases that are reinforced by wearable technologies, EEG-based devices in particular? Existing work on ethical and societal implications of such technologies can suggest possible answers. For example, Melissa Littlefield relies on a historical approach to analysis of technology to question what stands behind our desires to visualize and control the brain and to rely on technology such as PET, fMRI and EEG to for self-knowing and behavioral change [21]. Lucy Suchman contends that human-machine interfaces participate in obscuring the productive asymmetries of human and machine by placing wisdom with the machine and valorizing technology-meditated knowledge [40]. Drawing on a phenomenological tradition, actor-network theory (ANT) and choreography-based approach, Jaana Parviainen explores biomonitoring digital devices through the perspective of the gap that arises between the lived body experience and body as measured and quantified by technology [30]. She argues that this gap is dangerous as it reduces possibility for people to engage with lived and immediate experiences of their bodies (ibid.) In a paper on neuro-enchancements, Jonna Brenninkmeijer and Hub Zwart [3] borrow from Lacan to argue that enhancement gadgets are situated at the boundary between the friendly and the scary, between technologies of the self and, in Foucaultdian terms, technologies of control.

This brief overview of selected works on wearable technologies highlights the complexity and broad range of ethical and philosophical concerns that arise with proliferation of the said technologies. In what follows, we build up on the works of these authors to present a case study of meditating with Muse headband.

3   The Case of MUSE and the Lightness of Quantified Well-Being

Muse product website[2] presents the headband as a "brain fitness tool that measures signals much like a heart rate monitors your heartbeat". The device integrates 7 sensors: 2 on the forehead, 2 behind the ears; plus 3 reference sensors. With the promises of "More calm. Sharper focus. Better sleep", Muse is primarily marketed to individual users who wish to improve their sleep and meditation practices and their general sense of well-being and work productivity. User-friendliness and mobility make Muse for one of the popular off-the-shelf EEG-based wearables; as well as one of the most commonly deployed BCI in artworks [32].

The commercial success of Muse is barely a surprise when we consider the increasing popularity of the Quantified Self movement [24]. Indeed, in line with the core idea of the movement - self-knowing and self-management through quantified data - one of the main features of Muse is not only that it tracks users' bodily activity (i.e., heart-rate, electrical activity of the brain; breathing) and provides real-time feedback in the form of the changing soundscape, but that it also stores, scores and displays the data for the user to track their progress. Already at the level of supporting environments of the device (i.e., Muse meditation app), we are presented with a curious paradox: an open-ended process of meditation is cast as something that is to be measured, scored (e.g., rate of calmness) and optimized. In this process, the bodily activity of the user is captured by the sensors, transformed algorithmically and represented in graphs and figures that users can access through the Muse app. The emphasis on the "machine-mediated seeing" (as opposed to "embodied feeling") [9] is not only reflective of the "scopophilic tendency" [15, p.37] characteristic of the contemporary Western societies [9,21] but suggests a certain epistemological deficiency of the user: the workings of one's body are understood as obscure and inaccessible to us unless they are tracked, measured and displayed with a help of a machine.

Through the tracking and labeling of cognitive states (i.e., "calmness", "deep focus") and discarding of others as data noise, further normalization of the said states takes place. In this process, stress management and pursue of an increased productivity (narrowly defined by association with the state of "deep focus") become almost a prerogative, an ethical obligation and an important part of a self-care routine that an individual is to undergo to remain a productive and desirable worker and citizen [23]. Normalization of selected cognitive and affective states through the technical features of the Muse headset are reflective of a

---

[2] https://choosemuse.com/.

particular view on emotions and affect characteristic of the socio-economic structures that arise in the transition from Fordist economies to the so called service economies [31], wherein not only manual skills of workers but their entire personhood are called for and approached as something that can be instrumentalized and capitalized. Emotions are thus treated as resources that can be optimized and managed. This explains why commercial brain wearables have found their way into workplace environments. Take Muse' competitor Emotiv Epoc that is actively promoted for the use in companies where it is promised to "help to measure and analyze the changes in your employees' levels of stress and attention using EEG and EMOTIV's proprietary machine learning algorithms"[3].

Above, we briefly spoke that the brain activity that resists tracking and labeling by the device is subtracted from the lived corporeal experience and is discarded as noise of artifact. In the case of Muse, the sources of noise are plentiful: from muscular movements, blinking and clenching, to more nuanced affective dynamics that the device cannot decipher [2]. From this perspective, Muse establishes a new kind of meditation ritual where the steps that the user is to take in preparation to and during the meditation must also adapt to the workings of the device. Through the app-display one must first verify that the headband is in a correct position so that the data can be retrieved. While the guided sessions themselves are fairly standard, the meditation, however, can be interrupted if the device loses the connection. In this case, the user must pause the session and to adjust the headband/the positioning of their body for the device to work again.

In our experience of meditating with the device, the more time one spends with the device, the more they learn to better adapt not only at navigating the device to make sure it stays connected, but also to generate the states that device classifies as "calmness" and rewards with scores and the sounds of birds signing. Thus, the focus of the meditation now is directed at improving the calmness score, also by means of performing certain activities that correlate with "calmness" state (i.e. a simple form of hacking of the device that is often used by gamers [39]). We argue that this process of learning and adapting to the device can happen at the expense of genuine engagement with one's corporeal experience in the moment. Meditating with the device transforms an inherently intimate, embodied, dynamic communication with oneself into a machine-based practice where the device determines criteria of success and "choreographs" the cognitive and bodily aspects of the meditation [6,30].

Furthermore, normalization of selected affective states through the design of the device also invites a question concerning the very appropriateness of these states as a response to the idiosyncratic circumstances of one's life. Let us take a closer look at one of the meditation sessions available in the Muse app and titled "Burnout Self-Assessment". In a relatively short time of 8.09 min, the user is asked to reflect on where they are with respect to: a) the energy level ("in the current state of exhaustion"), b) depersonalization ("a sense of being dehumanized yourself, or diminishment of connection with others"), c) self-efficacy ("how

---

[3] https://www.emotiv.com/workplace-wellness-safety-and-productivity-mn8/.

would you rate yourself with respect to your capacity to influence your environment today?"). Once the (self-)rating of these three components of burnout is complete, the user is invited to rate themselves with respect to the "four pillars of resilience": self-awareness, level of autonomy ("what is your frustration level with respect to the sense of agency?", relaxation ("how are you doing with opportunities to rest, to decompose, to sleep?"), and, finally, community ("how much opportunity do you have for authentic connection?"). Setting aside the complexity of each of these questions, and the oxymoron that is the request to rate one's self-awareness level, the point we want to highlight here is that while these arguably non-trivial questions are asked, the device continues measuring and scoring the activity of the user, with an implicit assumption of the "deep restful focus" as the goal state of the meditation. In this context, complex existential and affective states such exhaustion, lack of authentic connection to others are cast as a kind of local problem that is - while unpleasant indeed - can be operationalized and efficiently "fixed", not without the help of the device. Notably, the idea of a "quick fix" is omnipresent in the wide selection of meditation practices: from meditation for the sense of purpose in healthcare profession to cancer comfort and baseball.

Interim Conclusion. Drawing on our experience of meditating with Muse and on the works of scholars such as Feenberg, Parviainen, Littlefield, Luton and others, we have illustrated how commercial BCI incorporate in their designs and supporting commercial environments particular understandings of well-being, emotions and how to access and manage these with a help of technology. We argue that these understandings are shaped (and in turn, continue to reinforce) what Feenberg refers to as "rationality" hegemony: the dominant socio-economic and cultural structures wherein values of managerial control, knowledge as equal to quantification and narrowly understood efficiency and productivity prevail. In the discussion on how the technical features of Muse are reflective of the rationality hegemony, we focused on the themes of: individual responsibility for mental and physical well-being as assisted by technology; normalization of selected few affective states as part of the promoted self-care routine; the assumption of epistemological insufficiency that is supposedly solved with technological mediation; and, last but not least, the general orientation toward visuality and knowing through data that devices such as Muse promote.

4   BCI Art as a Form of Critical Engagement and Subversion

4.1   Art as Technology Re-interpretation Domain

In Sect. 2, we suggested that art and artistic engagements with technologies such as BCI and other body wearables constitute an important part of exploring and expanding the field of interpretative flexibility of technical objects. Through this process, art participates in challenging established practices and values that are ingrained in existing designs of technologies and their promoted use cases, renegotiates the problem space that these technologies are supposed to address, and has a potential to propose new ways of engaging with technology and each other through technological mediation. Before we proceed to present selected case studies of BCI artworks that critically engage with the themes we highlighted in Sect. 3, we would like to say more on the relationship between art and technological emancipation, and how we approach it within the artistic research space of the Neuromatic GameArt Project.

From the perspective of critical constructivist framework, the neat delineation between art and technology can only exist as a theoretical abstraction. In contrast to the abstractly topological view on art, technology - and politics! - that assumes that these practices exist within their dedicated domains that sometimes interact, we follow Feenberg in espousing the view that both technology development and artistic practices with technology are inherently political. Both in art and in technology design, ideologies, values, different actors and social forces compete for which ideas get represented and further sedimented as a part of a hegemonic order. When we recognize the inherently political nature of art and technology design, we also see that art can be a force of change; be it incremental change through redefining of the socio-cultural horizon of technology [12], or a more radical change through explicit acts of resistance and political activism [11, 27, 34].

Instead of defining art as political or non-political (i.e., all art is political in that it either reinforces or challenges hegemony), Belgian political theorist Chantal Mouffe proposes that the political efficacy of art is better understood through examining artistic practices that she coins as *critical*. Critical art per Mouffe "makes visible what the dominant consensus tends to obscure and obliterate. [...] [and] participates in dislocating and destabilizing of "established orders" and instituting of aspects of society anew" [26]. From this perspective, we argue the political potency of BCI art with respect to technology (and decision-making about technology) emancipation can be enacted through:

- Making visible and challenging the assumptions and ideologies that are imprinted in technical designs and commercial environments of BCI.
- Extending socio-cultural horizon of BCI through exploration of new aesthetic forms and expressions with BCI.
- Proposing and exploring alternative realities and radically new forms of spacio-temporal arrangements [34] that lead to enable new subjectivities [26].

Of course, the neat delineation between these forms of enacting political through art are also an abstraction that we adopt for the purposes of structured discussion. In reality, and as we will also show through case studies of BCI art, these activities (implicitly or explicitly enacted by artists) cross-cut. Moreover, sometimes the challenging and the reinforcement of dominant values and practices can co-exist within the space of one artwork. That being said, in what follows, we draw on these three categories to support our discussion of how artists critically engage with the assumptions and biases of BCI and reflect on the possible ethical and social implications of these technologies.

4.2   Making the Codes of the Device Visible

To begin our discussion on how artists can make visible the values, established practices and dominant socio-cultural narratives that are hidden behind the seemingly neutral technical designs and environments of BCI, we would like to introduce the reader to an artwork that we developed within the Neuromatic Game Art project titled "Neuromatic Gan Portrait Game: the Artist is Measured" first presented at Parallel Vienna in September 2020[4]. This interactive installation combines elements of game design, interactive art, surveillance technology, AI-based image processing methods and neuroimaging technology to invite the audience to reflect on the role of these technologies as expressive of socio-political forms characteristic of what Deleuze referred to as "societies of control" [8]. The thematic core of the installation is the concept of technology mediated portraiture. Within the installation space that stretches out across three conjoint rooms, the visitor is invited to have their "portraits" created, first, by a software based on a Chinese facial recognition system and, second - by a Generative adversarial network (GAN) that reconstructs the visitor's face based on a set of human faces that was used to train the neural network. Similarly to how meditation with a Muse device is a ritual wherein one must accommodate themselves to meet the "expectations of the device", in this installation, to have the portrait taken the visitor must follow the commands of the system and to find a position where their face can be recognized as such by the surveillance system. This little dance choreographed by the machine [6] frequently results in portraits that are taken not when the visitor expects it, which makes for an ambivalent experience of performing work while simultaneously having one's agency and control over the outcome diminished. The theme of the (voluntarily) submission to the machines - to be observed, captured and scored by them - is also emphasized by the "experiment participation contract" that the visitors are invited to sign before they enter the space of the installation. The score that the visitor sees once the process of the portrait generation is completed represents portrait generation efficiency based on the visitor's face: the time that it took GAN to reconstruct the visitor's face from the training data. The part of the installation that is especially relevant in the context of this paper transpires in the second room where visitors encounter the Artist who is wearing an EEG headset, and where the activity of the Artist brain - as captured by the device - is screened real-time on a monitor for the visitors to see. Connected and also "observed" and measured by the device, the Artist is looking at the visitors' portraits generated by the machines. By recasting the artist as simultaneously an active onlooker but also - similarly to the audience - the subject of a scientific experiment wherein their inner process is represented through waves of electrical activity of the brain, the installation invites the audience to question what it means to be looked at by a person and what it means to be "looked at" by a machine? Can machines read minds? What can they tell - if anything - about personhood [10], subjectivity and creative process, and what is the meaning of the automated portraiture?

---

[4] https://neuromatic.uni-ak.ac.at/blog/eeg-stylegan-installation-at-parallel-vienna/.

Outside of the Neuromatic Project, many artists working with BCI have also engaged in critically reflecting on the role of technology in reinforcing the hegemony and normalization of values that characterize what Winograd refers to as the Western rationality paradigm [41]. For instance, "Naos" (2008), the installation by Carlos Castellanos, Philippe Pasquier, Luther Thie, Kyu Che stems from the ethical concerns about technology use for profiling and behavior prediction. The installation consists of a "bio-pod" where participants are presented with visual stimuli with affective content; meanwhile their physiological response, including brain activity, is being measured. Based on the measurements, the algorithm determines in real-time both the succeeding image, but also classifies the participant into one of four categories: passive, aggressive, loyal and subversive.

Another work, this time by Alberto Novello, titled "Fragmentation" (2014) is especially interesting in how the author creates a space for critical reflection that is also charged with affect. "Fragmentation" is a brain-wave controlled performance, combing dance, video, theater and gamification, that, in the words of the author, explores "frustration and stress of the postmodern life"[5]. On stage we see a naked man - a dancer impersonating a "post-modern man" - moving slowly through a maze while simultaneously controlling his avatar through the same maze projected above the stage. The control of the movements through the maze is executed through an EEG-based headset that the dancer is wearing: depending on the state that the device picks up on, the avatar can move to the right, to the left or straight. At the same time, sounds and flickering images are generated, again as triggered by the brain activity of the dancer. Taken together, the performance construes a somewhat dystopian scenery where a man - exposed and vulnerable in his nakedness, foregrounding the background of visual data waterfall - moves slowly, as if under an invisible weight, towards a metaphoric escape. By combining different expressive elements and mediums within one work, "Fragmentation", in our view, is a good example of how artists can engage with the ethical and political themes surrounding BCI technology in a manner that is both emotionally touching and conceptually thought-through (see [29]).

It is worth mentioning that in order for an artwork to make visible assumptions behind technical objects, the authors do not necessarily have to engage in the construction of complex narratives nor explicitly address political and ethical issues in their work. At times, a rather (conceptually) straightforward - if not simplistic - work nevertheless reveals what the technical codes of the devices tend to obscure. For example, consider the installation "Brain Noise Machine" by Gregg Kress (2010). Created in collaboration with Santhi Elayaperumal and Joel Sadler, this work is, as the authors refer to it, "a mind-controlled kinetic sculpture". In fact, the sculpture is an assemblage of old kitchen utensils connected to a Neurosky headset. In the absence of the "focused mental energy", the sculpture creates a continuous stream of chaotic noise[6]. The installation falls silent when mental focus is detected and it remains silent as long as the user

---

[5] https://vimeo.com/36403730.

[6] http://glkress.com/art-and-design/brain-art/brain-noise-machine/.

maintains the state that is deciphered as "focus". While the intent of the author is open to interpretation, for us the literal noise that the installation produces whenever its "expectations" of "focus" are not met by the user is revealing the limitations of BCI in the face of complexity of human affective and cognitive processes [10].

4.3   Challenging Technical Rationality

Subverting Hegemony by Creating Alternative Practices. In the introduction to this section we pointed out that the importance of artistic practices in (re-)shaping of the techno-social horizon also includes art works that explore different technological imaginaries and ways of engaging with technology outside of commercially promoted scripts. To illustrate, again, we would like to refer to our experience within the Neuromatic GameArt project, specifically, to one performance that took place in June 2020 as a culmination of a series of weekly Neuromatic Broadcasts[7]. In this online performance[8], we built up on the idea of a technologically mediated "quick fix" - an idea, as we discussed in 3, that is implicit in many commercial applications of BCI. Artistically, this work is inspired by and extends on the traditions of situationism [7] and the concept of ludic interfaces (e.g., [13]). We draw on situationism and play to create playful interactions with technology by taking existing structures and recontextualizing them in a different, unexpected way. Through this modification, different effects can be achieved. In this performance, developed by Charlotta Ruth, in collaboration with Margarete Jahrmann, Stefan Glasauer and Anna Dobrosovestnova - two "players" wearing Muse and Neurosky headsets - participated in a so called "quick fix brain focus training" that was broadcast live on Youtube. During the training, the players (Jahrmann and Glasauer) were instructed via text appearing on the screen to perform a series of seemingly absurd and unrelated tasks: from writing down what they wish to do in the next 50 years to circling their eyes ten times and eating nuts as a part of a "healthy diet". While the tasks flirted with the absurdity of fast meditations as remedies for every occasion, the brain data visualization reflected only the most perceptible changes in the players' brain activity. For instance, when asked to balance on one foot, the data turned into a very dense concentrated small ball. Simultaneously, the chat was open to anyone to participate by inserting poetic associations and/or questions that sometimes translate real-time into new "quick fix" instructions.

Today, we continue experimenting with how existing commercial BCI environments can be deconstructed and recontextualized and rearticulated [26] anew outside of their commercial environments. Currently, we are working on developing a series of "meditations" - short playful sessions that use the structure of meditations on the Muse app to create experiences and emotional states that are uncommon for the commercial meditations (e.g., scary meditation).

---

[7] https://neuromatic.uni-ak.ac.at/blog/neuromatic-broadcast-compilation-document ary-research-film-release-online/.

[8] https://www.youtube.com/watch?v=PAZG5BU-JaU&feature=youtu.be.

The "meditations" will be offered as regular interactive live sessions to Muse community and anyone willing to participate, with and without the device.

4.4 Creating Alternative Imaginaries

Needless to say that one of the critical potential of art is to go to the fringes of what is possible and imaginable to speculate about possible near and distant futures with technologies. One way to achieve this is through re-imaging the aesthetics and functionalities of BCI of the future. Consider, for example, the series of drawings titled "Helmets of the Near Future" by the contemporary Russian artist Pavel Pepperstein (2018). Pepperstein draws on the popular science-fiction narratives and imaginaries of neuroimaging technologies as one step that brings us closer to mind-reading to imagine and depict a collection of futuristic BCI-like devices that can visualize user's abstract (i.e. shapes and colors) and concrete (e.g. an image of themselves being crucified) thoughts.

If Pepperstein chooses to imagine BCI anew, existing devices can also be used to expand on their functionalities through metaphors and particular spacial and aesthetic re-arrangements. For example, artist Lisa Park in the work titled "Eunoia ii" (2014). This installation consists of 48 water bowls that represent 48 categories of affect, as inspired by the writings on emotions by Spinosa. The water in the bowls vibrates in response to the brain activity of the artist who is wearing an Emotiv Epoc headset while she's moving slowly around the bowls. The vibrations of the water create a mesmerizing soundscape that, together with the visual aspects of the installation, come together in a unique audio-visual representation of the artist affective dynamic.

The reason we highlight this performance here is because, in our view, it represents perfectly the ambivalence that is common to many BCI artworks: on the one hand, this work engages and reaffirms the assumption that a BCI can pick up on the complex affective states (which, as we discussed in Sect. 3 is not the case, at least not considering the state-of-the-art of BCI technology). By representing affect metaphorically with the 48 vibrating water bowls (in contrast to selected and labeled states such as "deep focus", "mind wandering" etc.), Park creatively extends the functionality of BCI beyond what the devices can in fact do. And, importantly, by translating the output of the device into aesthetic forms, she in turn invites an affective experience in the audience. In this process, an emotional connection is established between the artist and the spectator, with the device participating in creation of a kind of contact zone where elements and actors come together and exchange information and through this form what Munoz refers to as an "infraface" [28].

4.5 Extending Technology Horizon Through Exploration of Aesthetic Forms and Expressions

We contend that part of artistic practice is a search of relationship between senses and meaning. This relationship needn't necessarily be open to articulation in language. Moreover, an artist will not always be in control of how a particular relationship emerges. In BCI art, an important category of works are the works where brain activity of the artists and/or audience is translated into an audio or visual output [32], similarly to "Eunoia ii" installation that was described above. In these "experiments", artists often remain unaware how the outcomes of an experiment will look/sound like. The latter are constrained but not determined by the conditions that set the experiment: in some sense, like Pollock spilling paint over canvas - with only limited control over how the emerging shapes the patterns will look - in BCI art, brain activity is a material that is algorithmically sculpted. In this process, the artist is also a participant in witnessing, perceiving her works; moreover, the outcomes also generate an affective response that is further "fed" into the system.

In the Neuromatic Game Art research project, we have been using Muse device outside of its intended context of use. Every Friday, at 7 pm, Jahrmann and Glasauer put on Muse headbands and transmit the data real-time on Youtube. As part of the process of choosing how the data are being represented each session, the brain data are rendered and visualized with the math lab Psych tool box written from scratch by Glasauer. At the same time, live audio is generated out of these data via a reactor path written by Thomas Wagensommer. In each session, a "research question" - a special focus on how to represent the data in a unique manner - is pursued. The central element in these broadcast has never been to communicate "brain states" to the audience, but to explore the multiplicity of aesthetic forms that corporeal existence can be translated into through technological mediation. At the initial stages of the broadcasts, the brain data were visualized into a unique dance of dots on the screen. Sometimes dots come together, sometimes the organism shaped by the data of Jahrmann's brain is embracing that of Glasauer's. One is invited to lean back and observe the visual choreography or hang out in the chat with the two brain broadcasters. BCI art often suffers from a disconnection between what is actually happening and what is easily grasped by the audience. To find formats of expression where the link between what is technically happening and what is expressed and received by the audience remains one of the most difficult tasks. Often BCI art requires technical explanations and stays more in the realm of research. In contrast, in the Neuromatic Broadcast series we decided to emphasize the affective dimension of "broadcast brains" and create an experience where the visuals themselves become tactile and invite kinetic empathy in the viewers without necessarily having a clear reference to the "state" that gave rise to them.

From this perspective, the BCI artworks that explore the aesthetic dimension - intentionally or unintentionally - tap into the theme of what (brain) data can tell us about ourselves and others. What can we really learn about another person? Can brain data communicate subjective experience? The work by by Alan Dunning and Paul Woodrow, who are members of The Einstein's Brain Project[9] titled "Shape of Thought" (2010)[10] is a notable example. In this work, participants monitored by EEG and EKG sensors, are asked to recall a traumatic event

---

[9] https://people.ucalgary.ca/einbrain/new/main.html.
[10] https://bci-art.tumblr.com/post/172883734132/the-shape-of-thought.

from their past as they are being hypnotized. In the words of the authors, these "hypnotic recollections of the participants, their mental re-visualizations of traumatic events, produce effects on the body that are then imaged and examined, providing us with ways to investigate the workings of the body-mind through these mental images."[11]. In this work, the tension between the subjective experience of reliving a traumatic experience and an attempt to understand this experience from the third person perspective - by looking at the resulting visualizations - is perhaps the most evident. On the one hand, through technology, we do indeed get access to the private space of one's inner world. On the other hand, simultaneously, it remains as inaccessible - a kind of lacanian Object petit a [18] that we may come closer to but never really reach and grasp.

5   Conclusion and Future Work

This paper introduced our ongoing work within the interdisciplinary Neuromatic GameArt Project that brings together a team of artists, neuroscientists, game designers and philosophers of technology to critically examine ethical and societal implications of brain-computer interfaces, both by the means of philosophical inquiry and artistic practices with the devices. We discussed how philosophically, we position our research within the critical constructivist framework in philosophy of technology and laid out some key implications of the said framework for our work. These include, but are not limited to assuming that: (i) technology design, as artistic practices, are inherently political; (ii) individual and collective agency outside of expert communities can and should have a place in decision-making about technology; (iii) artistic engagements with technology participate in shaping of socio-cultural horizon of technology. We proceeded to introduce some critical perspectives on BCI and other wearable technologies and built up on these to support our analysis of the commercial headband Muse and accompanying meditation app. In this analysis, we focused on highlighting assumptions about self-knowledge, the role of quantification as an epistemic tool, emotions and well-being that are hidden behind the seemingly neutral design features of Muse.

In the second part of the paper, we turned to the discussion on how art participates in technology (re-)interpretation. By examples of our artistic work in Neuromatic GameArt Project and selected work by our colleagues in the BCI art communities, we illustrated how this can happen, among other, through: i) making the hidden assumptions and biases of technology visible (conceptually and on the level of sensory experience); ii) creating and exploring alternative practices and imaginaries with BCI that transcend commercially promoted use cases; iii) extending on interpretative flexibility of BCI by means of exploring aesthetic forms.

By casting art as political, our intention is not to idealize artistic practice by assigning it a unique role in the critique of hegemony or by assuming that it is immune to hegemony. If anything, we hope that our discussion of different BCI

---

[11] https://people.ucalgary.ca/einbrain/new/main.html.

artworks also showed that the relationship between art, technology and society is not straightforward and that - when it comes to art where technology is used but also criticized - there is no "pure" position of critique "out of nowhere". Art is not apolitical. In the words of Gene Ray: "All productions of spirit in class society are entanglements of truth and untruth, freedom and unfreedom, promise of happiness and marker of barbarism. Critique confronts the social untruth embedded in cultural artefacts in order to set free the potential truth that is also latent in them" [35, p.80]. Indeed, artistic practices can take a distance to the hegemonic socio-cultural structures by exploring new spacial, temporal and relational configurations outside of the established institutions and models; however, such distancing is never fully "outside" and is never fully divorced from the existing dominant socio-cultural and technical discourses.

Indeed, within the project we are continuously challenged by the question whether our engagements with technology further validate and reinstate the hegemony that gives rise to the idea that our utmost intimate self-practices need to be mediated by a machine. In the end, we did purchase the devices and we use them regularly as a part of artistic displays. Through the project, we inadvertently participate in promoting these devices, as well as we do - to extent - participate in reaffirming the assumption that technology can tells us something about our most intimate experiences. That is, the production of critical art with technology is inherently challenging as it is always tempting to get enamoured with technology and to take the assumptions related to it for granted. We do not know how to avoid this challenge. In this struggle, we side with Stavrakakis [38] when he draws on Lacan in acknowledging that the first step toward subjective and collective change is to "assume responsibility for our direct and indirect, conscious and unconscious, cognitive and affective implication in our symptom" [38, p.565]. For us, this means to remain sensitive to and self-critical in the face of near-impossibility to resist "playing by the rules" of the devices.

We also recognize that we are only in the beginning of the exploration of how technology and art can inspire, inform and challenge each other. From a theoretical/philosophical perspective, more work is needed to flesh out the mechanisms of subversive rationalization [11] and examine the ways in which artistic practices can feed back into technology designs. In particular, we invite cultural studies and historians to investigate these mechanisms through the prism of culture theory and the idea of incremental changes in socio-cultural sphere that accompany paradigmatic shifts (e.g. [22]). Another direction of research might take a more STS approach: given that artists who practice BCI art are quite frequently also academics and scientists, STS methods offer a toolkit and conceptual frameworks to study empirically how artistic work feeds back into scientific research, and vice versa. Inspired and challenged by our experiences with BCI, we also invite our colleagues in the art field to reflect on their use of technology in art: Which assumptions are taken for granted? Where do these assumptions come from? Who benefits from these? Most importantly, from a critical and political perspective, we encourage BCI artists to also consider how artistic engagements with BCI can give voice and explore conditions that help to empower those who are usually outside of the target group of the commercial BCI. Artists are invited to explore how they can think of brains (rather than brain) and bodies (rather than body) [36] as part of their artistic work.

Acknowledgements. This research paper is supported by the Austrian Science Fund (FWF): AR 581 Programm zur Entwicklung und Erschließung der Kunste (PEEK).

The first author extends her gratitude to Charlotta Ruth, Tim Reinboth and Baris Acar for their thoughtful comments to an earlier draft of the manuscript.

References

1. Acabchuk, R.L., Simon, M.A., Low, S., Brisson, J.M., Johnson, B.T.: Measuring meditation progress with a consumer-grade EEG device: caution from a randomized controlled trial. Mindfulness **12**(1), 68–81 (2021)
2. Bashivan, P., Rish, I., Heisig, S.: Mental state recognition via wearable EEG. arXiv preprint arXiv:1602.00985 (2016)
3. Brenninkmeijer, J., Zwart, H.: From 'hard' neuro-tools to 'soft' neuro-toys? Refocussing the neuro-enhancement debate. Neuroethics **10**(3), 337–348 (2017)
4. Coeckelbergh, M.: Hacking Feenberg. Symploke **20**(1), 327–330 (2012)
5. Coeckelbergh, M.: Introduction to Philosophy of Technology (2019)
6. Coeckelbergh, M.: Moved by Machines: Performance Metaphors and Philosophy of Technology. Routledge (2019)
7. Debord, G.: Society of the Spectacle. Bread and Circuses Publishing (2012)
8. Deleuze, G.: Postscript on the societies of control. **59**, 3–7 (1992)
9. Dror, O.Y.: The scientific image of emotion: experience and technologies of inscription. Configurations **7**(3), 355–401 (1999)
10. Dumit, J.: Picturing personhood: biomedical scans and personal identity (2004)
11. Feenberg, A.: Subversive rationalization: technology, power, and democracy. Inquiry **35**(3–4), 301–322 (1992)
12. Feenberg, A.: Between Reason and Experience: Essays in Technology and Modernity. MIT Press (2010)
13. Gaver, W.W., et al.: The drift table: designing for ludic engagement. In: CHI'04 Extended Abstracts on Human Factors in Computing Systems, pp. 885–900 (2004)
14. Geuss, R., et al.: The Idea of a Critical Theory: Habermas and the Frankfurt School. Cambridge University Press (1981)
15. Gregg, M.: Inside the data spectacle. Telev. New Media **16**(1), 37–51 (2015)
16. Kavoulakos, K.: Philosophy of praxis or philosophical anthropology? Andrew Feenberg and Axel Honneth on Lukács's theory of reification. In: Arnold, D.P., Michel, A. (eds.) Critical Theory and the Thought of Andrew Feenberg, pp. 47–69. Springer, Cham (2017). https://doi.org/10.1007/978-3-319-57897-2_3
17. Kirkpatrick, G.: Transforming dystopia with democracy: the technical code and the critical theory of technology. In: Arnold, D.P., Michel, A. (eds.) Critical Theory and the Thought of Andrew Feenberg, pp. 117–138. Springer, Cham (2017). https://doi.org/10.1007/978-3-319-57897-2_6
18. Lacan, J.: Les formations de l'inconscient. Bulletin de psychologie **6**, 519–539 (2011)
19. Laclau, E., Mouffe, C.: Hegemony and socialist strategy: towards a radical democratic politics. Verso Trade (2014)

20. Latour, B.: Science in Action: How to Follow Scientists and Engineers Through Society. Harvard University Press (1987)
21. Littlefield, M.M.: Instrumental Intimacy: EEG Wearables and Neuroscientific Control. JHU Press (2018)
22. Lotman, J.: Culture and Explosion, vol. 1. Walter de Gruyter (2009)
23. Lupton, D.: Critical perspectives on digital health technologies. Sociol. Compass **8**(12), 1344–1359 (2014)
24. Lupton, D.: The diverse domains of quantified selves: self-tracking modes and dataveillance. Econ. Soc. **45**(1), 101–122 (2016)
25. Meyer, U., Schulz-Schaeffer, I.: Three forms of interpretative flexibility. Sci. Technol. Innov. Stud. **2** (2006)
26. Mouffe, C.: Art and democracy: art as an agnostic intervention in public space. Art as a Public Issue. Open Mag. (14), 6–15 (2008)
27. Mouffe, C.: Agonistics: Thinking the World Politically. Verso Books (2013)
28. Muñoz, M.: Infrafaces: Essays on the Artistic Interaction (2013)
29. Novello, A.: A combination of gamification and DSP analysis to expose brain activity in EEG performances: the case of fragmentation-a brain-controlled performance
30. Parviainen, J.: Quantified bodies in the checking loop: analyzing the choreographies of biomonitoring and generating big data. Hum. Technol. **12**(1), 56–74 (2016)
31. Penz, O., Sauer, B.: Governing affects. Neo-Bureaucracies, and, Neoliberalism (2020)
32. Prpa, M., Pasquier, P.: Brain-computer interfaces in contemporary art: a state of the art and taxonomy. Brain Art, 65–115 (2019)
33. Radevski, S., Hata, H., Matsumoto, K.: Real-time monitoring of neural state in assessing and improving software developers' productivity. In: 2015 IEEE/ACM 8th International Workshop on Cooperative and Human Aspects of Software Engineering, pp. 93–96. IEEE (2015)
34. Rancière, J.: Aesthetics and its Discontents. Polity (2009)
35. Ray, G.: Toward a critical art theory. Fly, 79 (2009)
36. Spiel, K.: The bodies of TEI-investigating norms and assumptions in the design of embodied interaction (2021)
37. Spüler, M., Krumpe, T., Walter, C., Scharinger, C., Rosenstiel, W., Gerjets, P.: Brain-computer interfaces for educational applications. In: Buder, J., Hesse, F.W. (eds.) Informational Environments, pp. 177–201. Springer, Cham (2017). https://doi.org/10.1007/978-3-319-64274-1_8
38. Stavrakakis, Y.: Challenges of re-politicisation: Mouffe's agonism and artistic practices. Third Text **26**(5), 551–565 (2012)
39. Stober, J.M.: Hacking as a playful strategy for designing the artistic and experimental BCI-VR game: ride your mind (2018)
40. Suchman, L., Suchman, L.A.: Human-Machine Reconfigurations: Plans and Situated Actions. Cambridge University Press (2007)
41. Winograd, T.: Computers and rationality: The myths and realities "." Morelli, Ralph/Brown, W. Miller/Anselmi, Dina/Haberlandt, Karl/Lloyd, Dan (Hg.) Minds, Brains, and Computers: Perspectives in Cognitive Science and Artificial Intelligence, pp. 152–167. Ablex Publishing Corporation, Norwood (1992)

The Solitary Connected. Media Places and New Emotional Flows in the Platform Society

Mauro Ferraresi[✉]

IULM – International University of Languages and Media, Milan, Italy
mauro.ferraresi@iulm.it

Abstract. In a perspective that, as stated by Shaun Moores (2012), can start from media studies and somehow overcome them, the concept of media environment, namely the idea that the media create environments where to be and places where to live experience, can be enhanced with new elements. Through an analysis that differentiates places from experiencing places of affection, the hypothesis that moves us, and that we will try to demonstrate, is that there are digital places of affection, that is, web environments capable of developing affection like in certain places in the real world. According to the definition, and according to common sense, an affection is a constant sentimental inclination towards a person or thing for which one has, nurtures, conceives positive emotions.

To this end, we will start from some sociological concepts such as media environment, trust, meme, magnetic digital places.

Following this, we will briefly discuss some social consequences of pandemic periodization and then we will conclude with an exposition of the results of a survey conducted in the late spring of 2021 on these same topics.

Keywords: Media environment · Trust · Magnetic digital places · Digital emotions

1   Media Environment

The study of the environment in sociology comes from the studies of urban sociology inaugurated at the beginning of the 20th century by the Chicago school. From that moment onwards, the concept of environment has often been discussed by sociologists, until the idea that even the media are an environment and that a true ecology of the media can be elaborated. (Granata 2015).

The literature on the authors who have spent themselves in the study of media environments has grown considerably. Starting from the early works of Harold Innis (1951, 1952) and Marshall Mc Luhan (1962, 1964), and then Lewis Mumford (1967), Neil Postman that first in 1968 gave a lecture on the media ecology (2000), Gregory Bateson (1972) and others, the concept of media environment has proven to be a fruitful, idea. According to Luca de Biase, "Postman responded with the idea of media ecology to Marshall McLuhan's solicitation that media create a real environment in which people then live and develop, adapting to its characteristics." De Biase adds that it is useless to

© Springer Nature Switzerland AG 2021
C. Stephanidis et al. (Eds.): HCII 2021, LNCS 13096, pp. 575–584, 2021.
https://doi.org/10.1007/978-3-030-90328-2_39

consider the media environment as not natural and therefore not entirely real. Truth is that digital can be seen as less then real at the time of Mcluhan and Postman, but today the distinction between natural and artificial tends to fade: "Someone may be tempted to say that the media environment is a perceived environment, not natural, and therefore a little less than real. But if this was a debatable idea in the days of McLuhan and Postman, today in the digital world it is less and less difficult to digest: after all, the distinction between natural and artificial is less and less useful." (De Biase 2018).

The consequences can be numerous. An environment is what needs to be taken care of, as ecology teaches, likewise the media environment cannot be left to the constant pollutions of fake news and filtering bubbles (Eli Parisier 2012) It is necessary to work to keep the media environment clean since it is now highly polluted in ways and characteristics befitting the network. (Colombo 2020).

Numerous rhetorical and linguistic elements confirm this ascertained equalization between physical places and digital places. It is actually a metaphor that is no longer a metaphor but a precise denotation that explains an important characteristic of the media.

In the digital world we speak of virtual space, of electronic frontier, cyberspace and information highways; and then again of cafes, dungeons and virtual offices. These are just a few of the spatial and environmental definitions we refer to when describing websites and, generally speaking, what we do with the web (Adams 1997). Not to mention the surfing metaphor, and the poetics that accompany it. Manovich states that the fundamental characteristic of virtual space is the web surfing. This concept is inextricably linked to that of space and is so popular because space is always a subjective space "whose architecture reacts to the movements and emotions of the subject." (2001, 332) Manovich is helped by Baudelaire (1986) and Walter Benjamin (1986). Baudelaire wrote about the figure of the flâneur, who enjoys the crowd and its anonymity; that is, he enjoys his unknown presence among the people who act as a curtain, veiling and hiding the city, transforming the city as a consequence of the emotions felt. The figure of the flâneur, of the explorer, of the navigator is a whole on the web, so that Geert Lovink can speak of "data Dandy", i.e. a subject whose paths and surfing on the web become a mirror of his subjectivity and of his emotions. (Manovich 2001, 333 and following) We prefer to rename him: Digital Dandy. The Digital Dandy navigates gracefully among sites and transforms the architecture of digital spaces thanks to his emotional flow. If the nineteenth-century European dandy played the role of *lèche-vitrine*, the Digital Dandy plays the role of *lèche-website*.

As in certain semantic word clouds, some sites in fact react to navigation and increase their size and emotional importance at the detriment of others, acting as powerful attractors.

The Meyrowitz sense of place is now involved with virtual reality (1985). Mutual integration between places is underway whereby our experiences of real places are also inexorably borrowed from media; and vice versa. (Relph 2007).

Our physical environment plays a significant role in the development of our identity and perceptions, as well as the relationships we have with others. The space, as semiotics suggests, is always a space-of-meaning where relationships are structured "among practices, objects and subjects" and thus continuous negotiations are constructed among social actors, transforming the given space into lived space. (Pezzini 2020; Giannitrapani 2013, Ferraresi 2009).

To bring an example: a university professor organizes himself in different ways within the lived space of the university if he is in the classroom, in the university coffee shop, or in the Dean office. That is, the space takes on different actantial roles, whether Object of Value (the Dean office), Helper (the university bar), or Destinant (the university classroom). These are different actantial roles that have different interactional performances, that is, different organizations of their own social practices and interactions with other subjects in the space.

Similarly, we can argue that electronic artifacts also provide the structure for a potential organization of new social interactions (Ponti and Ryberg 2004).

2 Trust

The roots of the trust relationship can be found in at least three different soils. The first ground is that of competence and knowledge. The subject who "knows what he is saying and takes responsibility for what he is saying" is considered credible and trustworthy. (Belardinelli and Gili 2020). This is what in English terms is called confidence. The second ground is that of values. In this case, trust and credibility rely on the value system expressed. Sometimes those values are not exactly in tune with our own, but they still seem right and desirable, and above all consistent with the conduct exhibited. (ibid.)

The third ground is of relevance for our paper. In this third plot of land the roots lie in affectivity and in the relationship of trust and credibility that "is based on a positive and wellbeing-giving bond with the other as occurs in the relationship between mother and child, in the friendship or in the relationship between leaders and followers" (Gili, 2005; Gili and Panarari 2020).

The relationship of trust can be interpersonal but also institutional and in this case arises trust towards specific institutions, entities, sites, and it can be systemic. One trusts a system - the educational system, the health system, the system of government institutions, the media system - since one believes that it works exactly as one expects it to work.

In spite of the pollution mentioned above, in spite of the increasing sensationalism of the news to the detriment of its seriousness and credibility, in spite of the continuous search for sensationalism, in spite of the deficient gatekeeping work that denotes a lack of professionalism, in spite of the low budgets that lead to a decline in journalists' ability to find out the news, notwithstanding the raging of opinions instead of facts and, finally, notwithstanding the bandwagon effect whereby there are not too many discordant opinions on what is economically, politically and culturally relevant and desirable but, on the contrary, only a falling blob of dominant opinions are treated; Italians, according to a 2019 research conducted by the Demopolis institute on the under 30s and commissioned by the Italian Order of Journalists, continue to feed their media diet for 66% with television information and even with 63% with social media, Facebook, You tube and others, despite the growing contagion of fakes now appearing in exponential growth (Demopolis 1919).

What reasons do they keep high confidence in the information and media system, including digital media, despite the problems listed? And what trust do they drive towards social networks?

It is important to remember that the relationship of trust is always a mediation result and, normally, grows or diminishes because of the positive or negative experiences that a subject lives in the encounter with that particular institution, with that particular system (Berardinelli, Gili, ivi).

The hypothesis we advance, and which will be tested by the exploratory research we will discuss in the last paragraph of this paper, is that the roots of this credibility do not lie in competence or even in values, but rather in affectivity. (This truth also emerges from the Demopolis research when to the precise question: "Do you happen to doubt the credibility of the news?" the majority, 56% of respondents, answered yes and, nevertheless, the dependence on social media remains strong as much of the media diet continues to rely on them despite the lack of credibility they suffer. To another precise question: "What tools do you use to inform yourself?", 63% of respondents say they continue to use Facebook, Youtube and other social networks. (See Di Fraia 2015) Everything happens as if we were in the presence of a kind of oblative attitude such as that of the mother towards her son to whom she gives attention and affection with generosity and with minimal expectations of compensation (Fig. 1).

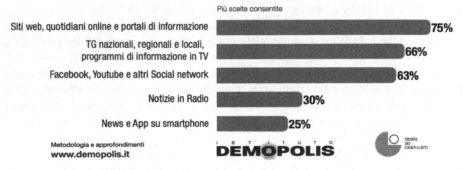

Come si informano gli under 30 in Italia: indagine Demopolis per l'Ordine dei Giornalisti

Per informarsi sull'attualità, quali strumenti utilizza?

Fig. 1. How Italians under the age of 30 get informed.

3 Magnetic Digital Places

In Spreadable Media the authors analyze the case of the spontaneous diffusion of Susan Boyle's video that "(…) attracted 103 million hits on 20 different websites within the first nine days of its publication" and they finally affirm that this is an active form of participatory culture, and that it is not, as most believe, the passive reception of viruses or memes. (2013, 23).

If Jenkins, Ford and Green are right, it must be admitted that there are places on the net that attract customers like magnets. On the net there is not only the contamination of a video, a photograph, a phrase that spreads like wildfire. It is reductive to understand these types of phenomena in this way. As Jenkins rightly reiterates, a place on the net does not seem to simply behave like a virus or a meme that spreads by contagion or imitation (Jenkins 2006).

There is an active and irresistible attraction towards certain websites even when moving from different platforms. Basically, users move towards the network sites, and not viceversa.

Those desirable places, that web surfers do things with, excite, create interest, entertain and drive more clicks. That's how you create that surplus of audience, the same surplus that marketers look for attracting customers to their flagship stores and retail stores creating a desire to stay as long as possible.

If attracting rather than spreading is the key verb, then one can liken the experiential marketing to those aspects of digital places that are under investigation here.

According to experiential marketing, stores are not only places to be, they are desirable and pleasant places: the difference is substantial. A precise distinction can be made moving from the concept of consumption mix (Ferraresi 2016). The place, in fact, can be affectively neutral, but when it is innervated by affective flows, which is what experiential marketing incessantly seeks with its desire to put the customer and his lifestyle at the center, then it is transformed into an easy space crossed by euphoric rather then dysphoric feelings. In marketing, this concept provides a sort of affective mark-up. (Ferraresi and Schmidt 2018).

4   The Pandemic Acceleration

During the pandemic acceleration, all of humanity experienced the lockdown. Staying at home implied a strong limitation to the outside world and the implement of the so-called work from home with negative repercussions on people's mobility, sociality and psychology.

But Covid 19 has generated, among other things, the definitive launch of smart working. The latter is the result of an agreement between company and employee whereby, depending on the work being done, the modalities are adapted.

Fundamentally, this is an agreement between company and employee that allows part of the work to be done at home, part at the company headquarters and part, perhaps, in a third location. The smart working is not the death of mobility, but reasoned mobility; it is not the death of sociality, but a less invasive sociality; it is not, finally and necessarily, damaging to the psychology of individuals. The pandemic periodization has forced a rapid and inevitable literacy that has left us at the mercy of radical technologies, (Greenfield 2017) making partially true some of Turkle's theories regarding the hypothesis of technologies capable of completely replacing human relationships. (2011 and 2015) Even following Turkle's idea, however, we have not reached the death or sunset of reality as Baudrillard predicted so many years ago, (1993) or as, in more recent times and with other language and tone, Codeluppi has somehow taken up (2018).

The acceleration of the pandemic has therefore accelerated all processes of digitization by developing even more the society of platforms (Van Dijck et al. 2018), meaning by this term not only the platformization of the web or society, but the platformization of individuals who have increased the rate of web surfing by continuously discovering new digital places where to invest their affectivity. The individual-platform is subject to algorithms and their incessant search for what we like, what we desire (Finn 2017). Thanks or because of the algorithms we are able to strengthen and shape our customs, habits.

Work, information, leisure, urban transport, health, education friendships, loves are developed with and through platforms, sharing and putting into circulation thoughts, feelings, emotions, needs, purchases. Participating in this universe of enormously smeared media (Jenkins et al. 2013), the individual-platform, or the Solitary Connected, inhabits virtual places investing affectivity.

Thus the big five platforms, namely Alphabet (Google), Amazon, Apple, Facebook, and Microsoft, thanks to the trojan horse of algorithms, operate to make currency out of the data they collect, but also out of user attention, money, and finally out of the users themselves. To these currencies discussed in Platform Society (2018, 83), we add a fifth currency: the emotional pleasure that makes people stay longer in virtual places filled with affective flows.

Some in-depth interviews conducted at IULM University, followed by a research carried out in spring 2021, seem to show that platforms are environments full of euphoric or dysphoric emotions which, through user navigation and thanks to the incessant work of algorithms, thicken into affective places.

The affective place of the network means the ease or the difficulty of the body and mind, in a formula: digital living.

We like to conclude this paragraph with a sentence of Tuan: "When space feels thoroughly familiar to us, it has become place." (1977).

5 The Survey

In late spring 2021, questionnaires were distributed in May and June to a panel of young Italians aged 19-37, more than 70% of whom were between the ages of 19 and 20. The distribution of the questionnaire took place online and 83 responses were collected. (See below)

This exploratory research made use of a random sample of students of the Fashion and Creative Industries course at the IULM University of Milan. The main region of origin of the respondents was Lombardy with more than 50% of the respondents, but there were also eight other Italian regions in the sample. The sample was predominantly female (96%). 57.8% of respondents said they belonged to the middle class, 31.3% to the upper-middle class.

The questionnaire asked about the affective investment of digital sites with particular attention to fashion and fashion accessories sites. The intent was to understand if and how affective investments also included corporate sites and not just social networks. That is, we wanted to investigate the online integrated creativity, i.e. the digital form of construction of the advertising discourse nowadays. (Ferraresi 2016, 2017) Within the online integrated advertising discourse do the affective mark-up happens as on certain social platforms?

The network advertising communication implemented through websites is responsible for one of the social ways of using the network: shopping. The others being gaming, information search (for example on Wikipedia) and social network (Bennato 2011).

The question regarding what reasons drive one to browse to fashion sites allowed for two answers, and the desire to shop online was indicated by 71% of respondents as the motivational drive to visit online fashion sites, immediately followed by the desire to learn about new trends (56%) and, finally, 44% of respondents said they were driven by curiosity and the desire to have fun (44%).

The pleasure in visiting a site also consists in the interest and fun it provides, and this drives 53% of respondents to return to visit it, while more than 50% still want to gather ideas and suggestions. This question also allowed for two responses.

The next question investigated the connection to the emotional investment provided by visiting these sites. 41% of those interviewed answered that there is indeed an emotional investment generated by the care and beauty of the site but, above all, 41% affirmed that in this way an important emotional bond is created with the brand; and 31% affirmed that in this way they live new experiences while more than 30% accept the analogy with the pleasure one gets from visiting certain places in the real world.

The last question of the questionnaire tried to investigate which aspects of a website are able to arouse emotions. In the first place, and for 71% of respondents, the graphics with which the site presents itself is sensation generator, then the products it displays (54%) and, finally, the storytelling (47%).

The reflection that emerges from the answers to this question suggests that it is the brand discourse that builds emotions, even more than the products.

Survey on affective and cultural investment in digital sites

*Campo obbligatorio

1. Age *

Seleziona tutte le voci applicabili.

- [ ] 19
- [ ] 20
- [ ] 21
- [ ] 22
- [ ] Other

2. Gender *

Seleziona tutte le voci applicabili.

- [ ] Woman
- [ ] Man
- [ ] Other

3. Region of origin *

   _____

4. Country of origin

   _____

5. What class do you think you belong to? *

   Seleziona tutte le voci applicabili.

   ☐ Lower class
   ☐ Middle-low class
   ☐ Middle class
   ☐ Middle-high class
   ☐ Upper class

6. What does motivate you to search for the website of a fashion, sportswear or streetstyle brand? (max two answers) *

   Seleziona tutte le voci applicabili.

   ☐ Curiosity and\or amusement
   ☐ Online shopping
   ☐ Looking for new trends
   ☐ Professional / study reasons
   ☐ Sense of belonging

7. When you find a fashion website you like, what do you do? (max two answers) *

   Seleziona tutte le voci applicabili.

   ☐ I surf it thoroughly
   ☐ I share it with friends
   ☐ I will enjoy visiting it again in the following days/months.
   ☐ I look for similar websites
   ☐ I do shopping
   ☐ I add it to my favourites
   ☐ I take ideas and suggestions

8. Visiting a fashion site you like, does it give you strong emotions? (max two answers) *

Seleziona tutte le voci applicabili.

- [ ] Yes, like visiting a place I love
- [ ] Yes, because I can create an emotional bond with the brand / griffe
- [ ] Yes, because I can create an emotional tie with the products (material culture)
- [ ] Yes because I find care and beauty
- [ ] Yes, whenever I can do shopping (consumption culture)
- [ ] Yes, because I enjoy new experiences
- [ ] Yes, because it makes me feel special
- [ ] Irrelevant
- [ ] Other...

9. What aspects of a fashion website evoke emotions to you? *

Seleziona tutte le voci applicabili.

- [ ] Products
- [ ] Website layout
- [ ] The storytelling
- [ ] The luxury experience
- [ ] The possibility to easily buy in just one click
- [ ] The possibility of interaction (chatbot, games, contest, ...)
- [ ] Other...

Questi contenuti non sono creati né avallati da Google.

Google Moduli

References

Adams, P.C.: Cyberspace and virtual places. Geogr. Rev. **87**, 155–171 (1997)

Bateson, G.: Steps to an Ecology of Mind. University of Chicago Press, Chicago (1972)

Baudelaire, C.: The Painter of the Modern Life. Soho Book Company, London (1986)

Baudrillard, J.: Symbolic Exchange and Death, SAGE, London (1993)

Belardinelli, S., Gili, G.: Fidarsi. Cinque forme di fiducia alla prova del Covid-19. Mediascapes J. **15**, 80–98 (2020)

Benjamin, W.: Paris, Capital of the Nineteenth Century Reflections. Schocken Books, New York (1986)

Bennato, D.: Sociologia dei media digitali. Laterza, Roma (2011)

Codeluppi, V.: Il tramonto della realtà, Carocci, Roma (2018)

Colombo, F.: Ecologia dei media. Manifesto per una comunicazione gentile, Vita e Pensiero, Milano (2020)

De Biase, L.: Homepage. https://blog.debiase.com/2018/10/03/media-ecology-fuor-metafora/. Accessed 6 June 2021

Demopolis Homepage. https://www.odg.it/wp-content/uploads/2019/01/grafica-sinottica.pdf. Accessed 6 June 2021

Di Fraia, G. (ed.): Social Media Marketing. Strategie e tecniche per aziende B2B e B2C, Hoepli, Milano (2015)

Ferraresi, M.: Luoghi del consumo: una nuova organizzazione dello spazio. Sociologia del lavoro 116 (2009)

Ferraresi, M. Le nuove leve del consumo, Carocci, Roma (2016)

Ferraresi, M. (ed.): Pubblicità: teorie e tecniche. Carocci, Roma (2017)

Ferraresi, M., Schmidt, B.: Marketing Esperienziale. Come sviluppare l'esperienza di consumo, FrancoAngeli, Milano (2018)

Finn, E.: What Algorithms Want: Imagination in the Age of Computing. MIT, Cambridge (2017)

Giannitrapani, A.: Introduzione alla semiotica dello spazio. Carocci, Roma (2013)

Gili, G.: La credibilità. Quando e perché la comunicazione ha successo, Rubettino editore, Catanzaro (2005)

Gili, G., Panarari, M.: La credibilità politica, Marsilio, Venezia (2020)

Granata, P.: Ecologia dei media, FrancoAngeli, Milano (2015)

Greenfield, A.: Radical Technologies. The Design of Everyday Life, Verso, London-New York (2017)

Jenkins, H.: Convergence Culture. New York University, New York (2006)

Jenkins, H., Ford, S., Green, J.: Spreadable media. New York University, New York (2013)

Innis, H.: The Bias of Communication. University of Toronto Press, Toronto (1951)

Innis, H.: The Strategy of Culture. University of Toronto Press, Toronto (1952)

Manovich, L.: The Language of New Media. MIT, Cambridge (2001)

McLuhan, M.: The Gutenberg Galaxy: the Making of Typographic Man. Routledge & Kegan Paul, London-New York (1962)

McLuhan, M.: Understanding Media. The Extensions of Man. McGraw Hill, New York (1964)

Meyrowitz, J.: No sense of Place. Oxford University Press, New York (1985)

Moores, S.; Media, Places and Mobility. Palgrave Macmillian, New York (2012)

Mumford, L.: The Myth of the Machine. Harcourt, New York (1967)

Parisier, E.: The Filter Bubble. What the Internet is Hiding from You. Penguin Press, New York (2012)

Pezzini, I. (ed.): Dallo spazio alla città, Mimesis, Milano (2020)

Ponti, M., Ryberg T.: Rethinking virtual space as a place for socialization. In: Fourth International Conference on Networked Learning Lancaster, pp. 332–339, United Kingdom. hal-00190156 (2004)

Postman, N.; The Humanism of Media Ecology. In: Keynote Address Delivered at the Inaugural Media Ecology Association Convention, Fordham University, New York (2000)

Relph, E.: Spirit of place and sense of place in virtual realities. Soc. Philos. Technol. Q. Electron. J. 10(3) (2007)

Tuan, Y.F.: Space and Place: The Perspective of Experience. University of Minnesota Press, Minneapolis (1977)

Turkle, S.: Reclaiming Conversation. The Power of Talk in a Digital Age. Penguin Press, New York (2015)

Van Dijck, J., Poell, T., de Waal, M.: The Platform Society. Oxford University Press, New York (2018)

Design of Wearable Digital Enhancement for Traditional Musical Instruments

Jiaqi Jiang[1], Qiong Wu[1]([✉]), and Wenlin Ban[2]

[1] Tsinghua University, Beijing 100084, People's Republic of China
`qiong-wu@tsinghua.edu.in`
[2] China Conservatory of Music, Beijing 100084, People's Republic of China

Abstract. This paper introduces a wearable electronic music controller, which enables the performer to play the musical instrument shakuhachi and control electronic music at the same time alone. We also exaggerate finger movements through visual feedback, help the audience understand the relationship between gesture and electronic music. It combines movement and stillness, and also tradition and modernity (Fig. 1).

Keywords: Interactive electronic music · Digital music instrument · Visual feedback · Wearable

1 Introduction

In interactive electronic music, there is a form of performance that a performer plays a musical instrument on the spot, and the sound is transferred to computer music software through real-time recording, and then the composer operates music software, deforms the sound into electronic music. So the audience will hear the superposition of musical instrument sound and electronic music, which brings a richer auditory experience than simple music instrument performance.

Fig. 1. The wearable electronic music controller with visual feedback

© Springer Nature Switzerland AG 2021
C. Stephanidis et al. (Eds.): HCII 2021, LNCS 13096, pp. 585–599, 2021.
https://doi.org/10.1007/978-3-030-90328-2_40

This kind of collaboration between the performer and the composer makes it necessary for the performer to consider the cooperation with others when performing, which, to some extent, limits the improvisation. In addition, in practice or composition scenarios, the presence of both the performer and the composer is required, making it difficult to compose and rehearse alone.

Using wearable devices to capture body movements and thus control electronic music is a better idea. Wearable devices have the advantages of flexibility and freedom.

Musicians do not need to consider the location of the computer, controller circuit, and other hardware issues. They only need to focus on sensing body movements and can move freely on the stage to perform more exaggerated performances. Cases such as MyoSpat system [1], Lady's Gloves [2], MiMu Gloves [3] all use wearable devices to control the music.

However, in these cases, the performer usually only operate this one instrument on the stage, and can use exaggerated body movements to generate various kinds of music, when the body movements also become a part of the musical performance. But this paper hopes that the wearable device can control electronic music while playing a traditional instrument, which is equivalent to, playing two instruments at the same time (Fig. 2). In this situation, in order to ensure that the playing actions of the traditional instrument are not deformed, it is inevitable that exaggerated body performance cannot be used to control electronic music, so the visibility of the triggering gesture is poor.

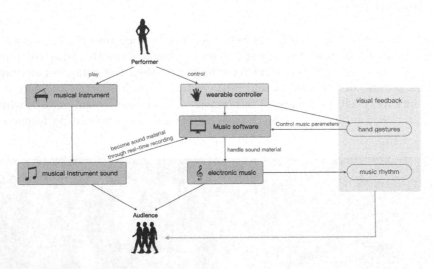

Fig. 2. A performer is able to play musical instrument and control electronic music at the same time alone through the wearable controller

Electronic musical instruments produce sound after processing and transforming sound materials by computers or electronic devices. This kind of sound can not be directly related to the way performers operate musical instruments, so the audience can be confused about how the sound is produced, not knowing which action triggers which sound, which is a transparency [4] issue discussed in the field of digital musical instruments. Several researchers [5,6] have found that it is effective to use visual feedback to help audiences establish this mental mapping between control input and sound output. Therefore, this paper uses wearable lighting to visualize and enhance the gestures and the rhythm of electronic music.

This paper suggested that using a wearable device to collect finger movements can make control over electronic music while playing a musical instrument normally, and visualize finger movements through light, so as to help the audience understand the generation of electronic music and enhance the stage effect. We choose the Chinese traditional musical instrument shakuhachi to perform with a sensor-enhanced glove. The shakuhachi, is a bamboo-made musical instrument with a desolate and vast sound that brings a unique mysterious, cool, and ethereal feeling. It has the Oriental Zen temperament, which is completely different from the modern sci-fi feelings brought by electronic music. The combination of the two is a collision between tradition and modernity.

In addition, during the performance of the shakuhachi, the performer stands or sits, and his body basically remains still, which is a very "quiet" state. We hope that through the visual feedback of the wearable device, to add a kind of dynamic to the "quiet" state to combine dynamic and static.

2   Related Works

2.1   Control Interfaces in Interactive Electronic Music Performance

Electronic music was born in the mid-20th century when composers evolved from "organizing notes" to directly "organizing concrete sounds" [7]. And with the development of recording and computer technology, composers began to explore the adjustability of live performances, introducing more uncertainties into musical performances, resulting in interactive electronic music [8].

Interactive electronic music creators use a variety of software tools, including Max/MSP [9], which is a graphical music and multimedia programming software.

Interactive electronic music attaches importance to the interactivity of the performance site and the resulting unfixed effects, an important aspect of which is the control of the computer software at the site. Different control interfaces will bring different effects to the stage performance:

- Some creators have **modified the traditional musical instruments** and added the electronically controlled sound generator to enable the performers to use a way similar to the original playing action, which can produce richer sound effects, such as [11,12];
- Some creators have introduced **interfaces typically used in other fields** to music stage performances, such as composer Jeffrey Stolet who has used devices such as the Wacom digital tablet, the Nintendo Wii GamePad, and the virtual golf game device Gametrak to control interactive music. And the

Stanford Laptop Orchestra has used 20 MacBook laptops for musical performances [13]. These controllers themselves have the ability to input parameters in multiple dimensions, enabling both rich musical control effects and the creation of an unexpected experience for the audience, giving the musical performance a sense of performance art.

- Some artists have designed completely **new forms of digital musical instruments**, which have unique shapes and control modes that do not resemble any existing traditional instruments. The generation principle of electronic music provides a wide space for the design of electronic musical instruments. Artists can design the appearance and control mode of musical instruments entirely from personal artistic goals and the dramatic effect, creating a unique visual language, like Laetitia Sonami's performance SPRING SPYRE [14]. This kind of electronic instruments attach importance to the stage performance effect and adopt exaggerated interactions.
- There are also artists who use **wearable devices** to control electronic music, which has the advantages of flexibility, portability and concealment, and the ability to bring body data into the music, such as instruments based on Myo armband, like interactive performance system SALTO [15] and interactive sound-visual image system MyoSpat [1], and instruments based on gloves like Lady's Glove [2], MiMu gloves [3] and so on. These wearable devices are mainly used alone, if used together with other musical instruments, they may interfere with each other. For example, Eleanor Turner used the MyoSpat system to perform the work "The Wood and the Water" [16], she uses Myo armband to generate electronic music while playing harp, but it is clear that she is doing the two alternately, because using Myo armband to generate music will actually affect the performance of the harp.

The application scenario proposed in this paper lies in the fusion of the two musical instruments, that is, when playing a traditional musical instrument, a wearable device is used to control electronic music, and this two do not interfere with each other.

This scene will also bring about a problem. Restricted by the performing actions of the traditional musical instrument, the interactive actions of the electronic musical instrument will be relatively hidden, because exaggerated body movements will interfere with the performance of the traditional instrument. Therefore, the stage performance will be relatively monotonous (compared with those electronic instruments that rely on exaggerated body movements), and other ways can be introduced to enhance the stage effect, such as the wearable interactive lighting adopted in this paper.

2.2   Using Visual Feedback to Solve Transparency Problems

Compared with the traditional musical performance like "musicians playing on the stage and audience appreciating under the stage", interactive electronic music performance emphasizes more on the interaction between performers and audiences. Therefore, during the performance process, how the audiences perceive music is particularly important.

However, electronic music does not rely on the physical structures of instruments to produce sound, so audiences often have difficulty understanding how electronic music is generated. Digital music instruments emerge one after another, mostly new in appearance, and audiences have no clue as to the way they will sound. This situation is called the transparency problem by Fels et al. [4] That is, the extent to which the audience can understand which control produces which sound [17].

In particular, in the scenario presented in this paper, the performer himself is playing a traditional instrument, which can easily lead the audience to believe that the electronic music they hear is triggered and controlled by someone else behind the scenes, or even it is a pre-recorded accompaniment. In this context, the issue of "transparency" is particularly salient. This problem can be improved by adding visual feedback.

Some researchers try to help the audience build their cognition of the way electronic music is generated through visual feedback. For example, the research of Olivier Perrotin et al. hopes to make the control gesture visible [5]. Their research shows that adding visual feedback can help the audience understand the playing mode and add expressiveness to the performance.

Researchers Florent Berthaut et al. further argue that specialized graphical interfaces should be developed for the audience [6]. They designed a set of 3D visualization applications that can amplify the musician's gestures and the connection with the sound. The feedback proved that the audience was highly enthusiastic about the visualization approach and believed that it could indeed help them understand the structure of the music instrument and the musician's behavior.

In summary, it makes sense to use visual feedback to help audiences understand the forms of control in electronic music.

Visual feedback is an effective means of addressing the transparency of the audience, which itself enhances the overall experience of the musical performance. Whether in electronic or traditional music, the visual component is a heavily engineered aspect of the stage.

Schloss points out the importance of visual clues in music performance [18], studies have shown that observers can perceive the expected expression of music just like actually listening to music performances only by watching videos [19]. Live music performance is a multi-modal experience. Sensory and non-musical factors deeply affect the audience's perception [17].

The use of visual feedback to enhance the music stage can take many forms, such as:

- **Making instruments glow with the action,** such as Christos Michalakos' Augmented drum kit [11], which embeds lights on the instruments, and each strike will light up the corresponding instrument.

- **Performers' costumes glow interactively:** Kicking the Mic project [20] includes a dress with built-in LEDs that match the performers' tap dance moves and rhythmic percussion to change the lighting.
- **Stand-alone interactive stage installations:** Stand-alone installations for visual feedback are free from the customization of specific instruments and people. ORBIS is a large transparent enclosure embedded with LEDs, in which the performer sits and uses sensors to collect the frequency of the music and the performer's body data, reflecting to the lights, so that each performance's visual effect is unique.
- **Interactive morphing device:** A physical morphing device may be better in daytime performances, compared to linghting. For example, Korean cellist Seunghan Sung placed 40 white rods around himself and controlled these rods to sway left and right by monitoring the rhythm of the music in real time, effectively enhanced the viewer's feeling of the music.

3   Design of the System

We chose a traditional musical instrument shakuhachi to perform with the controller glove. Shakuhachi is a bamboo-made musical instrument, whose tone is desolate and vast, bringing people a unique feeling of mystery and emptiness. It originated from China and later developed in Japan, with Oriental Zen temperament, the combination is a collision between tradition and modern.

During the performance of shakuhachi, the performer stands or sits, and his body basically remains still, which is a very "quiet" state. We hopes that through the visual feedback of wearing equipment, adding dynamics to this kind of "quietness".

The wearable device consists of the following parts, as shown in Fig. 3.

- **Finger motion capture:** detect finger bending degrees through strain sensors based on carbonized silk, and transmit the data to computer music software;
- **Finger light feedback:** there is a LED at the top of each finger, and the gesture changes of the finger are directly fed back by the light changes;
- **Arm wearing interactive light:** After the finger light is lit up, the optical fiber pattern on the arm will shine in a certain mode, mapping the rhythm of music.
- **Controller, Power supply and Bluetooth:** sensor data reading, data bidirectional transmission and lighting control.

3.1   Convert Finger Movements to Music Parameters

We use high-performance wearable strain sensors based on Carbonized Cotton Fabric to detect the bending degree of fingers. This sensor was proposed by Mingchao Zhang et al. [21]. It has a large workable strain range, high sensitivity

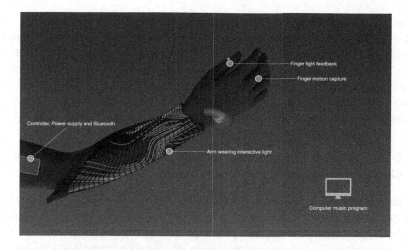

Fig. 3. The wearable device consists of the these modules

and long-term stability, and is simple and low-cost to prepare. From the design point of view, it is thin and light in texture, has almost no restriction on human movement, and has great potential for application in wearable devices.

We use 706 silicone rubber to paste the strain sensor on the high elastic fabric (Dupont Lycra), 706 silicone rubber is elastic after curing, therefore, the sensor can maintain the tensile capacity, making DuPont Lycra fabric into gloves and wearing them on fingers, the surface of the sensor can be protected by the coating of the fabric, it can also keep the sensor in the original position every time it is worn (Fig. 4).

Since the fingers also move and bend in their normal state, the differentiation of data changes was not obvious when the sensor covered only one joint of the finger. Therefore, we increased the length of the sensor to wrap two joints, then the values had obvious changes.

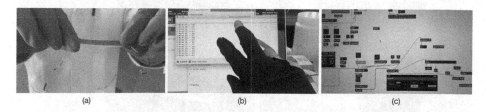

Fig. 4. a) using the strain sensor based on Carbonized Cotton Fabric to detect the bending degree of fingers; b) monitoring bending degree of fingers by the glove with sensors; c) controlling Music Parameters in MaxMsp

The gestures control the music in two ways:

The first one is to send a single signal using a specific gesture (finger bent to a certain degree) to control the switching of the music program. So the performer can use a free finger to make the gesture to switch the program at a time he or she deems appropriate. The second one is to map the finger movements during the performance to musical parameters, so that the motions of the fingers playing shakuhachi continuously control some musical effects.

3.2   Using Wearable Lights as Visual Feedback to Exaggerate Gestures and Music Parameters

In an interactive electronic music performance, The visualization objects can be action parameters like performer's control gestures, or musical parameters such as the musical characteristics like pitch, pitch length, intensity, rhythm, and so on. Perrotin notes that audiences are more interested in visualizations related to musical parameters because of the ability to highlight the performer's musical intent [5].

In this paper, two sets of visual feedback are designed, one to visualize the finger bending action by lights on the fingertips; the other one to visualize the music rhythm by wearable lights on the arm - including visual enhancements of both action parameters and music parameters.

According to different control modes of music programs, the controller has two forms of visual feedback.

Mode 1: There are multiple preset music programs, and the switching of programs is controlled by gestures. When a finger bends to the preset degree, it will trigger the changes in Max [9] on the computer, and at the same time trigger the LED on the corresponding finger to light up, A luminous area on the back of the hand will also be lit up, and then the optical fiber pattern on the arm will shine with the rhythm of the music for a period of time, exaggerating the movement of fingers to enhance the audience's perception (Fig. 5).

Fig. 5. Mode 1: When a finger bends to the preset degree, it will trigger the changes in Max, and at the same time trigger the LED on the corresponding finger to light up, then the pattern on arm will shine with the rhythm of the music.

Mode 2: map the bending degree of each finger to music parameters. The bending degree value of each finger is introduced into the software to control multiple music parameters, generating a kind of music performance "based on the performer's body", and the bending degree value also controls the brightness of the finger light, helping the audience to intuitively perceive the music changes brought by gestures. A luminous area on the back of the hand and arm will be used to enlarge these changes, guiding the audience to perceive the existence and triggering mode of electronic music (Fig. 6).

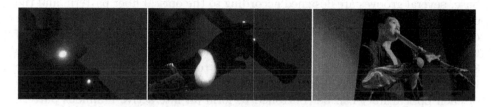

Fig. 6. Mode 2: map the bending degree of each finger to music parameters.

3.3   Using Optical Fiber, LED, Parameterized Modeling and 3D Printing to Construct Forms

We used optical fiber, LED and 3D printed nylon material base to complete the production of the wearing interactive lighting part, and the shape was designed by the method of parametric modeling.

Optical fiber is divided into end-face luminescent optical fiber and all-body luminescent optical fiber. The advantage in design is that, compared with LED strip, it can complete finer modeling (the diameter of a thin optical fiber is 0.25 mm, and the width of the dense LED strip which can control the color is about 7 mm), which is suitable for the modeling of small area. The brightness and color of the optical fiber can be changed by controlling the light source. The optical fiber itself does not heat up, and there is no need to install power supply, so the volume of the work can be relatively small.

Considering the limited surface area of the arm, we hope the shape can be more delicate, so we use the all-body luminous fiber material to make the pattern with line sense.

The inspiration source of modeling is as follows:

- **Sound wave:** it fits the use scene of music performance and emphasizes the characteristics of sound. The morphological feature is a fluctuating curve, which can be superimposed by multiple lines.
- **Karesansui:** shakuhachi develops and flourishes in Japan, and is used for religious rites and music. It has the meaning of Zen culture. Karesansui(dry landscape) is the classic representative of Japanese aesthetics, and also has the meaning of distant Zen, it fits the cultural meaning of shakuhachi. The morphological characteristics are shown as many parallel and curved lines, rounded corners, whirlpool, tortuous rotation and ripple feeling.

- **3D printing base:** starting from the "cylindrical" shape characteristic of arms, we hope the device to fit with the arm as much as possible. We also consider to introduce sense of technology and modernity to the modeling, therefore, 3D printing is chosen as the base of wearable equipment modeling.

Use Rhino and Grasshopper to finish the modeling design of optical fiber pattern and base. We tried 3D printing of resin and nylon material, and finally chose black nylon material because it has certain elasticity so is easy to wear or take of and the surface texture is also more beautiful. When modeling the base, several grooves are designed according to the optical fiber pattern, and the optical fibers are embedded into the grooves according to the pattern so they can be fixed to the position. We made a space in the base near the upper part of the arm, in which a 7mm wide LED strip is hidden as the light source. We made 3–4 optical fibers as a beam, and adhere them to different LED of the strip. The brightness of each LED can be controlled through arduino, so the brightness of each optical fiber can be controlled to form an interactive luminous pattern (Fig. 7–8).

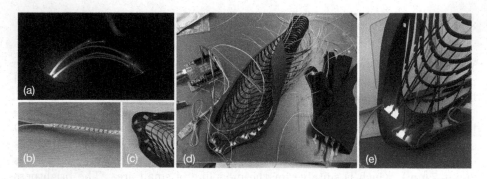

Fig. 7. a) the all-body luminescent optical fiber; b) the LED strip as the light source; c) making 3–4 optical fibers as a beam; d e) manufacturing process

3.4   Communication and Control

Portability and freedom are crucial to wearable devices, so we adopt Bluetooth wireless communication. Two-way data sending and receiving is conducted between the MAX/MSP program on the computer and the arduino uno on the wearable device. The MAX/MSP program receives the sensor data on the glove and generates the music effect. The arduino uno on the glove is responsible for reading the sensor data and controlling the light changes on fingers and arms, and the arm light needs to receive music rhythm data from MAX/MSP for control.

The light on the fingertip is directly controlled by arduino uno. For the interactive light on the arm, we use fiddle command to decompose the music rhythm data in the sound output of MAX/MSP, and use Bluetooth (HC-06) to

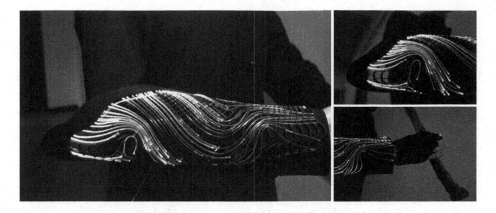

Fig. 8. Arm wearing interactive light

send it to arduino uno. The light source of the wearable light on the arm is an RGB LED strip containing 32 LEDs, and the LEDs are arranged into several groups, each contains about 8 LEDs. Every time the rhythm signal output by MAX/MSP is received, a group of LEDs will be lit up and controlled by the command of fastLED Library.

4   Evaluation

We organized the subjective user evaluation from two perspectives: performer and audience, and invited two performers (one male and one female, aged 20 and 39 respectively) and six audiences (two males and four females, aged between 23–37, four of whom had no musical foundation and two can play musical instruments) to participate in the evaluation. The participants watched three performances, no visual feedback, mode 1, and mode 2, followed by a 7-point scale rating and an interview. Table 1 and Table 2 shows the scoring results, and based on the user ratings and interviews, we report the following findings

First, from the perspective of performers:

- **Low cognitive burden:** performers were introduced the goals and operating methods of the wearable device before evaluation. Both of them understood the usage of the wearable device at the first introduction, and there was no wrong understanding in the subsequent experience.
- **Ease of learning:** In Mode 1, both performers learned to use it within 10 min, but one said they "easily forgot to bend his fingers and needed some time to adapt"; in Mode 2, there were no special operations to learn, and both performers said they did not need to spend extra time practicing.
- **Low interference to shakuhachi performance:** The way of controlling the electronic music did not conflict with the shakuhachi movements, but in Mode 1, the user was required to make specific gestures, which were slightly

more intrusive than in Mode 2, and participants reported that "it took some effort to remind myself to make control gestures".
- **Wearing comfort:** Both performers said that after wearing this equipment, they "can perform shakuhachi as usual", with no obvious burden and restrictions on the body, but they also raised some small issues, such as "the best the glove to reveal a little more fingers, or press the sound hole is easy to leak" "my hands are relatively large, the glove was a little tight when wearing for a long time" "a little worried about my movement will tear the circuit".

Table 1. Subjective evaluation results from the perspective of performers

Evaluation dimensions	Mode 1	Mode 2
Low cognitive burden	6.0 (SD = 0)	6.5 (SD = 0.71)
Ease of learning	5.5 (SD = 0.71)	6.5 (SD = 0.71)
Low interference	5.5 (SD = 0.71)	6.5 (SD = 0.71)
Wearing comfort	6.0 (SD = 0)	6.0 (SD = 0)
Overall satisfaction	5.5 (SD = 0.71)	6.0 (SD = 0)

On the other hand, from the perspective of the audiences:

- **Cognitive difficulty:** 1) Understanding of "finger movements triggering electronic music": both mode 1 and mode 2 with visual feedback outperformed the situation without visual feedback (mode 1 5.5, mode 2 4.33, no visual feedback 1.5), with some participants saying "the light made me notice the finger" and "I thought the electronic music was a recorded accompaniment when there was no light", indicating that visual feedback effectively helped the audience understand the principle of electronic music generation through gestures. The light makes the change more obvious. 2) Understanding of the connection between "finger lights and gestures": Both visual feedback modes helped users pay attention to gestures better, and some participants said "I pay extra attention to that action when his finger lights up". 3) Understanding of the connection between "arm lights and electronic music": Participants were able to understand the connection between arm-worn interactive lights and electronic music (mode 1: 5.17, mode 2: 4.83), which met the design expectation, but some participants said that "sometimes the lights did not match the rhythm of the music I understood, which caused some confusion", and this needs to be improved in the follow-up study.
- **Aesthetics:** The performance with lights was significantly better than the one without visual feedback in terms of aesthetics (mode 1: 5.5, mode 2: 5.83, no visual feedback: 2.67), and some participants said "with these lights it looks more technological" and "the stage has more changes and is richer and more beautiful than a simple shakuhachi performance".

Table 2. Subjective evaluation results from the perspective of audiences

Evaluation dimensions	Descriptions	non visual	Mode 1	Mode 2
Cognitive difficulty	Gestures triggers music	1.5 (SD = 0.84)	5.5 (SD = 0.84)	5.0 (SD = 1.26)
Cognitive difficulty	Finger lights & gestures	–	5.8 (SD = 0.75)	4.3 (SD = 0.82)
Cognitive difficulty	Arm light & music	–	5.2 (SD = 0.75)	4.8 (SD = 0.75)
Aesthetics	Overall visual effects	2.7 (SD = 0.52)	5.5 (SD = 0.55)	5.8 (SD = 0.41)

5 Discussion

The main contribution of this paper lies in: proposing to use wearable devices for electronic music control in the scenario of "traditional musical instrument performance and electronic music control are completed by one person". Because in this scene, the control action of electronic music is limited by the performance action of traditional musical instruments, and the "transparency" of electronic musical instruments to the audience is relatively low, this paper proposes to introduce visual feedback to exaggerate and enhance the performers' gestures and the generated electronic music, so as to deepen the audience's cognition of the generation mode of electronic music and improve the stage expressiveness.

The two interaction and feedback modes currently designed for the hand-worn controller are proposed from the perspective of music program creation, in the form of switching between multiple modes (mode 1) and mapping finger movements directly to musical parameters (mode 2), and there may be more interaction and feedback methods in the future from the perspective of human-computer interaction. This device can be applied not only to ensemble playing with the shakuhachi, but also to other instruments in the performance scenario.

Thanks to the light material and the mapping mode of "body movement-visual feedback", this work can also be applied to other fields, such as assisting the rehabilitation training of body parts such as fingers.

The disadvantage of this paper lies in: The control gestures are relatively single, and we hope to introduce more control gestures in the future, and further study the mapping relationship between music parameters and control gestures, in order to design more natural, easy to understand and operate control gestures. On the other hand, it lies in the diversity of visual feedback and the ability to guide the audience. In addition, the equipment currently has poor universality for hands of different sizes, different users need to modify the mapping range of parameters in advance, which is also a problem that needs to be improved in the future.

6 Conclusion

This paper introduces a wearable electronic music controller, which enables the performer to play the musical instrument shakuhachi and control electronic music at the same time alone. We also exaggerate finger movements through visual feedback, help the audience understand the relationship between gesture and electronic music. We proposed two interaction modes and corresponding visual feedback forms, and organized user evaluation. It is hoped that this work can provide some ideas for the design of digital musical instruments with more audience participation.

Acknowledgement. This research was supported by 2019 Beijing Social Science Foundation Project "Research on Digital Experience Design for Chinese Excellent Traditional Culture", the number is 19YTB022.

References

1. Di Donato, B., Dooley, J.: MyoSpat: a system for manipulating sound and light through hand gestures. University of Leicester (2017)
2. Lady's Gloves. https://www.youtube.com/watch?v=nEkufXDb-Ro. Accessed 6 June 2021
3. MiMu Gloves. https://mimugloves.com/. Accessed 6 June 2021
4. Fels, S., Gadd, A., Mulder, A.: Mapping transparency through metaphor: towards more expressive musical instruments. Organised Sound **7**(2), 109 (2002)
5. Perrotin, O., d'Alessandro, C.: Visualizing gestures in the control of a digital musical instrument. In: 14th International Conference on New Interfaces for Musical Expression (NIME 2014), pp. 605–608, June 2014
6. Berthaut, F., Marshall, M., Subramanian, S., Hachet, M.: Rouages: revealing the mechanisms of digital musical instruments to the audience. In: New Interfaces for Musical Expression, 6-pages, May 2013
7. Zhang, X.: The concept definition of electronic music. J. Central Conservatory Music (2002). (in Chinese)
8. Fan, L.: Conceptual definition of interactive electronic music. Collection (2017). (in Chinese)
9. Max. https://cycling74.com/products/max. Accessed 6 June 2021
10. Ban, J.: Research and application of interactive electronic music: an example of Pierre Boulez's work "Anthemes". Sound Yellow River (2016). (in Chinese)
11. Michalakos, C.: The augmented drum kit: an intuitive approach to live electronic percussion performance. In: ICMC 2012: International Computer Music Conference, pp. 257–260. Michigan Publishing (2012)
12. McPherson, A.P., Kim, Y.E.: Augmenting the acoustic piano with electromagnetic string actuation and continuous key position sensing. In: NIME, pp. 217–222 (2010)
13. Stanford Laptop Orchestra. http://slork.stanford.edu/media/. Accessed 6 June 2021
14. Sonami's performance SPRING SPYRE. https://youtu.be/aMYYbelPTuc. Accessed 6 June 2021
15. Rose, C.: Salto: a system for musical expression in the aerial arts. In: NIME, pp. 302–306 (2017)
16. The Wood and the Water by Eleanor Turner. https://vimeo.com/231523917. Accessed 6 June 2021
17. Bin, S.A.: The show must go wrong: towards an understanding of audience perception of error in digital musical instrument performance (2018)
18. Schloss, W.A.: Using contemporary technology in live performance: the dilemma of the performer. J. New Music Res. **32**(3), 239–242 (2003)

19. Davidson, J. W.: What does the visual information contained in music performances offer the observer? Some preliminary thoughts. In: Steinberg, R. (ed.) Music and the Mind Machine, pp. 105–113. Springer, Heidelberg (1995). https://doi.org/10.1007/978-3-642-79327-1_11

20. Kicking the Mic. http://www.helliontrace.com/projects/hellion/. Accessed 6 June 2021

21. Zhang, M., Wang, C., Wang, H., Jian, M., Hao, X., Zhang, Y.: Carbonized cotton fabric for high-performance wearable strain sensors. Adv. Func. Mater. **27**(2), 1604795 (2017)

Rehabilitate Sustain from Earth to Sea: A Design Study on Interplaying Biosocial Sculpture In-Between the Intertidal Zone

Jui-Yang Kao[1]([✉]), Shu-Wen Chang[1], Po-Wen Yu[1], and Wang-Chin Tsai[2]

[1] Yuanpei University of Medical Technology, Hsinchu, Taiwan
paul.you@msa.hinet.net
[2] Department of Creative Design, National Yunlin University of Science and Technology, Yunlin, Taiwan

Abstract. Obey the traditional idea of "Tian-Fu Di-Zai" (The Heaven Overspreads and Earth Sustains All, 天覆地載) in Chinese culture, this monography focuses on "Rise above both Self and Matters" (物我相忘) of Taoist by "Rehabilitate Sustain from Earth to Sea" (地載海涵). It cumulated subtly into consciousness of release-and protect lives. The motive of teapot craft design originated from unconsciously kill-and-persecute to environ-ecology by human self-centeredness since the Anthropocene. Sustainability become one of the most thematic of recent artistic creation, comparing to black-faced spoonbill pottery as one of the themes in this thesis, it is found that ecology is mostly an expression of creative skills in earlier artists' works than the social responsibility not shown, although. Thus, this paper precipitate-and-transform from "The Identity about the Matter and Me" (物我合一) firstly, then represent the (Bio)Social Sculpture among human and wildlife in the intertidal ecosystem by "Sociological Imagination". Aquatic system intertwining mountains, creeks, lakes, rivers into sea, which continued those real stories like starved Buffalos of cold highland, Bear strayed into boar trap, Leopard cat road killed, Elephant died of pineapple bomb, Whale fall organism and wisdom of Octopus. That constituted a discourse subjects of ceramic art compounded by such endless tragedies under the high and low tides. In the "Di-Zai" (Earth Sustain, 地載) series, which succeeding created 10 items of works and named respectively as: (1) Break off the shell; (2) Survival of the fittest; (3) Mimicry and camouflage; (4) Gaze with longing eyes; (5) Habitat restoration; (6) Fight for the foods with human; (7) Community symbiosis; (8) At the mercy of nature; (9) Epimeletic incubation, and; (10) Flight of ideas, etc. Another "Hai-Han" (Sea Rehabilitate, 海涵) series of 10 items, respectively named: (1) Deep-sea submergence; (2) Benthic organisms; (3) Pandora's box, origin of species; (4) Semi-biological mug; (5) Implements of waste antiquity; (6) Petrochemical disposal creation; (7) Co-synthesis tea pot; (8) Relationship in reflexivity; (9) Earth grow myriads of objects, and; (10) Mental image of representation, etc. Inclusion, after the social practice throughout crafts design and creation, this article suggests a new methodology of "Biosocial Sculpture" plays a comprehensive role of 'interactive design' to eco-artistic creation", that is, approaching Gesamtkunstwerk of the Sociological Imagination between humans and marine creatures. It reinterpret-and-transform the delicate "Human-Matter" (人物) relationship, reappear the form of ideas originate from the ceramic art creators. Furthermore, these works not only initiate

C. Stephanidis et al. (Eds.): HCII 2021, LNCS 13096, pp. 600–614, 2021.
https://doi.org/10.1007/978-3-030-90328-2_41

popular to pay attention to the human selfishness and disregard to biology, but also transform the social relationship to the environmental art education. It highlights a "social interaction design" engaging popular praxis based on daily tea wares with art education influence directly, keeping on recreation for a "surpass selfhood" (自我超越) endlessly in future.

Keywords: Teapot craft design · Ceramic art · Social sculpture · Participative interaction · Anthropocene

1 Introduction

1.1 Anthropocene and Human-Wildlife Conflict

Argument of Anthropocene is still in dispute on the road, its connotation for human treat the planet has stood on a common ground indeed, though. No matter what the Agricultural Revolution, the Industrial Revolution or the Great Acceleration After WWII, irreversible built environment has exhausted the world and made global climate change. Simultaneously, more and more disruptive innovation aroused human-wildlife conflicts like farmer traps, fisher drift netter and governor industrial zoning for habitat. Due to antecedent, belief and consequence for such different developers, there were miserable elegies (as Fig. 1) far and near as: starving buffalos forbidden in fence to attack the National Park travelers [1], elephants died after biting pineapple filled with explosives [2], Taiwan black bear trapped in "Boar Lasso" [3] and leopard cat was attacked to death

Fig. 1. Elegies of human-wildlife conflict for example.

by stray dogs or road killed [4], etc. Wherever human footprint goes there will be a lot of lonely animal caps bereaved, including the coldest Russian forest and the hot-and-humid Costa Rican rainforest. For the sake to raise those young kid animals on earth, there were 5 animal orphanage have been set up at least like rhino orphanage in South Africa, sloth orphanage in Costa Rica, brown bear orphanage in Russia, elephant orphanage in Sri Lanka and black bear and leopard cat orphanage in Taiwan [5], etc.

1.2   Ambition of Environmental Art Education

From a post-colonialism perspective by cultural study, the development of Taiwan traditional crafts aims to connect history with local cultural movement amid local communities in this island. So that crafts tradition, crafts historical writing, and crafts design education are the three significant topics to explore those colonial influences to crafts development. Return to the "Human-Matter" of social-cultural design to enrich art science by environmental education [6]. While thinking of integration solution to art, an actually breakthrough is established by art educators from their long-term experience and theoretical practice. Gather contemporary trends and information, it will be more effective to achieve the purpose of integrating various issues with art learning [7]. The "New Genre Public Art" developed in the 1970s, USA, based on public issues, public interests, and community to criticize the phenomenon of art isolation. After 2000, it appeared in the related discourses of Taiwan public art by introduced with "Mapping the Terrain: New Genre Public Art" (1995) publication. This words includes several art practices developed in different contexts of West, such as community art, artivism, participatory art, dialogue art and social engagement [8], etc. This article takes eco-craft design of enviro-art education as thematic subjects, hoping to reflect on the current enviro-ecological dilemma and return to traditional artistic conception of harmonious coexistence among heaven, earth and people with ceramic art craft. The shape of Taiwan Formosa is very similar to a big fish around this planet, such kind of new public art also contribute toa whale-fall-like Apocalypse in aesthetics.

1.3   Total Recall on Social Interaction

By way of Taiwanese New Genre Public Art, action in this thesis follows a three "R" steps as:

1. Recall to above miserable stories as subject-matter;
2. Reflexivity of daily life utensil like tea ware, and;
3. Reaction with social interaction to popular culture.

That is, this paper aim to employ Taiwanese New Genre Public Art to three interests as:

1. Recall the elegies of human-wildlife conflict in "dialogue art";
2. Reflexivity from visceral, behavioral and reflective level of emotional design in popular "artivism", and;
3. Reaction to interactive design for participants in "social engagement".

2 Theoretical Background

2.1 Eco-ethic and Way of Heaven

When it comes to ontological metaphysical thinking, Ancient Chinese philosophy is completely different from the "being" concept of ancient Greek philosophers. Instead, it takes the concepts of "heaven" and "human" as the main ideological discussion to the Confucianism and Taoism, the "heaven" and "human" concept is the first "primitive problem" that must be addressed. In terms of ecology, three extinction aesthetic forms as: original nature, co-ecological nature and humanized nature. A class hierarchy society constructed by Confucianism starts from individual, family, country to world, until be able to influence the forces of creation of the Universe, which was in the humanized nature state of ethical order. Axis on the affective life of aesthetic, Taoism adopting the natural inaction of Qi-Wu (adjustment of controversies, 齊物) or equal rights to coexist with other species. Therefore, it is interdependent on the co-ecology dimension of aesthetic form. Although both show respect for nature, the significant difference between Confucianism and Western weak anthropocentrism is that their starting point of respect is dissimilar. Confucian adopts an ethical hierarchy or religious sentiment for things are harmoniously self-sufficient with people, heaven and earth coexistence, while weak anthropocentrism take advantage on making use of resources by modern science and technology with rational management. Taoist Lao Tzu holds "Dao" (道) as a metaphysics above heaven and human, as the total source of the universe that integrates heaven, earth, and man into an organic wholeness. Rather than Confucianism talking about two levels of workings and morality of the nature, Taoism is completely different from the orientation of living in peace and inaction to open up the space of personal life. So that whether you are in an interpersonal or a human-matters relationship, you will be able to face and perceive the situation in indifferent and detached attitude. Creating an atmosphere of harmony and interdependence between the two creatures, and finally reach a state of inseparability of the unity of everything. It is just the same as the contemporary West "non-anthropocentrism" scholars' emphasis of eco-ethics [9]. The notions engaged to this artistic creation article, inherited the social ministry-based Confucian co-ecological nature to promote social responsibility on the one hand, and enlightened by the spiritual ministry-based Taoism to open an unlimited imagination from its humanized nature on the other. In a certain way, it also reconciles the Western "weak anthropocentrism" and "non-anthropocentrism" on the environmental reflexivity between felt preference and considered preference. And expect to build a fundamental to uncover the sociological imagination and social sculpture of the "human-matter" relationship in the next stage.

2.2 Taoism and Selfness Shift

By drawing on the philosophies of Taoist Zhuangzi and Friedrich Nietzsche for their undermining of anthropocentrism, the nature category obtains rehabilitate. Theorists posit four main approaches or "framing devices" for discourse: moral responsibility, empirical objectivity (natural sciences), aesthetic judgment, and radical anti-anthropocentrism that breaks through such framing devices and leaves anthropocentrism behind. As Taoism more generally teaches: the significance of any particular phenomenon is dependent on Its context. In general, the most important role played by the distinction between what comes from Heaven and the human is in the fatuous debate, still continuing in some benighted quarters, over anthropogenic global warming [10]. Taoist teachings that are friendly toward nonhuman animals on philosophy and central concepts as "Ci, Jian, Bugan Wei Tianxia Xian" (一曰慈, 二曰儉, 三曰不敢為天下先), and "Wuwei" (無為), as well as understandings of unity, harmony, and ultimate integrity. It teaches people neither to harm, nor to kill, and therefore anticipates a vegan diet. Taoism encourages people to love deeply and live compassionately (Ci, 慈), to exercise restraint and frugality (Jian, 儉), to seek harmony, and practice Wuwei. It teaches that the great transformation brings about a Great Unity, in which all things are part of one organic whole. Zhuangzi highlights basic similarities between humans and nonhumans, and encourages people to treat other beings thoughtfully [11]. Zhuangzian individualism has unique characteristics, which distinguish it from the various other individualist thoughts emerged in the West, who has a dynamic and open view on individual "self," considering individuals as changing and unique beings rather than fixed and interchangeable "atoms". Zhuangzi sets the unlimited Dao as an ultimate source for individuals to conform to, thus releasing individual mind into a realm of infinite openness and freedom. The Zhuangzian individualism is "inward" rather than "outward," concentrating on each one's spirit neither material interests nor rights in social reality, providing a spiritual space for the development of individuality in ancient China [12]. Zhuangzi posited kinds of "selfness" like, eliminate selfness (去己), without selfness (無己), forget selfness (忘己), bereave of oneself (吾喪我), unoccupied oneself (無我), coexist oneself with heaven and earth (天地與我並生), and all within oneself as one (萬物與我為一) etc., which can be induced into three drivers as: (1) dispositional driver in the centerless world with objective self; (2) reflective driver in the reflexive world with adaptive self, and; (3) transcendent driver in the chaos world with roaming self [13]. The journey of craft creation in this article follows a three-step self-exploration from inward to outward as mentioned above. First, liberating a lean self-centered subject by dispositional driver become an objective self. Then, respond a human-matter dilemma by reflective driver to the real object. Engage the transcend driver to reshape a new self, recreating the roaming self from the deconstructed order of human-matter subjects.

2.3 Eco-Aesthetics and Social Sculpture

Solute to Charles Wright Mills's call for a "Sociological Imagination", another book named "A Multi-Sociological Imagination in Taiwan" has been written and published in 2019. In which, meaning to think personal experience of surroundings connect with society, what individuals do and social structure change are affected interrelating each other. Social structure and changes affect individual behavior and vice versa, especially in the 7th chapter of "Sociological Imagination" devoted to "the Human Variety", Mills emphasized the vision of sociology should integrate society, biology and history. So that individuals construct social environment based on a broad and diverse society [14]. In general definition, while individual behaviors cause the consequence of societal becoming that means a great social interaction design. In the 21st Century, Sociology-Biology relations bring us to focus at the outset something that seems to ourselves one of the very sources for problematic. As sociologists think of when they say the word "biology" both as a way of conceiving vital processes in its manifold dynamics and/or a form of expertise in an academic discipline. People are standing at a critical point in remaking of biology/social sciences border exactly, what prompted this call for various contributors to such collection. There were two approach to shape the biosocial topography, first attempts to overcome a conventional separation of social from biological along with the biosocial outside sociology, second against social constructionist to reduce the body to a mere effect of language or power-structure with the biosocial turn in sociology. Between these two key areas of the new biosocial engagement, it can be divided into three sections as: (1) It rise of the new biology by implications for the social sciences; (2) It's thinking biosocially of promises, problems, and prospects, and; (3) It's biosocial challenges and opportunities to epigenetics and neuroscience [15].

Respectively, creativity in this monography takes three thematic materials as: (1) Hundred years of whale fall ecosystem to react new biological implication; (2) Black-faced Spoonbill haunt about intertidal zone to rethink biosocially, and; (3) Biosocial provocation in contact with neuroscience of deep sea octopus. The detail methodology about biosocial interaction design will be introduced in next section. Human-wildlife conflicts cause damage to eco-habitat but built environment, the unbalance man-matter relationship motivate a series of protesting artivism like the New Genre Public Art mentioned before. Joseph Beuys is one of the most well-known artists of origin to the New Genre Public Art, who is grounded in humanism, anthroposophy, and an expanded view of pedagogy through art. Beuys developed his practice during history when political alliances were questioned, derived from his involvement with Fluxus, the theories of anthroposophist Rudolf Steiner, and his radical pedagogical approach at the Dusseldorf Academy of Art toward a theory of Social Sculpture. Beuys' ideas embody his desire to seek an alternative to the chaotic political, economic, and social life of post-war Germany through works of art with holistic and spiritual intentions [16]. Contribute from inter-disciplines have paved a way for an open, participated, and responsible innovation approach, which is presently triggering the transition toward a non-exploitative human development. An anticipation of this conceptual framework can be found in Joseph Beuys' art, which can still represent a source of inspiration for innovators, entrepreneurs, economists, and community leaders [17]. Through an exploration of work undertaken by artist and a discussion of influence of Goethe on Beuys' practice, it will explore a way in whose approach to art was informed by methodologies which saw inward of human life and the outward world with ones' engagement profoundly linked in both physical and psychic terms. Beuys' work points out artist's will to the potential for a myth of fieldwork and communication of results, that suggest places anthropologist within a constantly changing world of matter that she or he shapes and transforms and is, in turn, transformed by [18].

2.4 Application of Medical Chatbot System

Smart phones are often used as the medium for mobile devices. The main reason is that smart phones are the items that people are used to carrying with them, and people are dependent on mobile phones. Mobile phones can also provide instant messaging functions, which can help patients or obtain health-related information in real time (Klasnja and Pratt 2012). Therefore, this study focused on smartphones to make chatbots on the

LINE APP platform. Jiang (2019) pointed out that the design of chatbot service models should consider the ease of use, usefulness, trust, system characteristics, compatibility and production quality of the system as well as the explanatory results, which are all the factors that will affect the user's intention. When designing a chatbot, we must consider whether the system operation, information and screen meet the ease of use, and whether the use of it is effective, can shorten the time, improve the quality, and meet the principle of usefulness. Users will trust the medical robots developed due to the medical institutions or correct medical information that they trust, thereby increasing their use intention. However, there were too many types of mobile phone applications in the past, and it takes some time for middle-aged and elderly people to operate new programs and adapt to new interfaces. But, the LINE chatbot enables users to familiarize themselves with the interface operation, which can reduce the time to adapt to the interface and achieve the purpose more efficiently. Also, the degree of completion after the system is executed, and whether there is any positive help after using the chatbot need to be considered. The chatbot's system features are not confined by any time and place or personalized information. The above considerations are used as a reference for building a chatbot system.

3 Methodology

3.1 Comparative Cases Study and Thinking Biosocially

More than half black-faced spoonbills of world population are winter residents in Taiwan. In 2020, the total number has reached record high at 4,864, even though the threat of global Covid-19 pandemic. According to the published results of "International Black-faced Spoonbill Census Report 2020" by Hong Kong Bird Watching Society (Table 1). There were 2,785 migrant birds in Taiwan accounting for 57.4% of the global black-faced spoonbills. winter. Mainly 1,839 concentrated in Tainan wetland habitats, continuing next to be Chiayi 550, Kaohsiung 241, and Yunlin 102, totally increased 401 for 8.7% than last year. Although the worldwide population has increased, but number of the Deep Bay, Macau and Vietnam has dropped significantly, threat to the global habitat hasn't been diminished, and eco-preservation still needs to be stepped up [19].

Table 1. World population of black-faced spoonbills in last 3 years.

Amount / Region	2018 No.	2018 %	2019 No.	2019 %	2020 No.	2020 %	Trend against 2019 Number	Trend against 2019 %
Taiwan	2195	55.7	2407	53.9	2785	57.4	+378	+15.7
Deep Bay (Hong Kong & Shenzhen)	350	8.9	383	8.6	361	7.4	-22	-5.7
Mainland China	744	18.9	990	22.2	1034	21.3	+44	+4.4
Japan	508	12.9	538	12.1	544	11.2	+6	+1.1
Vietnam	65	1.6	65	1.5	60	1.2	-5	-7.7
Macau	50	1.3	53	1.2	40	0.8	-13	-24.5
South Korea	26	0.7	23	0.5	24	0.5	+1	+4.3
Philippine	3	0.1	3	0.1	3	0.1	—	—
Thailand	0	0	1	0.02	0	0	-1	-100
Cambodia	0	0	0	0	0	0	—	—
Total	3941	—	4463	—	4851	—	+388	+8.7

(Data from: Liao, J. H., 2020)

Due to the highest number of planetary black-faced spoonbills, they have become Taiwan identity while haunting around intertidal wetlands or fish farms as living habitats. Biosocially (re)thinking of eco-conservation promises, environmental problems, and prospect to sustainability. More and more domestic artists start to develop their work with thematic black-faced spoonbills (Fig. 2, on the top upside from left to right), like local-related ceramic craftsmen as: the tea pot of Fan, Jhong-De in Tainan [20], the tea cup of Wang Ming-Fa in Kaohsiung [21], and the pottery plate of Li, Guo-Cin in New Taipei City [22]. Those artists' cases copied black-faced spoonbills' appearance perfectly, illustrated very nice solid-shapes or picture-compositions with outstanding skills of master. Beside well outward imitating expression with gas or electric kiln, the inward affection had been hidden obscurely. In different way, we dedicated to recall social responsibilities to promise human-wildlife conflict problem being solved. So, the black-faced spoonbills in this monography had transformed into childlike Anthropomorphic out of sociological imagination (Fig. 2. on the bottom side from left to right). Following the nature rule, all pieces challenged wood-fired kilns skills and lend a unique patina to finished ceramic products, furthermore.

Fig. 2. Comparative cases study on anthropomorphic sociological imagination for example.

3.2 Ceramic Craft Design and Octopus Discovery

Under a ceramic craft baseline of black-faced spoonbills, the most important purpose of handicraft design is responding to a friendly equity for human-matter harmony. Second purpose attempt to improve craft industry technology to meet needs of modern life, so that handicrafts design can be integrated to convenience, comfort and therapeutic of role play following principles to be: (1) Positioning of practical functions; (2) Evaluation of material applicability; (3) Usability of material characteristics; (4) Choice during processing technique, and; (5) Expression of ingenuity, etc. Because the perfect combination of "functional" and "aesthetic" is the highest level of crafts art, how to find the preferred substances for appropriate utensils is the top priority of craft design [23]. Analogy to design, craft and art, an unstable territory can be occupied for permanently shifting allegiances of these three sets of practices and families of discourses surrounding them. The evolving nature of design practice on the part of some leading exponents defies categorization: the designed goods of groups demonstrate a concern for allusive and narrative qualities beyond functionalism. Existing debates have centered on liaisons between practices and objects as subject to a conventional hierarchy of visual arts with fine art as the dominant partner. It is necessary to interrogate mutually informative relationship between practice and discourse, while appreciating the significance of liaisons among design, craft, and art. The principles that define the differences and relations among them are subject to historical change and vary regionally and culturally [24]. After Impressionism, supports of artist's thinking were replaced by four theories as: (1) the human finitude; (2) the empirical & transcendental corroboration; (3) the cogito & unthought, and; (4) the origin & history etc., which constituted a quadrilaterals framework of modern thought. Although these four theories seem to be independent on epistemology, they actually complement each other, although [25].

Aesthetics thinking chain system of designs, crafts, and arts by octopus that despised "human center" in contact with its neuroscience of biosocial provocative challenge. Rather to be invertebrates, octopus has 500 million nerve cells than vertebrates up to mankind. In addition, the magical creature actually has two memory systems. One is the brain, the other is located on the eight arms and feet, directly connected to the suction cups. All know, if humans want to complete a complex action, it relies on the brain to control specific operations and steps. But octopus is different with its eight arms (or tentacles) have independent nerve cords. As long as the brain gives an abstract command to the arms and legs, the brachiopods of octopus can "think" on its own and "decide" to take needed steps to complete tasks [26]. Due to its high dexterity, variable stiffness, and very complex behaviors, if compared with its position in the evolutionary scale, the octopus considered as an interesting model of robotics inspiration. The design of an artificial muscular hydrostat for developing an octopus-like robot [27]. Multidisciplinary projects worked alongside biologists to develop a soft robotic arm where mechatronic engineers that captures key features of octopus's anatomy and neurophysiology. Dynamic coupling embodiment between sensory-motor control, anatomy, materials and environment that allows for animal to achieve adaptive behaviors is used as a starting point for the design process but tempered by current engineering technologies and approaches [28].

3.3   Naming and Whale Falls Storyline

Taiwan island called Formosa by Western world, its shape is very similar to a big fish with a total area of 36,188 square kilometers, length to 394 km from north to south, width to 144 km from west to east, stretch to 1140 km of coastline, and over 200 mountains above 3000-m altitude. There are many rivers in territory, important ones under official governance among them reach to 118 (Table 2) [29]. Such magnificent mountains and rivers are skeleton, flesh, meridian, and blood vessels of this big fish, making it swim flexibly all around the planet. These important streams have also become pipelines connecting ecological cycle between island and ocean through such liquid trickles. Slowly transition by flowing water to convey nutrients of buffalo, elephant, black bear, stone tiger… and others that unfortunately died in human-wildlife conflicts from land to intertidal zone. It turns food material for aquatic creatures such as deep sea octopus, then octopus, fish, shrimp, and shellfish also become a delicacy for black-faced spoonbill. Like Twain island like fish, Black-faced spoonbill and Octopus stand out because of association with water.

Table 2. Important rivers under official governance in Taiwan.

Official Area Region	Central Gov.		Local Government										Total
	MOEA & COA	Provincial & Municipal	Northern				Central			Southern	Eastern		
			Yilan	New Taipei	Taoyuan	Hsinchu	Miaoli	Taichung	Yunlin	Pingtung	Taitung	Hualien	
Amount	24	2	6	19	7	1	4	1	1	12	29	12	118
Sum	26		33				6			12	41		

(data from: MOEA, 2009)

Water and Fish recall to Miserable Facts as Subjects. Which represented in the 'Yi Sing' (易性) of Laozi: "The highest good is like water. Water is good at benefiting the ten thousand things and it does not contend, residing in what the masses of people dislike. Thus it is close to the way." (上善若水, 水善利萬物而不爭, 處為人之所惡, 故幾於道。) Water has generative powers, like the way. It works without struggle and by going toward what is low and obscure; it is weak and soft, but "nothing is better at overcoming what is hard and strong." Water association is built into key concepts, as terms for pure (qing, 清), deep (shen, 深), profound (yuan, 淵), and overflow (fan, 氾) of the Dao, as in another excavated text called "The Great Oneness Gives Birth to Water" (Taiyi Sheng Shui, 太一生水) in which the "Great Oneness" generates water, then assists in heaven and earth generation. In 'Enjoyment in Untroubled Ease' (逍遙遊) of Zhuang Zhou addressed limitations of perspective appear in a different way in the fish story that begins the text: "The North Sea has a fish, whose name is "Minnow." Minnow is large, no one knows how many thousands of miles." (北冥有魚, 其名為鯤。鯤之大, 不知其幾千里也。) [30] Articulate to sociological imagination by forming from fish Taiwan, the ancient fantasy of whale fall has been implicated to be biological ecosystem interactively.

Wild Lifecycle Reflexive to People Daily Life. Whale-falls, which are thought to have habitat conditions which overlap seep ecosystems, may be used as a model system to explore the evolution of dispersal strategies and interactions between hosts and their symbiont microbes. Discovery of whale fall fauna at a whale carcass sunk at shelf depth contrasts the apparent lack of specialized organisms from shallow water seep environments. Include bacterial mat feeding dorvilleid annelids and whale-bone eating pogonophoran worm are maintaining whale-fall fauna alive in aquaria, that suggest an endless reproduction life-history strategy. To date more than 400 species found associated with whale-falls among [31].

The falls of large whales (30–160 t adult body weight) yield massive pulses of labile organic matter to the deep-sea floor. Long speculated on ecological observations accumulated since 1850s suggest that support a widespread characteristic fauna. Recent time-series studies of natural and implanted deep sea whale falls indicate that bathyal carcasses pass through at least three successional stages: (1) A mobile-scavenger stage lasting months to years, during which aggregations of sleeper sharks, hagfish, rat-tails and invertebrate scavengers remove whale soft tissue at high rates (40–60 kg d-1); (2) An enrichment opportunist stage (duration of months to years) during which organically enriched sediments and exposed bones are colonized by dense assemblages (up to 40 000 m-2) of opportunistic polychaetes and crustaceans; (3) A sulphophilic ("or sulphur-loving") stage lasting for decades, during which a large, species-rich, trophically complex assemblage lives on the skeleton as it emits sulphide from anaerobic breakdown of bone lipids; it includes a chemoautotrophic component deriving nutrition from sulphur-oxidising bacteria. Local species diversity on large whale skeletons during this stage (mean of 185 macrofaunal species) is higher than any other deep-sea hard substratum community. Global species richness on whale falls (407 species) is also high compared with cold seeps and rivals that of hydrothermal vents, even though whale-fall habitats are very poorly sampled [32]. In this lifecycle of whale, all the substances from its dead body faded away gradually, but livable martials and necessary nutrition yield to the ocean to breed the others. This evokes people to rethink their value of life if they can be touched everyday with daily utensil like tea pottery.

Reaction with Biosocial Interaction to Popular Culture. Formerly known as "Min-now Island" (鯤島), that meant Taiwan island like exactly a giant whale and also been estimated as the birthplace of Austronesian people. Since Orogeny movement on earth, Taiwan has been a "whale falling" phenomena in the northern hemisphere by biosocial application by sociological imagination. reflect on the island as. The whale falling systematic eco-settlement influenced not only migration of Austronesian people in human suspect, but also followed three periods of mobile-scavenger stage, enrichment opportunist stage, and sulphophilic stage for global contribution to habitats by the island Taiwan. This thesis addressed black-faced spoonbill as thematic subject and create 10 items of tea wares in series about: Break off the shell (破殼而出), Survival of the fittest. (優勝劣敗), Mimicry and camouflage (擬態偽裝), Gaze with longing eyes (心靈凝望), Habitat restoration (棲地復育), Fight for the foods with human (與人爭食), Community symbiosis (同體共生), At the mercy of nature (生死由命), Epimeletic incubation (孵育護佑), and Flight of ideas (意念表出) etc. These ceramic crafts set serial "Di-Zai" topic to demonstrate the aesthetic thinking of earth's selfless bearing everything through river flowing to sea in between inter-tidal zone as scenes of plot (Table 3 left side). Then, addressed octopus on sea floor as medium to restore a scene of ecosystem where whale fell, plot underwater as scene and create in sequence with: Deep-sea submergence (潛返大海), Benthic organisms (底棲生態), Pandora's box, origin of species (物種源始), Semi-biological mug (人造假物), Implements of waste antiquity (生活棄物), Petrochemical disposal creation (石化造物), Co-synthesis tea pot (生物映象), Relationship in reflexivity (反思意象), Earth grow myriads of objects (土生土長), and Mental image of representation (相由心生) etc. These 10 items of tea ware, designed to highlight an aesthetic thinking of "the highest good is like water", which nourishes all things on the theme of "Hai-Han" (Table 3 right side).

Table 3. Serial ceramic crafts of tea ware on "Di-Zai" and "Hai-Han"

Photography	Title/Function	Photography	Title/Function
	Break off the shell. Vase decoration.		Deep-sea submergence. Tea storehouse.
	Survival of the fittest. Tea storehouse.		Benthic organisms. Vase decoration.
	Mimicry and camouflage. Tea storehouse.		Pandora's box, origin of species. Tea storehouse.
	Gaze with longing eyes. Tea storehouse.		Semi-biological mug. Vase decoration.
	Habitat restoration. Tea tray.		Implements of waste antiquity. Vase decoration.
	Fight for the foods with human. Vase decoration.		Petrochemical disposal creation. Vase decoration.
	Community symbiosis. Vase decoration.		Co-synthesis tea pot. Tea pot.
	At the mercy of nature. Tea pot.		Relationship in reflexivity. Vase decoration.
	Epimeletic incubation. Tea pot.		Earth grow myriads of objects. Tea tray.
	Flight of ideas. Tea pot.		Mental image of representation. Vase decoration.

4 Conclusion

4.1 Theoretical Application

Based on "Recall, Reflexivity and Reaction" as 3R steps, the above works in this monography borrows Gesamtkunstwerk of social sculpture by Joseph Beuys first, then associates biosocial reflexivity of ecological viewpoint through relationship of objects and selfness hetero-associatively led by sociological imagination. A holistic "social interaction design" has been extended from craft design into a brand-new conceptual vision and techniques, which backwashed the realization of human-wildlife conflict in Taiwan island. Where 118 rivers and 1140 km of coastline converge of the intertidal zone, its eco-sensitivity reshape black-faced spoonbill and octopus into anthropomorphic forms with childlike transformation to "human-matter" interpretation.

4.2 Social Practice

Constantly selfness shifts of "beyond themselves" to pottery artists, clearly projecting into an inner creativity form expression of object and subject as one. An external childlike form cannot only further lead audiences to perceive how human beings destroy eco-habitats with "I alone" disregard reality of wildlife casualties. The influence of art-and-environment educations has shown out and expands "social interaction design" engaging popular praxis. In addition, based on the daily tea utensils of this study that can be used to drink tea every day, what constantly contacting on its social sculpture concepts to "wake up" to take altruistic actions of nursing wildlife That is the style of this thesis for what it differs from the other ceramic artists nowadays.

5 Prospect and Future Study

(1) **The continuous voice of the "Tian-Fu" series.** This article agrees with and quotes its animal right claims of Taoism. It hopes to eliminate human-wildlife inequity in the world by self-reflection and cultivation to look forward establishing a balance of relative differences. Taoism takes "Dao" as root of man and all things where "Dao begets everything". In such ideological context, humans and all things are on equal but oppose humans to dominate animals, then put forward the fifth animal rights of "interests account" [33]. In order to initiate and maintain the animal rights, the "Tian-Fu" series completed after "Di-Zai" and "Hai-Han" will be produced later. It focuses on terrestrial ecology with birds and beasts, and address craft design approach with social sculpture of pottery tea ware for life cares in the same way.

(2) **Good Ending of laboratory animals.** For scientific and technological needs of human medical development, the use of laboratory animals for academic or training has a long history. The "3R" specifications of replacement, reduction, and refinement have been proposed as experimental consideration for practitioners, even though, the "humane ending" techniques and procedures as the baseline of refinement [34]. These animals will never escape to death by sacrificed for human welfare. Therefore, since such inevitable evils are, more necessary "Rs" have been

proposed, such as: responsibility, rehabilitation, release, rehoming, retirement etc. In addition, 5 freedoms, including: free from hunger and thirst, free from discomfort, freedom from pain, injury and disease, freedom to express natural behavior, and free from fear and pain etc. [35]. This monography supplements two agencies of "restraint" during experiment and "remember" after death. In particular, that can address social sculptures to be designed to commemorate laboratory animals by ceramic craft design, just like pets at home. It advocates a "10Rs + 5Fs" code of care for laboratory animals indeed.

References

1. Apple Daily: Another buffalo died in Qingtiangang, Taipei Yangmingshan, Apple Daily News (2021). https://tw.appledaily.com/life/20210114/KEBU3YXXGBBAHA6QYHYS7AHT2A/
2. Naha, A.L.: Elephant's death kicks up a row, The Hindu News (2020). https://www.thehindu.com/news/national/kerala/elephant-death-kicks-up-a-row/article31741930.ece
3. You, C.S.: Wailing 6 hours for rescue, Taiwan black bear trapped in "Boar hanging lasso", UDN News (2020). https://udn.com/news/story/7470/4904374
4. Hu, P.S.: Cub leopard cat was attacked by dogs and died, UDN News (2021). https://udn.com/news/story/7324/5176025?from=udn-referralnews_ch2artbottom
5. Bai, S.Y.: Catch Sight of Love in the Animal Orphanage. Forward Publishing Ltd., New Taipei City (2020)
6. Lin, P.Y.W.: Taiwanese crafts and its research issues-a post-colonial perspective. J. Des. 9(2), 1–12 (2004)
7. Jhao, H.L., et al.: Assistant Teaching Reference of High School Art Field Curriculum Manual 1, pp. 117–118. National Taiwan Arts Education Center, Taipei (2006). https://ed.arte.gov.tw/ch/content/m_book_content_1a.aspx?AE_SNID=1454
8. Lyu, P.Y.: Translation of new genre public art in taiwan and its local transformation. ACT 47, 76–86 (2001)
9. Lin, C.M.: A philosophical discourse of the confucianism's and Daoism's eco-ethics. J. Dharma Seals 6, 51–71 (2016)
10. Parkes, G.: Zhuangzi and Nietzsche on the Human and Nature. Environ. Philos. 10(1), 1–24 (2013)
11. Kemmerer, L.: The great unity: daoism, nonhuman animals, and human ethics. J. Crit. Animal Stud. 7, 63–83 (2009)
12. Keqian, X.: A different type of individualism in Zhuangzi. Dao 10, 445–462 (2011)
13. Yearley, L. H., Zhuangzi's understanding of skillfulness and the ultimate spiritual state. Kjellberg, E. P. Ivanhoe, P. J. (eds.) Essays on skepticism, relativism, and ethics in the Zhuangzi, pp. 152–82. Albany: State University of New York Press (1996)
14. Tsai, H.J.: A Multi-Sociological Imagination in Taiwan. Tonsan Publication, Taipei (2019)
15. Meloni, M., Williams, S., Martin, P.: The biosocial: sociological themes and issues. Sociol. Rural. 64(1), 7–25 (2016)
16. Jordan, C.: The evolution of social sculpture in the United States: Joseph Beuys and the work of Suzanne Lacy and Rick Lowe. Public Art Dialogue 3(2), 144–167 (2013)
17. Montagnino, F.M.: Joseph Beuys' rediscovery of man-nature relationship: a pioneering experience of open social innovation. J. Open Innov. Technol. Market Complex. 4(4), 1–17 (2018)

614   J.-Y. Kao et al.

18. Walters, V.: Working 'in the opposite direction': Joseph Beuys in the field. Anthropol. J. Eur. Cult. **19**(2), 22–43 (2010)
19. Liao, J.H.: The critical fish farms reserved 4,864 black-faced spoonbills in global winter population. Environment Information Center, Taiwan Environment Information Association (TEIA) (2020). https://e-info.org.tw/node/223961
20. Huang, W.F.: Stunning pottery integrated the monuments into the food container. China Daily News (2013/3/28). https://tw.news.yahoo.com/%E5%8F%A4%E8%B9%9F%E8%9E%8D%E5%85%A5%E9%A3%9F%E5%99%A8-%E8%8C%83%E4%BB%B2%E5%BE%B7%E9%99%B6%E8%97%9D%E9%A9%9A%E8%89%B7-141300229.html
21. Pan Z.C.: Bloody red sky! Poinciana blossoms at "Tomato Club" in Hunei, Kaohsiung. The Liberty Times (2018/5/18). https://playing.ltn.com.tw/article/9709
22. Cultural Affairs Department, NTCG: Artist of Luzhou District: Li Guo-Cin. New Taipei City Artists Map (2020/6/9). https://artist-map.ntpc.gov.tw/xmdoc/cont?xsmsid=0H0766439667 18246116&sid=0H294559172941081625
23. Liou, J.J., et al.: Assistant Teaching Reference of High School Art Field Curriculum Manual 5: Craft Art. Taipei: National Taiwan Arts Education Center, pp. 176–189 (2006). https://ed. arte.gov.tw/ch/content/m_book_content_5a.aspx?AE_SNID=1458
24. Lees-Maffei, G., Sandino, L.: Dangerous liaisons: Relationships between design, craft and art. J. Des. History **17**(3), 207–219 (2004)
25. Zeng, C.S.: Critical Thinking of Western Aesthetics. Wu-Nan Book Inc., Taipei (2020)
26. SME, Weird Science Research Institute: 42 interesting scientific stories with open minds. China Times Publishing Company, Taipei (2020)
27. Cianchetti, M., Arienti, A., Follador, M., Mazzolai, B., Dario, P., Laschi, C.: Design concept and validation of a robotic arm inspired by the octopus. Mater. Sci. Eng. C **31**(6), 1230–1239 (2011)
28. Kang, R., Guglielmino, E., Zullo, L., Branson, D.T., Godage, I., Caldwell, D.G.: Embodiment design of soft continuum robots. Adv. Mech. Eng. **8**(4), 1–13 (2016)
29. Ministry of Economic Affair (MOEA): Announcement of rivers management division into Central Government, Provincial & Municipal Government, and County/City Government. National Central Library Gazette Online (2009). https://gazette.nat.gov.tw/EG_FileManager/ eguploadpub/eg015068/ch04/type3/gov31/num9/Eg.htm
30. Perkins, F.: Of fish and men: species difference and the strangeness of being human in the Zhuangzi. Harvard Rev. Philos. **17**(1), 118–136 (2010)
31. Dahlgren, T.G., Wiklund, H., Källström, B., Lundälv, T., Smith, C.R.: A shallow-water whale-fall experiment in the north Atlantic. Cah. Biol. Mar. **47**(4), 385–389 (2006)
32. Smith, C.R., Baco, A.R.: Ecology of whale falls at the deep-sea floor. Oceanogr. Mar. Biol. **41**, 311–354 (2003)
33. Wu, H.L.: Research into animal ethics in taoist thought mainly based on Laozi and Zhuangzi. Appl. Ethics Rev. **55**, 30–50 (2013)
34. Chinese-Taipei Society of Laboratory Animal Science. Laboratory Animal Science (Technical Chapter). Taipei: Council of Agriculture, Executive Yuan (2020)
35. Chinese-Taipei Society of Laboratory Animal Science. Laboratory Animal Science (Basics Chapter). Taipei: Council of Agriculture, Executive Yuan (2020)

DeepDive: The Use of Virtual Worlds to Create an Ethnography of an Ancient Civilization

Thomas Palazzolo[1], Ashley Lemke[2], Chencheng Zhang[1], Sarah Saad[1], Robert G. Reynolds[1,3(✉)], and John O'Shea[3]

[1] Wayne State University, Detroit, MI 48202, USA
robert.reynolds@wayne.edu
[2] University of Texas, Arlington, TX 78712, USA
[3] University of Michigan, Ann Arbor, MI 48109, USA

Abstract. The DeepDive System is a tool built to assist with the testing of archaeological hypotheses, the visualization of complex data, and the archiving of archaeological and ethnographic data. As such, it allows modern day archaeologists to recreate aspects of ancient cultural behavior through digital time travel. This paper describes how a researcher can configure a version of an ancient Land Bridge landscape and present it to selected participants. Their behavior can then contribute to the development of a hypothetical ethnography. A program that is potentially able to connect the actions of an ancient culture with the ecosystem that it is embedded in. The results of preliminary application of this system with hunters from a similar sub-Arctic landscape is described.

Keywords: Artificial ethnographies · Virtual Reality · Big data · DeepDive · Cultural algorithms · Archaeology · Ancient Engineering

1 Creating an Artificial Ethnography for an Ancient Civilization

The early goals of HCI were related to improving efficiency and user performance [1]. Recently there has been increased interest in the exploration of the emotional and aesthetic impact of a user's interaction with the technology [2]. John McCarthy and Peter Wright proposed a four-part framework with which to describe the subjective experience of users with a virtual world [3]. If the virtual world were a world that no longer existed, this collective user experience would count as a hypothetical ethnography about how the inhabitants could have interacted with each other and their environment in the past. An ethnography is the description of a particular human society within a given ecosystem, including customs and cultures.

McCarthy and Wright proposed a four-part framework through which to interpret the users' subjective experiences:

1. The impact of the experience on the senses. The experience's concrete and visceral impact.
2. The emotional and affective impact of the experience.

© Springer Nature Switzerland AG 2021
C. Stephanidis et al. (Eds.): HCII 2021, LNCS 13096, pp. 615–629, 2021.
https://doi.org/10.1007/978-3-030-90328-2_42

3. The composition of the sequence of actions that comprise an event.
4. The spatial and temporal context of the experience.

In this paper we focus on the impact that the spatial temporal context has on the everyday life of people in a society. The society of interest is one associated with a civilization long since vanished. Evidence for its existence is the focus of archaeological investigation here.

Submerged prehistoric archaeology is a sub-discipline of archaeology that deals with the discovery of ancient, submerged landscapes. In Europe alone over 3,000 submerged ancient sites have been recorded [4]. While there is a number of submerged sites North America, the emphasis has been on the study of shipwrecks and historical questions related to nautical issues [5–7]. As a result, underwater archaeology has not contributed as much to anthropological theory there, especially when it comes to broader theoretical issues [8]. The goal of this study is to use Artificial Intelligence techniques, machine learning, and virtual reality to recreate an ancient, submerged landscape. The Virtual Landscape is then used as a vehicle for archaeologists to test theories and validate hypotheses about ancient civilizations. Ultimately, the goal is to recreate the ethnography of the ancient society based upon the embodied spatial and temporal virtual ecosystem using a software tool, DeepDive.

The capabilities of the DeepDive tool are illustrated here with the specific example of the Alpena-Amberley Land Bridge. The Land Bridge is in Lake Huron, one of the Great Lakes in North America. Although submerged today, it was above water for approximately 2,000 years, from 10,000 B.P. to 8,000 B.P. because of glacial movements during the Ice Age. It spans the distance between modern-day Alpena, Michigan in the United States and Amberley, Canada. Logistically, it was up to eight miles wide and over 80 miles long as shown in Fig. 1. The insert within the figure shows the location of the Land Bridge relative to Michigan and the Great Lakes.

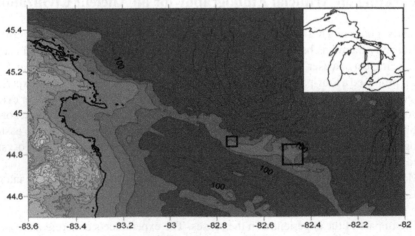

Fig. 1. The location of the US-side of the Alpena Amberley Land Bridge. The explored areas are denoted as squares on the map.

During the period during which the Land Bridge was above-water, it served as a landscape for prehistoric hunters to target migrating caribou that used the land for seasonal migrations [9]. These hunters constructed several structures using material available to them on the given terrain, stone. The Land Bridge has been submerged for thousands of years. This has helped to preserve these ancient structures, as they were shielded from modern human development by their relatively inaccessible location, 35–50 miles offshore and 80–130 feet deep.

The DeepDive system is designed to allow an archaeologist to configure the ancient environment by altering its physical and biological components. The result is to produce a model of the ecosystem that is given to the Virtual Reality system. Herd movements will be precomputed, and waypoints set up to choreograph the herd flow dynamics across the land bridge. Participants then utilize the ecosystem and their experiences recorded. These recordings are the basis for the construction of a hypothetical ethnography of the ancient people.

2 Researcher Interface Support

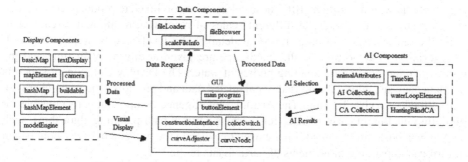

Fig. 2. Basic land bridge DeepDive system configuration

The DeepDive system provides a laboratory through which the archaeologist can reconstruct versions of the ancient landscape. The ecosystem of the AAR was sub-arctic in nature and most similar to modern-day Alaska [9]. It contains both static and dynamic aspects of the ancient landscape. The static component consists of the bottom topography, standing bodies of water, and rock formations. The dynamic component consists of sub-arctic plants and animals, and a unique composition of those elements during the Terminal Pleistocene. The major game available to ancient hunters was likely caribou. It was hypothesized that the Land Bridge was used by caribou to cross the lakes that separated what is now Michigan from Canada. The DeepDive system employs Artificial Intelligence to model the movement of caribou across the Land Bridge.

Three different algorithms were used to simulate the movement of caribou across the Bridge by computing optimal paths for the caribou under different assumptions about herd movement. One approach assumed that the herd moved optimally as a single unit, A*. A second approach allowed the herd to move optimally across the landscape in waves of animals, A*mbush. In the third approach the herd was allowed to optimally fission into subgroups and subsequently fuse back together, Dendriform A*.

The Archaeologist researcher first creates a version of the virtual ecosystem using the Interface presented in this section, based on recovered archaeological materials and paleoenvironmental samples and modeling. Figures 2 through 4 represent the controls that the researcher can use to dial up a version of the embedded ecosystem. The researcher was able to adjust several features including lake level, biomes, herd sizes, and visible structures. Next, the simulated ecosystem is given to the VR subsystem and used as a vehicle to collect information about the behavior of participants in the study. The results of participant movement can be recorded and played back in order to develop a more comprehensive assessment of the ethnography that emerged from the collective behavior of users.

Figure 2 shows a component diagram of the DeepDive System. The Data Component subsystem consists of information about the elevation of all 1 × 1 meter cells on the Land Bridge, over three trillion pieces of data provided by the National Oceanographic and Atmospheric Administration [10]. These cells can be combined to produce an embodied representation of the bridge at different scales of resolution to allow a researcher to view the landscape at different levels of detail. Lake levels can be adjusted as well to determine what portions of the landscape are given at any point in time and the corresponding location of standing bodies of water. The Display Component supports the data analysis, taking the myriad of calculated data and providing the researcher with a modifiable 2D visualization. The Artificial Intelligence component is responsible for modeling intelligent caribou behavior. Various optimal path-planning algorithms, such as A*, A*mbush, and Dendriform are used to generate the movement of caribou, which in turn can impact the movements of participants in the VR.

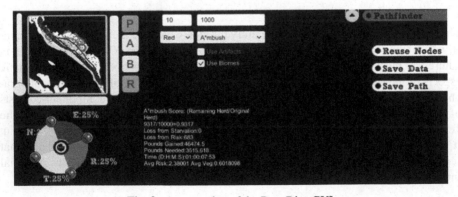

Fig. 3. A screenshot of the DeepDive GUI.

Figure 3 shows a screenshot of the **DeepDive GUI**. The upper-left corner contains a map which the researchers can scale and scroll to view the data at various levels of detail. The map is currently displaying an animated path that shows the calculated results of a researcher's request to view 10 waves of 1,000 caribou moving along an A*mbush formation. The herd's movements dictated by the wheel in the lower-left corner which weights the optimal pathfinding by Nutrition, Risk, Effort of Movement, and Time to Reach the Goal. In addition to the results of the pathfinding, the researcher can choose to display various pieces additional information, such as the presence of known archaeological structures which appear as pulsating red rings, and environmental biomes which appear as large swathes of color on the landscape. Patches of blue represent standing bodies of water. Different levels of vegetation are indexed different colors of green, with darker colors reflecting more vegetation than lighter ones.

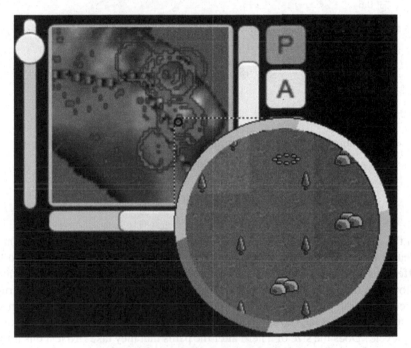

Fig. 4. A screenshot of the DeepDive's archaeological structure interface.

The visual interface is designed so that a researcher can quickly load, save, and alter data produced for a given version of the ecosystem, so it is flexible to incorporate new data and/or models. This version is then given to the VR system for the participants to interact with. In Fig. 4, the archaeological structure interface is displayed. The system's display can be reconfigured by the researcher based on which mode they choose to examine data in. In this situation, the archaeologist can not only place new structures onto the simulated landscape, but also view an enlarged view of the area with the structures shown relative to one another. As part of the system's goal to be an archive of discovered information, archaeological records can be quickly updated using new data which can then be placed in the simulation denoting its real-world location and structure type. This information can then be quickly stored for later retrieval.

3   Modelling Caribou Herd Dynamics

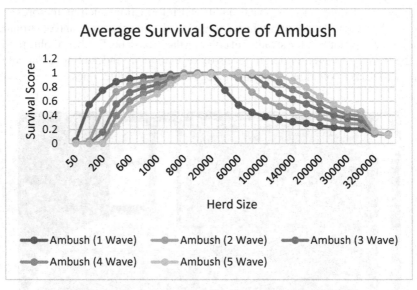

Fig. 5. Recorded survival rates of simulated caribou herds

In the previous section the researcher was able to adjust the physical and botanical landscape. In this section the researcher can simulate the movement of caribou herds of different sizes across the given landscape. Such simulations can be used to answer questions like the following: how many caribou could migrate near a hunting structure repeatedly without exhausting their supply of resources? How many caribou need to travel to ensure that a large enough number remains to repopulate the herd on the next mating cycle? Does the size of a herd alter the paths that they take? To test this information, the researcher can use the pathfinding system shown in Fig. 3. The roulette wheel allows the researcher to dial up the relative impact that each one of several factors will have on herd movement. The four factors shown there are: N (nutrition); E (effort); T (speed of movement); and R (risk). The larger its area under the wheel the more of an impact that it will have on selecting an optimal route for the herd. In addition to simulating the caribou herd's movements over the terrain, the system also keeps track of their survival rate based on two major detrimental factors. Death due to starvation (a lack of nutritional input sufficient based on the herd's size) and death due to risk (a factor based around predation, injury, and disease.)

Figure 5 is a collection of saved data from multiple runs of the A*mbush pathfinder technique, where multiple waves of caribou of steadily increasing sizes proceed across the simulated Land Bridge. Their survival score is displayed as a percentage of the initial herd size. It was possible to note from this gathered information that the simulated caribou appeared to reach a survivability plateau between herd sizes of approximately 8,000 and 20,000 caribou for this pathfinding mechanism, with herds surviving longer when the herd was broken into additional subsequent waves.

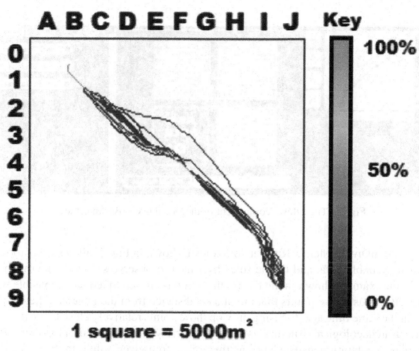

Fig. 6. Generating a herd density map for dendriform pathfinding

After completing a simulated run, the system also generates and stores information for the researcher. Figure 5 shows what could be done using the various survival metrics produced by the system, and Fig. 6 shows another way information can be displayed. Dendriform A*, a pathfinding system in which the simulated caribou can divide themselves and branch out over the landscape, generates waypoints where subheads need to split and then converge to manage bottlenecks and hazardous terrain. In the figure, the maximum herd density, representing the bulk of migrating herd, is shown as a bright red, which quickly splits apart into smaller percentages as the herd divides itself up repeatedly seeking resources. It is possible to see a bright red streak in the visualized grid at position F4, where there is a dramatic convergence bringing nearly the entire herd back together at a small stretch of land.

4   Data Analytics: Using Rulesets to Filter Data Display

The DeepDive System can display herd movement information, archaeological data, environmental biome information, vegetation density, terrain height, and the position of standing bodies of water, etc. This amount of information might be intimidating for the average researcher to analyze when attempting to test a given hypothesis. Ideally, the system needed to be powerful but exceedingly user friendly, such that any hypothesis could be tested relatively quickly and with minimal effort on the part of the archaeologist.

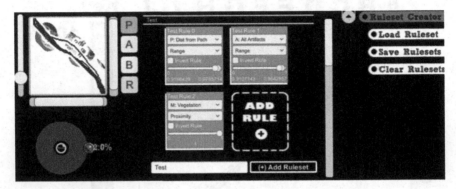

Fig. 7. The ruleset component of the DeepDive's user interface.

The DeepDive System's Ruleset component, shown in Fig. 7, allows users to select amongst available data, and define rules by which to observe selected patterns in that data. In the example shown in the figure, the user has chosen to reduce the visible scope of the data to just those points that are at a set distance from the generated herd's path, while at the same time also focusing only on those points relatively close to the positions of known archaeological structures. Within this narrowed scope, the user has then chosen to display vegetation density values as they relate to a given value. In this case, those areas with the highest vegetation scores are being displayed as a bright red color, with low scores being displayed in dark blue. The white sections of the map image indicate areas excluded from consideration via the filtering rule set.

Figure 8 shows an example where the user activated a Dendriform A* migration, and then wanted to see only those points on the map where herds converged with respect to their relative herd density values. The cluster of red points in the middle correspond with the information seen in Fig. 6, at location F4 on the grid.

In some cases, the user may be hoping to find an optimal solution for the given data. In Fig. 3 it was shown how the user can arbitrarily weight the different factors affecting optimization. The system is also able to compute the optimum set of pathways for a given herd size. Weighting caribou movement realistically, testing if a generated path can approach points of interest, and testing the validity of a hypothetical hunting structure location are all tests the system can perform for the user using the Cultural Algorithm, a data intensive evolutionary algorithm. The Cultural Algorithm is a powerful optimization tool which can take user input for a given task and adjust the system's elements around

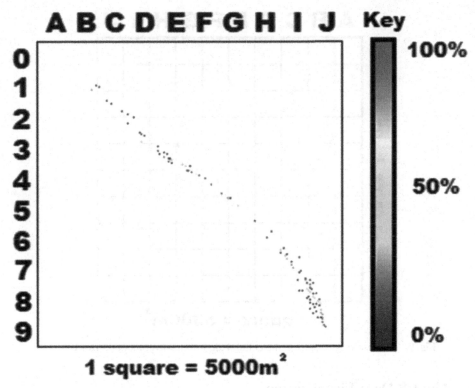

Fig. 8. A sample ruleset for herd converge and herd density

it using iterative evolution of agents as well as their knowledge sources which influence their growth [11].

Figure 9 shows the result of the Cultural Algorithm optimizing the A* pathfinder's weighting system, seen in Fig. 3, to match a user's specifications. In this case, the user selected the positions of the known archaeological structures, depicted in Fig. 9 as black circles clustered mainly in regions C2, G3, and G4. By clicking on the map and placing desired waypoint markers, the CA then adjusted the weights such that the A* path came as close to these points as possible, without being directly forced to reach them. It was then possible to examine this data for how survivable this path would be for a realistic herd as well.

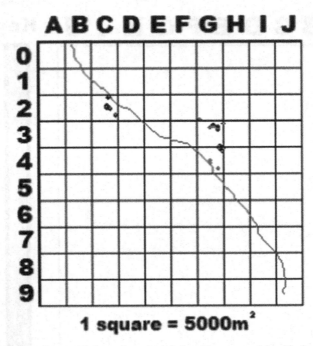

Fig. 9. The resulting path from the cultural algorithm waypoint optimizer for A*.

5   The VR Data Visualization

Fig. 10. A simulated herd moving across the landscape in Virtual Reality.

The results of the ecosystem simulation conducted by the researcher can then be transferred to the VR system and used as the basis upon which to compile a hypothetical ethnography based upon the interaction of selected participants. The simulation system sends a set of herd movement information including waypoints for fission and fusion to the VR system. Figure 10 shows a caribou migration path, generated by the system's pathfinder, being visualized as animated caribou models moving across the landscape. The landscape itself is generated from the height, water, and vegetation data, and on the right-hand side of the image a model of a known archaeological structure is displayed using three-dimensional scan data (in this case a photogrammetric model of the structure.)

The VR simulation is also interactive, allowing participants to move throughout the environment, hide within hunting structures, stalk caribou among the trees, and even record their own movements and verbal comments. While exploring in this portion of the simulation, participant movement and audio can be captured by the system, saved, and encoded as additional data for researcher to assemble a hypothetical ethnography for that landscape. Ethnographic records can have hunters exploring the landscape, and describing techniques they would use for the given terrain, archaeological records can describe the details of the expedition that led to the discovery of a given artifact, and participant records can provide insight into the function of the system as well as ways in which the system can be improved.

Fig. 11. Replicating user hand movements and teleportation in VR

Participants are also able to utilize their hands within the simulation, to grasp objects of interest, gesture towards given objects, and bring up additional options, such as a lexicon of available data. Names of plants, animals, and biomes can be readily accessed by pointing towards an object and making a simple hand gesture. Grasping a spear, the user can attempt to hunt a caribou provided they are able to remain out of the creature's line of sight. Figure 11 shows the VR system displaying a participant's hand, matching the real hand's position and gesture. By pointing to a particular location, a researcher can teleport to that position as well, without having to traverse on foot.

Fig. 12. Opening the option panel in VR

Participants are also able to access a host of optional features in VR, as shown in Fig. 12. This lets them to do the following: view their current position on the two-dimensional map; select a new position to move to from the map; activate the ability to hunt caribou; return themselves to a position they had previously moved from; and adjust their point of view for greater comfort in VR. These features can also be disabled for a more realistic and immersive experience for the participant.

Fig. 13. Herd density data displayed in the VR simulation.

In addition to the realistic landscape, any rules that the researcher generates in the DeepDive System's ruleset component can be visualized in the simulation as well. Figure 13 shows the herd density data displayed in Fig. 6, spread across the landscape.

Participants can watch the realistic models of caribou travel along the data points they established in their tests in the system.

6   Conclusion: Creating an Emergent Ethnography

Fig. 14. Ethnographic data being played back through the JAKE avatar.

The DeepDive system is now able to compile a virtual ethnography for a given landscape. The system was used with a group of hunters from Kotzebue, Alaska. Kotzebue was selected since the environment was sub-arctic and similar in principle to the ancient Land Bridge environment.

The DeepDive System can configure its data to adhere to any related hypothesis the archaeologist could wish to examine. That data is then displayed in a series of statistics and visuals that the researchers can proceed to analyze, present as evidence for the viability of a possible expedition, or utilize to explore additional hypotheses based on their discoveries. It also allows for users to share their information quickly with one another. In Fig. 14, an ethnographic recording is being played back, which lets users listen to the commentary of a native hunter from Kotzebue, Alaska, while following his movements across the land in the form of the JAKE avatar, which is modeled on the real-life remotely operated vehicle the archaeologists use.

Figure 15 gives a path followed by one hunter. It starts near the northern edge near a boulder field and moves down to the south passing by several known hunting structures. The hunter was not specifically aware of them but the path that they followed took then by each of them. Their path stops in front of the region with the highest density of caribou found in the simulation. The caribou were not visible yet when he stopped his path. In principle the path illustrates how the actual structures were influenced by and connected to caribou flow. Also, the path suggests that individuals can select to occupy to occupy one or more structures opportunistically dependent on current herd flow. This illustrates the basis for a simple but effective herd procurement system, something that might be a prime example of ancient engineered system.

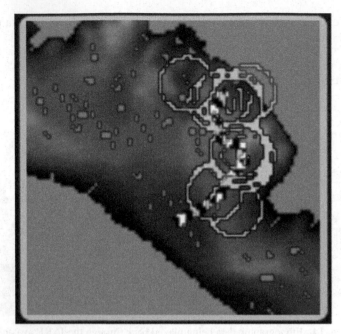

Fig. 15. A mapping of the ethnographic path data displayed as a black and white line.

The DeepDive system has the capabilities to allow anthropologists to develop hypothetical ethnographies. The information can be used to fuel new hypotheses and further the potential understanding of ancient civilization by making within the digital reach of archaeologists.

References

1. Bardzell, S., Odom, W.: The experience of embodied space in virtual worlds: an ethnography of a second life community. Space Cult. **11**(3), 239–259 (2008)
2. McCrickard, D.S., Jones, M., Stetler, T.L.: HCI Outdoors: Theory, Design, Methods and Applications, Springer (2020). https://doi.org/10.1007/978-3-030-45289-6
3. McCarthy, J., Wright, P.: Technology as experience. Interactions **11**(5), 42–43 (2004)
4. Bailey, G., Galanidou, N., Peeters, H., Jöns, H., Mennenga, M. (eds.): The Archaeology of Europe's Drowned Landscapes. CRL, vol. 35. Springer, Cham (2020). https://doi.org/10.1007/978-3-030-37367-2
5. Faught, M.: The underwater archaeology of paleolandscapes. Am. Antiquity **69**, 275–289 (2017)
6. Faught, M.: Remote sensing, target identification, and testing for submerged prehistoric sites in Florida: process and protocol in underwater CRM projects. In: Prehistoric Archaeology on the Continental Shelf, pp. 37–52 (2014). https://doi.org/10.1007/978-1-4614-9635-9_3
7. Halligan, J., et al.: Pre-Clovis occupation 14,550 years ago at the Page-Ladson Site, Florida, and the peopling of the Americas. Sci. Adv. **2**(5), e1600375 (2015)
8. Bailey, G.: New developments in submerged prehistoric archaeology: an overview. In: Prehistoric Archaeology on the Continental Shelf, pp. 291–300 (2014). https://doi.org/10.1007/978-1-4614-9635-9_16

9. O'Shea, J.M., Lemke, A.K., Sonnenburg, E.P., Reynolds, R.G., Abbott, B.D.: A 9,000-year-old caribou hunting structures beneath Lake Huron. In: Proceedings of the National Academy of Sciences of the United States of America (2014)

10. NOAA National Geophyiscal Data Center: Bathymetry of Lake Huron. In: NOAA National Centers for Environmental Information (1999)

11. Reynolds, R.G.: Cultural algorithm framework. In: Cultural on the Edge of Chaos, Springer, Cham, pp. 13–25 (2018). https://doi.org/10.1007/978-3-319-74171-0_2

12. McCrickard, D.S., Jones, M., Stelter, T.L, Editors: HCI Outdoors: Theory, Design, Methods and Applications, Springer (2020). https://doi.org/10.1007/978-3-030-45289-6

A Study of Framework Development and Research of Jewelry Design, Based on Pattern Egyptian Culture (Lotus Flower) Used in Culture Product Design

Eman Ramadan[1,2]([✉]) [iD] and Yu Wu[1]

[1] School of Art and Design, Wuhan University of Technology, Wuhan, China
eman.salah@fsed.bu.edu.eg, wu.yu@whut.edu.cn
[2] Department of Art Education, College of Specific Education, Benha University, Benha, Egypt

Abstract. Industrial design has played a crucial role in the integration of cultural elements into products and in increasing their cultural value in the competitive global marketplace. Nowadays there is a shortage of design studies and products that dealt with the Egyptian styles. Even though, the ancient Egyptian civilization is full of patterns and symbols that we can exploit, develop, and manufacture with different products. Lotus flower one of the most important symbol in the antient Egypt, it was associated with Egyptian gods because of the way in which the Lotus emerged from the water. The Ancient Egyptians believed that Lotuses were symbolic of creation, rebirth, strength. This article aims to clarify the true meaning of the Lotus flower pattern and how to transform this cultural feature into innovative jewelry designs under the framework of culture-oriented design. The main contribution of this work is to explore the old Egyptian styles and convert them into designs that are compatible with this era to spread the culture attractively. This process is done firstly through a detailed explanation of this pattern, this phase consists of cultural features, literature reviews, and concepts. Secondly, used some design programs such as Auto CAD and Render software to transform this pattern into jewelry designs. Finally, this paper establishes a cultural product jewelry design model that is meant to provide designers with valuable research that can be applied in many artistic fields like clothing design, fashion, decoration, and modern designs for this pattern.

Keywords: Cultural product · Design framework · Egyptian culture

1 Introduction

In the global market-local design era, connections between culture and design have become more closely. When we think about the "globalization", we must consider "localization" for the market first (Designers need a better understanding of cross-cultural communications not only for the global market but also for the local cultural) [1]. Design and transformation local cultural features into products appear to be more and more important in the global market. Cultural features are unique characters to be embedded

© Springer Nature Switzerland AG 2021
C. Stephanidis et al. (Eds.): HCII 2021, LNCS 13096, pp. 630–645, 2021.
https://doi.org/10.1007/978-3-030-90328-2_43

into a product both for the enhancement of its identity in the global market and for the fulfilling of the individual consumer's experiences [2]. Also, using local features in design fields as a strategy to create product identity worldwide, the designers have noted the importance of associating products with cultural features to enhance the product value [3].

The field of industrial design has played an important role in embedding cultural elements into products and in increasing cultural value in the global competitive product market. Therefore, designing a product with local features to emphasize its cultural value has become a critical issue in the design process, further explore how to integrate the local cultural features into the product design. Also, try to build a conceptual framework of design transformation [4]. The design is an important medium of communication, which is popularized in the culture of the earth to integrate the historical value with modern life. To make some contributions to the inheritance of Egyptian cultural heritage and the economic value of cultural products, the traditional Lotus flower pattern can be applied better to the cultural product design for modern life [5]. This paper aims to design the Egyptian culture as the Egyptian civilization is full of distinctive and wonderful patterns where the goal is to apply the famous Lotus flower pattern in ancient Egypt in modern jewelry designs, as jewelry making was very important in ancient Egypt. By creating modern jewelry designs to convey cultural traits in the form of a modern product [6], Through creating a framework for design and consumer opinions, also using CAD programs to transform the design into products closer to reality.

Culture as a form of creative resources can assist designers in catalyzing innovative product design. Based on the research conducted by Gaidysheva and Parnyakov, they illustrate the development of decorative handicrafts through the indigenous peoples of the far east, where the author incorporated elements of the Nanai shaman's culture into the design of modern things and transformed the culture into a cultural product [7]. Based on the research of Professor Rung-Tai Lin, he stated that connections between culture and design have become increasingly evident in this global market-local design era. Besides, designing culture into products will become a trend in the global market. The researcher aims to propose a cultural product design model, where the author transferred Taiwan's culture to modern design and product elements to enhance its design value as the results presented demonstrate the intertwining experience between design and culture. There is a need for a better understanding of cross-cultural communication to participate in the global market and develop a local design. As a result, cultural issues become essential for product design in the global economy. The intersection of design and culture becomes a vital issue making both local design and the global market worthy of further in-depth study [8]. Based on Ser's research, the researcher stated how to transform cultural features into design elements under the framework of culture-oriented design. The researcher plays a role as an explorer to generate a product design based on the cultural product design model [9]. Other researchers used gardenia flower as a basis to transfer the local culture of Taiwan's community (Fuzhou area) into a series of gardenia-inspired cultural products, where three levels of design thinking were used to translate gardenia and design cultural products based on it, this study incorporated code design methods and the three levels of design thinking to develop cultural product designs [10].

2   Culture Features and Product Design

2.1   Three Cultural Levels

Culture generally refers to patterns of human activity and symbolic structures, Moreover, culture has been described as the evolutionary process that involves Language, customs, religion, arts, thought, and behavior [11, 12]. From a design point of view, suggested a multi-layered cultural architecture including "artifacts", "value" and the 'basic assumptions' that defined key design features such as 'functional', Aesthetic and symbolic [13, 14], developed a framework for the study. Cultural objects have three special levels: the external "physical" level, the intermediate "behavioral" level, and the internal "intangible" level. As shown in Fig. 1, the culture can be categorized into three Layers: (1) Physical culture, including food, clothing, and transportation relevant things, (2) Social or behavioral culture, including human relations and social organization, and (3) Spiritual or idealistic culture, including art and religion [15]. These Three culture layers can be installed in the above three Leong culture levels., and they can be three design features it has been defined as follows: (1) The internal level that contains special content such as stories, emotion, cultural characteristics, (2) the intermediate level that contains the function, and operational concerns, usability, and safety, (3) the external level dealing with color, texture, shape, decoration, surface pattern, line quality, and details.

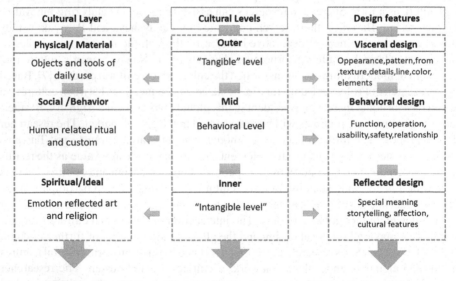

Fig. 1. Three layers and levels of cultural objects and design features [8].

2.2 Fundamental Cultural Resources of Ancient Egyptian Civilization

Designing culture, improving quality, and adding additional value to the product is essential for designing a cultural product and improving product performance. Egypt has strong potential to innovate and develop important cultural products [16]. Three basic resources for innovation and development as follows (1) The culture of the ancient Egyptian people in the ancient Egyptian civilization,(2) The ancient Egyptian civilization arose on the banks of the Nile River nearly 7,000 years ago and is the first and oldest civilization in history, (3) The multiplicity of patterns, symbols, and arts in which the ancient Egyptian artist created crafts and handicrafts that the ancient Egyptian civilization was famous for, such as the manufacture of jewelry and the multiplicity of Egyptian antiquities that are present in all museums inside and outside Egypt, Among these three resources [17, 18], the ancient Egyptian culture already has a unique and great inspiration with its primitive arts and handicrafts, therefore, the investigation of the ancient Egyptian culture as it has different arts and styles that distinguish it from any culture in the world [6]. For example, the art of making jewelry in which the ancient Egyptians excelled, as jewelry was an important method through which the ancient Egyptians tried to attract the attention of the gods (according to their belief). They believed that the more jewelry they wore, God's attention increased to them, As the ancient Egyptian culture and arts in Egypt are wonderful and their beautiful handicrafts have great potential to enhance the value of product design and thus increase its recognition in the global market [19].

2.3 Overview of the Lotus Flower Pattern and Jewelry Making in Ancient Egypt

The flower was known as Seshen and was associated with Egyptian gods. Because of the way in which the lotus emerged from the water, the Ancient Egyptians believed that lotuses were symbolic of creation, rebirth, strength [20]. The lotus flower was sacred in the life of the ancient Egyptian since the beginning of the ancient Egyptian history in the third millennium B.C., the lotus flower was not an aesthetic decorative element that the Egyptian depicted on the walls of temples only or used in the manufacture of perfumes or jewelry but was the title of creation among the ancient Egyptians [21]. The manufacture of jewelry was very important in ancient Egypt, and the evident greatness of the ancient Egyptian civilization in the handicrafts and artifacts. Jewelry was an important means by which the ancient Egyptians tried to attract the attention of their deities (according to their belief) [6]; they believed that the more jewelry they wore, God's attention increased to them. In ancient Egypt, women, men, and children, from poor families to royalties, wore the best colored jewelry they could afford, the materials from which the jewelry was made differ according to their wealth and stature, however, necklaces, bracelets, neck collars, pendants, earrings, arm, rings, and amulets adorned their necks, wrists, ears, fingers, and ankles [22, 23]. One example of this is the amulet, many ancient Egyptians wore jewelry for many different reasons, as shown in Fig. 2.

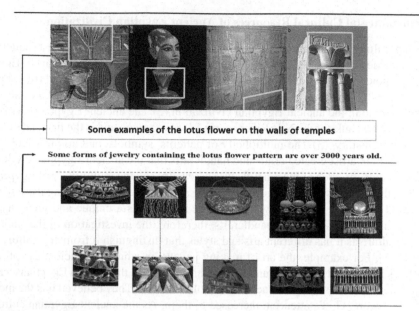

Fig. 2. Illustration of examples of the Lotus flower in ancient Egyptian life and ornaments

2.4   Cultural Attributive Analyses and Design Concepts Table

In Egypt, cultural has awareness initiatives to promote the Egyptian product attracted the design research community and then the handicrafts in ancient Egypt that disappeared due to the lack of a new generation of cultural craftsmen, [13] the transfer of local culture to younger generations has been retreated, studies show positive results, as Egyptian culture is a great value and deserves to be incorporated into the current daily products through the new design [24]. At this point, we focused on collecting data from the culture in terms of materialism, habits, and spirituality, then the data collected was matched with different data based on the civilization, the name of the object, the type, the image, the material, the color [19], the feature, the function, the style, the shape of the rules form composition, Cultural importance. These elements covered three levels of cultural and basic characteristics. [25]. We suggest that this information serve as a reference for designers during the product design phase. Table 1 illustrates an example of cultural design features.

Table 1. Example of a cultural attributive analyses and design concepts table

Analysis of Cultural Attributes		Interpretation of Culture	Features of Product	Category of Products
Cultural	Ancient Egyptian civilization	Wear, status symbol, jewelry decorative, arrangement also followed special rules, symmetrical	shading effects, decorative, extension of personal particularity	jewelry, Ornament, fashion, furniture
Object	Necklace a lotus flower			
Type	Ornament			
Image				
Material	glass beads shell pieces metal• gold.			
Color	The solid colored beads in blue, green, white and black. The shell pieces are white.	Sketch of Design Concept as Metaphor, Features of Product: extension of personal particularity, jewelry, wear		
Characteristic	These were precious jewelry worn by kings and queens and written on it the name of her lamb and buried with him when he died, and it was always made of precious metals such as gold and precious stones			
Operation	The manifold stones were often used together, such as in multiple-strand ornaments. were worn at the chest or around the neck.			
Pattern	Each type of traditional bead had a different name, and associated legend.			
Form grammar	The order of arrangement also followed special rules.			
Form construct	The lower part is characterized by its large size and always contains a symbol of the symbols of the gods and mostly the lotus flower, and it consists of multi-colored beads, and the lower part is the precious and unique part of completely decorated with pieces of green and blue gemstones, and made of gold			
Formation	This neckline is a ribbon consisting of a main part in the middle with three or more strands of chains. The branches have large colored beads and small beads and shells of one color.			
Using scenario	This type of neck necklace will only be worn by the king at ceremonies And when he dies, he is placed with him			
Cultural content	They would be used as wedding gift to the bride . In addition, also were believed to bring luck, And protection.			

3   Methodology

This research consists of two parts: primary data and secondary data. The primary data was conducted on the study of the lotus flower pattern and the analysis of this pattern with the expectation that it will be a framework for the design process. Secondary data we Are practicing design and creating a cultural product based on the design framework, process, and design concepts through jewelry design CAD software [26].

3.1 Design Framework and Process

Culture plays an important role in the field of design, and cultural design will become a key point in design evaluation in the future. Incorporating cultural features into the product design process will become a new design trend in the global market, [27]. Apparently, we need a better understanding of cultural communications not only for taking part in the global market, but also for developing local design, the cultural product design is a process of rethinking or reviewing the cultural features and then redefining them to design a new product to fit into society and satisfy consumers through culture and esthetic. [28]. Designing new products by adding unique cultural features would not only benefit economic growth, but also promote unique local culture in the global market. Therefore, transforming cultural features into a cultural product becomes a critical issue. [14] In order to facilitate the understanding of the cultural product design process, The author has suggested a framework and process are proposed for combining consumer attitudes, cultural levels, cultural attributes, transformation, product semantics and design features as shown in Fig. 3. A good understanding of the cultural attributes will benefit articulating the context between the culture and product design and therefore accelerate concept development, based on the cultural product design framework and process, the cultural product is designed using scenario and semantics approaches. In a practical design process four phases are used to design a cultural product, namely: definition (telling a situation), knowledge (setting an objective), fulfilment (writing an analysis), and Implementation (designing a product) as shown in Fig. 3, In addition, consumer needs, cultural content and design theories.

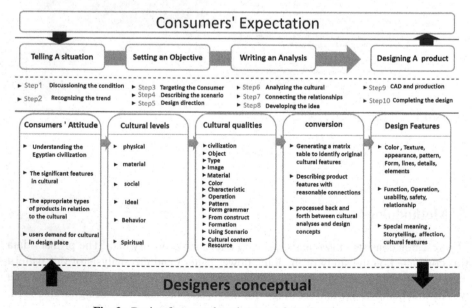

Fig. 3. Design framework and process for cultural products.

Ten steps of design procedure would provide designers or students a systematic method to designing a cultural product. The four phases and ten steps of the cultural product design process are further described accordingly as follows:

Definition/Telling a Situation:

1. Discussing the condition: Understanding cultural products through discussions. Designers must have a clear understanding of design aspirations and develop of attributes hierarchy.
2. Recognizing the trend: Based on cultural attributes, Integration of technological applications into the design of the new product.

Knowledge/ Setting an Objective:

3. Targeting the consumer: Explore the consumer community to define a product image using meaning and style derived from the concerns of the features of culture.
4. Describing the scenario: this step allows designers to describe scenarios of users who prefer a particular style and identify with the features, meaning, category, and appropriateness of the product.
5. Design direction: this step establishes a design specification, which will identify the goal, function, target group, and limitation of the design.

Fulfilment/ Writing an Analysis:

6. Analyzing the culture: based on cultural layers, generate a matrix table as shown in Table to identify original cultural features including civilization object, type, image, material, color, characteristic, operation, pattern, form grammar, form construct, formation, using scenario, cultural content, and resource.
7. Connecting the relationships: describe product features and develop a product with these cultural attributes. The analysis and synthesis will be processed back and forth between cultural analyses and design concepts as shown in Table.
8. Developing the concept: this step is the concept development and design realization, to transform the cultural meaning into a logically correct cultural product.

Implementation/Designing a Product:

9. CAD and production: in this step we used the CAD design software to form a surface by drawing lines, then formed a body by these surfaces we got.
10. Completing the design: examining the details and integrity of the cultural product as product features, supply cultural attributes to transform them reasonably into the product performance.

3.2 Quantitative Analysis

Design a questionnaire about creating a cultural product in the form of modern jewelry and consumers' awareness of the ancient Egyptian culture in designing a cultural product.

The questionnaire design perceptions regarding three aspects- appearance, function, and emotion. Viewer and consumer perceptions were identified from survey results to design-related cultural products, The questionnaire design is shown in Table 2, and the conclusions are as follows:

1. People who respond to attitudes towards ancient Egyptian culture believe that products with designs of Egyptian culture can enhance positive qualities and value-added value in life and competitively increase product value in the market.
2. People who respond to the most important features of the ancient Egyptian culture agree on the following order of importance: jewelry design, decoration, clothing design as these parts give a unique style to contemporary product and design, as jewelry, decoration and clothing design are among the favorites of most consumers. Because these parts are related to fashion and in our time, they represent great importance to most people and a product that facilitates exchange between people.
3. Topics that respond to appropriate product types in relation to ancient Egyptian culture the culture believes that jewelry, fashion decoration, and handicrafts, innovation will be improved through the unique style and contemporary design.
4. The topics that respond to users' demand for the ancient Egyptian culture in place of design are cultural features, texture, shape, color.

Table 2. Questionnaire design for lotus flower-inspired cultural products

Dimension	Operational aspect	Question
Tangible level	Perceptions of appearance	Q1. Does this product appropriately use the outer shape of the Lotus Flower to form its overall form? Q2. Can these products clarify the culture meanings of the Egyptian civilizations? Q3. What are the appropriate products that show the ancient Egyptian culture and can spread quickly?
Behavioral level	Perceptions of function	Q4. Do the functions of this product fit the requirements of modern individuals? Q5. Are these products look suitable for use? Q6. Are these products with Egyptian cultural designs can increase the value of the product?
Intangible level	Perceptions of emotions	Q7. Does this product touch you emotionally? Q8. Do you like these new products designs?
Assessment level	Overall perceptions	Q9. Do you find these products creative and ingenious? Q10. Do products with Egyptian cultural designs could increase the value of product?

The study used a questionnaire to analyze and compare perceptions and feelings regarding the lotus flower- inspired cultural product designs. The questionnaire results may serve as a reference for future studies in designing related products.

4 Design Practices in Innovation Jewelry Designs

Based on the study stage, we now propose a cultural product design process, which proves the effectiveness of this systematic approach in designing culture. The design practice in this study is the result of integrating literature reviews and design concepts from the ancient Egyptian civilization, and creating cultural products related to life now [29]. Despite the multiplicity of the ruling families, the jewelry industry in Egypt was a very important and distinctive industry in each of these families, and the lotus flower pattern remained engraved on these jewelry, as it represented an important pattern in the lives of Egyptians as it was involved in many industries such as the perfume industry. Moreover, these are distinctive features to demonstrate their application in the design of cultural products that consumers can easily identify, Through the design framework and design practices, the culture of the original cultural object and the analysis of cultural attribution were recorded in the design concepts table (Table 1), and cultural products were created in the form of jewelry bearing the cultural features of the original being through the steps that we mentioned and explained before, And we created three designs inspired by the Egyptian lotus flower [30], and it is a simple product that meets the requirements of the consumer and thus is a product that is able to compete in the global market and carries the cultural features of the original organism, and finally the practices were completed using CAD programs to simulate the display of the actual product, as shown in Fig. 4, where lotus flower jewelry was a valuable thing and was worn by royalty and used as gifts on occasions, and the stones used in the manufacture of these jewelry were based on the status of the wearer, and the social status, using design practices three designs were created in the form of jewelry (Figs. 5 and 6).

Where the first figure expresses the shape of a clock inspired by the shape of the lotus flower in a modern design that is able to compete in the global market, and the second shape expresses the lotus flower in the form of a simple necklace, and the third shape also expresses the lotus flower also, but in a different way that opens and closes in the form of a necklace, As cultural products are innovated using cultural features as examples to explore the relevance of the design reference to cultural features, it provides designers with a valuable reference for creating successful products.

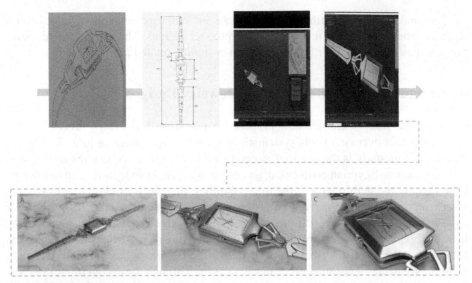

Fig. 4. The first design, wristwatch, innovating the design from Lotus flower by using Render software.

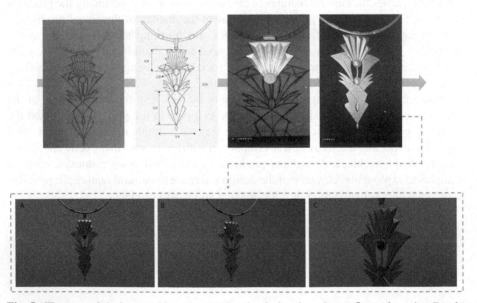

Fig. 5. The second design, necklace, innovating the design from Lotus flower by using Render software.

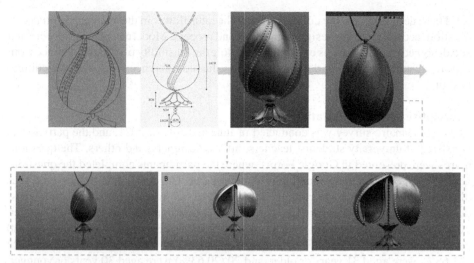

Fig. 6. The third design, necklace (chain), innovating the design from Lotus flower by using Render software.

4.1 Design Practices in Innovation Cultural Product Designs

The framework can also be applied outside jewelry design for other cultural products by incorporating cultural features into the product design process, combining consumer needs, cultural levels, design theories. Also, applying the four stages of cultural product design, namely definition, knowledge, fulfillment, and implementation, where the author implemented the framework on some other products, creating cultural products capable of competing in the global market. Figure 7 shows some cultural products inspired from the Lotus flower designed by using Auto CAD and Render software.

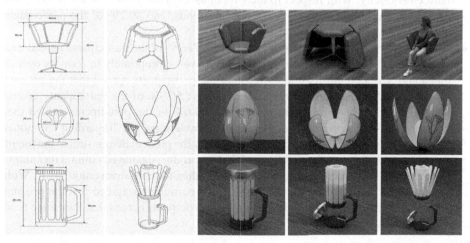

Fig. 7. Some cultural products are inspired by the Lotus flower pattern (chair, lighting unit, and water filtration cup, appeared from top to down).

These designs reveal the cultural form of the lotus flower in the ancient Egyptian civilization, according to the design framework and process. Modern products were created and designed using culture as examples to explore the feasibility of design reference from cultural features, providing designers with a valuable reference for successful cultural design.

Descriptive of the Quantitative Analysis

The questionnaire survey was conducted in June and July of 2021, and the participants consisted of university students, teachers, artists, designers, and others. The questionnaires were presented in Google Forms, where the participants completed the questionnaires based on their understanding of the questions. The questionnaire measured four dimensions; each dimension contained two or three questions; an analysis of the questionnaire participants demonstrated the following distributions. (a) Regarding gender, 70 participants (72.92%) were women, and 26 (27.08%) were men (b) Regarding age, 30 participants were (30.92%) aged 20–40 years, 25 (25.77%) were aged 30–40 years, 22 (22.68%) were aged 31 years or older, and 20 (20.63%) were aged 30 years or younger. (c) Regarding their professional backgrounds, 25 people (23.36%) had an art-related background, 17 (15.89%) had a design-related background, and 65 people (60.75%) had other learning backgrounds. The participants' opinions about the lotus flower-inspired cultural products were as follows:

- Lotus flower watch: In terms of appearance, 70.2% of the participants agreed that the product used the appearance of the lotus flower Concerning function, 59.3% of the participants agreed that the product looked beautiful and unpretentious, 88.2% of the participants agreed that the product was convenient to use, and 70.8% of the participants agreed that the functions of the product met the needs of modern people. Regarding emotional perceptions, 52% of the participants agreed that the product displayed cultural meanings, and 65% of the participants agreed that the product touched them emotionally. With respect to the overall assessment, 64.4% of the participants agreed that the product was creative and ingenious, and 80.2% of the participants agreed that they were fond of the product.
- Lotus flower necklace: In terms of appearance, 71.2% of the participants agreed that the product used the appearance of the lotus flower appropriately to form its overall appearance Concerning function, 80.5% of the participants agreed that the product looked beautiful and unpretentious, respectively; 56.9% of the participants agreed that the product was convenient to use, and 60.6% of the participants agreed that the functions of the product met the needs of modern people. Regarding emotional perceptions, 74.1% of the participants agreed that the product demonstrated the fun of history, 60.7% of the participants agreed that the product displayed cultural meanings, and 59.8% of the participants agreed that the product touched them emotionally. With respect to the overall assessment, 59.1% of the participants agreed that the product was creative and ingenious, and 67.6% of the participants agreed that they were fond of the product.

- Lotus flower chain: In terms of appearance, 60% of the participants agreed that the product used the appearance of the lotus flower appropriately to form its overall appearance, concerning function 80% of the participants agreed that the product looked beautiful and unpretentious, 60.8% of the participants agreed that the product was convenient to use, and 57.9% of the participants agreed that the functions of the product met the needs of modern people. Regarding emotional perceptions, and 77.6% of the participants agreed that the product touched them emotionally.62% of the participants agreed that the product displayed cultural meanings, with respect to the overall assessment, 65.2% of the participants agreed that the product was creative and ingenious, and 63.5% of the participants agreed that they were fond of the product.

5   Conclusion and Recommendations

The diversity of Egyptian styles and the uniqueness of the ancient Egyptian culture provides a potential application in the field of design. By enhancing the original meaning and images of cultures and making use of new production technology. The culture of the ancient Egyptian civilization in Egypt will have great potential to enhance the value of product design, thus, increasing the identification of Egyptian products in the global market. The framework design and the development process of the innovation of cultural products are established through the analysis of cultural attribution and the table of design concepts, through the integration of all the information. We provided a method for designing culture through cultural features and product features the importance of a product with cultural features to enhance the value of the product and meet the needs of the user. Ancient Egyptian patterns were simple symbols but had great meanings, so the investigation of the ideal product for the consumer always produced as things to use the results showed the potential for enhancement and uniqueness through product design, for cultural creativity and for products inspired by culture.

The study results and recommendations for future research directions are as follows.

- This study included cultural analyzes, design concepts, literature review, and through the integration of all this, we provided a framework that combines cultural features, product features, creating jewelry designs, also the importance of the product with cultural features to enhance the value of the product and meet user needs.
- Future studies can reference this study to devise framework to design their cultural product and apply the framework in the creative design of cultural products, assets of intangible value in Egypt, such as historical buildings, unique handcrafts, and historical monuments. All of this will preserve the Egyptian culture enable the development of cultural products, facilitate local industry development, and driving the regional economy.

References

1. Gilal, F.G., Zhang, J., Gilal, N.G., Gilal, R.G.: Integrating self-determined needs into the relationship among product design, willingness-to-pay a premium, and word-of-mouth: a

cross-cultural gender-specific study. Psychol. Res. Behav. Manag. **11**, 227–241 (2018). https://doi.org/10.2147/PRBM.S161269

2. Hung, Y.-H., Lee, W.-T.: The need for a cultural representation tool in cultural product design. Springer Singapore (2018). https://doi.org/10.1007/978-981-10-8189-7-9

3. Yousif, T.: The reflection of culture features on product design Tamer Yousif. Online J. Art Des. **8**, 215–222 (2020)

4. Shin, M.J., Cassidy, T., Moore, E.M.: Design reinvention for culturally influenced textile products: focused on traditional Korean bojagi textiles. Fash. Pract. **7**, 175–198 (2015). https://doi.org/10.1080/17569370.2015.1045354

5. Kathy, J.: Secrets of the Ancient Egyptian Sacred Blue Lotus. pp. 1–3 (2015)

6. Atherton-Woolham, S., McKnight, L., Price, C., Adams, J.: Imaging the gods: animal mummies from Tomb 3508, North Saqqara, Egypt. Antiquity **93**(367), 128–143 (2019). https://doi.org/10.15184/aqy.2018.189

7. Gaidysheva, M., Parnyakov, A.V.: Design of applied and decorative art elements based on the example of Nanai shaman's culture. Pacific Sci. Rev. **16**, 140–147 (2014). https://doi.org/10.1016/j.pscr.2014.08.025

8. Lin, R.T.: Transforming Taiwan aboriginal cultural features into modern product design: a case study of a cross-cultural product design model. Int. J. Des. **1**, 45–53 (2007)

9. Ser, S.: On culture-oriented product design: a study to transform cultural features to design elements. Int. J. Creat. Futur. Herit. **6**, 163–197 (2018)

10. Trapani, P.: Designing co-design: addressing five critical areas to increase the experience of participants and facilitator in a co-design session. In: Rau, P.-L. (ed.) HCII 2019. LNCS, vol. 11576, pp. 79–93. Springer, Cham (2019). https://doi.org/10.1007/978-3-030-22577-3_6

11. Qian, J., Xiao, A., Xin, X., He, M.: Pattern primitive library construction and feature analysis of kirgiz textile pattern. Human. Soc. Sci. **7**(6), 191 (2019). https://doi.org/10.11648/j.hss.20190706.11

12. HeMin, D.: Cultural creative product design from the perspective of chinese ancient ware modelling. E3S Web Conf. **179**, 02033 (2020). https://doi.org/10.1051/e3sconf/202017902033

13. Lin, R., Cheng, R., Sun, M.-X.: Digital archive database for cultural product design. In: Aykin, N. (ed.) UI-HCII 2007. LNCS, vol. 4559, pp. 154–163. Springer, Heidelberg (2007). https://doi.org/10.1007/978-3-540-73287-7_20

14. Chai, C., Shen, D., Bao, D., Sun, L.: Cultural product design with the doctrine of the mean in confucian philosophy. Des J **6925**, 1–23 (2018). https://doi.org/10.1080/14606925.2018.1440842

15. Qin, Z., Ng, S.: Culture as inspiration: a metaphorical framework for designing products with traditional cultural properties (TCPs). Sustain **12**(17), 7171 (2020) https://doi.org/10.3390/su12177171

16. Berk, G.G.: A Framework for Designing in Cross-Cultural Contexts: Culture-Centered Design Process a Dissertation Submitted to the Faculty of the Graduate School of the University Of Minnesota. pp. 1–287 (2013). https://doi.org/10.11299/155725

17. Allen, J.P.: The ancient egyptian pyramid texts. Anc. Egypt Pyramid Texts **33**, 182–193 (2017). https://doi.org/10.2307/j.ctt14jxv34

18. Troalen, L., Guerra, M.F., Maitland, M., et al.: Analytical study of the Middle Kingdom group of gold jewellery from tomb 124 at Riqqa. Egypt. X-Ray Spectrom. **48**, 586–596 (2019). https://doi.org/10.1002/xrs.3026

19. Li, H., Yi, X., Chen, M.: Symbolic meanings of Pharaoh 's false beard in ancient Egypt. pp. 352–359 (2017).https://doi.org/10.25236/ssah.2017.77

20. Hedegaard, S.B., Delbey, T., Brøns, C., Rasmussen, K.L.: Painting the Palace of Apries II: ancient pigments of the reliefs from the Palace of Apries, Lower Egypt. Herit. Sci. **7**(1), 1–32 (2019). https://doi.org/10.1186/s40494-019-0296-4

21. Al-gaoudi, H.A.: Painted ancient Egyptian mummy cloth of Khonsuemrenep from Bab EL-GASUS excavation: scientific analysis and conservation strategy. Sci. Cult. **6**, 49–64 (2020). https://doi.org/10.5281/zenodo.3724852
22. Ulusman, L., Bayburtlu, C.: Paradigm for art education; creation story of jewels, theme, design, artwork, 3D. Procedia – Soc. Behav. Sci. **51**, 284–288 (2012). https://doi.org/10.1016/j.sbspro.2012.08.160
23. Jassawalla, A.R., Sashittal, H.C.: Cultures that support product-innovation processes. Acad. Manag. Exec. **16**, 42–54 (2002). https://doi.org/10.5465/AME.2002.8540307
24. Efimova, A.: Masterpieces of Jeweller's Art in the Egyptian Style Made by Cartier in the Period of Art Deco. vol. 103, 16–17 (2017). https://doi.org/10.2991/iccese-17.2017.101
25. Hu, Y., et al.: Transforming chinese cultural features into modern product design. In: Rau, P.-L. (ed.) HCII 2020. LNCS, vol. 12192, pp. 313–324. Springer, Cham (2020). https://doi.org/10.1007/978-3-030-49788-0_23
26. Siriwattanasakul, K., Boonyongmaneerat, Y., Chandrachai, A., Anuntavoranich, P.: Creating effective and innovative cooperation between Universities and SMEs: a case study of the Thai Jewellery industry for design skill development. In: ISPIM Conference Proceedings, pp. 1–15 (2020)
27. Hidayat, J., Tjakra, G., Darmawan, R., Dharmawan, C.: Hybrid Design Model in Cross Cultural Collaboration: Case Study - Contemporary Bamboo-Ceramic-Batik-Silver Crafts Made by Indonesian and Japanese Artists. pp. 394–399 (2020). https://doi.org/10.5220/0008885703940399
28. Gao, Y., Fang, W., Gao, Y., Lin, R.: Conceptual framework and case study of china's womanese scripts used in culture product design. J. Arts Human. **7**(3), 57 (2018). https://doi.org/10.18533/journal.v7i3.1363
29. Johnson, M.J.: Art and architecture. Brill's Compan. Eur. Hist. **9**, 350–389 (2016). https://doi.org/10.1163/9789004315938-015
30. Elhabashy, S., Abdelgawad, E.M.: The history of nursing profession in ancient Egyptian society. Int. J. Africa Nurs. Sci. **11**, 100174 (2019). https://doi.org/10.1016/j.ijans.2019.100174

Relationship Between Human-Computer Interaction Features and Players' Decision-Making in Music Games

Gongli Wang[1], Guoyu Sun[1], Tianqi Xie[1], and Yiyuan Huang[2(✉)]

[1] Communication University of China, Beijing, China
gysun@cuc.edu.cn
[2] Beijing Institute of Graphic Communication, Beijing, China
yiyuan.huang@bigc.edu.cn

Abstract. Music games provide a series of frequent, accurate, powerful, and rhythmic interactions for players via unique game mechanics and rule settings, guiding them to use auditory and visual cues in the scene. The development of entertainment industry promotes the research on Human-Computer interaction of music games. This paper will focus on the relationship between the Human-Computer interaction mechanism of music games and players' game behavior decisions, and analyze the causes. Firstly, this paper reviews the theoretical and experimental researches on HCI in music games, references and analyzes the existing representative cases of music games, and constructs a relational model consisting of music game mechanics and players' decision making. Then, we introduce the music game *Don't Be Popcorn* designed by the authors. It describes the design and implementation of game mechanics and rules, interaction, and art effects. Finally, the experimental analysis is carried out to verify the relational model by inviting some participants to experience our game, analyzing the data of the test results. The results show that the behavioral decisions made by professional players are more radical than amateurs. Moreover, there is a Non-linear correlation between changes in the extent of player level performance and adjustments in behavioral decisions. Therefore, the proposed relational model can further provide references for game designers and researchers to analyze the interaction between players and music games.

Keywords: Music game · Video game · Human-computer interaction design · Players' Decision-Making

1 Introduction

Music games is a significant genre in video games. Since the release of *BeatMania DX* by Japanese video game designers in the 1990s, music games have completed the iteration through various interactive devices such as arcade devices, home consoles, computers, mobile devices, physical devices, and virtual reality [1]. In the process of forming mutual interaction between players and music game scenes, the visual, auditory

© Springer Nature Switzerland AG 2021
C. Stephanidis et al. (Eds.): HCII 2021, LNCS 13096, pp. 646–664, 2021.
https://doi.org/10.1007/978-3-030-90328-2_44

and interactive actions achieve interoperability and mutual sensation, mobilizing players' sensory stimulation, thus enhancing the fun of music game experience. Nowadays, music games have gradually come out from the niche. With various forms of interaction and unique themes, music games such as *Beat Saber*, *Taiko Drummer*, *Just Shapes and Beats*, *Geometry Dash*, *Sayonara Wild Hearts* and *Just Dance* are popular with numerous players.

Analyzed from the perspective of creation, music games can be defined as "a class of video games in which players use interactive input devices to follow the rhythm and melody of the background music while interacting with the game scene, and follow the sound and screen tips to complete frequent, accurate, powerful and rhythmic interactive operation simultaneously to achieve the game goal".[2] Compared with other types of electronic games, music is the core of the design and experience in this genre. Therefore, the interaction mechanism, interaction rules, operation performance evaluation and other modules are closely related to music elements and also play an essential role in advancing the game process, regulating the rhythm of interaction, creating an atmosphere of experience, highlighting the use of skills, and stimulating emotional resonance, etc. [3].

Music game has gradually improved with the innovation of software and Hardware-Related technologies such as interactive devices. At the same time, HCI theories are combined and explored in the field of video games, which also promotes more attention to the research of HCI design concepts and features for music games. There are many disciplines involved in the study of music games, most of them are Cross-Fertilized. At present, the research related to HCI design in music games mainly combines and applies theories of game psychology, computer graphics, ergonomics, and musicology [4, 5]. Among the academic results focusing on the HCI design of music games, scholars have studied the factors related to the interaction design of music games and the factors that affect the players' performance, the form of music interaction atmosphere shaping, the regularity of interaction spectrum generation, and other related aspects [6, 7].

In the actual experience of any video games, players follow the game mechanics and rules, receive feedback and evaluation, master and apply operational skills, and develop and adjust their strategies according to the change of perception process. This process can be described as the correlation between the interaction characteristics shaped by the game and players' behavioral decisions. Based on this, this paper aims to analyze the association between the HCI features of music games and players' Decision-Making and summarize the relationship model accordingly. We hoped this theoretical model could be used as a reference for music game developers and related researchers to conduct subsequent research on the Human-Computer interaction between players and music games.

This paper adopts case study and game experiment research as the research methods. The subsequent chapters are organized as follows: Sect. 2 is a review of the current research status, which will sort out and analyze the current academic research results and case studies from the aspects of game mechanics and rules design, operation behavior design, and players' Decision-Making of music games. Sect. 3 introduces the relationship model between Human-Computer interaction features and user behavior decisions in music games and initially analyzes the association of each module in this model. In Sect. 4 we introduce *Don't Be Popcorn*, a music game designed by our team. The design of this game will be guided by the view of interaction design features presented in the previous chapters and will be related to the preparation for the subsequent experimental study. In Sect. 5, we conduct an experimental study and verify in more detail the relevant ideas in the relational theoretical model with the results of the playtest and data analysis, and provide a more profound explanation of the model. Finally, Sect. 6 summarizes our research and make suggestions.

2   Relative Works

2.1   Game Mechanism Design

In the book Game Mechanics: Advanced Game Design, Ernest Adams and other authors suggest that "game mechanics are the rules, processes, and data at the heart of the game". Therefore, music game mechanics is the first framework that needs to be built for a music game design. The rules and gameplay in music game mechanics distinguish it from other video games and make a unique connection between player interaction and the feedback effect of the game scene [8].

According to traditional music games' primary mechanism and rules, many note indicators are generated in the level scene orderly and move from top to bottom according to the specified trajectory. When the note indicators move to the interactive judgment area at the bottom of the interface, the player needs to interact with the note indicators instantly to complete an effective operation. Repeat the above actions in the level and keep accumulating the score until the score reaches the requirement of passing the level. The above descriptions of the core gameplay and rules of music games form a music game interaction mechanism with the core elements of "Note Indicator", "Moving Track" and "Judgment Area", called "Dropping Interaction" (see Fig. 1).

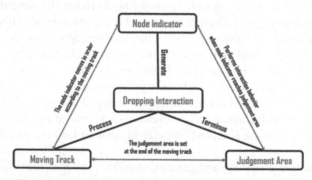

Fig. 1. Diagram of the "Dropping Interaction" mechanism.

Early music games such as *Rhythm Master* and *o2jam* are based on "drop interaction" as the core gameplay, which is used in setting the interaction mechanism and rules of the game. The current iteration and innovation of the traditional music game "falling interaction" mechanism usually involves changes in the visualization of note indicators, judgment areas, moving tracks, and movement rules. For example, the level of difficulty of the arcade music game *Maimai DX* is related to the layout of the interaction sequence composed of many note indicators. The interactive symbols such as slide, tap, Re-tap, long press is generated in an orderly manner along with the Fast-Paced music, guiding the player to tap on the touch screen inside the physical arcade or on the buttons along the outer edge. *Cytus II* levels will no longer move visually in terms of note indicators. However, they will instead scan up and down the previously fixed lines of the judgment area, with the rate and period of scanning adjusted to the soundtrack's mood (see Fig. 2).

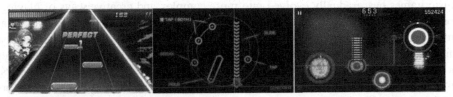

Fig. 2. Reference to the use of "Dropping Interaction" mechanism in music games (Left: *Rhythm Master*. Mid: *Maimai DX*. Right: *Cytus II*).

In the generation of note indicators in the "Dropping interaction" mechanism, Kagawa Toshimune et al. [9] focus on the technical principles of game interaction and propose the use of the "suffix tree" data parsing technique (Suffix Tree) to effectively extract the features of the background music of the level in music games, and use an adapted extraction and analysis algorithm to control the timing of game interaction and the critical sound timing, to achieve reasonable adjustment of the complexity of player interaction and the challenge of the game in music games, and provide effective guarantee for the procedural generation of the score composed of a large number of interactive notes in music games. As one of the elements of Drop-Based interaction, Jeong-up Lim and other authors [10] propose that "note indicators" are essentially a series of musical visualization symbols that can be realized through manipulation of devices by game designers by combining music theory, the thematic style and mechanics rules of music games, the data representation of sound, the use of MIDI standards, etc. The game designer combines music theory, music game thematic style and mechanics rules, sound data presentation, and MIDI standard application to create a series of music visualization symbols that manipulation devices can interact with them.

The design and application of music visualization elements are also critical to realize mutual interaction between players and music games under mechanism and rules. The use of sound visualization technology module for service video game development can effectively help to improve the quality and efficiency of music game development [11]. Timing synchronization among game music tracks, game scenes and players' interactive behaviors enables players to fully experience the rhythmic atmosphere of the "Dropping Interaction". With audio visualization technology, the information of game music tracks such as beat and pitch is transformed into a large amount of data. Then the designer constructs association rules between visual content and valuable data features to generate regular and distinctive visual elements [12]. Tzu-Chun Yeh [13] and other authors designed a music game *AutoRhythm* in such research, and by introducing the music data analysis in it and the structured generation method of the interaction spectrum in the game, and carrying out relevant experimental tests, they proposed a quality improvement scheme for the spectrum generation of music rhythm games. This scheme can effectively improve the quality of the player, background music, and game. This scheme can effectively improve the synchronization and harmony among the player, background music, and game interaction operations and provide positive effects for improving the quality of music game development.

With the continuous innovation of the concept of music game mechanism design and the use of new game interaction devices, the "Dropping Interaction" mechanism of music games has gradually evolved into more complex and creative ways of playing. For the convenience of description, this paper refers to games that combine traditional music games with other types of game mechanics as "hybrid music games", which adjust some of the interaction mechanisms of traditional music games and incorporate other video game mechanics, and change the figurative forms of the original note indicators, movement trajectories, and judgment areas to a greater extent. The game also incorporates the mechanics of other video games. For example, *Geometry Dash* combines parkour elements with flat scrolling interaction mechanism, in which the note indicators change into obstacles to be avoided or springboards to be touched, etc. The player has to complete the effective interaction operation of avoiding obstacles according to the movement speed of the character and the current movement form of the character when the music beat is synchronized with the location where the interaction should be made. *Mush Dash* incorporates the Non-Turn-Based boss battle mechanism of Role-Playing games, in which players follow the rhythm of the music and quickly and accurately hit the monsters sent by the boss to survive and try to fight against the boss (see Fig. 3).

Fig. 3. *Geometry Dash* level scene (left) and *Mush Dash* boss battle level scene (right).

The interaction mechanism and rules of many music games make the players' action not only rhythmic but also generally reflect the features of "high interaction frequency and quick response", "appropriate timing and standard action", and "high strength and intensity of interaction". The Above-Mentioned common points and differences between traditional music game "falling interaction" and "hybrid music game" in terms of core gameplay, game rules and interaction mechanism can be summarized as follows: the main feature of music games is that "players can quickly perceive and adapt to the relationship between the rhythm of interaction and the rhythm of music within a period of time, and complete a series of specific action sequences with frequent, accurate, powerful and rhythmic feeling," which is the main feature that distinguishes music games from other electronic games in terms of game mechanics.

Another book by Ernest Adams, Fundamentals of Game Design, mentions that game mechanics will present players with "Active Challenges" and "Passive Challenges." Active Challenges are formed according to the game mechanics, while Passive Challenges do not require game mechanics and are avoided by the player character [14]. In the context of the analysis of the interaction mechanism of music games, "Active Challenges" refers to the players' ability to follow the rhythm of the music and the synchronized visual cues to perform the interaction to ensure that the game passes and achieves a high rating. "Passive Challenge" means that the user needs to avoid the rhythm of the music and the synchronized visual cues, overcome the distracting factors that lead the player to fail the game, and perform the interaction according to the actual situation to avoid reaching the failure condition. The combination of "Active Challenges" and "Passive Challenges" in music games affects the deployment of the players' interactive behavior decisions. Combining the two types of challenges in the music game requires players to fully consider and use their decisions in the deployment of the "Active Challenge" and "Passive Challenge" corresponding to the corresponding play style.

Take the VR music game *Beat Saber* as an example. The game's different level objectives, pass restrictions and game mode diversity with the player needs to use the "Active Challenge" or "Passive Challenge". Players with the VR handle to cut the operation of the music cubes has different color distinctions. The arrow on the block indicates the direction of cutting. Their generation and movement patterns will be synchronized with the background music beat to achieve the timing. If there is no arrow, it means that the player can cut them from any direction, with the corresponding color of the "Lightsaber" cutting cubes can score points. Players need to face many music blocks in the level and "Grid Barriers", "Bombs", and other objects that players need to avoid. These objects, which pose a threat to the player, will appear along with the music cubes and be interspersed (Avoiding the grid and avoiding cutting into bombs). In addition, some of the levels in *Beat Saber* Campaign mode have conditions that limit the intensity and frequency of positive interactions, such as limiting the maximum number of consecutive hits and limiting the cumulative distance that players can move with their hands (see Fig. 4).

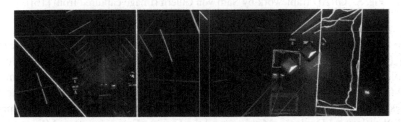

Fig. 4. *Beat Saber* music cube with bombs (left) and electrified grid barriers (right).

2.2 Gamer Behavioral Decision

The Fast-Paced, interactive type of music games need to be designed in such a way that they can keep the player focused for a long time while continuously gaining a sense of excitement and satisfaction, providing the conditions to stimulate the player to shape a positive mind flow experience in the game interaction [15]. Along with the increase of difficulty in the levels of music games, the number of note indicators increases and the frequency of appearance accelerates, and the complexity of note indicators of different interaction types increases, which requires players to have faster Pre-judgment reaction, more accurate operation timing, and more ruthless action intensity to improve the quality of interaction operations. In the face of this change, players need to combine their assessment of operational proficiency and level performance to develop and always adjust their strategies for passing the levels and the quality of their pursuit of completing the level objectives. In this paper, we refer to this part as players' behavioral decisions in music games.

Players make behavioral decisions in games based on a variety of factors. Sam von Gillern [16] from Iowa State University of Science and Technology has proposed a behavioral framework for interpreting players' experiences in video games, The Gamer Response and Decision Framework, GRAD framework for short (see Fig. 5).

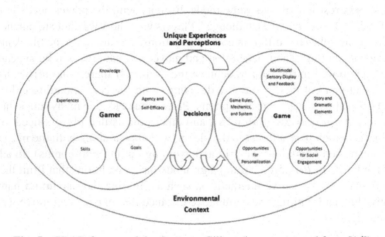

Fig. 5. GRAD framework by Sam von Gillern (image captured from [16]).

The author indicates that the framework is based on Rosenblatt's Reader Response Theory (1995), game research and psychology, and other related theories to understand and explain the learning process and players' Decision-Making process in the game. The GRAD framework is structured as a circular structure in which the gamer and the video game use the game scenario as the environmental context to drive the game process through the players' Decision-Making, and the Unique Experiences and Perceptions of the game feedback to influence the players' adjustment to the decision, thus forming a circular structure. In this way, the players' experiences, knowledge, skills, agency and Self-Efficacy, and goals are linked to the multimodal sensory display and feedback, game rules, mechanics and systems, Story and dramatic elements, Opportunities for personalization. The author has mentioned in the concluding statement of the GRAD model study that applying the concept of the GRAD model to the context of a specific game classification helps to highlight the exploration of connections related to the gameplay mechanics, player interaction behaviors for such games.

For the influence and causes of players' behavioral decisions in music games, Luisa Jedwillat et al. proposed the influence of background music in games on players' manipulative behaviors, arguing that the emotions brought by the soundtrack style in players' game experience can influence the way players to manipulate the game and make the interaction behavior harmonious with the music style theme [17]. Through an experimental study, Amanda C. Pasinski et al. [18] compared three groups of players, including formally trained musicians, Long-Term music game players, and general players, and analyzed and showed that the difference in the presentation of level scores of the music game *Rock Band 2* by different player groups influenced players' perception of music in music games to the operation degree of precision judgment, which in turn affects players' interactive performance ability. Joseph D. Chisholm et al. [19] compared two groups of Action Video Game Players (AVGPs) with Non-Video-Game Players (NVGPs) by conducting experiments related to eye movements and interaction responses. AVGPs are more focused, have faster response times, and have more skills and experience with these games.

3 Construction of HCI Features and Players' Decision-Making Framework in Music Games

The interaction and feedback results between different players and the game program often differ significantly in music games. The game designer takes the expected experience goal and feasible pass method as the main idea to guide and shape the game mechanism, play method, rules and other modules. However, because players have different operating abilities, interaction habits, and fitting degree, some players' interaction decisions do not faithfully reflect the game's original experience goals and design intentions, thus reducing the fun of the game.

Among the existing studies focusing on music games, few results correlate and combine the mechanisms and rules of music games and players' behavioral decisions, so this paper proposes the following hypothesis: players' behavioral decisions for music games are related to the unique game mechanisms and rules of music games, and accordingly proposes the relationship model between Human-Computer interaction features and players' decisions in music games. The proposed model can effectively clarify the factors related to the formulation and adjustment of players' behavioral decisions in music games (see Fig. 6).

The relationship model consists of three main elements: "Gamer" (same meaning as "Player"), "Gamer Behavior Decision" and "Music Game". Each of these elements contains several Sub-elements. Arrows indicate the interconnection between them (solid arrows show those directly or primarily related, indirectly or partially related are shown by dashed arrows). The specific form of their interconnection is described.

The unique game mechanics of music games determines how the player performs the "Active Challenge" or "Passive Challenge" mode of play. The various settings and rules of different music game levels will also guide players to focus more on one of the two modes of interactive play, making it more conducive for players to make reasonable

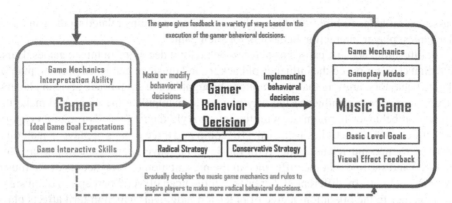

Fig. 6. HCI feature and gamer behavior decision relation model in music games.

behavioral decisions to achieve the pass conditions. Before players start to play a new music game, they will make initial behavioral decisions based on their previous proficiency in similar music games, their interpretation of the rules and mechanics of the new music game, their ideal performance and evaluation expectations. The game gives feedback in Real-Time game screen effects, score situation, scene element changes, etc., based on the operation situation established by the player's specified decision. Combined with the game pass target, these feedbacks will influence the player to adjust or decide details in the next part of the game process. After further understanding of the game objectives, gameplay mode, and their operational performance, players will decide to make more conservative strategies to reduce the risk of operational errors by tending to achieve the primary conditions of the game objectives in the following game decisions or to make more aggressive strategies to face more complicated and more likely to lead to the risk of failure by attempting more challenging game objectives by challenging higher pass conditions.

One should emphasize that for any music game, the "Active Challenge" and the "Passive Challenge" of the gameplay model do not necessarily have to coexist in the Above-Mentioned relational model, and the player may use both at some point in the process of the game. Players may use both active and passive challenges at certain times during the game level, so the two are not necessarily independent of each other. In addition, the "Conservative" or "Aggressive" strategy in the player's behavioral decisions is evaluated regarding the player's proficiency, experience, and expectations of the game's goals (Including the fixed goals set by the game and the player's own desired goals).

4   Application

Don't Be Popcorn is a game based on the Unity3D engine, combining the core mechanics, rules and play methods of Pop-Up shooting and music rhythm. In terms of theme creativity, the author's creative team planned and set the game style of 8 Bit and pixel, with anthropomorphic corn kernel characters resisting turning into popcorn in the pot as the story's background. The game mechanics, game rules, score calculation and accumulation logic, music score generation, and other game design aspects follow the "Game

Mechanics and Rules" point of view in the previous relationship model and guide. The production of this game provides a vehicle for subsequent player testing experiments. It provides an effective guarantee for subsequent data analysis and experimental verification of the relationship model between Human-Computer interaction characteristics and user behavior and Players' Decision-Making in music games.

4.1 Behavior Decision and Game Mechanics Design

The game mechanics and rules design module of this game contain four main parts: the player's interactive movement control of the corn kernel character, the information collection and data transformation of the music, the synchronization setting of the fireball launch and the music track, and the dynamic adjustment and encouragement mechanism of the level difficulty.

Interactive movement control is an essential part of the game behavior decision in the execution process, determining the external representation of the Players' Decision-Making behavior and decision mode. The game program sets up the interactive input interface of the Body-Sensing device, and gets the player's hand movement information by using external Body-Sensing devices such as Kinect, and binds the position of the corn kernel in the scene with the player's hand movement position information by using the camera ray collision function so that the corn kernel can move flexibly in the game scene. The game also sets up interaction mechanisms that support mouse operation so that the game can be played using the PC client without the hardware of a somatosensory device. The somatosensory device requires players to pay extra learning costs to cooperate with the physical and dynamic elements, which makes behavioral decisions more challenging and playable but difficult. The mouse interface is the usual control mode for players, which is relatively easy to operate, and players will spend more learning costs on strategic thinking and more rational behavioral decisions.

Music data processing and information collection provide necessary guarantees for the regular operation of music game mechanics and provide accurate guidance for players to interpret the music game mechanics and make behavioral decisions following the game mechanics and rules. The music played in the level scenes will be analyzed by the program in Real-Time. The data will be processed to form a synchronization between launch and movement patterns of fireballs in the game and changes in the pitch of the music and other information. Fireball movement and pitch show a close positive correlation, so the player can predict the changes of other elements by any fireball, thus choose the corresponding Decision-Making behavior to contribute to the challenge of the level and the realization of the music style. The data results obtained from the program's analysis of pitch properties are highly compatible with the changing pattern of pitch felt by people, which helps to improve the quality of automatically generated spectral effects in music games synchronized with background music, increase the emotional impact of music, and indirectly influence the style of players' behavioral decisions. In addition, using the sound spectrum sampling function in Unity, we mainly sample the pitch information of the game sound source in Real-Time and generate the sample data required by the program. These data are grouped and integrated, processed according to specific setting requirements of the game rules to provide support for some mechanisms such as the firing of fireballs in the game scenes.

The synchronization of the fireball obstacle generation with the music will influence the Players' Decision-Making behavior during the game. Fireball will generate from 20 launch pads at the edge of the scene and move towards the center of the screen. The launch pads' launch commands are programmatically controlled. Each launchpad is numbered from 1 to 20, and the number corresponds to the range of pitch data sampled in the soundtrack, with the numbered numbers ranging from small to large, indicating the sampling of different ranges of pitch attribute parameter values for the music from small to large. The lower pitch values correspond to the melodies that make the player feel low and rough in the music, corresponding to the low part of the music. In this stage, the number of fireballs launched is low and the threat of damage to the character is low, so players can adjust their behavioral decisions during this period to score as many points as possible in the scene, while preparing for the greater threat brought by the increase in pitch. The player has to decide whether to adjust to a conservative decision to avoid the threat, or to maintain an aggressive decision to meet the challenge according to his own operational ability. These samples are collected by the program, and the fluctuation of the data value will be close to synchronization with the music beat cycle. The game uses this relationship to achieve the synchronization of the control of fireball launcher with the music beat change and climax change, allowing players to switch between different psychological states and behavioral decisions, guiding players' emotions to rise and fall, dramatically shaping the narrative and rhythm of the game.

Dynamic difficulty adjustment and interactive encouragement mechanisms ensure that players continue to have a positive experience and are motivated to change their strategies to achieve better results. [20] The game uses a dynamic difficulty adjustment mechanism, which varies significantly from level to level and dynamically adjusts the degree of difficulty in the same level according to the player's stage performance. The fireball launch control will be subject to the change of sound sampling value, at the same time, after processing the sampling value and the player's operation performance will further affect the fireball launch frequency, movement speed, the probability of aiming at the player launch, the maximum number of simultaneous presences in the scene, to achieve the dynamic adjustment of the game difficulty. At the beginning of the game, fireballs have a long interval time, slow movement speed and low accuracy in targeting players. Suppose the player insists on staying unharmed for a long time during the game. In that case, the above parameters about the fireballs will gradually change. The player will gradually face a more significant number of fireballs with higher speed and accuracy, testing the player's ability to avoid obstacles. Once hit by the fireball, these parameters will immediately reset to the initialization stage, reducing the difficulty dynamically. This mechanism ensures the timeliness of the player's decisions and gives a progressive difficulty increase. On the one hand, it ensures that the player's strategy is feasible. On the other hand, it ensures that the chosen strategy can inspire the player to appropriate challenges. The work achieves a continuous appeal of the game by grasping the dependency between achievement and challenge and motivates the player to conceive more affluent behavioral strategies continuously.

In addition, in order to guide players to develop a clearance strategy more in line with their operating skills and proficiency, the game scene area is divided into a "Scoring Zone" and a "Recovery Zone" (see Fig. 7).

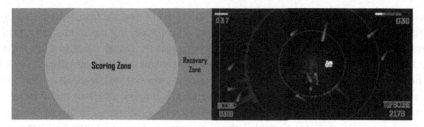

Fig. 7. The "Scoring Zone" and "Recovery Zone" (Left: Sketch. Right: Actual scene).

The "Scoring Zone" is located in the circle area in the center of the screen, insisting that the corn kernels move in the center area of the screen where fireballs easily hit them can accumulate points. As the cumulative damage received increases, the corn kernels will change shape and gradually puff up into popcorn. At this point, the collision volume of the character will become larger, more vulnerable to fireball damage, resulting in the risk of failure to enhance the pass. Players facing this situation to avoid the risk need to leave the "Scoring Zone" as soon as possible to avoid the "Recovery Zone". The "Recovery Zone" is located in the edge area outside the screen circle. Character in this area is less threatened by fireball damage. If the corn grain character's lifetime value is not full, move to the "Recovery Zone" will recover the health point. The lower the current life value, the faster the recovery efficiency, but the character will not accumulate points during the "Recovery Zone". This situation leads the player to return to the "Scoring Zone" to get a score.

These areas are designed to allow players to adapt to the game's difficulty, indirectly control the game's difficulty, and try new Decision-Making behaviors by adjusting their behavior and patterns. This setting avoids the game to win or lose binary mode to give players the blow of losing. under the premise of ensuring players' survival, it promotes players to adjust their behavioral decisions in the dynamic process to pursue higher scores. Then, the remaining life value will not be counted as an additional score when the game is paused bonus.

The mechanism as mentioned above of interaction incentive mechanism in this game on the dynamic change of level difficulty, the division of different functions in the interaction area, as well as the settings of score and life recovery mechanism, aim to jointly influence the player's behavioral decision and guide to adjust the player's interaction behavior. The change of music climax and the character's state will also prompt the player to make timely conservative low score behavior decisions, aggressive high score behavior decisions or custom behavior decisions in line with the player's operation level. The game is also a great way to ensure that the player is satisfied with the score and stimulates the player's sense of strategic behavior, thus effectively adding to the game's fun.

4.2 Behavior Decision and Art Effects Design

The game's art and effects design also play an essential role in shaping and deploying the player's behavioral decisions. In the GRAD framework, visual elements such as art and effects will act as "Multimodal Symbols" to the players, responding to game mechanics and rules and providing visual feedback to the players' interaction behavior. Players will repeatedly receive these static or dynamic symbols during the game and gradually understand the relationship between the symbols and the game's performance. At the same time, the storytelling relationship between different symbols and the player's role also helps players interpret the meaning of art elements and visual effects, which helps players to use a more accurate grasp of the game mechanics, and thus make behavioral decisions more clearly implemented and adjusted during the game. In this game, players will take on the role of "Corn Kernels", the character has to avoid contact with the source of damage "Fireball" to prevent excessive heat in the "Passive Challenge" part. In the "Active Challenge" part, corn kernels need to touch the bonus prop "Water drops" to get extra points while recovering from their health point. Therefore, "Fireball" and "Water Drops" will become essential art design elements in the game scene.

In terms of visual design, the design uses the metaphor of corn kernels and fire for the character part. The player controls the character as a corn kernel, which needs to avoid becoming an expanding popcorn and therefore avoid touching the fireball generated with the music rhythm. Corn kernels and fireballs are used as visual symbols, and through graphical representation, the player's experience of the popcorn making process is integrated into the understanding of the game rules. By extension, the fireball serves as an obstacle to be avoided in the game. The water droplet correspondingly conveys the opposite concept of the fireball, symbolizing a prop that is beneficial to the player. In the center of the screen, a Ring-Like pattern of the fire circle changes with the rhythm to divide the "Scoring Zone" and the "Recovery Zone". The circular shape of the fire ring reminds the player of the top view of a stove, using the stove metaphor to convey to the player the more dangerous hints represented by the center part of the screen as the "Heat Source".

In addition, the art design also uses rapid and intense visual changes to provide players with feedback on the interactive behavior, suggesting whether the interaction made by the player is in line with the interactive features and rules of the music game, and help the implementation and advancement of the pass decision. For example, the player manipulates the role of "Corn Kernels" in the fireball damage, the screen produces a momentary white splash screen effect. At the same time, the current life value of the character dynamically changes the puffed state of the corn kernels, adding to the expressive effect of the character's damage cue. When the player's health point is 0, the popcorn will be fully expanded and turned into ashes. Its visual representation can quickly identify the character's life state. In addition, the music in the climax of the drumbeat will drive the screen to produce a perspective shaking effect, shaping a more dynamic game scene Audio-Visual experience to help players control the law of interactive action (see Figs. 8, 9, 10 and 11).

Fig. 8. Corn kernel character in different life states.

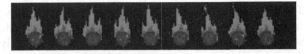

Fig. 9. Fire ball obstacle (Sequence frame animation display).

Fig. 10. Bonus item – water drop (Sequence frame animation display).

Fig. 11. Popcorn turned into ashes (Sequence frame animation display).

5   Experiment and Result Analysis

Following the relationship model proposed in the previous section and the specific implementation of each element in the model in the game design, this study will further explore the following elements in the game test, questionnaire feedback, and data analysis phases: the specific implementation of interaction decisions in *Don't Be Popcorn*. The relationship between game proficiency and willingness to challenge for higher scoring goals.

5.1   Experiment Design for Game Test

In selecting the experimental group for the game test, the participants invited to this experiment came from the college students in the author's university, and their ages ranged from 18 to 28 years old. The experimental population was divided into two groups according to whether they had played music games in the past year or not: the experimental group was the group of players who had played music games (n = 22), and the control group was ordinary players (n = 16) Participants have generally played music games such as *Taiko Drummer*, *Cytus II*, and *Rhythm Master* within the past year.

The test process will be conducted in both online and offline formats. The offline test will directly invite players to play *Don't Be Popcorn*. It will focus on observing the specific operation of the players' strategy, adjusting the strategy and performance of the level score during the game, and providing feedback on the performance and operation evaluation through a questionnaire after the game experience. In the online testing session, the researcher encapsulated the game program, uploaded it to the online network cloud and provided a sharing link. The players downloaded the game and started to play it directly through the PC client. The research questionnaire mainly asked the test players whether they had experience in playing music games and their evaluation of the difficulty of each level, as well as objective data such as the number of attempts required to pass each level for the first time and the score of each level.

38 questionnaires were collected from which 23 valid questionnaires were screened through the valid responses, including 14 for the experimental group and 9 for the

control group. After counting, we conducted a preliminary analysis of the questionnaires in a traditional nonquantitative method, and the statistical results tentatively showed that players with music game experience (experimental group) generally scored higher than the average players (control group), but there was no significant difference in the "Number of Attempts" and "Level Difficulty Rating" between the two groups of players. To demonstrate the experimental results' generalizability and significance and verify whether there is a more complex correlation between Decision-Making behavior and game mechanics, we further quantitatively analyzed and evaluated the test papers.

5.2 Questionnaire Research Analysis

The questionnaire results study will be carried out using SPSS 19.0 for data analysis. The results of the questionnaire analysis will be used to summarize the players' scores and difficulty ratings in the game experience sessions, and this will lead to further analysis of the players' characteristics in terms of their operational performance and Decision-Making strategies for interactive behaviors in music games.

The reliability test used the alpha coefficient model, and the results showed that Cronbach's alpha coefficient is 0.750. the KMO and Bartlett's sphericity tests were performed on this questionnaire (Sig. < 0.001, KMO $= 0.649$). The overall reliability of all questions involved in the data analysis was acceptable.

The relationship between the dependent variable "Score of Each Level" and the independent variable "Possess Experience of Music Games" was examined using the mean analysis method. The results showed that players with music game experience performed better than the average players in any level, and the difference between the scores of the two types of players in each level was about 209 points. In addition, comparing the score difference between the two types of players in different levels, it can be concluded that the average score of the second level is the highest, and the average score of the third level is the lowest (see Table 1). These results tentatively show that players with experience in music games can more easily use their previously acquired operational experience to decipher the game mechanics and master the skills of passing the game faster when experiencing the operational aspects of new music games. Moreover, the game's difficulty was negatively correlated with the performance of the player's pass score, and increasing the difficulty of the level reduced the performance of the player's pass score in general.

The relationship between "Attempts Required to Pass the Level", "Level Difficulty Rating", and "Possess Experience of Music Games" was analyzed using biased correlation. "Possess Experience of Music Games" was set as a control variable to exclude the interfering factors that affect the difficulty of this game according to the players' previous proficiency in playing music games. The two variables were tested for Two-Tailed significance using game level 1 as an example. The results showed that the partial correlation coefficient Correlation is 0.589 and the Two-Tailed significance is 0.004, indicating that there is a significant correlation between the number of first pass attempts in level 1 and the level difficulty evaluation, and this correlation coefficient is significant (see Table 2). It can be tentatively concluded that players' evaluation of the game's difficulty increases with the gradual increase in the number of passes required.

Table 1. Mean and standard deviation of the score of each level for different players.

Possess experience of music games		Score level1	Score level2	Score level3
Yes	Mean	1984.44	2116.25	1655.44
	N	16	16	16
	Std. deviation	834.357	827.630	817.357
No	Mean	1755.43	1957.14	1415.00
	N	7	7	7
	Std. deviation	934.388	900.951	839.385

Table 2. Skewed correlation analysis of the pass attempts and difficulty evaluation (level 1).

Control variables			Attempts required to pass the level	Level difficulty rating
Possess experience of music games	Attempts required to pass the level	Correlation	1.000	.589
		Sig. (Two-tailed)		.004
		df	0	20
	Level difficulty rating	Correlation	.589	1.000
		sig. (Two-tailed)	.004	
		df	20	0

Linear regression analysis was used to explore whether there was a linear relationship between the number of attempts required to pass different levels and the level score. Take level 1 as an example, set the independent variable as "Attempts Required to Pass the Level" and the dependent variable as "Level Score", and obtained the regression coefficient table of the first level score (see Table 3).

Table 3 gives the unstandardized coefficient constant value (B = 1576.336, Sig. = 0.025), and the corresponds value of passes required as the independent variable (B = 181.007, Sig. = 0.596). Based on the above data analysis results, it is assumed that as the number of first pass attempts increases while the player is playing the first level, the final score of the pass will also increase. However, since the significance of the unstandardized coefficient of the independent variable (sig > 0.05), it is denied that the linear regression results present a correlation. The above hypothesis needs rejected.

Table 3. Regression coefficients result for the score in level 1.

Model	Unstandardized coefficients		Standardized coefficients	t	Sig.	95% Confidence interval for B	
	B	Std. error	Beta			Lower bound	Upper bound
(Constant)	1576.336	654.559		2.408	0.025	215.105	2937.566
Attempts required to pass the level	181.007	336.553	0.117	0.538	0.596	518.894	880.907

6 Discussion

There is a linear relationship between the number of attempts required to pass different levels and the level score from the test results. However, this linear relationship should be denied from the significance analysis. After different players have a preliminary understanding of the difficulty of the music game levels and the focus of the play mode, players' clearance strategies will be evaluated and adjusted. In the process of repeatedly failing to pass the game, players accumulate skills and experiences that help them succeed in passing the game, and at the same time, the differences in frustration and Self-Confidence brought by repeated failures also affect the results of players' decisions to adjust their behaviors.

In addition, the scoring incentive mechanism and dynamic difficulty changes in this music game will also cause significant differences in the behavioral decisions of different players. Players are willing to adopt a higher risk of failure to pursue higher scores, trying to make aggressive game decisions and move within the "Scoring Zone" as much as possible. While other players chose to make relatively conservative decisions, giving priority to maintaining a safe life state for their characters, wandering between the "Scoring Zone" and the "Recovery Zone" more frequently, and even move directly to the "Recovery Zone" at the risky period of the game level, in which to avoid the threat of fireball obstacles and give up scoring more points.

The above experimental analysis and data research results show that players' behavioral decision making and adjustment in music games are related to the difficulty level of different interactive game modes, players' ability to master music game skills, and their ability to interpret and implement game mechanics and rules, etc. The results of players' strategies and behavioral decision making and adjustment are not only influenced by the game performance, but also include various factors such as players' tendency to pursue certain types of the gameplay experience and changes in skill mastery.

7 Conclusion

This paper combines theoretical research and case studies of works on game mechanics, rules and interaction of music games. With analyzing the context of music games, we propose a model of HCI characteristics and user decision relationship based on music games, sorting out the characteristics and interactive relationship of player experience of music games. The proposed model explores and sorts out the correlation and influencing factors between game mechanism and players' Decision-Making in the music game context. The model is proved through case studies of existing music game works and experimental tests of game projects.

Due to the technical environment of game development, our game needs further iteration and optimization in terms of the accuracy of temporal synchronization and the design of rhythmic interactive operation. Besides, fewer samples were available for experimental data analysis in this game test session. The analysis results were not entirely sufficient to verify the association between players' interaction behavior characteristics and music game design strategies in music games in general. Further research is needed to explore in more detail the Sub-Characteristics of the "Mechanics and Rules of Music Games" module of the proposed model, and to analyze how these Sub-Characteristics affect the formulation, execution, and adjustment of players' game behavior decisions at a deeper level. The model will be further explored and refined by conducting more extensive and targeted experiments on music games.

Acknowledgements. This study was supported by the National Key Research and Development Program of China (No. 2020AAA0105200).

References

1. Jenson, J., De Castell, S., Muehrer, R., Droumeva, M.: So you think you can play: an exploratory study of music video games. J. Music Technol. Educ. **9**(3), 273–288 (2016)
2. Heon, S.D., Baek, K.K., Hee, L.J.: Analysis and evaluation of mobile rhythm games: game structure and playability. Int. J. Electr. Comput. Eng. **9**(6), 5263–5269 (2019)
3. Cohan, T.D.: Rhythm quest: creating a music video game. Bard Undergraduate Senior Projects Fall **2019**(51), 115 (2019)
4. Huang, S.-Y., Zhang, L.: Interaction design of music mobile games from the perspective of emotional experience. Design **34**(05), 72–75 (2021)
5. Ni, H.: Critical elements analysis of music game design for user experience. China Collect. Econ. **2018**(35), 62–64 (2018)
6. Song, D.H., Yoo, J.Y., Lee, J.H.: Comparative analysis of mobile rhythm game user interface and control. Int. Conf. Future Inf. Commun. Eng. **10**(1), 315–318 (2018)
7. Jing, J., Yi, Z., Xin-yuan, H.: Music visualization-based game design and research. J. Comput. Appl. **32**(5), 1481–1483 (2013)
8. Sedig, K., Parsons, P., Haworth, R.: Player-Game interaction and cognitive gameplay: a taxonomic framework for the core mechanic of videogames. Informatics **4**(1), 4 (2017)
9. Kagawa, T., Tezuka, H., Inaba, M.: Frequency-based key component extraction-automatic generation of instruction scores for music video games. In: Proceeding of Conference on Entertainment Computing, pp. 326–333 (2015)
10. Up, L.J., Jieun, K., Gyuhwan, O.: A study on music visualization method in game with musical note. J. Korean Soc. Comput. Game **14**, 267–281 (2008)
11. Lipscomb, S.D., Zehnder, S.M.: Immersion in the virtual environment: the effect of a musical score on the video gaming experience. J. Physiol. Anthropol. Appl. Hum. Sci. **23**(6), 337–343 (2004)

12. Lopes, A.M., Machado, J.A.T.: On the complexity analysis and visualization of musical information. Entropy **21**(7), 669 (2019)
13. Yeh, T.C., Jang, J.S.R.: AutoRhythm: a music game with automatic hit-timing generation and percussion identification. IEEE Trans. Games **12**(3), 291–301 (2020)
14. Ernest, A.: Fundamentals of Game Design, 2nd edn. New Riders, Berkeley (2010)
15. Hrabec, O., Chrz, V.: Flow genres: the varieties of video game experience. Int. J. Gaming Comput. Mediated Simul. **7**(1), 1–19 (2015)
16. Gillern, S.V.: The gamer response and decision framework: a tool for understanding video gameplay experiences. Simul. Gaming **47**(5), 666–683 (2016)
17. Jedwillat, L., Nowack, N.: A game with music or music with a game? about the video game karmaflow. Nauka Televideniya - Art Sci. Telev. **16**(4), 85–108 (2020)
18. Pasinski, A.C., Hannon, E.E., Snyder, J.S.: How musical are music video game players. Psychon. Bull. Rev. **23**(5), 1553–1558 (2016)
19. Chisholm, J.D., Kingstone, A.: Action video games and improved attentional control: disentangling selection- and response-based processes. Psychon. Bull. Rev. **22**(5), 1430–1436 (2015)
20. Zohaib, M.: Dynamic difficulty adjustment (DDA) in computer games: a review. Adv. Human Comput. Interact. **2018**, 1–12 (2018)

Author Index

Printed in the United States
by Baker & Taylor Publisher Services